Studying Diversity in Teacher Education

Studying Diversity in Teacher Education

Edited by
Arnetha F. Ball and Cynthia A. Tyson

Published for the
American Educational Research Association

ROWMAN & LITTLEFIELD PUBLISHERS, INC.
Lanham • New York • Toronto • Plymouth, UK

Published for the American Educational Research Association

Published by Rowman & Littlefield Publishers, Inc.
A wholly owned subsidary of The Rowman & Littlefield Publishing Group, Inc.
4501 Forbes Boulevard, Suite 200, Lanham, Maryland 20706
http://www.rowmaneducation.com

Estover Road, Plymouth PL6 7PY, United Kingdom

British Library Cataloguing in Publication Information Available

Library of Congress Cataloging-in-Publication Data

Studying diversity in teacher education / edited by Arnetha F. Ball and Cynthia A. Tyson.
    p. cm.
ISBN 978-1-4422-0440-9 (cloth : alk. paper) -- ISBN 978-1-4422-0441-6 (pbk. : alk. paper) -- ISBN 978-1-4422-0442-3 (electronic)
  1. Teachers--Training of--United States. 2. English language--Study and teaching--United States--Foreign speakers. 3. Linguistic minorities--Education--United States. 4. Bilingual education--United States. I. Ball, Arnetha F., 1950- II. Tyson, Cynthia A., 1957-
  LB1715.S798 2011
  370.71'1--dc22   2010030526

Contents

Foreword

STUDYING DIVERSITY IN TEACHER EDUCATION

Dealing with diversity is one of the central challenges of twenty-first-century education. It is impossible to prepare tomorrow's teachers to succeed with *all* of the students they will meet without exploring how both students' and teachers' learning experiences are influenced by their home languages, cultures, and contexts; the realities of race and class privilege in the United States; the ongoing manifestations of institutional racism within the educational system; and the many factors that shape students' opportunities to learn within individual classrooms. To teach effectively, teachers need to understand how learning depends on their ability to draw connections to what learners already know, to support students' motivation and willingness to risk trying, and to engender a climate of trust between and among adults and students.

Teachers bring very different perspectives to this process of learning to teach, shaped by their own experiences as students. This question, asked by a student teacher in the early months of a yearlong program, will sound familiar to many teacher educators: "Ok, ok. We've talked enough about the diverse kids. When are we going to start talking about the 'normal' kids?" While most prospective teachers are eager to learn about the range of children and youth they will be working with, there are still many who want to focus on the "normal" kids: white, middle class, heterosexual, and at least outwardly well-adjusted to school—the presumed majority. Others are frustrated at the fact that there is a lot of talk about diversity, but there often seems to be little apparent action to remedy the achievement gap between the educational haves and the have-nots: the so-called *normal* kids and those who are *different*. Addressing the long apprenticeship of observation and the experience bases and perspectives of prospective teachers in preparing them to teach in diverse classrooms is a critical issue for teacher educators.

As a predominantly white, middle-class, suburban America is becoming less and less the norm, what some think of as the "good old days"—and others recollect as the days of separatism and vastly differential access to school—are fast disappearing. In a typical urban classroom in the heart of the Silicon Valley, where my colleague Arnetha Ball and I live and work, fewer than half of the students will usually have been born in this country. In addition to historical minority groups such as African Americans, Mexican Americans, and Chinese Americans, there are likely to be students from places like Russia, Bosnia, Guatemala, El Salvador, Brazil, Cambodia, Vietnam, Samoa, Tonga, Iraq, Iran, India, Zambia, South Africa, and the Philippines, among many more. Diversities in learning styles, interests, developed abilities, sexual orientations, and socioeconomic status will also be evident for teachers who have developed eyes to see the many facets of each of their students' lives and identities.

Teachers unaware of cultural influences on learning—as well as the structure and substance of inequality—will find it difficult to understand students whose experiences do not resemble what they remember from their own necessarily limited experience. New teachers need strategies to address language learning needs and sensitivity to cultural modes of communication as well as awareness of the psychological dimensions of learning—for example, the many ways in which students' construct knowledge from their very different life experiences and prior learning opportunities, as well as the ways in which students' beliefs about intelligence mobilize or paralyze their efforts. Developing an "equity pedagogy," as preeminent scholar James Banks puts it, will also often mean confronting injustices that shape students' self-esteem and opportunities to learn in both society and schools.

This book frames all of these issues of student and teacher learning with a powerful set of essays that will help researchers and teacher educators take up the critical questions of our time—questions like: What is diversity? What are the implications for students and teachers of the treatment of diversity issues in the classroom? What are the potential outcomes and side effects of teaching with an awareness of diversity? How can new teachers transmit not only skills and knowledge but also self-awareness and respect for others? What do teachers need to know and be able to do to teach diverse learners effectively, and how can they learn this? What do teacher educators need to know and be able to do to take up this important work?

Readers will find this volume a treasure trove of perspectives, answers, and provocations that should stimulate further the essential discussions we must have to create schools that can someday provide all children—and teachers—with the right to learn what they need and deserve.

Linda Darling-Hammond
Stanford, California
November 24, 2009

Introduction and Overview

Cynthia A. Tyson and Arnetha F. Ball

Studying Diversity in Teacher Education highlights scholarship by researchers who are seeking to celebrate and create room for deeper knowledge about one of the most important issues facing education today: diversity in teacher education. This volume foregrounds contributions by scholars from diverse backgrounds and identifies key epistemological, methodological, and sociopolitical issues related to diversity in teacher education. It has three main objectives. First, the volume illuminates historically persistent, yet unresolved, issues in teacher education from the perspectives of a remarkably diverse and eminent group of scholars in the field and presents research that is currently being done to address these issues. Second, it centers research on diverse populations, bringing together both research on diversity and research on diversity in teacher education, and presents frameworks, perspectives, and paradigms that have implications for the reconceptualization and reframing of research on complex issues that are oftentimes ignored or treated too simplistically within teacher education literature. The third aim of the volume is to analyze the sociocultural and sociopolitical consequences of the ways in which research on diversity and diversity in teacher education are conceptualized theoretically and operationalized and presents an agenda for future research that is imperative to meet the challenges facing our profession.

The volume is divided into three sections. Each section responds to one of these three important questions: (1) Where have we been in the research on diversity in teacher education, and what are pressing challenges that must be addressed in order for the field to move forward? (2) Where are we now as we consider the perspectives of current researchers who are challenging the rethinking and reconceptualization of the research on diversity in teacher education? (3) Where should we be going, and what is the nature of the work that still needs to be done in order to address the challenges currently facing our field? Within the context of these overarching challenges, contributing authors explore questions that include (but are not limited to) the following: What are some of the major contributions that have been made to the field on the topic of diversity in teacher education? What new insights can we gain by explicitly pulling the two components together: research on diversity and research on diversity in teacher education? What are critical issues that must remain in sight as we chart directions for future research? How might we rethink research frameworks, perspectives, and paradigms articulated on issues of diversity in teacher education so our theories and practices enable us to prepare teachers for effective classroom practices? How can we interrogate the myths that emerge from the research—myths that underlie and drive many of the ineffective curricular and pedagogical routines that take place in teacher education programs when it comes to discussions about diverse student populations? How can research support a reframing of the way we prepare teachers—or fail to prepare teachers— to create inclusive classrooms for all students in an increasingly diverse society? As contributing authors address these and other issues, they contribute to a rethinking and diversification of the intellectual underpinnings of the research in teacher education and focus attention on the most important issues challenging the field in these days and times.

This volume poses questions on the location of issues of diversity within the literature on teaching and teacher education and the types of research conducted in the name of "diversity" in this field. Researchers in teacher education are aware that while changes in student demographics have been dramatic, changes in the demographics of the teaching force have been slow. Since the mass exclusion of black educators following the *Brown v. Board of Education* decision, most teachers continue to be white, female, monolingual, and middle class. In 2005, Hollins and Torres-Guzman (2005) noted that the research on diversity in teacher education confirmed that many of the teachers assigned to teach diverse students in urban schools are concerned because they lack confidence in their ability to do well in diverse classroom settings, feel uncomfortable interacting with parents from diverse backgrounds, and feel inadequately prepared to teach students from culturally and linguistically diverse backgrounds. They further confirmed that few non-classroom-based or longitudinal studies existed and that diversity had been neither a priority for funding agencies nor a focus of well-supported programmatic research up to that time (Hollins & Torres-Guzman, 2005, p. 480). A recent online search of the data-bases containing research on teacher education was conducted using the key terms *teacher education*, *studies*, and *diversity*. That search revealed that, when the key terms *studies* and *teacher education* and the years *2005 to 2008* were entered, the number of studies found was 5,715. However, when the terms *diversity* and *teacher education* were entered for the years 2005 to 2008, the number of studies found was only 713. Even though Hollins and Torres-Guzman had challenged the field to conduct more research on *diversity in teacher education* in their 2005 seminal publication, our review search revealed that their challenge has not yet been adequately addressed by 2009. And while our search revealed that the number of research studies focusing on *diversity in teacher education* during 2005 was 147, that number had increased to only 169 in 2006, and to a mere 182 studies in 2007. While there exists a substantial body of research on diversity in education, the research focusing on diversity in teacher education is sparse. Perhaps a contributing factor to this minimal increase in the number of research studies on *diversity in teacher education* was the fact that there was a low number of researchers who were interested in conducting research on this topic because it was not viewed as an important area of study, or perhaps because this topic was not seen as a viable area of research. Perhaps the increase in the number of research studies on *diversity in teacher education* was so small because this topic was not seen as a prestigious area of research or because of the lack of funding that is available to support sustained or large-scale studies in this area. Perhaps the minimal increase in the number of studies on diversity in teacher education was because research on diversity in education was viewed as a stand-alone area rather than as part of a dual agenda that included research on diversity in education *and* research on diversity in teacher education. Regardless of the reason why there has not been more substantive research on diversity in teacher education, the fact remains that the need for further information in this area is great. The need for that research is made more evident by the continuing achievement gap between low-income students from culturally and linguistically diverse backgrounds and those from middle- and upper-class white and Asian backgrounds.

The compilation of this volume was made possible because there now exists a substantial number of critical-thinking scholars who are working diligently and successfully as researchers on issues of diversity in teacher education and because of their professional commitment to working *in, for,* and *with* diverse communities. In this volume we present the work of such scholars and the issues they are confronting. The research reported on in this volume reflects the work of a much more diverse group of scholars than is presented in most volumes that report on the research in teacher education. This volume demonstrates that when a significant accumulation of scholars from diverse backgrounds come together with or as scholars who are committed to the communities they *work in, work for, write with and about, and sometimes live in,* significant insights can be added to the field. Building on Makoni, Smitherman, Ball, and Spears (2003), the following are three important principles that undergird the work of scholars who work *in, for,* and *with* diverse communities:

1. Many of these researchers have an anthropological membership in a sociological affiliation and/or life experiences with the communities they research, analyze, and work in.
2. Diversity is often seen as one of the defining features of their scholarly research.
3. These scholars often draw on ideological orientations designed to analyze and expose the workings of ideology in research *on, about,* and *for* diverse populations.

In keeping with what Makoni, Smitherman, Ball, and Spears (2003) have said, the scholars in this volume demonstrate that there is a tendency to describe and analyze the ways in which inside members of communities who relate to the research and the researchers often build upon insider knowledge in ways that researchers who rely exclusively on outsider knowledge or who may take a detached or outside perspective are unable to do.

Many of the researchers contributing to this volume are working as scholars who are anthropological members in the communities they study and feel some sociological affiliation to the communities they are working in. They sometimes hold anthropological memberships and/or epistemological alignments that make it possible for them to offer alternative perspectives on the research on diversity in teacher education. These scholars often seek to impact not only the theoretical, ideological, and methodological aspects of scholarship but also to impact positively on the educational quality of the lives of students and teachers in the community. That impact might range from raising awareness about the basis of educational discriminatory practices to descriptions of teaching and learning practices in classrooms that serve diverse student populations to explanations about how teacher education programs might use that information in the preparation of quality teachers. The insider membership impacts on different facets of what they do, ranging from the selection of the topics to be investigated to how they analyze the data and even disseminate the results. Like the scholars in Makoni, Smitherman, Ball, and Spears (2003), these researchers are also seeking to contribute new insights from the research they conduct.

For such researchers, the selection of their topics of inquiry is not an academic exercise only: it is motivated by what the communities themselves see as key problems that need to be confronted. The research question is not only defined in collaboration with communities directly affected; the research results are also validated through the participation of the communities. For example, in Kinloch's chapter she engages in collaborative research as teacher-researcher with preservice teachers and urban high school students—crossing boundaries to engage in classroom discussions on meanings and perceptions of teaching, teachers, and students in urban public schools. The implications of her work in the community and with literacy include authoring new ways of learning that speak against inequitable educational practices and institutional structures; refiguring school spaces from sites where *banking* forms of education are experienced to sites of inquiry, exchange, and experimentation; and conceptualizing teaching and learning in frameworks that theorize equity pedagogy, multiculturalism, and social change. As is demonstrated in Kinloch's chapter, it is important that the communities feel the research results resonate with their experiences. Because many of the researchers contributing to this volume are both scholar researchers and members of the communities they work in, their scholarship provides insights as members of local communities as well as nuanced general knowledge for the field. Building on the work of such scholars, an overview of the chapters in this volume follows.

Part I

Part I of this volume provides insights on the historical context surrounding the research that has been conducted on the topic of diversity in teacher education and illuminates persisting challenges that continue to face our field. In other words, it provides the reader with a context concerning "where we've been"—at least as that phrase relates to the research on diversity in teacher education. Looking at diversity issues from the perspective of their respective areas of specialization, we have asked eminent scholars in the field to provide background knowledge and historical contextualization related to what is presently known about diversity in teacher education and remaining challenges to the profession.

With this challenge in mind, Carl Grant and Melissa Gibson and colleagues begin part I by setting a historical context for the volume. Although teacher education is a relatively young field—with research on diversity in teacher education only appearing since the 1980s—these scholars realize that several historical reviews have appeared in recent years. Rather than replicate the format of these prior reviews, these scholars take on the questions of "where we have been," "where we are now," and "where we are going as a field" from a rather unique perspective. In chapter 1 these authors review the research on diversity in teacher education from the perspective of the research that has been conducted by sixteen committed scholars in the field. Working in collaboration with research assistants Aaliyah Baker, Stefan Brueck, Phillip Caldwell, Lauren Gatti, Kerry Kretchmar, Alison Leonard, Cate Pautsch, Katie Payne, Mary Perkinson, and Melissa Sherfinski, Grant and Gibson look across the work of sixteen selected scholars to describe the rich and thoughtful literature that has been produced on the ideas of teacher education for diversity. Because of the important contributions of the scholars highlighted in this chapter, teacher education scholars are now able to draw much inspiration—both ideologically and methodologically—from the work compiled by the scholars included in this chapter. Using methodology that surveys contributions from these scholars, the authors are able to explore issues like the field's lack of a solid empirical base for its findings and the need for ideological and methodological work in the future. After exploring the recommendations, practices, and findings of the literature reviews and self studies that populate the field, they document the ways in which policy has constructed the questions of diversity and teacher education and offer suggestions for moving the field of diversity and teacher education forward into the twenty-first century and into the policy arena.

Leaders in the field of research on diversity in teacher education, Valerie Pang and Cynthia Park illustrate in their chapter the continued tenacity that is needed in order to move scholarship in the field to the next level. These scholars accomplish this by continuously challenging the field and by their persistence in raising serious questions about lingering challenges that face those who conduct research on diversity in teacher education. Refusing to allow teacher education researchers to ignore "the elephant that is standing in the middle of the room," Pang and Park's chapter focuses on the development of courageous leadership in the field as a means of advancing issues of equity in teacher education. Based on analyses using a historical and cross-disciplinary research approach, this study challenges teacher educators to create a new, interdisciplinary paradigm for multicultural teacher education—an educational field that should be cultivated as a discipline in its own right where issues of equity are at its core. As in the emergence of any new field of study, multicultural teacher education must be informed by appropriate knowledge, theories, principles, and practice. According to these authors, accomplishing this goal requires the academy's support for institutional change, comprehensive curricular integration rather than a fragmented approach, conversations among practitioners, local community activists and university professors, and a research agenda based on cross-disciplinary inquiry. Care must be taken that the content of this emerging field of study not be usurped by any one discipline or set of stakeholders. Thus, the authors encourage representation in this conversation of practitioners and local community activists as well as university professors.

In chapter 3 Christine Sleeter and Rich Milner raise questions that go to the heart of teacher education by focusing on successful efforts for diversifying the teaching force. The authors conduct a review of the literature on the diversification of the teaching force and conclude that there are four interrelated areas of concentration that can move the field forward: (1) more and deeper situated internal self studies; (2) more and deeper contextualized external evaluations; (3) more and deeper long-term and longitudinal studies; and (4) studies that investigate linkages between teacher ethnicity and student learning. Based on their review, the authors suggest implications for both practice and research. They emphatically state, "We are past the time when teacher education programs can assume that little can be done to diversify the teaching population." Their review suggests several models that have been used with success, and they suggest that there are several options that teacher education programs can try to guide them in new directions for the work of teacher education.

In chapter 4 Etta Hollins moves the conversation forward by initiating a discussion concerning one of the most fundamental challenges facing the profession—the central role of identity formation in preparing teachers to work with diverse student populations. Using identity formation as a proxy for culture, Hollins forwards an argument that culture is central to social interaction, communication, and cognition, and it forms the basis of teaching and learning. The focus of this chapter is the content and process of identity formation for the majority of those entering teacher preparation programs, its relationship to the appropriation of *knowledge for practice*, and the implications for constructing *knowledge in practice*. In this discussion, identity formation is used as a proxy for culture. This discussion is based on the premise that culture is central to social interaction, communication, and cognition that form the basis for teaching and learning.

Part II

Part II of this volume provides insights on current research that is being produced to address persisting challenges to the field. The purpose of this section is to showcase current trends and innovations in research on diversity and their implications for teacher education. The authors in this section center research on diverse populations and apply that research to what is presently known about teacher preparation while exploring the strengths and limitations of existing trends in the research on teacher education. Perhaps most important, the scholars in this part present promising frameworks, perspectives, and paradigms in research on diversity and point out their implications for research in teacher education, which can challenge the field toward new directions for future research on the preparation of teachers for diverse and underserved populations.

Looking at diversity issues from the perspective of their areas of specialization, we have asked this group of scholars—all rising stars in the field—to discuss promising practices at the heart of their work that has the potential to give direction for the research on diversity in teacher education—that is, possibilities for rethinking and reconceptualizing the profession. In response to that request, the contributing authors developed chapters in their specific areas of specialization that explore current research issues and illuminate the strengths and limitations of existing research on diversity and on diverse populations and applied the implications of that research to the research on teacher education. Each chapter in this section is structured to provide a brief overview of the background literature, showcases exemplary research that they themselves are conducting on issues of diversity, and shares the author's perspectives and recommendations on how that research applies to issues of diversity in teacher education. To this end, the scholarship on diversity in teacher education has been divided into two areas:

1. Current trends and innovations in research on diversity and their implications for research in teacher education, and
2. Frameworks, perspectives, and paradigms in research on diversity and their implications for research in teacher education

A. Centering research on diverse populations in teacher education

In chapter 5, Therese Quinn and Erica Meiners survey the persistent attempts to erase lesbian, gay, bisexual, transgender, and queer (LGBTQ) subjects from teacher education programs. They also examine the shifting role of the "state" in erasing LGBTQ lives. In addition, the authors of this chapter survey strategies that have been historically used to exclude particular communities from equal access to education. They argue for a shift in teacher education from teaching tolerance of difference to developing political clarity and competency and suggest a research agenda that prioritizes examining barriers to the implementation of that shift.

Written by Valerie Kinloch, chapter 6 discusses a student-teacher inclusive model that should be considered when framing standards on the types of relationships that can exist between minority youth who are participating in the research process and the researcher. In this chapter the author considers research on "homeplaces" (hooks, 1990) and urban struggles within African American communities (Haymes, 1995; DuBois, 1899). The author employs critical pedagogy (Freeman, 2006; Giroux & McLaren, 1994) to examine debates over the "white-ification" of—or the increasing presence of white residents within—historic African American communities undergoing gentrification. The chapter introduces readers to Phillip and Khaleeq, two African American youth from New York City's Harlem, whose multimodalities, linguistic codes, and voluntary writings on the community's visible realities compare with "white-ification." Consideration of these issues provides insights into youth literacy practices for research on diversity in teaching and teacher education. The chapter concludes by critically considering the implications of these and other students' insights in the preparation of teachers to teach in diverse settings. This chapter describes lessons that emerged when two groups of students—preservice teachers and urban high school students—crossed boundaries to engage in classroom discussions on meanings and perceptions of teaching, teachers, and students in urban public schools. The questions that guide the encounter between these two groups are: In what ways can preservice and high school students from racially and culturally different backgrounds engage in critical discussions about teaching and learning, and what are specific lessons that can emerge? Drawing on Greene's (2000) belief that young learners need to be noticed and consulted in the research process, the author provides a framework that can be used when teaching and researching with urban youth. This framework leads into the chapter's methodological design, which employs a teacher-researcher reflexive lens to investigate how two racially different groups of students engaged in boundary crossings to critique assumptions about teaching, diversity, and urban students. Based on the findings, implications for urban teaching and teacher research in a multicultural society emerge. In this chapter, Kinloch demonstrates how brief engagements between preservice teachers and urban youth can (1) help us to question public assumptions of urban students and their academic abilities and performances and (2) promote critical approaches to working with urban students in ways that do not silence them or ask them to abandon their critical voices.

In chapter 7, Patricia Quijada Cerecer provides a critical examination of how Indigenous youth discuss learning in and out of a rural public high school through their relationships with adults. Using a qualitative research design and Tribal Critical Race Theory, the author explores how participants negotiate their Indigenous cultural scripts, familial responsibilities, and power-status as young people, generating a complex relational learning process that problematizes and challenges how adults think about youth and build relationships with them. The chapter closes with reflections on what teacher education needs to take into account when serving Indigenous youth populations. This information serves as a model of the research that every teacher educator and every teacher education candidate needs to be exposed to in order to be prepared to teach effectively in diverse classrooms.

In chapter 8, "'Something to Brag About': Black Males, Literacy, and Teacher Education," David Kirkland explores the relationship between black language, black literacy, and black male identity. Here, the author addresses two questions: What is literacy to the making of the black male, and what is the black male to the making of literacy? To answer these questions, Kirkland analyzes the spoken and written discourse of a group of young black males, the "cool kids" in an after-school mentoring program, to better understand the relationship among black males, African American language, and literacy. This examination serves dual purposes: First, it seeks to advance a conversation on black male literacy as a critical context for research on preparing teachers for diversity, situating the specific literacy practices of the cool kids within black modes of discourse. Second, it seeks to add to what we know about black males and literacy, providing an empirical portrait of what he sees as black masculine literacies. The lack of understanding concerning these discourses when they arise in classroom settings is a site of great anxiety for many new teachers. To reduce these anxieties, Kirkland's chapter serves as a model of the kind of research that every teacher education candidate must be exposed to in their teacher education programs. The new insights gained from this research, if considered seriously, have the potential to extend the research agenda on race, gender, literacy, and diversity in teacher education in ways that might ultimately expand and offer innovative frameworks that include the sociolinguistic realities that are more familiar to urban youth, particularly young black men.

Chapter 9, by Michelle Trotman Scott and Donna Ford, focuses on the need to prepare teachers to work with students with disabilities and the gifted and talented—a significant part of our schools' diverse student populations. These programs are designed for children whose educational needs are not well met in regular classrooms. The authors note that these programs have been populated with a disproportionate representation of racial and ethnic minority students since their inception. Thus, the authors focus specifically on scholarship related to the topic of special education overrepresentation and gifted education underrepresentation, address factors that contribute inequitable and indefensible referral and placement, and draw implications for teacher practice and preparation. The chapter reviews the research on students with disabilities and the gifted as a part of the body of literature on diversity in education and addresses lingering questions about the causes of the disproportionate referral and placement of students from diverse backgrounds. The chapter concludes with a discussion of the implication of this phenomenon for teacher preparation and recommendations for future research on diversity in teacher education.

In chapter 10, Mandie Uys, Maryna Reyneke, and Kotie Kaiser discuss a collaborative approach to professional development for teachers who are speakers of nondominant languages that taps into perceived barriers to strengthen teaching and learning within a very diverse South African context. A descriptive study of a professional development program serves as a case for considering not only how English may be perceived as a benefit rather than a barrier within this context but also illustrates how in-service training can be used to enable teachers to tap into the strengths that students bring into diverse classrooms. The authors propose a model for sustainable and fluid workshops that can allow for lifelong training of teachers in a dynamic and linguistically complex educational environment. In this chapter, the authors discuss the development of a focused and socially responsible approach for research on diversity in teacher education. This model is useful for considering future work with teachers who are Indigenous language speakers, which can be useful in developing a framework for future research with populations from diverse linguistic backgrounds within a global context.

B. Frameworks, perspectives, and paradigms in research on diversity: Implications for research in teacher education

Thandeka Chapman begins this section with a chapter that focuses on critical race theory as a framework for research on diversity in teacher education. This chapter provides a review of the literature on critical race theory (CRT) in educational research, particularly as it pertains to teachers and teacher education. Her review includes a brief history of CRT in education, a review of CRT applications to K–12 and teacher education classrooms and programs, and an application of CRT to a current research project. Chapman draws on CRT to provide an analysis of past and present institutional processes and policies that continue to produce underprepared teachers for students of color and children living in poverty. Using the tenets of critical race theory, the author explores how current and historical contexts of higher education and teacher education policies limit the reform of teacher education in order to maintain the core assimilationist principles of whiteness and middle-class morality. Chapman proposes that these cherished and embedded limitations are the reason why programs continue to produce teachers who marginalize children of color, particularly poor children of color, in public schools and fail to recruit students of color and nontraditional white students into these programs. The author concludes by turning a critical eye toward issues of praxis and CRT as a framing for social justice research on teaching and learning in racialized classrooms and teacher education and proposes new possibilities and a promising framework for the research on diversity in teacher education that is more productive than prior approaches.

In chapter 12, Brad Olsen focuses on identity as a framework for teacher education research and argues that teacher identity can be situated as a useful framework for researching diversity in teacher education. Olsen engages several research tradi-

tions to put forward *teacher identity* as recent descendant of a theoretical genealogy
with roots in philosophy, socioculturalism, and critical theory. Introducing identity
as a conceptual tool that considers how the self continually develops in practice, the
chapter offers discussions of diversity, teacher identity, and recent teacher identity
studies. Olsen delineates five foundational tenets to explain what teacher identity
is and illuminate its value as a viable methodology for research and a beneficial
pedagogy for teacher education. Related to diversity, its primary usefulness is twofold: teacher identity productively captures the diversity of all teachers, and it offers
a holistic framework for engaging teachers in issues of diversity. Although teacher
identity is a paradigm in progress, this chapter attempts to move it forward as a useful way to think about and study the diversity of teachers, teaching, teacher learning,
and teaching careers in situ.

Chapter 13, authored by Tiffany Lee, proposes the use of culturally responsive
schooling as a framework for research on teaching and teacher education. Here, Lee
focuses on teaching Native youth, teaching about Native peoples and the shifting
paradigms used to reclaim Native ways of living in the educational context. This
chapter begins with a review of the research literature that has been published on
this topic by recognized scholars in the field and situates the work of this chapter
within the existing literature. Lee focuses on rethinking teacher education for indigenous education that involves interrogating the dilemma regarding Native peoples'
lived experiences and influences. The dilemma is twofold: one facet is pedagogical—how to best educate teachers of Native students in schools that largely fail
them. This involves understanding teacher-student relationships that are influenced
by Native students' cultures and that affect classroom practices and expectations
in schools that are largely driven by Western institutional structures and values.
The second facet of this dilemma is curriculum and content—how to best educate
teachers to teach *all* students about Native peoples by incorporating Indigenous
worldviews, knowledge, and contemporary lifestyles without relying on stereotypes
and other historical misperceptions of who Native people have been and who they
are today. In effect, this approach calls for teachers to reenvision their roles and,
in turn, allows Native peoples to reclaim themselves. A common thread in this research has been the resistance to Western cultural assimilation and resistance to the
abandonment of one's Native heritage. Examples from Montana and New Mexico
demonstrate the transformative change efforts by and on behalf of Native peoples'
education and education about Native peoples. Drawing on these cases, Lee offers
three compelling and critical areas for further research. First, in the area of professional development, research is needed on how culturally responsive schooling can
be taught to teachers of Native students given its contextually, politically, culturally,
and linguistically based nature. Second, research is needed on how we can convince
educators that cultural assimilation at the expense of Native students' heritage and
life ways is not the answer for improving educational achievement. Third, research
is needed on how we can engage Native students educationally when Native people
still live in a colonized state and attend schools that represent Western worldviews
and white mainstream ideologies. Building on the common thread that runs
throughout this research—resistance to Western cultural assimilation—serves as a
model of the complex issues that warrant further investigations in the research on
diversity in teacher education.

In chapter 14 Maisha Winn and Joseph Ubiles elaborate on a teacher-researcher collaborative process called "worthy witnessing," which can serve as a model that forms the basis for a responsible methodological approach to research on and in diversity communities. In this chapter the authors, a university researcher-teacher educator and a classroom teacher, discuss their process for collaborative research in urban public high schools. More specifically, the authors use their research together to form the bases for a multiage writing seminar for ninth–twelfth graders as well as their work with preservice and in-service teachers—a process they refer to as "worthy witnessing"—to demonstrate four phases in the collaborative research process that include admission, declaration, revelation, and confidentiality. Ultimately the authors seek to provide a critical lens for teacher researchers and university researchers to engage in responsible research in ethnically diverse schools and classrooms that honor students and teachers.

In chapter 15, Jeffrey Duncan-Andrade ends this section by contributing to a rethinking of teacher education by strategizing an approach that develops educators who are better equipped to respond to their "socially toxic environments" (Garbarino, 1995) that emerge from racism, poverty, and other forms of oppression. The chapter begins by examining recent research breakthroughs in fields that are rarely discussed in teacher education: public health, medicine, community psychology, and social epidemiology. These fields have increasingly turned their attention to identifying and understanding the social indicators of health and well-being—for education, this is the idea that "place," the conditions in which our students live, must be understood for teachers to be effective (Adelman, 2008). This research reveals clearly identifiable social toxins that many diverse young people face in the broader society, and these are the "principal facts" for teacher education to confront. Drawing from these analyses, this paper presents a pedagogical framework for educators to respond, treating the classroom as a microecosystem committed to "radical healing" (Ginwright, 2009) and "critical hope" (Duncan-Andrade, 2009). The chapter concludes with a discussion of pragmatic steps to be taken by teacher education to develop teachers that can meet the challenge of delivering this type of pedagogy. This analysis serves as a model of the research that every teacher educator and every teacher education candidate needs to be exposed to in order to teach effectively in diverse communities and classrooms.

Part III

Part III provides insights on future trends and directions for the research on diversity in teacher education and provides an agenda for the work that still needs to be done. This section focuses on *what works* and the nature of the research that is needed in order for our profession to address the persisting issues that currently perplex our field. These chapters challenge the profession from different perspectives with the goal of providing a focused and socially conscious research agenda for the twenty-first century.

This section begins with chapter 16, written by Kenneth Zeichner. In this chapter, Zeichner reflects back on the work he has completed over the past few years, on what we have learned about the state of research on teacher education, and on research on diversity in teacher education in particular. This chapter focuses specifically on two aspects of the research on multicultural teacher education: the need to connect individual studies to one another in programs of research within communities of researchers in ways that enable the accumulation of knowledge over time and the need to design research in ways that reflect the complexity of what is being studied. The chapter concludes with a discussion on what we still need to know in order to address the challenges that we must face as a profession.

Chapter 17, written by Marilyn Cochran-Smith and Kim Fries, acknowledges the fact that although a consensus has emerged in the United States and elsewhere that teacher quality matters, there is no such consensus about what "teacher quality" actually means, how exactly it matters, how it should be assessed, whether and how it depends on teacher preparation, and how it is enhanced or diminished by other factors, such as teachers' characteristics, licensing and credentialing regulations, the cultures and conditions of schools, and the broader social, political, and socioeconomic contexts of schools and society. Given this lack of consensus, the authors go on to examine the controversies surrounding teacher quality and teacher preparation with a particular focus on diversity, based on critical analysis of key recent documents, including policies or proposed policies, position papers, critiques, commission reports, research reviews, testimony, and other public discourse. The authors analyze the major approaches being proposed and/or implemented regarding teacher quality and preparation, the theories of action behind these, and the larger political agendas and educational theories, traditions, and ideologies to which the reforms are attached. They also assess the implications of these for diversity and for reducing or maintaining educational inequities. Cochran-Smith and Fries argue that underlying differences and similarities in the policy discourse lead to sharply different conclusions in the policy arena that have serious implications for diminishing or maintaining educational inequities in the nation. Drawing on a larger analysis of policy documents and other materials produced between 2005 and 2009, this chapter identifies and unpacks five major discourses that are currently shaping policy and policy controversies in the United States regarding teacher quality and teacher preparation. The authors suggest that differences in these five discourses are not simply the result of different conclusions about how best to reach certain goals, but rather that these discourses are based on different ideas about what the goals should be in the first place. Embedded in these different constructions of "the problem" of teacher quality and teacher education are different values and assumptions about diversity and diverse groups. The authors suggest that different outcomes and consequences emerge from particular constructions of the problems to be solved and the larger agendas to which they are attached.

In 2000, Sonia Nieto wrote an article for the *Journal of Teacher Education* titled "Placing Equity Front and Center: Some Thoughts on Transforming Teacher Education for a New Century." In it, she suggested how teacher education programs could "place equity front and center" by reconceptualizing teacher preparation curricula and pedagogy, changing the nature of faculty work and rewards, and promoting collaborative relationships among faculty. In chapter 18 of this volume, Nieto and her coauthor, Kathy McDonough, review some recent efforts to do these things and discuss whether recent changes have been sufficient to prepare preservice teachers to work in diverse settings. Within the context of this discussion, Nieto and McDonough focus on one of the most fundamental challenges facing the profession—the field's inability to resolve persistent and lingering problems related to preparing teachers for diverse classrooms. These authors question whether the profession has the heart to put diversity where it actually belongs in our efforts to prepare teachers for twenty-first-century classrooms. In this chapter, Nieto and McDonough challenge the profession to reconceptualize teacher preparation curricula and pedagogy, to alter the kinds of field placements in which students are placed, and to change the nature of faculty work and rewards to prioritize collaborative relationships. The authors revisit Nieto's earlier thoughts on transforming teacher education for a new century and discuss whether such changes were sufficient to prepare preservice teachers to work in diverse settings today. Given the current sociopolitical context, they also suggest some future directions for teacher education programs in the coming years.

In chapter 19 Gloria Ladson-Billings notes that teacher education institutions, educators, and researchers must continue to examine their programs and research agendas to ensure that today's and tomorrow's teachers can meet the complex challenges of teaching in today's diverse contexts. Since teacher educators cannot teach what they do not know, they must themselves develop the skills and knowledge that will be required of their students. Ladson-Billings further notes that as we create a research agenda for the twenty-first century the field must explore questions such as the following: What are good models for cooperation between school districts and colleges or universities in providing field experiences for preservice and beginning teachers? What is a good balance of subject matter expertise methods classes and practicum experiences in preparing new teachers? What should be the distribution of these elements throughout the teacher education program? What are appropriate goals, modes of delivery, and instructional methods for preparing preservice teachers for diversity, equity, and teaching for social justice in their classrooms? What approaches to continuing education and graduate study will keep in-service and preservice teachers engaged in lifelong learning throughout their professional lives? As she considers these issues, Ladson-Billings presents a research agenda for diversity in teacher education.

The final chapter of this volume is authored by Arnetha Ball and Cynthia Tyson and focuses on preparing teachers for diversity in twenty-first-century classrooms within a global context. The fact that today's educational institutions face similar challenges globally in their efforts to prepare teachers to teach diverse and underserved populations underscores the need for inquiry into the best methodologies, techniques, conditions, and materials for bringing equity and social justice to student populations in classrooms across the globe. The chapter further emphasizes the fact that we are citizens of a global community, which requires that we reevaluate the notion of "scholar-activist"—scholars who are truly activists and who are about the business of changing the global patterns of persistent underachievement while seeking to further develop educational processes, practices, and policy making in order to address the pressing challenges facing our field. This will require the recasting of issues of research on diversity within a global context where people of color are the majority population. A realization that people of color are the majority population can serve to increase motivation and a sense of urgency concerning research on the role of generativity in the development of research on preparing teachers for culturally and linguistically complex classrooms. This realization can also motivate a recasting of the negative image of scholar-activist into a more positive light. An important ideological orientation that researchers on diversity in teacher education must embrace is a global and comparative perspective. Because of historical and political factors of oppression, unequal access to education, and increased migration from rural to urban areas, diverse populations are dispersed across the globe. The need to prepare more researchers from diverse communities around the globe is a growing phenomenon because these researchers will bring with them diverse perspectives that grow out of their circumstances and experiences. These perspectives will allow a new generation of scholars and researchers to look at global issues with multiple local visions. The authors conclude by calling for scholar activists that do the following:

- Cultivate a network of global scholars, researchers, and practitioners interested in working within cross-national collaborations on the study of diversity in teacher education,
- Challenge the field to identify generativity in teacher thinking and teacher practices as a primary goal for the profession to work toward,
- Advance the quantity and quality of research in the field by strengthening global collaborations on setting a mutually beneficial research agenda and by broadening the methodological approaches used in the field,
- Identify "innovative research activities" that can advance the research on diversity in teaching and teacher education.

CONCLUSION

This volume seeks to make a groundbreaking contribution to the field—taking discussions on diversity in education and diversity in teacher education to the next level. By explicitly bringing the two components together, the contributing authors raise ontological, epistemological, and ethical questions necessary for the exchange of new ideas to take place concerning the nature, purposes, and directions for research on diversity in teacher education. Together, these chapters provide a necessary foundation that new scholars can build on as each contributing author brings attention to research that can support teachers who are preparing to teach students in poor, marginalized, and underachieving schools. These chapters invite multiple readings for scholars to explore new terrains and for scholars who are interested in understanding and conducting new research on diversity in teacher education. It is hoped that this work can serve to accelerate educational parity across sociocultural and sociopolitical barriers and chasms and that the legacy of academic failure that plagues so many diverse students can be overcome through the expanded understanding that this volume will bring.

REFERENCES

Adelman, L. (executive producer). (2008). *Unnatural causes: Is inequality making us sick?* [Television Series]. San Francisco, CA: California News Reel.

DuBois, W. E. B. (1899). *Philadelphia negro.* Philadelphia: University of Pennsylvania.

Duncan-Andrade, J. M. R. (2009). Note to educators: Hope required when growing roses in concrete. *Harvard Educational Review, 79(2)*, 181–94.

Freeman, D. (2006). Teaching and learning in the 'age of reform': The problem of the verb. In Gieve, S., & Miller, I. (Eds.), *Understanding the language classroom*. Basingstoke, UK: Palgrave Macmillan.

Garbarino, J. (1995). *Raising children in a socially toxic environment*. San Francisco: Jossey-Bass Publishers.

Ginwright, S. A. (2009). *Black youth rising: Activism and radial healing in urban America*. New York: Teachers College Press

Giroux, Henry A., & McLaren, P. (1994). *Between borders: Pedagogy and the politics of cultural studies*. New York: Routledge.

Greene, M. (2000). *Releasing the imagination: Essays on education, the arts, and social change*. San Francisco: Jossey-Bass.

Haymes, S. N. (1995). *Race, culture, and the city: A pedagogy for Black urban struggle*. New York: State University of New York Press.

Hollins, E., & Torres-Guzman, M. W. (2005), Research on preparing teachers for diverse populations. In Chochran-Smith, M., & Zeichedern, K. (Eds.) *Studying teacher education: The report of the AERA Panel on Research and Teacher Education*. Hahwayh, NJ: Lawrence Erlbaum Associates.

hooks, bell. (1990). *Yearning: Race, gender, and cultural politics*. Boston, MA: South End Press.

Makoni, S., Smitherman, G., Ball, A., & Spears, A. K. (Eds.) (2003). *Black linguistics: Language, society and politics in Africa and Americas*. New York: Routledge.

I

HISTORICAL CONTEXT AND PERSISTING CHALLENGES

Preparing Teachers for Diversity

> Where have we been in the research on diversity in teacher education, and what are the pressing challenges that must be addressed in order for the field to move forward?

Part I of this volume provides insights on the historical context surrounding the research that has been conducted on the topic of diversity in teacher education and illuminates persisting challenges that continue to face the field. In other words, it provides the reader with a context concerning "where we've been" in the research on diversity in teacher education.

Authors in this section, including Grant and Gibson and colleagues, Pang and Park, Sleeter and Milner, and Hollins, review the historiography of teacher education and diversity in teacher education from the perspective of the research conducted by sixteen committed scholars in the field, draw on a historical cross-disciplinary approach to challenge teacher education to create a new interdisciplinary paradigm for multicultural teacher education, examine research on teacher education's efforts to diversify the teaching population and provide five issues that should be addressed in the training of educators, and provide a historical analysis and exploration of the process of identity formation for those entering the teacher profession as a proxy for investigating the influence of culture and social ideology on learning to teach. These eminent scholars provide a review of and inquiry into issues of diversity in teacher education from their respective areas of specialization and, in doing so, provide background knowledge and historical contextualization related to what is presently known about diversity in teacher education and the remaining challenges to the profession.

1

Diversity and Teacher Education

A Historical Perspective on Research and Policy

Carl Grant and Melissa Gibson *

Questions about diversity and education—including teacher education—are not new questions. In fact, in the United States, the intersection of diversity and education has been a source of inquiry for decades. As successive waves of migrants have entered schools, as groups previously excluded have gained educational access, as classrooms increasingly reflect the heterogeneity of American society, and as the world grows interdependent and globalized, questions of whether and how American education—including teacher education—should address student diversity have been at the forefront.

What it means to address diversity varies greatly, but several key questions endure. For example, Woodson (1933/2008) wondered whether white teachers could successfully teach black students. Although he concluded that "there is no particular body of facts that Negro teachers can impart to children of their own race that may not be just as easily presented by persons of another race if only they have the same attitude as a Negro teacher" (p. 28), this remains hotly debated. Who should teach particular groups of students, and are disposition and ideology—or "the same attitude"—enough? The flipside of this is the teaching of white students by black teachers. Jackson Coppin (Sigerman, 2000) is cited as perhaps the first African American to teach both black and white students: "I felt I had the honor of the whole African race upon my shoulders. I felt that should I fail, it would be ascribed to the fact that I was colored" (p. 264). Who should teach different groups of children, and what are the implications of these demographic (mis)matches?

Phillips (1940) raises another enduring question, arguing that black teachers need additional qualifications to teach black students: "keen insight into the current social, economic, and political issues in relation to the problems peculiar to minority groups, vocational opportunities for one's group, and a willingness to assume educational leadership" (p. 485), raising the question, is content knowledge alone enough qualification?

In *A Talk to Teachers*, James Baldwin (1963) raises a third enduring question in the teacher education discourse. Baldwin tells teachers that, as educated people, they have the ability to create social change in their classrooms. He argues that teachers should teach the truth, not sugarcoated history, and should acknowledge that America has often perpetuated segregation and discrimination in order to keep marginalized peoples, such as African Americans, in their place. Here, Baldwin raises essential questions about what and how students should be taught as well as the role of the school in social reconstruction.

These questions, while historically situated, are debated today. Of course, they assume that schools and teachers *should* address student diversity. But this very assumption is also interrogated. What, precisely, do we mean by diversity? And what is the role of diversity in American society? These questions are closely associated, for example, with the turn of the nineteenth century, when unprecedented waves of immigrants were seen as a threat to the American way of life (see Banks, 2005; Jacobson, 1998; Montalto, 1982; Olneck, 2004). Debates around who should be considered "diverse" and whether to accommodate that diversity in schools continue today, whether in disagreements about the nature of a multicultural curriculum (see Buras, 2008; Sleeter, 1995) or in describing diversity as evidence of "cultural deprivation" (e.g., Clark & Plotkin, 1972; Lewis, 1966).

Obviously, these questions about diversity, education, and teaching are not new. Despite the youth of the field, its questions are enduring: What do we mean by diversity? What is and what should be the role of diversity in American society and schools? Why does diversity matter? Who should teach diverse groups of children? What should diverse groups of children learn and how should they be taught? What does a teacher need to know, believe, and do in order to teach diverse groups of children? These questions remain at the heart of research, public policy, and debate. Their endurance is both reassuring and worrying—Why are we still asking the same questions? Has anything at all changed?

While there have been many literature reviews of research on diversity and teacher education (e.g., Cochran-Smith, Davis, & Fries, 2004; Grant & Secada, 1990; Hollins & Guzman, 2005; Ladson-Billings, 1995b; Sleeter, 2001), this chapter takes a somewhat different approach. This prior work has been essential for setting a course for the field—in drawing attention to gaps in the research, in describing the central areas of inquiry, and in directing future research agendas. We will not attempt to rehash these findings—although we will, undoubtedly, repeat some of them. Instead, we don the hats of historians: "History has the special obligation to recall, reassess, and re-interpret the past, bringing it to bear on the present and translating it into a form each new generation can use" (Nye, 1960, p. 2). Historians study the past to understand how institutions, programs, and societies have evolved to their present state and to understand how contemporary conditions have come to be defined and perceived as they are. Our aim is not to tell a comprehensive history of diversity and teacher education but to gauge where we are today, how we have come to be here, and where we need to go in the future. To do that, we begin by surveying research on teacher education and diversity conducted by committed scholars: How do those who have made the field define, describe, and problematize it? Given concern for diversity in public discourse, we also look to public policy as a way of understanding the role of diversity in teacher preparation: How is attention to and consideration of diversity in teacher education framed by policy makers, and how does this discourse compare to scholarship? Where public policy and teacher education research meet is, we believe, where we can gain future direction and also gain understanding about why we have not gone there yet.

In taking this tack, we also don the hats of detectives. We approach the field like a crime scene, where clues might lead to the solution of the crime. Good observation and analysis can lead detectives to an understanding of the crime, the perpetrator, and the victim. And although no pun is intended, it's clear that at this crime scene, "diversity" has been the victim. In our historical detective work, we hope, as Nye (1960) describes, to bring the past to bear in such a way that it is of use to future generations. Like solving any complicated crime, however, this historical detective work follows a long and murky path.

WHERE HAVE WE BEEN? SCHOLARLY RESEARCH ON DIVERSITY AND TEACHER EDUCATION

To understand where the field has been and to *define* the field, we have looked to scholars whose primary chain of inquiry has focused on diversity and teacher education. Each of the researchers included in our review is a committed scholar in the field. This is not to discredit the work of other scholars, nor is it to ignore research on diversity issues in other areas of education. Rather, because we are interested in understanding broadly where we have been as a field and because we have been charged with telling the history of the field, we have focused our review on those who have historically *made* the field.

We are, in essence, conducting a conceptual literature review. In defining our research this way, we borrow from Mary Kennedy's (2007) typology. Unlike a systematic literature review, which focuses on an empirical question and gathers all available literature, a conceptual review is concerned with "gaining new insights into an issue" (p. 139). This kind of review may be theoretical, historical, methodological, or integrative in nature. Conceptual reviews, rather than asking what we know empirically, set out to ask why we don't know more. Our conceptual review is historical in nature: Over time, how has diversity and teacher education, as an area of inquiry, constituted itself through *research*? In looking across this research, what new directions are scholars pointed in?

To answer these questions, we have looked at the research of sixteen scholars of diversity and teacher education[1]—a total of 152 articles, chapters, reports, and books. We focused our review on *research* rather than on theoretical, editorial, or conceptual pieces—although these pieces are drawn on when appropriate. When surveying *research* on diversity *and* teacher education by senior scholars, what composite is painted of the field?

The State of the Field: Thirty Years of Research

Grant and Secada (1990) noted twenty years ago the dearth of empirical research on diversity and teacher education. While attention to diversity has ballooned since then (an ERIC search today using the descriptors "diversity" and "teacher education" returns 960 records!), when looking at the research reviewed here, one realizes that Grant and Secada's critique still holds weight. A full sixty-nine of the research pieces included here—almost half—are literature reviews, or synthetic research. What these syntheses repeatedly note—and as borne out by our own review of the research on diversity and teacher education—is that the field lacks a strong empirical base for its claims, findings, and recommendations about multicultural teacher education (see Grant, Elsbree, & Fondrie, 2004; Grant & Tate, 1995; Hollins & Guzman, 2005; Ladson-Billings, 1994b, 1995b, 1999a, 1999b; Sleeter, 1985, 2001).

Of the eighty-three pieces that are not literature reviews, only three include longitudinal or large-scale data (Ball, 2006; Pagano, Weiner, Obi, & Swearingen, 1997; Villegas & Clewell, 1998a) and only two employ primarily quantitative analysis (Darling-Hammond, 2000b; Gollnick, 1978). Few studies at all deal with assessing program effectiveness or looking at the outcomes of teacher education in K–12 classrooms. There is limited empirical research on teacher education and diversity. The majority of research, after literature reviews, is practitioner inquiry or self-study (n = 23), program description (n = 20), case study (n = 14), and survey/self-reporting (n = 15), with these genres frequently overlapping: for example, eight of the program and case studies are also practitioner inquiry (Cochran-Smith, 2003a, 2004; Cochran-Smith & Lytle, 1993; Irvine, 2002, 2003; Ladson-Billings, 2001; Sleeter et al., 2005; Villegas, 2007). While this research enriches the field and offers a strong anecdotal base for recommendations, practices, and further research, it does not necessarily constitute an empirical base.

What is striking about this body of research is not its prioritizing of self-reflective and narrative inquiry over empirical research. After all, qualitative research is primarily "concerned with moral discourse [that] asks . . . the social sciences and the humanities [to] become sites for critical conversations about democracy, race, gender, class, nation-states, globalization, freedom, and community" (Denzin & Lincoln, 2007, pp. 3–4). Indeed, the preferred research methods of teacher educators—from case study and practitioner inquiry to narrative inquiry and literature reviews—afford a critical and reflexive means of interrogating the field. These methods are a good fit for the type of questions asked.

What *is* surprising, however, is the exclusion of empirical approaches. Certainly, empiricism has been used as a hegemonic tool to "deflect attention away from deeper issues of value and purpose" and to "make radical critiques much more difficult to mount" (Smith & Hodkinson, 2007, p. 431). That said, empirical research plays an important role in speaking back to power because empiricism is quote often the tool of the powerful: "One makes one's way through universes in which more and more technical, rational justifications will be necessary in order to dominate and in which the dominated can and must also use reason to defend themselves against domination" (Smith & Hodkinson, 2007, p. 431).

And therein lies the tension of research on diversity and teacher education. On the one hand, it sets out to challenge dominant ideologies, and it must employ methods—such as practitioner inquiry and critical synthesis—that allow it to do so by bringing out the nuanced and perspectival meanings of students and educators. On the other hand, such research is not often generalizable—and policy makers look to generalizable research to inform decisions. While self-study can be a transformative experience for educators, it does not often impact policy—and without a clear line of inquiry within and the continual building off other self-studies, it will continue to fail to do so (Zeichner, 2007).

Certainly, teacher education is a young field. The earliest articles reviewed here date from the 1970s and early 1980s (e.g., Gollnick, 1978; Grant, 1981; Grant & Sleeter, 1985; Hollins, 1982; Sleeter, 1985; Zeichner & Grant, 1981), with many other scholars not writing about teacher education and diversity until the late 1980s and early 1990s (e.g., Cochran-Smith & Lytle, 1993; Haberman, 1988a, 1988b; Haberman & Post, 1990; Irvine, 1988, 1989, 1990; King, 1991; King & Ladson-Billings, 1990; Ladson-Billings, 1991; Villegas, 1988; Villegas et al., 1993). What's more, research on diversity and teacher education is an area that has rarely been funded for large-scale research (Grant & Millar, 1992).

While the youth of the field and the lack of funding certainly *explain* the state of research, they do not excuse it. Repeatedly, scholars call for more research examining the effectiveness of teacher education programs and connecting university-based teacher education to K–12 classrooms (e.g., Cochran-Smith, 2003b; Cochran-Smith & Fries, 2005; Cochran-Smith, Davis, & Fries, 2004; Gollnick, 1978; Gollnick, Osayende, & Levy, 1980; Grant & Agosto, 2006; Grant & Tate, 1995; Hollins, 1993; Hollins & Guzman, 2005; Ladson-Billings, 1998; Sleeter, 2001; Zeichner et al., 1998). Yet these forays are limited. Of the 152 research pieces, 16 heed this call (Ball, 2006; Cochran-Smith, Barnatt, Friedman, & Pine, 2009; Cochran-Smith et al., in press, 2009; Pagano, Obi, Weiner, & Swearingen, 1995, 1997; Sleeter, 1989, 1992a, 1992b, 1992c, 2004; Valli, 1995, 1996a, 1996b; Villegas & Lucas, 2002; Weiner, 1993a). Even program research is often an analysis of one's *own* program—with the work of Gollnick, Villegas, and Zeichner as notable exceptions (Gollnick, 1978; Gollnick et al., 1979; Gollnick, Osayenda, & Levy, 1980; Melnick & Zeichner, 1997, 1998; Tabachnik & Zeichner, 1993; Villegas & Clewell, 1998a; Villegas et al., 1993; Zeichner, 1995; Zeichner & Melnick, 1996a, 1996b). Self-study and program description are valuable—but they alone do not constitute an empirical base. Sleeter (2001) even argues that they lead to a repetitive knowledge base that fails to offer new findings.

Defining Our Terms: What Do We Mean When We Say Diversity?

What is meant by diversity and teacher education? In this body of research, diversity is largely synonymous with race, ethnicity, and/or culture, with these terms frequently overlapping or conflated (n = 103). Given that attention to diversity and multiculturalism in education stems, in part, from racial and ethnic struggles for justice (see J. Banks, 2004)—and given the public attention to the achievement gap between different races and ethnicities—this conception of diversity is logical. It also makes sense given the oft-cited "demographic imperative" facing teacher education: K–12 classrooms are increasingly heterogeneous, with growing numbers of students of color in U.S. schools, while those entering teaching are overwhelmingly white women (see Banks et al., 2005; Cochran-Smith, 2004; Nieto, 2005; Sleeter, 2001; Valli, 1996a; Villegas & Davis, 2008; Weiner, 2002). How can teacher education prepare these candidates for the children who will be in their classrooms? And how can it do so in meaningful ways that embody a specific commitment to diversity *beyond* the platitudes of educating "all children"?

It is worth noting the frequent conflation of race-ethnicity-culture in the research as well as the infrequent discussion of what distinguishes them or how they impact learning. In this, the field's conception of diversity is open to critique: Hollins (2008) challenges such an approach with her theorization of "deep" cultural knowledge, in which she argues that we need to move beyond a static or simplified understanding of culture as entirely social or political to an understanding that sees culture abstractly and flexibly as the nexus of affect, behavior, and intellect. Scholars are not always explicit about "deep culture" and how it impacts learning. Similarly, King (1997, 2004) argues that, too often, the white or Euro-American experience is not recognized as a cultural experience; teacher education must help preservice teachers relearn their understanding of race, ethnicity, and culture through a "pedagogy of transmutation," or a culture-centered pedagogy that pushes back against hegemonic miseducation. To engage in this counterhegemonic education, however, requires that teacher educators themselves deeply understand what constitutes culture, how it is distinguished from race, and how it impacts and is integral to learning (Hollins, 1990, 1999; King, 1994, 2004). More important, teacher educators must understand the dehumanizing effects of a singular focus on race and ethnicity—particularly the black/white binary—on *all* students and to understand the ways in which attention to 'diversity' can obscure the workings of oppression and hegemony (King, 2004, 2005).

While most of the research reviewed defines diversity in terms of race, culture, and ethnicity, there is frequent mention of the need to prepare teachers to be successful with "all students" (a problematic phrase that we will return to later in this chapter). Many scholars attend to "all children" by naming socioeconomic stratification (n = 51) and linguistic diversity (n = 37) along with race-culture-ethnicity (n = 98) as diversity, but there is little research examining what it takes to prepare excellent teachers for *all* students, truly—for diversity that encompasses gender (n = 22), religion (n = 6), (dis)ability (n = 8), sexuality (n = 1), and ideology (n = 1). While literature undoubtedly exists, it is not necessarily at the heart of research on diversity and teacher education.

Orientations to Diversity: Why Does Diversity in Schools Matter?

There are several orientations from which teacher educators answer, "Why does diversity matter?" One approach looks at diversity in relation to urban schooling (e.g., Clewell & Villegas, 1999; Haberman, 1996; Nieto, 2003b; Valli, 2000; Weiner, 1993b, 2002). The nexus of racial discrimination, the effects of living in ghettoized poverty, the lack of adequate material support for schools, the centralized and bureaucratic nature of large urban districts, the prevalence of "street culture" (Haberman & Post, 1998), and the high turnover rate of urban teachers—coupled with overwhelmingly white, upper- and middle-class, suburban and rural female teachers, who live in different "existential worlds" than their potential students (Gay, 1993)—warrants changes in teacher education. Teaching marginalized student populations requires different dispositions, beliefs, training, and practices than traditionally conveyed in teacher education—including the need to address institutional factors such as bureaucracy, time demands, class sizes, and emotional strain that too often send teachers fleeing (Haberman, 1995b; Irvine, 1990; Villegas & Davis, 2008; Villegas & Lucas, 2004; Weiner, 2000). Traditional teacher education is failing urban students, as evinced by the high turnover rate of urban teachers, the poor achievement of urban students, and the lack of qualified teachers (Haberman, 1994, 1995a): "Something other than conventional preparation is necessary" (Ladson-Billings, 1994b, p. 138).

A second approach looks at training teachers to be successful educators of specific student populations, such as African American students (e.g., Ball & Lardner, 1997; Hollins et al., 2004; Hollins & Spencer, 1991; Irvine, 1990; King, 1991; Ladson-Billings, 1994b) or English Language Learners (e.g., Grant, 1982; Lucas, Villegas, & Freedson-Gonzalez, 2008). Teachers must understand how culture impacts learning, and they must also understand the way that this culture is traditionally assimilated or ignored in schooling. To be a successful teacher of African American students, for example, requires that teachers not only value African American culture but they must also understand its role in learning, particularly as an asset to students' achievement, identity, and sense of self (see King, 1994). Teacher education, then, must help preservice teachers gain cultural knowledge; it must help them connect that culture to their classroom practice and it must challenge teachers to reject deficit views. It must also help teachers differentiate among race, ethnicity, and culture and to see how social hierarchies and constructions of race dehumanize (King, 2004, 2005).

A third approach attends to diversity from a multicultural, social justice orientation. Schools are envisioned as pluralistic and democratic places that honor and accommodate diversity; they are also seen as vital for promoting social justice, for furthering social reconstruction, and for cultivating pluralistic dispositions and commitments among future citizens (e.g., Cochran-Smith, Davis, & Fries, 2004; Grant & Agosto, 2008; Nieto, 1999; Sleeter & Grant, 1999; Valli, Cooper, & Frankes, 1997). Teacher education, in turn, helps to instill multicultural perspectives, values, and practices; it encourages preservice teachers to develop a multicultural knowledge base; it cultivates a commitment to social justice; and it encourages teachers to question the purposes of education and who education serves and to enact an alternative vision in their classrooms and schools. A multicultural approach asks teachers and teacher educators to move beyond simply naming the "demographic imperative" and demographic differences in achievement, retention, and engagement. Instead, a multicultural approach begins by asking what the purposes of schooling are in a pluralistic society and to work backward to articulate what and how students should be taught and what corresponding skills, dispositions, and knowledge teachers need. In many ways, a multicultural, social justice orientation subsumes other approaches to diversity.

Diversity and the Teaching Force: Who Will Teach Diverse Groups of Children?

When teacher educators talk about diversity, they are generally referring to the diversity of K–12 students—and not necessarily the diversity of educators. Given the aforementioned "demographic imperative," or the cultural and demographic mismatch between white, middle-class teachers and students of color from a variety of socioeconomic backgrounds, this emphasis on student diversity is logical. Teacher education *must* be concerned with better preparing these teachers for the students they will teach and for helping them to bridge their different "existential worlds" (Gay, 1993).

However, several scholars question this emphasis (e.g., Haberman, 1991a, 1991b; Ladson-Billings, 1999a; Zeichner, 1995). Can teacher education really shape beliefs and dispositions, and can coursework really instill the attitudes and perspectives that enable teachers from dominant backgrounds to successfully teach all students? There is evidence to suggest it cannot. For example, Haberman (1991a; Haberman & Post, 1992) found that coursework intending to educate about culture, inequality, and diversity often ended up reinforcing rather than challenging stereotypes. Likewise, Weiner (1993a, 1993b) found that teachers' class, race, and gender indelibly shaped their perspectives, beliefs, and practices. As Gay (1993) points out and as others have echoed (e.g., Haberman & Post, 1998; Villegas & Clewell, 1998b), demographic differences often result in different lived experiences, ideologies, and cultural norms—demographic differences often indicate that individuals live in different "existential worlds." Can these differences be bridged?

This question is at the heart of research on diversity and teacher education: *How* do we bridge these differences? There is, however, a strong subset of teacher education research arguing that the recruitment and retention of teachers who share experiences, perspectives, backgrounds, and ideologies with diverse groups of students are just as important as trying to bridge cultural differences (e.g., Haberman, 1988a; Hollins, 1990; Irvine, 1988, 2002; Irvine & Fraser, 1998; Villegas & Clewell, 1998a, 1998b; Villegas & Davis, 2008; Villegas et al., 1993; Villegas & Lucas, 2004; Weiner, 1993b, 2002).

For example, Haberman (1993, 1995b, 1996; Haberman & Post, 1998) argues that the best predictor of success in urban schools is not teacher preparation; rather, it is teachers' life experiences, their attitudes and dispositions toward inequality and difference, and their reasons for teaching. In a thumbnail sketch of successful urban teachers, Haberman and Post (1998) found these teachers were generally over thirty years of age and not white, had lived in poverty at some point in their lives, had experienced living "normally" in the midst of violence, had extensive experience with children, were themselves urban residents, and had firsthand knowledge of social injustice. These characteristics—including a predisposition to a multicultural curriculum—were not taught. They were, however, characteristics that could be selected for, leading Haberman and Post (1998) to argue that "selection is more important than training" (p. 102). Similarly, Villegas (Villegas & Clewell, 1998a, 1998b; Villegas & Lucas, 2004) has argued that—while a teacher's race and ethnicity do not guarantee success and while *all* teachers can be better prepared for diverse classrooms—the cultural and experiential match between teacher and student can lead to increased success. Villegas (2007) also notes that the commitments and dispositions such programs try to instill are, in part, determined by the teacher candidate's preexisting beliefs and life experiences.

Research on the pedagogy of African American teachers supports this view. From the well-known practice of Marva Collins (Hollins, 1982) to the African American teachers researched by Irvine (2003), it is clear that African American teachers and other teachers of color often enact a culturally specific pedagogy, a pedagogy of cultural translation (Irvine, 1989) and a pedagogy of caring, other mothering, believing, demanding, and disciplining (Irvine & Hill, 1990). These teachers of color and their pedagogies have often been silenced in teacher education research (Irvine & Hill, 1990)—and yet their culturally specific practices embody the ways that identity indelibly shapes teaching and learning. Indeed, Irvine (2002) argues that teachers' understanding of their roles and of the purposes of education are based on unique cultural and historical perspectives.

To this end, several scholars advocate diversifying the teaching force by recruiting more teachers of color and by making the beliefs, ideologies, attitudes, and dispositions of teacher candidates part of the screening and selection process for teacher education programs (Haberman, 1988a, 1988b, 1991b; Haberman & Post, 1998; Irvine, 1988; Ladson-Billings, 2000; Sleeter, 1992a, 2001; Sleeter et al., 2005; Zeichner, 1995; Zeichner & Hoeft, 1996; Zeichner et al., 1998). In fact, traditional screening and selection factors, such as grades and standardized test scores, seem to have little correlation to a teacher's eventual success in diverse and/or urban classrooms (Haberman, 1988b; Sleeter, 2001; Villegas et al., 1993). More indicative is a candidate's proven commitments to a diverse student population. Villegas and Clewell (1998a, 1998b) advocate tapping the paraprofessional pool as a more reliable and diverse source of teachers than the typical undergraduate population. Rethinking who is allowed to become a teacher may be just as important as how we train teachers. Valli (1995), however, challenges this view. While she acknowledges the need for greater diversity, she also argues that emphasizing recruitment alone can abdicate teacher educators of their responsibility to better educate the teacher candidates in front of them and "that the quest for the *ideal* candidates will function as an excuse for those of us responsible for teacher education" (Valli, 1995, p. 128).

Visions of K–12 Schooling: How Should Diverse Groups of Children Be Taught?

Sleeter (2001) argues that, in order to improve multicultural teacher education, we need to start with an end result in mind: What is successful, meaningful, equitable, and just education for all students, and what does teaching look like in the context of this vision? Several teacher educators have articulated just such a vision (e.g., Cochran-Smith, 2008; Haberman, 1991b; Irvine, 1990; King, 1994, 2004; Ladson-Billings, 1994a; Lucas, Villegas, & Freedson-Gonzalez, 2008; Nieto & Bode, 2008; Sleeter & Grant, 1999; Valli, 1996a, 1996b; Villegas & Lucas, 2002). However, these visions of culturally relevant, multicultural, equitable, and socially just education are not always explicitly woven into research on teacher education. In fact, most of the 152 pieces reviewed are quite disconnected from K–12 classrooms and learning: Only ten offered a vision for teacher education based on an explicit vision of K–12 schooling (Cochran-Smith et al., 2009b; Haberman, 1995a; Irvine, 1990; King, 1994, 2004; Lucas, Villegas, & Freedson-Gonzalez, 2008; Nieto & Bode, 2008; Valli, 1996a, 1996b; Villegas & Lucas, 2002); only 16 explicitly connect to K–12 students' learning (Cochran-Smith, Barnatt, Friedman, & Pine, 2009; Cochran-Smith et al., 2009b; Darling-Hammond, 1997; Grant, Elsbree, & Fondrie, 2004; Grant & Tate, 1995; Haberman, 1993; Horowitz, Darling-Hammond, & Bransford, 2005; Irvine, 1990; Ladson-Billings, 1998, 1999a; Lucas, Villegas, & Freedson-Gonzalez, 2008; Villegas & Davis, 2008; Villegas & Lucas, 2002; Weiner, 2000, 2002, 2003); and only 23 conducted research primarily in K–12 classrooms and then linked this classroom-based research to teacher education (e.g., Ball, 2006; Ball & Lardner, 1997; Cochran-Smith, Barnatt, Friedman, & Pine, 2009; Cochran-Smith et al., 2009b; Darling-Hammond, 2004a, 2004b; Haberman, 1993, 1995; Haberman & Post, 1990; Hollins, 2006; Hollins et al., 2004; Nieto, 2003a, 2003b, 2005b, 2009; Sleeter, 1989, 1992a, 1992b, 1992c; Valli, 1995, 1996a, 1996b; Villegas & Lucas, 2002).

While it is important to note the limited connections between this vision of K–12 schooling and research on diversity and teacher education, it must also be noted that there is a strong vision of what a just and equitable multicultural education for all students is. First and foremost, it considers the multiple purposes of education— and it rejects the narrowing of education solely to employment preparation. Instead, it looks to the role of schooling in a democratic society, in helping students find personal happiness and fulfillment, in cultivating curiosity and a love of learning, and in engendering social critique (e.g., Grant, 1991; Grant & Agosto, 2008; Grant & Tate, 1995; Haberman, 1995b; King, 1994; Ladson-Billings, 1994a; Sleeter, 2008a). Multicultural education is also committed to antiracist and antisexist pedagogies (Cochran-Smith, Davis, & Fries, 2004; Gollnick et al., 1979; Irvine, 2003; Nieto, 1994, 1999; Sleeter et al., 2005) and social justice (Cochran-Smith, 2004, 2008; Grant & Agosto, 2008; Irvine, 2003; Ladson-Billings, 2006b; Nieto, 1999, 2000a, 2005b; Sleeter & Grant, 1999; Sleeter et al., 2005; Valli, Cooper, & Frankes, 1997).

Two frameworks help define multicultural education. In Sleeter and Grant's (1999) typology, there are five approaches to multicultural education: (1) teaching the exceptional and culturally different, (2) human relations, (3) single group studies, (4) multicultural education, and (5) education that is multicultural and social reconstructionist. It is this last level—education that is multicultural and social reconstructionist—that is most closely aligned with a social justice or critical multicultural approach (e.g., Grant, 1991; Irvine, 2003; Nieto, 2009; Nieto & Bode, 2008; Sleeter, 2004a; Villegas, 1988; Villegas & Lucas, 2002a; Zeichner et al., 1998). In education that is multicultural and social reconstructionist, educators are committed to the elimination of oppression, to cultivating students' sense of hope and agency, to connecting critical pedagogy and Freire's notion of *conscientização* to multicultural theories and practices, to teaching resistance and social responsibility, and to enacting a curriculum that privileges knowledge construction, relevance, critical thinking, and democratic practices. Banks's (2004) five dimensions of multicultural education complement the Sleeter and Grant (1999) typology by describing five different ways that multicultural education is enacted: (1) through knowledge construction, (2) content integration, (3) prejudice reduction, (4) equity pedagogy, and (5) empowering school climates and social structures.

Together, these typologies of multicultural education help to define a vision of education that is about far more than the equitable distribution of test scores; rather, "multicultural education is an idea, an educational reform movement, and a process whose major goal is to change the structure of educational institutions so that male and female students, exceptional students, and students who are members of diverse racial, ethnic, language, and cultural groups will have an equal chance to achieve academically in school" (Banks & Banks, 2001, p. 1). Multicultural education is concerned with identifying and theorizing practices that will achieve these ends, with an emphasis on humanizing, constructivist, and equity pedagogies, such as culturally relevant and responsive teaching (Gay, 2000; Ladson-Billings, 1995b; Sleeter & Grant, 1999; Villegas & Lucas, 2002a).

Culturally relevant pedagogy (Ladson-Billings, 1995b)—or culturally responsive teaching (Gay, 2000; Villegas & Lucas, 2002), cultural synchronization (Irvine, 1990), and culture-centered education (King, 1994, 2004)—is one instantiation of equity pedagogy (J. Banks, 2004). In a culturally relevant approach, teachers use their knowledge of students' cultures—not only their race and ethnicity but also the nexus of their identities, in as local and specific of a way as possible—to shape their pedagogical practices and to make curricular decisions. In addition, culturally oriented approaches reframe the purposes of education. For example, in a culturally relevant classroom, students engage in social critique, they achieve academically and are engaged in authentic learning, and they develop cultural competence in both their own and the dominant culture (Ladson-Billings, 1995c). Similarly, in a culture-centered approach, "the purpose, methods and content of education are all involved in preparing African American students to understand, preserve and *use* their cultural knowledge and competence to achieve academic and cultural excellence. From this perspective, education should help students develop a 'relevant personality' that includes a collective identity, the skills, knowledge, vision, and motivation to challenge societal injustice and join with others to reinvent the society" (King, 1994, p. 28).

Both multicultural education and culturally relevant pedagogy are radically different than the developmentalist, psychologized approach to learning traditionally emphasized in teacher education; they also fly in the face of neoliberal reforms that emphasize standardized tests and global competition as the primary purpose of education. This differing vision of education inevitably produces different visions of successful teaching, and it inevitably leads to different visions of teacher preparation.

Teacher Education in Practice: What Does a Teacher Need to Know, Believe, and Do?

Preparing teachers to enact these visions of education requires, first and foremost, an ideological commitment to multiculturalism and against hegemonic forces that define difference as a problem (Hollins, 2008; Irvine, 1990; King, 1994; Ladson-Billings, 2006a; Villegas, 1988; Weiner, 2003). The research on diversity and teacher education is virtually unanimous that ideology, dispositions, and beliefs matter (see Grant & Secada, 1990)—and that no teacher can enact a multicultural education without a commitment to it. However, as King (1991) points out, many teacher candidates espouse such commitments while clinging to beliefs that leave unquestioned structural racism, white privilege, and the normative narratives of American identity. To King (1997) and others, undoing such "miseducation" and "dysconscious racism" is at the heart of teacher education (e.g., Ball, 2000; Cochran-Smith, 2000; Grant, 1991; Haberman, 1993; Hollins, 1990; Irvine, 2003; King & Ladson-Billings, 1990; Ladson-Billings, 1994b, 2001; Nieto, 2005; Pagano, Weinter, Obi, & Swearingen, 1995; Sleeter, 1985, 1989, 2004; Valli, 1996a, 1996b; Villegas & Lucas, 2002; Weiner, 2003; Zeichner & Grant, 1981; Zeichner & Hoeft, 1996).

Generativity

According to Ball (2009), *generativity* also plays a critical role in the preparation of teachers to work effectively in multicultural classrooms. Generativity refers to a teachers' ability to add to what they learn within teacher education programs by connecting that knowledge to personal-, professional-, and student-centered knowledge in ways that enable them to produce new knowledge that is useful in curriculum planning and pedagogical problem solving in diverse classrooms. Ball argues that, using generativity, teachers can envision their classrooms as *communities of change* where transformative teaching and learning takes place—where teachers model generative thinking in their teaching so their students will, in turn, use generativity in their classroom and community practices as well.

The social context of schooling. Teacher educators recommend that preservice teachers study structural inequality to analyze sociopolitical structures and then use this understanding of the social context of schooling as the backdrop for pedagogical decision making (Darling-Hammond, 1995; Grant, 1991; Irvine, 2003; King & Ladson-Billings, 1990; Villegas, 1988; Villegas & Lucas, 2002; Zeichner & Liston, 1990). However, such experiences must be carefully scaffolded (King, 1991; Sleeter, 1992b, 1996)—otherwise they can foster resistance and hopelessness, particularly among preservice teachers from privileged backgrounds (Sleeter, Torres, & Laughlin, 2001; Zeichner & Liston, 1990). Examples of how teacher educators "scaffold *conscientização*" abound (Sleeter, Torres, & Laughlin, 2001; Hollins, 1990; King, 1997; Sleeter, 1996; Sleeter, Torres, & Laughlin, 2001).

Cultural knowledge. Teacher educators also advocate a focus on cultural knowledge (Banks et al., 2005; Darling-Hammond & Bransford, 2005; Hollins, 2008; Irvine, 2003; King, 1994; Tabachnik & Zeichner, 1993; Zeichner, 1995, 1996). After all, if preservice teachers will be teaching students who come from a different cultural background than their own and if preservice teachers are to enact a culturally relevant pedagogy, they must have knowledge of their students' culture(s). This recommendation, however, comes with important caveats. For one, there is a danger in teaching *about* culture, which can lead preservice teachers to essentialize cultures and cultural difference (Cochran-Smith, 2004; Grant, 1991; Haberman, 1991a; Hollins, 2008; Ladson-Billings, 2000; Zeichner, 1996) or to ignore the complex intersections of identity (Grant & Agosto, 2006; Grant & Sleeter, 1985). There is also the danger that a cultural component to teacher education will be relegated to a single course or to a curricular add-on; to be effective and transformative, culture must be woven throughout the entire program (Cochran-Smith, 2000; Sleeter, 2001; Tabachnik & Zeichner, 1993; Zeichner, 1996). Preservice teachers need to see culture as integral to learning—and that can only be accomplished if culture is made integral to their own learning (Hollins, 1997, 2008; King, 1994). While cultural coursework is certainly important, preservice teachers also need to engage in cross-cultural and community-based field experiences from the beginning of their teacher education program (Ladson-Billings, 2001; Sleeter, 2001; Sleeter & Boyle-Baise, 2000; Pagano, Weiner, Obi, & Swearingen, 1997; Zeichner, 1995, 1996; Zeichner & Melnick, 1996a, 1996b). Again, though, these recommendations come with a caveat: Without reflective coursework and supervision to help scaffold these experiences, they can end up reinforcing stereotypes and misconceptions (Cochran-Smith, 2003a; Grant, 1981; Grant & Secada, 1990; Haberman & Post, 1992; Sleeter, 1992a, 1992b, 2001; Sleeter & Boyle-Baise, 2000; Zeichner, 1995).

The purpose behind culturally based teacher education is not to produce static cultural knowledge. Rather, it is to help preservice teachers learn how to apply and connect cultural knowledge to the specific students in one's classroom (Ball, 2009; Banks et al., 2005; Grant, 1991; Hollins, McIntyre, et al., 2004; Hollins, 2008; Irvine, 2002; King, 1994; Ladson-Billings, 2001). Preservice teachers need to learn there are no magic formulas for good teaching; it is context-specific and unique to the classroom and culture in which it is situated (Grant & Agosto, 2006; Hollins, 1999; Irvine, 2002; Ladson-Billings, 1994b). The instructor's job is not only to serve as a bridge between students' cultures and the academic world but also to see students as *individuals* situated within particular cultures and communities and impacted by particular pedagogies (Hollins, McIntyre, et al., 2004; Irvine, 2002; Irvine & York, 1995).

Self-knowledge. One of the dangers in teaching about culture is that it becomes something that belongs to "others" while whiteness is seen as "just normal" (Ladson-Billings, 2006a). Thus, self-examination becomes vital to the scaffolding of *conscientização* regarding culture and the social context of schooling (Cochran-Smith, 2000; Darling-Hammond & Bransford, 2005; Hollins, 1999, 2008; King, 1994, 1997; Sleeter, 1996; Sleeter, Torres, & Laughlin, 2001; Zeichner, 1995; Zeichner & Grant, 1981; Zeichner & Hoeft, 1996). If preservice teachers can see their own ethnic and cultural heritage—if they can begin to understand that their "just normal" whiteness is in fact a culture, and a privileged culture—then they can begin to explore the complex ways that culture functions in learning (Grant, 1991; Hollins, 1990, 1997, 1999, 2008; King, 1991, 2004; Ladson-Billings, 2006a; Tabachnik & Zeichner, 1993). Self-awareness can build understanding of the role that our autobiographies play in perpetuating inequality (Grant, 1991; King, 1997). Again, this self-exploration must be scaffolded—otherwise, privileged and oppressive dominant cultural narratives can be reinforced (King, 1991). Starting with preservice teachers' autobiographies and personal conceptions of culture allows teacher educators to engage in a constructivist task, to start where preservice teachers are and move them forward on a continuum of social and cultural awareness (Valli, 1996a, 1996b).

Habits of mind. Ultimately, the purpose of this vision of teacher education is not to instill objective knowledge but to cultivate particular "habits of mind" (Hollins, McIntyre, et al., 2004) that enable teachers to assimilate cultural knowledge, knowledge of the social context, content knowledge, and pedagogical tools into an analysis and improvement of practice (Cochran-Smith, 2004; Cochran-Smith & Lytle, 2009; Hollins, 1999, 2008; Irvine, 1990; King, 1994; Weiner, 2002; Zeichner & Liston, 1990). Such a vision of teacher education eschews the "methods fetish" (Bartolome, 1994), instead promoting "inquiry as stance" (Cochran-Smith, 2003a; Cochran-Smith & Lytle, 2009) or a reflective approach to teaching that always considers how any tools and practices can be used to further justice and equity (Valli, Cooper, & Frankes, 1997). Such an approach sees the work of teacher education as having less of a content and technical focus than having a learning and political focus (Cochran-Smith, 2004). As Nieto (2003a) argues, teacher preparation needs to shift its initial focus from questions of what and how to questions of why. In fact, Nieto summarizes the purposes of this kind of teacher education well: Preservice teachers need to be taught to face and accept their own identities, become learners of their students' realities, develop strong and meaningful relationships with students, become multilingual and multicultural, learn to challenge racism and bias, and develop a community of critical friends in order to refocus attention to issues of access, equity, and social justice in multicultural education.

Reflective communities of practice. Such work cannot happen in the isolation of a traditionally run university classroom. Rather, it requires reflective communities of practice—not only among preservice teachers but also among cooperating teachers, university supervisors, and school-site professionals (Ball, 2009; Cochran-Smith, 2003a, 2004; Cochran-Smith & Lytle, 1993; Hollins, McIntyre, et al., 2004; Hollins, 2006; Ladson-Billings, 2001; Nieto, 2000; Zeichner & Melnick, 1996a, 1996b). These reflective communities become a generative, metacognitive space for teachers (both pre- and in-service) to think together about the role of diversity and culture in their classrooms and to work together to develop pedagogies for the students with whom they work. These reflective communities, when supported by critically conscious teacher education, have the power to impact teachers' ideology and beliefs about diversity (Ball, 2000, 2009); they also have the power to cultivate the "habits of mind" (Hollins, McIntyre, et al., 2004) teachers need to successfully teach all students and to make apparent the rigorous, intellectual work of praxis (Cochran-Smith, 2004). Reflective communities of practice also extend teacher education throughout the professional lifespan (Ball, 2009; Cochran-Smith & Lytle, 1993; Darling-Hammond, 2004a; Hollins, 1993; Irvine, 1990, 2002, 2003; Nieto, 2009; Sleeter, 1992a, 2008b).

These reflective communities of practice—if they are to truly impact learning—require close collaboration between the university and the communities with which the university works. Whether through school-based cross-cultural field experiences (Grant & Koskela, 1986; Ladson-Billings, 2001; Pagano, Weiner, Obi, & Swearingen, 1997; Valli, 1996a, 1996b; Zeichner & Melnick, 1996a, 1996b), community-based service learning experiences (Sleeter & Boyle-Baise, 2000), professional development schools (Valli, Cooper, & Frankes, 1997), rethinking the supervisor-student teacher-cooperating teacher triad (Cochran-Smith, 2004), or making the school the primary site of teacher education (Ball, 2009; Haberman, 1994, 1995a; Haberman & Post, 1998), these communities of practice require embedding teacher education in the school site and then creating the space for all of the educators involved to reflect together on how best to educate the students before them (Sleeter, 2001). Indeed, the success of teacher education for diversity requires close university, school, and community partnerships (Banks et al., 2005; Villegas & Clewell, 1998a, 1998b; Weiner, 1993b; Zeichner, 2003; Zeichner & Hoeft, 1996).

Field experiences. Field work matters. Yet research is overwhelmingly focused on the university and *not* on the field experience, whether on teacher education courses (n = 52), program structures (n = 32), or pedagogies that challenge preservice teachers' identities, dispositions, and ideologies (n = 76). While many researchers assert the importance of the field experience—and particularly the importance of the cooperating teacher—in teacher education (n = 38), there is little research on this. Only 15 of the 152 pieces systematically studied the field experience and/or the cooperating teacher (Cochran-Smith, 2003a; Grant & Koskela, 1986; Grant & Zozakiewicz, 1995; Haberman, 1991a, 1994, 1995a; Haberman & Post, 1990, 1998; Ladson-Billings, 1999b, 2001; Valli, 1996a, 1996b, 2000; Zeichner & Melnick, 1996a, 1996b). A broader review of literature on diversity and teacher education echoed this finding (Grant, Elsbree, & Fondrie, 2004).

This is a particularly glaring hole given that much of the work of teacher education falls on the shoulders of university supervisors and cooperating teachers. The cooperating teacher, in particular, has the potential to be a coinvestigator of praxis (Cochran-Smith, 2004); the cooperating teacher also sets the tone of the field experience, particularly through his or her disposition toward multicultural education

(Grant & Zozakiewicz, 1995; Haberman & Post, 1990; Pagano, Weiner, Obi, & Swearingen, 1995) or by modeling emancipatory pedagogy (King & Ladson-Billings, 1990). In fact, from Dewey (1904) to Haberman (1995a; Haberman & Post, 1998), teacher educators recognize that the primary site of teacher learning is the school, particularly one's first school with one's first mentor. This is where the habits of "star teachers" are potentially cultivated (Haberman, 1995b; Haberman & Post, 1998)—or where stereotypes are reinforced (Haberman & Post, 1992). Yet there is little research on—or programmatic monitoring of (King & Ladson-Billings, 1990; Sleeter, 2001; Valli, 1996a, 1996b)—field experiences and cooperating teachers. This area begs for research (Cochran-Smith, 2003a; Grant, Elsbree, & Fondrie, 2004; Hollins & Guzman, 2005; Pagano, Weiner, Obi, & Swearingen, 1995; Sleeter, 2001; Sleeter & Boyle-Baise, 2000). In particular, Ladson-Billings (2000) and Irvine (2002) urge returning to the classroom of experts, where transformative pedagogies are enacted and where teacher educators and preservice teachers alike can rethink and reshape practice.

Assessing teacher competencies. What kind of pedagogy do teachers educated in programs concerned with diversity enact in their classrooms? How will we assess their competency and our success as teacher educators? As several scholars caution (Cochran-Smith et al., 2009a; Grant & Secada, 1990; Sleeter, 2001; Villegas, 2007; Weiner, 2002), focusing on beliefs is not enough; we must also articulate and measure what competent multicultural teachers *do*, and teacher education programs must then measure their success based on whether or not their graduates actually do these things. Particularly in our era of accountability, reclaiming what constitutes a "highly qualified teacher" for diverse classrooms is important to teacher education. After all, at most institutions, preservice teachers are still being prepared to teach in "idealized schools that serve white, monolingual, middle-class children from homes with two parents" (Ladson-Billings, 1999b, p. 87), where teacher quality is measured by a basic skills test and a liberal arts degree.

Yet teacher educators concerned with diversity agree that these indicators do not guarantee that a teacher is highly qualified to teach in diverse classrooms (Darling-Hammond, 1995, 2004a; Darling-Hammond, Wise, & Klein, 1999; Haberman, 1988a, 1988b, 1991b, 1993, 1996; Haberman & Post, 1998; Hollins & Guzman, 2005; Irvine, 1988; Villegas & Clewell, 1998a). Such indicators do not, for example, account for teachers' pedagogical content knowledge, nor do they account for teachers' beliefs about their diverse students (see Enterline, Cochran-Smith, Ludlow, & Mitescu, 2009; Irvine & Fraser, 1998; Ladson-Billings, 2000). If multicultural education requires pedagogical and cultural-content knowledge, if it requires habits of mind that enable teachers to critically analyze the social context and to make pedagogical decisions based on this analysis, and if it requires teachers to develop authentic and respectful relationships with students across differences, how will those competencies be measured? How can we measure teachers' ability to apply what they know about content, pedagogy, and culture to the specific children in their classrooms? How can we use those assessments to evaluate teacher education programs?

The challenge, of course, is assessing teacher competencies in culturally relevant and context-specific ways, without penalizing teachers for practices situated in their community and culture, as Ladson-Billings's (1998) and Irvine and Fraser's (1998) research on the National Board of Professional Teaching Standards showed happened to some African American teachers. The challenge is to assess competency while also honoring the context- and culture-specific practices of good teaching (Ladson-Billings, 1995a).

One approach is the performance assessment, or using observations and portfolios to measure whether practice has changed or grown in relation to a program's objectives (Cochran-Smith et al., 2009a; Darling-Hammond, Wise, & Klein, 1999; Enterline, Cochran-Smith, Ludlow, & Mitescu, 2009; Grant & Agosto, 2008; Hollins, 2006; Sleeter, 1985; Zeichner & Wray, 2001). Another approach ties teacher competency to K–12 students' learning (Cochran-Smith et al., 2009a, 2009b; Darling-Hammond, 1997; Hollins, 1993; Hollins & Guzman, 2005). Haberman (1994, 1995a) advocates longitudinal assessment—based on the proven and persistent success of a program's graduates in urban schools. After all, just looking at retention rates, it seems that teacher education as currently constructed does not produce effective urban and multicultural teachers. As such, Haberman (1995a) and others (Cochran-Smith, 2003a; Grant & Agosto, 2006; Zeichner, 2003) recommend rethinking teacher educators' qualifications and competencies: Instead of selecting teacher educators based their graduate degree, they should be selected and judged based on their own proven success in urban and multicultural classrooms.

Institutional Support for Diversity: Teacher Education Programs in Practice

Teacher education does not occur in isolation. Commitments to diversity, equity, and multiculturalism are also impacted by the university at large, by K–12 school structures and climates, and by policy at the local, state, and federal level. Acknowledging the interconnectedness of teacher education and these other factors is essential.

For example, in addition to recruiting more diverse teacher candidates, teacher education programs and universities must be structured to make it feasible for more diverse students to attend. Program *structures* impact who can participate: programs that offer teacher education coursework at different hours of the day are more likely to attract candidates who need to work; increasing financial aid and scholarships can help support teacher candidates who might not be able to afford full-time study; multicultural mentoring programs have proven successful at retaining students of color (Darling-Hammond, 1995, 2004a; Gollnick, 1978; Haberman, 1988b; Price & Valli, 1998; Sleeter et al., 2005; Villegas et al., 1993; Villegas & Lucas, 2004). Even rethinking certification has impacted teacher diversity—whether it be by recruiting from the paraprofessional pool and then decreasing time to certification (Villegas & Clewell, 1998a, 1998b) or condensing the field experiences into a one-year, paid internship in a school setting (Darling-Hammond, 1997).

This kind of work must also be supported at the university level through the recruitment and retention of a more diverse university faculty and student body (Gollnick, 1978; Grant & Secada, 1990; Ladson-Billings, 2000; Price & Valli, 1998; Villegas et al., 1993; Zeichner & Hoeft, 1996). Within the university curriculum, multiculturalism must be moved from the margins to the mainstream. Rather than approaching ethnic studies requirements as an add-on, multicultural studies must be seen as central to the work of preparing tomorrow's thinkers, leaders, entrepreneurs, and teachers (Gollnick, 1978; Price & Valli, 1998; Sleeter et al., 2005; Zeichner & Hoeft, 1996; Zeichner et al., 1998).

Policy—at the local, state, and federal levels—indelibly impacts these commitments (Cochran-Smith, Davis, & Fries, 2004; Cochran-Smith & Fries, 2008; Darling-Hammond, 2004a; Gollnick, 1995; Villegas & Lucas, 2004; Weiner, 2000; Weiner et al., 2001; Zeichner & Liston, 1990). For example, the funding and regulation of teacher education is impacted by state and federal legislation; such funding and regulation has a direct effect on not only the amount of financial aid and scholarships a program can offer to its students but also on the resources available to develop a culturally responsive teacher education program. Policy also affects schools themselves, which are structured to be resistant to the kind of education promoted by teacher educators concerned with diversity. Educating teachers for diversity requires restructuring schools themselves—partly through policy mandates—in order to foster high-quality education for all students (Darling-Hammond, 2004a; Grant, 1991; Haberman, 2000; Ladson-Billings, 1995b, 1999a; Sleeter, 1992a, 1992c). Yet, Ladson-Billings (1995b) argues, "Too many teacher educators (and teachers) believe that they can implement an effective multicultural education program without effective fundamental change in the classrooms and schools in which they teach" (p. 755).

WHERE ARE WE NOW? DIVERSITY IN EDUCATION AND TEACHER EDUCATION POLICY

In the introduction to the *Handbook of Education Policy Research*, the editors state:

> Education is no longer just about what happens in classrooms and schools, but increasingly about rules and regulations promulgated in state capitals and the federal government designed to improve student academic performance. . . . As "policy" has assumed an increasingly pivotal role in the educational system, a growing number of scholars have turned their attention to the process through which rules and regulations are adopted and the consequences they have on teaching and learning. (Sykes, Schneider, & Ford, 2009, p. 1)

Indeed, a growing number of scholars have also turned their attention to examining and *critiquing* the very "rules and regulations promulgated in state capitals and the federal government," as well as the ensuing mandates generated by professional associations. As we shall see, policy at all levels has been instrumental in shaping the national educational agenda, an agenda that does not pay attention to diversity in the way that scholars of teacher education do. Yet, many who study policy are centrally concerned with diversity—particularly its role beyond citing the achievement scores of students of color or the resegregation of schools (Cochran-Smith & Fries, 2001; Grant & Chapman, 2008). Instead of relegating diversity to mere demographic statistics, these scholars and critics argue that Diversity (big D) in education has to do with the multilayered and complex intersections of identity; how these dimensions of identity are privileged and marginalized in schools; what role these identities play in making sense of the world, in learning, and in choosing a life path; and how systemic responses to these identities play out in schools.

Teacher educators concerned with diversity are among these critics because their work is deeply impacted by policy. In fact, the 152 pieces reviewed here are littered with references to policies and initiatives that have shaped teacher education—from national agendas set by the Coleman Report (1969) and A Nation at Risk (1983) to the standards and competencies set by organizations like NCATE and AACTE. More recently, these scholars have engaged with national debates about "highly qualified teachers" and the impact of accountability and alternative certification on teachers and classrooms. Common to all is the observation that most policies about education, generally, and teacher education, more specifically, ignore multicultural and culturally relevant teacher education.

How and to what extent has policy—and the professional mandates that have grown from it—addressed diversity in teacher education? What connections are there between policy and research? To explore these connections, we look at touchstone policies of the last forty years—the Elementary and Secondary Education Act (1965), A Nation at Risk (1983), and No Child Left Behind (2001). We then turn to a current policy debate, deregulation versus professionalization. As we will see, the enduring questions—What do we mean by diversity? What should be the role of diversity in schools? Why does diversity matter? Who should teach diverse groups of children? What should diverse groups of children learn and how should they be taught? What does a teacher of diverse groups of children need to know, believe, and do?—are answered quite differently by policy makers.

Federal Policy Initiatives: Shifting Attention Away From Diversity

At least as far back as the early nineteenth century, educators have been concerned with the sociopolitical dimensions of diversity in education. Take the following statement from William Hamilton (1827) regarding white teachers' capacity to teach black children:

> It has been a policy of white men to give you a high opinion of your advancement when you have made but smattering attainments. They know that a little education is necessary for better accomplishing the menial service you are in the habit of performing for them. They do not wish you to be equal with them—much less superior . . . They will take care you do not rise above mediocrity. (Mabee, 1997, p. 95)

What does it mean to equitably educate all children? What is a socially just education? These sociopolitical questions, of central concern to Hamilton, could have been at the heart of late-twentieth-century federal educational policy—particularly in light of the civil rights movement and *Brown v. Board of Education* (1954). As the United States began to imagine what a multiracial and multiethnic democracy might look like, it might have also imagined the role of race and ethnicity in schooling. Would its commitments to diversity be in name only—simply guaranteeing equal access to educational opportunities without reconsidering what those educational opportunities were and who they privileged? Or would its commitments be deeper and more enriched—reconsidering, for example, the role of education in a pluralistic democracy and rethinking teaching and learning in light of student diversity?

Federal educational policy had the opportunity to take seriously the sociopolitical dimensions of diversity and to set an equitable and just reform agenda. Instead, policy answers the enduring questions of diversity and teacher education in quite narrow ways: What do we mean by diversity? *Demographic statistics.* What should be the role of diversity in schools? *It should not impact learning.* Why does diversity matter? *Because differing outcomes according to race, ethnicity, and class impedes global competition and status.* Who should teach diverse groups of children? *Content-area experts.* What should diverse groups of children learn and how should they be taught? *Basic content knowledge, taught in ways proven successful by scientifically based curriculum.* What does a teacher of diverse groups of children need to know, believe, and do? *Teachers need to know their subjects.* While diversity rhetorically matters, it seems that federal educational policy—as shaped by the Elementary and Secondary Education Act (1965), A Nation at Risk (1983), and No Child Left Behind (2001)—has done little to rethink education in light of diversity.

The Elementary and Secondary Education Act

The role of diversity in education had the potential to truly flourish with the Elementary and Secondary Education Act, or ESEA (1965)—the most far-reaching federal education legislation ever written and one of the cornerstones of President Lyndon B. Johnson's War on Poverty. ESEA was born of an era when diversity was at the fore of public consciousness, particularly the relationship among poverty, race, and political marginalization. Race riots were plaguing U.S. cities, and the *Report on the National Advisory Commission on Civil Disorders* (1968) concluded that they had resulted from black frustration at a lack of economic opportunity. The Commission expressed an outcry for diversity: "Our nation is moving toward two societies, one black, one white—separate and unequal" (p. 1). Educators and politicians could no longer ignore the increasing number of social movements based on gender, ethnicity, sexuality, and (dis)ability swirling around them. In fact, on many occasions, schools were the very site of protest. In the era from which ESEA was born, questions about the role of diversity in U.S. society and about racial and economic equity and justice were central.

Yet ESEA was largely silent about diversity. As the touchstone federal education legislation of the civil rights era, it had the potential to invigorate a national commitment to diversity, but it did not. While it directed more resources to low-income students, it did not take a stand on any of the sociopolitical dimensions of diversity. This stands in stark contrast to other policy documents of the era, particularly those published by professional organizations. While none were as politically significant as ESEA, they were nevertheless significant in number, and they included mandates from educational associations (e.g., American Association of Colleges for Teacher Education [AACTE], Association for Supervision and Curriculum Development [ASCD]) urging for increased diversity and multicultural efforts in teacher education.

The era of ESEA was marked by attention not only to diversity but also to the failures of teacher education. Koerner (1963), for example, severely criticized teacher education. He argued that there was little connection between teacher preparation and job performance, that education lacked a common body of knowledge, that there were too few academic requirements for teachers, that there was intellectual weakness among education faculty and students, particularly in graduate programs, and that educational coursework was "puerile, repetitious, dull, and ambiguous" (p. 18). Koerner recommended closing teacher-training colleges and doing away with the undergraduate education degree, instead having preservice teachers major in an academic subject supplemented by professional courses. Conant (1963) offered another vision. He argued that courses in pedagogy be eliminated in favor of field-based training and that states should require teacher candidates to hold a bachelor's degree, to fulfill student-teaching requirements in state-approved placements, and to hold a teaching certificate endorsed by the university.

Many of Koerner's and Conant's recommendations were taken up by later policies, but—along with diversity—they were largely ignored by ESEA. For legislation that was ostensibly concerned with the elimination of poverty and the resolution of racial issues through the improvement of teachers and teaching for low-income students, ESEA was remarkably silent about diversity and about how to prepare teachers for diversity. This is particularly disappointing given that ESEA—in both its original 1964 legislation and its 1978 reauthorization—devoted significant federal resources to the improvement of the pedagogy in urban and rural schools. Yet the type of pedagogical questions asked by teacher educators—How should diverse groups of students be taught? What do teachers of diverse groups of students need to know, believe, and do?—were for the most part ignored.

A Nation at Risk. The National Commission on Excellence in Education (NCEE) released A Nation at Risk (1983) nearly twenty years after ESEA. In it, NCEE claimed widespread failure in American schools, linking this failure to the nation's economic challenges and to global competition: "If an unfriendly foreign power had attempted to impose on America the mediocre education performance that exists today, we might well have viewed it as an act of war" (p. 1). To this, President Reagan added, "I believe that parents, not government, have the primary responsibility for the education of their children. Our agenda is to restore quality to education by increasing competition and by strengthening parental choice and local control" (Carroll, 2008). The reverberations from these statements can be felt today, with emphases on global competition and marketized solutions to school failure.

While A Nation at Risk commented on the importance of equal educational opportunity—"All, regardless of race or class or economic status, are entitled to a fair chance and to the tools for developing their individual powers of mind and spirit to the utmost" (p. 2)—it ignored the sociopolitical dimensions of diversity. It ignored *equity* of educational opportunities. Instead, it simplistically attributed failure to teachers and teacher education: too many teachers drawn from the bottom of high school and college classes; teacher preparation curriculum weighed down with courses in educational methods; low teacher salaries deterring candidates; and poorly qualified teachers in math, science, and foreign languages. Schools were failing due to poorly qualified teachers, where poor qualifications were equated with a lack of content knowledge. Its recommendations for reform included higher education standards for teachers, increased professionalization (e.g., performance-based teacher salaries; upward career ladders; incentivizing career entry; teacher-driven career preparation), and the recruitment of content "'experts.'" In these recommendations, we hear echoes of Koerner's (1963) and Conant's (1963) critique of teacher education, but we hear nothing about diversity. Although A Nation at Risk was ostensibly concerned with school failure—a concern that, in many ways, has sparked our obsession with the achievement gap—it does not consider the sociopolitical dimensions of educational success and failure. It does not consider the ways that schooling and education are culturally based or privilege some groups and marginalize others. A Nation at Risk reduces the problem of educational failure to a technical, professional problem—exactly what Cochran-Smith (2004) argues culturally relevant teacher education is not.

In that, A Nation at Risk marked a neoliberal shift. The Reagan administration essentially redirected attention *away* from diversity—not only with A Nation at Risk but also with the passage of the Bilingual Education Act (1984), which watered down federal attention to bilingual education—and instead toward accountability and deregulation. Yet as a result of midcentury social movements, at the time there was actually *increased* attention to diversity and multiculturalism in education—particularly where the diversification of the nation's classrooms was experienced firsthand. But A Nation at Risk and the neoliberal era of educational reform it ushered in hampered that attention.

No Child Left Behind. The No Child Left Behind Act—the 2001 reauthorization of ESEA—was ostensibly engineered to improve education and achievement in America's schools, particularly schools serving low-income students and students of color. NCLB states, "In America, no child should be left behind. Every child should be educated to his or her potential" (U.S. Department of Education, 2004, p. 3). According to proponents, this statement recognizes and affirms the diversity in America's schools by acknowledging the importance of educating *all* students. But what, exactly, does it mean to educate *all* children to their potential? According to the federal law, there are two key components: student outcomes associated with accountability standards and the closing of the achievement gap between students of different socioeconomic backgrounds, ethnic groups, language statuses, and (dis) abilities. To do this, NCLB addresses four areas: (1) mandating teacher and principal accountability for student outcomes; (2) implementing scientifically based curriculum; (3) increasing parental involvement and choice; (4) and expanding local control and flexibility in the management and administration of schools. NCLB promises to focus resources on students poorly served by the existing educational system and to develop more reliable data-tracking and reporting systems.

In all of this, NCLB places great importance on the teacher's role in public education. As such, it requires that all pupils are taught by a "highly qualified teacher," where a "highly qualified teacher" has a bachelor's degree, holds a state teaching license, and has proven that he or she knows the subject(s) he or she teaches by either passing a content-knowledge test or through coursework. In this definition, a teacher's high qualifications are largely determined by content knowledge, particularly as evaluated by paper-and-pencil tests. In fact, almost a decade after its authoring, there are now more than 600 tests used to measure teaching candidates' basic skills and content knowledge (Cochran-Smith & Zeichner, 2005). When coupled with its emphasis on scientifically based curriculum resources—which, in reality, are often teacher-proof, direct instruction curricula—it seems that NCLB finds pedagogical content knowledge and culturally based pedagogy to be of little significance. In fact, in its more than 600 pages, NCLB is silent about multiculturalism and diversity, about the need for culturally competent teachers and about the role of a multicultural curriculum in improving student learning (Day-Vines & Patton, 2003). Despite its rhetorical commitment to diversity and equality, NCLB ignores diversity.

Professionalization v. Deregulation: Today's Teacher Education Policy Debate

In all three of these federal policy initiatives, we see two common threads: a generic emphasis on better educating "all children" and a focus on teacher quality. Since the middle of the twentieth century, the American public has been increasingly concerned with the performance of "all students" in schools—whether out of a concern for civil rights and social justice (ESEA), as a result of cold war posturing (A Nation at Risk), or out of a concern for global economic competition (NCLB). Regardless of the political reasons why, diversity in schools—particularly as connected to low achievement—was a problem to be dealt with. And given that teachers themselves were the constituency failing to "deal with" the problem of diversity, the solution also apparently rested with teacher quality.

While these emphases are shared with teacher educators, policy does not consider these from the same perspective. Instead, policy initiatives argue that diversity should *not* have an impact on student learning—"all students" should achieve equally, if only they are provided with teachers who know their subject matter. This contrasts with those who argue that differential achievement is directly connected to the melting of diversity into an amorphous group of "all students" and that teachers need a specific set of skills, knowledge, and dispositions to teach diverse groups of students—which includes deep understanding of how social stratification and racial hierarchies have served to oppress and dehumanize *all* students. Nevertheless, the policy presence of these issues ensured that teacher quality and the better education of "all students" were front and center in education reform. After all, with attention focused on the failures of teacher education—with, for example, A Nation At Risk (1983) declaring that "too many teachers are being drawn from the bottom of high school and college classes" and that teacher education was weighted down with courses in educational methods instead of insisting teachers "meet high educational standards" (p. 3)—the handwriting was on the wall for immediate and deep reform in teacher education.

Teacher educators were forced to respond to issues of teacher quality and student diversity, and respond they did: They formed a series of professional organizations and committees that offered their own reform recommendations. For example, the Holmes Group in *Teachers for Tomorrow's Schools* (1986), and the Carnegie Forum on Education and the Economy's Task Force on Teaching as a Profession in *A Nation Prepared: Teachers for the 21st Century* (1986), both argued that teachers' knowledge should be grounded in the humanities and sciences, that the undergraduate teacher education program should be eliminated, and that teacher education should become a postbaccalaureate program. However, they remained committed to the important role of teacher education in teachers acquiring the skills, knowledge, and dispositions necessary to better educate all students.

Not all reformers agreed. The Thomas B. Fordham Foundation, in *The Teachers We Need and How to Get More of Them: A Manifesto* (1999), argued that teacher education was an unnecessary hurdle that deterred the best and the brightest from entering the profession. In fact, this disagreement is at the heart of the teacher education policy debate today. Dill (1996) refers to it as the teaching-as-profession versus teaching-as-craft debate, Rotherham and Mead (2003) describe it as the teacher professionalism versus competitive certification debate, and Cochran-Smith and

Fries (2001) call it the professionalization versus deregulation debate. In essence, it is a debate about whether to establish stronger professional standards for teachers or whether to do away with institutionalized teacher preparation. In other words, is teacher education part of the solution to the "problem" of teacher quality and student diversity, or is it itself the problem? While this is at the heart of contemporary policy debate, we would argue that it still ignores fundamental questions about the sociopolitical dimensions of diversity in schools and learning.

Teacher educators and the professionalization agenda. The Holmes Group—a consortium of ninety-six universities responding to critiques of teacher education such as that in A Nation at Risk (1983)—sought to advance teaching as a true profession and not a "semi-profession" (e.g., Etzoni, 1969; Lortie, 1975) by improving both the preparation of teachers and the quality of K–12 schooling. Their recommendations, based on scholarly research, focused on strengthening connections between schools of education and the rest of the university, particularly the colleges of arts and sciences, and strengthening links with educational allies and partners, such as K–12 schools and teachers (Holmes Group, 1986).

The efforts initiated by the Holmes Group, along with those of the Carnegie Forum on Education and the Economy's Task Force on Teaching as a Profession (1986), formed a community of scholars, organizations, and teachers devoted to reforming teacher education policy and procedures. The key members of this community of reformers have included Judith Lanier, Dean of Education at Michigan State University and president of the Holmes Group, and Linda Darling-Hammond, Executive Director of the National Commission on Teaching and America's Future (NCTAF), as well as the National Council for the Accreditation of Teachers (NCATE), the National Board for Professional Teaching Standards (NBPTS), and the Interstate New Teacher Assessment and Support Consortium (INTASC). This reform community receives support from the Carnegie Corporation, the Pew Charitable Trusts, the Ford Foundation, and the DeWitt Wallace Reader's Digest Fund.

Together, this association of reformers—particularly NCTAF—has issued a series of reports and recommendations for the professionalization of teacher education. In these, one sees repeated calls for more detailed teacher competency standards, a restructuring of teacher education, and increased attention to the achievement of "all students." Yet while diversity is named as part of the reform vision for teacher education, it is often done so in ways that do little to advocate for multicultural and culturally relevant teacher education.

National Commission on Teaching and America's Future. A blue-ribbon panel issued the NCTAF report, *What Matters Most: Teaching for America's Future* (1996). According to *What Matters Most*, the mission of NCTAF was "to provide an action agenda for meeting America's educational challenges, connecting the quest for higher student achievement with the need for *teachers who are knowledgeable, skillful, and committed to meeting the needs of all students*" (emphasis added; NCTAF, 1996, p. 4). *What Matters Most* intended to offer what NCTAF considered "the single most important strategy for achieving America's educational goals: A blueprint for recruiting, preparing and supporting excellent teachers in all of America's schools," with this blueprint focused on "ensuring that all communities have teachers with the knowledge and skills they need to teach so that all children can learn and that all school systems are organized to support teachers in this work" (NCTAF, 1996,

p. 3). *What Matters Most* identified several key barriers to sound teaching and learning, including low expectations for student performance, unenforced standards for teachers, major flaws in teacher preparation, slipshod teacher recruitment, inadequate induction for beginning teachers, lack of professional development and rewards for knowledge and skill, and K–12 schools that were structured for failure rather than success.

In calling attention to teacher quality and by connecting teacher quality to "recruiting, preparing, mentoring and retaining" teachers, the report argued that teacher quality was a key factor in improving American education and that teacher preparation—*professionalization*—was highly correlated with improving student learning. Throughout most sections of the report, NCTAF called attention to diversity, as expressed by the phrase "all students," in relation to teachers' knowledge, skills, and dispositions. In that, *What Matters Most* goes farther than the federal policy documents that were its impetus in tackling the learning and achievement of "all students." For example:

> Concern about "at risk" children—those who drop out, tune out, and fall behind—cannot be addressed without teachers who know how to teach students who come to school with different learning needs, home situations, and beliefs about what education can mean for them (NCTAF, 1996, p. 10).
>
> Teaching in ways that help diverse learners master challenging content is much more complex than teaching for rote recall or low-level basic skills. Enabling students to write and speak effectively, to solve novel problems, and to design and conduct independent research requires paying attention to *learning,* not just to "covering the curriculum." (NCTAF, 1996, p. 38)

A follow-up document, *Doing What Matters Most: Investing in Quality Teaching* (Darling-Hammond, 1997), reported on progress toward having a high-quality teacher in every classroom. *Doing What Matters Most* drew on data about the conditions of teaching that had recently become available and examined policy changes that had occurred. The report addressed diversity in a similar manner to *What Matters Most:*

> However, few teachers have had any opportunity to learn how to teach students with disabilities . . . just one-fourth of the teachers serving these [limited English proficient] children had received any training in strategies or teaching new English language learners . . . today's teacher will serve at least four or five students with specific educational needs that she has not been prepared to meet. In addition, she will need considerable knowledge to develop curriculum and teaching strategies that address the wide range of learning approaches, experiences, and prior levels of knowledge the other students bring with them as well. And she will need to know how to help these students acquire much more complex skills and types of knowledge than ever before (Darling-Hammond, 1997, p. 7).
>
> Reforms, we have learned over and over again, are rendered effective or ineffective by the knowledge, skills, and commitments of those in schools. Without know-how and buy-in, innovations do not succeed (Darling-Hammond, 1997, p. 7).
>
> Recruitment needs to focus not only on ensuring that we have enough teachers, but also on recruiting a diverse teaching force that represents the American population if majority and minority students are to experience diverse role models. (Darling-Hammond, 1997, p. 15)

Certainly and as demonstrated, the professionalization argument as articulated by NCTAF addresses diversity in education, even paying explicit attention to low-income students, students of color, English language learners, and "at-risk" students. In addition, NCTAF advocates paying far more attention to diversity than the deregulation camp, as we shall see—going so far as to build professional competency standards around diversity.

That said, while NCTAF is clear as to who should teach diverse students— "teachers who are knowledgeable, skillful, and committed to meeting the needs of all students" (Darling-Hammond, 1997, p. 4)—it deals with the other enduring questions regarding diversity and teacher education more implicitly than explicitly. In other words, when reading through both *What Matters Most* and *Doing What Matters Most*, it is often left up to the reader to decide in teaching "all children" what the role of diversity is, why diversity even matters to education, what diverse groups of children should learn and how they should be taught, and what, specifically, a teacher needs to know, believe, and do in order to teach diverse groups of students. Answers to these questions are alluded to with statements like, "Concern about 'at risk' children . . . cannot be addressed without teachers who know how to teach students who come to school with different learning needs, home situations, and beliefs about what education can mean for them" (NCTAF, 1996, p. 10), or, the teacher "will need considerable knowledge to develop curriculum and teaching strategies that address the wide range of learning approaches, experiences, and prior levels of knowledge the other students bring with them as well" (Darling-Hammond, 1997, p. 7). Something different is clearly needed, but what that different preparation is remains vague—NCTAF does not connect the professionalization of teacher education for the benefit of "all students" with multicultural and culturally relevant research or practice.

National Council for the Accreditation of Teacher Education (NCATE). The professional accrediting organization for schools, colleges, and departments of education in the United States, NCATE is a nonprofit, nongovernmental alliance of thirty-three professional, education, and public organizations representing millions of Americans who support quality teaching (NCATE, 2009). NCATE is one of the profession's primary mechanisms for establishing high-quality teacher preparation, doing so via six professional standards used to accredit teacher preparation institutions. Standard 4 specifically attends to diversity:

> The [program] designs, implements, and evaluates curriculum and provides experiences for candidates to acquire and demonstrate the knowledge, skills, and professional dispositions necessary to help all students learn. Assessments indicate that candidates can demonstrate and apply proficiencies related to diversity. Experiences provided for candidates include working with diverse populations.
>
> In addition, the language of social justice and diversity is used throughout descriptions of NCATE's aims: "NCATE standards require that professional education programs prepare candidates who operationalize the belief that all students can learn; demonstrate fairness in educational settings by meeting the educational needs of all students in a caring, non-discriminatory, and equitable manner." (NCATE, 2009, pp. 6–7)

Given that one of NCATE's six professional accreditation standards is the "diversity standard" and given the emphasis on preparing teachers to teach "all students,"

NCATE's attention to diversity seems obvious. However, even in an explicit "diversity standard," the details of what it means to educate all students, what it means to "operationalize the belief that all students can learn," and what it means to "demonstrate and apply proficiencies related to diversity" is open to interpretation. Does this mean that teachers should engage in culturally relevant pedagogy? Does it mean that they should teach a multicultural curriculum or a mastery-driven approach to basic skills? Does it mean teachers work from a color-blind perspective or a culturally centered one? While a certain amount of vagueness certainly provides "wiggle room" for the demonstration of the "knowledge, skills and professional dispositions" required in a particular teaching context—in other words, a certain amount of vagueness honors the context-specific nature of good teaching—such vagueness (including the use of platitudes like "all students can learn") also allows for the superficial treatment of diversity. It allows teacher educators to deal with the demographic statistics of diversity without grappling with the sociopolitical dimensions.

National Board for Professional Teaching Standards (NBPTS). National Board certification is intended to measure a teacher's practice against high and rigorous standards. NBPTS was created in 1987 after the Carnegie Forum on Education and the Economy's Task Force on Teaching as a Profession released *A Nation Prepared: Teachers for the 21st Century.* Shortly after its release, NBPTS issued its first policy statement in the form of teacher competency standards, *What Teachers Should Know and Be Able to Do* (1987). These standards are NBPTS's vision of master teaching. There are five core propositions that serve as the foundation for National Board for Certified Teachers' (NBCTs) knowledge, skills, dispositions, and beliefs, with diversity addressed in Proposition 1: "Teachers are committed to students and their learning." The following statements are taken from Proposition 1:

- NBCTs are dedicated to making knowledge accessible to all students. They believe all students can learn.
- They treat students equitably. They recognize the individual differences that distinguish their students from one another and they take account for these differences in their practice.
- NBCTs understand how students develop and learn.
- They respect the cultural and family differences students bring to their classroom.
- They are concerned with their students' self-concept, their motivation and the effects of learning on peer relationships (NBPTS, 1987, p. 1).

Diversity as expressed in proposition 1 of *What Teachers Should Know and Be Able to Do* is narrowly conceived. Again, the NBPTS standard flattens out diversity to platitudes: "all students can learn"; "treat students equitably"; "respect cultural and family differences"; and "concerned with their students' self-concept." Such vagueness makes it difficult to understand what teacher education for diversity actually looks like—in some cases, even leading successful, culturally relevant pedagogues to be denied National Board certification (see Irvine & Fraser, 1998; Ladson-Billings, 1998).

Interstate New Teacher Assessment and Support Consortium (INTASC). According to INTASC's website, it is "a consortium of state education agencies and national educational organizations dedicated to the reform of the preparation, licensing, and on-going professional development of teachers." INTASC believes that "an effective teacher must be able to integrate content knowledge with the specific strengths and needs of students to assure that *all* students learn and perform at high level." *Model Standards for Beginning Teacher Licensing, Assessment and Development: A Resource for State Dialogue* (1992) articulates a common core of teaching knowledge and skills that should be acquired by all new teachers, followed by specific standards for eight disciplinary areas and/or levels of schooling. Although all of the standards are not yet available online, for the three standards where information is available (art, foreign language, and special education), one principle in each standard deals with diversity: "Principle #3—The teacher understands how students differ in their approaches to learning and creates instructional opportunities that are adapted to diverse learners" (INTASC, 2007, p. 22). Both NBPTS and INTASC are united in their view that the complex art of teaching requires performance-based standards and assessment strategies that are capable of capturing teachers' reasoned judgments and that evaluate what they can actually do in authentic teaching situations.

INTASC's *Model Standards for Beginning Teacher Licensing, Assessment and Development* does not address diversity so much as it addresses "diverse learners." Conflating diversity with "diverse learners," however, essentializes diversity by ignoring students' group history and cultures. What's more, there is little mention of the role of culture in teaching and learning or how teachers use cultural and contextual knowledge to make their reasoned judgments and pedagogical decisions in authentic teaching situations.

Policy reformers and the deregulation agenda. It is reasonable to argue that seeds were planted for the deregulation agenda with the release of the Coleman Report (1966). The U.S. Office of Education commissioned a study of the equality of educational opportunities, particularly in light of ESEA's (1965) emphasis on increasing funding and other educational inputs for low-income schools. Were inputs equalizing? If they were, what were the effects? What the study found was that equality of inputs did not have as strong of an effect on outputs as policy makers hoped. The ramifications of this finding continue to resonate in today's professionalization and deregulation policy debate:

> The major virtue of the study as conceived and executed lay in the fact that it did not accept [the input] definition, and by refusing to do so, has had its major impact in shifting policy attention from its traditional focus on comparisons of inputs (the traditional measures of school quality used by school administrators: per-pupil expenditures, class size, teacher salaries, age of building and equipment, and so on) to a focus on output. (Coleman, 1972, p. 149)

The Coleman Report (1966) shifted attention from inputs to outputs. A Nation at Risk (1983), in particular, sounded the alarm regarding America's educational failures, not only reenergizing the emphasis on outputs but also narrowing input attention to teacher quality—equity in funding, curriculum, and school structures were not nearly as important as a teacher's content knowledge. Teacher quality was at the heart of the report's urgent and sharp rhetoric: "A nation at risk . . . [whose] educational foundations . . . are presently being eroded by a rising tide of mediocrity that threatens our very future as a nation and a people" (NCEE, 1983, p. 1). This sharp rhetorical flourish around "a rising tide of mediocrity" led to unprecedented pressure on policy makers and politicians to improve achievement and to do so by improving teacher quality. Manno (1994) describes this time:

> The nation's states became hotbeds of education reform. Elected officials (such as governors, legislators, and mayors) and lay people (such as business leaders and newspaper editors) set out to wrest control of education from the education experts (school superintendents, school boards, and other members of the education establishment). These "civilians" began to demand that the "education experts" make themselves accountable to the public. (p. 3)

Both implicitly and explicitly, A Nation at Risk (1983) argued that the input-focused and resource-based strategies of President Johnson's War on Poverty—as implemented through ESEA (1965)—had failed to improve the outputs of American education and that it was time to shift educational policy in a new direction. Moreover, setting this new direction would not be left up to "educational experts" who had allowed the rising tide of mediocrity to consume American education on their watch (Manno, 1994). Proponents of this new direction in educational reform argued that, in order to engender globally competitive student achievement, education had to be wrested free from the grips of mediocre educators: Policy makers needed to focus on promoting more choice in school selection (e.g., voucher programs) as well as the deregulation of principal and teacher selection and licensure. In relation to teacher education, this approach specifically advocated that teachers not be prepared at teacher education institutions; instead, people should be allowed to teach if they knew their subject, if they had a desire to teach, and if they were willing to work and learn the *craft*—instead of the *profession*—of teaching from master teachers. Stoddard and Floden (1995) describe this impetus toward deregulation:

> The movement towards school district-based teacher education followed a decline in the public's confidence that colleges can recruit and adequately prepare enough effective teachers. Critics argued that teacher education programs had little substance and that their lack of rigor and low academic standards actually discourage talented individuals from entering the teaching profession . . . From this perspective, college-based programs of teacher preparation are viewed as barriers to raising professional standards in teaching and need to be bypassed. Alternate route programs are designed to provide an alternative means of entry into teaching for individuals who do not wish to take the college route and to offer school districts the freedom to recruit, hire and train teachers. (p. 3)

Additionally, some states (e.g., New Jersey, California) argued that they were experiencing a shortage of qualified teachers that university teacher education programs were unable to rectify. In 1983, New Jersey created the first alternative pathway to certification to "attract a new market for teaching—liberal arts graduates—and transition them into elementary and secondary teaching without going through a traditional college teacher education program. This solution to teacher quantity and quality demands began the alternative teacher certification movement, and the nation took notice" (Feistrizer, 2008, p. 7). Feistrizer, a major proponent of deregulation, also notes that during this same period, Texas justified its recently developed alternative certification pathways by arguing that they would bring more black and Latino college graduates into teaching. Proponents of choice and/or deregulation include Chester Finn (2003), Dale Ballou and Michael Podgursky (1997, 1999, 2000), Emily Feistrizer (2008), the Fordham Foundation (1999), the Heritage Foundation (2009), the Pioneer Institute (2006), and the Manhattan 31 Institute (2000).

Our review of the writings by proponents of deregulation shows little attention to diversity—neither the demographic statistics of diverse classrooms and their achievement levels nor the sociopolitical dimensions of diversity and learning. Moreover, when answering the enduring questions about teacher education and diversity, proponents of deregulation do so with little attention to diversity: The content of schooling, the training of teachers is color-blind and subject-specific. Diversity appears to have little bearing on teaching or learning and little if any bearing on improving American education.

If addressed at all, diversity is invoked when arguing for reform in the selection of teachers. Unencumbered by having to jump through the hoops of schools of education, alternative routes would better attract high-quality teachers to teach (poor and urban) students and they would better attract highly qualified minorities to teaching (Shen, 1997; Wilson, Floden, & Ferrini-Mundy, 2001). In fact, much of the writing in the deregulation camp critiques the recommendations and findings of professionalization advocates. For example, Ballou and Podgursky (1997) challenge statements such as the following:

> The findings of both qualitative and quantitative analyses suggest that policy investments in the quality of teachers may be related to improvement in student performance . . . this analysis suggests that policies adopted by states regarding teacher education, licensing, hiring, and professional development may make an important difference in the qualifications and capacities that teachers bring to their work. (Darling-Hammond, 2000a, p. 1)

However, Ballou and Podgursky (1997) argue:

> The commission overstates policy implications, ignoring critical limitations of the research. In many instances, the commission flatly misreports and misrepresents what these studies show. . . . [T]he commission's statement that teacher qualifications account for 40% of the measured variance in student scores is flatly incorrect: indeed, it is a statistical solecism. (pp. 8, 13–14)

While the professionalization camp bases its arguments regarding the importance of teacher education on the quality of classroom teachers, the deregulation camp summarily dismisses these findings. Whether related to diversity and the achievement of "all students" or not, deregulation advocates argue that teacher education does not affect teacher quality.

Learning from the debate. What is immediately obvious from looking across the professionalization and deregulation debate is that each side is grounded in an ideological point of view. Professionalization advocates believe strongly that controlling quality of inputs—particularly teacher quality—is in the public interest and that this public interest is best protected by stronger regulation, standardization, and professionalization. Deregulation advocates believe just as strongly that attention to outputs is best for the individual and that this individual interest is protected by doing away with regulation and the monopoly of education experts. In many ways, the deregulation and professionalization debate falls along traditional dividing lines in American political thought. Cochran-Smith (2001) summarizes the difference between deregulation and professionalization:

> Many of the most contentious debates about the outcomes question in teacher educa-
> tion stem from two fundamentally different approaches to teacher education reform
> and from two fundamentally different views of the purposes of schooling. The first,
> which is intended to reform teacher education through professionalization so that all
> students are guaranteed fully licensed and well-qualified teachers, is based on the belief
> that public education is vital to a democratic society. The second, which is intended
> to reform teacher education through deregulation so that larger numbers of college
> graduates (with no teacher preparation) can enter the profession, is based on a market
> approach to the problem of teacher shortages that feeds off erosion of public confidence
> in education. (p. 527)

WHERE ARE WE GOING? CONNECTING RESEARCH TO POLICY

In *What Matters Most: Teaching for America's Future*, NCTAF (1996) makes five recommendations for improving education, in general, and the quality of teaching, in
particular. It recommends that teacher educators and education professionals:

1. Get serious about standards, for both students and teachers
2. Reinvent teacher preparation and professional development
3. Fix teacher recruitment and put qualified teachers in every classroom
4. Encourage and reward teacher knowledge and skill
5. Create schools that are organized for student and teacher success (p. 11).

In many ways, these echo the research on teacher education and diversity. Reinventing teacher preparation is what scholars recommend when they argue that
teacher education is failing urban schools (Haberman, 1994) and that "something
other than conventional preparation is necessary" (Ladson-Billings, 1994b, p. 138).
Fixing teacher recruitment is what Villegas and Clewell (1998a, 1998b) and Haberman and Post (1998) recommend when arguing for a more diverse teaching force.
Creating schools that are organized for success is what Ladson-Billings (1995b)
calls attention to when warning educators that they cannot "implement an effective multicultural education program without effective fundamental change in the
classrooms and schools in which they teach" (p. 755).

What distinguishes the research of teacher educators concerned with diversity from
the recommendations of NCTAF and other policy-minded organizations is their
explicit commitment to and concern with multicultural education and culturally
relevant pedagogy, the cultural dimensions of learning, the social context of schooling, and the sociopolitical dimensions of diversity and identity in pluralistic and
democratic education. These explicit and nuanced commitments are missing from
policy discourse—even among advocates of improving education for "all children."
In policy discourse—whether in federal policy initiatives or the professionalization-
deregulation debate—there seems to be no mention of preparing "the teacher as
activist, as agent for social change, as ally in anti-racist initiatives" (Cochran-Smith

& Fries, 2001, p. 5). Without this explicit vision, however, the commitment to "all children" threatens to become nothing more than an empty slogan.

This, then, is the challenge for scholars of teacher education and diversity: To bring these explicit commitments into the policy arena, where the path for teacher education is shaped, mandated, and financed; to bring them to bear in such a way that their centrality to our pluralistic and democratic society is obvious and that makes clear that a just, equitable education for "all students" cannot be realized without them:

> As we establish the grounds and groundwork for the outcomes question, one of the challenges we face is how to keep social justice—particularly issues of race, class, and language background—on the agenda. At the same time that a professional consensus has emerged around an image of the professional teacher as knowledgeable, reflective, and collaborative, another image has emerged of the effective teacher of children of color and of children whose first language is not English and/or whose culture is not Western European in origin. This other image of the professional teacher is of one who constructs pedagogy that is culturally relevant, multicultural but also socially reconstructionist, anti-racist, anti-assimilationist, and/or aimed at social justice. In short, the professional teacher is one who teaches in a way that bell hooks has called emancipatory or "transgressive." (Cochran-Smith & Fries, 2001, p. 6)

There is a rich body of scholarship putting forth this vision of the professional teacher, a body of scholarship speaking directly back to the policies of teacher quality, deregulation, accountability, and standardization. This scholarship speaks back to policy—but policy makers don't seem to be listening. If they were, wouldn't the research and recommendations of those truly committed to better educating "all children"—research that even includes documentation of successful practices in schools and communities usually deemed as failing and as "the problem"—be a part of the policy conversation?

There is a clear disconnect between policy and the research on teacher education and diversity. What is the reason? Of course, there is a political dimension—this research stands in clear opposition to the neoliberal reforms, including the deregulation agenda, perpetuated by federal policies since A Nation at Risk. But even among allies, such as professionalization advocates, there seems to be scant attention to the work and recommendations of scholars of teacher education and diversity. Perhaps this disconnect stems from the limitations of this body of research mentioned earlier: A thin empirical base; a lack of longitudinal and large-scale studies; few connections between teacher education and the K–12 classroom and student learning; a lack of research on how specific components of teacher education (e.g., the field study, the cooperating teacher) impact teacher learning; a vague vision for assessing teacher education's effectiveness in terms of multicultural outcomes; a lack of exemplars or programs that are successfully educating teachers for diversity; and a still somewhat narrow conception of diversity in education.

If "education is no longer just about what happens in classrooms and schools, but increasingly about rules and regulations promulgated in state capitals and the federal government" (Sykes, Schneider, & Ford, 2009, p. 1), and if scholars of teacher education and diversity are truly committed to enacting a more just and equitable education, then they must find a way to be heard. Where, then, must the field go in order to impact policy and to be heard by policy makers? Based on the conceptual review conducted here—of both research and policy—there are several areas that need further research, in addition to the need for more empirical, longitudinal, and large-scale studies:

- How do we assess high-quality teacher education for diversity? What competencies and "standards"—what multicultural outcomes—are we measuring our work against, and what tools will we use to assess? How does this assessment connect to K–12 teaching and learning?
- What are the roles of supervisors and cooperating teachers—the teacher educators who, arguably, have the largest impact on preservice teachers, and yet are undertrained and understudied? How do restructured field experiences (e.g., community-based field experiences, cultivating reflective communities of practice) align and improve these teacher education influences? What impact does this improvement have on K–12 teaching and learning?
- What do we find when we follow multicultural teacher education program graduates into their classrooms? What does their practice look like? What impact does the ideological work of teacher education—the cultivation of "habits of mind"—have on K–12 classroom practice and student learning?
- How do we connect individual teachers' and teacher educators' work to larger systemic forces—to programmatic structures, to bureaucratic pressures, to sociopolitical forces? How do we help our preservice teachers to navigate and push back against these forces in order to endure and be successful in urban and multicultural schools?
- What effect does the deregulation of teacher education have on the quality of multicultural and culturally relevant teachers? Do alternative pathways attract more diverse teacher candidates? Are alternative pathways more or less successful at meeting the needs of urban and underserved schools? What is the connection between deregulation and the practices of culturally relevant pedagogy and multicultural education? How does the training provided in alternative pathways impact teachers' multicultural competencies? How does deregulation impact the learning and achievement in multicultural and urban schools?
- What programs and pathways are successful at educating culturally competent teachers? What distinguishes these programs and pathways?
- What can be learned from global and transnational teacher education work on diversity and equity?

Some scholars of teacher education and diversity are already heeding these calls. Cornbleth (2008), for example, followed preservice teachers into their student-teaching classrooms in order to understand how their beliefs about diversity both shaped and were shaped by their student teaching experience. Similarly, Anderson and Olsen (2006) followed graduates of an urban teacher education program into their first year of teaching in order to ascertain their experiences with professional development, particularly how professional development—when combined with their preservice preparation and school setting—shaped these teachers' attitudes about their profession and their career trajectories. Ball's (2006, 2009) decade-long cross-national study followed South African and U.S. teachers who completed a professional development course into schools where diverse students from poverty backgrounds were clustered in order to ascertain what happened to these teachers in the teacher education course that significantly developed their teaching. It demonstrates how teacher education can foster generative thinking and positive attitudes about diversity among teachers using writing as a pedagogical tool to facilitate and document teacher change. Finally, Watson et al. (2006) surveyed first-year urban teachers on their understandings of effective urban teaching versus effective teaching in order to gauge their dispositions about and attitudes toward urban students. What they found was a deficit-laden view—a finding that has deep implications for teacher preparation. From all of this research following program graduates into their classrooms, these researchers are able to make recommendations for improving teacher education and, ultimately, improving K–12 education and student learning.

In fact, these studies point the way toward the direction that research on diversity and teacher education needs to heed if it wants to impact not only the policy conversation but also the quality of K–12 students' education and learning. These are the questions that research on teacher education and diversity needs to ask if it wants to, as Ladson-Billings (1999a) describes, help "students to move out of categories and into their full humanity":

> What kinds of knowledge, skills, and abilities must today's teacher have? How are we to determine teaching excellence? Is a teacher deemed excellent in a suburban, middle-income white community able to demonstrate similar excellence in an urban, poor community? How do we educate teacher educators to meet the challenges and opportunity diversity presents? How do we deconstruct the language of difference to allow students to move out of categories and into their full humanity? (Ladson-Billings, 1999a, p. 242)

NOTES

*With research contributions by Aaliyah Baker, Stefan Breuck, Phillip Caldwell, Lauren Gatti, Kerry Kretchmar, Alison Leonard, Cate Pautsch, Katherina Payne, Mary Perkinson, and Melissa Sherfinski.

1. The sixteen scholars are Arnetha Ball, Marilyn Cochran-Smith, Linda Darling-Hammond, Donna Gollnick, Carl Grant, Martin Haberman, Etta Hollins, Jacqueline Jordan Irvine, Joyce King, Gloria Ladson-Billings, Sonia Neito, Christine Sleeter, Linda Valli, Ana Maria Villegas, Lois Weiner, and Ken Zeichner.

REFERENCES

Anderson, L., & Olsen, B. (2006). Investigating early career urban teachers' perspectives on and experiences in professional development. *Journal of Teacher Education, 57(4)*, 359–77.

Baldwin, J. (1963). A talk to teachers. *Saturday Review*, 42–44.

Ball, A. (2000). Preparing teachers for diversity: Lessons learned from the U.S. and South Africa. *Teaching and Teacher Education, 16(4)*, 491–509.

Ball, A. (2006). *Multicultural strategies for education and social change: Carriers of the torch in the U.S. and South Africa.* New York: Teachers College Press.

Ball, A. (2009). Toward a theory of generative change in culturally and linguistically complex classrooms. *American Educational Research Journal, 46(1),* 45–72.

Ball, A., & Lardner, T. (1997). Dispositions toward language: Teacher constructs of knowledge and the Ann Arbor Black English case. *College Composition and Communication, 48(4),* 469–85.

Ballou, D., & Podgursky, M. (1997). Reforming teacher training and recruitment: A critical appraisal of the recommendation of the National Commission on Teaching and American's Future. *Government Union Review, 17(4),* 1–53.

Ballou, D., & Podgursky, M. (1999). Teacher training and licensure: A layman's guide. In Karstoroom, M., & Finn, C. (Eds.), *Better teacher, better schools* (pp. 31–82). Washington, DC: Thomas Fordham Foundation.

Ballou, D., & Podgursky, M. (2000). Reforming teacher preparation and licensing: What is the evidence? *Teachers College Record, 102(1),* 5–27.

Banks, C. (2005). *Improving multicultural education: Lessons from the intergroup education movement.* New York: Teachers College Press.

Banks, J. (2004). Multicultural education: Historical development, dimensions, and practice. In Banks, J., & Banks, C. (Eds.), *Handbook of research on multicultural education* (2nd ed.), (pp. 3–29). San Francisco: Jossey Bass.

Banks, J., & Banks, C. (Eds.) (2001). *Multicultural education: Issues and perspectives,* fourth edition. Boston: Allyn & Bacon.

Banks, J., Cochran-Smith, M., Moll, L., Richert, A., Zeichner, K., LePage, L., Darling-Hammond, L., Duffy, H., & McDonald, M. (2005). Teaching diverse learners. In Darling-Hammond, L., & Bransford, J. (Eds.). *Preparing teachers for a changing world: What teachers should know and be able to do.* San Francisco: Jossey Bass.

Bartolome, L. (1994). Beyond the methods fetish: Toward a humanizing pedagogy. *Harvard Educational Review, 64(2),* 173–94.

Bilingual Education Act. (1984). Pub. L. No. (98–511), 98 Stat. 2370.

Brown v. Board of Education of Topeka, Kansas. (1954). 347 U.S. 483.

Buras, K. (2008). *Rightist multiculturalism: Core lessons on neoconservative school reform.* New York: Routledge.

Carroll, C. (2008). Morning bell: "An act of war." Retrieved July 24, 2009, from http://blog.heritage.org/2008/04/22/morning-bell-an-act-of-war/

Clark, K., & Plotkin, L. (1972). A review of the issues and literature of cultural deprivation theory. In Clark, K. et al. (Eds.). *The educationally deprived: The potential for change* (pp. 47–73). New York: MARC.

Clewell, B., & Villegas, A. (1999). Creating a nontraditional pipeline for urban teachers: The pathways to teaching careers model. *Journal of Negro Education, 68(3),* 306–17.

Cochran-Smith, M. (2000). Blind vision: Unlearning racism in teacher education. *Harvard Educational Review, 70(2),* 157–90.

Cochran-Smith, M. (2001). The outcomes question in teacher education. *Teaching & Teacher Education, 17(5),* 527–46.

Cochran-Smith, M. (2003a). Learning and unlearning: The education of teacher educators. *Teaching and Teacher Education, 19,* 5–28.

Cochran-Smith, M. (2003b). The multiple meanings of multicultural teacher education: A conceptual framework. *Teacher Education Quarterly, 30(20),* 7–26.

Cochran-Smith, M. (2004). *Walking the road: Race, diversity, and social justice in teacher education.* New York: Teachers College Press.

Cochran-Smith, M. (2008). Toward a theory of teacher education for social justice. Paper prepared for the annual meeting of the American Educational Research Association, April 2008, New York City.

Cochran-Smith, M., Barnatt, J., Friedman, A., & Pine, G. (2009). Inquiry on inquiry: Practitioner research and students' learning. *Action in Teacher Education, 31(2),* 17–32.

Cochran-Smith, M., Davis, D., & Fries, K. (2004). Multicultural teacher education: Research, practice, and policy. In Banks, J., & Banks, C. (Eds.), *Handbook of research on multicultural education* (2nd ed.), (pp. 931–75). New York: Macmillan.

Cochran-Smith, M., & Fries, M. K. (2001). Sticks, stones, and ideology: The discourse of reform in teacher education. *Educational Researcher, 30(8)*, 3–15.

Cochran-Smith, M., & Fries, K. (2005). Researching teacher education in changing times: Politics and paradigms. In Cochran-Smith, M., & Zeichner, K. (Eds.), *Studying teacher education: The report of the AERA panel on research and teacher education* (pp. 69–110). Mahwah, NJ: Lawrence Erlbaum Associates.

Cochran-Smith, M., & Fries, K. (2008). Research on teacher education: Changing times, changing paradigms. In Cochran-Smith, M., Feiman-Nemser, S., McIntyre, J., & Demers, K. (Eds.), *Handbook of research on teacher education: Enduring questions in changing contexts* (3rd ed.), (pp. 1050–93). New York: Routledge.

Cochran-Smith, M., & Lytle, S. (1993). *Inside/Outside: Teacher research and knowledge.* New York: Teachers College Press.

Cochran-Smith, M., & Lytle, S. (2009). *Inquiry as stance: Practitioner research in the next generation.* New York: Teachers College Press.

Cochran-Smith, M., Mitescu, E., Shakman, K., & the Boston College TNE Evidence Team (in press). Just measures: Social justice as a teacher education outcome. *Teacher Education and Practice.*

Cochran-Smith, M., Shakman, K., Jong, C., Terrell, D., Barnatt, J., & McQuillan, P. (2009). Good and just teaching: The case for social justice in teacher education. *American Journal of Education, 115,* 347–77.

Cochran-Smith, M., & Zeichner, K. (2005). *Studying teacher education: The report of the AERA panel on research and teacher education.* Mahwah, NJ: Lawrence Erlbaum Publishers.

Coleman, J. (1966). *Equal educational opportunity.* Cambridge, MA: Harvard Educational Review.

Coleman, J. (1972). The evaluation of "Equality of educational opportunity." In Mosteller, F., & Moynihan, D. (Eds.), *On equality of educational opportunity* (pp. 149–50). New York: Vintage Books.

Conant, J. (1963). *The education of American teachers.* New York: McGraw-Hill.

Cornbleth, C. (2008). *Diversity and the new teacher: Learning from experience in urban schools.* New York: Teachers College Press.

Darling-Hammond, L. (1995). Inequality and access to knowledge. In Banks, J., & Banks, C. (Eds.), *Handbook of research on multicultural education* (pp. 465–83). New York: Simon & Schuster Macmillan.

Darling-Hammond, L. (1997). *Doing what matters most: Investing in quality teaching.* Kutztown, PA: National Commission on Teaching and America's Future.

Darling-Hammond, L. (2000a). *Solving the dilemmas of teacher supply, demand, and standards: How we can ensure a competent, caring, and qualified teacher for every child.* New York: National Commission on Teaching & America's Future.

Darling-Hammond, L. (2000b). Teacher quality and student achievement: A review of state policy evidence. *Educational Policy Analysis, 8(1).* Retrieved from http://epaa.asu.edu/ojs /article/view/392.

Darling-Hammond, L. (2004a). The color line in American education: Race, resources, and student achievement. *Du Bois Review, 1(2),* 213–46.

Darling-Hammond, L. (2004b). Standards, accountability, and school reform. *Teachers College Record, (106)6,* 1047–85.

Darling-Hammond, L., & Bransford, J. (2005). *Preparing teachers for a changing world: What teachers should learn and be able to do.* San Francisco: Jossey-Bass.

Darling-Hammond, L., Wise, A., & Klein, S. (1999). *A license to teach: Raising standards for teaching.* San Francisco: Jossey-Bass.

Day-Vines, N., & Patton, J. (2003). The perils, pitfalls, and promises of the No Child Left Behind Act of 2001: Implications for the education of African American and other minority learners. *T/TAC Link Lines*, 1–5.

Denzin, N., & Lincoln, Y. (2007). Introduction: The discipline and practice of qualitative research. In Denzin, N., and Lincoln, Y. (Eds.), *Collecting and interpreting qualitative materials* (pp. 1–55). Thousand Oaks, CA: Sage Publications.

Dewey, J. (1904). *Democracy and education: An introduction to the philosophy of education*. New York: MacMillan.

Dill, V. (1996). Alternative teacher certification. In J. Sikula (Ed.), *Handbook of research on teacher education* (2nd ed.), (pp. 932–60). New York: MacMillan.

Enterline, S., Cochran-Smith, M., Ludlow, L., & Mitescu, E. (2009). Learning to teach for social justice: Measuring change in the beliefs of teacher candidates. *New Educator, 4*, 1–24.

Etzoni, A. (1969). *Semi-professions and their organization: Teachers, nurses, social workers*. New York: Free Press.

Feistrizer, E. (2008). *Alternate routes to teaching*. New Jersey: Pearson Education.

Gay, G. (1993). Building cultural bridges: A bold proposal for teacher education. *Education and Urban Society, 25(3)*, 285–99.

Gay, G. (2000). *Culturally responsive teaching: Theory, research and practice*. New York: Teachers College Press.

Gollnick, D. (1978). *Multicultural education in teacher education: The state of the scene*. Washington, DC: American Association of Colleges for Teacher Education.

Gollnick, D. (1995). National and state initiatives for multicultural education. In Banks, J., & Banks, C., (Eds.), *Handbook of research on multicultural education* (pp. 44–64). New York: Simon & Schuster Macmillan.

Gollnick, D. et al. (1979). *Analysis of teacher education's need for materials and training related to sex equity: Final report*. Washington, DC: American Association of Colleges for Teacher Education.

Gollnick, D., Osayende, K., & Levy, J. (1980). *Multicultural teacher education: Case studies of thirteen programs*. Washington, DC: American Association of Colleges for Teacher Education.

Grant, C. (1981). Education that is multicultural and teacher preparation: An examination from the perspectives of preservice students. *Journal of Educational Research, 75(2)*, 95–101.

Grant, C. (1982). Educational research and teacher training for successfully teaching LEP students. In *Proceedings of the second national research symposium on limited English proficient student issues: Focus on evaluation and measurement* (Vol. 2) (pp. 431–55). Washington, DC: U.S. Department of Education Office of Bilingual Education and Minority Languages Affairs.

Grant, C. (1991). Culture and teaching: What do teachers need to know? In Kennedy, M. (Ed.), *Teaching academic subjects to diverse learners* (pp. 237–56). New York: Teachers College Press.

Grant, C., & Agosto, V. (2006). What are we tripping on?: Transgressing the fault lines in research in the preparation of multicultural educators. In Conrad, C. & Serlin, R. (Eds.), *The Sage handbook for research in education* (pp. 95–115). Thousand Oaks, CA: Sage.

Grant, C., & Agosto, V. (2008). Teacher capacity and social justice in teacher education. In Cochran-Smith, M., Feiman-Nemser, S., Demers, K., & McIntyre, D. (Eds.), *Handbook of research on teacher education: Enduring questions in changing contexts* (pp. 175–202). Mahwah, NJ: Lawrence Erlbaum Associates.

Grant, C., & Chapman, T. (2008). *History of multicultural education*. New York: Routledge.

Grant, C., Elsbree, R., & Fondrie, S. (2004). A decade of research on the changing terrain of multicultural research. In Banks, J. & Banks, C. (Eds.), *Handbook of research on multicultural education* (2nd ed.) (pp. 184–207). San Francisco: Jossey-Bass.

Grant, C., & Koskela, R. (1986). Education that is multicultural and the relationship between preservice campus learning and field experience. *Journal of Educational Research, 79(4),* 197–204.

Grant, C., & Millar, S. (1992). Research and multicultural education: Barriers, needs and boundaries. In Grant, C. (Ed.), *Research & multicultural education: From the margins to the mainstream.* London: Falmer Press.

Grant, C., & Secada, W. (1990). Preparing teachers for diversity. In Houston, W. (Ed.), *Handbook of research on teacher education* (pp. 403–22). New York: Macmillian.

Grant, C., & Sleeter, C. (1985). The literature on multicultural education: Review and analysis. *Educational Review, 37(2),* 97–118.

Grant, C., & Tate, W. (1995). Multicultural education through the lens of the multicultural education research literature. In Banks, J., & Banks, C. (Eds.), *Handbook of research on multicultural education* (pp. 145–66). New York: Macmillan.

Grant, C., & Zozakiewicz, C. (1995). Student teachers, cooperating teachers, and supervisors: Interrupting the multicultural silences of student teaching. In Larkin, J., & Sleeter, C. (Eds.), *Developing multicultural teacher education curricula* (pp. 259–78). Albany: Sate University of New York Press.

Haberman, M. (1988a). Proposals for recruiting minority teachers: Promising practices and attractive detours. *Journal of Teacher Education, 33(4),* 38–44.

Haberman, M. (1988b). *Recruiting and selecting teachers for urban schools.* New York: ERIC Clearinghouse on Urban Education.

Haberman, M. (1991a). Can cultural awareness be taught in teacher education programs? *Teaching Education, 4(1),* 25–31.

Haberman, M. (1991b). The rationale for training adults as teachers. In Sleeter, C. (Ed.), *Empowerment through multicultural education* (pp. 275–97). Albany: SUNY Press.

Haberman, M. (1993). Predicting the success of urban teachers (The Milwaukee Trials). *Action in Teacher Education, 15(3),* 1–5.

Haberman, M. (1994). Preparing teachers for the real world of urban schools. *Educational Forcum, 58,* 162–68.

Haberman, M. (1995a). Dimensions of excellence in programs preparing teachers for urban poverty schools. *Peabody Journal of Education, 70(2),* 24–43.

Haberman, M. (1995b). *Star teachers of children in poverty.* West Lafayette, IN: Kappa Delta Pi.

Haberman, M. (1996). Selecting and preparing culturally competent teachers for urban schools. In Sikula, J., Buttery, T., & Guyton, E. (Eds.), *Handbook of research on teacher education: A project of the Association of Teacher Educators* (2nd ed.), (pp. 747–60). New York: Simon & Schuster Macmillan.

Haberman, M. (2000). Urban schools: Day camps or custodial centers? *Phi Delta Kappan, 82(3),* 203–8.

Haberman, M., & Post, L. (1990). Cooperating teachers' perceptions of the goals of multicultural education. *Action in Teacher Education, 12(3),* 31–35.

Haberman, M., & Post, L. (1992). Does direct experience change education students' perceptions of low-income or minority children? *Midwestern Educational Researcher, 5(2),* 29–31.

Haberman, M., & Post, L. (1998). Teachers for multicultural schools: The power of selection. *Theory into Practice, 37(2),* 96–104.

Heritage Foundation. (2009). *The Carte: How special interests block real education reform.* Washington, DC: Heritage Foundation.

Hollins, E. (1982). The Marva Collins story revisited. *Journal of Teacher Education, 32(1),* 37–40.

Hollins, E. (1990). Debunking the myth of a monolithic white American culture; or, moving toward cultural inclusion. *American Behavioral Scientist, 34(2),* 201–9.

Hollins, E. (1993). Assessing teacher competence for diverse populations. *Theory into Practice, 32(2),* 93-99.

Hollins, E. (1997). Directed inquiry in preservice teacher education: A developmental process model. In King, J., Hollins, E., & Hayman, W. (Eds.), *Preparing teachers for cultural diversity* (pp. 97-112). New York: Teachers College Press.

Hollins, E. (1999). Relating ethnic and racial identity development to teaching. In Sheets, R., & Hollins, E. (Eds.), *Racial and ethnic identity in school practices: Aspects of human development* (pp. 183-93). Mahwah, NJ: Lawrence Erlbaum Associates.

Hollins, E. (2006). Transforming practice: Structured dialogue spurred educators at two underachieving schools to fuel their own professional development. *Educational Leadership, 63(6),* 48-52.

Hollins, E. (2008). *Culture in school learning: Revealing the deep meaning* (2nd ed.). Mahwah, NJ: Lawrence Erlbaum Associates.

Hollins, E., & Guzman, M. (2005). Research on preparing teachers for diverse populations. In Cochran-Smith, M. & Zeichner, K. (Eds.), *Studying teacher education: The report of the AERA panel on research and teacher education* (pp. 477-548). Mahwah, NJ: Lawrence Erlbaum Associates.

Hollins, E., McIntyre, L., DeBose, C., Hollins, K., & Towner, A. (2004). Promoting a self-sustaining learning community: Investigating an internal model for teacher development. *International Journal of Qualitative Studies in Education, 17(2),* 247-64.

Hollins, E., & Spencer, K. (1991). Restructuring schools for cultural inclusion: Changing the schooling process for African American youngsters. *Journal of Education, 172(2),* 89-100.

Holmes Group. (1986). *Teachers for tomorrow's schools.* East Lansing, MI: Holmes Group.

Horowitz, F., Darling-Hammond, L., & Bransford, J. (2005). Educating teachers for developmentally appropriate practice. In Darling-Hammond, L., & Bransford, J. (Eds.), *Preparing teachers for a changing world: What teachers should learn and be able to do.* San Francisco: Jossey Bass.

Interstate New Teacher Assessment and Support Consortium. (2009). INTASC Standards development. Retrieved July 12, 2009, from http://www.ccsso.org/projects/interstate_new_teacher_assessment_and_support_consortium/Projects/Standards_Development/

Irvine, J. (1988). An analysis of the problem of disappearing black educators. *Elementary School Journal, 88(5),* 503-13.

Irvine, J. (1989). Beyond role models: An examination of cultural influences on the pedagogical perspectives of black teachers. *Peabody Journal of Education, 66(4),* 51-63.

Irvine, J. (1990). *Black students and school failure: Policies, practices, and prescriptions.* New York: Praeger.

Irvine, J. (2002). *In search of wholeness: African American teachers and their culturally specific classroom practices.* New York: Palgrave.

Irvine, J. (2003). *Educating teachers for diversity: Seeing with a cultural eye.* New York: Teachers College Press.

Irvine, J., & Fraser, J. (1998). "Warm demanders": Do national certification standards leave room for culturally responsive pedagogy of African American teachers? *Education Week, 17(35),* 56-57.

Irvine, J., & Hill, L. (1990). From plantation to schoolhouse: The rise and decline of black women teachers. *Humanity and Society, 14(3),* 244-56.

Irvine, J., & York, D. (1995). Learning styles and culturally diverse students: A literature review. In Banks, J., & Banks, C. (Eds.), *Handbook of research on multicultural education* (pp. 484-97). New York: Macmillan.

Jacobson, M. (1998). *Whiteness of a different color: European immigrants and the alchemy of race.* Cambridge, MA: Harvard University Press.

Kennedy, M. (2007). Defining a literature. *Educational Researcher, 36(3),* 139-47.

King, J. (1991). Dysconscious racism: Ideology, identity, and the miseducation of teachers. *Journal of Negro Education, 60(2)*, 133–46.

King, J. (1994). The purpose of schooling for African American children: Including cultural knowledge. In Hollins, E., King, J., & Hayman, W. (Eds.), *Teaching diverse populations: Formulating a knowledge base* (pp. 25–59). Albany: State University of New York Press.

King, J. (1997). "Thank you for opening our minds": On praxis, transmutation, and black studies in teacher development. In King, J., Hollins, E., & Hayman, W. (Eds.), *Preparing teachers for cultural diversity* (pp. 156–69). New York: Teachers College Press.

King, J. (2004). Culture-centered knowledge: Black studies, curriculum transformation, and social action. In Banks, J., & Banks, C. (Eds.), *Handbook of research on multicultural education* (2nd ed.), (pp. 349–78). San Francisco: Jossey-Bass.

King, J. (2005). A transformative vision of black education for human freedom. In King, J. (Ed.), *Black education: A transformative research agenda* (pp. 3–17). Mahwah, NJ: Lawrence Erlbaum.

King, J., & Ladson-Billings, G. (1990). The teacher education challenge in elite university settings: Developing critical perspectives for teaching in a democratic and multicultural society. *European Journal of Intercultural Studies, 1(2)*, 15–30.

Koerner, J. (1963). *The miseducation of American teachers.* New York: Harper & Row.

Ladson-Billings, G. (1991). Beyond multicultural illiteracy. *Journal of Negro Education, 60(2)*, 147–57.

Ladson-Billings, G. (1994a). *The dreamkeepers: Successful teachers of African American children.* San Francisco: Jossey-Bass.

Ladson-Billings, G. (1994b). Who will teach *our* children? Preparing teachers to successfully teach African American students. In Hollins, E., King, J., & Hayman, W. (Eds.), *Teaching diverse populations: Formulating a knowledge base* (pp. 129–58). Albany: SUNY Press.

Ladson-Billings, G. (1995a). But that's just good teaching! The case for culturally relevant pedagogy. *Theory into Practice, 34(3)*, 158–65.

Ladson-Billings, G. (1995b). Multicultural teacher education: Research, practice, and policy. In Banks, J., & Banks, C. (Eds.), *Handbook of research in multicultural education* (pp. 747–59). San Francisco: Jossey-Bass.

Ladson-Billings, G. (1995c). Toward a theory of culturally relevant pedagogy. *American Educational Research Journal, 32(3)*, 465–91.

Ladson-Billings, G. (1998). Teaching in dangerous times: Culturally relevant approaches to teacher assessment. *Journal of Negro Education, 67(3)*, 255–67.

Ladson-Billings, G. (1999a). Preparing teachers for diverse student populations: A critical race theory perspective. *Review of Research in Education, 24*, 211–47.

Ladson-Billings, G. (1999b). Preparing teachers for diversity: Historical perspectives, current trends, and future directions. In Darling-Hammond, L., & Sykes, G., (Eds.), *Teaching as the learning profession: Handbook of policy and practice* (pp. 84–123). San Francisco: Jossey-Bass.

Ladson-Billings, G. (2000). Fighting for our lives: Preparing teachers to teach African American students. *Journal of Teacher Education, 51(3)*, 206–14.

Ladson-Billings, G. (2001). *Crossing over to Canaan: The journey of new teachers in diverse classrooms.* San Francisco: Jossey-Bass.

Ladson-Billings, G. (2006a). It's not the culture of poverty, it's the poverty of culture: The problem with teacher education. *Anthropology and Education Quarterly, 37(2)*, 104–9.

Ladson-Billings, G. (2006b). "Yes, but how do we do it?" Practicing culturally relevant pedagogy. In Landsman, J., and Lewis, C. (Eds.)., *White teachers/diverse classrooms: A guide to building inclusive schools, promoting high expectations, and eliminating racism* (pp. 29–42). Sterling, VA: Stylus.

Lewis, O. (1966). *La vida: A Puerto Rican family in the culture of poverty.* New York: Random House.

Lortie, D. (1975). *Schoolteacher: A sociological study.* Chicago: University of Chicago Press.

Lucas, T., Villegas, A., & Freedson-Gonzalez, M. (2008). Linguistically responsive teacher education: Preparing classroom teachers to teach English language learners. *Journal of Teacher Education, 59(1),* 361–73.

Mabee, C. (1979). *Black education in New York State: From colonial to modern times.* New York: Syracuse University Press.

Manhattan Institute. (2000). New York City conference on school choice event transcript. Retrieved August 15, 2009, from http://www.manhattan-institute.org/html/huber.htm

Manno, C. (1994). *Outcome-based education: Has it become more affliction than cure?* Retrieved July 12, 2009, from http://www.americanexperiment.org/main.php

Melnick, S., & Zeichner, K. (1997). Teacher education for cultural diversity: Enhancing the capacity of teacher education institutions to address diversity issues. In King, J., Hollins, E., & Hayman, W. (Eds.), *Meeting the challenge of diversity in teacher preparation* (pp. 23–39). New York: Teachers College Press.

Melnick, S., & Zeichner, K. (1998) Teacher education's responsibility to address diversity issues: Enhancing institutional capacity. *Theory into Practice, 37(2),* 88–95.

Montalto, N. (1982). The intercultural education movement, 1922–1941: The growth of tolerance as a form of intolerance. In Weiss, J. (Ed.), *American education and the European immigrant: 1840–1940* (pp. 142–60). Urbana: University of Illinois Press.

National Board for Professional Teaching Standards. (2002). *What teachers should know and be able to do.* Arlington, VA: NBPTS.

National Commission on Excellence in Education. (1983). *A nation at risk.* Washington, DC: U.S. Department of Education.

National Commission on Teaching and America's Future. (1996). *What matters most: Teaching for America's future.* New York: National Commission on Teaching and America's Future.

National Council for the Accreditation of Teacher Education. (1979). *Standards for the accreditation of teacher education.* Washington, DC: NCATE.

National Council for the Accreditation of Teacher Education. (2009). *Professional standards for the accreditation of teacher preparation institutions.* Washington, DC: NCATE.

Nieto, S. (1994). Lessons from students on creating a chance to dream. *Harvard Educational Review, 64(24),* 392–426.

Nieto, S. (1999). *The light in their eyes: Creating multicultural learning communities.* New York: Teachers College Press.

Nieto, S. (2000). Placing equity front and center: Some thoughts on transforming teacher education for a new century. *Journal of Teacher Education, 51,* 180–87.

Nieto, S. (2003a). Challenging current notions of "highly qualified teachers" through work in a teachers' inquiry group. *Journal of Teacher Education, 54,* 386–98.

Nieto, S. (2003b). *What keeps teachers going?* New York: Teachers College Press.

Nieto, S. (2005). *Why we teach.* New York: Teachers College Press.

Nieto, S. (2009). From surviving to thriving. *Educational Leadership, 66(5),* 8–13.

Nieto, S., & Bode, P. (2008). *Affirming diversity: The sociopolitical context of multicultural education* (5th ed.). Boston: Pearson.

Nye, R. (1960). *The cultural life of the new nation, 1776–1830.* New York: Harper Row.

Olneck, M. (2004). Immigrants and education in the United States. In Banks, J., and Banks, C. (Eds.), *Handbook of research on multicultural education* (2nd ed.), (pp. 381–403). San Francisco: Jossey-Bass.

Pagano, A., Weiner, L., Obi, R., & Swearingen, J. (1995) How student teaching in an urban setting affects teacher candidates' career motivations. *Urban Review, 27(1),* 51–76.

Pagano, A., Weiner, L., Obi, R., & Swearingen, J. (1997). How teaching in the urban setting affects career motivations of beginning teachers: A longitudinal study. Paper presented at the annual meeting of the American Educational Research Association, Chicago.

Phillips, M. R. (1940). The Negro secondary school teacher. *Journal of Negro Education, 9(3),* 482–97.

Pioneer Institute for Policy Research. (2006). *Charter school facts: Paper No. 1.* Boston, MA: Pioneer Institute.

Price, J., & Valli, L. (1998). Institutional support for diversity in preservice teacher education. *Theory into Practice, 37(2),* 114–20.

Rotherham, A., & Mead, S. (2003). *Teacher quality: Beyond No Child Left Behind—A response to Kaplan and Owings (2002).* Reston, VA: NASSP Bulletin.

Shen, J. (1997). Has alternative certification policy materialized its promise? A comparison between traditionally and alternatively certified teachers in public schools. *Educational Evaluation and Policy Analysis, 19,* 276–83.

Sigerman, H. (2000). An unfinished battle, 1848–1865. In Cott, N. (Ed.), *No small courage: A history of women in the United States.* New York: Oxford University Press.

Sleeter, C. (1985). A need for research on preservice teacher education for mainstreaming multicultural education. *Journal of Educational Equity and Leadership, 5(3),* 205–15.

Sleeter, C. (1989). Doing multicultural education across the grade levels and subject areas: A case study of Wisconsin. *Teaching & Teacher Education, 5(3),* 189–203.

Sleeter, C. (1992a). *Keepers of the American dream: A study of staff development and multicultural education.* Washington, DC: Falmer Press.

Sleeter, C. (1992b). Resisting racial awareness: How teachers understand the social order from their racial, gender, and social class locations. *Educational Foundations, 6* (Spring), 7–32.

Sleeter, C. (1992c). Restructuring schools for multicultural education. *Journal of Teacher Education, 43(2),* 141–48.

Sleeter, C. (1995). An analysis of the critiques of multicultural education. In Banks, J., & Banks, C. (Eds.), *Handbook of research on multicultural education.* San Francisco: Jossey-Bass.

Sleeter, C. (1996). *Multicultural education as social activism.* Albany: SUNY Press.

Sleeter, C. (2001). Preparing teaching for culturally diverse schools: Research and the overwhelming presence of whiteness. *Journal of Teacher Education, 52(2),* 94–106.

Sleeter, C. (2004). Critical multicultural curriculum and the standards movement. *English Teaching: Practice and Critique, 3(2),* 122–38.

Sleeter, C. (2008a). Equity, democracy, and neoliberal assaults on teacher education. *Teaching and Teacher Education, 24,* 1947–57.

Sleeter, C. (2008b). Preparing white teachers for diverse students. In Cochran-Smith, M., Feiman-Nemser, S., Demers, K., & McIntyre, D. (Eds.), *Handbook of research on teacher education: Enduring questions in changing contexts* (pp. 175–202). Mahwah, NJ: Lawrence Erlbaum Associates.

Sleeter, C., & Boyle-Baise, M. (2000). Community service learning for multicultural teacher education. *Educational Foundations, 14(2),* 33–50.

Sleeter, C., & Grant, C. (1999). *Making choices for multicultural education: Five approaches to race, class, and gender* (3rd ed.). Upper Saddle River, NJ: Prentiss Hall.

Sleeter, C., Hughes, B., Meador, E., Whang, P., Rogers, L., Blackwell, K., et al. (2005). Working an academically rigorous, multicultural program. *Equity and Excellence, 38(4),* 290–98.

Sleeter, C., Torres, M., & Laughlin, P. (2001). Scaffolding conscientization through inquiry in teacher education. *Teacher Education Quarterly, 31(1),* 81–96.

Smith, J., & Hodkinson, P. (2007). Relativism, criteria, and politics. In Denzin, N., and Lincoln, Y. (Eds.), *Collecting and interpreting qualitative materials* (pp. 411–34). Thousand Oaks, CA: Sage Publications.

Stoddard, T., & Floden, R. (1995). *Traditional and alternative routes to teacher certification: Issues, assumption and misconceptions.* East Lansing, MI: National Center of Research on Teaching.

Sykes, G., Schneider, B., & Ford, T. (2009). *Handbook of education policy research.* New York: Routledge.

Tabachnick, B., & Zeichner, K. (1993). Preparing teachers for cultural diversity. *Journal of Education for Teaching: International Research and Pedagogy, 19(4)*, 113–24.

Task Force on Teaching as a Profession. (1986). *A nation prepared: Teachers for the 21st century.* Washington, DC: Carnegie Forum on Education and the Economy.

Thomas B. Fordham Foundation. (1999). *The teachers we need and how to get more of them: A manifesto.* Washington, DC: Thomas B. Fordham Foundation.

U.S. Department of Education. (2004). *A guide to education and No Child Left Behind.* Jessup, MD: Education Publications Center.

U.S. Kerner Commission. (1968). *Report of the National Advisory Commission on Civil Disorders.* Washington, DC: U.S. Government Printing Office.

Valli, L. (1995). The dilemma of race: Learning to be colorblind and color conscious. *Journal of Teacher Education, 46(2)*, 120–29.

Valli, L. (1996a). Learning to teach in cross-cultural settings: The significance of personal relations. In Rios, F. (Ed.), *Teacher thinking in cultural contexts* (pp. 282–307). New York: SUNY Press.

Valli, L. (1996b). Trusting relations, preservice teachers, and multicultural schools. In McIntyre, D. J., & Byrd, D. (Eds.), *Preparing tomorrow's teachers: The field experience* (pp. 26–40). Thousand Oaks, CA: Corwin Press.

Valli, L. (2000). Facing the urban, diversity challenge: Teacher education in the United States. In Scott, A., & Freeman-Moir, J. (Eds.), *Tomorrow's teachers: International and critical perspectives on teacher education* (pp. 123–42). Christchurch, New Zealand: Canterbury University Press.

Valli, L., Cooper, D., & Frankes, L. (1997). Professional development schools and equity: A critical analysis of rhetoric and research. In Apple, M. (Ed.), *Review of Educational Research, 22*, 251–304. Washington, DC: AERA.

Villegas, A. (1988). School failure and cultural mismatch: Another view. *Urban Review, 20(4)*, 253–65.

Villegas, A. (2007). Dispositions in teacher education: A look at social justice. *Journal of Teacher Education, 58(5)*, 370–80.

Villegas, A., & Clewell, B. (1998a). Increasing the number of teachers of color for urban schools: Lessons from the Pathways National Evaluation. *Education and Urban Society, 31(2)*, 42–61.

Villegas, A., & Clewell, B. (1998b). Increasing teacher diversity by tapping the paraprofessional pool. *Theory into Practice, 37(2)*, 121–30.

Villegas, A., & Davis, D. (2008). Preparing teachers of color to confront racial/ethnic disparities in educational outcomes. In Cochran-Smith, M., Feiman-Nemser, S., Demers, K., & McIntyre, D. (Eds.), *Handbook of research on teacher education: Enduring questions in changing contexts* (pp. 583–605). Mahwah, NJ: Lawrence Earlbaum & Associates.

Villegas, A., et al. (1993). *Teaching for diversity: Models for expanding the supply of minority teachers. A policy issue perspective.* Princeton, NJ: Educational Testing Services.

Villegas, A., & Lucas, T. (2002). *Educating culturally responsive teachers: A coherent approach.* Albany: SUNY.

Villegas, A., & Lucas, T. (2004). Diversifying the teacher workforce: A retrospective and prospective analysis. In Smylie, M., & Miretzky, D. (Eds.), *Developing the teacher workforce* (pp. 70–104). Chicago: University of Chicago Press.

Watson, D., Charner-Laird, M., Kirkpatrick, C., Szczesiul, S., & Gordon, P. (2006). Grappling with definitions, grappling with difference. *Journal of Teacher Education, 57(4)*, 395–409.

Weiner, L. (1993a). Choosing teaching as a career: Comparing motivations of Harvard and urban college students. Paper presented at the Conference of the Eastern Educational Research Association.

Weiner, L. (1993b). *Preparing teachers for urban schools: Lessons from thirty years of school reform.* New York: Teachers College Press.

Weiner, L. (2000). Research in the 90s: Implications for urban teacher preparation. *Review of Educational Research, 70(3)*, 369–406.

Weiner, L. (2002). Evidence and inquiry in teacher education: What's needed for urban schools? *Journal of Teacher Education, 53*, 254.

Weiner, L. (2003). Why is classroom management so vexing to urban teachers? *Theory into Practice, 42(4)*, 305–12.

Weiner, L., Rand, M., Pagano, A., Obi, R., Hall, A., & Bloom, A. (2001). Illuminating the impact of state educational policy promoting school reform on curriculum and instruction programs. *Educational Policy, 15*, 644–73.

Wilson, S., Floden, R., & Ferrini-Mundy, J. (2001). *Teacher preparation research: Current knowledge, gaps, and recommendations.* Seattle: Center for the Study of Teaching & Policy.

Woodson, C. (1933/2008). *The mis-education of the Negro.* New York: Classic House Books.

Zeichner, K. (1995). Preparing educators for cross-cultural teaching. In Hawley, W., & Jackson, A. (Eds.), *Toward a common destiny: Improving race and ethnic relations* (pp. 397–419). San Francisco: Jossey-Bass.

Zeichner, K. (1996). Educating teachers for cultural diversity in the United States. In Craft, M. (Ed.), *Teacher education in pluralistic societies: An international review* (pp. 141–58). New York: Routledge.

Zeichner, K. (2003). The adequacies and inadequacies of three current strategies to recruit, prepare, and retain the best teachers for all students. *Teacher's College Record,* 105(3), 490–515.

Zeichner, K. (2007). Accumulating knowledge across self-studies in teacher education. *Journal of Teacher Education.* 58(1), 36–46.

Zeichner, K., & Grant, C. (1981). Biography and social structure in the socialization of student teachers: A re-examination of the pupil control ideologies of student teachers. *Journal of Education for Teaching, 7(3)*, 298–314.

Zeichner, K., Grant, C., Gay, G., Gillette, M., & Valli, L. (1998). A research informed vision of good practice in multicultural teacher education: Design principles. *Theory into practice, 37(2)*, 163–211.

Zeichner, K., & Hoeft, K. (1996). Teacher socialization for cultural diversity. In Houston, R. (Ed.), *Handbook of research on teacher education* (pp. 525–47). New York: Macmillan.

Zeichner, K., & Liston, D. (1990). Teacher education and the social context of schooling: Issues for curriculum development. *American Educational Research Journal, 27(4)*, 610–36.

Zeichner, K., & Melnick, S. (1996a). Community field experiences and teacher preparation for diversity: A case study. In McIntyre, D., & Byrd, D. (Eds.), *Preparing tomorrow's teachers: The field experience* (pp. 41–61). Thousand Oaks, CA: Corwin Press.

Zeichner, K., & Melnick, S. (1996b). The role of community field experiences in preparing teachers for cultural diversity. In Zeichner, K., Melnick, S., and Gomez, M. (Eds.), *Currents of reform in preservice teacher education* (pp. 176–96). New York: Teachers College Press.

Zeichner, K., & Wray, S. (2001). The teaching portfolio in U.S. teacher education programs: What we know and what we need to know. *Teaching and Teacher Education, 17(5)*, 613–21.

2

Creating Interdisciplinary Multicultural Teacher Education

Courageous Leadership Is Crucial

Valerie Ooka Pang and Cynthia D. Park

INTRODUCTION

Our progress as a nation is dependent not only upon an informed citizenry but also on one that is willing to take responsibility to protect the rights of a diverse people to life, liberty, equality, and the pursuit of happiness (Zinn, 1990). The sustainability of our democracy is dependent upon the capacity of citizens of varied backgrounds to work together with respect and collaboration in addressing social problems (Dewey, 1916). The public educational system provides opportunities through the teaching and learning processes not only to replicate the social system as it stands but to also reform society as an agent of social change. In support of these social goals, it is the responsibility of teacher educators engaged in multicultural education to provide the leadership to strengthen the role of equity as a guiding force in teacher education (Gay, 2005).

However, the cultural characteristics and lived experiences of the majority of new teachers coming into the system continue to be dissimilar to those of many students from low-income and underachieving schools. This divergence continues to widen. Teachers who have little knowledge about their students—how the students are brought up at home, how they speak to one another outside formal academic settings, and the cultural-knowledge base their students bring to school—face extraordinary challenges in knowing how to create an effective learning environment. This disparity is further exacerbated because schools and colleges in charge of teacher preparation also seem to be determined to maintain an organizational and philosophical structure that supports the nineteenth-century industrial factory model and mainstream cultural orientation. Research points to this lack of cultural and linguistic continuity between teachers and students. The results of large-scale surveys of newer teachers in Texas and New York City (Darling-Hammond, Chung, & Frelow, 2002; Zeintek, 2007) underscore the need for renewal in teacher preparation. They found that teachers trained in both traditional teacher certification and alternative teacher credentialing programs did not feel prepared to develop multicultural curriculum that addressed the learning needs of their students. When teachers believe they do not have the ability to create effective instruction for all children, how possible can it be to achieve equity in education?

Therefore, multicultural teacher education, a field dedicated to providing equity in education, should be in the vanguard of professional development efforts not only for teachers but also for instructional leaders, principals, teacher educators, staff developers, community activists, and others whose charge it is to improve learning. Placing multicultural teacher education front and center in the enterprise of teacher development will take courage—the social and political courage necessary to construct and apply a new interdisciplinary paradigm based on a strong cross-disciplinary knowledge base that will reinforce equity and cultural diversity as the core of teacher education and will ensure that equity becomes an integrated value among those charged with training teachers, instructional leaders, and professional developers.

Gaining credibility for the emerging discipline of multicultural teacher education will demand research that is more reliable and valid than has been the case (Zientek, Capraro, & Capraro, 2008). In addition, those engaged in multicultural teacher education must create structural institutional changes that encourage their peers to hire culturally and linguistically diverse teacher educators (Gay, 2000). An increase in diversity among a new generation of teacher educators will bring new orientations, understandings, and ways of knowing that are essential to meeting the mission, goals, and study of multicultural teacher education. Courageous leadership is crucial in this endeavor, for as Gay (2005) has written, change is difficult due to the pervasive and perennial presence of status quo political influences in both teacher education and in schools.

In this study we examine the impact that cross-disciplinary scholarship related to multicultural concerns has had and could have on the theory and practice of teacher education. We utilize historical data that presents a case study of a federal initiative designed to infuse multicultural education into teacher education. The case study will identify lessons learned about the infusion process. We also present a new interdisciplinary paradigm for multicultural teacher education that addresses the challenges of education's ever-changing social contexts. This paradigm includes change on three specific levels: organizational change in colleges and schools of education, curricular change throughout the professional development of teachers, and individual change in educators. Our discussion begins by addressing five issues critical to ensuring that equity is infused into all aspects of teacher education. Our theoretical understanding of equity includes the social context of race, culture, religion, class, gender, language, sexual orientation, and disabilities.

In order for a new paradigm for multicultural teacher education to be developed, we believe the following issues must be addressed.

Issue 1. Educators must continue to question the traditional focus of schooling from transmission of cultural knowledge to "informed social criticism" (Vinson, 1998). A more effective paradigm of multicultural teacher education would substantially improve how teachers themselves become more reflective thinkers willing to challenge social adaptation (Hahn, 1996; Nofke, 2000; Ross, 2001; Stanley & Nelson, 1994), and how they commit to the struggle of moving beyond the status quo to address and take action on complex contemporary social issues surrounding race, racism, gender bias, disabilities, religion, language, culture, immigration, and classism. In order for teachers to be reflective educators in a democracy committed to infusing equity into schools, they must be informed critical thinkers and effective curriculum and instruction specialists. They also must be empowered to work collaboratively to engender a genuine sense of community among culturally diverse people. In this regard a useful conceptual framework to guide the work of schools and colleges of education begins with a clear understanding of issues related to equity.

Issue 2. Given the present-day conservative political climate, it is more important than ever that teacher educators address the criticisms (Bloom, 1988; D'Souza, 1991; Ravitch, 1990, 1991, 1997) of a multicultural approach to diversity in education. Teacher educators and their students must be trained to engage their critics in an ongoing, well-articulated dialogue based on content that speaks to weaknesses found in the field (Sleeter, 1995). "Too PC" has become part of common usage but is often used in inaccurate contexts, and such explanations do not include the value of equity.

Issue 3. The multicultural teacher educator of the future must be able to marshal in-depth content from a variety of pertinent disciplines and must be able to integrate this knowledge appropriately in the training of future educators. By using data from multiple disciplines, future teacher educators and their students will gain a comprehensive understanding of the complexity of contemporary social issues, such as how the biological and political constructs of race impact school-based teaching and learning (Omi & Winant, 1994; Pang & Valle, 2004).

Issue 4. The principle goal of multicultural teacher education must be to address the achievement gap between ethnic "minority" students and their mainstream peers. Fostering change in teacher education as a whole requires a redefinition of the appropriate content of multicultural teacher education. Care must be taken that no one group of stakeholders be the center of this reform process; rather, issues of equity must define the "center." Additional needed research would include understandings of the orientations and ways of knowing of students from underrepresented groups (Grant & Brown, 2006). In order to create effective learning environments, teachers of the future must have the competencies and dispositions to discover and understand the differing ways of life and knowledge bases multicultural students bring with them to the public school classroom (Gay, 2005).

Issue 5. Multicultural teacher education has arisen out of several movements. First it is an extension of multicultural education, a field arising out of both the intercultural education and the civil rights movement. The intercultural education movement was seen in schools primarily as the addition of curriculum focusing on cultures from other countries (Pak, 2006), while the civil rights movement was a political call for social change. Multicultural education, as we know it today, was developed originally by curriculum specialists in the early 1970s such as James A. Banks, Geneva Gay, Carl A. Grant, and the historian, Carlos Cortez. It was through their intellectual efforts that the field of multicultural education has developed and progressed from the early 1970s to the present time. It is time now to cultivate emerging scholarship in related disciplines and integrate it into the established base.

We believe that a discipline devoted to multicultural teacher education will more fully align the professional development of teacher educators and teachers with our national ideals of equity and social justice. The next section will begin to raise critical questions about the need for and the identification of a new paradigm for multicultural teacher education.

IMPLICATIONS AND IMPACTS FOR IMPROVING PRACTICE

To begin discussing new ways of thinking about multicultural teacher education, we have identified questions to frame the conversation. These questions reinforce the importance of developing multicultural teacher education as a cross-disciplinary field. Those questions ask:

1. In what ways would the development and implementation of a new interdisciplinary paradigm for multicultural teacher education increase the numbers of new teachers who embrace informed social criticism based on research?
2. In what ways do the results of new studies about race gleaned from the interdisciplinary intersections among such fields as anthropology, biology, ethnic studies, evolutionary biology and ecology, history, and paleontology substantively challenge assumptions based on today's prevalent sociopolitical scholarship promulgated by some multicultural teacher educators (Gould, 1996; Graves, 2001; Olson, 2002)?
3. How would making high-quality interdisciplinary research more widely known among veteran and emerging multicultural teacher educators improve the quality of multicultural research they do?
4. How does a new cross-disciplinary paradigm for multicultural teacher education relate to multicultural education's historical precedents?
5. How can the answers to these questions impact educational policy so that multicultural teacher education will improve over the next quarter century?

We assume that teacher educators, themselves, must have the courage to engage in "informed social criticism" toward Dewey's goal of a creation of a strong citizenry (1916). Teacher educators must also be individuals who believe in equity and take the inherent risks of incorporating critical thinking and collaboration in teacher education programs. A more effective paradigm for multicultural teacher education must begin with courageous teacher educators with strong moral convictions (Gay, 2005; Welch & Pollard, 2006).

We propose that effective multicultural teacher education requires all participating faculty and administrators to have a cognate area in equity and that this training should begin with those faculty in charge of training the teacher educators of tomorrow, who would in turn be equipped to prepare future teachers and other educational practitioners through graduate education. Professional development for existing faculty would consist of the appropriate knowledge, theories, principles, and practice to support equity over the entire spectrum of our educational system from kindergarten through graduate school. In what follows we present a case study as an example of professional development for teacher educators. This national initiative was designed to infuse multicultural and bilingual education into the curriculum of colleges of education. The lessons learned from this experience provide the groundwork for a new paradigm in multicultural teacher education.

A CASE STUDY: LESSONS LEARNED FROM
A MULTICULTURAL TEACHER EDUCATION INITIATIVE

In the 1990s, the U.S. Department of Education Office of Bilingual Education and Minority Language Affairs (OBEMLA) sponsored a national competitive grant initiative to establish three national centers for training practicing teacher educators in multicultural and bilingual education. One of those centers was awarded to a large urban university on the West Coast. OBEMLA built into the grant solicitation the requirement that teacher educators, themselves, be engaged in a three-year professional development experience so that the infusion of multicultural and bilingual education would become an integral part of the teacher credentialing and graduate programs of universities and colleges around the nation. The goals of the West Coast center were (1) to improve the skills of both tenured and tenure-track faculty and their administrators in preparing teachers to incorporate issues of equity and principles of bilingual education relative to language and cultural heritage into the existing regular education curricula and (2) to facilitate the necessary systemic change in college organizations so that the infusion of cultural and language acquisition principles and skills into both preservice and in-service teacher education would become a reality.

The professional development program created by the West Coast center rested on the assumption that successful realization of the infusion of the principles and practices of equity in education required the participation of both college administrators and their teacher education faculty. Participation of administrators would encourage the systemic change necessary to ensure that issues of equity, race, culture, and language would be infused into the entire professional development experience of prospective public school educators. The required participation of a dean or assistant dean from each participating college or university became a signature characteristic of the West Coast center's program.

ORGANIZING FOR INSTITUTIONAL CHANGE

A team of three to four faculty members, including at least one administrator, represented each participating university. Each team was involved in summer professional development experiences for several years. A second signature characteristic of the West Coast center's program was a roundtable of deans. Forty-two deans participated in the inaugural nationwide meeting of the roundtable. Discussion centered on support for policy changes in multicultural and bilingual teacher training at their respective universities and colleges, which demonstrated their high level of commitment to the goals of the innovation. The designers of the program assumed that lasting change would only occur if administrators believed in the change; if the proposed change were embraced for primarily "political" reasons, that is, to please the whims or desires of those in power at the time, change would not last and therefore would not act as a catalyst for institutional systemic change. Each university team created an institutional plan.

Training for Teacher Educators and College of Education Administrators

The West Coast center supported instructional change at the participating universities through a series of training experiences. First, an intensive, two-week, residential workshop was conducted for the university teams. The team interacted with and learned from noted consultants in the field, such as Shirley Brice Heath, Geneva Gay, Robert Rueda, Christine Sleeter, Carl Grant, and Henry Trueba. These experts shared their knowledge, models, and theories about teaching in multicultural, bilingual classrooms. They trained professors in alternative educational environments, the development of inclusive syllabi, and the formulation of an action plan that would bring out systemic structural changes in their colleges of education.

Second, miniconferences throughout the three years provided university teams opportunities to come together to share their experiences in the infusion and systemic change process. Several conferences were held to provide information on the development of California's Bilingual Cross-cultural, Language, and Academic Development Emphasis. Miniconferences also gave participants the opportunity to identify strategies that were effective and those that were not. These sessions also provided continuity to the infusion process.

Lessons Learned

Through long-term reflection upon the training experiences and responses of participants, lessons learned from this initiative that helped inform the development of a new paradigm for multicultural teacher education. These lessons provide important insights into the education of existing faculty charged with the development of multicultural teacher education.

Lesson 1. For systemic change to occur, institutional teams must be composed of both administrators and faculty. Supporting the infusion of equity in teacher training for preservice and in-service teachers requires organizational change in colleges and schools of education. In addition, both faculty and administrators must agree to infuse a clear theoretical framework for multicultural and bilingual education into their regular education curricula.

Lesson 2. Like the students in their classes, faculty respond best to environments that are built on trust, respect, and genuine collaboration. They need an atmosphere where they feel safe in asking questions and providing comments without being ridiculed. Faculty were most open to dialogue when they felt validated as thinkers and educators by the leaders of the training.

Lesson 3. Experiential learning is essential; faculty must engage in hands-on, real-world learning such as discussing prejudice in schools, visiting urban schools, asking questions of highly effective urban public school administrators and teachers, and learning a second language (Pang, Anderson, & Martuza, 1997). Several trainers utilized Cantonese and Spanish to demonstrate the frustrations, confusion, and isolation that English learners often face in classrooms across the country. Trainers realized that professors, like others, needed a point of reference for understanding basic affective and cognitive challenges of English learners and other underrepresented students.

Lesson 4. Dialogue is a key instructional strategy for faculty that includes heterogeneous grouping. Listening to continual lectures does not change attitudes. Rather, faculty were most reflective in open-ended, problem-posing, and issues-centered seminars. Having individuals tackle authentic social issues is an important approach to instruction and their development of a strong philosophical foundation (Freire, 1970). One of the discussions in which faculty were seriously engaged was a dialogue on the resistance of universities to change (Pang, Anderson, & Martuza, 1997). Faculty dialogue where participants felt they had equal status with one another and with the leaders of the training resulted in collaboration, clarification of values, and the creation of team action plans.

Lesson 5. For faculty to infuse multicultural and bilingual education into their own classes, they needed baseline knowledge of philosophies, theoretical frameworks, goals, and bridging theory with practice in multicultural teacher education. The knowledge shared dealt with progressive education, social reconstruction, critical theory, sociocultural theory of learning, language acquisition, and the ethic of caring. In this way faculty wrestled with identification of a philosophical and theoretical framework for their own teaching and their institution. From these discussions, faculty restructured individual course syllabi and worked collaboratively on the institutional action plan.

Lesson 6. Informal networking became an important aspect of the training. Since teams of faculty participated in a two-week residential training program, individual members were able to establish long-lasting collegial relationships; some are still vibrant currently after more than a decade. This way collaborations and relationships were not contrived or manufactured due to institutional needs; rather, faculty found others with similar discipline backgrounds and common course loads.

Any initiative or program also uncovers various impediments that arise during the course of the process. The following limitations provide information that new programs developing multicultural teacher education as a field of study should consider.

Limitation 1. Many institutions are gatekeepers for the status quo, and these organizations were slow to change. "Issues of equity and culture are complex and the power structure of colleges and schools [of Education] is built upon a social hierarchy of exclusion. Although professors of color may be recruited or new books with cultural content added to the bookstore shelves, the power structure remains solidly in place; this structure is based on the legitimacy of the Western construction of knowledge, value orientation, and historical tradition" (Pang, Anderson, & Martuza, 1997, p. 55).

An example of how the power struggle between administrators and faculty can create tension within the professional development program occurred. A participating faculty member during the residential two-week training identified the oppression she felt from one of the lead administrators of the West Coast center:

> Multicultural education celebrates diversity and cultural differences: communication styles and approaches should all be welcomed and discussion time and group process should be facilitated. Unfortunately, this did not happen in the townhall meetings. Like we say in Spanish, "No podemos enseñar la moral en calsonsillos." "You cannot preach, what you don't model." The incident between Dean [name] and Dr. [name] was living proof of what happens to our children (minority and language minority student) in our American classroom. We stop listening to their messages and the minority child becomes voiceless. If we want to empower our minority, LMS children, we need to start looking and working within our professional circles. This was a very sad experience, and it does not validate this effort. Are things really going to change? (Pang, 1993, p. 1)

Limitation 2. Another substantial barrier to the inclusion of equity issues and content into teacher education is the promotion and tenure process. Some faculty felt that they could not speak up at the training when their dean or other deans were present because that might influence their ability to secure future tenure and promotion. In one instance, a dean publicly admonished all faculty including other administrators present at a session for not adhering to the defined workshop sched-ule. This dean also reprimanded faculty participants for not wearing their name tags. When faculty did not want to be identified as speaking out, they engaged in a strat-egy of passive resistance. Spontaneously, associate deans and professors exchanged name tags. They were all wearing names, but someone else's tag. This way the ad-ministrator who had scolded them called faculty by erroneous names. This strategy was one avenue professors felt they could engage in without being individually targeted. The power of oppression even at a training session focusing on equity and social justice was in play. Below is a comment written by a faculty member about what would prevent him from implementing the knowledge and strategies gained in the professional development training. He was concerned that time taken away by studying and implementing issues of equity in his teaching would hamper his ability to continue with his research and publishing agenda. This is what he wrote after the two-week, residential training session:

> With regard to institutional change: (1) the snail's pace at which my university seems to move; (2) the limited time and energy that I, personally, can commit due to pressures to publish (Pang, 1993, p. 8).

In addition, tenure at a university can also become an obstacle for change in that faculty may feel free from pressures to reflect upon their views about teacher educa-tion. Faculty who are tenured have job security and academic freedom, and these elements can insulate them from modifying their course content.

Limitation 3. Administrators and the institutions of higher education they repre-sent must be committed to multicultural teacher education in order for long-term change to occur; for example, training for teacher educators. The need for profes-sional development for faculty was echoed by an associate dean of education in the final evaluation of the two-week seminar:

> Whether my institution has a commitment to multicultural education is unclear so our team will have to work to get institutional commitment. Faculty members in some cases do not have much background. (Pang, 1993, p. 8)

It is important to expand on the comments and experiences of the West Coast center on professional training for teacher educators. Building upon the successes of this initiative can provide important elements for a model for future programs to address the importance of placing equity at the forefront of teacher education.

EXTENDING THE TEACHER EDUCATION INITIATIVE: RECOMMENDATIONS FOR DEVELOPING A NEW PARADIGM IN MULTICULTURAL TEACHER EDUCATION

The lessons learned from the case study suggest that the implementation and adop-tion of any innovative paradigm for multicultural teacher education must involve change on three levels. First, the organization must make changes in its policies and structures to support and integrate multicultural teacher education. This includes administrative support for equity in all aspects of teacher training. Second, there must be curricular change where issues of equity are discussed in all course work and field experiences from educational philosophy courses to math education methods. In addition, every member of the faculty must gain a cognate area in equity. The multidimensional paradigm change will support the integration of equity as a permanent element in teacher education from course work to field experiences. Faculty also must be engaged in highly supportive and ongoing training that facilitates their reflection on their own teaching and discussion of new cross-disciplinary issues. Yearly retreats where faculty and administrators can review organizational action plans also will assist in making sure that equity becomes part of the university structure in teacher education from the recruitment of underrepresented faculty to the recruitment of culturally and linguistically diverse students.

Current cross-disciplinary research suggests that content and structural elements must also be included in a new multicultural teacher education paradigm. We suggest the following:

1. Teacher educators in a college or department should work toward consensus on a theoretical framework that provides cohesion across the components of the professional development process of credentialing and graduate programs; consensual approaches to decision making may draw out the change process;
2. Integration of appropriate equity issues and concepts in course work would be facilitated through the adoption of a spiral curriculum design for multicultural teacher education in which the scope and sequence of concepts, knowledge, attitudes, and skills are clearly listed and reiterated throughout the phases of the training program. Adoption of a spiral design encourages faculty to utilize interdisciplinary content in teacher education courses. This design would expand the understandings of prospective teachers about complex issues of equity such as racism (Frederickson, 2002) and immigration because they would see core concepts and skills in different contexts (King, Hollins, & Hayman, 1997); faculty must continually address teacher prejudice since teachers will need repeated opportunities to reflect on their own, institutional, and cultural discriminatory practices (Banks & Banks, 2004; Gay, 2002; Goodwin, 1997; Pang, 2005); finally faculty should engage in high-level research to strengthen the discipline of multicultural teacher education (Goodwin, 1997). For example, a perennial issue in education that must be a component within this spiral curriculum is to identify what is meant by equity in education and how to address the achievement gap between children of color and their mainstream peers.

• **Theoretical Framework**

A strong theoretical framework is a crucial component of multicultural teacher education because it will act as a cohesive force across departmental programs and disciplines. A theoretical framework is a comprehensive framework of the educational philosophy, principles, goals, educational competencies, ways of assessment, and courses of study that together define the new multicultural education paradigm. Scholars such as Zeichner, Grant, Gay, Gillette, Valli, and Villegas (1998) have identified important principles for a strong system of beliefs. To achieve a strong collaborative team, faculty must work collegially to develop the details of the theoretical framework in a way that produces a shared direction for the department. When differences of opinion arise within the department, faculty can return to the theoretical framework to ensure that all individuals are working toward the community's common goals. This process should be informed by the work of multicultural teacher education scholars such as Cherry McGee A. Banks, James Banks, Christine Bennett, Jim Cummins, Paulo Freire, Eugene Garcia, Geneva Gay, A. Lin Goodwin, Carl A. Grant, Jacqueline Jordan Irvine, Joyce King, Sonia Nieto, Valerie Ooka Pang, Robert Rueda, and Christine Sleeter. Teacher educators must be clear about the philosophical and psychological foundations that will serve as the foundation for the theoretical framework. The foundation may include critical theory (Freire, 1970; Sleeter & Bernal, 2004), progressive education (Dewey, 1916), learning theory (Lev Vygotsky), sociocultural theory of learning (Moll, 1992), caring-centered multicultural education (Pang, 2005), and culturally relevant education (Gay, 2000; Gay, 2005; Irvine, 2003).

- **Spiral Scope and Sequence**

Following the identification of the theoretical framework for the organization, the faculty will also need to develop a well-defined spiral scope and sequence so they understand how their teaching builds upon and reinforces the principles of the framework throughout. This scope and sequence may also be founded on standards such as those described by organizations of accreditation, such as National Council for Accreditation of Teacher Education (NCATE). This curricular framework will include principles, knowledge, skills, processes, and attitudes for teacher development such as integration of culture-specific knowledge, culturally relevant education, the impact of immigration on schools, and institutional change theory in teacher education. The scope and sequence must address the issue of the achievement gap between students from low-income and more affluent communities focusing on what must be done at all levels of schooling to create more effective schools.

- **Advancing an Interdisciplinary Approach to Multicultural Content**

With the increased use of technology and the ability to communicate in a moment to countries around the globe, knowledge continues to escalate. Teacher educators must be aware of this explosion in cross-disciplinary research. For example, in the discussion of racism, recent research in biomedical sciences, especially the burgeoning of DNA studies, underscores the potential importance of such studies in defining and refining what the accepted stance should be regarding the biological bases for racial distinctions. For example, in this discipline one of the most important questions to be discussed should be: How real is race?

The concept of race is complex as it involves information from various disciplines such as history, biology, evolution, genetics, and paleontology. Teacher educators and teachers must make decisions about complex social issues concerning race and racism. Race is often talked about not only as a political construct but also as if it were a proven biological concept based on physical differences (Pang, 2005, p. 88). The taxonomy of racial classification was originally created by Carolus Linneaus, a Swedish naturalist (Gould, 1996). Linnaeus first developed the classification system that is, in large measure, still used by biologists today to categorize plants and animals. In his system, he placed humans in the order of primates, the genus given was *Homo*, or man, and the species name was *sapiens*, which means wise. In his quest to further categorize humans, Linnaeus extended his classification to include a four-race system that was primarily based on geography and three characteristics of people: physical color, disposition, and posture (Gould, 1996). Linneaeus's work was then expanded upon by J. F. Blumenbach, an eighteenth-century German naturalist. Blumenbach identified people who lived near Mount Caucasus as the ideal in physical beauty and named this group Caucasians (Gould, 1996). During Blumenbach's lifetime many Europeans tended to believe in their own superiority over other groups. Blumenbach's work reinforced this tendency with his suggestion that people could be classified into various "categories." In the twentieth century Boaz, a respected anthropologist, cast doubt on the biological reality of racial differences among people (Boaz, 1931; Boaz, 1940). He wrote more than seventy-five years ago about his belief that the concept of race was not accurate:

> It is a fundamental characteristic of all local populations that the individuals differ among themselves, and a closer study shows that this is true of animals as well as of men. It is therefore, not quite proper to speak in these cases of traits that are hereditary in the racial type as a whole, because too many of them occur also in other racial types. Hereditary racial traits should be shared by the whole population so that it is set off against others. (Boaz, 1931, p. 5)

It has become clear that racial distinctions are socially constructed rather than biologically based. Asa Hilliard III reminded his audience at the 2002 American Educational Association Conference that "racism is real; race is not." However, many teachers still believe that race is an accurate biological construct. It is important, therefore, to include in the curriculum for teacher education information from the Human Genome Project to understand the large degree of similarity across different "racial" groups. Researchers mapped the human genome; this study was not called the African Genome Project or the American Indian Genome Project, but they were all involved in the Human Genome Project. Researchers in labs across the world worked collaboratively to identify the approximately 30,000 genes that make up our human DNA (Ridley, 2000). DNA analysis of our genetic makeup across so-called racial divisions shows that we humans as a group are more biologically the same than different. We do, however, represent diverse cultural orientations whose differences are based in learning rather than heredity. Therefore, race is not real in the biological sense; however, racism is real in the political and sociological arenas. This distinction suggests that prejudice and discrimination as socially learned attitudes must be continually reviewed throughout a multicultural teacher education professional development sequence. The training of prospective teacher educators must include increasing awareness of how prejudice is reinforced in society, including schools and psychosocial strategies on how prejudice can be reduced.

TEACHER PREJUDICE REDUCTION

An effective multicultural teacher education program must deal with how teacher prejudice can be ameliorated through the credentialing process (Sleeter, 1992). Necessary to this process is an awareness of how stereotyping can sustain negative racial attitudes. The results of the intersect between sociology and learning psychology has resulted in research on the positive effects of self-regulation training as a mechanism for improving racist attitudes in adults (Monteith, Voils, & Ashburn-Nardo, 2001; Pang & Park, 2003; Pang & Sablan, 1998; Stephen, 1999).

Psychological studies on stereotyping as it interacts with race and social class have yielded reliable and valid instruments to identify racism using implicit assessment techniques whose methods are either not well known or not frequently used by teacher educators; however, these techniques could provide new understandings about teacher prejudice. Devos and various colleagues have used implicit (rather than explicit) measures of stereotyping on perception that have yielded insights into the nature of cross-gender, cross-cultural relationships, and role modeling among protégés and their mentors (Devos, 2006; Devos & Cruz Torres, 2007; Devos, Diaz, Viera, & Dunn, 2007; Devos & Ma, 2008). This research has implications for the student teacher–cooperating teacher relationship in highly diverse schools. It also provides a highly reliable and valid way to monitor the attitudes prospective teachers have about racial groups. The line of research pursued by Devos and Monteith and their collaborators gives teacher educators new tools and strategies to establish reliable and valid baselines and to detect perceptible changes among pertinent "isms" that the credentialing process should seek to address (Larke, 1992; McAllister & Irvine, 2002; Pang, 2005; Sleeter, 1992; Stephen, 1999).

- **Research Conducted by Teacher Educators**
Robust, high-quality research will strengthen the development of multicultural teacher education. Such research will also provide models to assist the field in intellectual rigor and quality of its emerging interdisciplinary scholarship. Researchers such as A. Lin Goodwin, Joyce E. King, Carol D. Lee, Luis Moll, Gary Orfield, Stephen Raudenbush, and Audrey Thompson provide a strong knowledge base. In addition, research involving large samples of novice teachers can inform teacher educators about the relative effects of formal training. Darling-Hammond, Chung, and Frelow (2002) surveyed almost 3,000 teachers in New York City with fewer than four years of teaching experience who had graduated either from traditional university credential programs or nontraditional programs such as Teach for America or Teacher Opportunity Corps. In their sample, 65 percent were white, 15 percent were Hispanic, 13 percent were African American, 4 percent were Asian American, and 3 percent identified themselves as other. Irrespective of the type of training the teachers had experienced, they reported that they did not feel adequately prepared to create multicultural curriculum or to teach English language learners (Darling-Hammond et al., 2002, p. 290), even though they were teaching in some of the most culturally and linguistically diverse schools in our nation. Zeintek (2007) replicated this study in Texas and analyzed a sample of 1,197 surveys from teachers with three years of teaching or less. These teachers also revealed that they did not feel prepared to create multicultural curriculum (p. 995). The large sample sizes and the replication of the study in two disparate geographical areas lend credibility to the finding that teacher education programs tend not to inspire confidence among their graduates to teach effectively in multicultural settings nor to address the needs of second-language English learners.

RESEARCH IN CURRICULUM STUDIES
LINKING THEORY WITH PRACTICE

Multicultural teacher education will gain credibility as a discipline in so far as a strong link between theory and practice is established. Research conducted by Gonzalez, Moll, and Amanti (2005) has fruitfully employed the intersects among educational, anthropological, and psychological research methods to establish the curriculum and instructional strategies pertinent to culturally relevant teaching, especially among emergent bilingual populations. Their work, known as the Funds of Knowledge project, is based primarily on the theories of Vygotsky. Gonzalez, Moll, and Amanti propose that children arrive at school with a "bank" of knowledge that teachers can build on in their schooling. Educators who are cued into the sociocultural background of students know how to scaffold learning by carefully linking instruction to students' lived experiences. These researchers demonstrated that a holistic orientation toward teaching is more effective than teaching skills in isolation. This pedagogical approach is informed by the research of James Greenberg, C. Vélez-Ibáñez, and Luis Moll, who studied the cultural knowledge of family relationships and social networks of thirty-five Mexican families in a working-class community (Moll & Greenberg, 1990). The study was expanded to include teachers who were taught anthropological skills that were utilized in the community. Gonzalez, Moll, and Amanti extended elementary school teachers' knowledge of students and their families. The teachers themselves then created writing lessons using their students' own experiences of their family members and the careers they were engaged in, as well as their visits to Mexico to see relatives.

Carol D. Lee has also successfully translated theory into effective practice through the Cultural Modeling Project. Building on Vygotsky's theories, Lee has focused on signifying, which many African American and other students engage in, such as "ritual insult" and "rapping, loud talking, and marking" (Lee, 2001, p. 100). Lee taught students and teachers to look below the surface interpretation of students' use of black English vernacular to discover underlying meanings. Lee had high school students identify elements of metaphors, irony, and satire in their own expressions and discussions. She taught them to transfer these skills to literature taught in their English classes. After three years, all of the English teachers at this high school taught Cultural Modeling Project strategies (Lee, 2001). By affirming the students' lived experiences and incorporating their ideas and "funds of knowledge" into the instruction, Lee engaged low-achieving freshmen in discussions where they identified specific literary elements in novels and other creative writings. Initially students were resistant to participating in class; however, as Lee taught, students became more involved in intellectually rigorous discussions and their skill levels dramatically increased. The students' own expectations about their abilities rose, and the teacher's views of students also changed.

POLICY IMPLICATIONS

This review of the intersection of quality interdisciplinary studies with substantive philosophical and curriculum research on multicultural education implies a number of policy recommendations necessary to develop and improve multicultural teacher education as we progress toward the midpoint of the twenty-first century. They are:

1. A paradigm shift must occur in the structural organization in higher education. In the past, universities have developed on the belief that an organization must be grounded on rational and linear orientations. Scholars in organizational theory have posited a shift that describes the process of change that is nonlinear and dynamically complex, moving toward the construction of learning communities in contrast to hierarchical models (Beer, Eisenstatdt, & Spector, 1990; Bergquist, 1993).

2. Educating effective future teachers to meet the challenges of an increasingly diverse public school student population will require a substantive change in the present-day relationship between multicultural teacher education and teacher education as a whole. Developing a new discipline dedicated to multicultural teacher education must be accomplished to fill the needs of a strongly immigrant and pluralistic nation as we move into the twenty-first century. This will require open dialogue among teacher educators and their constituencies to create a set of common goals toward enhancing the place and importance of multicultural education, including bilingual education in the teacher education curriculum. This dialogue should serve first to identify appropriate theoretical frameworks but also the inclusion of representatives of community activist and parental organizations. Input from diverse constituencies will help identify research agendas examining multicultural teacher development programs that are authentic to cultural, linguistic, racial, class, gender, sexual orientation, religion, and disabilities concerns prevalent in public schooling.

3. To ensure that all prospective teacher educators and administrators gain sufficient capacity to infuse multicultural issues within a teacher education program, a cognate area in multicultural and bilingual education should be required as part of their advanced degrees. Without enhancing the educational background and training of prospective teacher educators and administrators in this way, the credential programs and graduate education of the prospective teachers and administrators they train will lack issues of equity for differing cultures, races, and linguistic groups throughout the curriculum.

4. Addressing the issues set forth in this study will also require high-profile political initiatives on a national scale. Members of national professional organizations such as the American Educational Research Association (AERA), the American Association of Colleges for Teacher Education (AACTE), and the National Council for Accreditation of Teacher Education (NCATE) could spearhead such an initiative. This leadership should also include consultation with key members of Congress and their staffs. These groups would come together regularly to make and widely disseminate policy recommendations about federal or state policies that impact issues pertinent to multicultural education, including those surrounding the recruitment of a diverse teacher workforce. Examples include the No Child Left Behind legislation, which many educators feel is too narrow in its goal, forcing a "testing as accountability" orientation toward schooling that is counterproductive to the development of the whole child.

5. Finally, integrating the principles and practice of multicultural teacher education into the field of teacher education as a whole, and increasing the numbers of professionals in teacher education from underrepresented backgrounds, will require a transformation not only in the ways schools and departments of teacher education construct and deliver teacher education curriculum and training but also in the expectations of teacher educators as they interact with school district personnel, cooperating guide teachers, principals, and superintendents: "This would include mak[ing] all faculty members accountable and [would] counteract the tendency to marginalize issues of diversity in the education process" (Gay, 2005, p. 224).

CONCLUSION

The establishment of multicultural teacher education as a discipline in its own right will increase the probability that faculty and administrators in colleges and schools of education are more fully prepared to train prospective teacher educators, credentialed teachers, and graduate students for effective service in schools; equity must be at its core and must be valued for education to improve. The new paradigm places multicultural teacher education at the forefront of teacher education and posits that the establishment of multicultural teacher education in its own right will act as a driving force to cement holistic change in teacher education. The new paradigm conceives the identification of a multidimensional model where reform requires structural changes in higher education, necessitates continual professional development aimed at the creation of a spiral curriculum, and involves the importance of individual development. As part of that change, a shared theoretical framework based on tested sociocultural learning theories and the results of cross-disciplinary research on issues pertinent to equity must be included. This paradigm works to create an institutional orientation to equity; we do not believe that isolated and fragmented pieces are effective in a teacher education program. The status quo offering of many universities of one or two classes in diversity and language lack coherence in providing a comprehensive teacher education program dedicated to achievement of all children. Placing equity front and center in teacher education will take courageous leadership and the moral commitment to serve all students. Improving the capacity of emerging teachers to deal with the ever-growing multicultural nature of our schools will require teacher educators to move beyond politics, their own personal agendas, and the status quo of university structures and to embrace a collaborative approach to teaching and learning where the needs of children are at its core.

REFERENCES

American Association of Colleges of Teacher Education. (2006). Defining dispositions. Retrieved November 20, 2007, from http://www.aacte.org/Programs/TEAMC/teamc_disposition_definitions.pdf

Banks, J. A., & Banks, C. M. (2004). *Handbook of research on multicultural education*. New York: Macmillan.

Beer, M., Eisenstadt, R., & Spector, B. (1990). Why change programs don't produce change. *Harvard Business Review, 68(6)*, 158–66.

Bennett , W. J. (1994). *The de-valuing of America: The fight for our culture and our children.* New York: Simon & Schuster.

Berquist, W. H. (1993). *The postmodern organization: Mastering the art of irreversible change.* San Francisco: Jossey-Bass.

Bloom, Allan. (1988). *The closing of the American mind: How higher education has failed democracy and impoverished the souls of today's students.* New York: Simon & Schuster.

Boaz, F. (1931). Race and progress. *Science, 74*, 1–8.

Boaz, F. (1940). *Race, language, and culture.* New York: Macmillan Company.

Darling-Hammond, L., Chung, R., & Frelow, F. (2002). Variation in teacher preparation: How well do different pathways prepare teachers to teach? *Journal of Teacher Education, 53*, 286–302.

Devos, T. (2006). Implicit bicultural identity among Mexican American and Asian American college students. *Cultural Diversity and Ethnic Minority Psychology, 12*, 381–402.

Devos, T., & Cruz Torres, J. A. (2007). Implicit identification with academic achievement among Latino college students: The role of ethnic identity and significant others. *Basic and Applied Social Psychology, 29*, 293–310.

Devos, T., Diaz, P., Viera, E., & Dunn, R. (2007). College education and motherhood as components of self-concept: Discrepancies between implicit and explicit assessments. *Self and Identity, 6*, 256–77.

Devos, T., & Ma, D. (2008). Is Kate Winslet more American than Lucy Liu? The impact of construal processes on the implicit ascription of a national identity. *British Journal of Social Psychology, 47*, 191–215.

Dewey, J. (1916). *Democracy and education.* New York: Free Press.

D'Souza, D. (1991). *Illiberal education: The politics of race and sex on campus.* New York: Free Press.

Fredrickson, G. M. (2002). *Racism: A short history.* Princeton, NJ: Princeton University Press.

Freire, P. (1970). *The pedagogy of the oppressed.* New York: Continuum.

Gay, G. (1994). *A synthesis of scholarship in multicultural education.* North Central Regional Educational Laboratory. www.ncrel.org/sdrs/areas/issues/educatrs/leadrshp/le0gay.htm

Gay, G. (2000). *Culturally responsive teaching: Theory, research, and practice.* New York: Teachers College Press.

Gay, G. (2002). Preparing for culturally responsive teaching. *Journal of Teacher Education, 53*, 2, 106–16.

Gay, G. (2005). Politics of multicultural education. *Journal of Teacher Education, 56(3)*, 221–28.

Gonzalez, N., Moll, L., & Amanti, C. (2005). *Funds of knowledge: Theorizing practices in households, communities, and classrooms.* Mahwah, NJ: Laurence Erlbaum Associates.

Goodwin, A. Lin. (1997). Multicultural stories: Preservice teacher's conceptions of and responses to issues of diversity. *Urban Education, 32(1)*, 117–45.

Gould, S. J. (1996). *The mismeasure of man* (Rev. ed.). New York: W. W. Norton & Co.

Grant, C. A., & Brown, A. L. (2006). Listening to African American males' conceptions of high-stakes tests. In Pang, V. O. (Ed.), *Principles and practices of multicultural education* (pp. 103–23). Westport, CT: Praeger Publishers.

Graves, J. L. (2001). *The emperor's new clothes: Biological theories of race at the millennium.* New Brunswick, NJ: Rutgers University Press.

Hahn, C. (1996). Research on issues-centered social studies. In Evans, R. W., and Saxe, D. (Eds.), *Handbook on teaching social issues* (pp. 25–41). Washington, DC: National Council for the Social Studies.

Irvine, J. J. (2003). *Educating teachers for diversity: Seeing with a cultural eye.* New York: Teachers College Press.

King, J. E., Hollins, E., & Hayman, W. C. (1997). *Preparing teachers for culturally diversity.* New York: Teachers College Press.

Larke, P. (1992). Effective multicultural teachers. *Equity and Excellence, 25,* 133–39.

Lee, C. D. (1993). *Signifying for a scaffold for literary interpretation: The pedagogical implications of an African American genre.* Urbana, IL: National Council of Teachers of English.

Lee, C. D. (1995). A culturally based cognitive apprenticeship: Teaching African American high school students skills in literary interpretation. *Reading Research Quarterly, 30,* 508–631.

Lee, C. D. (2001). Is October Brown Chinese?: A cultural modeling activity system for underachieving students. *American Educational Research Journal, 36,* 97–143.

Moll, L. (1992). *Vygotsky and education: Instructional implications and applications of sociohistorical psychology.* New York: Cambridge University Press.

Moll, L., & Greenberg, J. (1990). Creating zones of possibilities: Combining social contexts for instruction. In Moll, L. (Ed.), *Vygotsky and Education* 319–48. New York: Cambridge University Press.

Monteith, M. J., Voils, C., & Ashburn-Nardo, L. (2001). Taking a look underground. Detecting, interpreting, and reacting to implicit racial biases. *Social Cognition, 19(4),* 395–417.

Noddings, N. (1984). *Caring: A feminine approach to ethics and moral development.* Berkeley: University of California Press.

Nofke, S. (2000). Identity, community and democracy in the new social order. In Hursh, D. W., and Ross, E. W. (Eds.), *Democratic social education: Social studies for change* (pp. 73–83). New York: Flamer.

Olson, S. (2002). *Mapping human history: Genes, race, and our common origins.* Boston: Houghton Mifflin.

Omi, M., & Winant, H. (1994). *Racial formation in the United States: From the 1960's to the 1990's* (2nd ed). New York: Routledge.

Pak, Y. (2006). Multiculturalism matters: Learning from our past. In Pang, V. O. (Ed.), *Principles and practices of multicultural education* (pp. 3–22). Westport, CT: Praeger.

Pang, V. O. (1993). *Compilation of final evaluation forms: Second session 1993.* Technical Report. Multicultural Education Infusion Center.

Pang, V. O. (2005). *Multicultural education: A caring-centered, reflective approach* (2nd ed.). Boston: McGraw-Hill.

Pang, V. O., Anderson, M., & Martuza, V. (1997). Removing the mask of academia: Institutions collaborating in the struggle for equity. In King, J. E., Hollins, E., & Hayman, W. C. (Eds.), *Preparing teachers for culturally diversity* (pp. 53–70). New York: Teachers College Press.

Pang, V. O., Gay, G., & Stanley, W. B. (1995). Expanding conceptions of community and civic competence for a multicultural society. *Theory and Research in Social Education, 23,* 302–31.

Pang, V. O., & Park, C. D. (2003). Examination of the self-regulation mechanism: Prejudice reduction in pre-service teachers. *Action in Teacher Education, 25(3),* 1–12.

Pang, V. O., & Sablan, V. (1998). Teacher efficacy: How do teachers feel about their ability to teach African American students. In Dilworth, M. (Ed.), *Being responsive to cultural differences: How teachers learn* (pp. 39–58). Washington, DC: American Association of Colleges for Teacher Education.

Pang, V. O., & Valle, R. (2004). A change in paradigm: Applying contributions of genetic research to the teaching about race and racism in social studies education. *Theory and Research in Social Education, 32(4),* 503–22.

Ravitch, D. (1990). Multiculturalism: E pluribus plures. *American Scholar, 34(3),* 337–44.

Ravitch, D. (1991). A culture in common. *Educational Leadership, 49(4),* 8–11.

Ravitch, D. (1997). How affirmative action harms minorities. *Forbes, 160(11).*

Ridley, M. (2000). *Genome: The autobiography of a species in 23 chapters.* New York: Perennial Publishers.

Ross, E. W. (2001). The struggle for the social studies curriculum. In Ross, E. W. (Ed.), *The social studies curriculum: Purposes, problems, and possibilities* (Rev. ed.) (pp. 19–41). Albany: SUNY Press.

Sleeter, C. (1995). An analysis of the critiques of multicultural education. In Banks, J. A., and Banks, C. M. (Eds.), *Handbook of research on multicultural education* (pp. 81–94). New York: Macmillan.

Sleeter, C. E. (1992). *Keepers of the American dream: A study of staff development and multicultural education.* Washington, DC: Falmer.

Sleeter, C. E., & Bernal, D. D. (2004). Critical pedagogy, critical race theory, and antiracist education: Implications for multicultural education. In Banks, J. A. and Banks, C. A. (Eds.), *Handbook of research on multicultural education* (2nd ed.) 240–58. San Francisco: Jossey-Bass.

Stanley, W. B., & Nelson, J. L. (1994). The foundations of social education in historical context. In Martusewicz, R., and Ryenolds, W. (Eds.), *Inside/out: Contemporary critical perspectives in education* (pp. 266–84). New York: St. Martin's.

Stephen, W. (1999). *Reducing prejudice and stereotyping in schools.* New York: Teachers College Press.

Thompson, A. (1998). Not the color purple: Black feminist lessons for educational caring. *Harvard Educational Review, 68(4),* 522–53.

Vinson, K. (1998). The traditions' revisited: Instructional approach and high school social studies teachers. *Theory and Research in Social Education, 26,* 50–82.

Welch, O., & Pollard, D. (2006). *From the center to the margins: The importance of self definition in research.* Albany: SUNY Press.

Zeichner, K. M., Grant, C., Gay, G., Gillette, M., Valli, L., & Villegas, A. M. (1998). A research informed vision of good practice in multicultural teacher education: Design principles. *Theory into Practice, 37(2),* 163–71.

Zientek, L. R. (2007). Preparing high quality teachers: Views from the classroom. *American Educational Research Journal, 44(4),* 959–1001.

Zientek, L. R., Capraro, M. M., & Capraro, R. M. (2008). Reporting practices in quantitative teacher education research: One look at the evidence cited in the AERA panel report. *Educational Researcher, 37(4),* 208–16.

Zinn, H. (1990). *Declarations of independence.* New York: Harper Collins.

3

Researching Successful Efforts in Teacher Education to Diversify Teachers

Christine E. Sleeter and H. Richard Milner IV

INTRODUCTION: A DEMOGRAPHIC URGENCY

Who teachers are in terms of their cultural, gendered, racial, ethnic, cultural, socioeconomic, and linguistic background is an important issue because research suggests that an overwhelmingly white teaching force cannot meet the needs of increasingly diverse P–12 students (Gay & Howard, 2000; Milner, 2006; Sleeter, 2001). The demographic divide imperative (Banks, 2003) and what we are calling a demographic urgency is present in an important body of literature that makes a case for the preparation of teachers for the diversity they will face in P–12 educational contexts (cf. Gay & Howard, 2000; Sleeter, 2008; Zumwalt & Craig, 2005). Emphases on demographics in teacher education and subsequently P–12 operate on at least two levels: (1) teachers in teacher education programs (who are mainly white and female) need to be (better) prepared to meet the needs of racially and ethnically diverse learners; and (2) teacher education programs need to be more persistent and innovative in selecting, recruiting, and inducting a more diverse teaching force.[1]

While current teacher education demographic data that are available suggest that the teaching force is diversifying slightly, the rate and consistency of its diversification remains a serious problem. Almost a decade ago, analyzing statistics from the U.S. Department of Education, Gay and Howard (2000) found that

> 86% of all elementary and secondary teachers are European Americans. The number of African American teachers has declined from a high of 12% in 1970 to 7% in 1998. The number of Latino and Asian/Pacific Islander American teachers is increasing slightly, but the percentages are still very small (approximately 5% and 1% respectively). Native Americans comprise less than 1% of the national teaching force. (pp. 1–2)

The demographics of teachers between 2007 and 2008 are captured in table 3.1. The data in the table represent the most current statistics available at the time of this review. As it shows, there has been fairly little change in the demographics of the teaching force over the last decade.

Table 3.1   Teaching Demographics in Public Elementary and Secondary Schools (in percent)

	Elementary	Secondary
White	82.7	83.5
Black	7.1	6.9
Hispanic	7.5	6.8
Asian	1.2	1.3
Pacific Island	0.2	0.2
American Indian/Alaska Native	0.4	0.5
More Than One Race	0.9	0.9

Source: NCES (2009).

VALUE OF TEACHERS OF COLOR[2]

There are at least two lines of thinking regarding the diversification of the teaching force. These lines of thinking are not mutually exclusive—both are important. One line of thinking suggests that where the real emphasis should be placed is on the better preparation of teachers, regardless of their racial and ethnic background, for the students they will face. This line of thinking sometimes builds on the compelling qualitative research of Ladson-Billings (1994), who found that teachers from any racial and ethnic background could learn to be successful pedagogues of African American students. In this sense, what teachers know and have the skills to learn about themselves, their students, the contexts in which they teach, their curriculum development, and their teaching matter more than teachers' racial and ethnic backgrounds. Another line of thinking suggests working to recruit and retain teachers of color for the benefit of the diverse students teachers will encounter. Following the latter line of thinking, cultural and racial congruence and incongruence (Irvine, 2003) are often used as frames to discuss the complexities embedded in the urgency to prepare teachers to meet the needs of *all* students. Because white teachers and students of color often possess different racialized and cultural experiences and repertoires of knowledge and knowing both inside and outside the classroom, racial and cultural incongruence may serve as a roadblock for academic and social success in the classroom (Foster, 1997; Irvine, 2003; Nieto, 2000).

For instance, research suggests that teachers of color can have a positive influence on the achievement among students of color, especially when teachers and students share the same racial background (Irvine, 2003; Nieto, 1999). Irvine (2003) reported on the research of Meier, Stewart, and England (1989), who investigated the impact of African American educators on African American students' success and found that in contexts with high percentages of African American teachers: "fewer African American students were placed in special education classes. Fewer African Americans were suspended or expelled. More African Americans were placed in gifted and talented programs. [And] more African Americans graduated from high school" (p. 54).

Teachers of color can be invaluable for student success in the classroom (Siddle-Walker, 2000) because they can serve as role models for students (Cole, 1986; Milner & Howard, 2004; Villegas & Clewell, 1998) and understand and respect the cultural knowledge students possess, and they use this knowledge as a foundation for their teaching practices (Irvine, 1988; Siddle-Walker, 2000). In their observations on why teachers of color are needed, Villegas and Clewell (1998) wrote:

> If children do not see adults of color in professional roles in schools and instead see them overrepresented in the ranks of non-professional workers, they are taught implicitly that white people are better suited than racial/ethnic minorities to hold positions of authority in our society. (p. 121)

Pang and Gibson (2001) maintained that "Black educators are far more than physical role models . . . they bring diverse family histories, value orientations, and experiences to students in the classroom, attributes often not found in textbooks or viewpoints often omitted" (pp. 260–61). Teachers of color are valuable to the teaching profession, not only because students of color benefit but all students can benefit from what the teachers bring into the learning environment. Villegas and Clewell (1998) also stressed how important is for white students to have teachers of color: "By seeing people of color in professional roles, white youngsters are helped to dispel myths of racial inferiority and incompetence that many have come to internalize about people of color" (pp. 121–22).

Building from her research as well as that of others, Irvine (2003) formulated three central propositions related to the importance of a diversified teacher force. She explained that teachers of color (1) serve as "cultural translators" (p. 55) in the classroom, (2) have high expectations for their students, they are reliable mentors for their students and advocate for them, and (3) provide a culturally based teaching approach in the classroom. Teachers of color are likely to deeply understand students of color and their cultural references because teachers of color experience life outside of the classroom in ways similar to many of their students. Teachers of color, for instance, understand some of the problems students face because they grapple with similar issues with their own children. In terms of building and establishing racial and cultural knowledge about their students, teachers of color sometimes attend the same church as their students, frequent the same beauty and barber salons (also see Siddle-Walker, 2000), and understand the structural challenges that their students face, such as being followed around in a department store due to their racial and ethnic background. Experiences outside of the classroom allow teachers to build on and from these experiences for opportunities to connect and learn in the classroom. Such experiences allow teachers to empathize with, not pity, their students (McAllister & Irvine, 2002). Thus, students do not want to let their teachers down because the teachers are concerned for the students (Foster, 1997), and this concern has been described as other mothering (Collins, 1991). The teachers want for their students the best—just as they would want for their own biological children.

We also see teacher race and ethnicity as an indicator of the worldviews available within any school's professional teaching corps. The more homogenous the teachers, the more homogenous the worldviews that are likely to be used to analyze teaching and student needs, which is particularly problematic when those worldviews and the experiences underlying them diverge from those of students.

It is important to note that while we believe that diversifying the teaching force is a critical component to student success, we are not asserting that such diversification is a panacea for increasing student achievement and student-learning opportunities. Rather, we understand that teachers operate within and through systems and institutions that shape their work with students. A teacher's racial or ethnic background does not determine a teacher's ideology, shared background with a particular group of students, or ability to teach. Further, the systemic and institutional support or lack thereof that teachers receive can sometimes serve as roadblocks for teachers of color in their work with students.

Buendia, Gitlin, and Doumbia's (2003) research about English language learning students and teaching highlighted tensions between established discourses in a context and the pedagogical, as well as philosophical, beliefs teachers of color brought into the school. In short, the discourse in the school context carried "deficit views of immigrant students" (p. 315). Teachers in the study believed that the immigrant students needed to be "socialized . . . into things like being responsible . . . [and] how to handle all of the freedom" (p. 302) in the new context. The ingrained discourse of the school seemed to convey the message that the students did not bring intellectual and social assets and capital to the learning environment. Moreover, the teachers of color in the study struggled to develop and implement curricular and pedagogical strategies that, from their experiences, could more appropriately meet the needs of English language learners—in opposition to the permeating dominant discourse in the school. Although teachers of color may find racial and cultural conditions and experiences appropriate and relevant because of their personal experiences of racism and sexism, for instance, the pervasive (and white) belief systems, goals, missions, and discourses of the school can circumvent highly capable teachers' desires to transform the curriculum. Buendia, Gitlin, and Doumbia (2003) declared that "the present-day contexts of schools may push critically minded teachers of color in ways that undermine their desires" (p. 317). Consequences of common expectations and practices of colleagues and administration in a school could cause teachers of color to revert to or to fall in line with the common practices established in a school.

Still, the research on the value of diversifying the teaching force is too compelling to ignore the potential benefits for students of color and all students. Thus, because of its value, it is urgent that attention be given to diversifying the teaching force itself. In what follows, we review programs to recruit and prepare teachers of color. We then critically examine the nature of research reported on such programs, and sketch out what a research agenda might look like to advance the area. We conclude with implications for policy, practice, and research.

PROGRAMS TO RECRUIT AND PREPARE TEACHERS OF COLOR

Programs that have been designed to recruit and prepare teachers of color usually take into account at least some of the following factors related to the teaching workforce and reasons why there are relatively few teachers of color. (1) Most teachers prefer to teach close to home; "growing your own" teachers of color has been recommended as a promising strategy for that reason (Boyd, Lankford, Loeb, & Wyckoff, 2005). (2) At the P–12 levels, students of color are sometimes not well prepared for higher education or receive much guidance about navigating into higher education. (3) Related, teacher testing disproportionately washes out teachers of color (Alberts, 2002). (4) Research focusing on black teachers suggests that, while teaching used to be seen as a profession to gain entry into the middle class, with the increase in job prospects, university students of color are often selecting different careers instead (Foster, 1997; Milner & Howard, 2004; Zumwalt & Craig, 2005). (5) Some university students of color are put off by the whiteness and irrelevance of teacher education programs they see.

We divided programs we reviewed into two categories: those that bring candidates of color into and through existing teacher education programs and those that tailor teacher education programs specifically for racially and ethnically diverse working adults. We began by seeking published journal articles or book chapters that had substantive descriptions, if not actual empirical studies, about specific programs; we excluded those in which descriptions were very brief (such as one page). We searched several databases (such as ERIC), not limiting our search to any particular years or journals. To keep our review manageable, we limited it in three ways. First, we limited the review to preservice level programs, although we recognize that there are also efforts to retain teachers of color at the professional development level. Second, we limited it to programs in the United States, although we recognize that similar efforts are taking place elsewhere (c.f., Solomon, 1997; Wang, 2001). Third, we limited it to programs that have been intentionally designed to diversify who goes into teaching, rather than including those with relatively diverse student populations achieved by virtue of location.

Bringing Candidates of Color Into and Through Existing Teacher Education Programs

Many programs attempt to build the pipeline of potential teacher candidates of color either prior to or while they are in the university. Such programs do not attempt to change teacher education programs but rather to build support systems into, around, and through them. Pipeline programs work with youth to demystify higher education and increase the likelihood that youth will be prepared academically for college, while also exposing them to experiences that may attract them into teaching. Programs to support university students of color typically offer financial and academic support as well as social and cultural support to combat alienation on predominantly white campuses.

Pipeline programs. Pipeline programs involve collaboration between university-based teacher education programs and feeder institutions, mainly secondary schools. Magnet high school programs for potential teachers of color are an intensive kind of pipeline program that has been implemented in a few cities. For example, the Teaching Professions Program at Coolidge High School in Washington, D.C., was designed to build interest of African American students in teaching (Hunter-Boykin, 1992), and the Socratic Institute at Riverside High School was designed in collaboration with the University of Texas at El Paso to interest Latino students in teaching (Oliva & Staudt, 2003, 2004). Both programs, which serve grades 9–12, recruit academically capable students, add coursework related to teaching (such as Orientation to Teaching) to their academic curriculum, and involve participants in tutoring younger children. As of 1992, the Teaching Professions Program had about

130 students, with a fairly high retention rate; all fifteen graduates that year had been accepted into universities (Hunter-Boykin, 1992). The more recent Socratic Institute reported having eighty-two students in 2004, 98 percent of whom were Latino; none had yet reached graduation (Oliva & Staudt, 2004).

Less intensive pipeline programs to build interest in teaching typically include activities such as bringing secondary students onto a college campus, strengthening their academic skills, and involving them in tutoring younger children. Project FUTURE at Texas Tech University works with cohorts of students from sixth grade through their first year of college. Between 2005 and 2006, 440 students, over 80 percent of whom were of color, participated. Activities include a day-long conference on the university campus, other events on campus throughout the school year, and mentoring by a Texas Tech student (Stevens, Agnello, Ramirez, Marbley, & Hamman, 2007). Much smaller projects with high school students included the Teacher Track Project at California State University at Fullerton (Yopp, Yopp, & Taylor, 1992) and "Project: I Teach" at the University of Texas at San Antonio (Zapata, 1988).

Connecting prospective teachers of color with excellent mentors appears to be a critical component to recruitment success. Padak, Stadulis, Barton, Meadows, and Padak (1994) described the results of mentoring in the Urban Teachers Project that was designed to recruit future urban teachers. The partnership (which still exists) represented participation of school personnel, Kent State University, and the project staff. Like the programs above, this one supported high school students interested in education and urban teaching with a Saturday program to assist students with building knowledge about education and teaching and also in-school academic support through tutoring. A third component of support was mentoring, which was the main focus of the study. The authors summarized the success of the mentoring component of the project, stating:

> The development and maintenance of mentoring relationships may offer a partial solution to the problem of encouraging talented minority students to become teachers in urban settings. Our experience suggests that mentoring focused on professional socialization can be successful while future teachers are still in high school. Becoming a well-prepared and committed teacher involves professional socialization . . . mentor teachers can effectively support students' [mentees'] transition into college and ultimately into the teaching profession. (p. 351)

Programs to support university students of color. Programs designed to support university students of color who may be interested in completing teacher certification typically offer scholarships (often with the expectation that graduates will teach in local schools) and additional academic and cultural support. The nature of the support differs somewhat depending on whether the program targets mainly traditional-age students or working adults.

The University of Texas at San Antonio, in collaboration with San Antonio College, developed the Academy for Teaching Excellence, a large, comprehensive program to support Latino college students interested in becoming teachers. A central feature is the Teacher Academic Learning Community, which recruits mainly Latino freshmen, then offers them summer bridging and other academic support (particularly for passing academic proficiency exams), personal support (such as cultural seminars and life-planning assistance), and professional support (such as mentoring in field experiences). As of 2006, about 750 students, mostly Latino, had participated, with a very high retention rate (Flores, Clark, Claeys, & Villarreal, 2007). Hopi Teachers for Hopi Schools, which involved collaboration between Northern Arizona University and the Hopi Nation, one of twenty similar projects funded by the Office of Indian Education, served two cohorts of about twenty students each between 2000 and 2006. In addition to financial support, it offered academic advising, tutoring, monthly meetings, and workshops designed to help participants negotiate challenges at the university. As of 2006, it had certified thirty-eight Hopi teachers (White, Bedonie, de Groat, Lockard, & Honani, 2007).

The Freshman/Sophomore Minority Teachers Grant Program involved collaboration among a university and two community colleges in Arkansas to help African American students navigate the transition from a community college to a four-year institution as an education major. Students were supported through stipends, mentoring, and various community-building activities (Holmes & Couch, 1997). Similarly, the Career Opportunity Program 2000 in Des Moines, Iowa, involved collaboration between a school district, a community college, and a private four-year college; most of its students were non-traditional-age African Americans. Although about 130 students participated, as of 1998 only twelve had completed the program, probably due to the cost of tuition and the traditional nature of the four-year college (Hall Mark, 1998). Project TEAM (Transformative Educational Achievement Model) at Indiana University, which began in 1996, successfully served cohorts of fifteen to twenty students of color per year, beginning with the freshman year. In addition to financial support, a key feature of this program was its honors seminar that addressed concerns of students of color that are often ignored in predominantly white programs, such as how teachers of color can negotiate predominantly white schools (Bennett, 2002; Bennett, Cole, & Thompson, 2000). Many fairly small programs incorporate features of some of the larger programs described above but support fewer than a dozen students at any given time. Project TEACH, which involved collaboration among a four-year college, a community-based organization, and a school district, brought in one or two students of color per year for twelve years, supporting the education and certification of eighteen teachers of color (Irizarry, 2007). A collaborative effort between the Marietta City School District in Georgia and Kennesaw State College brought in two new freshmen per year, assisting a total of seven scholars of color with completing their degrees in education (Fielder, 1996).

The importance of linking identities of students of color with teaching and academic research cannot be underestimated. For example, Dillard (1994) reported on an eight-week summer research institute, Opening Doors: The Worlds of Graduate Study for Minority Students in Education, that occurred in the summer of 1992. She planned and directed the institute for twenty-one undergraduate students of color interested in careers in education and graduate school. Results pointed to the importance of teacher identity and the maintenance of teachers' ethnic identities in particular. The idea that programs in education and also educational contexts expect teachers to divorce themselves from their racial and ethnic identities was problematized and used as a site of critique and discussion in the institute.

Programs aimed toward working adults take into account not only ethnic identity and cultural support but also pragmatic concerns associated with adults' need to continue to work and barriers adults may experience in higher education institutions. Two California State University Teacher Diversity Projects that were described in published articles served paraprofessionals, most of whom were Latino and bilingual, and whose education levels ranged from high school through university graduates. At California State University at San Bernardino, the Excellence and Equity in Teaching Project collaborated with community colleges. Participants were selected based partly on their commitment to teaching. Academic counselors monitored their progress through coursework and helped them navigate the transfer from the community college to the CSU campus. Support groups at the community colleges offered academic and cultural support. As of 1996, the project had forty participants (Gutiérrez, 1992; Gutiérrez & Murphy, 1996).

Similarly, the Teacher Track Project at California State University at Fullerton, in collaboration with two community colleges and three school districts, recruited and supported instructional aides, most of whom were Latinos and some of whom were credentialed teachers from other countries. Support included advisement on course taking, monthly meetings, small financial stipends, and occasional special events such as guest speakers. At the time of writing, sixty-six instructional aides were involved (Yopp, Yopp, & Taylor, 1992). Newcomers Entering Teaching involves collaboration between the University of Southern Maine and the Portland, Maine, public schools to help immigrant university-educated adults, most of whom had been teachers in their home countries, to complete the university's certification program. The program helps them navigate university bureaucracies, develop their use of academic English, prepare for the GRE, and meet entry requirements of the certification program. It also offers financial help to those who need it and an internship during the final semester. At the time of writing, six immigrant teachers had completed the program (Ross, 2001).

In summary, programs that are designed to bring candidates of color into and through teacher education tend to share several features. They build an interest among students of color in a teaching career, often taking steps to link students' racial or ethnic identities with teaching, such as by connecting them with mentor teachers from their same background or engaging students in projects that are culturally relevant to them. Such programs also offer academic support as well as support navigating college requirements. Programs aimed toward secondary education students attempt to demystify college by bringing students to the college campus; programs aimed toward college students offer scholarships as well as other support that will enable them to successfully enter and succeed within the teacher education program.

Redesigning Teacher Education Programs

Ultimately, we believe that teacher education programs themselves should be transformed to attract, welcome, and prepare diverse teachers. Implicitly, most programs are designed mainly with traditional-age white students in mind, a reality that may be invisible to those in such programs but is visible to those who sense not belonging. In Agee's (2004) study, she explained that "the teacher education texts used in the course made recommendations for using diverse texts or teaching diverse students based on the assumption that preservice teachers are White" (p. 749). This assumption could alienate preservice teachers of color. What about the curricular and instructional needs of Asian or Latino teachers, for instance?

The Multilingual/Multicultural Teacher Preparation Center (M/M Center) in the Bilingual/Multicultural Department at Sacramento State University, which is more than twenty years old, is an excellent example of a program designed around student diversity. About 75 percent of its candidates are of color and most are bilingual, a mix the program attracts because of its focus, its very diverse faculty, and its commitment to working with communities of color and for social justice. Outsiders to California may assume that teacher education programs in California are routinely diverse, but such is not the case. Wong and colleagues (2007) explain, "Race-conscious . . . and language-conscious policy-making and program development characterize the program's history and current operations" (p. 9). The M/M Center actively recruits, advises, and mentors undergraduates of color on its campus, and over time has developed a network of outreach into schools serving students of color. Its curriculum features multicultural content and the application of theory into practice through extensive field experiences in schools serving low-income and culturally and linguistically diverse students and English language learners.

Unlike the M/M Center, most redesigned university teacher education programs are alternative versions of existing traditional programs, reworked to serve adults who wish to become teachers—paraprofessionals or other noncertified school district employees, emergency certified teachers, and career-changers—but who generally cannot stop working to return to college.[3] In addition, such programs often capitalize on experiences that adults who are already working in classrooms have. While a higher percentage of teachers of color than white teachers are certified through some kind of alternative program (Shen, 1998), the fact that a program is "alternative" does not necessarily mean that it was designed to appeal to prospective teachers of color. For example, about 75 percent of new teachers certified through Teach for America (TFA) are "caucasian, middle-class, female, monolingual English speakers" (Veltri, 2008, p. 522); while TFA may attract a somewhat more diverse population than many other teacher education programs, we do not see it as designed specifically to recruit and prepare a diverse population. Similarly, some urban alternative programs (such as one operated by Los Angeles Unified School District) have quite diverse populations due to location. Partly because nonuniversity alternatives have been reviewed elsewhere (c.f., Zeichner & Conklin, 2005) and because they tend not to present themselves as having been designed explicitly to diversify the teaching population, we do not review them here.

The DeWitt Wallace–Reader's Digest Fund launched Pathways into Teaching Careers, the largest cluster of such programs, in 1989; eventually there were forty-one sites around the United States. Pathways programs shared several features: (1) they involved partnership between a teacher education institution and local school districts; (2) partnering districts actively helped to recruit and select participants; (3) the selection process combined traditional and nontraditional criteria (such as commitment to teaching in urban schools); (4) the teacher education curriculum was modified to meet participants' needs; and (5) the program offered a system of academic support, social support, and financial support (Clewell & Villegas, 1999). Several Pathways programs have been described in published articles.

The Pathways program at Armstrong Atlantic State University (in collaboration with Savannah State University and Savannah-Chatham County Public Schools) was developed to respond to the immense need for teachers of color in Georgia.

Designed mainly for paraprofessionals, it successfully certified about ninety African American teachers (Lau, Dandy, & Hoffman, 2007). Dandy (1998) proposed targeting the paraprofessional pool, including "teaching assistants, clerks, and other school employees with or without baccalaureate degrees" (p. 89). A central focus, however, was the recruitment of these individuals who actually live and work in the community of students being taught. The success of the program was credited to (1) strong collaboration between local schools and the universities involved; (2) leadership by university representatives committed to the objectives of the program; (3) program standards that "begin with a strategic selection process and provide financial, emotional, and academic support" (p. 101); and (4) curricular modification.

Other Pathways programs made use of similar ideas. The program at Norfolk State University, also designed for paraprofessionals, had certified sixty teachers as of 1997 (Littleton, 1998). The Alternative Pathways to Teaching Program at Wayne State University served mainly noncertified school district employees and career-changers. A track of that program, funded partially by the National Science Foundation, certifies minority math and science teachers who already have a degree. At the time of writing, forty-one candidates (mainly African American) had either completed or were about to complete it (Cavallo, Ferreira, & Roberts, 2005). "Project 29" at the University of Illinois at Chicago was designed to prepare bilingual teachers for Chicago Public Schools. Its name was taken from a provisional teaching certificate (Type 29) that was about to expire. Although it began as a Pathways program, partly because one of its codirectors became dean and the other became a full-time faculty member, it has become institutionalized within the college where it has influenced other teacher education programs; for example, graduate elementary teacher candidates across the college are now interviewed as part of the admissions process. As of 2006, Project 29 had produced 145 teachers, three-fourths of whom are Latino (Sakash & Chou, 2007).

Many other colleges and universities have had alternative programs with similar characteristics to Pathways programs. Two that have been in existence since the mid-1990s and have certified hundreds of teachers, the majority of whom are teachers of color, are the Latino Teacher Project (now called the Latino and Language Minority Teacher Projects) in Los Angeles and the Metropolitan Milwaukee Teacher Education Program. The Latino Teacher Project, established through a partnership among four higher education institutions, three school districts, the county office of education, and labor unions representing paraprofessionals, certifies bilingual teachers for southern California schools. The project first selects schools that have bilingual paraprofessionals and a commitment to working with the project; the schools then nominate paraprofessionals who are already bilingual and committed to becoming certified bilingual teachers. The curriculum is much the same as it is for the traditional university program but made more accessible to participants primarily by scheduling and by allowing participants to student teach in their own classrooms. The project offers financial, academic, and social support (e.g., grouping participants into cohorts, assigning on-site faculty mentors, and providing regular seminars) (Genzuk & Baca, 1998).

The Metropolitan Milwaukee Teacher Education Program was established through collaboration between Milwaukee Public Schools, the teachers union, and the University of Wisconsin at Milwaukee. Using a structured interview and observing candidates working with urban children over a summer, university faculty select candidates on the basis of their perceived ability to succeed in urban schools. Unlike most other programs we review, this one expects participants to pay the $10,000 program fee; assistance is available for those in need. Also unlike most other programs, this one is not only classroom-based but also designed and staffed mainly by outstanding urban teachers. Participants teach in their own classroom under the guidance of veteran teachers. Supporting classes and workshops focus on expectations for teachers working in the district; the curriculum, which is aligned with state standards, was developed by urban teachers. The only full-time faculty members who teach in the program are outstanding classroom teachers who are on leave. A separate group of assessors assess participants' classroom performance; those who demonstrate that their students are learning are recommended for certification (K–9, with a bilingual endorsement option), and those who do not are dropped from the program. Completers earn licensure but no college credits or degrees (Haberman, 2001).

Many other small and more temporary programs have also existed. Elementary Certification for Ethnic Colleagues for the Elementary School (EC3) in Wisconsin was created through collaboration between two universities and a local school district, mainly for adult career changers. The curriculum was adapted from that of both universities, with courses meeting during the evenings; stipends supported students during full-time student teaching. The program successfully certified three cohorts of teachers of color, mainly African Americans (Shade, Boe, Garner, & New, 1998). Similarly, the LeMoyne-Owen Teacher Education Program in Tennessee was designed for adult career-changers through collaboration with four school systems, a local Head Start, private day care facilities, and local businesses. Classes were held in evenings and on weekends, and financial support was available during the student-teaching semester. The program also offered tutorial services, and workshops addressed needs such as test preparation and resume preparation. As of 1995, it had certified seventy-five teachers of color (Love & Greer, 1995). The Teacher Opportunity Program in Kentucky was formed through collaboration between a university and a school district. It compressed coursework from the traditional teacher education program, and it included intense fieldwork in which candidates were hired as teaching assistants; additional scholarship funds were located for candidates who needed them. Over a three-year period, the program certified twenty-two teachers of color (Brennan & Bliss, 1998). The Teacher Early Entry Paraprofessional training program in Texas was designed to assist bilingual paraprofessionals who had completed two years of college in finishing their degree and teacher certification. Participants were placed as interns with experienced classroom teachers and then offered university classes in evenings and on weekends (Torres-Karna & Krustchinsky, 1998).

Table 3.2 summarizes key features programs share in relationship to partnerships between universities and school districts that serve students of color, such as selection criteria into teacher education programs, support students are offered, features of coursework and field experiences, and ways of linking students' racial and ethnic identities with teaching.

An important consideration that captures our attention is that while some programs we reviewed were temporary, others have become institutionalized. The M/M Center, Project 29, the Latino and Language Minority Teacher Projects, and the Met-

Table 3.2   Common Features Programs Share

Dimension of Teacher Ed. Program	Common Features
Partnership between university program and school districts that serve students of color	• Candidates recruited through partnership • Partnership develops school placements, recruits teacher mentors • Districts hire interns if possible • Districts hire graduates of program
Selection into the program	• Traditional academic criteria • Ability, interest, experience working with children or youth of color • Second language competence, where relevant
Student support	• Academic: preparation for tests, intensive work in other academic skills as needed; navigation through college requirements and transfer requirements • Financial: scholarships, stipends common; programs for adults assume candidates need income while earning teaching credential • Personal: life planning as needed • Cultural: activities, seminars that acknowledge and build on candidates' cultural backgrounds in relationship to teaching
Coursework	• Accessibility: scheduling and location tailored to working adults • Relevance: builds on knowledge and experiences candidates already have
Fieldwork	• Acknowledges candidates' experiences • Paraprofessionals student teach in own classroom • Paid internships where possible
Link student identity with teaching	• Mentors who are teachers of color • Culturally relevant projects, curriculum that use scholarship by educators/researchers of color • Significant proportion of teacher education faculty are of color

ropolitan Milwaukee Teacher Education Program have all existed for more than a decade (in some cases, two decades), and have each produced hundreds of teachers. From our perspective, they illustrate that it is possible to redesign university-based teacher education, working in collaboration with school districts, to substantially diversify the teaching population.

NATURE OF THE RESEARCH

Programs designed to recruit and prepare teachers of color have been in existence for a long time but are not well researched and consequently are not well known. Thus, successful efforts as well as challenges that programs face are not reported very much in journal articles, which makes it difficult to draw definitive conclusions about the nature, structure, and progress of such work. We examined the nature of research that has been done on the programs above. Three categories of research emerged: narrative descriptions written by those who participated in running a program, internal evaluations by those working in a program, and external evaluations.

Program Description Only

About one-third of the programs we reviewed report only program descriptions, narrated by someone working in the program (Cavallo, Ferreira, & Roberts, 2005; Fielder, 1996; Genzuk & Baca, 1998; Gutierrez, 1992; Holmes & Couch, 1997; Littleton, 1998; Love & Greer, 1995; Ross, 2001; Shade, Boe, Garner, & New, 1998; Torres-Karna & Krustchinsky, 1998). One might classify these loosely as narrative research, in that they offer "inside stories" by those involved with specific programs, providing testimonial that such programs are possible. For the most part, these narratives are contextualized within conceptual frameworks that help readers interpret the program. However, they suffer limitations common to insider stories: selective perception by virtue of the writer being immersed in a program one often has had to fight for, and in some cases an absence of data (such as numbers of program completers) that would help readers develop their own analysis. Moreover, such narratives usually fail to critique their own programs in ways that can provide insight into the pervasive struggles and mistakes that shape them.

Internal Program Evaluations

About two-thirds of the programs reported not only descriptions but also internal evaluations. The great majority used data gathered through interviews and/or surveys with program participants, either while they were in the program or shortly after completing it, to find out how well the program worked for them, how it addressed their needs, and any other information that might help to strengthen the program. For example, Lau, Dandy, and Hoffman (2007) surveyed graduates of the Pathways program at Armstrong Atlantic State University to identify factors that led to its high retention rate during the program and after the teachers were hired. Yopp, Yopp, & Taylor (1992) surveyed instructional aides in the Teacher Track Project to find out how it had addressed their needs, looking particularly at needs of reentry women who felt insecure about their academic abilities but took their studies very seriously. Irizarry (2007) interviewed Project TEACH participants to find out why they entered teaching and identified ways in which the project helped and supported them. Dillard (1994) used interactive journals, videotaping, and interviews to gauge participant growth in the Opening Doors Project.

Such internal evaluations only rarely included data provided by someone external to the program about graduates' performance in the classroom. An example of using some external data is Haberman's (1999) evaluation, which included not only telephone surveys of graduates but also principals' ratings of graduates' performance in the elementary classroom. Although program reports that include internal evaluation data offer more information that helps readers analyze the program, these studies are still limited. Data about graduates' quality of teaching is limited when it takes the form of general ratings of teachers as excellent, satisfactory, or less than satisfactory, as did Haberman's study. External evaluators often ask questions and bring perspectives that may complement, but are not identical to, those of insiders. Longitudinal studies where program participants are interviewed, surveyed, and/or observed in naturalist settings and studies that are ongoing and that take place over longer periods of time may add to the literature through these internal program evaluations, particularly if some data can point to the attrition or academic success of students.

External Program Evaluations

An external program evaluation offers a perspective by someone who was not involved in the work of a program. External evaluators may bring questions, considerations, or points of view that differ from those of program insiders. This does not necessarily make external evaluations inherently better than internal descriptions or internal evaluations, but they do help to counterbalance internal accounts. If we are to claim that teacher education can and should work more actively to diversify the teaching population, we need external evaluations of existing programs as well as the important accounts offered by internal evaluations.

We found very few external evaluations of such programs. The largest was for the Pathways into Teaching Careers program (Clewell & Villegas, 1999, 2001; Villegas & Clewell, 1998). Clewell and Villegas gathered data over a six-year period by surveying Pathways participants, staff, teacher supervisors, principals, and teacher evaluators. By the year 2000, Pathways had recruited and served 2,593 participants nationally, which was 18 percent more than its original goal. Sixty-three percent of its participants were teachers of color. According to Clewell and Villegas (2001), Pathways participants completed teacher certification at a higher rate (75 percent) than that of traditional teacher education students (60 percent). At the end of their first year of teaching, Pathways graduates were rated more highly by their principals and by an external assessor using Praxis III than were their traditional counterparts. Clewell and Villegas conclude that it is possible to diversify the teaching force while improving its quality and retention rate in urban schools, using programs like those that had been funded under Pathways. For example, targeting the paraprofessional pool through university- and school-district partnerships has been seen as a logical way to tap prospective teachers of color (Dandy, 1998; Milner & Howard, 2004). Based on their evaluation, Villegas and Clewell (1998) identified five strategies to increase the number of teachers of color through the recruitment of paraprofessionals: (1) the establishment of partnerships with school districts; (2) the use of multiple sources of information in the selection of teacher candidates; (3) the providing of academic and social support services; (4) the modification of teacher education programs (such as when courses are offered); and (5) the availability of tuition assistance.

We located a few other smaller external evaluations, in which data consisted of interviews with program participants and others, as well as examination of documents. González (1997), for instance, evaluated six programs in three regions of the United States that had been funded by the Ford Foundation. Through site visits, he sought to find out students' perceptions of program features that best met their needs. Across all six programs, he found that students appreciated the personal care that they received and the comprehensive services that were designed to address the variety of their needs. González noted that these programs went beyond a remedial approach, viewing the preparation of teachers of color as a developmental process that cultivates what they bring into the learning contexts in addition to addressing needs and deficits. He noted that these services cost money but argued that investing in teachers of color is worth the cost.

In Brennan and Bliss's (1998) evaluation of the Teacher Opportunity Program in Kentucky, an external evaluator collaborating with a faculty member found that the school district appreciated the maturity and experience of the candidates and the quality of their work in schools; candidates appreciated program support, including involvement of minority teacher mentors. They also found some problems: most candidates needed more content coursework for elementary teaching, which lengthened time of completion; and the school district's commitment to hire graduates of this program was resented by some white graduates of the traditional program. Beckett (1998) studied the Latino Teacher Project in Los Angeles and the Navajo Teacher Preparation Program at Fort Lewis College, Colorado, in order to identify factors that were responsible for the programs' initiation and continuing success. She found that both programs had dedicated leaders who were able to develop collaborative relationships with other institutions and to involve skilled professionals in the design and work of the program.

RESEARCH WE NEED

We are suggesting that the literature available regarding the diversification of the teaching force has been an important body of work that has contributed to what we know about this topic. However, based on our review, four interrelated areas of focus can move the field forward: (1) more and deeper situated internal self-studies; (2) more and deeper contextualized external evaluations; (3) more and deeper long-term and longitudinal studies; (4) studies that investigate linkages between teacher ethnicity and student learning; and (5) studies that investigate factors beyond instructional considerations.

Situated Internal Self-Studies

The internal evaluation studies that we reviewed in this chapter—those where someone was involved in program development and implementation—need to be more solidly situated in the broader self-study literature. We are calling for researchers who engage in internal evaluations of their own programs to situate their studies in the broader self-study discourse because without such grounding it will be difficult for the broader field of teacher education to build knowledge in the area, hopefully for systemic changes in the field. In *The Report of the AERA Panel on Research and Teacher Education*, Cochran-Smith and Zeichner (2005) emphasized that researchers in the field of teacher education need to situate their research and conceptual discussions more solidly in theory and the broader literature in the field. They wrote, "Without locating empirical studies in relation to appropriate theoretical frameworks regarding teacher learning, teacher effectiveness, and pupil learning, it will be difficult to explain findings about the effects of particular teacher education practices" (p. 32). The self-study strand of teacher education is a logical site for the internal evaluation studies on recruitment and retention of teachers of color, particularly because so many of the studies are conducted by someone very close to the program, such as the project director, planner, or facilitator. In addition, these self-studies need to engage in the difficult work of critiquing these programs as well as reporting the testimonies and successes of them. Without posing the difficult questions about the programs, about those in them, and about those who develop and implement them, it will be difficult for improvement on a broader scale, especially in terms of subsequent and transferable practices in teacher education.

Contextualized External Evaluations

In addition to what we are calling situated internal self-studies, external evaluations should also include broader and deeper contextual features. It would be very useful if studies not only provided superficial descriptions of participants in schools after participants have graduated or reports from principals of teachers who have experienced these programs but also deep descriptions about the kinds of places in which these teachers are placed, the milieu, the support or lack thereof of parents and colleagues in the school, and so forth. Such findings, emerging from an external evaluator, would provide a deeper sense of the effectiveness of the programs themselves and their ability to prepare teachers to succeed in a range of contexts. What types of programs seem to best prepare teachers for urban schools, for instance? We are also calling for external evaluators to provide more context-rich evaluations of the programs themselves in teacher education in order to provide insight into the successful and unsuccessful practices of those participating and facilitating the programs.

Long-Term and Longitudinal Studies

Research programs also need to be long-term and longitudinal. For instance, as revealed in this review, the field only benefits intermediately by studies that capture the beginning of a program or programs that are someplace in the middle of implementation. Reports are needed that capture the (long) range of the program, from program development through years when teachers are actually in the classroom with students. We see these longitudinal studies involving at least three related phases—program development, program implementation, and program evaluation. Early questions that may emerge in program development might include: How did and has the program developed? Who was involved with the program development? What kinds of philosophical and theoretical grounding shaped the program? What challenges did those involved encounter? How did those involved work through the difficulties? Program implementation would allow for continued study of what is working and not during program evaluation. We see this process as one where those involved in facilitation as well as participants are being evaluated and questioned both by internal and external investigators. In addition, documents and policies, such as the curriculum, course offerings, professional development workshops, funding, mentoring opportunities, and so forth would also be consistently evaluated over long periods of time and adapted where needed. Finally, a third phase of long-term study is program evaluation, where teachers are actually evaluated in their actual teaching practices with overt attention placed on program objectives. Germaine to the third phase of teachers' work in P–12 is student learning, an area to which we turn next.

Teacher Ethnicity with Student Learning

Perhaps the most important and pressing question about recruiting and retaining teachers of color is whether student learning increases when they are taught by a teacher of color and the extent to which matching teacher and student ethnic or racial identity matters. This has been studied, but not extensively (cf. Dee, 2004). Research should continue to focus on, to the extent possible, whether student learning is enhanced or not by being taught by a teacher of color. As mentioned in previous sections of this chapter, researchers have investigated links between student achievement and teachers of color (c.f., Irvine, 2003; Meier, Stewart, & England, 1989). We recognize that there is an uncountable number of other factors that will influence student learning and that it would be very difficult to determine the extent to which a teacher's racial and ethnic background might influence student learning. However, the posing of such a question has to be incorporated in studies in order to gain perspective around how students of color fare with teachers of color.

From our view, this line of research should not be atheoretical. Theories, used as analytical and conceptual tools to help explain and elucidate the complexities of studying matters related to diversifying the teaching force—matters such as race, ethnicity, contexts, student learning, and achievement—are needed to continue building the field. Useful theoretical tools about how and why diversifying the teaching force is important can shed light on the empirical literature. For instance, sociocognitive theories might address the question of whether teachers of color make better role models and advocates for students of color. Sociocultural theories might assist researchers in unpacking the learning milieu and how it shapes the teaching and learning exchange. Moreover, theories such as culturally relevant pedagogy (Ladson-Billings, 1994) and culturally responsive pedagogy (Gay, 2000) may prove to be useful tools in understanding what teachers of color bring into the classroom and are able to transfer into their practices. These and other innovative theoretical frames are essential to building a more robust literature base related to the importance of diversification in the teaching force.

We also believe that studies should investigate factors other than student test scores, which is why we deliberately focus on "student learning" in this section and not student achievement (although we recognize that these two areas are not mutually exclusive). There is a body of research that is beginning to investigate, for instance, connections between African American teachers and the reading scores of African American students in comparison to students' reading scores who do not have African American teachers (Easton-Brooks, Lewis, & Yang, 2010). If there are powerful effects, the literature should reflect the features of these successful teachers of students of color such that others in teacher education can learn and benefit (Ladson-Billings, 1994; Milner, 2006).

Factors Beyond Instructional Considerations

While our preference is for studies to focus specifically on educational outcomes, namely student learning and student achievement, we also recognize that research needs to occur related to diversifying the teaching force apart from instructional considerations. For example, studies are needed that

- investigate matters of equity in district hiring practices, recruitment efforts, and retention policies with an intense eye toward teachers of color;
- study the recruitment and retention patterns and practices of districts and states;
- consider, qualitatively speaking, the ways in which teachers of color are "socialized" into hostile teaching environments on the district, school, and classroom levels; and
- research connections between and among school- and district-level administrators, such as school-level principals and district-level personnel, and their recruitment and retention of teachers of color.

In addition, research should examine the extent to which schoolwide responses to academic needs of students of color are affected by the composition of professionals within the school. Do schools serving a high proportion of students of color analyze and respond to their students more effectively when a high proportion of the teachers are from similar backgrounds as their students? Finally, research teasing out interactions between teacher and student ethnicity should also examine to what extent social-class background of students and teachers might mediate the impact of racial and ethnic background.

IMPLICATIONS AND CONCLUSIONS

This review suggests implications for both practice and research. We are past the time when teacher education programs can assume that little can be done to diversify the teaching population. This review suggests several models that have been used with success. Although some models may prove more successful and longer-lasting than others, it is still safe to say that there are various options teacher education programs can try and descriptions of what others have done that can guide new trials. External evaluations, although limited, offer useful information. They consistently find a high degree of satisfaction on the part of school-district personnel with teachers of color certified through programs like those in this review. Evaluations have also found that programs with comprehensive services that take into account the lives and needs of candidates of color, particularly older candidates who are already working, are probably more effective than those with more limited services.

In addition, we believe that institutions that serve highly diverse populations of students should continue working to build programs and to attract students into teacher education. Historically black institutions, for instance, may be good sites for more innovation in terms of recruiting undergraduate students into teacher education and also for partnering with local school systems. Historically black institutions and their long-standing commitment to and practices of preparing large numbers of African American students was compromised, according to Clark (1988), when the HOLMES/Carnegie reports pushed for fifth-year programs for teacher education programs. Black colleges and universities have relied on undergraduate teacher education programs (and undergraduate programs more generally) for financial vitality, and a good number of these institutions did not have, and still do not have, graduate-level programs for any discipline—consider private institutions such as Fisk University in Nashville, Tennessee.

Despite the large number of programs to recruit and prepare teachers of color that have existed, however, research on them has been sparse. Because of a dearth of follow-up studies on pipeline programs, for example, we do not have a clear picture of their impact and what features are most essential to a program's success. We know very little about how well graduates of redesigned programs teach in the classroom after they are hired, and virtually nothing about the quality of their teaching in relationship to that of teachers certified through traditional programs. It appears that externally funded programs that do not become institutionalized last only as long as the funding and/or the employment of committed individuals. One might ask to what extent programs that become institutionalized not only last but also change how the institution recruits and supports its students and what factors enable and support institutionalization.

Finally, we found very little conceptual work embedded within many of the studies reviewed. The literature takes more of a reporting format than an intellectually situated one. Deeper, more nuanced questions need posing about not only how to increase the number of teachers of color but also about the very essence of their presence in the classroom with students. Dillard (1994) asserted that

> to address the inadequate numbers of teachers of color in our public schools today, we must move the discussion beyond simple numerics [*sic*]. Solely focusing the work of recruitment on increasing the numbers of people of color denies the very essence of being for those who embrace and love their ethnicity . . . The question should be: what is it that the teacher of color brings to the teaching and learning setting which is qualitatively different and inherently of value in our increasingly diverse schools? (p. 16)

Future studies might continue examining ways to increase the number of teachers of color in public schools and also pose deeper questions about what it means for teachers of color to teach increasingly diverse students; how well these teachers fare with all their students, including white ones; what support structures enable and hinder their success; and what qualities about these teachers ensure meaningful learning opportunities for their students.

NOTES

1. We understand that every person represents racial, cultural, and ethnic diversity, although white people usually are classified as the norm and others are considered diverse. We understand that there is a great deal of diversity among people from every racial, cultural, and ethnic background. However, for the purpose of this discussion and due to page restrictions, we are defining racially, culturally, and ethnically diverse groups of people as those groups that are not white or European American.

2. Throughout this chapter, we use *people of color* to refer to those individuals who are not white. We realize that this use is problematic because there is variance between and among individuals of color. However, the use of people of color seems to be the most appropriate language at this time as *minority* is also an inappropriate word choice.

3. The term *alternative* means a wide variety of program configurations. Generally it refers to either university-based programs that are alternative to the regular program(s) or alternative route programs that are only loosely connected to universities or not connected at all.

REFERENCES

Agee, J. (2004). Negotiating a teaching identity: An African American teacher's struggle to teach in test-driven contexts. *Teachers College Record, 106(4)*, 747–74.

Alberts, P. (2002). Praxis II and African American teacher candidates (or, "Is everything black bad"?). *English Education, 34(2)*, 105–25.

Banks, J. A. (2003). *Teaching strategies for ethnic studies* (7th ed.). Boston: Allyn & Bacon.

Beckett, D. R. (1998). Increasing the number of Latino and Navajo teachers in hard-to-staff schools. *Journal of Teacher Education 49(3)*, 196–205.

Bennett, C. I. (2002). Enhancing ethnic diversity at a Big Ten university through Project TEAM: A case study in teacher education. *Educational Researcher, 31(2)*, 21–29.

Bennett, C., Cole, D., & Thompson, J. (2000). Preparing teachers of color at a predominantly white university. *Teaching and Teacher Education, 16(4)*, 445–64.

Boyd, D., Lankford, H., Loeb, S., & Wyckoff, J. (2005). The draw of home: How teachers' preferences for proximity disadvantage urban schools. *Journal of Policy Analysis and Management, 24(1)*, 113–32.

Brennan, S., & Bliss, T. (1998). Increasing minority representation in the teaching profession through alternative certification: A case study. *Teacher Educator 34(1)*, 1–11.

Buendia, E., Gitlin, A., & Doumbia, F. (2003). Working the pedagogical borderlands: An African critical pedagogue teaching within an ESL context. *Curriculum Inquiry, 33(3)*, 291–320.

Cavallo, A. M. L., Ferreira, M. M., & Roberts, S. K. (2005). Increasing student access to qualified science and mathematics teachers through an urban school-university partnership. *School Science and Mathematics, 105(7)*, 363–72.

Clark, V. L. (1988). Teacher education at historically black institutions in the aftermath of the HOLMES/CARNEGIE reports. *Teacher Education Quarterly, 15(2)*, 32–49.

Clewell, B. C., & Villegas, A. M. (1999). Creating a nontraditional pipeline for urban teachers: The Pathways to Teaching Careers model. *Journal of Negro Education, 68(3)*, 306–17.

Clewell, B. C., & Villegas, A. M. (2001). *Absence unexcused: Ending teacher shortages in high-need areas. Evaluating the Pathways to Teaching Careers program.* Washington, DC: Urban Institute. ERIC Document ED460235.

Cochran-Smith, M., & Zeichner, K. M.(2005). Executive summary. In Smith, M. C. & Zeichner, K.M. (Eds.), *Studying teacher education: The report of the AERA panel on research and teacher education* (pp. 1–36). Mahwah, NJ: Lawrence Erlbaum Associates.

Cole, B. P. (1986). The black educator: An endangered species. *Journal of Negro Education, 55(3)*, 326–34.

Collins, P. H. (1991). *Black feminist thought: Knowledge, conscious, and the politics of empowerment: Perspectives on gender*, vol. 2. New York: Routledge.

Dandy, E. B. (1998). Increasing the number of minority teachers: Tapping the paraprofessional pool. *Education and Urban Society, 31(1)*, 89–103.

Dee, T. S. (2004). Teachers, race and student achievement in a randomized experiment. *Review of Economics and Statistics, 86(1)*, 195–210.

Dillard, C. B. (1994). Beyond supply and demand: Critical pedagogy, ethnicity, and empowerment in recruiting teachers of color. *Journal of Teacher Education, 45(1),* 9–17.

Easton-Brooks, D., Lewis, C., & Zhang, Y. (2010). Ethnic-matching: The influence of African American teachers on the reading scores of African American students. *National Journal of Urban Education & Practice. 3(1),* 230–43.

Fielder, D. J. (1996). Diversifying from within: the minority teacher scholarship program. *Phi Delta Kappan, 77(6),* 445–6.

Flores, B. B., Clark, E. R., Claeys, L., & Villarreal, A. (2007). Academy for teacher excellence: Recruiting, preparing, and retaining Latino teachers through learning communities. *Teacher Education Quarterly, 34(4),* 53–70.

Foster, M. (1997). *Black teachers on teaching.* New York: New Press.

Gay, G. (2000). *Culturally responsive teaching: Theory, research, & practice.* New York: Teachers College Press.

Gay, G., & Howard, T. (2000). Multicultural teacher education for the 21st century. *Teacher Educator, 36(1),* 1–16.

Genzuk, M., & Baca, R. (1998). The paraeducator-to-teacher pipeline. *Education and Urban Society, 31(1),* 73–88.

González, J. M. (1997). Recruiting and training minority teachers: Student views of the preservice program. *Equity & Excellence in Education, 30(1),* 56–64.

Gutierrez, J. (1992). Expanding the teacher pool. *School Community Journal, 2(2),* 23–30.

Gutierrez, J. M., & Murphy, J. A. (1996). Persistence and impediments in minority students becoming teachers. *School Community Journal, 6(1),* 113–25.

Haberman, M. (1999). Increasing the number of high-quality African American teachers in urban schools. *Journal of Instructional Psychology, 26(4),* 208–12.

Haberman, M. (2001). The creation of an urban normal school: What constitutes quality alternative certification? *Educational Studies, 32(3),* 278–88.

Hall Mark, D. L. (1998). Growing our own: A three-way partnership. *Urban Education, 32(5),* 591–615.

Holmes, B. D., & Couch, R. (1997). Seamless collaboration for student success: Effective strategies for retaining minority students. *Michigan Community College Journal, 3(2),* 43–51.

Hunter-Boykin, H. (1992). Responses to the African American teacher shortage: "We grow our own" through the Teacher Preparation Program at Coolidge High School. *Journal of Negro Education, 61(4),* 483–95.

Irizarry, J. G. (2007). "Home-growing" teachers of color: Lessons learned from a town-gown partnership. *Teacher Education Quarterly, 34(4),* 87–102.

Irvine, J. J. (1988). An analysis of the problem of the disappearing Black educator. *Elementary School Journal, 88(5),* 503–14.

Irvine, J. J. (2003). *Educating teachers for diversity: Seeing with a cultural eye.* New York: Teachers College Press.

Ladson-Billings, G. (1994). *The dreamkeepers: Successful teachers of African-American children.* San Francisco: Jossey-Bass.

Lau, K. F., Dandy, E. B., & Hoffman, L. (2007). The Pathways Program: A model for increasing the number of teachers of color. *Teacher Education Quarterly, 34(4),* 27–40.

Littleton, D. M. (1998). Preparing professionals as teachers for the urban classroom. *Action in Teacher Education, 19(4),* 149–58.

Love, F. E., & Greer, R. G. (1995). Recruiting minorities in to teaching. *Contemporary Education, 67(1),* 30–32.

McAllister, G., & Irvine, J. J. (2002). The role of empathy in teaching culturally diverse students: A qualitative study of teachers' beliefs. *Journal of Teacher Education, 3(5),* 433–43.

Meier, K. J., Stewart, J., & England, R. E. (1989). *Race, class, and education: The politics of second generation discrimination.* Madison: University of Wisconsin Press.

Milner, H. R. (2006). The promise of black teachers' success with black students. *Educational Foundations, 20(3–4)*, 89–104.

Milner, H. R., & Howard, T. C. (2004). Black teachers, black students, black communities and *Brown*: Perspectives and insights from experts. *Journal of Negro Education, 73(3)*, 285–97.

Nieto, S. (1999). *The light in their eyes: Creating multicultural learning communities.* New York: Teachers College Press.

Nieto, S. (2000). Placing equity front and center: Some thoughts on transforming teacher education for a new century. *Journal of Teacher Education, 51(3)*, 180–87.

Oliva, M., & Staudt, K. (2003). Pathways to teaching: Latino student choice and professional identity development in a teacher training magnet program. *Equity & Excellence in Education, 36*, 270–79.

Oliva, M., & Staudt, K. (2004). Latino professional identity development. *Kappa Delta Pi Record, 41(1)*, 38–41.

Padak, N. D., Stadulis, J. D., Barton, L. E., Meadows, F. B., & Padak, G. M. (1994). Mentoring with future urban teachers. *Urban Education, 29(3)*, 341–53.

Pang, V. O., & Gibson, R. (2001). Concepts of democracy and citizenship: Views of African American teachers. *Social Studies, 92(6)*, 260–66.

Ross, F. (2001). Helping immigrants become teachers. *Educational Leadership, 58(8)*, 68–71.

Sakash, K., & Chou, V. (2007). Increasing the supply of Latino bilingual teachers for Chicago Public Schools. *Teacher Education Quarterly, 34(4)*, 41–52.

Shade, B. J., Boe, B. L., Garner, O., & New, C. A. (1998). The road to certification: A different way. *Teaching and Change, 5(3–4)*, 261–75.

Shen, J. (1998). Alternative certification, minority teachers, and urban education. *Education and Urban Society, 31(1)*, 30–41.

Siddle-Walker, V. (2000). Valued segregated schools for African American children in the South, 1935–1969: A review of common themes and characteristics. *Review of Educational Research, 70(3)*, 253–85.

Sleeter, C. E. (2001). Preparing teachers for culturally diverse schools: Research and the overwhelming presence of whiteness. *Journal of Teacher Education, 52(2)*, 94–106.

Sleeter, C. E. (2008). Preparing white teachers for diverse students. In Cochran-Smith, M., Feiman-Nemser, S., & McIntyre, J. (Eds.), *Handbook of research in teacher education: Enduring issues in changing contexts*, 3rd ed. (pp. 559–82). New York: Routledge.

Solomon, R. P. (1997). Race, role modeling, and representation in teacher education and teaching. *Canadian Journal of Education, 22(4)*, 395–410.

Stevens, T., Agnello, M. F., Ramirez, J., Marbley, A., & Hammer, D. (2007). Project FUTURE: Opening the door to West Texas teachers. *Teacher Education Quarterly, 34(4)*, 103–20.

Torres-Karna, H., & Krustchinsky, R. (1998). The early entry program. *Teacher Education and practice, 14(1)*, 10–19.

U.S. Department of Education, Institute of Education Sciences, National Center for Education Statistics. (2009). *Percentage distribution of school teachers, by race/ethnicity, school type, and selected school characteristics: 2007–08.* Retrieved from nces.ed.gov/pubs2009/2009324/.../ sass0708_2009324_+12n_02.asp.

Veltri, B. T. (2008). Teaching or service? The site-based realities of Teach for America teachers in poor, urban schools. *Education and Urban Society, 40(5)*, 511–42.

Villegas, A. M., & Clewell, B. (1998). Increasing the number of teachers of color for urban schools: Lessons from the Pathway national evaluation. *Education and Urban Society, 31(1)*, 42–61.

Wang, J. (2001). The training of ethnic minority teachers: The NNU model. *Asia–Pacific Journal of Teacher Education and Development, 4(2)*, 73–88.

White, C. J., Bedonie, C., de Groat, J., Lockard, L., & Honani, S. (2007). A bridge for our children: Tribal/university partnerships to prepare indigenous teachers. *Teacher Education Quarterly, 34(4)*, 71–86.

Wong, P. L., Murai, H., Berta-Ávila, M., William White, L., Baker, S., Arellano, A., et al. (2007). The M/M Center: Meeting the demand for multicultural, multilingual teacher preparation. *Teacher Education Quarterly, 34(4),* 9–26.

Yopp, R. H., Yopp, H. K., & Taylor, H. P. (1992). Profiles and viewpoints of minority candidates in a teacher diversity project. *Teacher Education Quarterly, 19(3),* 29–48.

Zapata, J. T. (1988). Early identification and recruitment of Hispanic teacher candidates. *Journal of Teacher Education, 39(1),* 19–23.

Zeichner, K. M., & Conklin, H. G. (2005). Teacher education programs. In Cochran-Smith, M., & Zeichner, K. M. (Eds.), *Studying teacher education* (pp. 645–736). Mahwah, NJ: Erlbaum.

Zumwalt, K., & Craig, E. (2005). Teachers' characteristics: Research on the demographic profile in studying teacher education. In Smith, M. C., & Zeichner, K. M. (Eds.), *The report of the AERA panel on research and teacher education* (pp. 111–56). Mahwah, NJ: Lawrence Erlbaum Associates.

4

The Meaning of Culture in Learning to Teach

The Power of Socialization and Identity Formation

Etta R. Hollins

Teaching and learning are cultural constructs influenced by social norms, values, and practices that are evident in the curriculum and everyday social discourse in formal education from preschool through graduate school. These everyday practices in schools serve many purposes, including socialization and identity formation for the young. School practices help the young find their place in society—to come to understand their social identity and that of "others." During this socialization process some students are prepared for positions of power and privilege and others for positions of subordination.

The culturally constructed teaching and learning practices in schools provide greater access to academic learning for the privileged than for those from disenfranchised cultural and ethnic groups. This is evident in the academic performance of students in the nation's elementary and secondary schools, especially when comparing the performance of those attending urban schools with the national averages. For example, Lutkus, Grigg, and Donahue (2007) in the National Assessment of Educational Progress (NAEP) for urban school districts reported that at the fourth grade, in reading 32 percent of students across the nation performed at proficient as compared to 22 percent of urban students. The performance of fourth-grade students nationally is unacceptable, but it is even more ominous for urban students. The majority of students in urban schools tend to be from ethnic minority groups and include a higher percentage of low-income students. Much of what students learn in school is influenced by the quality of the preparation their teachers received in their preservice teacher preparation programs (Darling-Hammond, 2000).

The purpose of this discussion is to examine learning to teach as a complex sociocultural process that builds upon a socialization process that begins in the home culture and extends to formal education in school, and for the majority of those entering teacher preparation programs, is grounded in an ideology of power and privilege (Helms, 1990). This is particularly important and challenging given the fact that those entering the profession are mainly white, middle class, female, and grew up in a suburban community or small town where there was little contact with those different from themselves (Zumwalt & Craig, 2005). Most of these individuals have been socialized into a culture of privilege in a pluralistic society that is stratified by race and social class. Additionally, the majority of teacher educators have been socialized in much the same way as the candidates in their teacher preparation programs. Yet, teacher educators are charged with the responsibility of preparing preservice teachers for schools and classrooms that serve students from diverse cultural and experiential backgrounds and for promoting the basic societal values of equity and social justice. The focus of this discussion is on understanding the identity formation process for the majority of those entering teacher preparation programs, the relationship between identity formation and the appropriation of knowledge for practice, and the implications for constructing *knowledge in practice* for teaching students from diverse and underserved groups. For the purposes of this discussion, identity formation is used as a proxy for culture.

The basic premise of this discussion is that culture is central to social interaction, communication, and cognition (Swidler, 1986). It is the lens through which groups and individuals interpret, understand, and respond to the social, physical, and spiritual worlds. It is within the context of culture and socialization that social identity is formed, and values, perceptions, habits of mind, and propensities for learning develop. Cultural beliefs and values emerge as the *ideology* that frames policies and institutions that govern and serve society. In this context, ideology is defined as a "set of beliefs (either factual or evaluative), [that comprise] . . . a system of comparatively stable basic assumptions that inform human perceptions of and attitudes toward physical or social reality" (Shkedi & Nisan, 2006, p. 690). Many schools, in their present form, are social institutions grounded in the prevailing social ideology of power and privilege and house the profession into which teachers are socialized.

THE CONTEXT AND PROCESS OF IDENTITY FORMATION

Social identity formation is a developmental process that enables one to position self in the world in relationship to others—to know who one is. Social identity formation is based on a myriad of factors. Smedley (1998) pointed out that "until the rise of market capitalism, wage labor, the Protestant Ethic, private property, and possessive individualism, kinship connections also operated as major indices that gave all peoples a sense of who they were" (p. 691). Other indices of social identity in this historical period included place of birth, male or female line of ancestry, language spoken, occupation, and lifestyle or social position. Occupations often determined how people were viewed and how their contributions were valued by the society. During this time, phenotype variations among people did not influence social identity formation.

Phenotype, or racial classification based on specific physical features, became the focus of human difference in the American colonies and spread to Western Europe during the eighteenth century. Two prevalent examples of ways racial classification affected social identity formation in the American colonies include subordinating, isolating, and separating Africans who were enslaved and Indians who had been colonized from European settlers. Justification for the inhumane treatment of African slaves and disenfranchised Indians was based on a theory of racial inferiority and savagism. This historical and social construction of race became an important aspect of social stratification and social identity formation in the United States.

Adams (1996) provides an example of the role of schools and classroom teachers in the assimilation of Indian children into the culture of the European immigrants during the early twentieth century. The process entailed creating boarding schools to isolate Indian children from traditional social networks for identity formation and enculturation; elimination of traditional cultural practices including language, clothing, and other aspects of physical appearance; and indoctrination with European values of Protestantism, individualism, and the work ethic to replace Indian values of spiritualism, communalism, and respect for nature and the land. Classroom practices used to carry out this process included Bible reading, the recitation of scriptures from the Bible, classroom prayers, and hymn singing. Additionally, the boys were taught the skills of self-sufficient farming and the girls were taught the domestic skills of housekeeping. Through this process Indian children were to take on a new identity crafted by settlers that entailed new social networks formed among those with shared experiences, new political alignments, and a new ideological frame for explaining their existence and relationships in the world. Aspects of this example are quite similar to contemporary practices in federally controlled schools for Native Alaskan and Navajo children where an assimilationist agenda included elimination of the home language and cultural heritage (Lipka & McCarty, 1994).

The process of identity formation in the example Adams (1996) provided is complex. Identity formation has interrelated social, political, and intellectual dimensions that coalesce to support a view of self in relationship to others and a commitment and loyalty to those perceived as being like one's self. Identity formation involves socialization as a member and participant in a particular ethnic, racial, or cultural group. Individuals learn the language, behavior, beliefs, and practices of the group and form social networks within the group. The political dimension of identity formation introduces group boundaries and identifies outsiders. This dimension encourages participation in the management and maintenance of the social position of the group. The intellectual dimension of identity formation involves the development of an ideology that explains social and political actions and relationships. The young are socialized into the group through interaction with a network of individuals and institutions that reinforce the different dimensions of their identity and that foster a particular worldview and ideology. This discussion will focus on schooling as a primary vehicle for identity formation.

K–12 School Practices and Social Identity Formation

The example of the assimilation of Indian children into the culture of their oppressors provides evidence of the role of school as a primary institution in identity formation and the socialization of the young into group membership. Schools are places that validate, reinforce, and socialize children into many of the values of the larger society using the basic principle in the example with the Indian children, but using different practices and tools. In public schools today, children are not deliberately isolated from family and social networks; however, the cultural context of school imposes rules and procedures designed to push students to conform to an idea of who they "should" and "should not" be. Schools both repress the identification practices of some students while valorizing those of others. For example, dress codes are often enforced that eliminate certain ethnic attire. The curriculum influences identity formation by presenting an essentially Eurocentric perspective that emphasizes many of the same values as found in the Indian boarding schools; and classroom practices such as power relationships and the relationships among students reflect values of the majority culture. The social stratification based on race and social class is evident in schools and classrooms in the relationships between teachers and students and among students.

The elementary and secondary school curriculum. Fundamentally, the school curricula are about the social construction of knowledge and the content and values that comprise the socialization of the young as members of the larger society. The examples in this discussion will provide evidence that the curriculum and school practices serve an essential function in identity formation and the maintenance and perpetuation of the prevailing social ideology that supports social policies and in-stitutional practices. At times, this process has been very contentious.

For example, during the 1990s there was a great deal of controversy over the social studies curriculum and social studies textbooks. Critics like Diane Ravitch (1990, 1991/1992) argued for teaching the common culture and for avoiding *particularism* with a focus on developing ethnic and racial pride among students. In contrast, Thomas Sobol, New York Commissioner of Education, argued for a mul-ticultural approach to the curriculum. After a very contentious struggle over social studies textbooks in New York, Sobol (1993), in a recommendation to the New York Regents, stated:

> What I propose is a curriculum which will tell more of the truth about more of our history to all of our children. It is a curriculum based on fact, faithful to historical pro-portion, and grounded in the democratic and moral values of our common American culture. It is a curriculum which informs young people fully of the ideals and struggles that have shaped our nation, which gives young people a reason for believing that they have a stake in its success, and which prepares young people to participate effectively in an increasingly diverse society and an increasingly shrinking world. (p. 265)

Like Sobol, Joyce King called for a more authentic representation of the history of the diverse populations in the United States. King (1992) focused attention on the ideological representation and depiction of the Middle Passage and slavery in textbooks. King argued for a more authentic representation of historical events based on a deeper understanding of the cultural signs and symbols of the people presented in history textbooks. King's discussion of the representation of slavery in textbooks is consistent with Banks's (1996, 2002) argument for a more careful ex-amination of knowledge construction and the purposes and interests served in the school curriculum. Banks traced the academic development of the concept of racism and introduced the concept of transformative knowledge—primarily the work of oppressed groups within the society—as a way to advance the democratic principles of equity and social justice.

Teachers are responsible for implementing the curriculum mandated by state departments of education and local school districts. This provides opportunities for reinterpretation of mandates and curriculum content. Cornbleth (1998) reported a study of teaching practices in the fifth, seventh, eighth, and twelfth grades, where it was found that students were provided multiple, partial, and often conflicting images of the history of the United States. However, among the consistent themes that emerged in the study were that the United States was viewed as imperfect but still the best country in the world; social injustices were viewed as historical and not contemporary; and sameness and homogeneity were emphasized. In discussing observations in three of the classrooms in her study, Cornbleth pointed out:

> All three of these teachers seemed to be encouraging, and students seemed for the most part accepting, identification with mainstream white America as if there were few if any significant social divisions. Teachers may have been attempting to maintain classroom peace by suggesting agreement across racial-ethnic and other differences or trying to position their students and themselves as progressive "good guys." (p. 634)

These practices can be viewed as a more subtle approach to the assimilation of minority students into mainstream values and the maintenance of white privilege than that employed with Indian children in boarding schools at the beginning of the twentieth century. However, Cornbleth's findings support King's (1992) caution:

> What is at stake is not just that all students are expected to internalize the Euro-immigrant ideological perspective and identity insisted upon in the approved textbooks. Nor is it just that questioning this assumption has generated alarm and countercharges of "disuniting" racial separatism. More, this ideological perspective, and school texts that endorse and promote it, obviate the need for any social analysis of the persistent racial inequality that already disunites America. Such textbooks cannot enable black students or others to understand the root causes of the historical and contemporary injustices people continue to endure, nor can they prepare them to participate in the continuing struggle for social transformation." (p. 328)

Additionally, curriculum content is presented within the social context of a classroom with implications for relationships among students and between teachers and students. The curriculum content and social arrangements in the classroom legitimate particular ideological perspectives, societal values, and the relative position of groups in the society. Classroom practices together with the social context in the classroom affirm or disconfirm the social identity students bring to school.

Social context in elementary and secondary school classrooms. The social context in elementary and secondary school classrooms is an important aspect of social identity formation for children and youth. Here, students learn their social position in relationship to that of their peers and the extent to which they are valued by their teachers. This is a process of social enculturation that can last as long as fifteen years and begins as early as three years of age for many children. For mainstream white children, school is in many ways a continuation of learning initiated at home. A social identity associated with power and privilege is already underway for many mainstream white children, and many children of color have begun to internalize this perspective as well as their own subordinate position. By the time many children enter school they have developed a complex understanding of relationships among and between individuals and groups in the society. For example, Van Ausdale and Feagin (2001) reported in a year-long study at a preschool where children as young as three years old understood the status of white people in relationship to other people in the society, and they understood what should and what should not be shared with adults. These researchers discussed the extent to which the preschool children in their study understood, had internalized, and practiced aspects of racism in their discourse and interaction with other children. These authors explained:

> In our analysis of the preschool data, we have delineated a number of important dimensions of racial and ethnic relationships—often, relations of oppression. These dimensions include (1) concepts and thinking, (2) spoken discourse, (3) everyday practices and performances that restrict or privilege, and (4) identities and psychological (and physical) embodiment. We see these various aspects of what might be called the "racializing process" in the accounts of our children. (pp. 35–36)

Race, ethnicity, and social class are complex issues that are pervasive in the larger society of the United States. Young children learn the discourse of racism early and incorporate the beliefs, behaviors, and practices into their daily lives (Van Ausdale & Feagin, 2001).

The socialization process described by Van Ausdale and Feagin (2001) continues into elementary school. Lewis (2003) reported a study conducted at three elementary schools where she documented the interplay of race, status, and power among groups of students and the reluctance of teachers and administrators to discuss issues associated with race or to acknowledge and intervene to protect children victimized by their peers. Lewis described the ways in which the curriculum privileged white, middle-class students and disadvantaged others. She described the systematic categorization of individuals or groups as white or not white based on "language, accent, cultural performances, and other signals of social location. . . . These various markers of otherness operate interactively to move people further or closer on the continuum of difference" (p. 132).

This systematic categorization was documented by Katz (1999) in a study of the relationships and perceptions of immigrant Latino middle-school students and their teachers. Katz found that while the Latino students felt that their teachers discriminated against them as a single group regardless of their academic performance by giving preferential treatment to Asian students, teachers stated that they treated the students as individuals. The teachers acknowledged that they assessed students differently, provided support differentially based on their behavior in the classroom, perceived peer pressure as a negative factor for Latino students, and tried to "separate out higher achieving students from the group" (p. 830). That is, teachers tried to intentionally reconstruct the social identity for Latino students—to make them more like their ideal white mainstream students. This seems to have been an unspoken condition for teachers to care about Latino students' academic success. However, such social isolation might not be the most comfortable situation for the Latino students. Katz (1999) pointed out:

> Two essential elements of a productive teacher-student relationship are high expectations mixed with caring. High expectations without caring can result in setting goals that are impossible for the student to reach without adult support and assistance. On the other hand, caring without high expectations can turn dangerously into paternalism in which teachers feel sorry for "underprivileged" youth but never challenge them academically. High expectations and caring in tandem, however, can make a powerful difference in students' lives. (p. 814)

In this situation teachers seemed to hold low expectations and to distance themselves from students who presented themselves as culturally Latino—who spoke Spanish and socialized with other Latinos (Katz, 1999).

Proweller (1999) investigated racial identity formation among white girls at Best Academy, an elite private high school. This researcher found that when

> asked to locate themselves racially, white youth construct their analyses through a language of othering, decidedly positioning themselves in relation to an "other." In order to articulate whiteness as a lived part of their everyday experience, they must find a language that inscribes *who they are* racially in terms of *who they are not*. ([emphasis in original] p. 781)

This approach to positioning self within a social context had the effect of maintaining a white social identity, establishing boundaries and defining outsiders. However, within the context of the school, students were socialized into what Proweller referred to as "liberal discourses that set the terms for negotiating cultural difference" (p. 786). This amounted to a containment of difference such that most students across ethnic and racial lines internalized the discourse of liberal ideology projected through a rhetoric of color blindness and sameness that allowed white privilege to go virtually unchallenged.

The studies reviewed on K–12 schools provide evidence of the socialization of students into the ideology of power and privilege through the school curriculum (Adams, 1996; Cornbleth, 1998; King, 1992; Lewis, 2003), the social dynamics in the classroom (Katz, 1999; Lewis, 2003; Van Ausdale & Feagin, 2001), and in relationships among students and between students and teachers (Katz, 1999; Lewis, 2003; Van Ausdale & Feagin, 2001). This socialization process supports white children in developing a social identity associated with power and privilege. Students of color are socialized to accept the position of whites as superior and to accept an identity of subordination for themselves.

University Practices and Social Identity

At the university level social identity is maintained in much the same way as in elementary and secondary schools. However, in addition to providing knowledge and training for students, universities are places for legitimizing and producing knowledge. Banks (2002) pointed out that knowledge reflects the social context and the social and political interests of its creators. Much of the knowledge created within a society reinforces the prevailing ideologies and social arrangements. This is the case with much of the knowledge that constitutes the subject matter in many university courses. For example, Fishkin (1995) discussed how prior to and during the 1980s and 1990s university courses titled American Literature and The Modern Novel almost exclusively included elite white male authors and how the work of these authors promoted the prevailing ideology of intellectual exclusiveness. However, during the 1990s transformative scholars began to increasingly challenge the privilege of whiteness in American literature. One example is Toni Morrison's book *Playing in the Dark: Whiteness and the Literary Imagination*. Here, Morrison challenged the idea that white authors created powerful literary works in a culturally diverse society without the influence of people of color as well as the idea that people of color have not created powerful literary works. Yet, the absence of literary works by people of color in American literature courses taught in universities reinforced beliefs about the superiority of white authors.

The privileged status of white authors in American literature courses reinforced the privileged status of white students in university classrooms and supported behavior that disenfranchised students of color. For example, Diangelo (2006) conducted a study of the production of whiteness in a graduate-level course in a college classroom where more than half of those enrolled were students of color and the majority were Asian international students. At this particular class meeting, the topic focused on conducting research studies, and the guest speaker was a white, female anthropologist. A group dynamic was observed that marginalized students of color and privileged the white students. More important, Diangelo observed:

> Domination in the classroom is more than just a matter of who speaks and how often; those who speak have the power to direct the course of the discussion. The white students essentially controlled the class and tailored the learning that took place. This learning met their needs as they directed the material to their own research questions and interests. Furthermore, they were affirmed as learners on multiple levels; their participation style was affirmed, their research interests were affirmed, their questions and comments were affirmed, *and ultimately, their lack of any attempt to include the perspectives of the international students of color was affirmed* ([emphasis in original], pp. 1991–93).

This is a powerful example of the ways in which white power and privilege are legitimized, the associated behaviors and practices reinforced, and the low status of people of color is affirmed.

The discussion to this point has focused on the process and context for social identity formation from early childhood to university-based graduate courses. It has been pointed out that the curriculum content and the social arrangements in classrooms at each level of schooling support and reinforce group status, power, and privilege (Diangelo, 2006; Lewis, 2003; Proweller, 1999; Van Ausdale & Feagin, 2001); and that the identity formation process inculcates in the young a particular ideological perspective that encourages group adherence and the maintenance of status, power, and privilege (Diangelo, 2006; Proweller, 1999; Van Ausdale & Feagin, 2001). The next part of the discussion is focused on the impact of this process on teacher candidates' appropriation of *knowledge for practice*.

SOCIAL IDENTITY FORMATION AND
THE APPROPRIATION OF *KNOWLEDGE FOR PRACTICE*

This discussion will examine the impact of social identity formation and life experiences on the appropriation of knowledge for professional practice through researched examples of approaches employed in courses aimed at preparing candidates to teach students from diverse cultural and experiential backgrounds. This discussion will take into consideration pedagogical content knowledge and socialization into the profession.

Pedagogical Content Knowledge in Preservice Teacher Preparation

Candidates enter preservice teacher preparation with a major or minor in a particular discipline or subject matter that is a regular part of the K–12 school curriculum. In preservice teacher preparation programs this subject matter knowledge is reorganized conceptually to support teaching and learning and combined with appropriate instructional strategies to form pedagogical content knowledge. The way candidates understand subject matter and the appropriateness of pedagogy when learning to teach is influenced by their early education and socialization and influences their readiness for different conceptualizations and perspectives.

In a discussion of concept development in learning to teach, Smagorinsky, Cook, and Johnson (2003) draw on Vygotsky's notion of two types of concepts, scientific and spontaneous. Spontaneous concepts are "generalizations learned informally through practical activity and everyday social interaction . . . [that] . . . tend to be situated in the context in which they are learned and are thus less amenable to abstraction to new situations" (p. 1403). In contrast, a scientific concept is learned "through formal, systematic instruction . . . [which] enables one to reapply it to a new situation" (p. 1403). However, scientific concept development is mediated by spontaneously developed concepts and the social context in which learning takes place, and it can serve to constrain or enhance scientific concept development. The earlier discussion of elementary, secondary, and university-based curriculum content and the social context for learning provided evidence of the consistency between formal and informal concept development related to identity formation and the supporting ideology for mainstream white students and ways in which this constrained understanding the experiences of social and cultural outsiders. These constraints in understanding extend beyond social and cultural experiences to include subject matter. These constraints to conceptual understanding are evident in views of the world as an extension of self and views of knowledge as neutral and universal.

The world as extension of self in learning to teach. The research we have examined in this chapter suggests that embedded in the social ideology that supports identity formation for white mainstream students is a sense that their way of being in the world is normative and that other ways of being and doing are less than desirable. A particular social dynamic in teacher preparation enables and maintains this perspective and influences ways of making sense of other peoples' experiences as well as concepts in the academic disciplines.

Studies of approaches to race and racism in teacher preparation reveal aspects of the dynamic that enables and maintains this perspective of the world as an extension of self. Additionally, related research provides evidence that the social context in university classrooms can reinforce and maintain white privilege and superiority. For example, Haviland (2008) investigated how white teachers approached issues of race and racism in two white-dominated educational settings, an eighth-grade classroom and a university student-teaching seminar. Two characteristics of whiteness were identified along with their particular maintenance strategies. First, whiteness was characterized as "powerful yet power-evasive" (p. 44), with maintenance strategies that included avoiding words, false starts in conversations about race and racism, safe self-critique that maintained the appearance of the "good" white person, asserting ignorance or uncertainty even in the presence of compelling evidence, letting others off the hook for having committed offenses involving race or social class, citing authority, silence, and changing the topic. Second, "whiteness employs numerous techniques to maintain its power" (p. 47) and the cohesiveness of group members including affirming sameness, joking, agreeing with and supporting each other, praising and encouraging, caring about each other, socializing and sharing personal information, and focusing on barriers to multicultural education.

Haviland (2008) acknowledged that while she was able to observe this process, her own socialization into whiteness inhibited her from redirecting or disrupting this process during class discussions. This study provides evidence that teacher educators who share similar backgrounds as the candidates may experience personal feelings of conflict when attempting to redirect conversations or thought processes that enable and maintain white power and privilege. The findings from this study indicate the power of early life experiences and socialization, the extent to which candidates from privileged backgrounds in teacher education can resist alternative explanations for the role of individual effort and values in their own success, as well as alternative explanations for the lack of success of those with different life and educational experiences.

The resistance to ideas that challenge views of the world as an extension of self and of the legitimacy of different perspectives are manifest in specific behaviors. For example, Ladson-Billings (1996) discussed her experience as an African American professor at a predominantly white, private, elite university teaching a multicultural education course. She observed how white students used silence as a way to retreat and "defy and deny the legitimacy of the teacher and/or the knowledge" (p. 82). Ladson-Billings pointed out that silence can have many different meanings, including feelings of discomfort, oppression, and embarrassment. She suggested that faculty need to probe and explore student silence around issues of diversity to better understand the sense that students make of their own lives and the lives of other people.

Consistent with Ladson-Billings' suggestion, Mueller and O'Connor (2007) investigated how candidates in a teacher preparation program processed their own autobiographies when confronted with data each collected from personal interviews with individuals different from themselves. The participants (fourteen white and one black) were enrolled in a course that focused on understanding how systemic inequities and sociocultural contexts influenced the lives and educational trajectories for themselves and those different from themselves. The researchers found:

> By the end of the semester most of the students had developed a set of narratives that maintained the logic of their original assumptions about why they succeeded in school. In the process they silenced and muted interview data that contradicted their assumptions. They contradicted their own data analysis in their efforts to conclude that their life story, and that of the other, was more alike than different. In the process of erasing the differences that existed between them and their interviewees, they nullified how they benefitted as members of structurally privileged groups. (p. 852)

These candidates seemed to have developed a habit of mind that permitted them to reinterpret other people's experiences to support their own views and that confirmed their identity and perceived position in the society in relationship to others.

Another important aspect of the study by Mueller & O'Connor (2007) was the identification of "a set of beliefs that were common across students, irrespective of their stated political or ideological orientations" (p. 853). There were differences among the students in the liberal or conservative sentiments they expressed. The more liberal student was more likely to acknowledge that race matters in the society. However, these researchers found that:

> These ideological dispositions, though, were inconsequential in the face of what seemed to be an unwavering ethnocentrism. For the most part, students seemed to unreflexively maintain the "rightness" or "goodness" of their own ways of being and ways of understanding the world. Rather than altering their world views or shifting in their understandings of culture, they twisted information that was incongruent with their own ethnocentric beliefs to fit their already established frames of reference. (p. 853)

In this example, an assignment intended to help candidates learn about those with cultural and experiential backgrounds different from their own was mediated through the ideology of power and privilege into which candidates had been socialized. Instead, candidates used the assignment to controvert differences as a way to reinforce their belief in the ideology of power and privilege and to protect their identity.

In some instances white candidates called upon myths and stereotypes to protect their identity and to preserve the ideology of power and privilege. McIntyre (1997) reported a study of the process of constructing an image of a white teacher in a student teaching seminar with thirteen middle- and upper-middle-class female undergraduate students at a private university in the northeastern United States. At the beginning of the seminar the participants were concerned about their ability to be effective teachers for students of color and about how their students would perceive them as teachers. These candidates were concerned that they had not experienced inner-city life and did not understand the culture and experiences of the students they would teach. However, they wanted their students to accept them as teachers (colorless) who were there to help them rather than as white teachers. McIntyre found that there were multiple ways that the candidates protected their white identity and preserved the ideology of power and privilege while teaching students of color. For example, the "inability to situate racism and whiteness within multicultural education distanced the participants from thinking that we, as whites, are implicated in the kind of educational system that continues to privilege white students" (p. 662). These candidates distanced themselves from dominant group oppression, disassociated themselves from a minority status, and in the process they "reify the (re)production of myths and stereotypes while simultaneously sustaining the image of the 'good white knight teachers' rescuing students from bad lives and from bad white classroom teachers who are part of 'the problem'" (p. 665). These candidates characterized themselves as "caring and benevolent teachers" (p. 667) while they stereotyped their students as coming from dysfunctional families and communities and lacking ability and motivation. These ideas were often reinforced by the discourse and actions of their cooperating teachers.

In contrast, Gomez, Black, and Allen (2007) described how Alison, a white, female, undergraduate teacher candidate engaged in a four-semester field experience, where she moved through a progression of experiences that supported the development of new insights and a transformation of the social ideology she brought to the program. Transition points in Alison's development included moving from a view of the surface features of cultural difference to understanding a deeper meaning of culture; from viewing science as neutral to viewing science as socially constructed knowledge; from awareness of the need for culturally relevant curriculum to the ability to make linkages between students' interests and experiences and curriculum content; coming to understand how race and ethnicity provide people with a sense of community and how identity can create boundaries that exclude other people; and moving from the belief that race is a needed and natural construct to the realization that race is a social construct. Toward the end of her program the researchers found that "Alison articulated how the social languages of her teacher education program collided with and provided her with new ways to think about the social languages and ideology that she brought to teaching from her childhood, from the books she read and movies she watched, and from her general socialization as a White U.S. resident" (p. 2128).

The studies described in this section provide evidence that the view of the world as an extension of self may be reinforced through course content and the social dynamic among white students and between white students and students of color in university classrooms. Many white students have developed a variety of strategies for maintaining their identity with power and privilege when confronted with disconfirming information, including reinterpreting other people's experiences to fit their own ideological perspective (Mueller & O'Connor, 2007), the use of silence against professors who present information that conflicts with their own identity with power and privilege (Ladson-Billings, 1996), and distancing themselves from racism and oppression while simultaneously calling upon myths and stereotypes to support their ideological orientation (Gomez et al., 2007). These strategies allow many white students to maintain their own sense of identity as normative and the world as an extension of self.

Teacher educators socialized into the power and privilege ideology may have difficulty disrupting this perspective for candidates in the teacher preparation program (Haviland, 2008). This is particularly important given that the study reported by Gomez and colleagues (2007) suggests that the design of the teacher preparation program is important in determining what candidates learn about themselves and about teaching those different from themselves.

Knowledge as neutral and universal in framing curriculum content. In their elementary and secondary schools, candidates have learned to view knowledge as neutral and universal when in reality this is not the case. This perspective is directly linked to views of the world as an extension of self where one's own way of existing in the world is normative. This means that other ways of existing in the world are incorrect or inappropriate. This establishes the dualistic paradigm characterized by notions of good versus bad and right versus wrong found in perspectives on social practices and academic knowledge. In the study reported by Gomez and colleagues (2007), Alison's thinking was transformed from viewing science as neutral to viewing science as socially constructed knowledge and from viewing race as a needed and natural construct to the realization that race is a social construct. These are difficult transitions that do not occur in all teacher preparation programs for the majority of candidates. This is due in part to the ubiquitous ideology of power and privilege that undergirds the design of many courses. For example, in a process of deep introspection and self-criticism, Cochran-Smith (2000) pointed out:

> Reading between the lines of my own courses and of the larger teacher education curriculum revealed a white European American construction of self-identity and "other." "We" I came to realize, often referred not to "we who are committed to teaching elementary school differently and improving the life chances of all children," but to "we White people (especially we White women) who are trying to learn how to teach people who are different from us." (p. 181)

Learning to teach people different from ourselves requires moving beyond a view of the world as an extension of self to an openness to diverse perspectives and to views of knowledge as socially constructed and evolving. This is especially important given that teachers need to understand subject matter beyond what is required in other occupations and professions (Shulman, 1987). For example, Ball, Thames, and Phelps (2008) identified a distinctive "specialized content knowledge" needed by teachers, but not by others, who use mathematical knowledge (p. 401). This specialized content knowledge enables teachers to identify common student conceptions and misconceptions, quickly identify the source of errors in mathematical procedures and problem solving, and to identify other patterns in student thinking and problems of practice in teaching mathematics. This requires an openness regarding learners, learning, and pedagogical practices that many candidates in teacher education have not acquired.

It is difficult to overcome years of a socialization process that has been central to identity formation. This socialization process inculcates in individuals the beliefs and perspectives through which new knowledge and experiences are filtered and appropriated. This means that socialization and identity formation are powerful influences on concept development. For example, Southerland and Gess-Newsome (1998), in a study of a group of candidates consisting of twenty-two white and one ethnic minority, found that candidates held a positivistic view of knowledge and learners. This included "valuing one form of reasoning; understanding knowledge to be singular in voice; and deferring to authorities as ultimate sources of knowledge" (p. 139). Consistent with the positivistic view, candidates perceived knowledge to be universally accepted and unchanging, cognitive abilities to be fixed, and the role of teachers as that of guiding learners toward universally accepted truth. The positivistic perspectives these candidates displayed are consistent with earlier discussions of white mainstream perspectives that are incorporated into social identity formation and that devalue the knowledge students from diverse cultural and experiential backgrounds bring to the classroom.

Further, Southerland and Gess-Newsome pointed out that "the preservice teachers recognized the learners in their classrooms in terms of norms—deviations from the norm were understood to be inherently limiting. The goal to help students fit within a set of norms shaped the preservice teachers' reactions to inclusive science teaching" (pp. 142–43). Teaching to the norms did not include incorporating their students' prior knowledge. Teacher candidates framed meaningful achievement of their students in a particular way, and students from diverse backgrounds were less likely to display the behaviors that mainstream teacher candidates viewed as "smart" or "ready for school." Thus, when assessing their students' learning, the participants in this study resorted to measures of effort and interest rather than what students learned or understood.

The powerful influence of candidates' beliefs on setting teaching goals and identifying appropriate practices during student teaching was investigated in a study conducted by Kang (2008). In this study candidates' initial belief profiles were compared to subsequent data collected during student teaching. These profiles had two main dimensions: *ontological* (knowledge as representation of reality, science as a fixed body of knowledge, and learning as receiving knowledge) and *relational* (knowledge as multiple interpretations of reality, science as emerging knowledge, and "learning as answering one's own questions") (p. 484). Kang found that 48 percent of the candidates "kept their initial personal epistemological beliefs and teaching goals, and enacted their beliefs in teaching. These preservice teachers' learning outcome throughout the course, therefore, might have been developing ways of enacting their initial personal epistemologies and teaching goals" (p. 493). The data further revealed that "the [preservice] teachers negotiated their teaching practices with teaching conditions after filtering new approaches through their beliefs" (p. 496). This suggests that the beliefs candidates held prior to entering the teacher preparation program had more influence on their teaching goals and practices than did course work in the program and knowledge about their students in the classroom.

Consistent with Kang's (2008) findings, Rodriguez (1999) reported on two types of resistance candidates displayed in learning to teach students from diverse cultural and experiential backgrounds, resistance to ideological change and resistance to pedagogical change. Resistance to ideological change refers to "resistance to changing one's beliefs and value system," including making content socially and culturally relevant, and teaching for conceptual understanding. Pedagogical change refers to "resistance to changing one's perception of what constitutes being an effective teacher" (p. 616), including resistance to social constructivist and pupil-centered teaching and learning. Rodriguez employed counterresistance strategies that included dialogic conversation, authentic activity, metacognition, reflexivity, and placing candidates in diverse school contexts. Rodriguez observed:

> The tone of the students' discourse demonstrates how frustrating and uncomfortable it is for them as members of the culture of power to confront the social and political complexity of teaching, something that many of them did not expect (or want) to cover in a secondary science methods class. Some students resisted exploring how their actions (or inactions) contributed to the present educational hegemony by naming "the problem" as out of their control or too depressing. On the other hand, some students found the discussion and articles to be "eye opening." (p. 606)

It is important to point out that conceptualizations of knowledge for teaching are deeply embedded in a broader social ideology as indicated in the general reaction of the public to the role of black English in teaching African American students in the Ann Arbor court case in 1979 and in the Oakland, California, Ebonics controversy in the 1990s. Ball and Ladner (1997) identified positivistic views of African American language held by teachers and the general public that were similar to those regarding teaching and learning science held by candidates in the study by Southerland and Gess-Newsome (1998). However, it was more apparent that teachers' attitudes toward and resistance to using pedagogical practices that incorporated African American discourse patterns and rhetorical styles to facilitate students' learning was grounded in a race-based ideology of power and privilege. Ball and Ladner pointed out:

> Speech behavior is central to a full understanding of how a community expresses its realities, and research on teacher efficacy suggests that effective teachers develop strong human bonds with their students, have high expectations, focus on the total child, and are able to use communication styles familiar to their students. (p. 481)

Teachers' resistance to engaging, building upon, and extending the habits of mind students bring to school that are deeply embedded in the ways of learning and communicating in their home culture hampers the effectiveness of classroom instruction and student learning.

The resistance to incorporating into classroom practices the ways of learning and communicating that students bring from their home culture is documented in studies reported by Southerland and Gess-Newsome (1998), Rodriguez (1999), and Kang (2008) that provide evidence of the connection between social identity formation and the appropriation of knowledge for practice. These researchers are concerned with ideological perspectives and pedagogical practices in the preparation of candidates from white, mainstream backgrounds for teaching students different from themselves. This discussion makes apparent the power of multiple levels of enculturation over time and brings to the forefront the issue of socialization into the teaching profession. Ball and Ladner (1997) provided evidence of the entrenchment of the prevailing ideology. However, Rodriguez provided evidence that a well-designed, well-thought-out, theoretically grounded approach to support candidates in constructing pedagogical content knowledge can provide powerful learning opportunities. The counterresistance strategies Rodriguez used were clearly social constructivist in nature and drew upon the relationship among members of the cohort to facilitate constructing knowledge for practice.

The Socialization Process in Preservice Teacher Preparation

The process of identity formation provides strong evidence for the power of socialization in learning, internalizing, and adhering to group norms, practices, and values. This process occurs over time and in different contexts that include the family, a social network of individuals who are members and participants in the group, all levels of formal education, and other agencies and institutions. Building on knowledge of the process of identity formation suggests that teacher preparation programs need to be more intentionally designed such that all courses and field experiences are aligned to support a single vision and values and that collaboration among preservice and in-service teachers needs to be carefully planned.

The Holmes Group (1986) pointed out specific weaknesses in teacher preparation programs that included the absence of a carefully planned and interrelated sequence of courses, coherent and comprehensive curriculum content, targeted recruitment, and poor management of matriculation through the program. The Holmes Group recommended that students progress systematically through the program in a cohort. The third Holmes Group Report, *Tomorrow's Schools of Education* (1995), further supported cohorts as the desired structure for matriculation through a teacher preparation program. The cohort structure was viewed as the beginning of a teacher learning community that provided support for socialization into the profession and for career-long professional development.

Preservice Cohorts. Studies of the impact of cohorts reveal both strengths and weaknesses in the implementation. For example, Bullough, Clark, Wentworth, and Hansen (2001) found that on the one hand cohorts were "a support system and . . . a tool for building powerful and positive [shared experiences]" (p. 107); but on the other hand, the cohort provided less support for the development of shared personal and professional commitments focused on nurturing the development of children and investing in other teacher's professional development—the sort of values inherent in long-term growth as a classroom teacher. Additionally, candidates formed subgroups with subject matter specializations. Earlier findings by Radencich, Thompson, Anderson, Oropallo, Fleege, Harrison, and Hanley (1998) revealed even more serious weaknesses in the use of cohorts, including the formation of cliques, negative and sometimes vicious treatment of those perceived as outsiders (whether peers or faculty), pressure to conform to group norms, positive or negative impact on academic performance, the rigor of a course dependent on the orientation and leadership of the group, and inconsistent approaches used by cohort supervisors. Some participants benefitted from the cohort arrangement, while others were uncomfortable with it. Generally, Radencich and colleagues felt the cohort arrangement fell short of the primary goal of developing a social conscience that is "behavior guided by a sense of professionalism, a sense of morality and empathy for the needs of others" (p. 110). While these researchers supported the concept of cohorts, they concluded that much work needs to be done to better guide the process.

Ohana (2004) reported a study that compared students in two methods courses, one assigned to a cohort and the other to the regular program (RP). An important finding in this study was that:

> when students in the RP course saw a discrepancy between what they learned in methods and what they witnessed in their field experiences, they often used the course material as the authority or lens through which they characterized practice. The cohort students did not. They more often used each other as the authority in such matters. They were just as free in their criticism of classroom practice as the RP students, but, instead of consulting theory for clarification or interpretation, they went to their fellow students. (p. 249)

The findings from the three studies of cohorts presented here are representative of those from other studies (Brownell, Yeager, Sindelar, VanHover, & Riley, 2004; Mandzuk, Hasinoff, & Seifert, 2005; Sapon-Shevin & Chandler-Olcott, 2001). When taken together the findings from these studies present the strengths and weaknesses of cohort structures. The evidence from these studies indicates that cohorts provide more emotional than academic or intellectual support for candidates, and within cohorts candidates develop norms that influence the behavior and attitudes of members toward teaching, learning, and social relationships (Bullough et al., 2001). More important, the findings from these studies indicate that when allowed to develop naturally the socialization process in cohorts has aspects in common with that in identity formation. The identity formation process is characterized by adherence to group-established norms, values, and practices; group boundaries are clearly delineated, outsiders are clearly identified, and ways of interacting with outsiders are established and monitored (Radencich et al., 1998); and authority is intentionally maintained within the group (Ohana, 2004). Where cohorts engage in this process, there is evidence of resistance to learning to teach students from diverse backgrounds and rejection of faculty and peers viewed as outsiders (Radencich et al., 1998). Under these conditions, cohorts can maintain and reinforce the perspectives on teaching students from diverse cultural and experiential backgrounds reported by Southerland and Gess-Newsome (1998) and Rodriguez (1999). When assigned to low-performing urban schools as teachers, there is the risk that these candidates can easily become contributors and participants in the well-recognized *culture of practice* that maintains the low quality of teaching and student learning outcomes in these schools (Hollins, 2006).

Teacher Professional Communities. Teacher professional communities are places where novice teachers are socialized into the ideologies and practices common at a particular school site and that influence beliefs and practices throughout their careers. The ideology in a particular professional community is influenced by the prevailing ideology in the larger society, the social identity and value perspectives of the participants—especially those who provide formal and informal leadership—and the perceived social status of the students at the school site. This discussion examines the role of professional communities in maintaining the ideology of power and privilege and the quality of teaching for students from diverse cultural and experiential backgrounds.

In an investigation of a teacher community in a large urban high school, Abbate-Vaughn (2004) identified three distinct teacher ideologies. One group of teachers (the Quiet group) valued order, student docility, and the ability to follow rules over teaching and learning. For the Quiet group, the textbook defined knowledge worth teaching. These teachers valued the structure and repetition provided by textbooks and the accompanying workbooks. A second group (the Academic group) focused on academic goals with the aim of preparing students for pursuing higher education. Teachers in this group, like those in the Quiet group, subscribed to an "objective" source of knowledge that allowed for simplification and mastery. These teachers valued and privileged the mainstream curriculum that had proven meaningful in their own education with little attention to ways of making learning meaningful to the minority students who were the majority in their classrooms. The third group (the Effort group) valued skills and grounded instruction in students' prior knowledge and talents acquired outside of school. Teachers in this group questioned the design of the traditional school curriculum and its relevance to the majority of urban students in their classrooms. These teachers felt it was important to make connections between the mandated school curriculum and the prior knowledge and background experiences of the students. Instructional activities were grounded in meaning making by using students' prior knowledge to facilitate learning.

In summary, Abbate-Vaughn (2004) found:

For teachers operating from a Quiet stance, carrying an ideology that heavily relied on structuring lessons to standardize student behavior prevented them from exploring alternative options. They construed the TPC [teacher professional community] as the forum where the ideology of control . . . would be rightly valued. Their colleagues in the Academics group held high expectations for all students by relying on notions of mastery of the "traditional" curriculum as the ticket to college. Given the mismatch between the canon and their students' prior knowledge, their expectations were only occasionally materialized. Teachers clustered around the Effort ideology seemed best positioned to promote an understanding of the student population's strengths and joined the TPC with a relatively open agenda. Their reliance on establishing personal connections with the students was discredited by both teachers from the Academics and Quiet groups when results from standardized tests scores indicated little academic progress among students. During the study, however, there was not one instance in which teachers challenged the validity of those evaluation measures given their students' wide range of literacy and numeracy skills.

The first two groups of teachers in Abbate-Vaughn's study viewed schooling as an extension of their own socialization experiences and sought to engage familiar norms, values, and practices. The third group sought to contextualize their teaching practices and the school curriculum to facilitate learning for the urban students in their classrooms. Similar to the practices in the preservice cohort described by Radencich and colleagues (1998), the first two groups of teachers were able to establish and maintain norms for the teacher professional community by discrediting those who behaved as outsiders, thus, reinforcing and maintaining the low quality of teaching and student performance at the school. The approach used by the third group held unrealized potential but needed more work to produce the desired student learning outcomes.

Wilson, Corbett, and Williams (2000) reported on a community of practice at an urban junior high school that supported high expectations and exceptional academic performance for urban students that achieved the expected learning outcomes. In this community of practice, teachers worked together as a team for the core subjects for a specific group of students. The teachers set high expectations for students that included requiring that every student master all skills and subject matter as indicated by achieving a grade of B and assigning the student an incomplete (I) until this level of performance was reached. Teachers assumed responsibility for ensuring that students reached the desired level of performance by adapting instruction to the students' needs and incorporating prior knowledge and experiences, reteaching concepts that students did not understand when first taught, and when something did not seem to be working for a student, the team of teachers met with the student and the student's parents to develop a new approach or plan for the student. The day was structured to support students' academic performance. The last session of the day was devoted to reteaching and enrichment. This is when students who needed help received it from their regular teachers, and those who had achieved mastery could work on extensions that would allow them to earn an A grade.

The teacher community in the study reported by Wilson, Corbett, and Williams (2000) had a particular ideological perspective on teaching and learning that was very different from two of the groups in the study reported by Abbate-Vaughn (2004), candidates in the study reported by Radencich and colleagues (1998), and candidates in the study reported by Southerland and Gess-Newsome (1998). The teachers in Wilson, Corbett, and Williams's study had a plan and an established routine that supported students' learning and the socialization of new teachers into the community of practice in a way that enhanced professional growth and the ability to teach students from diverse cultural and experiential backgrounds and with a variety of academic needs. These teachers believed that there were two types of students, those who could do the work but had not and those who had not learned to do the work. The first group needed encouragement, and the second group needed additional instructional support.

Thus far, the discussion has been focused on observations in "naturally occurring" professional communities. This raises important questions about the potential of interventions for disrupting, redirecting, and transforming dysfunctional communities of practice that do not support student learning in urban schools. Hollins (2006) reported a study using structured dialogue as an intervention for transforming a culture of practice for teachers at a low-performing urban elementary school. Structured dialogue is a process of teachers engaging in conversation among peers for the purpose of addressing a particular problem or issue with a focus on what is working, the challenges faced, and the learners' responses to particular approaches. When the teachers began participating in structured dialogue, they held an ideological perspective on students, teaching, and learning and the relationship among peers. For example, in this community of practice, teaching was a private act and the number of years of teaching experience was valued over the quality of professional practice; teaching practices were viewed as generic and universal; the quality of students' efforts, family wealth or poverty, parental support, and intelligence were believed to account for learning outcomes; teacher talk about students, their parents, and their life conditions was negative, without sensitivity or understanding; and the enculturation of new teachers was automatic and without conscious thought or planning.

After three years of participating in structured dialogue, Hollins (2006) reported a substantial change in the ideology found in the teacher culture of practice and the academic performance of the students. Teaching had become transparent and practices were publicly disclosed; teachers openly acknowledged their own weaknesses and sought assistance from their colleagues; the relationship among instructional practices, learner characteristics and experiences, and learning outcomes was recognized and acted upon; teachers assumed responsibility for learning outcomes for their students, for their own learning, and for contributing to learning among colleagues; new standards for instructional practices included contextual validity—determining what worked for the students in their classrooms; teachers actively and consciously engaged in the systematic enculturation of new members into the professional community; and additionally, teachers addressed the tension between their efforts to improve classroom practices and public demand for accountability.

The ideology in the low-performing school at the outset of the study reported by Hollins (2006) had elements in common with those of the first two teacher groups in the study reported by Abbate-Vaughn (2004) and the preservice cohort reported by Radencich and colleagues (1998). Subsumed within the ideology of the transformed culture of practice Hollins (2006) described are the characteristics at the successful urban school described in the study reported by Wilson, Corbett, and Williams (2000) and in the Effort group described in the study reported by Abbate-Vaughn (2004). Hollins supports Rodriguez's (1999) finding that specific social constructivist strategies can be used to change personal perspectives, ideology, teaching practices, and, ultimately, to improve academic performance for urban students.

Summary of Findings from the Studies Reviewed

The studies reviewed in this chapter provide insights into the socialization process through which many white children are prepared for a position of power and privilege and many children of color to internalize a subordinate position. These studies revealed that: (1) socialization into the ideology of power and privilege is ubiquitous in the educational process in the United States from kindergarten through graduate school (Adams, 1996; Cornbleth, 1998; Diangelo, 2006; Fishkin, 1995; Katz, 1999; King, 1992; Lewis, 2003; Proweller, 1999; Sobol, 1993; Van Ausdale & Feagin, 2001); (2) many university faculty in different disciplines, including teacher education, have been socialized into the ideology of power and privilege and may have difficulty engaging in practices that challenge this ideology (Cochran-Smith, 2000; Diangelo, 2006; Fishkin, 1995; Haviland, 2008); (3) there are identifiable interpersonal and intrapersonal practices that maintain the ideology of power and privilege, including viewing the world as an extension of self (Diangelo, 2006; Ladson-Billings, 1996; Haviland, 2008; McIntyre, 1997; Mueller & O'Connor, 2007; Proweller, 1999); and (4) where candidates are organized in cohorts in their teacher preparation program there is the risk of reinforcing and legitimizing prior knowledge and experiences framed by the ideology of power and privilege (Bullough et al., 2001; Ohana, 2004; Radencich et al., 1998). Further, an examination of studies of teacher communities in urban school settings revealed that in low-performing schools, teachers have retained views characteristic of the power and privilege ideology, including that of knowledge as neutral and of minority students as deficit or not able to measure up to expectations (Abbate-Vaughn, 2004; Hollins, 2006). The remainder of this chapter will address the implications of these findings and their application in designing an approach for constructing *knowledge in practice* that will mitigate the influence of the ideology of power and privilege.

IMPLICATION FOR PRESERVICE TEACHER PREPARATION

A fundamental implication for preservice teacher preparation based on the findings from the studies reviewed here is the need for a process that will mitigate the influence of the ideology of power and privilege in learning to teach and that supports constructing authentic and contextualized *knowledge in practice* that will support learning for diverse and underserved students. This approach will need to replace particular habits of mind and circumvent the interpersonal and intrapersonal strategies employed to preserve and reproduce the ideology of power and privilege in the process of learning to teach.

The need for this approach is specifically supported by evidence from studies of how candidates appropriated knowledge for practice in courses (Kang, 2008; Rodriguez, 1999; Southerland & Gess-Newsome, 1998), the knowledge privileged when candidates were organized in cohorts in their teacher preparation programs (Bullough et al., 2001; Ohana, 2004; Radencich et al., 1998), and the discourse in teacher communities in low-performing urban schools as compared to high-performing urban schools (Hollins, 2006; Wilson et al., 2000). The findings from these particular studies have implications for the social context for learning to teach (the relationship among candidates, between candidates and faculty, and cooperating teachers and students in field experiences) and the process for learning to construct *knowledge in practice* (the relationship among pedagogy, learners, and learning outcomes). The focus of the discussion that follows is a proposition for changing the social discourse in learning to teach by addressing the social context and the process for constructing *knowledge in practice*.

PROPOSITION FOR CHANGING THE SOCIAL DISCOURSE IN LEARNING TO TEACH

The remainder of this discussion is focused on a proposition for changing the social discourse in learning to teach. This proposition is based on the research studies presented in this chapter that provided evidence of the influence of the ideology of power and privilege on learning to teach and the strategies used to preserve and perpetuate this ideology. This proposal presents counterstrategies built into the social context for field experiences and a process of structured dialogue situated in contextualized inquiry and problem solving.

The Social Context for Constructing *Knowledge in Practice*

The importance of the social context for constructing *knowledge in practice* is evident in research on candidates organized in cohorts in their preservice teacher preparation programs and in teacher communities of practice in urban school settings. When organized into cohorts, candidates provided emotional support for each other and privileged the experience and judgment of peers over knowledge for practice acquired in university courses (Bullough et al., 2001; Ohana, 2004; Radencich et al., 1998). This suggests that the social discourse among candidates can reinforce and maintain the ideology of power and privilege into which many candidates have been socialized and through which knowledge for practice may have been filtered. The social discourse that maintains the ideology of power and privilege in preservice programs, in part, accounts for its influence in low-performing urban schools where teachers form professional communities with shared beliefs about pedagogy and learners perpetuate students' low academic performance (Hollins, 2006; Wilson et al., 2000).

Changing the discourse in the social context for constructing *knowledge in practice* is important in mitigating the influence of the ideology of power and privilege in low-performing urban schools and for learning to teach students from diverse cultural and experiential backgrounds in preservice teacher preparation programs. In preservice teacher preparation, the social context for constructing *knowledge in practice* is the interface between participants in the university and the school setting for field experiences—the discourse among candidates, university faculty, cooperating teachers and their students, and other school personnel.

It is the discourse that occurs in the interface between participants in preservice teacher preparation at the university and in the school setting that can support constructing authentic and contextualized *knowledge in practice*; where candidates, faculty, and cooperating teachers can learn to rely on knowledge gleaned from the immediate classroom context combined with theoretical knowledge from the teacher preparation program to guide planning instruction and solving problems of practice. Here, the everyday classroom practices of teachers and candidates can constitute the subject matter for dialogue, inquiry, and problem solving. The relationship among participants needs to be one of shared observations, collaborative inquiry, and problem solving, where university faculty and cooperating teachers guide the focus of the dialogue and the application of *knowledge in practice* from coursework in the program.

The social context for constructing *knowledge in practice* differs significantly from traditional models of student teaching where the cooperating teacher is the expert, the candidate is an apprentice, and a university professor visits the classroom periodically to assess the candidate's progress in learning to teach (Feiman-Nemser, 2001). The social context for constructing *knowledge in practice* is a learning community where all participants are learners, including the candidates, university faculty, and the cooperating teachers and their students. The candidates, university faculty, and cooperating teachers collaborate in interrogating the relationship among learning, learners, pedagogy, and learning outcomes—where each works to develop inquiry as a habit of mind. In this social context, participants make their observations and thinking public and subject to interrogation by other members of the learning community. This is especially important in overcoming the influence of the ideology of power and privilege that is likely to have permeated the early education of many participants.

The Process for Constructing *Knowledge in Practice*

Constructing *knowledge in practice* refers to gaining an operational understanding of the relationship among pedagogy, learning, learners, and learning outcomes. This means understanding how knowledge about students' experiences, interests, preferences, and their prior knowledge can inform pedagogical practices—the design of learning experiences and how the curriculum is framed. It means understanding how pedagogical decisions that take into consideration the specific characteristics of learners influence learning outcomes.

Constructing *knowledge in practice* engages participants in making and documenting observations and raising questions about the relationship among learning, learners, pedagogy, and learning outcomes. In the context of classroom teaching, these questions may reveal the strengths and weaknesses of a particular lesson or learning experience by identifying the prior experiences, knowledge, and skills that helped some students succeed and not others. It might be observed that students were unable to apply the new knowledge in an unfamiliar situation, which could lead to identifying learning experiences that better support the application of new knowledge. In the context of these observations and questions, participants might use different theoretical perspectives on learning taken from coursework in the teacher preparation program to guide planning more productive learning experiences.

The consistent use of a particular theoretical perspective on learning to design instruction and to interpret students' responses supports developing inquiry as a habit of mind that deepens understanding of teaching and learning, and it enables powerful teaching to meet expected learning outcomes and standards. The use of a theoretical perspective on learning helps candidates develop a systematic way of thinking about and reflecting on the relationship among learning, learners, pedagogy, and outcomes and to rely less on prior personal experiences and preferences and the personal experiences and preferences of peers. This helps candidates construct authentic contextualized *knowledge in practice*.

An inquiry-based approach to constructing *knowledge in practice* using shared observations, collaborative problem solving, and a particular theoretical perspective on learning for planning instruction and interpreting students' responses requires a carefully designed format. This format brings together candidates, cooperating teachers, and university faculty in dialogue about the relationship among learning, learners, pedagogy, and learning outcomes with the immediate classroom context as subject matter. The observations, questions, and problems documented and presented in dialogue are from the immediate classroom practices of candidates and cooperating teachers. General questions can be developed to guide this dialogue, such as: What did you learn today about your students and pedagogy that will better inform your classroom practices? How does learning theory help you explain your observations? The ultimate goal for the dialogue is to increase the expertise of candidates and cooperating teachers in facilitating learning for diverse and underserved students.

CONCLUSION

The majority of candidates entering preservice teacher preparation programs are white, come from the middle class, grew up in the suburbs or a small town, and have had little contact with those from cultures different from their own. Many candidates have attended schools and universities with peers and teachers like themselves and where the social discourse and the curriculum content reinforced the ideology of power and privilege. The impact of this ideology is evident in candidates' views of the world as an extension of self and of knowledge as neutral and universal. In courses in their teacher preparation programs, many candidates resist evidence that conflicts with the ideology of power and privilege, which impedes their ability to learn to teach students from diverse and underserved groups. Many teacher educators and cooperating teachers share the background experiences and perspectives of the majority of the candidates entering the teacher preparation programs.

The challenge for teacher educators is to develop an approach that will engender habits of mind to mitigate or replace the ideology of power and privilege in learning to teach. This means changing the discourse that has perpetuated this ideology in professional communities of practice. One approach to changing this discourse is to involve candidates, cooperating teachers, and university faculty in a process of shared observations, collaborative inquiry, and problem solving based on evidence from classrooms with diverse and underserved students. In this dialogue the focus is on the relationship among learning, learners, pedagogy, and learning outcomes. Planning instruction and interpreting students' responses is guided by a particular theoretical perspective on learning included in coursework in the preservice teacher preparation program. The goal of this process is for candidates and cooperating teachers to develop authentic and contextualized *knowledge in practice* and for university faculty to gain new perspectives and insights into classroom practices. While the proposed practices require further investigation, existing evidence supports the potential for changing the discourse and for mitigating the influence of the ideology of power and privilege in learning to teach students from diverse and underserved groups.

REFERENCES

Abbate-Vaughn, J. (2004). The things they carry: Ideology in an urban teacher professional community. *Urban Review, 36(4)*, 227–49.

Adams, D. W. (1996). Fundamental considerations: The deep meaning of Native American schooling, 1880–1900. In Hollins, E. R., *Transforming curriculum for a culturally diverse society* (pp. 27–57). Mahwah, NJ: Lawrence Erlbaum Associates.

Ball, A., & Ladner, T. (1997). Dispositions towards language: Teacher constructs of knowledge and the Ann Arbor English case. *College Composition and Communication, 48(4)*, 469–85.

Ball, D. L., Thames, M. H., & Phelps, G. (2008). Content knowledge for teaching: What makes it special? *Journal of Teacher Education, 59(5)*, 389–407.

Banks, J. A. (1996). Multicultural education and curriculum transformation. *Journal of Negro Education, 64(4)*, 390–400.

Banks, J. A. (2002). Race, knowledge construction, and education in the USA: Lessons from history. *Race Ethnicity and Education, 5(1)*, 7–27.

Brownell, M. T., Yeager, E. A., Sindelar, P. T., VanHover, S., & Riley, T. (2004). Teacher learning cohorts: A vehicle for supporting beginning teachers. *Teacher Education and Special Education, 27(2)*, 174–89.

Bullough, R. V. Jr., Clark, D. C., Wentworth, N., & Hansen, J. M. (2001). Student cohorts, school rhythms, and teacher education. *Teacher Education Quarterly, 28(2)*, 97–110.

Cochran-Smith, M. (2000). Blind vision: Unlearning racism in teacher education. *Harvard Educational Review, 70(2)*, 157–90.

Cornbleth, C. (1998). An America curriculum? *Teachers College Record, 99(4)*, 622–42.

Darling-Hammond, L. (2000). Teacher quality and student achievement: A review of state policy evidence. *Education Policy Analysis Archives, 8(1)*. Retrieved at epaa.asu.edu

Darling-Hammond, L. (2006). Constructing 21st-century teacher education. *Journal of Teacher Education, 57(3)*, 300–314.

Diangelo, R. J. (2006). The production of whiteness in education: Asian international students in a college classroom. *Teachers College Record, 108(10)*, 1983–2000.

Feiman-Nemser, S. (2001). From preparation to practice: Designing a continuum to strengthen and sustain teaching. *Teachers College Record, 103(6)*, 1013–55.

Fishkin, S. F. (1995). Interrogating "whiteness," complicating "blackness": Remapping American culture. *American Quarterly, 47(3)*, 428–66.

Gomez, M. L., Black, R. W., & Allen, A. (2007). "Becoming" a teacher. *Teachers College Record, 109(9)*, 2107–135.

Grossman, P., Wineburg, S., & Woolworth, S. (2001). Toward a theory of teacher community. *Teachers College Record, 103(6)*, 942–1012.

Haberman, M., & Post, L. (1998). Teachers for multicultural schools: The power of selection. *Theory into Practice, 37(2)*, 96–104.

Haviland, V. S. (2008). "Things get glossed over": Rearticulating the silencing power of whiteness in education. *Journal of Teacher Education, 59(1)*, 40–54.

Helms, J. E. (1990). *Black and white racial identity: Theory, research, and practice.* New York: Greenwood Press.

Hollins, E. R. (2006). Transforming practice in urban schools. *Educational Leadership, 63(6),* 48–52.

Hollins, E. R. (2008). *Culture in school practice: Revealing the deep meaning* (2nd ed.). New York: Routledge.

Holmes Group. (1986). *Tomorrow's teachers: A report of the Holmes Group.* East Lansing, MI: Holmes Group.

Holmes Group. (1995). *Tomorrow's schools of education.* East Lansing, MI: Holmes Group.

Kang, N. (2008). Learning to teach science: Personal epistemologies, teaching goals, and practices of teaching. *Teaching and Teacher Education, 24,* 478–98.

Katz, S. R. (1999). Teaching in tensions: Latino immigrant youth, their teachers, and the structures of schooling. *Teachers College Record, 100(4),* 809–40.

King, J. E. (1992). Diaspora literacy and consciousness in the struggle against miseducation in the black community. *Journal of Negro Education, 61(3),* 317–40.

Ladson-Billings, G. (1996). Silences as weapons: Challenges of a black professor teaching white students. *Theory into Practice, 35(2),* 79–85.

Lewis, A. E. (2003). *Race in the schoolyard: Negotiating the color line in classrooms and communities.* New Brunswick, NJ: Rutgers University Press.

Lipka, J., & McCarty, T. L. (1994). Changing the culture of schooling: Navajo and Yup'ik cases. *Anthropology & Education Quarterly, 25(3),* 266–84.

Little, J. W. (1993). Teachers' professional development in a climate of educational reform. *Educational Evaluation and Policy Analysis, 15(2),* 129–51.

Lutkus, A., Grigg, W., & Donahue, P. (2007). *The nation's report card: Trial urban district assessment reading 2007* (NCES 2008–455). National Center for Educational Statistics, Institute of Education Science, U.S. Department of Education, Washington, D.C.

Mandzuk, D., Hasinoff, S., & Seifert, K. (2005). Inside a student cohort: Teacher education from a social capital perspective. *Canadian Journal of Teacher Education, 28(1/2),* 168–84.

McIntyre, A. (1997). Constructing an image of a white teacher. *Teachers College Record, 98(4),* 653–81.

Mueller, J., & O'Connor, C. (2007). Telling and retelling about self and "others": How pre-service teachers (re)interpret privilege and disadvantage in one college classroom. *Teaching and Teacher Education, 23,* 840–56.

Ohana, C. (2004). Extended field experiences and cohorts with elementary science methods: Some unintended consequences. *Journal of Science Teacher Education, 15(3),* 233–54.

Proweller, A. (1999). Shifting identities in private education: Reconstructing race at/in the cultural center. *Teachers College Record, 100(4),* 776–808.

Radencich, M. C., Thompson, T., Anderson, N. A., Oropallo, K., Fleege, P., Harrison, M., & Hanley, P. (1998). The culture of cohorts: preservice teacher education teams at a southeastern university in the United States. *Journal of Education for Teaching, 24(2),* 109–27.

Ravitch, D. (1990, Spring). Diversity and democracy: Multicultural education in America. *American Educator,* 16–20.

Ravitch, D. (December 1991/January 1992). A culture in common. *Educational Leadership,* 8–11.

Rodriguez, A. J. (1999). Strategies for counterresistance: Toward sociotransformative constructivism and learning to teach science for diversity and for understanding. *Journal of Research in Science Teaching, 35(6),* 589–622.

Sapon-Shevin, M., & Chandler-Olcott, K. (2001). Student cohorts: Communities of critique or dysfunctional families. *Journal of Teacher Education, 52(5),* 350–64.

Shkedi, A., & Nisan, M. (2006). Teachers' cultural ideology: Patterns of curriculum and teaching culturally valued texts. *Teachers College Record, 108(4),* 687–725.

Shulman, L. S. (1987). Knowledge and teaching: Foundations of the new reform. *Harvard Educational Review, 57,* 1–22.

Smagorinsky, P., Cook, L. S., & Johnson, T. S. (2003). The twisting path of concept development in learning to teach. *Teachers College Record, 105(8),* 1399–436.

Smedley, A. (1998). "Race" and the construction of human identity. *American Anthropologist, 100(3),* 690–702.

Sobol, T. (1993). Revising the New York state social studies curriculum. *Teachers College Record, 95(2),* 258–72.

Southerland, S. A., & Gess-Newsome, J. (1998). Preservice teachers' views of inclusive science teaching as shaped by images of teaching, learning, and knowledge. *Science Education, 83(2),* 131–50.

Stodolsky, S. S., & Grossman, P. L. (2000). Changing students, changing teachers. *Teachers College Record, 102(1),* 125–72.

Swidler, A. (1986). Culture in action: Symbols and strategies. *American Sociological Review, 51(2),* 273–86.

Van Ausdale, D., & Feagin, J. R. (2001). *The first R: How children learn race and racism.* New York: Rowman & Littlefield Publishers.

Wilson, B., Corbett, D., & Williams, B. (2000). A discussion of school reform—Case I: All students learning at Granite Junior High. *Teachers College Record,* October 30, 2000. Retrieved September 28, 2008, from http://www.tcrecord.org/Home.asp ID Number: 10619

Zumwalt, K., & Craig, E. (2005). Teachers' characteristics: Research on the demographic profile. In Cochran-Smith, M., & Zeichner, K. M. (Eds.), *Studying teacher education: The report of the AERA panel on research and teacher education* (pp. 157–260). Mahwah, NJ: Lawrence Erlbaum, Publishers.

II

CURRENT TRENDS AND INNOVATIONS IN RESEARCH ON DIVERSITY

Implications for Teacher Education

Where are we now as we consider the perspectives of current researchers who are challenging the rethinking and reconceptualization of the research on diversity in teacher education?

Part II of this volume focuses on current trends and innovations in the research on diversity in teacher education and sets in motion a dialogue on the interrogation of teacher preparation in the context of the diverse lives of the current student demographics. What new insights can we gain by explicitly pulling two historically separate components together: research on diversity and research on diversity in teacher education? Realizing that it is not enough to discuss the research on diversity in education as it relates to issues like the achievement gap, standardized measures of assessment, and the development of national curriculum standards, these authors provide perspectives and paradigms from the research on diversity that can be used when reconceptualizing and recentering the research on diversity in teacher education through existing and innovative frameworks.

Section A of part II centers on diverse populations with information that every teacher educator and every teacher candidate in a teacher education program must be exposed to in order to prepare them to teach diverse learners. Often the research on teacher education is criticized for being weak and for neglecting to provide teachers and teacher educators with sound research that can be used in the redesign and transformation of their programs. Teachers can be better prepared for the diversity they will find in their classrooms when teacher educators are provided with the research base they need to better prepare their students about issues of diversity. Quinn and Meiners's chapter on the lives of lesbian, gay, bisexual, transgender, and queer students, Kinloch's chapter on urban youths, Quijada Cerecer's chapter on Indigenous youth, Kirkland's chapter on black males, Scott and Ford's chapter on students with disabilities and gifts and talents, and Uys, Reyneke, and Kaiser's chapter on researching speakers of nondominant languages contribute to a foundational base of research about diverse populations to which every teacher educator and teacher candidate must be exposed in order to begin the journey toward preparing a force of teachers that are prepared to teach diverse learners.

In section B Chapman, Olsen, Lee, Winn, Ubiles, and Duncan-Andrade present frameworks, perspectives, and paradigms in research on diversity that seek to turn a critical eye toward issues of Critical Race Theory (CRT), teacher identity as a framework for research, practice, and diversity in education, Tribal Critical Race Theory, responsible research in ethnically diverse schools and classrooms, and responding to "socially toxic environments" that emerge from racism, poverty, and other forms of oppression. The authors in this section pore over what is presently known about research on diversity in education and explore the strengths and limitations of applying that to the research on diversity in teacher education. Perhaps most important, the scholars present research that has the potential to challenge the field to reposition itself to move in innovative directions for future research on the preparation of teachers for diverse and underserved populations.

Section A

Centering Research on Diverse
Populations in Teacher Education

5

Teacher Education, Struggles for Social Justice, and the Historic Erasure of Lesbian, Gay, Bisexual, Transgender, and Queer Lives

Therese Quinn and Erica R. Meiners *

At least twenty-five years of research documents the pedagogical, social, and economic value of incorporating lesbian, gay, bisexual, transgender, and queer (LGBTQ) content into curriculum and policies and using sexual orientation and gender identity as frameworks to seek educational and social justice (Blanchett, 2009; Casper & Schultz, 1999; Cosier, 2009; Epstein, 1994; Horowitz & Hansen, 2008; Jennings, 1994; Khayatt, 1992; Kumashiro, 2004; Mayo, 2009; McCready, 2009; Meyer, 2009; Pascoe, 2007; Smiler, 2009; Szalacha, 2005). Much research also emphasizes the centrality of locating LGBTQ lives and struggles for justice within an intersectional analysis, *always linking* LGBTQ to race, ability, gender, and more (Crenshaw, 1991; Diaz & Kosciw, 2009; Fine & McClelland, 2006; Kumashiro, 2004; North, 2008; McCready, 2009; Quinn & Meiners, 2009).

Yet, despite this research, LGBTQ–sensitive content and policies continued to be marginalized in teacher education (Macgillivray & Jennings, 2008). For example, even with research documenting that stemming LGBTQ-targeted violence in schools is central to creating safer learning contexts for all (Linville, 2009; Massachusetts Department of Education, 2002; Meyer, 2009), research highlighting that the lack of attention to LGBTQ-directed violence weakens students' positive feelings about school (Grossman, Haney, Edwards, Alessi, Ardon, & Howell, 2009), and research that documents that listening to the experiences of LGBTQ youth in teacher preparation programs positively informs educators' abilities to work effectively with LGBTQ youth and families (Stiegler, 2008), a 2009 audit of the online inclusion of sexual orientation and gender identity in the policies, conceptual frameworks, and curriculum of the fifty-seven teacher preparation programs in the state of Illinois documented that a majority of the programs failed to include references to LGBTQ lives (Duke, 2007; Fine & McClelland, 2006; *Visibility Matters*, 2009).

This inability of research on the centrality of LGBTQ lives in schools to transfer into teacher preparation programs pushed us to step back from scholarship that examined classroom life, or curriculum, and moved us to "study up" (Nader, 1974

[1969]), or to examine those with more power and privileges in social and political organizations and how these subjects and structures produce and maintain oppression and injustices.[1] Nader's challenge is epistemic and political. What we research—the fundamental unit of analysis—matters. We take up her challenge in this chapter by summarizing research that addresses factors affecting teacher education programs' inclusion of LGBTQ concerns and content. Specifically, we ask: What do we know about attempts to include LGBTQ lives and content in teacher education; how are these strategies related to, and dissimilar to, other educational justice histories—notably desegregation; to what extent are contemporary strategies for LGBTQ educational equity constrained by sociopolitical contexts, such as neoliberalism; and how have these sociopolitical contexts affected policy in the field? In what follows we provide an overview of these topics, necessarily abbreviated by length limitations.

TEACHER EDUCATION AND LGBTQ LIVES

The presence of nonheteronormative teachers has long incited political mobilizations against sexual minorities as "the expectation that educators act as exemplars for students has led to intense public scrutiny of teachers' personal lives and restricted professional autonomy" (Graves, 2009, p. 120; see also Blount, 2005). Shifting the lens from research on classroom-based practices and on curriculum, this chapter surveys how the field of teacher education continues to marginalize LGBTQ lives and content, and this requires sketching the history of teacher accreditation practices. While the field of teacher education has marginalized LGBTQ lives in varied ways, from active prohibition of sexual minority educators to erasure of LGBTQ content in teacher education curriculum, this chapter focuses on accreditation because this is the national and state policy framework within which public education programs must function.

Historically, teachers were "certified" by communities; no accreditation process existed (Tamir & Wilson, 2005). The main criterion for teachers was "moral values," and spiritual leaders vouched for the candidates (Tozer, Violas, & Senese, 1998, p. 59). These informal practices weeded out queer and other outsider educators (Blount, 2005). Vouching by spiritual leaders shifted to vouching by the state, and by the 1840s a majority of teachers in the United States received certificates from local officials based on an examination (Sedlak in Tamir & Wilson, p. 333). This allowed local control but also the pitfalls of "patronage" and nepotism; schools varied widely in quality (Tozer et al., 1998). The state stepped into the picture, developing licensure requirements as a form of quality control over the growing numbers of women working in school. Throughout the start of the twentieth century, state departments of education flourished and the first "normal" schools evolved into teachers colleges (Tamir & Wilson, 2005).

The profession has a history of constructing queers as deviants who are "unfit to teach" through informal prohibitions and formal discriminatory practices (Blount, 2005; Khayatt, 1992; Graves, 2009). Excluding queers from education was originally the function of the community, and historians note that in the early twentieth century "personal behavior weighed more heavily than personal professional competence in determining a teacher's fitness to serve in a given community. Documentary evidence combined with rich anecdotal data shore up this point" (Graves, 2009, p. 126). It is important to note that the conception of the "homosexual" is a relatively recent construct (Eskridge, 2000; Faderman, 1991; Katz, 2003; Somerville, 2000). Historian Canaday documents that modern conceptions of homosexuality developed at the same time as modern constructions of the U.S. bureaucratic state (2009, see also Epstein, 2009; Eskridge, 2000). This scholarship documents that prohibitions against queers are built into the developing nineteenth-century bureaucracies of the immigration, military, and welfare-state systems. Starting with explicit prohibitions against degenerate, "mannish" women and "perverted" and "feminine" men, these bureaucracies developed into the twentieth century, in concert with the production of the "homosexual." "The history of the modern American state is simultaneously a genealogy of what we now take to be homosexuality" (Epstein, 2009, p. 26).[2]

Into the twentieth century, while community scrutiny still played a significant role to regulate the sexual and moral fitness of educators, discourses and regulatory bodies changed. The category of homosexual became a public and marked figure that the state actively policed. Between the two world wars, teachers were "called upon to be 'hygienic models' for their students" (Graves, 2009, p. 127), and oversight of teachers' sexuality moved from community-led to administrative (Perrillo, 2004). Some historians suggest that the shift from community to primarily "professional" surveillance afforded teachers an increased measure of autonomy along with other aspects of professionalism, although this is also debated (Perrillo, 2004; Rousmaniere, 1997).

After World War II, many states possessed investigative bodies charged with identifying and terminating the employment of suspected homosexual educators. For example, Max Rafferty, California Superintendent of Public Instruction in the 1970s and chair of a credentialing commission that decided which teachers were fit to teach, stated: "And from the beginning, I do assure you, we took for granted the self-evident proposition that a homosexual in a school job was as preposterously out of the question as a heroin mainliner in the local drugstore" (as quoted in Blount, 2005, p. 142; Graves, 2009).

By the mid-twenty-first century, the regulation of teacher-training institutions was increasingly managed by quasi-public organizations. For example, NCATE was formed in 1954 by the American Association of Colleges for Teacher Education (AACTE) and four other educational organizations, including the National Education Association. By the 1960s, NCATE was the leading institution shaping teacher education. NCATE's power expanded in part due to alliances with state governments and the move to standardize the teacher education curricula at the state level. For example, in 1999, the New York State Education Department mandated that all state schools be accredited by a federally approved accreditor or by the New York Board of Regents, and as NCATE was at that time the only federally approved accreditor, fifty-eight institutions in New York moved to seek NCATE accreditation (Johnson, Johnson, Farenga, & Ness, 2005, p. 63).[3] Today NCATE accredits more than half of all schools providing teacher education, which have programs that prepare two-thirds of all new teachers. NCATE has built strategic partnerships with state boards of education who, in effect, "outsource" their review work to this organization (Johnson et al., 2005, pp. 3, 19).

Today NCATE has partnerships with fifty states, including the District of Columbia and Puerto Rico (NCATE State Partnership Program FAQs, 2008). Johnson and colleagues point out that while its tagline says, "'Helping all students learn' implies helping all women learn, helping all girls learn, and helping all citizens of a given country learn, regardless of their racial, ethnic, and religious backgrounds," NCATE accredits teacher education programs in countries that routinely exclude sectors of their population from access to education (Johnson et al., 2005, p. 88). Similarly, against scientific agreement, the organization accredits teacher education programs in schools that "support Biblical creationism" (Johnson et al., p. 4).

In fact, just as laws are embedded within social and political systems and reflect those standards, so do NCATE's practices; it mirrors social norms, including biases, perhaps more than it models laudable goals. In a post-9/11 context, following the second George Bush administration which courted conservative people of faith who were often openly hostile toward LGBTQ people and lives, it should be no surprise that, rather than "touch the third rail of sexuality politics," NCATE has chosen to *not* act, based on the quantity of research showing a persistent need for attention to LGBTQ content in schools by retaining the term *sexual orientation* and strengthening attention to both sexual orientation and gender identity in its professional standards (Lugg, 2004, 2006, p. 37).

The relative growth of accrediting organizations, such as NCATE, offers an opportunity to examine changing state functions and a window to look at strategies deployed by justice movements. Just as the state and nonstate agencies that regulated and legitimated teacher education shifted through the nineteenth, twentieth, and into the twenty-first centuries, the antigay movement has correspondingly retooled its strategies. Central to this work has been its move to concede the right to privacy for select queers while simultaneously restricting their access to the public sphere.

> [The antigay movement] defined privacy as a kind of confinement, a cordon sanitaire "protecting" public sensibilities. They attacked gay rhetorical claims for privacy-in-public and for publicizing the private, specifically, and worked to define the public sphere as an isolated, domestic site completely out of range of any public venue. (Duggan, 2003, p. 53)

Through the 1980s and 1990s, in public schools (for example), "No Promo Homo" regulations restricted the public, in the form of education funds, from being used to support positive discussions about queer sexualities in schools (Eskridge, 2000). In other words, teachers could be queer in private, but they would have no right to visibility or support in the public school. For example, the failed 1978 Briggs Measure in California aimed to bar all-out, not closeted homosexuals from teaching; more recently, a 1992 Oregon ballot measure stated, "All governments in Oregon may not use their monies or properties to promote, encourage or facilitate homosexuality, pedophilia, sadism or masochism. All levels of government, including public education systems, must assist in setting a standard for Oregon's youth which recognizes that these behaviors are abnormal, wrong, unnatural and perverse and they are to be discouraged and avoided" (Queer Planet, 1992, ¶43). Then, again in 2000, a reworded Measure 9 was introduced in Oregon, seeking to prohibit school employees from "encouraging, promoting, sanctioning homosexual, bisexual behaviors" among students; it, like the previous bill, was narrowly defeated ("Anti-Gay Measure," 2000).

While there have been changes in public policy and public sentiment surrounding LGBTQ rights, across the United States teachers are still expected to support the social-reproduction purposes of schools and are assumed to be heterosexual and "models of . . . values" (Khayatt, 1992, p. 146). However, by definition, queer teachers disrupt the assumption of values congruence or the idea that all teachers agree with and abide by social norms when they are known, or "out," in their schools. But even when unknown and unlabeled, queers can trigger "moral" or "sex panic" in schools (Rofes, 2005, p. 94). Heteronormativity, the structures and systems "that legitimize and privilege heterosexuality and heterosexual relationships as fundamental and 'natural' within society" (Cohen, 2005, p. 24), is pervasive in most institutions, including schools and teacher education programs (Blount, 2005; de Castell & Bryson, 1998; Rofes, 2005). Fear of the queer, and all the meanings and associations attached to nonheteronormativity, still leads schools to suppress teachers, teachers to censor students and themselves, and students to act in ways that often have disastrous results: In 2008 a student *killed* an out gay and non-gender-conforming same-sex peer who asked him to be his Valentine (Russell, 2008; Setoodeh, 2008). In 2009 at least three young men reportedly committed suicide after being subjected to school-based homophobic harassment (Chasnoff, 2009).

In particular, queer lives are increasingly vulnerable in the current neoliberal landscape, which aims at opening up all parts of society to the free market. NCATE, as a semipublic but opaque organization, is not an anomaly in education; the "public" is increasingly marginalized as bureaucratic and ineffective, and it is being replaced by a consortium of private market practices that are perceived as more efficient or more natural than the artificial monopoly. This reframing is a hallmark of contemporary neoliberalism—a framework aimed at opening up all parts of society to the free market and that is notable for these qualities: "competition, inequality, market 'discipline,' public austerity, and 'law and order'" (Duggan, 2003, p. x). In the United States, the neoliberal remaking of institutions and practices, from utility services to schools, continues, as David Harvey (2005) states, through the "long march" of corporations, media, think tanks, and other powerful private for-profit forces that have sought not only to change economic and political policies but also cultural understandings, such as who has access to public space and public support, that ground our relationship to democracy (p. 40).

Along with a reduction of support for "assistance" services, privatization means a loss of resources for elementary, secondary, and higher education and an erosion of the democratic possibilities of institutions that make decisions, set standards, and shape policy for the public educational system. Into this void enter foundations, nonprofit organizations, and some for-profit entities to form the *shadow state*, or the nongovernmental forces that essentially fulfill what were once posited as the responsibilities of the state (Gilmore, 2007; Scott, Lubienski, & DeBray-Pelot, 2009; Wolch, 1990).[4] Since the early 1980s, this shadow state has not only delivered central services, from health care and arts and museums, to education and housing, it is also increasingly accountable for making fundamental alterations to public institutions such as schools. Yet this trend is dangerous for queers. LGBTQ teachers were declared "not fit to teach" by communities in the twentieth century, and state professional panels and agencies also "rooted" out the queers from teaching in the twenty-first century, yet through democratic participation, such as in movements for justice and political engagement, sexual minorities have been successful in securing some rights to public access. However, the current neoliberal and political framework of shadow state control of formerly public institutions does not provide much means for democratic participation.

REPEATING HISTORIES OF EDUCATIONAL EXCLUSION

Erosion of the public through the support of the private is not a completely new phenomenon. In particular, when the public sphere expands to include people with new practices that challenge dominant ideologies—for example, African Americans integrating politics and neighborhoods during Reconstruction—those opposing such changes deploy new institutions and rhetoric, from laws and oaths to schools and organizations, that work to enforce the status quo. It is important to connect these struggles to include LGBTQ lives in teacher education curriculum to broader histories of struggles for educational equity. In particular, it is instructive to note how the strategies utilized to exclude communities from equal education are similar. The political life in schools is heavily regulated, as previously outlined, by communities and the state and increasingly by nonstate actors, and this regulation is reflected in the colleges and university programs that prepare educators.

In particular, we turn to examples when schools were "forced" to desegregate after the *Brown* decisions, "with all deliberate speed," and a strategy known as "massive resistance" was initiated by Virginia's senator Harry Byrd and authorized by the state's governor in which integrated public schools were shut down or defunded (*Yale Law Journal*, 1973, p. 1437). In Prince Edward County, Virginia, public schools were ordered padlocked by city supervisors and remained closed for five years, from 1958 to 1964, until the federal courts ordered tax collection to begin again and for *public* schools to be opened (Saxon, 1995; *Griffin v. School Board of St. Edward*, 1964). In fact, most southern states passed legislation that would allow or mandate closing schools that integrated while at the same time creating means to support "voluntary" private segregation schools, which opened across the south to cater to white children and to "private" beliefs held by white supremacists (Ryan, 2004). These schools were directly and indirectly supported by the government through tuition grants, the "transfer of facilities from closed public schools," and state and federal tax exemptions (*Yale Law Journal*, 1973, p. 1436; Andrews, 2002). Other resources and labor were provided by private economic, civic, and religious institutions such as the Baptist church, banks that provided start-up loans, and local groups including citizen's councils and parents' organizations. Code terms for white supremacy, such as claims to *tradition* and the *right to individual liberty*, in the form of politically and structurally supported "freedom of choice" plans, were the hallmarks of these segregatory initiatives (Ladson-Billings, 2004: Lassiter, 2006; Lipsitz, 1998; Ryan, 2004, p. 1636).

"Massive resistance" was not confined to K–12 institutions. Public institutions in the south, such as the University of Mississippi in 1962, desegregated after riots, under the presence of federal troops. For private postsecondary institutions, the process was slower. In 1970, the Internal Revenue Service (IRS) declared that private institutions claiming federal tax exemptions must comply with federal antidiscrimination standards. Perhaps the most visible case is Bob Jones University (BJU), which agreed to admit African American students in 1971; yet until 1975 all African American students that were admitted were required to be married. Although the school now avoids condemning interracial romance, it still bans same-sex love. In fact, in letters sent to former students in 1998, BJU announced that it would have gay alumni arrested for trespassing if they merely attempted to visit the campus, though the school later said queers could still visit the BJU museum so this museum wouldn't lose its tax-exempt status, held independently from the school ("Bob Jones University Tells Gay Alumni," 1998).[5]

Just as "maintaining tradition" was used as a code phrase when segregationist academies and postsecondary were created and maintained in the years after the *Brown* decisions, a similar sentiment is used to justify antiqueer educational institutions. These same strategies are used today to justify the exclusion of LGBTQ content and lives from private religious colleges that are accredited by the state to produce public teachers (Quinn & Meiners, 2009). Legally, the rights of LGBTQ individuals in schools are not as clear as those of racial minorities. Sexual identity is not a protected federal category, and private schools like BJU, along with other private entities such as the Boy Scouts, are free to ban both queer individuals and acts (Zehr, 2006). Further, in these private schools, speech and expression are also often regulated through the lack of employment protection and unionization for all staff. But public education is also, and perhaps increasingly, restrictive for queers, with the rise in charter and other privatized schools operating outside structures that provide workplace protection for employees (Quinn, 2007). And as recent as fall 2006, the National Council for the Accreditation of Teacher Education (NCATE)—the primary U.S. accreditation agency for colleges and programs of teacher education—asked for public feedback on proposed revisions to its "Professional Standards, 2002 Edition." The changes eliminated the phrase "social justice" and facilitated the de facto elimination of sexual orientation from the document (see Quinn & Meiners, 2007). As teacher educators and professionals in the field, we responded to NCATE's subsequent call for public comments on these changes by pointing out the continuing evidence that public schools are unsafe for sexual and gender identity minorities (Pascoe, 2007; Russo, 2006;), and therefore should be represented in the standards that shape both the profession of teacher education and what happens in our public school classrooms. We wrote a letter that included 300 of our colleague's signatures, documenting research that pointed to the persistent violence that LGBTQ youth experience in schools and the importance of including LGBTQ content in teacher preparation programs as one strategy to support educators to be able to create safer classrooms. We never received a response.

This broad overview is important because the specificities of queer lives in schools and in teacher education programs are located in social and political contexts. As we have worked to explicate in this chapter, schools and teacher education programs are not exempt from the effects of a changing sociopolitical landscape or from larger struggles about the place and rights of all minoritized individuals and communities in a participatory democracy. Although much research, including what is represented by the following statistics (see table 5.1), indicates that addressing sexual orientation (a person's emotional, romantic, and sexual attraction) and gender identity (a person's sense of being male or female, feminine or masculine) in our schools

Table 5.1   Statistics Concerning LGBTQ Lives in Schools

Schools are unsafe for lesbian, gay, bisexual and transgender (LGBT) youth because of their sexual orientation and/or gender expression	• 67.1% reported that hearing "gay" or "queer" used in a derogatory manner caused them to feel bothered or distressed • 64.3% reported feeling unsafe in their school • 45.5% reported being verbally harassed and 26.1% had experienced physical harassment in school because of their gender expression • 40.5% reported that teachers never intervened when hearing homophobic remarks • 18.6% reported hearing homophobic remarks from faculty or school staff frequently or often
Negative school climates affect LGBT youths' well-being and academic success.	LGBT students are more likely than the general student population to: • attempt suicide (32.7% vs. 8.7%), • skip school because they feel unsafe (17.7% vs. 7.8%).
Teachers are ill equipped to confront issues that contribute to anti-LGBT hostility.	• 81.7% of LGBT students reported that they had never learned about LGBT people, history, or events in any of their school classes • In a study of preservice teachers, 57% indicated that they needed more training or education to work effectively with LGBT youth and 65% reported that they needed more specific education to address homosexuality in their teaching • In a study of high school health teachers, two-thirds indicated that they had inadequate education about LGBT issues.

Data from Massachusetts Department of Education, 2002; Telljohann, Price, Poureslami, & Easton, 1995; Koch, 2000; Kosciw & Diaz, 2006.

is urgent, NCATE has resisted offering strong support for LGBTQ representation in teacher education programs (Horn & Szalacha, 2007; Quinn & Meiners, 2007).

As attempts to foreground and prioritize queer concerns in education trigger anxieties and oppositions that often, in turn, derail endeavors to put into practice what we have learned from research, we suggest a shift that may help address this problem.

FROM *TOLERANCE* TO *COMPETENCY* IN TEACHER EDUCATION PROGRAMS AND IN SCHOOLS: POLICY AND PRACTICE IMPLICATIONS

Queer-inclusive policies are important, but LGBTQ representation should not be our only goal in transforming teacher education programs. Rather, a focus on educating about rights, power, and as Amartya Sen describes, freedoms *to* (such as, to live the lives we choose) and freedoms *from* (e.g., discrimination) is also important (Unterhalter, 2007). As Lugg aptly notes, "Protection or nonoppression is not the same as social justice, or for that matter, education" (2003, p. 124). However, choosing a model to support educating about rights and representation for all can be difficult: the dustbin of educational theory and research is piled high with difference frameworks, including *teaching diversity, teaching so that all can learn, culturally relevant pedagogy, multiculturalism,* and *teaching for tolerance.* While these and other versions of diversity education have had various levels of popularity, based on the continuing marginalization of sexual orientation, gender identity, and related topics in teacher education, they have not been effective tools in ongoing work against homophobia and heterosexism in the field (Asher, 2007; Jennings & Sherwin, 2008; Lugg, 2003; Macgillivray & Jennings, 2008). However, difference matters because justice matters; attention to difference in education is important as a catalyst for social change.

When the goal of justice slips from view, diversity frameworks can be ineffective at fostering change. For example, when discussing "difference" in education, *tolerance* is a common orientation; this view promotes inclusion and tolerating all positions and views. However, this framework can translate as an inability to differentiate between claims and leads to "category confusion," where those who *name the problems* are perceived to *be the problems* (Jakobsen & Pellegrini, 2003, pp. 58–59). As a result, perpetrators of hate are obscured, and audiences are asked not to acknowledge hate but to "tolerate both sides of a conflict" (Jakobsen & Pellegrini, 2003, p. 59). In this way, the state—which once sanctioned race-based exclusionary initiatives that curtailed the movement, education, and other rights of people of color in the United States through social policies (not just individual acts) that continue to affect our communities—now allows institutions to exclude queers from education places under the rubric of tradition.

As an alternative to tolerance and other diversity frameworks in teacher education that both erase and fail to explicate queer lives, we are inspired by Beauboeuf-LaFontant's (1999) analysis of culturally relevant teaching, which she asserts should be recast as "'politically relevant' teaching, to emphasize the political, historical, social, as well as cultural, understandings that teachers bring to their profession" (p. 705). She explains that teachers who are imbued with "political clarity" (p. 705) and actively engaged in politically relevant teaching are aware that "both schooling for democratic citizenship and schooling for second-class citizenship have been basic traditions in American education" (Anderson, quoted in Beauboeuf-LaFontant, 1999, p. 705). Beauboeuf-LaFontant argues that although cultural congruence between educators and students is "certainly helpful," it is "not sufficient for remedying the contemporary problems" (p. 718). Instead, the goal should be to show that "there is a political history of striving to the practice of democracy in line with our founding ideals, and that this 'positive struggle' has included people of *various* cultural and social backgrounds" (Wills, quoted in Beauboeuf-LaFontant, 1999, p. 719; emphasis in original).

If taken up more broadly within teacher education, this move from cultural to political *clarity* (awareness of the relationship between education and society, and the educator's role as a political actor) could be paired with political *competency* (familiarity with collective histories and strategies of political action) to be parallel and interlocking goals. Together *political clarity and competency* as aims, dispositions, or standards in teacher education could foster more-aware teachers and more activist teacher educators and, ultimately, could help preserve a fully public education system. However, this raises the question of the relationship of our national education leadership to the field of teacher education.

It is unlikely that teacher candidates will be urged by their preprofessional preparation programs to develop and demonstrate clarity about the social impact of their
work, which includes taking action when possible, when our field's leadership organizations generally fail to demonstrate that clarity and also refrain from acting. Yet,
education policy-setting organizations could support educators by creating means
of democratic access to and foregrounding social justice in their institutional policies and practices and by acknowledging and using justice-focused research such as
we have referenced throughout this chapter. As we expect educators to grapple with
hard questions in their schools and communities, and not to shy away from the
uncomfortable questions and topics, our schools of education, accrediting agencies,
and professional organizations should also model this stance.

However, teachers are not waiting for their "leaders" to lead. Educators with clearly
articulated progressive political agendas and organizing strategies are emerging as a
national force, creating more and easier-to-access radical teacher and public education
activist groups across the United States and internationally, and coming together to
push for community-inclusive reform policies in public education—the Caucus of
Rank and File Educators (CORE) and Teachers for Social Justice in Chicago; Teachers
4 Justice in San Francisco; La Raza Educators in Los Angeles; and the New York Collective of Radical Educators (NYCORE) are just a few. Among the issues these groups
have addressed are access to equal school funding, support for improved workplace
conditions for teachers, alternatives to militarized public schools and programs, and
more. Members of these groups are changing classrooms, too, by producing and sharing progressive curriculums and resources. One recent example is *Planning to Change
the World: A Plan Book for Social Justice Teachers* (Mack & Picower, 2008) published
by NYCORE and the Education for Liberation Network. This teaching and teacher-
organizing practice is scaffolded by years of research on social justice in education, including that which specifically addresses LGBTQ concerns, from teacher preparation
and gender identity negotiation to classroom climate and much more (Ayers, Quinn,
& Stovall, 2008; Blackburn, 2007; Duke, 2007; McIntyre, 1997; Ng, Staton, & Scane,
1995; Nieto, 2003; Roberts, Allan, & Wells, 2007; Stiztlein, 2007).

How might these changes—claiming political clarity and competency as goals for
educators; activating an educational community leadership to make policy decisions
based on research showing the need for action on issues impeding the education and
experiences of LGBTQ students and teachers; and coalescing a radicalized and activist
teacher community—show up in and affect teacher education classrooms? First, we
expect that teacher educators, when charged with the goal of social justice, will make
powerful changes in their preprofessional preparation programs by revisiting the traditional teacher education canons; for example, instead of teaching about difference
and offering taxonomies of how to define and engage with difference, they might
flip this script to teach how difference is produced and, as Beauboeuf-LaFontant and
others point out, linked to power, and that the ways society delineates difference is
always political. They might continue to ask, "Who benefits?" (Gramsci, quoted in
Brantlinger, 2009, p. 1) from the way our educational system has been organized.
Posing and investigating these and similar questions with their students potentially
equips these new teachers with an understanding of how identity is not simply an
a priori category to engage with in schools but a system that is politically produced
in institutions, including the system of public education. This call for politically en-

gaged curricula in teacher education programs also presses scholars in teacher education to think about our research endeavors differently.

CONCLUSION: RECOMMENDATIONS FOR A RESEARCH AGENDA

Despite a growing body of research, teacher accreditation entities have historically and persistently viewed LGBTQ subjects and social justice as inflammatory and worked to eradicate or minimize these topics from accreditation documents and certification requirements in an effort to avoid controversy (Butin, 2007; Quinn & Meiners, 2007). In addition, in teacher preparation programs, also despite mounting scholarship, to date the connections between data and policies related to sexuality and gender identity remain unclear. Based on this track record, we have one primary recommendation for an ongoing research agenda aimed at advocacy for the lives and rights of LGBTQ individuals in public education: *Identify and examine barriers.*

Because the resistance to addressing queer content in education is persistent, more attention must be paid to the barriers to incorporating LGBTQ lives into curriculum and LGBTQ rights into policy and frameworks. As we have noted throughout this chapter, good research on these topics exists and already offers a range of solutions and directions, so it seems that the problem is less *what we don't know* than *what we don't do.* However, rather than simply proposing more "on-the-ground" research of local attitudes and prejudices, we again remind readers to study up by focusing on structures, systems, and power. For example, with an eye to studying up and attending to barriers, these and other currently underaddressed questions could be explored:

- What is the path of decision making through which policies related to LGBTQ content and rights in public education are determined?
- Where does the policy-level commitment to LGBTQ inclusion break down, and where can it be meaningfully shored up?
- What is the relationship of different theoretical diversity frameworks to the process of policy and agenda setting in public education?
- What effects do conditions of employment in school workplaces have on LGBTQ presence or absence in public education?
- Similarly, how are changes in the structures of teacher and public education, namely, calls for reduced teacher certification requirements and a continued move to "choice" systems, affecting LGBTQ presence or absence in schools?

Perhaps as important as studying up is studying ourselves; as teacher educators and researchers we advocate lateral investigation into the problem of implementation that we've identified by asking: What are our responsibilities as teacher educators? Are we posing the right questions to our students? Could we recommend and take up more relevant and urgent topics in our classrooms and research? And, finally, have we linked our and their work in teaching and knowledge production to the larger purpose of social justice? By studying up and studying ourselves, and pursuing projects with articulated social justice goals, we honor the labor of our historic forebears, education activists who, like Mary Church Terrell, Margaret Haley, Eric Rofes, and so many others, sought to align our national ideals of democratic participation and justice for all individuals, with the lived realities of children and teachers in schools.

NOTES

*This chapter was co-written and has no first author; the order of our names reflects a publishing rotation.

1. In her article *Up the Anthropologist*, Laura Nader (1974) [1969] reminds anthropologists of the importance of "studying up." She writes that researchers are conditioned to *study down* or to examine those with less power and privilege: children, prisoners, poor people, and so on. Yet, Nader writes, it is increasingly important for anthropologists to study up by focusing on "the colonizers rather than the colonized, the culture of power rather than the culture of powerlessness" (p. 289).

2. Mills (1997) and Pateman (1989) have made related arguments about the centrality of white supremacy in the United States and sexism to the formation of the modern "democratic" state.

3. While alternative, boutique, and online teacher education programs continue to emerge and often do not seek accreditation as they are shaped by political and economic "market" forces that do not necessitate accreditation and primarily research institutions can avoid the pressures of seeking national accreditation as their "brand" is often adequate to draw students, teacher education programs embedded in colleges and universities that lack a brand status, or a market, gravitate toward NCATE as the primary national legitimating organization (Johnson et al., 2005). As of 2009, the Teacher Education Accreditation Council (TEAC) is also active, but with only a few dozen institutions accredited through the TEAC process. The June 2009 TEAC minutes available on the TEAC website also state that TEAC is working with NCATE to explore the development of one "umbrella organization" (Teacher Education Accreditation Council, 2009, p. 2).

4. The shadow state is not accountable to any public, just to its unelected board members and donors. For example, in 2006 Bill Gates was identified by the Education Research Center in the report *Influence: A Study of the Factors Shaping Education Policy* as the most influential person in educational policy in the previous decade, surpassing then-president George Bush (Swanson & Barlage, 2006).

5. This record of exclusion has not hurt the school—BJU is not marginal; it is accredited by the Transnational Association of Christian Colleges and Schools (TRACS), which is recognized by the U.S. Department of Education and works with more than 100 institutions across the states, according to the school's and the organization's websites, and is a well-known pit stop for Republican presidential nominees and candidates, including Ronald Reagan, Bob Dole, Alan Keyes, and George W. Bush (Carlson, 2005).

REFERENCES

Andrews, K. (2002, March). Movement-countermovement dynamics and the emergence of new institutions: The case of "white flight" schools in Mississippi. *Social Forces, 80(3)*, 911–36.

Anti-gay measure has apparently failed. (2000, November 11). *USA Today*. Retrieved February 8, 2007, from http://www.usatoday.com/news/vote2000/or/gay.htm

Asher, N. (2007). Made in the (multicultural) U.S.A.: Unpacking tensions of race, culture, gender, and sexuality in education. *Educational Researcher, 36(2)*, 65–73.

Ayers, W., Quinn, T., & Stovall, D. (2008). Teachers' experiences of curriculum: Policy, pedagogy and situation. In Connelly, M., Ming, H., & Phillion, J. (Eds.), *Sage handbook of curriculum and instruction*, pp. 306-326. Thousand Oaks, CA: Sage Publications.

Beauboeuf-LaFontant, T. (1999). A movement against and beyond boundaries: "Politically relevant teaching" among African American teachers. *Teachers College Record, 100(4)*, 702-23.

Blackburn, M. (2007). The experiencing, negotiation, breaking, and remaking of gender rules and regulations by queer youth. *Journal of Gay & Lesbian Issues in Education, 4(2)*, 33-54.

Blanchett, W. (2009). HIV/AIDS prevention and sexuality education for *all* students: Critical issues in teaching for social justice. In Ayers, W., Quinn, T., & Stovall, D. (Eds.), *Handbook for social justice in education* (pp. 345-57). New York: Routledge.

Blount, J. (2005). *Fit to teach: Same-sex desire, gender, and school work in the twentieth century*. Albany: SUNY Press.

Bob Jones University tells gay alumni: Don't come back. (1998, October 24). *Amarillo Globe*. Retrieved June 9, 2008, from http://www.amarillo.com/stories/102498/new_bjuniv.shtml

Brantlinger, E. (2009). Impediments to social justice: Hierarchy, science, faith, and imposed identity (disability classification). In W. Ayers, T. Quinn, & D. Stovall (Eds.), *Handbook of social justice in education*, pp. 400-16. New York: Taylor & Francis/Routledge.

Butin, D. (2007, Summer). Dark times indeed: NCATE, social justice, and the marginalization of multicultural foundations. *Journal of Educational Controversy, 2(2)*. Retrieved September 21, 2008, from http://www.wce.wwu.edu/Resources/CEP/eJournal/v002n002/a003.shtml

Canaday, M. (2009). *The straight state: Sexuality and citizenship in twentieth century America*. Princeton, NJ: Princeton University Press.

Carlson, P. (2005, May 5). Taking the Bob out of Bob Jones U: Christian institution readies for the next generation. *Washington Post*, p. C01.

Casper, V., & Schultz, S. (1999). *Gay parents/straight schools: Building communication and trust*. New York: Teachers College Press.

Chasnoff, D. (2009, April 17). "Getting real" about bullying-related suicides. *Huffington Post*. Retrieved August 12, 2009, from http://www.huffingtonpost.com/debra-chasnoff/getting-real-about-bullyi_b_188043.html

Cohen, C. (2005). Punks, bulldaggers, and welfare queens: The radical potential of queer politics? In Johnson, P. & Henderson, M. (Eds.), *Black queer studies* (pp. 22-51). Durham, NC: Duke University Press.

Cosier, K. (2009). Creating safe schools for queer youth. In Ayers, W., Quinn, T., & Stovall, D. (Eds.), *Handbook for social justice in education* (pp. 285-303). New York: Routledge.

Crenshaw, K. (1991). Mapping the margins: Intersectionality, identity politics, and violence against women of color. *Stanford Law Review, 43(6)*, 1241-99.

de Castell, S., & Bryson, M. (1998). From the ridiculous to the sublime: On finding oneself in educational research. In Pinar, W. (Ed.), *Queer theory in education* (pp. 245-50). New York: Lawrence Erlbaum.

Diaz, E. M., & Kosciw, J. G. (2009). *Shared differences: The experiences of lesbian, gay, bisexual, and transgender students of color in our nation's schools*. New York: GLSEN.

Duggan, L. (2003). *The twilight of equality: Neoliberalism, cultural politics and the attack on democracy*. Boston: Beacon Press.

Duke, T. (2007). Hidden, invisible, marginalized, and ignored: A critical review of the professional and empirical literature (or lack thereof) on gay and lesbian teachers in the United States. *Journal of Gay & Lesbian Issues in Education, 4(4)*, 19-38.

Epstein, D. (Ed.). (1994). *Challenging lesbian and gay inequalities in education*. Philadelphia: Open University Press.

Epstein, S. (2009). A gross unfairness. *The Nation*. Retrieved August 10, 2009, from http://www.thenation.com/doc/20090817/epstein

Eskridge, W. (2000, November). No promo homo: The sedimentation of antigay discourse and the channeling effect of judicial review. *New York University Law Review, 75,* 1328–1411.

Faderman, L. (1991). *Odd girls and twilight lovers: A history of lesbian life in 20th century America.* New York: Columbia University Press.

Fine, M., & McClelland, S. (2006). Sexuality education and desire: Still missing after all these years. *Harvard Educational Review, 76(3),* 297–338.

Gay, Lesbian, Straight Educators Network. (2007). 2007 national climate school survey. Retrieved May 25, 2009, from http://www.glsen.org/binary-data/GLSEN_ATTACHMENTS/file/000/001/1306-1.pdf

Gilmore, R. (2007). In the shadow of the shadow state. In INCITE! Women of Color against Violence (Eds.), *The revolution will not be funded: Beyond the non-profit prison industrial complex* (pp. 41–52). Boston: South End Press.

Graves, K. (2009). *And they were wonderful teachers: Florida's purge of gay and lesbian teachers.* Champaign: University of Illinois Press.

Griffin v. School Board of St. Edward. (1964). Retrieved May 20, 2008, from http://afroamhistory.about.com/library/blgriffin_v_princeedward.htm

Grossman, A., Haney, A., Edwards, P., Alessi, E., Ardon, M., & Howell, T. (2009). Lesbian, gay, bisexual, and transgender youth talk about experiencing and coping with school violence: A qualitative study. *Journal of LGBT Youth, 6(1),* 24–46.

Harvey, D. (2005). *A brief history of neoliberalism.* New York: Oxford University Press.

Horn, S., & Szalacha, L. (2007). Chicago Public Schools youth risk behavior survey, 2005. Board of Education of the City of Chicago. Retrieved July 16, 2007, from http://209.85.215.104/search?q=cache:IQHvB8VMhlsJ:www.oism.cps.k12.il.us/pdf/2005yrbs.pdf+2003+Youth+Risk+Survey+CDS+Chicago+Public+Schools&hl=en&ct=clnk&cd=1&gl=us

Horowitz, A., & Hansen, A. (2008). Out for equity: School-based support for LGBTQA youth. *Journal of LGBT Youth, 5(2),* 73–85.

Jakobsen, J. & Pellegrini, A. (2003). *Love the sin: Sexual regulation and the limits of religious tolerance.* New York: University Press.

Jennings, K. (Ed.). (1994). *One teacher in 10: Gay and lesbian educators tell their stories.* Boston: Alyson.

Jennings, T., & Sherwin, G. (2008). Sexual orientation topics in elementary teacher preparation programs in the USA. *Teaching Education, 19(4),* 261–78.

Johnson, B., & Johnson, D. (2007). An analysis of NCATE's decision to drop "Social Justice." *Journal of Educational Controversy, 2(2).* Retrieved August 10, 2008, from http://www.wce.wwu.edu/Resources/CEP/eJournal/v002n002/a004.shtml

Johnson, D., Johnson, B., Farenga, S., & Ness, D. (2005). *Trivializing teacher education: The accreditation squeeze.* New York: Rowman & Littlefield.

Katz, J. (2003). *Love stories: Sex between men before homosexuality.* Chicago: University of Chicago Press.

Khayatt, M. (1992). *Lesbian teachers: An invisible presence.* Albany: State University of New York Press.

Koch, C. A. (2000). Attitudes, knowledge, and anticipated behaviors of preservice teachers of individuals with different sexual orientations. *Dissertation Abstracts International, 61(05),* 1797A. (UMI No. 9973083).

Kosciw, J. G., & Diaz, E. M. (2006). *The 2005 national school climate survey: The experiences of lesbian, gay, bisexual and transgender youth in our nation's schools.* New York: GLSEN.

Kumashiro, K. (2004). Against common sense: Teaching and learning toward social justice. New York: Routledge.

Ladson-Billings, G. (2004). Landing on the wrong note: The price we paid for *Brown. Educational Researcher, 33(7),* 3–13.

Lassiter, M. (2006). *The silent majority: Suburban politics in the Sunbelt south.* Princeton, NJ: Princeton University.

Linville, D. (2008). Queer theory and teen sexuality: Unclear lines. In Anyon, J. (Ed.), *Theory and educational research: Toward critical social explanation* (pp. 153–74). New York: Routledge.

Lipsitz, G. (1998). *The possessive investment in whiteness: How white people profit from identity politics.* Philadelphia: Temple University Press.

Lugg, C. (2003). Sissies, faggots, lezzies, and dykes: Gender, sexual orientation, and a new politics of education? *Educational Administration Quarterly, 39(1),* 95–134.

Lugg, C. (2004). One nation under God? Religion and the politics of education in a post-9/11 America. *Educational Policy, 18(1),* 169–87.

Lugg, C. (2006). Thinking about sodomy: Public schools, legal panopticons, and queers. *Educational Policy, 20(1),* 35–58.

Macgillivray, I. (2000). Educational equity for gay, lesbian, bisexual, transgendered, and queer/questioning students: The demands of democracy and social justice for America's schools. *Education and Urban Society, 32(3),* 303–32.

Macgillivray, I., & Jennings, T. (2008). A content analysis exploring lesbian, gay, bisexual, and transgender topics in foundations of education textbooks. *Journal of Teacher Education, 59(2),* 170–88.

Mack, T., & Picower, B. (2008). *Planning to change the world: A plan book for social justice teachers.* New York: New York Collective of Radical Educators and Education for Liberation Network.

Massachusetts Department of Education. (2002). 2001 youth risk behavior survey results. Retrieved October 10, 2008, from www.doe.mass.edu/cnp/hprograms/yrbs/01/results.pdf

Mayo, C. (2009). Access and obstacles: Gay-straight alliances attempt to alter school communities. In Ayers, W., Quinn, T., & Stovall, D. (Eds.), *Handbook for social justice in education* (pp. 319–31). New York: Routledge.

McCready, L. (2009). Social justice education for black male students in urban schools: Making space for diverse masculinities. In Ayers, W., Quinn, T., & Stovall, D. (Eds.), *Handbook for social justice in education* (pp. 332–44). New York: Routledge.

McIntyre, A. (1997). *Making meaning of whiteness: Exploring racial identity with white teachers.* Albany: SUNY Press.

Meyer, E. (2009). *Gender, bullying, and harassment: Strategies to end sexism and homophobia in schools.* New York: Teacher's College Press.

Mills, C. (1997). *The racial contract.* Ithaca, NY: Cornell University Press.

Nader L. (1974 [1969]) Up the anthropologist - Perspectives gained from studying up. In D. Hymes (Ed.). *Reinventing anthropology,* pp. 284–311. New York: Vintage Books.

National Council for Accreditation of Teacher Education. (NCATE). (n.d.). *Glossary.* Retrieved September 19, 2006, from http://www.ncate.org/public/glossary.asp?ch=143

National Council for Accreditation of Teacher Education. (NCATE). (2008, January 8). State Partnership Programs FAQs. Retrieved August, 2009, from http://www.ncate.org/states/partnershipFAQ.asp?ch=96

North, C. (2008). *Teaching for social justice? Voices from the front lines.* Boulder, CO: Paradigm Press.

Ng, R., Staton, P., & Scane, J. (Eds.). (1995). *Anti-racism, feminism, and critical approaches to education.* Toronto: OISE Press.

Nieto, S. (2003). *What keeps teachers going?* New York: Teachers College Press.

Pascoe, C. J. (2007). *Dude, you're a fag: Masculinity and sexuality in high school.* Berkeley: University of California Press.

Pateman, C. (1989). *The sexual contract.* Cambridge, MA: Polity Press.

Perrillo, J. (2004). Beyond "Progressive" reform: Bodies, discipline and the construction of the professional teacher in interwar America. *History of Education Quarterly, 44(3),* 337–63.

Queer Planet. (1992, December 6). *A human rights report.* Retrieved November 30, 2007, from http://www.qrd.org/qrd/world/1993/queerplanet/qpq-11.92a1

Quinn, T. (2007). "You make me erect!": Queer girls of color negotiating heteronormative leadership at an urban all-girls' public school. *Journal of Gay and Lesbian Issues in Education, 4(3)*, 31–47.

Quinn, T., & Meiners, E. (2007). Do ask, do tell: What's "professional" about taking social justice and sexual orientation out of public school classrooms? *Rethinking Schools, 21(4)*, 25–26.

Quinn, T., & Meiners, E. (2009). *Flaunt it! Queers organizing for public education and justice.* New York: Peter Lang.

Roberts, G., Allan, C., & Wells, K. (2007). Understanding gender identity in K–12 schools. *Journal of Gay & Lesbian Issues in Education, 4(4)*, 119–30.

Rofes, E. (2005). *A radical rethinking of sexuality & schooling: Status quo or status queer.* New York: Rowman & Littlefield.

Rousmaniere, Kate. (1997). *City Teachers: Teaching and school reform in historical perspective.* New York: Teachers College Press.

Russell, S. (2008, April 25). Remembering Lawrence King: An agenda for educators, schools, and scholars. *Teachers College Record.* Retrieved July 7, 2008, from http://www.tcrecord.org ID Number: 15236.

Russo, R. (2006). The extent of public education nondiscrimination policy protections for lesbian, gay, bisexual and transgender students: A national study. *Urban Education, 41(2)*, 115–50.

Ryan, J. (2004). *Brown,* school choice, and the suburban veto. *Virginia Law Review, 90,* 1635–47. Retrieved May 20, 2009, from http://64.233.167.104/search?q=cache:oXNyGnsMezoJ:www.virginialawreview.org/content/pdfs/90/1635.pdf+segregation+academies+tradition&hl=en&ct=clnk&cd=10&gl=us

Saxon, W. (1995, May 20). Albertis S. Harrison Jr., 88, dies: Led Virginia as segregation fell. *New York Times.* Retrieved May 20, 2009, from http://query.nytimes.com/gst/fullpage.htm l?res=990CE5D81E3EF936A15752C0A963958260

Scott, J., Lubienski, C., & DeBray-Pelot, E. (2009). The politics of advocacy in education. *Educational Policy, 23(1)*, 3–14.

Setoodeh, R. (2008, July 19). Young, gay and murdered. *Newsweek.* Retrieved August 13, 2009, from http://www.newsweek.com/id/147790/page/1

Smiler, A. (2009). Unintentional gender lessons in schools. In W. Ayers, T. Quinn, & D. Stovall (Eds.), *Handbook of social justice in education,* pp. 358–70. New York: Taylor & Francis/Routledge.

Sommerville, S. B. (2000). *Queering the color line: Race and the invention of homosexuality in American culture.* Durham, NC: Duke University Press.

Stiegler, S. (2009). Queer youth as teachers: Dismantling silence of queer issues in a teacher preparation program. *Journal of LGBT Youth, 5(4)*, 116–23.

Stitzlein, S. (2007). Skill and persistence in gender crossing and nonconformity among children. *Journal of Gay & Lesbian Issues in Education, 4(2)*, 13–32.

Swanson, C., & Barlage, J. (2006, December). Influence: A study of the factors shaping education policy. *Education Week.* Retrieved July 12, 2008, from http://www.edweek.org/media/influence_execsum.pdf

Szalacha, L. (2005). The research terrain: A brief overview of the historical framework for LGBTQ studies in education. In Sears, J. (Ed.), *Gay, lesbian, and transgender issues in education: Programs, policies, and practice* (pp. 77–88). New York: Routledge.

Tamir, E., & Wilson, S. M. (2005). Who should guard the gates? Evidentiary and professional warrants for claiming jurisdiction. *Journal of Teacher Education, 56,* 332–42.

Teacher Education Accreditation Council. (2009, June 20–21). Minutes, Teacher Education Accreditation Council Annual Board of Directors Meeting. Scottsdale, AZ. Retrieved July 31, 2009, from http://www.teac.org/wp-content/uploads/2009/03/board_minutes_june2009.pdf

Telljohann, S. K., Price, J. H., Poureslami, M., & Easton, A. (1995). Teaching about sexual orientation by secondary health teachers. *Journal of School Health, 65(1)*, 18–22.

Tozer, S., Violas, P., & Senese, G. (1998). *School and society: Historical and contemporary perspectives.* Boston: McGraw-Hill.

Unterhalter, E. (2007). *Gender, schooling, and global social justice.* New York: Routledge.

Visibility matters: Higher education and teacher preparation in Illinois: A web-based assessment of LGBTQ presence. (2009). Illinois Safe Schools Alliance. Retrieved June 30, 2009, from http://www.illinoissafeschools.org/page_attachments/0000/0030/VisibilityMatters_ReportCard.pdf

Wolch, J. (1990). *The shadow state: government and voluntary sector in transition.* New York: The Foundation Center.

Yale Law Journal. (1973, June). Segregation academies and state action. *82(7)*, 1436–61.

Zehr, M. (2006, May). A clear stand: Religious schools are being pressed to spell out their policies regarding gay students and the children of same-sex couples. *Education Week, 25(37)*, 27–30.

6

Crossing Boundaries, Studying Diversity

Lessons From Preservice Teachers and Urban Youth

Valerie Kinloch

> Yet the eager teachers do appear and reappear—teachers who provoke learners to pose their own questions, to teach themselves, to go at their own pace, to name their worlds. Young learners have to be noticed, it is now being realized; they have to be consulted; they have to question why.
>
> —Maxine Greene, 2000, p. 11

On a Tuesday night in the spring of 2007, I invited my seniors from an English language arts class that I was teaching in a Harlem high school to attend my teacher education graduate course at a local university. The graduate course, focused on diversity, difference, and multiculturalism in the teaching of English, was primarily comprised of white, female, preservice teachers—with a very small percentage of students of color and white males—who were nearing the end of their degree program and student-teaching placements in middle and high schools in New York City. For fifteen weeks, we came together to examine a variety of topics, including teacher knowledge, cultural and community practices, whiteness, white privilege, silence and action, and teaching multilingual and bidialectical students of color. These topics were framed around specific inquiry questions: How can we constructively interrogate meanings of diversity and difference as we examine current debates on language (e.g., variances, practices)? In what ways can conversations on "teaching for diversity" (see Center for Multicultural Education, 2001) include students' lived experiences and racial, ethnic, and cultural identities? How is *power* defined in the presence of categories (e.g., poor, working class, wealthy, white, of color), and what are the educative and political consequences of relying on these categories? How can we discuss multiculturalism by investigating culture and place and by interrogating teaching practices, experiences, and assumptions as related to research on diversity in teacher education?

These questions sparked various conversations on teaching in a multicultural society and its public schools, particularly in light of statistics that predict an increase in the number of immigrants in the United States (Rich, 2000) and the number of students of color in our classrooms (Holloway, 1993; National Center for Education Statistics, 1999–2000; Pallas, Natriello, & McDill, 1989; Pratt & Rittenhouse, 1998). At the backdrop of such statistics, our inquiry questions required examination of personal assumptions, pedagogical practices, and ideological belief systems in relation to teaching in diverse classrooms, communities, after-school programs, and summer enrichment workshops. It also required us to talk with and listen to the perspectives—cultural, social, community, ideological—of students (in this case, high school students) who are oftentimes left out of conversations on teaching and teacher education. As educators and researchers, I believe we must increase our current efforts to explicitly address the absence of youth voices in educational scholarship concerned with teaching, diversity, and difference. Only then will our work have a stronger impact on policy decisions and democratized forms of engagement among students and teachers in a variety of settings.

With these things in mind, this chapter describes lessons that emerged when two groups of students—preservice teachers and urban high school students—crossed boundaries to engage in classroom discussions on meanings and perceptions of teaching, teachers, and students in urban public schools and lays a foundation for future research in this area. The guiding research question is: In what ways can preservice and high school students from racially and culturally different backgrounds engage in critical discussions about teaching and learning, and what are specific lessons that can emerge? Drawing on Greene's (2000) belief that "young learners have to be noticed, it is now being realized; they have to be consulted; they have to question why" (p. 11), the chapter is framed in a brief review of literature in teacher research and on teaching and researching with urban youth. This framework leads into the chapter's methodological design, which employs a teacher-researcher reflexive lens to investigate how two racially different groups of students engaged in boundary crossings (i.e., ideologically; geographically; racially) to critique assumptions about teaching, diversity, and urban students. Through the findings, implications for urban teaching and teacher research in a multicultural society emerge. Such implications, as I will discuss, point to an ongoing need for teacher preparation programs to better prepare prospective teachers (who are mostly white) to work with various student populations (including urban and multilingual students of color).

LITERATURE REVIEW AND THEORETICAL FRAMING

On Teacher Research

In "The Teacher Research Movement: A Decade Later," educational researchers Cochran-Smith and Lytle (1999) examine the place of teacher research and practitioner inquiry in the United States. Arguing that teacher research is an embodiment of several intellectual traditions, they describe five specific trends that characterize teacher research as a movement. These trends include: the interconnections of teacher research to education, development, and reform measures; the emergence of critical theories and frameworks for research on teaching and teacher education; local and global effects of teacher education research; analyses of teacher research as a field and as a movement; and the impact of teacher research on universities.

Acknowledging the 1970s and 1980s paradigm shift that described teachers as thinkers and knowers, or, as Berthoff (1987) asserted, as "RE-searchers" who sought professional conversations on teaching with other teachers (see also Atwell, 1987), Cochran-Smith and Lytle also recognize teacher research designed as forms of "social action and social change" (p. 15). That is, in addition to a group of teachers and researchers representing school and university collaborations and progressive forms of education, there was a group of teacher educators and researchers "rooted in an ethnographic research tradition and a multi-disciplinary understanding of language, literacy, and pedagogy" (p. 16). These two groups and their differing approaches, traditions, and perspectives on teacher research are beneficial because they articulate new visions of teachers as researchers as opposed to technicians (Apple, 1986), or mechanical transmitters of knowledge.

Cochran-Smith and Lytle's (1990, 1993, 1999) scholarship is significant for many reasons, given its critique of the changing practice of teaching and its emphasis on teachers' knowledge production, power, agency, and voice. Their research serves as a foundation by which other studies on teaching and teacher education implicitly and/or explicitly rely. Clearly, the movement toward scholarship that positions teachers as active researchers is marked by important, contemporary work. In *Multicultural Strategies for Education and Social Change: Carriers of the Torch in the United States and South Africa*, Ball (2006) examines teacher education, teacher efficacy, and the teaching of racially and linguistically diverse students across two contexts. Doing so, Ball is able to conceive of expanded ways to successfully assist teachers in dealing with the demands of a changing world—demands that result from shifting school and community demographics, globalization, and the ongoing educational marginalization of disenfranchised people of color in the United States and South Africa. Important here is Ball's critical emphasis on the globalization and reformation of teacher research and teacher education in ways that privilege teacher perspectives in debates on teaching racially, linguistically, and ethnically diverse students. Hence, she engages in an important expansion of meanings of teaching, schooling, and social change that positions teachers as researchers (Berthoff, 1987; Cochran-Smith & Lytle, 1999; Lee, 1997, 2007). At the same time, Ball engages Sleeter's (2001) insistence "to focus on preservice teachers' classroom performance in schools in which children of color and children from poverty backgrounds get clustered and to investigate what happens in preservice programs that significantly develops their teaching" (pp. 219–20).

Ball (1995, 2003, 2006) is not alone in her efforts to present expansive viewpoints of educational research in teaching and teacher education. Other researchers have begun to investigate the nexus among teacher knowledge, pedagogy, and cultural practices in relation to pre- and in-service teachers and teacher researchers. At the same time, attention has been placed on how teachers academically prepare students for the world in which they live. Offering a critical perspective on improving urban youth literacy skills, Lee's (2007) *Culture, Literacy, and Learning: Taking Bloom in the Midst of the Whirlwind*, theorizes student engagements with familiar discourses and repertoires: African American English, hip-hop and popular culture, and forms of cultural knowledge from primary communities of socialization (see Gee, 2001). Such engagements, paired with her teaching practices and "Cultural Modeling Project," serve as the basis of collaborations across dimensions of learning (i.e., social; emotional; cognitive) that promote the place of cultural knowledge in the attainment of academic knowledge. Lee's scholarship, grounded in cultural modeling and learning sciences, critiques the role, knowledge, and problem-posing skills (see Shor, 1992) of teachers in relation to the education of diverse students.

In terms of connections between teacher knowledge and student academic achievement, educational scholars are also exploring how critical inquiry, methodologically, can challenge students and teachers working "toward an understanding of language, literacy, and pedagogy" (Cochran-Smith & Lytle, 1999, p. 16). Fecho (2004), for instance, believes that students and teachers should be able to experience risks as they collaboratively search for meanings related to language, power, boundary crossings, and schooling. In his timely book, *"Is This English?" Race, Language, and Culture in the Classroom*, Fecho powerfully states, "We who teach and learn in everyday classrooms fail to see the same need to call educational space into question, and, as anthropologists do, make the familiar strange" (p. 156). His attempts to "make the familiar strange" by transacting with students, colleagues, and texts respond to Cochran-Smith and Lytle's call for research that articulates new, expanded visions of teachers and teaching.

Additionally, there is a growing need for further research, grounded in a multicultural framework (see Banks, 1996; National Association for Multicultural Education, 2003), on teaching, teacher education, and teacher and student knowledge. Sleeter (2005), in *Un-Standardizing the Curriculum: Multicultural Teaching in the Standards-Based Classroom*, challenges educators to consider how multicultural curricula can be rigorously taught in light of current constraints posed by educational standards. In her promotion of high academic standards for teachers and students, Sleeter offers critical insights into the challenges faced by countless teachers and discusses the possibilities for teachers to make their practices and pedagogies more expansive. In many ways, I believe that Sleeter's (2001, 2005) research sets the stage for additional work in multicultural education and social justice. For example, Teel and Obidah's (2008) edited collection, *Building Radical and Cultural Competence in the Classroom*, takes up Sleeter's challenge for educators to "un-standardize" the curriculum through a multicultural framework. Contributors to Teel and Obidah's collection describe the influence that race and culture have on teaching, teacher quality, and academic achievement of students of color. They insist that if teachers strengthen their cultural competences, then students will receive more critical forms of education. Together, Sleeter's scholarship, Teel and Obidah's collection, and studies conducted by other researchers (Ball, 2006; Lee, 2007; Richardson, 1994) are not only responsive to Cochran-Smith and Lytle's (1999) call for work that articulates new visions of teachers and teaching. They also encourage us to draw on multiple frameworks, including multicultural education, to think of students as active learners.

On Teaching and Researching With Urban Youth

I believe it is essential for research on teaching and teacher education, particularly situated within a multicultural framework and in sociocultural theory, to account for students' academic interactions. Doing so poses the rich potential to understand the role played by teachers, schools, local communities, and family-peer networks in students' academic performances and cognitive, emotional, and social dimensions of learning. In other words, it is important to position both teachers and students at the center of discussions on knowledge, culture, literacy, and social change. For example, Morrell's (2008) *Critical Literacy and Urban Youth: Pedagogies of Access, Dissent, and Liberation* draws on the tradition of critical theory to discuss meanings of literacy education and social change in the lives of teachers and in the education of urban youth. To fulfill the promise of describing an extended, more inclusive definition of "critical," Morrell turns his attention to four case studies involving students and their teacher. They include popular culture in a secondary-level English class, cyberactivism and cyberspace, community research, and critical media literacy. These cases point to a grounded theory of literacy and critical literacy pedagogy that constructs classrooms, schools, and communities as democratic spaces (see Kinloch, 2005, 2009) for teachers and students. In this way, Morrell contributes to an expanded view of teaching and research that "respects teachers as agents and intellectuals" (p. 13), supports collaborative teacher networks, and encourages students to be actively involved in their own learning.

To further develop the idea of expansive learning in ways that position teachers and students as agents of social, political, and educative change, Fisher's (2007) *Writing in Rhythm: Spoken Word Poetry in Urban Classrooms* explores the power of literacy through the medium of spoken word poetry. Working with Joe, a language arts teacher, and African American and Latino youth in "Power Writers," an after-school writing program in Brooklyn, New York, Fisher describes classroom strategies that honor students' lived experiences and provides them with the academic tools to write and perform their stories. Similarly, Jocson's (2008) *Youth Poets: Empowering Literacies in and out of Schools* employs a sociocultural framework to discuss intersections of pedagogy and literacy on the one hand and the production of poetry and the attainment of academic literacies on the other hand. To do so, she investigates the writing lives of seven students who craft, perform, and publish poetry; acts that can find themselves inside of classrooms and that can contribute to a research tradition that articulates multiple approaches to teacher and student knowledge, literacy, and identity (Ball, 2006; Lee, 2007; Schultz, 2003).

There are countless other studies that support the call for expanded definitions of literacy for teachers and students. From Campano's (2007) literacy work with immigrant youth, Yagelski's (2000) questioning of the role of literacy's ambiguity in the lives of students and teachers, to Michie's (1999, 2005) strategies for teaching for social justice in an urban context, educational research has begun to account for the diverse, creative ways teaching connects to learning in multiple contexts and with multiple students. In my own research on the implications of race and place on youth narratives of community change (Kinloch, 2007a, 2007b, 2010), I describe an expansive vision of literacy that accounts for out-of-school spaces of learning (e.g., a gentrifying community, a tenants' association meeting). The students in that work draw on writing and multimodal forms of communication to produce literacy responses to spatial changes within their familial community. Doing so demonstrates their critical capacities that are often untapped in the space of schools, on the one hand, and describes the shifting roles played by students and teachers in a multicultural society on the other hand (see also Kinloch, 2009).

The aforementioned scholars and their scholarship contribute to advancing educational research, generally, and teacher education and literacy research, particularly, through diverse methodological approaches, theoretical perspectives, and spaces of learning. The study presented in this chapter contributes to this body of scholarship in its investigations of democratic engagements (Kinloch, 2010) between two groups of students—youth of color attending an urban high school; white preservice students in a teacher education program—and me, a university professor and a visiting high school teacher. Thus, this work serves as a model for the kind of scholarship that is currently needed on diversity in teacher education. This work extends the conversation from what we already *know* about diversity to what we now need *to do* to account for the perspectives of preservice teachers and urban youth in a climate of rapidly changing political and educational initiatives. More immediately, one thing we can do, as described throughout this chapter, is to work at accelerating educational parity across geographical, racial, and economic boundaries. Doing so requires us to account for expansive visions of teaching, understandings of diversity, and debates over differences as articulated not simply by what theory tells us but by what preservice teachers and high school students teach us.

METHODOLOGICAL APPROACH:
ON DATA COLLECTION AND ANALYSIS

This chapter reports on data collected during the 2006–2007 academic year when I was a teacher-researcher in a mandatory senior-level English class at Perennial High School in New York City. I first entered the high school in September 2006 to work with two students, Alexandria and Antonio, whom a handful of teachers described as "problematic," "loud," "unruly" (Alexandria), and "disengaged" (Antonio). My work with Alexandria and Antonio, however, revealed the opposite. Alexandria was an intense and active reader who devoured novels by Edwidge Danticat and Toni Morrison with deliberate speed; she was fascinated by genre studies, romantic drama, and street lit. Antonio displayed a critical capacity for literacy that oftentimes went untapped by his teachers. He shared stories with Alexandria and me about his participation in community events, his reading of magazines and newspapers, and his interest in solving mathematical problems. The identity markers placed on Alexandria and Antonio by their teachers, then, were not accurate depictions of their intellectual capacities, academic and personal interests, or attitudes toward schooling. Such observations, which disrupted how students were labeled and positioned in classes, specifically, and in school, generally, encouraged me to work with other students at Perennial in an effort to understand the conflicting ways in which teachers marked students. Thus, I accepted the principal's invitation to teach a mandatory senior English course at the school, which spanned from January to July 2007.

For five days a week, I taught a class of approximately thirty students on varying learning levels and with multiple literacy strengths and challenges. Various teachers at Perennial *warned* me that some students would not complete assigned work (in class or at home) and would resist being pushed in intellectually stimulating ways: "There's Christina, and she's always giving everyone a problem," shared one teacher. "Keep an eye out for Ramon because he won't write a sentence for you, but he'll act out at the drop of a pin," commented another teacher. Such remarks motivated me to employ a critical teacher-researcher self-reflexive lens to question such deeply rooted assumptions about urban students' abilities to not perform well, if at all. In so doing, I designed the course around themes of community and literacy, focusing heavily on the local community (Harlem) where students lived and attended school. We studied poets and poetry from the Harlem Renaissance, read articles and news stories about the history of Harlem, and examined books about urban schooling. Our critical readings were complemented by rigorous writing assignments that students and I oftentimes collaboratively designed. These included persuasive essays paired with original spoken-word poetry and performances, multimodal writing projects on a community topic, and, among other assignments, extended journal responses to course readings accompanied by original music lyrics performed on an electric guitar. Learning, in this academic context, was rich, reciprocal, democratic, and multiple.

Thus, the larger project engaged in critical analyses of students on the periphery of high school graduation and participation in a larger world that they questioned and that questioned them (e.g., racially, linguistically, culturally). Employing qualitative research methods (e.g., classroom-based student observations, class discussions, collected student writings, interviews) and using a critical teacher-researcher reflexive lens (Campano, 2007; Fecho, 2004; Michie, 2005), I observed students' active participation in their learning through processes involving reading, writing, questioning, and collaborating. At the same time that students critiqued negative depictions of their Harlem community (e.g., in disrepair, in need of gentrification), they rejected the attitudes of teachers that painted them as disengaged products of their familial communities. With this in mind, I wanted my preservice teacher education candidates to listen to (Schultz, 2003) my high school students talk honestly about needing teachers to reject negative characterizations of urban students' intellectual capacities. Therefore, the data presented in this chapter derive from a class session held at the university with my teacher education candidates (n = 18) and some of my high school students (n = 12). In addition to Khaleeq, a youth participant from my other, separate Harlem project,[1] one of the language teachers from Perennial, whom students highly respected, was also present. From the collection and analyses of video footage, teacher-researcher field notes, separate follow-up discussions with both groups of students, and a series of follow-up questions from my teacher education candidates and shared with my high school students, I examine the ways high school students crossed boundaries to critique meanings of and purposes of teaching for diversity (with future teachers) in an urban context.

To address my research question, I analyzed video and audio recordings of the class session and identified various perspectives, articulated by students, on teaching and learning. Other themes that I identified included fostering a learning community around texts and lived experiences, creating and supporting insightful meaning-making moments through critical literacy encounters, building trust through open student-teacher dialogue, and implementing an equity pedagogy in classrooms and schools. In what follows, I present the results of the class session, discuss its significance for what we know about teaching and teacher education, and describe its larger implications for studying and researching diversity.

Findings

The overarching goal of this study and its analysis is to describe lessons that emerged when two different groups of students gathered together at a local university to discuss perceptions of teaching, urban students, and diversity. To do this, I present two cases from my class session with high school students and preservice teachers. The first case presents data on how students grappled with meanings of equity and equality, which quickly led to a discussion of students' performances of routine academic tasks and the need for students and teachers to work interactively. The second case opens with a question posed by Ruth, a preservice teacher, on students and teachers collaborating, taking responsibility for learning, and creating supportive, critical classroom spaces. Her question leads to how Sharif, a high school student, demonstrates student work that can emerge from such an environment where students and teachers work toward "a common ground."

Confronting Differences, Making Meaning

I began our class session by writing two words on the blackboard:
  EQUITY
  EQUALITY
Underneath these two words I scribbled the term *pedagogy*. Hoping to establish connections across the individual lessons being taught to the two groups of students gathered in the room—my teacher education candidates and high school English seniors—I invited them to draw on prior knowledge, lived experiences, and specific course texts to think through these terms. In a matter of seconds, Yvette, an African American high school student sitting at the top of the room, turned around in her chair, stared at the board, and commented, "Well, IN-equality means unfairness, not equal, not enough, and from that we know what equality means!" Noticing others nodding their heads in agreement and shying away from the word *equity*, Yvette stared at me to call on someone else. "Can someone define equity?" I asked, which was followed by a lengthy bout of silence. I continued, "We've heard of schools encouraging 'Campaigns for Educational Equity,' right? So, tell me what this means." For the last five-to-six years, the local university where, on this spring evening, two racially and economically different groups of students crossed boundaries to discuss perceptions of urban teaching, teachers, and students, had increased its concentration on issues of educational equity. Committed to the advancement of "equity and excellence in education . . . [and] expanding and strengthening the national movement for quality public education for all," the university's attention to equity was commendable.[2] Yet understandings of equity and practices in equity pedagogy did not easily transfer into practical terms for my preservice teachers and high school students, which was evident in their hesitation to explain its meanings in a local or national context.

According to Banks and Banks (1995), equity pedagogy refers to "teaching strategies and classroom environments that help students from diverse racial, ethnic, and cultural groups attain the knowledge, skills, and attitudes needed to function effectively within, and help create and perpetuate, a just, humane, and democratic society" (p. 152). This conceptualization of equity pedagogy also refers to the ways in which students are taught to critique structures of power, "assumptions, paradigms, and hegemonic characteristics" (p. 152). Indeed, my students, particularly my urban youth, were readers and writers, critical of the world in which they lived and of dominant power structures that cultivated inequality. However, their intellectual abilities to read and write did not necessarily parallel a fundamental goal of equity pedagogy; that is, to transfer one's critical capacities into actions that could produce agents of social change in a democratic world. Hence, from my observations and conversations with both groups of students individually and in small groups, I believe their hesitation to address meanings of equity pointed to two possible factors. These included: (1) an initial resistance to talk about equity in a large group and across racial, economic, and geographical differences for fear of being "called out" or *Othered*, and (2) an initial resistance to articulate feelings on a topic that is oftentimes not explicitly discussed in classrooms where teachers and students are positioned as active learners instead of teachers as transmitters and students as receivers of knowledge. Both of these possibilities, in my opinion, speak to the historically naïve ways we, as a field, have engaged students and colleagues in pubic critiques about, across, and directly related to race, class, place, and educational equity. Instead of learning to talk (and listen), we have learned to remain silent in the presence of differences.

Taking seriously Banks and Banks's (1995) insistence that we do not overlook the critical lessons gained from engaging in equity pedagogy—critiquing assumptions about students, teachers, and learning; dismantling unbalanced and inequitable educational structures—I asked students to think and write about as well as offer detailed examples of equity and equality for our next class session. "Provide definitions, conceptualizations, examples," I asked, "because these two words are at the heart of what we're talking about when we examine stereotypes people have of certain students they consider to be *at risk* or *underprepared* or *developmental* or *remedial*. And then at the bottom of that list of labels tends to fall the word *urban*. Why's that?" By asking students to contemplate meanings of (in)equality and (in)equity, I was hoping to stimulate larger conversations in which students and preservice teacher candidates would collaboratively interrogate long-standing perceptions they had of each other, of schooling, and of urban teaching and urban education.

Mariana, a Latina high school student sitting on a table near the back of the room, asked to speak about the ways in which teachers are trained and how they interact with students, which, for Mariana, related to discussions on equality and equity. She commented: "I don't know if this the right way . . . But one way, maybe, to talk about this is by thinking about skills teachers got when they leave their ed program." One of her peers, Sophie, an African American student sitting close by, whispered, "Or skills they don't *got*" (speaker's verbal emphasis). Nodding in agreement, Mariana explained: "They [teachers] need to know reality, about how urban schools are, stop thinking we don't know how to read and write, give us more." In this case, the more that Mariana was referring to relates to Banks and Banks's (1995) argument that we critique assumptions we have of others as we engage an equity pedagogy, which can result in the eventual dismantling of inequitable educational practices, pedagogies, and institutional structures. In some ways, it also parallels Lee's (2007) insistence that we employ multiple dimensions of learning to yield educative collaborations between students and teachers and to promote cultural learning *and* the attainment of academic achievement.

Take the following exchange between high school students, Mariana and Sophie, and a preservice teacher of color, Imani, as an example:

Mariana: I'm serious 'cause some teachers just go and give us textbooks as the work and they don't do no work with you [students]. They don't interact with you and you don't learn nothing. And if you have a great teacher who interacts with you and makes the lessons fun and understand where you come from and the problems you face, then it makes everything much easier because kids would learn more and would want to come to school more. That's the way I see it.

Imani: By definition, what is a great teacher as opposed to one who's not?

Mariana: I mean, like, if you go to class and you have to be there by 9:15 and they put the Do Now and Aim on the board—and you have to do the Do Now on your own. And . . . then they give you book work and then after book work you gotta answer questions. And after the questions, you gotta do worksheets and after worksheets you gotta write essays. Now, a good teacher would make these things more interactive and base things on your real life and have students do related tasks. And I think that's a good teacher.

Sophie: And you're still doing the work.

Mariana: Exactly. You're getting more out of it and you're learning from all points of view.

Mariana's statements on how students routinely perform academic tasks assigned by teachers—"do the Do Now"; "after book work you gotta answer questions"; "after worksheets you gotta write essays"—points to Freire's (1997) concept of "banking education" in which "the teacher issues communiqués and makes deposits which the students patiently receive, memorize, and repeat" (p. 53). Here, Mariana and her high school peers resisted the act of *banking* after years of performing this act in countless classrooms. Her refutation of this educational approach paralleled her call for interactive teaching approaches where the "teacher would make these things [learning] more interactive and base things on your real life."

Contemplating meanings of equity and equality as a student in an urban high school and community, Mariana was reiterating a fundamental idea posited by Freire (1997). That is, "knowledge emerges only through invention and re-invention, through the restless, impatient, continuing, hopeful inquiry human beings pursue in the world, with the world, and with each other" (p. 53). In light of the rapidly changing, multicultural world in which we all live, Mariana's reading of school space, generally, and teaching, specifically, is important to critique because of its explicit assertion that "some teachers don't know us and really don't care. Then they get us doing routine work and that's unfair." Yvette returned to the discussion by stating, "That's an unequal balance." She then murmured, "Inequality, unequal, inequity are heavy words to think about by ourselves and to do it with different races like we doing. Interesting." Her confession that these words are "heavy" especially "with different races" has encouraged me to better engage an equity pedagogy in my ongoing work with preservice candidates (mostly white) and high school students (mostly African American and Latino). Doing so can move us closer to privileging the perspectives of both teachers and students in debates on teaching, learning, and knowledge (Ball, 2006; Cochran-Smith & Lytle, 1999; Lee, 2007). It can also encourage us to take seriously Mariana's feelings on teacher training, "banking" forms of education, and interactive teaching and learning approaches in our commitment to equitable pedagogic and institutional systems. Clearly, our work, as a field, is not done.

Student as Teacher: An Important Reversal of Learning

Ruth, a white, female, preservice teacher, commented: "I'm just wondering—if not every student has the kind of stability or whatever, like resources from home, and we're together in a class, is it just . . . the teacher's responsibility or can we help one another?" After pausing to acknowledge students' outbursts that served as initial responses to her query, Ruth continued, "How can it be, how can you help me help my students and how can I help my students help one another? You know, does that happen in the classes that you're in now and can you tell me what it looks like?" Sitting silently in a corner next to the classroom's entrance, Sharif, an African American high school student, asked to comment. Embodying a critical, self-reflexive disposition in his academic encounters and daily conversations with teachers and peers at Perennial High School, Sharif qualified his comments as "very simple." Then, he explained: "All your students gotta reach a common ground, you know. Like somebody said earlier, in school it's like a democracy, you know, if the kids have a voice. You can't just be enforcing rules out the blue and expect everybody to go peachy cream about it." Damya, an African American female from Perennial, was sitting close by and expressed her agreement with Sharif's point and encouraged him to elaborate. Sharif continued: "Try to talk to the kids, see their point of views, have everybody at a certain common ground. That's when you have success."

In this context, success, for Sharif, was measured by the ways in which teachers and students reached, understood, and enacted the principles of "a common ground" in their interactions with one another. Specifically, Sharif, after listening to others' reactions to Ruth's question and to his response to it, suggested that establishing "a common ground" could help us to better implement an equity pedagogy in our classrooms. In his own words, "Talking about, like, equity and equality is huge. Don't force the conversation just out the blue . . . Like at least once a week or whatever . . . say, 'What do y'all think about life?' or 'What's going on in the world and how do you feel?' 'How's life treating you?' Get students' point of views on things and maybe, like, topics of equity and equality might come up." Here, Sharif offered specific strategies by which teachers can engage students in readings of the world and of themselves in the world, which could lead to critical, timely discussions on equity and equality. He not only responded to Ruth's question but also reframed her question by considering the ways in which the topics "equity" and "equality" could emerge from teachers' purposeful interactions with students. In relation to the second part of Ruth's question, "Can you tell me what it looks like?," Sharif encouraged everyone to consider how such questions (e.g., "What's going on in the world and how do you feel?") connected to learning in and out of the classroom and how learning encompasses a continuum of ideas. According to Sharif, a teacher should "get everyone's view points. And as time goes by . . . people gon' be like 'Oh, I remember when you said this last week,' and then you can start building and getting a certain feel of people. Like, you gotta run with those learning moments."

Running with those moments and establishing "a common ground" can lead to democratic engagements (Kinloch, 2005, 2010) among students and teachers. Such engagements, I argue, are based in critical conversations, mutual exchanges, and reciprocal learning that people have in multiple spaces of interaction as they engage education as a social process. We—preservice teachers, high school students, and me—were participating in democratic engagements by exchanging ideas on teaching and learning. We were also imagining possibilities for implementing an equity pedagogy in our daily activities and conversations in the classroom and in our collaborative encounters in the larger world.

Conversations about teachers learning to help students, students learning to help their peers, and teachers making space in the curriculum to talk with students about the world in which they live relate to discussions on literacy, multiculturalism, and student-teacher interactions. When I asked my preservice teachers to explain to my high school students Moll and Gonzalez's (2001) "funds of knowledge" framework, Sarah, another white preservice teacher, and Ruth provided a combined response: "Students have their own knowledge from families, communities . . . that we should tap into and positively use and bring into the curriculum alongside classroom knowledge. It's along the lines of what Sharif said about building off each other and learning together." Sharif, Mariana, Sophie, and Damya, in particular, shook their heads in agreement. Then, I asked my high school students to explain to my preservice students what ethnographic research entails. After catching eyes with Rajon, an African American student from Perennial, I asked him to "take a shot at explaining ethnography." Hesitantly, he shared, "Like when somebody studies a group of people, more like a culture for a period of time." Sharif inserted, "We learned about that in our class 'cause we were talking about how people, you know, like from the outside could study something they're not part of over time. They could learn a lot of important information." He concluded, "That related to, like, where most of us live [Harlem] and the things we think's not fair for that community." Mart, a white preservice teacher, shared, "That takes you to talking about inequality, inequity, racism, and discriminatory practices. It stems from conversations and comments from students. Then, connect that to what you [pointing at me] said before about equity pedagogy and engagement."

Students agreed with the approach, as initially articulated by Sharif, for engaging students in conversations about the world, conversations that could lead to discussions about equity and equality. However, my preservice teachers seemed to be more interested in how such conversations on establishing "a common ground" and on equity and equality could translate into written assignments that are not confined within a five-paragraph structure. I explained that everything does not have to translate neatly into written products or minilessons, that the processes for engaging in honest discussions on (in)equity, (in)equality, and racism, for example, are significant in and of themselves. They still wanted specific practices and teaching ideas; therefore, I briefly talked about the work my high school students were doing. Damya shared one of her extended spoken-word poems and later explained that it has just as much to do with being a person of color reflecting on life as with critiquing racist practices in America. Rajon searched for his writings in his backpack, and upon discovering he did not have a copy with him, said, "I'm not a poet or writer or nothing, but I've been looking around me . . . and instead of just saying the world's unfair for people looking like me, you know, I turned to writing about it. I don't have my writing here, tho'." Finally, I glanced at Sharif, who glanced back at me and remarked, "Yeah, I got something. Basically, umm, recently, we had a project and I was just studying like three singers or poets that, basically, state like how I felt and stuff . . . it's been, like, a while since I did this assignment, so I'm not explaining it well."

Describing his interpretation of the assignment, Sharif talked about his decision to write a traditional persuasive essay on the relevance of hip-hop culture by focusing on three current artists: Jewel Santana, Nas, and Jay-Z. From the essay, he crafted five original poems on themes that emerged from his close readings of rap lyrics, investigations into the artists' lives, and from his thesis on the power of oral culture and performance in contemporary African American popular music. Following his essay and poems was a brief responsive journal entry on his understanding of the assignment and the writing choices he made in producing (and subsequently presenting to the class) his multigenre project. According to Sharif, "I basically wrote the paper and some poems that relate to music and poetry that have to do with my lifestyle and how people sometimes feel about the pains in the world and how it all connects." He talked about the meanings of three of his original poems, "Remember," "Questions," and "Because of This" before sharing them. Here is an extended excerpt from Sharif's poem, "Remember":

> Remember when ABCs were the only problems you had
> Remember the days of Tag and Skelly
> Remember wearing Fila and LA Gear on the first day of school
> Remember splitting 25¢ juices
> Remember blowing Gateway Cartridges
> Yeah, those were the good days.
>
> Don't you remember the first dollar that made you feel rich
> Remember having a small ass TV just to get a picture
> Remember giga pet and yo-yos
> Remember when your pet died giga pets and yo-yo broke
> Yeah, those the good times as well.
>
> Remember the days of Pokémon
> Remember when "Step-by-Step" was on TV, which made your family love you
> Remember "Growing Pains" which made you love your family
> Remember your 1st kiss which made you feel on top of the world
> Remember the days when you felt invincible . . . Remember.

After answering questions related to his writings, Sharif talked about the need to remember the past, whether playful or painful, as we think about where we are today and where we want to be tomorrow—"Remember." Insofar as teaching and addressing topics of equity and equality in schools are concerned, Sharif and his peers insisted that teachers make space in the classroom for students to experiment with texts, ideas, and experiences. His experimentation led him to wear an "interpretative attitude" (see Nino, 1996) to craft and present a multilayered assignment that featured his poem, "Remember." Supporting such encounters can lead to Mariana's interactive form of learning, can produce creative yet critical writings and readings about the world ("those the good times as well"), and can encourage others to see students as learners who "pose their own questions," "teach themselves," "name their worlds" (Greene, 2000, p. 11). These things can occur alongside our efforts to locate specific ways by which to implement aspects of Banks and Banks's (1995) equity pedagogy. Additionally, these things have the potential and promise to foster democratic engagements and critical inquiry moments among students and teachers in a variety of contexts.

CROSSING BOUNDARIES: DISCUSSION AND WORKING RECOMMENDATIONS

Undoubtedly, there is an urgent need for research on teacher preparation programs and their need to critically focus on the ways in which prospective teachers and the diverse students with whom they may work conceptualize meanings of equity, equality, and difference. In this chapter, I have demonstrated how brief engagements between preservice teachers and urban youth can help us to question public assumptions of urban students and their academic abilities and performances. Such interrogations, I believe, can lead to the promotion of critical approaches to working with urban students in ways that do not silence them or ask them to abandon their critical voices, creative choices, and lived realities. It can also encourage teachers to experiment, alongside students, with expansive meanings of teaching and learning as we work toward a "multi-disciplinary understanding of language, literacy, and pedagogy" (Cochran-Smith & Lytle, 1999, p. 16). Doing so requires that we listen to and talk with students about perceptions of teachers, teaching, and learning in this multicultural world.

Mariana's call for interactive learning moments between teachers and students is important, for it is rooted in collaboration, democratic forms of engagement, and reciprocal learning exchanges. Her call points to the need for additional research on students and teachers as educational collaborators who examine familiar and unfamiliar discourses (Lee, 2007) while working toward an equity pedagogy (Banks & Banks, 1995). Clearly, many teachers are working under constraints posed by educational standards, as Sleeter (2005) explains; however, we can make our practices and pedagogies more expansive. By encouraging critical engagements across groups (e.g., preservice teachers, high school students, researchers, parents, community members), we can "call educational space into question" (Fecho, 2004, p. 156), account for students' academic interactions, and suggest expanded definitions of literacy for students and teachers in this diverse, multicultural world. At the same time, we can propose new visions of teachers *and* students as "RE-searchers" (Berthoff, 1987), not technicians, transmitters, and passive receivers. The days of docile students, if ever they existed, are long gone. As a field, our actions—resulting from our pedagogic practices, research agendas, and ideological and epistemological stances—have implications for educational research, generally, and studies on diversity in teaching and teacher education, specifically.

Some of the implications of this work include: authoring new ways of learning and new selves that speak against inequitable educational practices and institutional structures; refiguring school spaces from sites where *banking* forms of education are experienced to sites of inquiry, exchange, and experimentation; and conceptualizing teaching and learning in frameworks that theorize equity pedagogy, multicultural-ism, and social change. These things are relevant for learning in the contexts of schools as well as local, national, and international communities. In particular, when I consider these implications, I return to that evening in the spring of 2007 when my preservice teachers and high school students came face-to-face. While we never came to an official agreement on meanings of equity and equality, we did struggle with these concepts beyond the allowed spatial-temporal configurations afforded by one shared class session. Through my students' processes of critical reflexivity, they began to articulate emerging thoughts and changing perspectives on urban teaching and students, supported by ongoing investigations of readings in multicultural education. My preservice teachers shared with me questions that emerged after our session with my high school students. In turn, I shared these ques-tions with my students at Perennial High School and observed them talking about "our time at [the university]" and how "we were doing some teaching that night and everybody was game" (Mariana). The list of follow-up questions included: How can teachers teach students and discuss with them ways to take responsibility for their learning? How do students respond to teachers who do not share their racial or ethnic background? How do you want your teachers to know you? Do they see everything you want them to see and know everything you want them to know? If not, is there something your teachers could do to get to know you better?

Thinking about these questions in relation to studying diversity in teaching and teacher education demonstrates the need to engage in an educational movement dedicated to the eradication of inequitable practices and committed to transcending the ascribed roles of teachers and students. Only then might we be able to envi-sion the extended meaning of Greene's (2000) assertion that "young learners have to be noticed . . . they have to be consulted; they have to question why" (p. 11). It is important for teachers and students to willingly cross boundaries as we study diversity and collectively question why or why not. This act of crossing can prove revolutionary for how we reimagine the position of "teacher" from a *trained* expert to a participant in a classroom of learners. My preservice teachers and high school students, for example, were shifting in and out of their assigned positions, at times unknowingly, and were experimenting with expanded meanings of teaching and teachers, on the one hand, and of students' and teachers' knowledge production, agency, and power on the other hand. On that spring evening, we were crossing boundaries as a way to study diversity and ourselves. Such acts have serious implica-tions for teacher education, teacher research, practitioner inquiry, and research with urban youth in a multicultural society.

The type of educational research that I am calling for privileges the voices, per-spectives, and critical insights of teachers (pre- and in-service) and students, even if those insights appear multiple, complex, contradictory, and divergent. Undoubt-edly, there is a pressing, most urgent need for scholarship that accounts for the real-ity of spatial-temporal differences, identity and power relations, shifting community and school demographics, globalization, and the rapid onslaught of technological advances. We live in an educational and a political era in which countless students, especially our urban youth of color, are negatively depicted in mass media as dis-engaged, disinterested learners. As educators and researchers, we cannot leave such depictions unchallenged, and we can neither engage in "educational" conversations nor teach in teacher preparation programs without listening to and including the actual voices and experiences of our students. What is needed in the field, then, is rigorous research that utilizes expansive theoretical frameworks and complex methodological designs, that is inclusive of a multivoice approach, and that provides specific yet critical directions for preparing teachers and students to live, work, and participate in a diverse, multicultural world. Only then can we expect our students, as they expect us, to engage in the world as active, democratic citizens.

NOTES

1. At the time of my teacher-research project at Perennial High School, I was also completing a research project with youth at a different high school. That project, spanning approximately three-and-one-half years and located in the Harlem High School of New York City and the local Harlem community, investigates youth narratives of race, place, and identity against the backdrop of gentrification and revitalization in a historically African and African American community.

2. Information retrieved from the university's website. Accessed April 2007 and February 2009.

REFERENCES

Apple, M. (1986). *Teachers and texts: A political economy of class and gender relations in education.* New York: Routledge & Kegan Paul.

Atwell, N. (1987). *In the middle: Writing, reading, and learning with adolescents.* Portsmouth, NH: Boyton/Cook.

Ball, A. F. (1995). Text design patterns in the writing of urban African-American students: Teaching to the strengths of students in multicultural settings. *Urban Education, 30(3),* 253–89.

Ball, A. F. (2003). U.S. and South African teachers' developing perspectives on language and literacy: Changing domestic and international roles of linguistic gatekeepers. In Makoni, S., Smitherman, G., Ball, A. F., & Spears, A. K. (Eds.), *Black linguistics: Language, society, and politics in African and the Americas,* 186–214. London: Routledge.

Ball, A. (2006). *Multicultural strategies for education and social change: Carriers of the torch in the United States and South Africa.* New York: Teachers College Press.

Banks, C. A. M., & Banks, J. A. (1995). Equity pedagogy: An essential component of multicultural education. *Theory into Practice, 34(3),* 152–58.

Banks, J. A. (Ed). (1996). *Multicultural education, transformative knowledge, and action. Historical and contemporary perspectives.* New York: Teachers College Press.

Berthoff, A. (1987). The teacher as RE-searcher. In Goswami, D., & Stillman, P. (Eds.), *Reclaiming the classroom: Teacher research as an agency for change* (pp. 28–38). Upper Montclair, NJ: Boynton/Cook.

Campano, G. (2007). *Immigrant students and literacy: Reading, writing, and remembering.* New York: Teachers College Press.

Center for Multicultural Education. (2001). *Diversity within unity: Essential principles for teaching and learning in a multicultural society.* Retrieved December 30, 2006, from http://education.washington.edu/cme/DiversityUnity.pdf

Cochran-Smith, M., & Lytle, S. (1990). Research on teaching and teacher research: The issues that divide. *Educational Researcher, 19(2),* 2–11.

Cochran-Smith, M., & Lytle, S. (1993). *Inside/outside: Teacher research and knowledge*. New York: Teachers College Press.

Cochran-Smith, M., Lytle, S. L. (1999). The teacher research movement: A decade later. *Educational Researcher, 28(7),* 15–25.

Fecho, B. (2004). *"Is this English?" Race, language, and culture in the classroom*. New York: Teachers College Press.

Fisher, M. (2007). *Writing in rhythm: Spoken word poetry in urban classrooms*. New York: Teachers College Press.

Freire, P. (1997/1970). *Pedagogy of the oppressed*. New York: Continuum.

Gee, J. P. (2001). Literacy, discourse, and linguistics: Introduction and what is literacy? In Cushman, E., Kintgen, E. R., Kroll, B. M., & Rose, M. (Eds.), *Literacy: A critical sourcebook* (pp. 525–44). Boston: Bedford/St. Martins.

Greene, M. (2000). *Releasing the imagination: Essays on education, the arts, and social change*. San Francisco: Jossey-Bass.

Holloway, K. (1993). Cultural politics in the academic community: Masking the color line. *College English, 55,* 53–92.

Jocson, K. (2008). *Youth poets: Empowering literacies in and out of schools*. New York: Peter Lang Publishers.

Kinloch, V. (2005). Poetry, literacy, and creativity: Fostering effective learning strategies in an urban classroom. *English Education, 37(2),* 96–114.

Kinloch, V. (2007a). "The white-ification of the hood": Power, politics, and youth performing narratives of community. *Language Arts, 85(1),* 61–68.

Kinloch, V. (2007b). Youth representations of community, art, and struggle in Harlem (NYC). *New Directions for Adult & Continuing Education, 116,* 37–50.

Kinloch, V. (2009). Suspicious spatial distinctions: Literacy research with students across school and community contexts. *Written Communication, 26(2),* 154–82.

Kinloch, V. (2010). *Harlem on our minds: Place, race, and the literacies of urban youth*. New York: Teachers College Press.

Lee, C. D. (1997). Bridging home and school literacies: A model of culturally responsive teaching. In Flood, J., Heath, S. B., & Lapp, D. (Eds.), *A handbook for literacy educators: Research on teaching the communicative and visual arts* (pp. 330–41). New York: Macmillan.

Lee, C. D. (2007). *Culture, literacy, and learning: Taking bloom in the midst of the whirlwind*. New York: Teachers College Press.

Michie, G. (1999). *Holler if you hear me: The education of a teacher and his students*. New York: Teachers College Press.

Michie, G. (2005). *See you when you get there: Teaching for change in urban schools*. New York: Teachers College Press.

Moll, L., & Gonzalez, N. (2001). Lessons from research with language-minority children. In Cushman, E., Kintgen, E. R., Kroll, B. M., & Rose, M. (Eds.), *Literacy: A critical sourcebook* (pp. 156–71). Boston: St. Martin's Press.

Morrell, E. (2008). *Critical literacy and urban youth: Pedagogies of access, dissent, and liberation*. New York: Routledge.

National Association for Multicultural Education. (2003). *Definition of Multicultural Education*. Retrieved February 1, 2009, from http://www.nameorg.org/aboutname.html#define

National Center for Education Statistics. (1999–2000). *School and staffing survey*. Washington, DC: U.S. Department of Education.

Nino, C. S. (1996). *The constitution of deliberative democracy*. New Haven: Yale UP.

Pallas, A. M., Natriello, G., & McDill, E. L. (1989). The changing nature of the disadvantaged population: Current dimensions and future trends. *Educational Researcher, 18(5),* 16–22.

Pratt, R., & Rittenhouse, G. (Eds.). (1998). *The condition of education, 1998*. Washington, DC: U.S. Government Printing Office.

Rich, M. F. (2000). America's diversity and growth: Signposts for the 21st century. *Population Bulletin, 55(2)*, 1–43. Washington, DC: Population Reference Bureau.

Richardson, V. (1994). Conducting research on practice. *Educational Researcher, 23(5)*, 5–10.

Schultz, K. (2003). *Listening: A framework for teaching across difference.* New York: Teachers College Press.

Shor, I. (1992). *Empowering education: Critical teaching for social change.* Chicago: University of Chicago Press.

Sleeter, C. E. (2001). Epistemological diversity in research on preservice teacher preparation for historically underserved children. *Review of Research in Education, 25*, 209–50.

Sleeter, C. E. (2005). *Un-Standardizing the curriculum: Multicultural teaching in the standards-based classroom.* New York: Teachers College Press.

Teel, K. M., and Obidah, J. E. (2008). *Building radical and cultural competence in the classroom: Strategies from urban educators.* New York: Teachers College Press.

Yagelski, R. P. (2000). *Literacy matters: Writing and reading the social self.* New York: Teachers College Press.

7

Power in Community Building

Learning From Indigenous Youth How to Strengthen Adult-Youth Relationships in School Settings

Patricia D. Quijada Cerecer

> We are not living in the White man's world . . . What we're learning in school is White man's education. If it wasn't for the White man to come to this land our way of learning would still be taking place . . . but that is a dream learning the way we used to learn.
>
> —Warren, eleventh grade

Warren passionately illuminates how school learning is politicized in U.S. schools. In fact, Warren's narrative reflects his understanding of how race plays a central role in determining whose knowledge is taught in U.S. schools. Moreover, he illuminates how Indigenous knowledge systems are omitted from the curriculum. Katrina, an eleventh grader, elaborated on Warren's point by sharing the following:

> I am just tired of always reading how history books talk about us [American Indians]. . . . It is a terrible feeling when you are in class and have to read books that describe us that way . . . my friends and I all look at each other and get really angry. . . . We wonder why the school continues to use the same books.

Warren, Katrina, and other youth poignantly express how they are problematizing learning in U.S. schools. In fact, Warren and Katrina's narratives echo the experiences and feelings of other Indigenous youth who participated in this project and who believe their cultural practices or Indigenous knowledge systems are not taught nor valued in school settings.[1] The aim of this chapter is to illuminate how Indigenous youth describe adult–youth relationships as an important part of their learning experiences and problematize the type of engagements they are experiencing in schools. By describing their experiences with adults in school settings, Indigenous youth link how knowledge, culture, and power are embedded in the formation and maintenance of relationships. Youth describe how these adult–youth relationships impact their day-to-day experiences in school settings and their motivation to further their education.

171

In this chapter I first review the literature on culturally responsive schooling and Indigenous knowledge in school contexts. Second, I discuss the methods, provide an overview of the youth who participated in the project, and describe the school context. Finally, I draw upon examples from my research in a rural public high school that illuminates how Indigenous youth describe their experiences in building and establishing community through schoolwide events and their relationships with teachers and adults at the high school.

UNDERSTANDING CULTURALLY RESPONSIVE SCHOOLING AND INDIGENOUS KNOWLEDGE SYSTEMS

To date an abundance of critical literature examines the plight of U.S. schools and its complex relationships with students of color (McWhorter, Noguera, & Akom, 2000; Delpit, 1995; Duncan-Andrade & Morell, 2008; Lee, 2006, 2007; Nieto, 1999, 2004; Nilles, Alvarez, & Rios, 2006; Noguera, 2003; Quijada, 2008, 2009; Quijada & Murakami-Ramalho, 2009; Suarez-Orozco, 2003; Valenzuela, 1999). A dimension of this literature that is central to this chapter is how culturally responsive schooling (CRS) for Indigenous youth can employ changes and transformations in how teachers engage in relationships with Indigenous students.

Gay (2000) advocates that culturally responsive education must value and affirm each student's background while simultaneously acknowledging the contributions and potentials of each student. CRS for Native students has been described as a means to connect a student's home culture to the school's culture in anticipation of improving learning and academic achievement (Pewewardy & Hammer, 2003). To engage in CRS, educators must not only understand and respect a student's historical, social, and cultural background and the multifaceted identities students embody, but also manifest this understanding and respect for the students cultural practices through their expectations of the students. Teachers who engage in CRS practices must embody a pedagogical philosophy and employ teaching practices that assert high expectations that are attainable by students. That is, CRS requires that educators and students be held accountable for the process to be truly optimal. Castagno & Brayboy (2008) assert that for this to be accomplished, educators must have attained a certain degree of cultural competence. In so doing, educators must understand and affirm the Indigenous knowledge that youth bring to the school context.

At the forefront of this process, educators must understand and position youth as being social change agents and knowledge producers (James & Prout, 1990; Lesko, 2001). This conceptual shift disrupts traditional developmental paradigms that position youth as struggling to achieve independence and autonomy and transitioning from childhood toward adulthood. This positioning of youth, at minimum, ceases to validate youths' knowledge, their positions in society, as well as the "adultlike" roles and responsibilities most youth of color, and in particular Indigenous youth, embody and carry out on a daily basis. In making this conceptual shift of how youth develop, educators validate the knowledge youth bring to a school context.

Brayboy & Maughan (2009) asserts how "Indigenous communities have long been aware of the ways that they know, come to know, and produce knowledge, because in many instances knowledge is essential for cultural survival and well-being" (p. 3). Warren, at the beginning of this chapter, illuminates this for us as he problematizes the type of knowledge that is being privileged in his school setting. In fact, Warren and many of the youth reinforce how teacher educators must remain conscious that Indigenous knowledge is part of an individual's lived experiences (Battiste, 2008; Battiste & Henderson, 2000).

Valuing, affirming, and understanding Indigenous epistemologies and the culture each student brings to the school and classroom setting is essential (Brayboy & Maughan, 2009; Okakok, 2008). Affirming and acknowledging how multiple knowledge systems exist and understanding youth as knowledge producers is central for teachers and other adults to be especially aware of as they form relationships with youth in school settings and build upon community–school relations. Linking knowledge, culture, and power to how relationships are formed and maintained with Indigenous students is critical for educators to understand. In fact it is through relationships that knowledge is exchanged and (re)produced, an essential point for future educators to understand.

Engaging in relationships in this manner will also illuminate for educators the importance in understanding and affirming diverse learning contexts. Understanding this will also allow educators to make connections between curriculum and the funds of knowledge that youth bring to the classroom. Doing so will begin the process of transforming teaching and leadership ideologies and practices in school settings, which will in turn enhance academic motivation and productivity.

At the core of enhancing academic productivity for this group of students is the development of strong healthy relationships with adults in school settings, reconfirming the importance of understanding and valuing Indigenous epistemologies. In fact, students are interested in building relationships with adults that are mutually reciprocal, affirmed their identities, and valued their knowledge. Such a relationship demonstrates an interest in understanding and valuing the individual youth, their respective families, and communities.

METHODS, PARTICIPANTS, AND SCHOOL CONTEXT

In this chapter I draw upon data from ethnographic interviews and participant observations to grapple with how youth reflect upon building community through their relationships with adults at their high school I refer to as "Hilltop High School." The study draws upon twenty-one participants (eleven female and ten male) who self identified as American Indian (or Native American) youth, lived on one of the nearby reservations, and attended Hilltop High School. Hilltop High School is located in a rural city in the southwestern part of the United States. At the time of the study, this small, rural public high school had an enrollment of 190 students. Hilltop High School reported 51.5 percent of the students attending were female and 48.5 percent were male. The racial and ethnic diversity of the school was 66 percent American Indian, 21 percent Latina/o, and 13 percent white.

Building Community Through School-Wide Events

Hilltop High School's small enrollment and close proximity to student's family–community should have facilitated building a tight campus community and strengthen family–community–school partnerships. While schoolwide events were ideal platforms for adults, students, and family–community members to nurture these coalitions, school administrators did not seize these opportunities. The annual students awards assembly was an example shared by many students as a missed opportunity to build family–school partnerships.

The majority of the Hilltop High School students' parents graduated from the school. Students proudly shared how their graduation would continue the legacy. The parents' commitment to their children's education was demonstrated by their eagerness to be involved in or attend school activities. Katrina, for example, shared the following:

> I really like when we have school-wide assemblies that include our parents and family members . . . the awards assembly was really cool because our families would see us receive awards. You know, it makes us proud to honor our parents and family this way.

Students shared how the schoolwide year-end awards ceremony was a central and important event in the students' lives. A majority of the students and families looked forward to this annual event as it honored not only the students' accomplishments, but also the families role in the process. In fact, in previous years it was the school's event most widely attended by family and community members. The awards ceremony generally consisted of a dinner to honor the students and their families followed by the dissemination of the awards. However, due to the present budgetary crisis, the high school eliminated the dinner and rescheduled the awards ceremony during regular school hours. Scheduling the ceremony during the day made it challenging for parents and community members to attend due to work responsibilities. The decision to reschedule the awards assembly to the day was very disappointing to the students and their families. Yet school administrators did not consider the disappointment or emotional impact students would experience by making this decision. Katrina, for example, shared the following:

> I worked so hard to get straight A's. I really pushed myself to get this. And now it is like not that exciting because my mom and sisters and brothers can't come. My mom is at work during the day and my brothers and sisters are in school. It just doesn't make sense. . . . I am really mad because my family encouraged me so much and pushed me to do well in school and now they can't be part of this celebration.

For Katrina and other students, rescheduling the awards assembly during the day was a huge disappointment. Katrina shared how her family played a pivotal role in motivating and encouraging her to persevere through her studies and obtain straight A's. In so doing, Katrina wants to share her award with them, yet cannot due to the administration's decision to change the assembly during the day time when her parents work. This schedule change sent a message to parents and family members that their active roles in ensuring their children were academically productive was not valued. This scheduling change further illuminates how administrators view the academic development of the youth as an individual process and their academic merits as individual accomplishments. The decision reflects an ideology that values individual merit and ignores the role and degree of importance community plays in the lives of youth. Yet as shared by Katrina and other youth their academic success was a family–communal accomplishment.

This example illuminates the importance for educators to understand Indigenous epistemologies. In so doing, educators would understand how central families and community are to the academic success. This is an example of how schools do not foster family–community–school partnerships. This situation also exemplifies why institutions need to transform the dominant ideologies that guide their leadership practices so that individuals such as the youth of this project feel welcomed and part of the school community.

Time and time again school administrators and some teachers did not seize the students' and parents' cultural assets to build a positive campus climate or strengthen family–community–school partnerships. While schoolwide events were ideal platforms for adults, students, and family–community members to build these coalitions, teachers did not seize these opportunities. For example, during the tribal school's elementary graduation, Mr. Johnson, an eleventh grade teacher, shared an instance of when only one student attended his class. Mr. Johnson shared his disappointment in the following way: "I don't get it. My entire class is absent. They are all at the head start graduation. Now you tell me what does an eleventh or twelfth grader have to do at a head start graduation?" Mr. Johnson locates the "problem" in the youth and centers his understanding of the youth as being deficient in their decision-making abilities rather that understanding the importance of this event for the youth, their family, and community. Missing from Mr. Johnson's worldview is the cultural importance of family and community events for Indigenous youth on this reservation. Like other adults at Hilltop he is challenged in understanding the relational and cultural connections Indigenous youth necessitate from community.

Salient in these examples became how school leaders missed opportunities to engage community and family members in important school events honoring students for their academic accomplishments. Such opportunities would have served as a catalyst toward building a coalition between the school, community, and family members. In fact these incidents combined demonstrate how the Indigenous epistemologies embodied by youth and their respective communities are not valued by the school's administration.

Building Community Through Teacher–Student Relationships

As described earlier, Hilltop's teacher–student ratio should have facilitated building relationships between students and teachers that were reciprocal and demonstrated a commitment and responsibility to each other, yet it did not. One of the youth, Erin, who is a ninth grader, reflected on her relationships with teachers this way:

> I wish we could get to know teachers, you know where they are from . . . things about how they grew up . . . why they are here teaching us. I want to learn from them but I also want to know them. . . . We invite them to our celebrations or feast days and sometimes they attend, but we don't really get to know them and what they are about. I feel like they are my teachers but I don't really know them.

Erin shared how important it is to know teachers and "what they are about" illuminating the importance of understanding who a teacher is outside of the school space. Erin later shared:

Our teachers see where we are from and visit us sometimes at our homes, but I rarely hear about how they grew up. It would be cool to know more about where my teacher grew up, where they went to college, what their families are like, but they just teach us and don't share much about themselves.

For Erin the adult–youth relationships at Hilltop High School were engaging and distant. In fact, Erin and other youth advocated to build relationships with teachers that were reciprocal and affirming of students' identities. Engaging in their subjectivities and demonstrating a commitment to each other was important for the youth and evident in how youth sought to form relationships with adults. For these youth establishing a trustworthy relationship with adults at the school site was essential. Indigenous youth embodied and identified with relationships that were reciprocal in the degree of care and authentic sharing that occurred. Warren described how he reflected upon relationships with teachers this way:

A teacher should be someone I trust that I believe what they tell me. You know someone, who is someone who I don't doubt what they are saying or why they are saying it. Here it is hard because sometimes I wonder why they are teaching us some of the stuff they do, like some of the information they teach us in history. It just isn't true so how can I trust my teacher. Then when I ask too many questions about it they get mad, not angry or yell at me, but I can tell that they don't want to hear it. (Warren, eleventh grade)

Warren shared how relationships with adults must be trustworthy and mutually reciprocal. In fact, Warren illuminates how his critical perspective of the subject matter marginalizes him in the classroom and distances him from establishing a closer trusting relationship with his teacher. Additional observations at Hilltop High school confirmed the challenges youth faced in identifying trustworthy adults.

Youth Suggestions on How to Improve Adult–Youth Relationships

We know what we have to do—we do the same thing every day—we sit and write our research paper, some days we can go to the library and do research—but we pretty much know what we have to do. . . . I wish Mr. Johnson would teach us . . . you know talk to us about what we are doing and learning and even about what we do outside of school. (Dawn, eleventh grader)

While Dawn and other students are discontent with the adult–youth relationships in school settings, they have not given up on learning. In fact, Dawn and the other youth offer teachers suggestions on how to build better relationships. For example, Dawn encourages teachers to "talk to us about what we are doing and learning and even what we do outside of school." These suggestions provide insight on what the students seek in learning and suggestions on how to create a more engaged pedagogy that builds adult–youth relationships. Laura shared how "debates would be fun and exciting to learn about how others see different issues" encouraging teachers to eliminate assignments that are more individualized. Students are interested in becoming actively involved in creating curriculum. The youth seek curriculum that is fueled by hands-on projects, discussions and debates, and that are student centered. It is important, however, for teachers to draw upon pedagogical techniques that integrate learning to the daily lives of students which are integral elements when engaging in CRS (Castagno & Brayboy, 2008).

Despite these suggestions made by students, teachers rarely integrated such suggestions into the curriculum. For example, Mr. Johnson, an English teacher, proudly described how his classroom promotes independence, critical thinking, and research skills. Mr. Johnson shared the following:

> I have designed my classes very similar to a university class. . . . I have students work independently on research projects that involve writing and expression of self. This prepares them for the niversity system where students are expected to do the work independently and progress is not monitored on a daily basis.

However, students felt that his class was monotonous and disconnected from their real world. As stated earlier, Erin and other students "sought to be taught" indicating an interest in having teachers engaging them in the learning process. Unfortunately, Mr. Johnson seems to embody a very traditional perspective of writing that includes isolation, seclusion, ignoring how writing can also be a social and interactive process. Dawn's observation and reflection is indicative of a student who understands this conceptually and is advocating for alternative ways to develop a relationship with her teacher.

Teaching, for Dawn and for other students, meant engaging students in critical dialogues and an opportunity to incorporate their lived experiences. Missing from Mr. Johnson's class was the mentorship and exchange of knowledge preferred by these students. In essence, missing was the formation of an authentic relationship with the youth. As the relationship is formed, it is important to foster a collaborative learning environment that helps build a classroom community and motivates students to excel (Deloria & Wildcat, 2001; Hilberg & Tharp, 2002; Swisher & Deyhle, 1989). Although Dawn shared how Mr. Johnson could improve his teaching by involving his students, she also recognizes the importance of what he is doing. She described it this way:

> He is preparing us for college. He tells us that this is the way college operates. So I do what he says because I want to go to college and am happy that he is doing this. I mean I want to work at something I really like and to do that I realize I need to go to college.

Dawn was quick to equate pedagogical practices with involvement and the acquisition of skills to get into college. She and the other participants understood how a college degree would open up career opportunities for them. Dawn offers a sophisticated analysis of teaching that promotes a more engaged and culturally relevant pedagogy. It is an analysis that situates learning within relationships, but also seeks to develop skills that will get her into college. Equally important, Mr. Johnson's cultural perspective of college fuels a particular type of knowledge that is reproduced, leaving the power in the instructor's hands to determine what kinds of knowledge and relationships are valid. However, youth are conscious of how certain knowledge is privileged over others. Earlier, William shared how he was aware that schools are teaching "white man's education" illuminating how youth are able to see how education is politicized and racialized.

For Dawn and other students, learning opportunities were enhanced and seized by the students when teachers established a relationship with the students. Dawn shared the following:

> I try my best because I know Ms. G. She has visited my house, knows by family, come to my house for birthday parties and I met her husband. I feel like she cares about my learning. She really pushes us to try our best.

> Teacher–student relationships that are reciprocal are critical to the learning development of indigenous youth. Teachers who engaged students in curricular activities that aimed to strengthen collaborative skills that indigenous students brought to the classroom were valued rather than ones that were centered on competition (Deloria & Wildcat, 2001; Hilberg & Tharp, 2002; Swisher & Deyhle, 1989).

IMPLICATIONS FOR EDUCATORS

Throughout the conversations with youth it became salient how adults' construction of youth and formation and maintenance of relationships with them had not been problematized by the adults. Youth do not feel legitimized and validated. So adult–youth relationships for Indigenous youth at Hilltop High School need to be more reciprocal and authenic.

Schools need to (re)read how relationships with Indigenous youth are formed and how Indigenous knowledge is affirmed. Youth provided an informed critique of how teachers and adults could improve pedagogical practices and schoolwide policies. The schools policies and rules (dis)engaged youth in relationships from personnel at the school site. For ndigenous youth, policy formation and decision-making opportunities demonstrate a schools' ability to foster better relationships with students. Yet it also presents an opportunity to dismantle relationships with students, families, and their community. In other words, from the youth's perspective these decisions and policies communicated specific messages to youth. Unfortunately for these youth the decisions made and policies formed disengaged youth from their learning process.

The type of engagement Indigenous youth seek with adults is one that is reciprocal. Indigenous youth narratives illuminate how they wished adults in school settings understood them as knowledge producers and active social agents (Cosaro, 1997; James & Prout, 1990; Lesko, 2001; Mayall, 2002; McRobbie, 1994; Amit-Talai & Wulff, 1995). Youth believed teachers and other adults in school settings should engage in more than a pedagogical relationship with students. Students yearned for activities at school that would build community.

These youth seek teachers who value the Indigenous epistemologies they each bring to the school setting. Equally important, youth seek teachers who are able to situate their lived experiences, share them, and incorporate them into their pedagogical practices. They also seek teachers who engage in the reciprocal transformative learning relationship with them. Central to youth development and identity is this process of relational engagement.

Youth in this project have provided us with a language to begin to (re)think our conceptualization of Indigenous youth, not as "deficient youth in need of treatment, but rather as youth in need of emerging opportunities" (Nakkula, 2003, p.

15). The emerging opportunities adults provide, however, need to be transformative in nature. Youth illustrated "how being engaged in learning the task of the moment instilled in them a desire to keep learning long after the completion" of the task or event (Nakkula, 2003, p. 15).

According to Nakkula (2003) "transformational learning occurs when students sense that they too have moved their teachers, through their efforts and accomplishments and through their deep engagement in the learning process," a "reciprocal ransformation" occurs (pp. 15–16). It is this reciprocal transformation that educators must embrace not just as individuals, but also as individuals who influence policy (Nakkula, 2003). It is important to keep in mind is how these policies engage and (dis)engage youth from the educational experience.

While adults at Hilltop High School suggest that youth are disconnected from school and school culture, participants offered an informed critique of how certain school decisions and policies disenfranchised them and their respective families and communities from the schooling experiences. This was evident in Warren's reflection at the beginning of the paper critiquing the xenophobic ideologies that are embedded in school policies and practices. They offer a sophisticated critique of school, which operationalizes changes in their educational experiences. Through these policies participants understood how institutions positioned youth against adults rather than build and reinforce adult–youth partnerships. It is this dialectical conversation between school and Indigenous youth that must be (re)examined so policies, administrators, teachers and pedagogical practices are transformed.

It is these differences, as revealed through the short but telling narratives, that unveil the complexity of Indigenous adult–adolescent relationships in school settings. Central for this study were the ways that participants forge youth–adult relationships that value their contributions as leaders. At school, youth could not engage their cultural practices, identity formations, or sense of community with adults in school settings. Participants did not feel valued as a source of knowledge or participant in the adult relationships they shared at school. Missing from such relationships was a sense of shared responsibility or commitment toward learning from each other. The positioning of youth in school settings is significant and affects the academic achievement of American Indian youth. In schools, adults failed to value participants' process in accomplishing tasks and instead valued outcomes that overlooked relationships that youth necessitate.

Participants explored their adult relationships by engaging in their subjectivities and gravitated toward relationships that were reciprocal. In this capacity they demonstrated how they care about school, community, and family despite age differences that emerged in such settings. Specifically, adolescents offered a sophisticated analysis for understanding how learning and teaching emerged in relationships with adults, establishing a context to rethink how we constructed and defined youth–adult relationships in school and family settings.

The points I have emphasized have been my attempt to engage in the lives of Indigenous youth and their understandings of youth–adult relationships. I have emphasized their voices and sought to move beyond theory in an effort to challenge our thinking about youth by first listening to their voices and now to question how we have developed our understandings about youth–adult relationships. This chapter begins that process for Indigenous youth as it illuminates how a particular group of American Indian youth who reside on a reservation establish and discuss relationships with adults in the home, community, and school settings. The study fosters an understanding of how youth express agency through the establishment of relationships with adults. In looking toward the future, several important and central questions for educators would be: How can educators in school settings forge alliances with youth to come together across differences to create learning relationships that (in)form, (re)form, and maintain cultural practices that are central to development and education? How can educators in school settings learn about and from the youths' cultural practices as a way to engage in culturally relevant relationships and teaching practices? How can educators strive to establish a reciprocal transformative learning relationship with youth in school settings?

NOTE

1. I use the term Indigenous, Native American, American Indian, and Native interchangeably when discussing Native people generally and/or outside of the participants. I also capitalize the terms as a proper noun, in line with the United Nations use of terms and out of respect for the unique cultural and political relationship Native people have with their homelands.

REFERENCES

Amit-Talai, V., & Wulff, H. (Eds.). (1995). *Youth cultures: A cross-cultural perspective.* London: Routledge.

Battiste, M. (2008). The struggle and renaissance of Indigenous knowledge in Eurocentric education. In M. Villegas, S. R. Neugebauer, & K. R. Venegas (Eds.), *Indigenous knowledge and education: Sites of struggle, strength, and survivance* (pp. 85–92). Harvard education review, no. 44. Cambridge, MA: Harvard Educational Review.

Battiste, M., & Henderson, J. Y. (2000). *Protecting Indigenous knowledge and heritage: A global challenge.* Saskatoon, Canada: Purich Publishing, Ltd.

Brayboy, B. (2005). Toward a tribal critical race theory in education. *The Urban Review, 37*(5), 425-446.

Brayboy, B., & Maughan, E. (2009). Indigenous knowledges and the story of the bean. *Harvard Educational Review, 79(1),* 1–23.

Castagno, A. E., & Brayboy, B. (2008). Culturally responsive schooling for Indigenous youth: A review of the literature. *Review of Educational Research, 78(4),* 941–93.

Collins, W. A., & Repinski, D. J. (1994). Relationships during adolescence: Continuity and change in interpersonal perspective. In R. Montemayor, G. R. Adams, & T. P. Gullotta (Eds.), *Personal relationships during adolescence* (pp. 7–36). Thousand Oaks, CA: Sage.

Cosaro, W. A. (1997). *The sociology of childhood.* Thousand Oaks, CA: Pine Forge Press.

Daniels, J. A. (1990). Adolescents' separation-individuation and family transitions. *Adolescence, 25(97),* 105–17.

Deloria, V., & Wildcat, D. (2001). *Power and place: Indian education in America.* Golden, CO: Fulcrum.

Delpit, L. (1995). *Other people's children: Cultural conflict in the classroom.* New York: New Press.

Duncan-Andrade, J., & Morell, E. (2008). *The art of critical pedagogy: Possibilities for moving from theory to practice in urban schools.* New York: Peter Lang.

Fiering, C., & Lewis, M. (1993). The transition from early childhood to middle adolescence. Sex differences in the social network and perceived self-confidence. *Sex Roles, 24,* 489–509.

Gay, G. (2000). *Culturally responsive teaching: Theory, research, and practice.* New York: Teachers College Press.

Gecas, V., & Seff, M.A. (1990). Adolescents and families: A review of the 1980s. *Journal of Marriage and Family, 52,* 941–58.

Grotevant, H. D., & Cooper, C. R. (1998). Individuality and connectedness in adolescent development: Review and prospects for research on identity, relationships, and context. In E. Skoe & A. von der Lippe (Eds.), *Personality development in adolescence: A cross national and life span perspective* (pp. 3–37). London: Routledge.

Hilberg, R., & Tharp, R. (2002). *Theoretical perspective, research findings, and classroom implications of the learning styles of American Indian and Alaska Native students.* Charleston, WV: ERIC Clearinghouse on Rural Education and Small Schools.

James, A., & Prout, A. (1990). *Constructing and reconstructing childhood: Contemporary issues in the sociological study of childhood.* New York: Falmer Press.

Lee, T. S. (2006, January). "I came here to learn how to be a leader": An intersection of critical pedagogy and Indigenous education. *InterActions: UCLA Journal of Education and Information Studies, 12(1),* article 3. Retrieved from http://repositories.cdlib.org/gseis/interactions/vol2/iss1/art3.

Lee, T. S. (2007). Connecting academics, Indigenous knowledge, and commitment to community: High school students' perceptions of a community based education model. *Canadian Journal of Native Education, 30(2),* 196–216.

Lesko, N. (2001). *Act your age!: A cultural construction of adolescence.* New York: Routledge-Falmer.

Mayall, B. (2002). *Towards a sociology for childhood, thinking from children's lives.* Philadelphia: Open University Press.

McRobbie, A. (1994). *Postmodernism and popular culture.* London: Routledge.

McWhorter, J. H., Noguera, P., & Akom, A. (2000). Explaining the Black education gap. *The Wilson Quarterly, 24(3),* 72–92.

Nakkula, M. (2003). Identity and possibility: Adolescent development and the potential of schools. In M. Sadowski (Ed.), *Adolescents at school: Perspectives on youth, identity, and education* (pp. 7–18). Cambridge, MA: Harvard Education Press.

Nieto, S. (1999). *The light in their eyes.* New York: Teachers College Press.

Nieto, S. (2004). *Affirming diversity: The sociopolitical context of multicultural education* (4th ed.). Boston: Pearson.

Nilles, V., Alvarez, L., & Rios, F. (2006). Preparing teachers to work with second language learners. In R. Jiménez & J. Pang (Eds.), *Race, Ethnicity, and Education,* Vol. 2 (pp. 39–54). Westport, CT: Praeger.

Noguera, P. (2003). *City schools and the American dream: Reclaiming the promise of public education.* New York: Teachers College Press.

Okakok, L. (2008). Serving the Purpose of Education. In M. Villegas, S. Neugebauer, & K.R. Venegas (Eds.), *Indigneous knowledge and education: Sites of struggle, strength, and survivance* (pp. 268–86). Harvard education review, no. 44. Cambridge, MA: Harvard Educational Review.

Pewewardy, C., & Hammer, P. (2003). *Culturally responsive teaching for American Indian students.* Charleston, WV: ERIC Clearinghouse on Rural Education and Small Schools.

Quijada, D. A. (2008). Marginalization, identity formation, and empowerment: Youth's struggles for self and social justice. In N. Dolby & F. Rizvi (Eds.), Youth moves: Identities and education in global perspective (pp. 207–20). New York: Routledge.

Quijada, D.A. (2009). Youth debriefing diversity workshops: Conversational contexts that forge intercultural alliances across differences. International Journal of Qualitative Studies, 22(4), 449–68.

Quijada, P. D., & Murakami-Ramalho, E. (2009). Who says I don't want to come to school? School policies disenfranchise American Indian youth's educational vision. *World Indigenous Nations Higher Education Journal*, 39–49.

Suarez-Orozco, M. (2003). Becoming somebody: Central American immigrants in U.S. inner-city schools. In E. Jacob & C. Jordan (Eds.), *Minority education: Anthropological perspectives* (pp. 129–43). Norwood, NJ: Ablex.

Swisher K., & Deyhle, D. (1989). The styles of learning are different, but the teaching is just the same: Suggestions for teachers of American Indian youth. *Journal of American Indian Education, August*, 1–14.

Valenzuela, A. (1999). *Subtractive schooling: U.S.-Mexican youth and the politics of caring.* Albany, NY: SUNY Press.

8

"Something to Brag About"

Black Males, Literacy, and Diversity in Teacher Education

David E. Kirkland

Any teacher educator serious about understanding the question of diversity in teacher education recognizes already that diversity in teacher education is much larger than the Ed School (Labaree, 2004). Therefore, you cannot study diversity in teacher education without studying first diversity outside it because "diversity" in teacher education is precisely connected to teachers gaining knowledge of the conditions and abilities of underrepresented and marginalized groups external to the homogene (Swartz, 2009). In this chapter, I explore black males, as an under-represented and marginalized group, and their literacy practices outside the context of school. In so doing, I provide an organic context for studying diversity in teacher education as the study of black males and literacy out of school presents an ethno-graphically real context for studying diversity writ large.

This chapter grows out of a desire to move forward conversations in teacher education on teaching black males in more positive directions. Rooted in a profit perspective, which begins with a deep respect for what people can do as opposed to what they cannot, the chapter is guided by two basic assumptions: (1) that the majority of black males are highly literate, yet in ways many of their teachers fail to recognize (Kirkland, 2006; Kirkland & Jackson, 2009), and (2) that teachers of black males benefit from understanding nuanced elements of black masculinity (Fashola, 2005; Hopkins, 1997; Kunjufu, 1995).

In keeping with these beliefs, the chapter seeks to answer the following questions: How does certain modes of black discourse as units of black masculinity help shape the ways in which young black men see themselves, participate in everyday life, and practice literacy (Alim, 2006; Kirkland, 2006; Kirkland & Jackson, 2009)? How might this knowledge of black masculinity offer teacher educators new insights on diversity in teaching? In answering these questions, the chapter hopes to speak more broadly about what teachers need to know in order to work with underrepresented populations, in this case young black male students.

BACKGROUND AND RATIONALE OF THE STUDY

Much of the conversation in teacher education surrounding young black men and literacy is guided by deficit perspectives. Even the most progressive ideas tend to lean toward models that diminish black males and the sociolinguistic wealth they bring into classrooms. Among these more "progressive" ideas are narratives that question young black males' desire to learn. In literacy scholarship, such narratives tend to condemn black males for being "too cool" and "too boastful" to learn and, therefore, "too resistant" to advance their literacy development (Davis, 2001; Majors & Billson, 1993; Taylor & Dorsey-Gainses, 1988).

There is also a second set of so-called progressive ideas that promotes "interventions" based on peculiar missionary metaphors (e.g., *reading recovery* as opposed to *reading discovery*). These ideas tend to promote narratives that chronicle an ironic story of "salvation" that some young black men endure, a journey toward a literacy that sits outside their sociolinguistic reach. We have come to know such stories well—"a hope in the unseen," "there are no children here," "the freedom writers"— the list goes on. While each narrative scribbles its own fanciful tale against the blank slate of our most desired academic norms, teachers of young black males often fatally fail to replicate such stories. In order to better prepare teachers to educate young black men, scholarship in teacher education needs to write new narratives that respect black males for who they are and link their experiences with literacy to the rich and vibrant elements of their real-life language experiences (Fashola, 2005; Haddix, 2009; Noguera, 2008).

While it lacks examples on how they succeed, the research literature on black males and literacy is replete with examples of how young black men fall short of proficiency, profiling "gaps" in achievement (Hilliard III, 2003; Noguera, 2003), entrenched forms of remediation (Milofsky, 1974), and chronic misbehavior (Jencks & Phillips, 1998; Meier, 1996). Given the portrait the scholarship paints, it is no wonder that young Black males in contemporary American society face major challenges to their development and well-being. Indeed, many of these challenges emanate from classrooms where teachers of black males view them through the deficit lens.

It should not be lost that national educational statistics backs this view of Black males. According to the National Assessment of Educational Progress (NEAP), nearly 70 percent of black fourth grade boys read below grade level, compared with 27 percent of white children. Many have observed that even Hispanic and Asian fourth graders fared better on reading exams than black males, although English is their second language (Fashola, 2005; Jackson & Moore, 2006; Noguera, 2003). The lists of troublesome comparisons go on. Given only these examples, it is not surprising that teachers find it difficult to teach or even understand their black male students.

While there are many ways to articulate how and why black males perform poorly in school in general and on "literacy" exams in particular, Jones (2002) offers what I find to be a useful explanation that is related to black male (language) identities. He explains, "One of the main reasons African-American youngsters do poorly in school is because of language differences between black and white children" (p. 1). As Smitherman (1977, 2006) and others (Hilliard, 1990; Moore, 1996;) have suggested, schools, and more specifically classrooms, penalize black students, black males in particular (Ferguson, 2000), who speak black language. It doesn't help either that reading and writing have been constructed as the province of white females (hooks, 2004b). This perception complicates the relationship between black males and literacy. For example, a black male who likes to read is often questioned, perceived "as on the road to being a sissy" (hooks, 2004b, p. 40). It is not only those surrounding black men who buy into this way of thinking. Black men, themselves, all too often carry the ideological baggage of self-denial and hatred (Kirkland, 2006; Young, 2007). According to Madhubuti (quoted in hooks, 2004, p. 36),

> No one actually told men "you should hate yourself." However, the images, symbols, products, creations, promotions, and authorities of white America all very subtly and often quite openly taught me white supremacy, taught me to hate myself.

Given the positionalities of the researcher and the researched, the concept and its context (Milner, 2007), the "literate" and the "illiterate" labels when attached to black males, are always politically charged. They encourage a dichotomous view of literacy that camouflages the sociolinguistic realities in which literacies are practiced. The events and activities that define them are "constitutive of and by material relations of discourse, power, and knowledge" (Luke, 1997, p. 3). Given to such power relations, the public image of the illiterate black male deeply obscures the literate lives of many young black men. It is in this way that Freire[1] (1982) suggests:

> These men, illiterate or not, are, in fact, not marginal . . . They are not "beings outside of"; they are "beings for another." Therefore the solution to their problem is not to become "beings inside of," but men freeing themselves; for in reality they are not marginal to the structure, but oppressed men within it. Alienated men, they cannot overcome their dependency by "incorporation" into the very structure responsible for their dependency. There is no other road to humanization—theirs as well as everyone else's—but authentic transformation of the dehumanizing structure. (p. 339)

The connections that Freire makes between freedom and oppression, between centers and margins is essential for understanding what Noguera (2008) sees as the "trouble with black boys." For black males, black masculine "identity is twin skin to linguistic identity" (Anzaldúa, 1987/1999). Therefore, the same social conventions and ideologies—what Smitherman calls black modes of discourse—that shape language also shape black masculinity. Hence, a disregard for black (male) language is equally a disregard for black males (Kirkland & Jackson, 2009).

This disregard for things—black males and black language—raises important questions about black males' intelligences and wills to learn. Do young black men lack literacy in ways that mainstream depictions suggest? If we insist no, then how might considering their sociolinguistic realities offer a new perspective on literacy in their lives? How might this new perspective help teacher educators reshape the discourse on literacy in ways that support and utilize the sociolinguistic tools that young black men bring with them to school? How might studying black males in teacher education help disrupt the fears, misunderstandings, and vile discriminations that work to perpetuate the trouble with black males?

METHODOLOGY: TOWARD AN ETHNOGRAPHY OF DISCOURSE

To address the above questions, this study blends two research traditions: critical ethnography and critical discourse analysis. This work is situated within the linguistic anthropological traditions of scholars such as Hymes (1993), Heath (1983), and Dyson (2003). While the general methodological focus of this work is language in use, the specific focus of investigation is language in the context of a group of young black men. I focus on the young men's bragging practices—what Smitherman (1977) sees as a black mode of discourse—as my central unit of analysis.

Building on Smitherman's notion of discourse, I view bragging in this study as socially and historically situated way of being as expressed through spoken or written *words*, emerging relative to one's culture, community, and communicative identity (Bakhtin, 1981; Gee, 1989, 1996, 2004; Smitherman, 1999, 2006). I use the phrase "ethnography of discourse" to shed light on bragging as black masculine language literacy practice. I have sought to capture this practice as discourse for the purpose of understanding it in the complexity and contexts in which it is performed.

Before analysis there exist the range of patterned complexities that influence human phenomenon, which in order to render meaning, requires capturing, which—in turn—requires contextualizing. In this way, an *ethnography of discourse* can be distinguished from more traditional approaches to discourse, as traditional approaches tend to pay particular attention to analyzing discourse as opposed to collecting it. To capture discourse, one needs to investigate directly what Gee (1996) calls "Discourse,"[2] with a capital *D*, in contexts of human situations, so as to discern how certain D/discourses have influenced and are influencing the processes, practices, and patterns that shape literacy. In this work, I seek to accomplish this task, as I have blended critical discourse analysis and critical ethnography.

Through this blending, certain forms of discourse (e.g., bragging) are contextualized for closer study. We begin to understand how forms of discourse such as bragging convey meanings beyond mere words (Smitherman, 1999). Unstable truths lie beyond words, in perceived experiences and movements of things and in contexts that give way to discursive messages. Bragging, for example, is concealed within highly sophisticated discursive conventions: "clever rhymes, puns, and culturally toned experiences and references from a fresh and new perspective" (Smitherman, 1999, p. 275). Story plots are interwoven within routine formulas and fixed sayings that grow out of the sociolinguistic situation, where "braggadocio is richly interwoven into the everyday AAL conversational context, and it is ritualized in the toasts, long-standing narrative epics from the oral tradition" (Smitherman, 1999, p. 275). Hence, an array of literate abilities, ranging from metalinguistic awareness to critical skills, derives from the cultural experience that is captured in a singular discursive expression.

Then to understand literacy more accurately, one must take as contexts various relational points (i.e., race, gender, geography) and social locations (e.g., classrooms, peer groups, communities), investigating specific forms of discourse in "all elements that constitute the characteristics that shape the practices of a group." In addition, analyzing certain forms of discourse, such as bragging, presents a fresh lens through which to identify and interpret ethnographic and sociolinguistic data. By blending research approaches, one can more accurately capture the complex sociolinguistic and cultural contexts of a given communicative event.

METHOD

The data for this study were collected from the "My Brother's Keeper" mentoring program (MBK) in Detroit, Michigan. MBK operated over a thirty-week expanse. Two or three times a month throughout the school year, MBK transported Michigan State University (MSU) mentors to the program site in Detroit to interact with a group of black male students. These sessions occurred on Saturdays and lasted for approximately three hours. Sessions were typically structured around the following activities:

1. Welcome and Project Pledges (10 minutes)
2. Current Events Activity (20 minutes)
3. Mentor-to-Student Sessions (30 minutes)
4. Lunch and Refreshment (30 minutes)
5. Mentor-Led Community Service-Learning/Literacy Projects (1 hour, 30 minutes)
6. Dismissal

In addition to mentoring sessions at Malcolm X Academy, students participated in two weekend mentoring retreats (one in the fall and one in the spring) in East Lansing, Michigan, on the campus of MSU. They also attended a one-week workshop during the summer, also at MSU. During their visits to campus, students explored details of collegiate life. They visited dorms and classrooms, learned about college majors and careers, and were introduced to numerous faculty, staff, and university and college students, who provided tips for making successful transitions to college and beyond.

At the time of this study, the MBK program enrolled sixteen young men, each of whom agreed to participate in this study. With their permission, I gathered data, focusing—among other things—on the young men's bragging practices to understand how black masculinity reconfigured literacy among the young men of MBK.

From September 2003 to June 2004, I collected four types of data, which included video recordings, field notes, interview transcripts, and student artifacts (i.e., clothing, students' work, program plans, textbooks, etc.).

Using an unmanned camcorder,[3] I captured videotapes of the young men's activities in the program's meeting room.[4] These records helped to document the performative aspects of students' interactions, as well as other important features such as the social situation of MBK and the young men's clothing and style. I also took detailed descriptive scratch notes that I later composed as formal field notes within an hour of leaving the program site (Emerson, Fretz, & Shaw, 1995).

I conversed regularly with the young men to record their perspectives. These conversations helped to clarify meanings for events that involved bragging and/or literacy. Conversations generally emerged organically except in needed cases where clarification to better understand the group's practices. All conversations were recorded and, for this chapter, selected episodes have been transcribed.

Finally, I obtained copies of students' records, students' academic and nonacademic writings, etc. In cases where documents could not be copied, I collected original sources with permission from students and their parents. All such artifacts were
labeled, dated, and organized in data folders.

To analyze data, I first coded them by themes and patterns based on the young
men's literacy practices. For analytic reasons, I have defined *literacy practice* as any
act of reading and composing (as opposed to writing), where the young men used
or interpreted symbolic materials in the process of constructing and making sense
of their social worlds. The second stage of analysis involved displaying data in a
set of matrices in order to make better sense of the themes and patterns that were
generated during the first stage of analysis. Finally, I drew conclusions to generate
theory as to how black males construct identities through their language and literacy
practices. My goal for this work has been to offer a humanizing view of Black males
from which teachers and teacher educators can learn from (Kirkland, 2009).

"IN ORDER FOR ME TO WRITE, I GOTTA HAVE SOMETHING TO BRAG ABOUT"

It was immediately revealing when Etherin, one of the study's participants, revealed
to me: "In order for me to write, I gotta have something to brag about." Etherin is
not talking out of turn. He is confessing a tradition of black masculine storytelling
that has reached back farther than "Shine," "Stag-o-Lee," "Dolemite," and "The Signifying Monkey." His discourse of braggadocio, of "braggin"—to us the young men's
terminology—gives many black male writers a kind of poetic prowess, the inexorable
permission, to tell stories without limits to how tall a tale can be. According to Smitherman (1999), "The toast-teller projects himself (or herself, but usually himself) as a
powerful, all-knowing, omnipotent hero, able to overcome all odds" (pp. 275–76).

In this section, I attempt to do two things: First, I seek to illustrate how rich description of underrepresented groups outside the classroom can be a worthy source
of scholarship for serious study of diversity in teacher education. Second, I seek to
illuminate the particular uniquenesses of black males through a conversation about
their literacy practices in order to bring their particular ways with words closer to
the teachers who will teach them. The description that follows serves dual purposes:
to make the case for studying underrepresented and marginal groups outside the
context of school and to describe the group, in this case a group of black males,
through their literacy practices. In this way, Etherin's comment about writing reveals
him in a way in which teachers must see their students. It also reveals something
about literacy in a way that humanizes young black men, a perspective that can be
helpful to teacher educators interested in diversity.

"LET'S TALK ABOUT SEX": SEX THEMES IN THE IDENTITY CONSTRUCTIONS AND LITERACY HABITS OF BLACK MALES

Sex was perhaps the most bragged about topic in the group. In addition to reading
and writing about it, they invented and appropriated language for it. During a group

discussion about "the social significance of hip-hop to contemporary thought and language," the program instructor, Mr. J, a staunch supporter of hip-hop culture, expressed his displeasure with rappers "overuse" of the words "bitches" and "hoes," particularly in reference to women. While the discussion caught their interest, the young men's attention veered into an interesting direction. Off to the side, Hakim tapped Larry, his close friend, on the arm:

Hakim: Mr. J [is] right . . ."cause nobody would want you callin' dey momma or sista a bitch or ho . . .

Larry: I'll kick somebody ass if they call my momma out her name. *[Pause. Moments pass. Hakim interrupts the silence.]*

Hakim: Hey man? I heard Robbie doin' Tricia. Dat true?

Larry: For real . . . you think he hittin that?

Hakim: E-ro sent me an e-mail. He said that he be with her all the time. I don't know. E-ro be lyin sometime. But Robbie, he a playa, so he might be hittin' it. 'Sides, she like that. If he ain't hittin' that, somebody else hittin' it . . . *[Interrupted.]*

Larry: He think he a playa. You know he tried to holla at Mr. J's daughter.

Hakim: She fine as hell, though. I would holla at her, too.

Larry: Me too. *[Both young men smiling.]*

Hakim: Nigga, what you talking about. You fuckin' around wit who, Trina. *[Smiling.]*

Larry: I can't help it if all the girls love me.

In this brief exchange, the dialogue between Hakim and Larry moved in competing directions. Their conversation began by acknowledging that something was wrong with describing females using derogatory language. By expressing their dissension to verbal put-downs against women in rap, the young men expressed critical awareness toward issues of misogyny that is pervasive in not just rap but also American mainstream culture. Hakim's statement, "Mr. J [is] right . . . 'cause nobody would want you callin' dey momma or sista a bitch or ho," suggests that he and his peers are somewhat aware of the problems related to describing women as objects for sexual exploitation.

As their conversation continued, however, the young men slipped into a familiar mode of talk that did not correspond with their earlier expressed beliefs. As they were interested in expressing their desire for sex and talking about "getting" not just one but multiple girls, they did so in language consistent with the misogynistic overtones of texts and verbiage borrowed from the cultures they previously critiqued.

For them, bragging about sex and women offered a way to author a desired self, whose value was measured uniquely by the tallness of the tale. That is, the young men, in boasting about sex, performed their identities, more or less, performing masculinity in hyperbole. For these young men, bragging was not only a socially accepted strategy, where exaggerated exploits were privileged in the linguistic playground of black masculinity; it also manifested make-believe yet desired selves that could be actualized simply through oral creations (Alim, 2006; Rickford & Rickford, 2000; Smitherman, 1977, 1999). According to Smitherman (1999), "While the speakers may or may not act out the implications of [bragging], the point is that the listeners do not necessarily *expect* any action to follow" (p. 207, emphasis in the original). It did not matter whether or not their tales were fact or fiction. What mattered was the entertainment the tale offered.

The young men's sexual boasts were not just spoken and listened to, they were also read and written. And while I do not argue that sexually explicit texts be allowed in classrooms, I do know that sex themes were part of the young men's literate realities.

When working with young men like the students of MBK, teachers must be prepared to not vilify such students or their language. Rather they must see that attention to sexual activity and the opposite sex is not only natural in the process of growing up but also necessary in the process of young black men's social development. The situation of "Sex Talk," then, not only presents opportunities for the young men to play with adulthood but also opens opportunities for them to find new and more productive ways to talk about sex. Perhaps most important, it offers their teachers opportunities to join and guide them in their quests to make sense of themselves and the world around them.

"I JUST LIKE LOOKING AT THINGS": VOYEURISM AS PRELITERACY AMONG BLACK MALES

The young men of MBK also *read* and *wrote* the world with their eyes. Their conversations were, in this way, motivated by peculiar viewings of the things around them, particularly famous females. These viewings were not simply the visual act of watching things. They involved active participation, such as "reading" pictures in magazines and books, which highlighted a new set of boastful conventions. For analytical purposes, I have characterized such viewings as *voyeurism*.

The young men's voyeuristic impulses, both youthfully naïve and childishly natural, revealed a lot about the ways in which they practiced literacy. After observing them looking through magazines, I asked the young men, what caught their interests in the magazines? Their responses were almost unanimous: "girls." I next asked them, how did they felt about looking at women in these books and magazines? The young men, responding to my question, insisted that "looking at females was natural," as it made them "feel like men." In their vernacular, "feeling like a man" was a synonym for being seen by other men (and sometimes women) as "normal" and "cool"—another form of exhibitionism propped up against their particular kind of voyeurism. Hence, the young men's pursuit for normalcy expressed though an exploitative act of viewing—pronounced in a sort of primitive, peepish reading practice, revealed a disturbing coming of age and coming to literacy story.

These stories were inspired not by the innocent sexual desires of a few young men but by peers and peer pressures to fit in and to belong. The young men of MBK engaged in voyeuristic acts, playfully thumbing through pictured texts with keen eyes and curious sensations. They were quite literally reading their worlds, engaging in a literacy practice inspired by an acute and ever-present pressure to see and be seen.

Hakim: There is a lot out here for us [men] to read. They make magazines in here for all of us to read. We men . . . We like women. If you don't, den you gay.

David: Is that a problem?

Hakim: Yeah, that's a problem. Being gay ain't cool. Men like women, so we read stuff like *Playboy*. They know what men like, and people make a lot of money because they know it. Even the women know.

Larry: I mean . . . I don't know about *Playboy*; I don't read it. I like to look at it, but I don't read it. *[Laughs.]* Not that I don't want to *[laughs]*, but in all the magazines I do read, you got women taking they clothes off. I pick 'em up partly 'cause of the woman in there. Fine, and they got dope ass bodies. So it's only normal to look at stuff like that. Nerdly little boys lookin at other stuff. We lookin at what we like, what men should like.

Hakim: Yup, 'cause in all the magazines—*XXL, Smooth, Vibe, Source, King,* all of them— 'cause they know men, real men *[laughs]*, like to look at that. We judge each other by whether or not your girl look like the girl in there. The truth is, it captures your attention, and we wanna read stuff that captures our attention.

This exchange demonstrates how the young men made specific connections to the *scenes* of their perceived masculinities, which offered a kind of *seen* manhood. Their lenses for "seeing" manhood, like the boasts that defined them, exaggerated popular notions of masculinity, dominated by hypermasculine, heteronormative models of pop culture. It is through this lens that the young men of MBK saw one another—behind a faint and skewed silhouette of masculinity usually expressed through their voyeuristic ways of reading and writing the world.

Their cleavage to seen-masculinity—both the act of viewing what they perceived men to view and the act of being viewed as men—sat at the center of the young men's views of themselves, which in turn helped to shape their performances of literacy.

Etherin: You ain't no man if you don't wanna see a pretty woman. You ain't gone be cool with me. I like women, Jack. You better like women, too, and I better know you like women.

Such expressions of seen masculinity—while dangerously problematic in many ways—were themselves boasts that, in turn, influenced what and the ways in which the young men read and write. Hakim explained:

[When] I started reading *King* . . . first I wanted to look at the girls. Then I started to see other stuff I like. They had rides in there that was off the chain. I read an interview they did with Nelly and found out about his sister having cancer. And how he [gave] a lot of money to charity to . . . cure . . . cancer. . . . Now, I can't pick up a magazine like this one [*King*] unless it got more than pretty girls in it. I'm interested in a lot of stuff they write. . . . I just like looking at things.

There was a development to Hakim's viewings. Not unlike an individual enticed to read an article because of an image associated with it, Hakim's literacy progression moved from viewing to the actual reading of texts. As "looking at [pictures of] girls" in magazines helped Hakim become interested in reading print, the world surrounding Hakim was based on such symbiotic associations. But given this, one wonders about the various associations that young black men make between the scenic world they view with incredible interest and the lettered one they make sense of through the scenes that surround them.

I do not expect educators to display provocative pictures of women in order to pique young black male interest. This would be inappropriate and is a lesson many of our young (and older) men must unlearn. Yet, I wonder about Hakim's interest in *King Magazine*: Was it primarily and profoundly influenced by his sexual and social development (i.e., need to conform to others)? If so, was he merely acting in ways that others saw as acceptable, as masculine? Whatever the answer, Hakim's reading of scenes preceded and perhaps coincided with his reading of print. There is the dynamic of the inverse other here, for being a man demands that which is not masculine and exemplars of the not cool, including ourselves when we inadvertently fail to keep up the pose, slipping in the eyes of others. This takes a lot from gaze theory, how identity construction is dependent upon self-presentations acknowledged by self and by others. Hence, this reading of the world should not be left without instruction, for young boys too often grow to be old men without critical viewing practices. Still, teachers of young black men should not misperceive the young men's viewing practices as laziness or as a distraction disassociated with literacy practice. Such viewings are part of a greater developmental process and, at least for these young men, are part of the literacy process itself.

"DOPE RIDES": THE ICONOGRAPHY
OF THINGS IN THE WRITING OF SELVES

There was no busing to MBK. So the young men received rides from parents, usually mothers or grandmothers. Many would arrive to the program early and wait in the parking lot for program meetings to begin. While waiting, they typically congregated to one side of the parking lot and talked about "dope rides"—their phrase for nice cars.

Hakim: Did y'all see [MTV's] *Cribs* last night?

Group: Yeah.

Larry: Yeah, I saw it.

Hakim: Did y'all see JD's [Jermaine Dupree] ride. He gotta a sweet ass Bentley. He got twenty-twos on it and everything. His grip so sweet.

Etherin: No doubt . . . but did y'all see how many rides Master P got. On that one episode . . . He got like two Benzes and Hum-D's. He collect cars. See what I'm sayin. He collectin' cars . . . real cars . . . expensive shit. An' I heard all of them got V6 or V8 engines under they hood. *[Pause.]* I bet they fast as hell.

The young men nodded their heads up and down in agreement. Fast cars, like "NASCAR fast," sparked interest among the group, and as Etherin—always astute to the ways of men—would later explain: "That's what men like . . . fast cars." The conversation continued:

Etherin: My Momma supposed to be gittin' one of those new trucks . . . you know . . . one of those . . . *[interrupted by Larry]*

Larry: Escalades?

Etherin: Yeah an Escalade, kinda like the one Silk [the Shocker] got . . . Man I hope ma momma lemme grip that.

Hakim: Man, an Escalade cost 'bout fifty, sixty Gs. You momma cain't buy that, even if they let her use her foodstamp card. *[Laughs.]* And fool, you cain't even drive yet. *[The group laughs. Smiles.]*

Etherin: *[Still smiling.]* I know, but sometime she be letting me start her car . . . *[Laughter.]*

There was more laughter, followed by more talk about cars, interspersed with more laughter and more serious thought about the world in general.

The young men were playing with masculinity, bragging about the cars they wanted but did not have. Their bragging about cars was something to be measured by. Etched in their own image of manhood, the young men coveted the strength of cars, to metaphorically and sometimes literally sit in the driver's seat, even if it meant starting up their mothers' cars as a way to seize the masculine spotlight. They imagining—making up an adult world, where they knowledgably and boastfully contributed to family work under the assumed masculine accomplishment of driving "dope rides" and discussing the ones they (or their mothers) were "supposed to be getting."

In their exposition of cars, the young men displayed clear yet complicated knowledge about vehicular traits—from the intricacies of rims (e.g., "twenties") to the velocity of engines (e.g. "V6," "V8," "fast as hell"). Such knowledge also demonstrated their "cool pose" (Connor, 1995; Kirkland & Jackson, 2009; Majors & Billson, 1993), which was on display, staged in the urban amphitheater of a fractured and tire-beaten parking lot. Importantly, it was also measured intensely against an audience of impressionable and eagerly listening peers.

Perhaps more important, conversations about cars showed up regularly in some of these young men's writings. "Dope rides" was a topic of social relevance (Ladson-Billings, 1995), a topic of expertise, and also "something to brag about." Etherin's response to a writing prompt about future careers helps to illustrate this point:

> I want to be a rapper, but they don't want us to be rappers because rappers ain't field nigga's. They won't do what they say do. Plus, rappers pull all the baddest women. They got the dopest rides with the V6 engines, twenty inch rims, and the banging sounds. And they do something I like to do—spit rhymes in order to get it . . . Although I like rappers because of the stuff they can get, especially the dope rides, I want to be one because the things they do . . .

Etherin's writing displays a level of social sophistication—both conscious and capitulatory. Embedded in his essay is a level of social commentary that educators commonly want students to achieve (Alvermann, 2003; Newkirk, 2002). Etherin did not write from the margins but from his own center, where items such as cars helped him understand the larger politics of social life.

Etherin's writing can be seen as an extension of his conversations with his peers. His interpretation of society's mechanisms of control was embedded in his ideal rapper, who "won't do what they say do." This social critique construct is significant because, beyond boasting, Etherin's discussion on "dope rides" acts as a form of *critical literacy*, a way of "writing" words to critique and make sense of an unjust social world (Gutierrez, 2008; Luke, 1997; Morrell, 2002).

His practice of literacy did not emanate from the MBK program but from the out-of-school positions of Etherin and his peers. Hence, bragging, for the young men, was itself a way of stepping outside norms in order to critique them. By boasting about what rappers possess, for example, Etherin was able to legitimate rap as a desirable occupation and critique a world that would suggest that it was not (e.g., "they don't want us to be rappers because rappers ain't field nigga's"). His boastful and critical discourse set in motion a number of literate stances, even overtly political ones, which enabled Etherin to articulate his complex and shared understandings of authority, resistance, and automobiles.

In his response to the same writing prompt, Larry also "bragged" about dope rides:

> You need a job that will give you the best chance to get what you want in life. If we can't get what we want in life, why live? Life is supposed to be about joy and the pursuit of happiness, not about struggling all the time. I need a job that will let me get a tricked-out Escalade with chrome spinners. With the right job and the right ride, you will be happy, but you need the right job to get the right ride. If you got the right job and the right ride, you get all the honeys too.

Larry shares a complex understanding of a material world where one should be given "the best chance to get what one wants in life." His social commentary quickly morphs into social critique: "If we can't get what we want in life, why live? Life is supposed to be about joy and the pursuit of happiness, not about struggling all the time."

Larry's question about life ("why live?") initiates another level of critique that I observed as alive in the young men's conversations with one another. Social questions about wealth and poverty, about social inequities, were always active in the young men's talk about "dope rides," debates on who could get them and who could not.

While his response had its critical moments, it also operated within the less-than critical stances that operated within bragging (i.e., bragging equates talking about being able to "get what you want in life" as opposed to "struggling all the time"). Larry's comments on "a tricked-out Escalade with chrome spinners" further situated his writing in the contexts of the boast. This black mode of discourse, as Smitherman (1977) would put it, may have capitulated to the capitalist establishment he was criticizing. But what some would view as capitulation may have been a kind of playful posing that helped the young men defer their dreams and cope with the self-doubt caused by pain and poverty (Kirkland, 2009). Hence, the ways in which Etherin, Larry, and their peers defined themselves, either by bragging about their desires or by expressing an interest in cars, greatly influenced the complex and sometimes difficult-to-understand ways in which the youth used the iconography of things to practice literacy and to brag.

DISCUSSION AND CONCLUSION

As I attempt to situate this research beyond the topics of black males and literacy, I do want to note that many claims that black males lack literacy are not only misleading but also threatening. Teachers interested in diverse perspectives on teacher education must be exposed to this line of thinking. They must also resolve particular questions that, if left unresolved, mandate various oppressions throughout our schools. Are black males less literate than other American youth? Of course, the answer is unequivocally no, but many novice teachers go into classrooms believing otherwise (Haddix, 2009).

By focusing on a single unit of discourse, I have observed a subtle, perhaps universal practice of literacy tied to how a group of young black males made sense of things. In this way, Dyson (2006) has suggested that the so-called literacy gap is an aberration that reflects more accurately cultural derisions in our society than achievement ones. The true crisis that young black males face deals more with power, authority, and a lack of understanding than it does with a lack of ability (Noguera, 2008). I agree here that their boast made them different not deficient. Researchers and educators then must be careful when making sweeping claims about the literate capabilities of any group, particularly black males, as these claims have historically worked to reinforce dangerous assumptions about the cognitive and linguistic abilities of oppressed people.

Therefore, studying diversity in teacher education is most meaningful when it challenges inaccuate assumptions about marginlized people (Lowenstein, 2009; Swartz, 2009). Too often such study, without real understandings of unique groups, works to reinforce stereotypes rather than eliminating them. We have seen this with black males, where the devaluing of black males has only helped to deepen beliefs that lead to further devaluing of black males (hooks, 2004b). Such cycles of discrimination have profound implications for shaping society and even more profound implications for undermining teacher education. For many Black males the consequence of misinformed teachers can be catastrophic. Moreover failures in teacher preparation leave young black men to flood our street corners, our prisons, and, worst, our cemeteries.

Teacher educators need to know that many black males come to school with existing relations to literacy. This does not mean that teacher educators should manufacture bragging curricula for black boys, simply fetishizing black masculinity. Nor does it mean that we should essentialize black males, as many of them may never brag, at least not in the same ways as the young men of MBK. What it does mean is that black males can and often do perform literacy in ways that somethings get vilified.

Therefore continued research is needed on underrepresented youth, for these embody are the diversity we seek to study in teacher education. This research, however, must hold back from selectively exemplifying particular youth, as such lines of inquiry will only serve as a new brand of discrimination (Gutierrez & Orellana, 2006). Instead, we need studies of youth that promote their voices and represent them in ways that allow teachers to understand the complexities of the students. We also need studies, like this one, that presents contextualized content knowledge about social and cultural phenomenon such as literacy that can help reconfigure pedagogy—a new sociocultural kind of pedagogical content knowledge for new century classrooms. Finally, we need studies in teacher education that explain learning outside classrooms so that we can recalibrate theories of teaching and learning within classrooms to better fit students and their development needs.

While our needs in teacher education are vast, I return to the particular question of black males. How do we prepare teachers to know them? For Black males, it might help if teachers were prepared to attend to the complexities of growing up black and male:

1. through courses that examine theories on black masculinities (cf., Brown, 1999; Young, 2007);
2. through targeted field experiences (within black neighborhoods as opposed to schools) working with young black men (cf., Morrell, 2005);
3. through research-training skills in ethnography and/or critical discourse analysis so that teachers can draw informed and systematic conclusions about their students to better teach them (cf., Alim, 2005; Heath, 1983; hooks, 2004a); and
4. through assessment tools that measure whether or not a teacher can adequately demonstrate complex and sophisticated cultural knowledge of her or his students. This assessment of social and cultural content and pedagogical knowledge must be matched equally with an assessment of culturally relevant content and pedagogies (cf., Dixson, 2003; Greene & Abt-Perkins, 2003; Irvine & Armento, 2001).

My point here is that teaching teachers about the complexities surrounding black males must go beyond the current crisis discourse. Black males are emerging, and my analysis of how they emerge as literate as evidenced in their boast exemplified this. Indeed, there is a good deal to learn in teacher education by listening to their social and cultural languages, to what they can do as opposed to what they cannot. Without such outreach, there is no studying diversity in teacher education.

NOTES

1. Freire is speaking specifically of Latin American men, but African American men, as there marginal counterparts, certainly apply in his argument. This connection is made visible later by Freire and Macedo (1995) in their article published in the *Harvard Educational Review*, which dealt with race, language, and the politics of education.

2. According to Gee (1996), "Discourses," with a capital *D*, are "the recognizable co-ordinations of people, places, objects, tools, technologies, and ways of speaking, listening, writing, reading, feeling, valuing, believing, etc." By contrast, "discourse," with a lowercase *d*, just stands for language in use. In this chapter, I do not make a distinction between the two usages, but I distinguish them here to shed light on a specific feature of discourse that relates to social ways of being and behaving.

3. While students were videotaped to desensitize students to the presence of a video recorder in the classroom at the very first program meeting, formal videotapes were taken after the third program meeting.

4. The meeting space was one of Malcolm X Academy's larger classroom spaces, with seats for forty students.

REFERENCES

Alim, H. S. (2005). Critical language awareness in the United States: Revisiting issues and revising pedagogies in a resegregated society. *Educational Researcher, 34(7)*, 24–31.

Alim, H. S. (2006). *Roc the mic right: The language of hip hop culture.* New York: Routledge.

Alvermann, D. E. (2003). U.S. middle years teaching education and youth literacies. *Teaching Education, 14(1),* 7–24.

Anzaldúa, G. (1987/1999). *Borderlands, La Frontera: The new mestiza* (2nd ed.). San Francisco: Aunt Lute Book.

Asher, N. (2005). At the interstices: Engaging postcolonial and feminist perspectives for a multicultural education pedagogy in the South. *Teachers College Record, 107(5),* 1079–106.

Bakhtin, M. M. (1981). *The dialogic imagination: Four essays.* Trans. M. Holquist & C. Emerson. Austin: University of Texas Press.

Brown, J. A. (1999). Comic book masculinity and the new black superhero. *African American Review, 33(1),* 25–42.

Connor, M. K. (1995). *What is cool? Understanding black manhood in America.* New York: Crown Publishers.

Davis, J. E. (2001). Black boys at school: Negotiating masculinities and race. In Majors, R. (Ed.), *Educating our black children: New directions and radical approaches* (pp. 169–82). London: Routledge/Falmer.

Dixson, A. D. (2003). "Let's do this!" Black women teachers' politics and pedagogy. *Urban Education, 38(2),* 217–35.

Dyson, A. H. (2003). Popular literacies and the "all" children: Rethinking literacy development for contemporary childhoods. *Language Arts, 81(2),* 100–109.

Dyson, A. H. (2006). Literacy in a child's world of voices, or, the fine print of murder and mayhem. *Research in the Teaching of English, 41(2),* 147–53.

Emerson, R., Fretz, R., & Shaw, L. (1995). *Writing ethnographic fieldnotes.* Chicago: University of Chicago Press.

Fashola, O. (Ed.). (2005). *Educating African-American males: Voices from the field.* Thousand Oaks, CA: Corwin Press.

Ferguson, A. (2000). *Bad boys: Public schools in the making of black masculinity.* Ann Arbor: University of Michigan Press.

Foster, K. M. (2005). Diet of disparagement: The racial experiences of black students in a predominantly white university. *International Journal of Qualitative Studies in Education, 18(4),* 489–505.

Freire, P. (1982). *Pedagogy of the oppressed.* New York: Continuum.

Freire, P., & Macedo, D. P. (1995). A dialogue: Culture, language, and race. *Harvard Educational Review, 65(3),* 377–402.

Gee, J. P. (1989). What is literacy? *Journal of Education, 171(1),* 5–25.

Gee, J. P. (1996). *Social linguistic and literacies: Ideology in discourses* (2nd ed.). Bristol, PA: Taylor & Francis.

Gee, J. P. (2004). Discourse analysis: What makes it critical? In Rogers, R. (Ed.), *An introduction to critical discourse analysis in education* (pp. 19–50). Mahway, NJ: Lawrence Erlbaum Associates.

Greene, S., & Abt-Perkins, D. (2003). *Making race visible: Literacy research for cultural understanding.* New York: Teachers College Press.

Gutierrez, K. D. (2008). Developing a sociocritical literacy in the third space. *Reading Research Quarterly, 43(2),* 148–64.

Gutierrez, K. D., & Orellana, M. F. (2006). The "problem" of English learners: Constructing genres of difference. *Research in the Teaching of English, 40(4),* 502–7.

Haddix, M. (2009). Black boys can write: Challenging dominant framings of African American adolescent males in literacy research. *Journal of Adolescent & Adult Literacy, 53(4),* 341–43.

Heath, S. B. (1983). *Ways with words: Language, life and work in communities and classrooms.* Cambridge, MA: Cambridge University Press.

Hilliard, A. G., III. (1990). Limitations of current academic-achievement measures. In Lomotey, K. (Ed.), *Going to school: The African-American experience* (pp. 135–42). New York: State University of New York Press.

Hilliard III, A. G. (2003). No mystery: Closing the achievement gap. In Perry, T., Steele, C., & Hilliard III, A. G. (Eds.), *Young, gifted, and black: Promoting high achievement among African-American students* (pp. 131–65). Boston: Beacon Press.

hooks, b. (1994). *Teaching to transgress: Education as the practice of freedom.* New York: Routledge.

hooks, b. (2004a). Culture to culture: Ethnography and cultural studies as critical intervention. In Hesse-Biber, S. & Leavy, P. (Eds.), *Approaches to qualitative research.* New York: Oxford University Press.

hooks, b. (2004b). *We real cool: Black men and masculinity.* London: Routledge.

Hopkins, R. (1997). *Educating black males: Critical lessons in schooling, community and power.* Albany: State University of New York Press.

Hymes, D. (1993). Toward ethnographies of communication. In Maybin, J. (Ed.), *Language and literacy in social practice.* London: Multilingual Matters.

Irvine, J. J., & Armento, B. (2001). *Culturally responsive teaching.* New York: McGraw Hill.

Jackson, J. F. L., & Moore, J. L. I. (2006). African American males in education: Endangered or ignored? *Teachers College Record, 108(2)*, 201–5.

Jencks, C., & Phillips, M. (Eds.). (1998). *The black-white test score gap.* Washington, DC: Brookings Institution.

Jones, L. (ed.). (2002). *Making it on broken promises: African American male scholars confront the culture of higher education.* Herndon, VA: Stylus Publishing.

Jones, S. (1997). *The archeology of ethnicity: Constructing identities in past and present.* Boston: Routledge & Kegan Paul.

Kirkland, D. E. (2006). *The boys in the hood: Exploring literacy in the lives of six urban adolescent black males.* Unpublished Dissertation, Michigan State University, East Lansing.

Kirkland, D. E. (2009). The skin we ink: Tattoos, literacy, and a new English education. *English Education, 41(4)*, 375–95.

Kirkland, D. E., & Jackson, A. (2009). "We Real Cool": Toward a theory of black masculine literacies. *Reading Research Quarterly, 44(3)*, 278–97.

Kunjufu, J. (1995). *Countering the conspiracy to destroy black boys.* Chicago: African American Images.

Labaree, D. F. (2004). *The trouble with ed schools.* New Haven, CT: Yale University Press.

Ladson-Billings, G. (1995). Toward a theory of culturally relevant pedagogy. *American Education Research Journal, 32(3)*, 465–91.

Lowenstein, K. L. (2009). The work of multicultural teacher education: Reconceptualizing white teacher candidates as learners. *Review of Educational Research, 79(1)*, 163–96.

Luke, A. (1997). *Critical literacy: An introduction.* St. Leonards, NSW: Allen & Unwin.

Luke, A., & Freebody, P. (1997). *Constructing critical literacies: Teaching and learning textual practice.* Cresskill, NJ: Hampton.

Majors, R., & Billson, J. M. (1993). *Cool pose: The dilemmas of black manhood in America.* New York: Lexington Books.

Meier, T. (1996). Never so truly free: Reading and writing about Malcolm in the community college. In Perry, T. (Ed.), *Teaching Malcolm X* (pp. 53–76). New York: Routledge.

Milner, H. R. (2007). Race, culture, and researcher positionality: Working through dangers seen, unseen, and unforeseen. *Educational Researcher, 36(7)*, 388–400.

Milofsky, C. (1974). Why special education isn't special. *Harvard Educational Review, 44(4)*, 437–58.

Moore, R. (1996). Between a rock and a hard place: African Americans and standard English. ERIC Document Reproduction Service No. ED 402 593.

Morrell, E. (2002). Toward a critical pedagogy of popular culture: Literacy development among urban youth. *Journal of Adolescent and Adult Literacy, 46(1)*, 72–77.

Morrell, E. (2005). Critical English education. *English Education, 37(4)*, 312–21.

Newkirk, T. (2002). Chapter 8: A big enough room. *Misreading masculinity: Boys, literacy, and popular culture* (pp. 169–91). Portsmouth, NH: Heinemann.

Noguera, P. A. (2003). The trouble with black boys: The role and influence of environmental and cultural factors on the academic performances of African American males. *Urban Education, 38(4)*, 431–59.

Noguera, P. A. (2008). *The trouble with black boys: And other reflections on race, equity, and the future of public education.* New York: Jossey-Bass.

Rickford, J. R., & Rickford, R. J. (2000). *Spoken soul: The story of black English.* New York: John Wiley & Sons.

Smitherman, G. (1977). *Talkin and testifyin: The language of black America.* Detroit, MI: Wayne State University Press.

Smitherman, G. (1999). *Talkin that talk: African American language and culture.* New York: Routledge.

Smitherman, G. (2006). *Word from the mother: Language and African Americans.* New York: Routledge.

Swartz, E. (2009). Diversity: Gatekeeping knowledge and maintaining inequalities. *Review of Educational Research, 79(2)*, 1044–83.

Taylor, D., & Dorsey-Gainses, C. (1988). *Growing up literate: Learning from inner-city families.* New York: Heinemann.

Young, V. A. (2007). *Your average nigga: Performing race, literacy, and masculinity.* Detroit, MI: Wayne State University Press.

9

Preparing Teacher Education Candidates to Work With Students With Disabilities and Gifts and Talents

Michelle Trotman Scott and Donna Y. Ford

To say that U.S. schools are becoming more racially and culturally different[1] on a daily basis is not an understatement, and this trend in student diversity is expected to continue. Conversely, teacher diversity or demographics has remained relatively stable, with little change expected. Despite this inverse patter between students and educators, unfortunately, gifted programs and AP classes are not increasing in diversity for at least three groups—Black, Hispanic, and American Indian students. At no time in our nation's history have these groups been proportionally represented in gifted education. Equally unfortunately, the reverse holds for special education—these same groups are overrepresented in high-incidence disability categories (i.e., learning disabilities, mild mental retardation, and emotional and behavior disorders).

Over five decades after the landmark decision of *Brown v. Board of Education* (1954) made school segregation illegal and sought to remedy historical inequities, African Americans are still fighting for equal and equitable rights in educational settings. Black and some other culturally different students continue to be denied access to gifted education programs, and many are misplaced in special education; a field whose labels and categories carry a great deal of stigma. Whether intended or not, gifted education, AP, and special education are riddled with injustices that hinder their educational well-being and future opportunities.

Several factors are at work that contribute to and maintain over- and underrepresentation in the above educational programs. First, it has been demonstrated that educators' attitudes and belief systems play a vital role in social injustices that exist in school settings (Ford, Grantham, & Whiting, 2008). Teachers overrefer Black students in particular for special education evaluation and underrefer them for gifted education evaluation. Given that many college and university programs do not require educators to take multicultural education classes, educators may harbor negative stereotypes and fears about Black and other racially and culturally different students. This lack of formal preparation does little to decrease deficit thinking about Black students; it fails to enlighten and empower educators to work competently or efficaciously with the diverse population of students that they serve. Furthermore, many educators are being taught by professors and instructors who, likewise, have little or no formal training and experience in multicultural education.

In this chapter, we discuss the status of gifted education, AP classes, and special education classes for Black and other culturally different students. We present an overview of major factors hindering equitable education for Black and some other culturally different students in these classes and programs. However, we devote most attention to Black students as they are the most disenfranchised students in U.S. schools. We also present characteristics of teacher education programs as they are and as they should be, competencies needed by all teachers of racially and culturally different students, summaries of three multicultural curriculum models, and recommendations for teacher preparation relative to multicultural education. In writing this chapter we are mindful that both the Council for Exceptional Children and the National Association for Gifted Children have, in recent years, adopted standards that highlight competencies needed by teachers to be effective with racially and culturally different students with disabilities and gifts and talents. Both standards include attention to cultural differences. This is, at last, recognition that a culturally competent teaching force may reduce the occurrence of mislabeling that can lead to the overrepresentation of culturally different students in special education and their underrepresentation in gifted education (Ford & Harris, 1999).

INEQUITY AT WORK IN GIFTED EDUCATION, AP, AND SPECIAL EDUCATION: TEACHER EDUCATION PROGRAMS MATTER

In 2006, the Office of Civil Rights presented data from its biennial Elementary and Secondary Civil Rights Survey of school districts nationally. Three data sets are relevant to this chapter—gifted education, AP classes, and special education results. The data are disturbing and unwarranted. When it comes to gifted education, Black students were underrepresented by 47 percent, which is tantamount to approximately 250,000 Black students not identified as gifted; for Hispanic students, some 40 percent were underidentified. Relative to AP, Black students were underrepresented by 50 percent; they represented 14 percent of the high school population, but only 7 percent were enrolled in AP classes.

When the population of students in special education programs is examined, the reverse was found (also see National Research Council, 2002). In terms of high-incidence disabilities, Black students are significantly overrepresented in the categories of mild mental retardation, emotional and behavior disorders, and learning disabilities. African American students were overrepresented in all of the areas that carried a highly stigmatized label (National Research Council, 2002) and produced the lowest high school graduation (U.S. Department of Education, 2003, 2009) and college attendance rates (Blackorby & Wagner, 1996; Horn & Berktold, 1999; Kauffman, 2002; U.S. Department of Education, 2009). Equally troubling, Blacks in special education had and have the lowest rates of inclusion in the general education classroom or setting (Trout, Nordness, Pierce, & Epstein, 2003). When all things are considered, students who are racially and culturally different, specifically those who are African American, will continue to face overrepresentation in special education programs (i.e., the high-incidence categories) and underrepresentation in gifted education programs and AP classes if focused, proactive, and aggressive steps are not taken in teacher education programs.

Contributing Factors: Inequity at Work

A number of factors contribute to the difficulties African American students confront relative to demonstrating their potential, achievement, and intellect. That is, several factors play major roles in gifted education and AP underrepresentation and special education overrepresentation. To change the aforementioned problems and trends, we contend that teacher education programs in gifted education and special education must set as a goal and priority that teachers leave their programs culturally competent (i.e., knowledge, dispositions, and skills). For teacher education candidates (preservice and in-service) to do so, teacher education programs must, at minimum:

- ensure that teacher candidates have consistent, multiple opportunities to examine their biases, stereotypes, and prejudices regarding Black and other racially and culturally different students; as well as critically explore how their beliefs and subjectiveness negatively affect Black students' achievement, placement, self-expectations, and more;
- ensure that its curriculum and materials (e.g., visual aids, displays, books, articles) are multicultural and culturally responsive—at the highest levels;
- require that field experiences take place in classrooms and communities that are racially and culturally different;
- ensure that theories and research assigned for reading and discussion are grounded in culture rather than being culture blind; and
- teach education candidates how to develop instruments and practice assessments that are culturally responsive (e.g., understanding, recognizing, and reducing test and instrument bias; nondiscriminatory assessment standards, principles, and practices).

These recommendations are expanded in the remaining sections of this chapter.

Teacher Expectations and Student Identification and Placement: The Need for Critical Self-Reflection

It has been our experience that teacher education candidates rarely engage in self-reflection or self-analysis relative to understanding how their beliefs and misperceptions contribute to poor or negative school experiences for Black students. Few will engage in such self-reflection on their own; and few teacher educators encourage, require, or provide them opportunities to do so. In terms of gifted education, AP, and special education, teachers in training *must* understand the powerful connection between their beliefs, attitudes, biases, and so on and the misidentification and misplacement of Black students.

Teacher referral ranks high among key factors contributing to overrepresentation and underrepresentation (Ford et al. 2008). At the heart of referral issues is deficit thinking—beliefs, attitudes, and values influence behaviors and practice. African

Americans and Hispanics have been designated to be "genetically inferior" and "culturally deprived" or "culturally disadvantaged" at some point in their past and current history. The more recent terminology is that these groups are "culturally different" (Gould, 1995; Valencia & Solórzano, 1997). Such notions about group differences in potential and ability influence definitions, policies, and practices designed to address such differences. Gould (1981, 1995) and Menchaca (1997) persuasively detailed how deficit thinking contributed to past and contemporary notions about race, culture, potential, and intelligence. Gould's work reinforced the reality that researchers are not objective, impartial, and bias free; instead, some have used miscalculated, dishonest, and prejudicial research methods, convenient omissions, and data misinterpretation to confirm their own and others' views. These prejudgments and attendant behaviors and practices have contributed to the widely held belief that human races could be ranked in a linear scale of mental worth (see Gould, 1981).

Menchaca (1997) placed in both historical and contemporary context the evolution of deficit thinking. His work shows how such thinking influenced past and current segregation in schools (e.g., *Plessy v. Fergusen*, 1896) and resistance to desegregation during the civil rights era and today. Unfortunately, educators continue to resist desegregation, using gifted education, AP, and special education to resegregate students along racial lines (e.g., Ford & Webb, 1994; Ford, Grantham, & Whiting, 2008; Losen & Orfield, 2002; Oakes, 1985).

Underlying the above decisions and actions is hesitance or resistance among some education candidates to examine the strong relationship among their beliefs, attitudes, and school practices and the resultant educational and social outcomes of Black and other racially and culturally different students (e.g., school failure, low grades, poor motivation, etc.). "Because educators do not view themselves as part of the problem, there is little willingness to look for solutions within the educational system itself" (Garcia & Guerra, 2004, p. 151).

Teacher education programs must consistently, openly, and proactively assign readings and hold discussions with teacher education candidates on their expectations and deficit thinking (fears, biases, stereotypes) and how these affect their behaviors, practices, and decisions, which are often discriminatory.

Underrepresentation and Overrepresentation: The Need for Culturally Responsive Testing and Assessment

In addition to educator biases that influence referrals to special education and underreferral to gifted education and AP, the use of high-stakes tests comes with much controversy. Utilizing tests to identify and assess students is a prevalent educational practice that has increased with recent federal legislation (e.g., No Child Left Behind, 2001). High-stakes testing is common practice, playing the decisive role in decisions made about students, including identification and placement decisions for gifted education, AP classes, and special education.

More than 90 percent of school districts use intelligence or achievement test scores for gifted education recruitment (screening, identification, and placement) (Davis & Rimm, 2003; National Association for Gifted Children, 2009). This extensive reliance on test scores for decision making negatively influences the demographics of gifted programs and AP classes by keeping them White and middle class. While traditional intelligence tests equitably identify and capture the strengths of middle-class White students, they have been less effective with African American and Hispanic students (e.g., Naglieri & Ford, 2005).

Similarly, in special education, tests are used for identification, labeling, and placement decisions. As an illustration, students who score low on intelligence tests run the risk of being labeled mentally retarded and those who show a discrepancy between intelligence and achievement are at risk for being labeled learning disabled. African American students face the greatest risk of such labeling, as previously noted.

The federal government's requirement that assessment be multidimensional and nondiscriminatory is vital, but it alone is not enough to redress inequities. This and other practices have not been enough to decrease the negative impact of testing on African American students and some other racially and culturally different students. These students face double jeopardy when it comes to testing—doors are closed to gifted education and AP, but open to special education. All of this discussion raises a fundamental question: Why do we continue to use these tests so exclusively or extensively if certain groups do not perform well on them (Ford & Whiting, 2006; Whiting & Ford, 2006)?

Given that tests are here to stay, it is imperative teacher education programs train teacher candidates in the responsible and equitable use of tests and instruments. Teacher education programs must, relatedly, teach candidates how to interpret scores and performance (especially IQ scores and scores from behavioral instruments) in responsible and professional ways. This is particularly important in special education and gifted education teacher education programs due to the extensive or exclusive reliance on test scores for identification and placement.

Educators must also be taught how not to limit themselves to "testing" students but, instead, to "assess" students. Assessment includes testing, but it goes further by being multimodal and multidimensional, which consists of administering more than one instrument and evaluating students in multiple ways (e.g., written, oral, performance, project) and using a combination of objective and subject information to make a comprehensive, informed, culturally centered decision.

Just as important, teacher education candidates must be taught about the principle and goal of nondiscriminatory and equitable assessment and evaluation (Ford & Whiting, 2006; Whiting & Ford, 2006). When assessment and evaluations of students are nondiscriminatory, teacher education candidates avoid using instruments found to be biased; when developing their own tests, they do so with the goal of avoiding bias against Black students with gifts and disabilities. Teacher education programs must teach candidates how to develop and use instruments that do not discriminate against Black students.

They must know that federal law stipulates and requires nondiscriminatory assessment in special education because it appears to miss a lot in translation and actual practice. Likewise, candidates ought to know that professional organizations (e.g., AERA, APA, NAGC, CEC, NCATE, ATE, NAME) all have position papers, principles or standards regarding equitable testing and assessment of racially and culturally different students. Teacher education students must be exposed to these papers, standards, and principles, along with test bias, test anxiety, and stereotype threat (see Perry, 2003; Steele, 2010), the limitations of tests, norming and validity issues, test interpretation or misinterpretation, and test use, misuse, or abuse.

Training teacher educators in culturally responsive assessment instruments and practices can have a positive impact on overrepresentation and underrepresentation. Regarding special education testing and assessment, teacher educators should be assigned readings by such scholars as Alba Ortiz, Russell Skiba, Jim Cummings, and Richard Figueroa, to name but a few. In gifted education, we recommend teacher educators be exposed to the *Naglieri Non-Verbal Abilities Test* (1 and 2), *Raven's Progressive MAT*, and *Universal Non-Verbal Intelligence Test*.

Culturally Responsive Curriculum: Increasing Teacher Candidates' Cultural Competence

Unlike special education, gifted education is not federally mandated. Thus, teacher educators who want to work with gifted students do not necessarily require formal training, unless mandated at the state level (National Association for Gifted Children, 2009). According to Van Tassel-Baska (2006), only 3 percent of colleges and universities offer coursework in gifted education. Hence, the majority of teachers working with gifted students have no formal preparation to do so.

Relatedly, too few schools seem to take seriously the need to prepare teacher educators to be culturally competent, even in special education with its large Black student population. Frequently, such preparation is limited to one course on "diversity" or on "at risk" students (Banks, 1994, 1997, 2007, 2008). This lack of preparation in the need and characteristics of gifted students dilutes the efficacy of teachers who do and will work with them. In other words, teacher education candidates who are ill prepared in gifted education are likely to be ineffective at identifying and serving them. This incompetence is particularly problematic when teacher educators use the behaviors of White students as the norm by which to understand, compare, evaluate, and make decisions about Black and other racially and culturally different students.

Essentially, teacher educators in higher education classrooms often matriculate with a Euro-centric or culture-blind curriculum that ill prepares them to understand, respect, and work efficaciously with students who are racially and culturally different. Subsequently, they fail to understand students who differ from them culturally relative to learning styles, communication styles, and behavioral styles. To repeat, the result is deficit thinking and a cultural mismatch between teacher educators and students; this fosters poor learning environments, low teacher expectations of students, poor student-teacher relationships, mislabeling, and misinterpretation of behaviors.

To address these shortcomings and, thus, prepare teacher educators for working responsively with Black students in gifted education, AP classes, and special education students, teacher education programs and faculty need to: (1) expose them to multicultural and culturally responsive education and curricular models, theories, and strategies in general, but also specific to special education and gifted education. In special education teacher preparation specifically, we recommend the works in the area of curriculum and instruction by Cathy Kea, Gwendolyn Cartledge, Gwendolyn Johnson, Gloria Campbell-Whatley, Debbie Voltz, Wanda Blanchett, James Patton, and Festus Obiakor, for example.

In gifted education, in addition to our own works, we recommend that of Alexinia Baldwin, Mary Frasier, Ernesto Bernal, Margie Kitano, Tarek Grantham, James Moore,

Gilman Whiting, Fred Bonner, Jaimie Castellano, Paula Olszewski-Kubilius, Sally Reis, Joe Renzulli, and Joyce Van Tassel-Baska.

In our own classrooms, we rely mainly on the multicultural model of James Banks to teach preservice and in-service teachers how to develop relevant, substantive, multicultural curriculum and materials for students in gifted education and special education.

In an effort to reach the goal of affirming individual differences and human diversity through the elimination of prejudices, biases, and stereotypes based on sociodemographic variables (Ford & Harris, 1999), a multicultural curriculum must be implemented. This type of curriculum allows teachers to provide an education that infiltrates all aspects of teaching and learning rather than providing an education that is narrow and only supplements a curriculum that is restrictive or forces culturally different populations to conform to the ideas and beliefs of a culture different from their own.

Davidman and Davidman (1994) summarized the goals of multicultural education as those that provide multicultural knowledge, educational equity, cultural pluralism, empowerment, and social relations. The first goal, multicultural knowledge, empowers students to develop cultural pluralism as well as think, work, and live with a multicultural perspective. Educational equity, the second goal, provides students with three fundamental conditions that give them an equal opportunity to learn, to reach individual and group positive educational outcomes, and affords them with equal physical and financial conditions that aid them as they strive to reach their fullest potential, both academically and affectivity.

The next goal, cultural pluralism, creates positive attitudes in all that work with students in diverse settings, while the goal of empowerment helps students and educators advocate for an education that provides culturally relevant teaching, culturally responsive classrooms, and promotes positive student outcomes. The last goal, social relations, enables educators to provide knowledge, skills, and a classroom environment that will prepare students to live and work in a very culturally different and diverse society.

Several strategies have been developed to meet the goals for multicultural education. Grant and Sleeter's model (1998) discusses five approaches to multicultural education. These approaches, teaching the culturally different approach, human relations approach, single-group studies approach, multicultural education approach, and education that is multicultural and socially reconstructionist, allow one to view multiculturalism in a more comprehensive way. They also make educators more aware of group similarities and differences, how cultures can interact together, and aid them in developing ways of thinking and analyzing so that they may be better able to become proactive and make positive change in society.

The Banks's model (1994, 2007, 2008) focuses on four levels of integrating multicultural content into the curriculum. The first level, contributions approach, provides a quick and easy way to put ethnic content into the curriculum by adding heroes, cultural components, holidays, and other discrete elements related to ethnic groups during special days, occasions, and celebrations. The second level, the additive approach, can be implemented using the existing curriculum without changing its structure by simply adding multicultural content, concepts, themes, and perspectives. Level 3, the transformation approach, is more complex in that the basic goals, structure, and nature of the curriculum are changed to enable different, alternative perspectives, concepts, events, issues, problems, and themes to be viewed and interrogated. The fourth and final level, the social action approach, enables students to identify, analyze, and clarify important social problems and issues and make decisions and take reflective actions to help resolve the issues or problems. In sum, the four levels help all students increase their motivation, learning, and knowledge about cultural and racial differences as well as to acquire a sense of social justice or activism (Gay, 1993, 2002).

The Ford-Harris model (Ford & Harris, 1999) combines Bloom's (1956) taxonomy of educational objectives and the works of Banks (1994, 2008) to provide educators with a multicultural education model that focuses on Banks's transformation and social activism levels and on Bloom's analysis, synthesis, and evaluation levels. A model such as this enables students to receive an education that includes products, content, and processes that reflect the goals, objectives, and perspectives of multicultural education (Ford & Harris, 1999). When used correctly, multicultural curriculums, such as those just briefly described, give Black students in gifted and special education opportunities to reach their potential as well as emerge in areas that the teacher educator may otherwise not be aware.

Characteristics of Students Who Are Culturally Different: Training in Culturally Responsive Instruction

It would be a disservice to African Americans and other racially and culturally different students to deny, minimize, or trivialize their heritage, culture, and history. Yet, this is done on a routine basis in far too many schools. Groups and individuals coming from different cultural backgrounds bring similar and different needs and styles to the learning environments. Teacher education candidates must not only learn about culturally responsive curriculum but also instruction.

Along with other scholars, Boykin (1994; Boykin, Tyler, Miller, 2005) has found that African Americans exhibit certain modal cultural styles. These particular styles are developed as one is nurtured within a particular familial and communal context. When individuals are placed in situations and contexts different than what they are accustomed to, they are likely to have difficulty making the necessary adjustments to be successful, a phenomenon known as *cultural shock* (Oberg, 1974).

We now use Boykin's research-based findings to demonstrate how teacher educators can misunderstand such differences, thus highlighting the need for formal multicultural educator preparation. Before doing so, a few caveats are in order. These data-based characteristics represent modal behaviors and beliefs, which is a statistical concept. Thus, not all African Americans will display all of the characteristics; they are not a homogeneous group. Further, other individuals and groups can and do display one or more of these characteristics. The model includes nine characteristics to utilize as a guide from which to begin acquiring a better understanding of African Americans, without turning the generalizations (model, guide, framework) into stereotypes (inflexible thinking; all-or-nothing thinking) (see Shade, Kelly, & Oberg, 1997).

Spirituality. Spirituality is prevalent within the African American culture. African Americans may believe that life's happenings are not automatic and that religious and higher forces influence people's everyday lives and all of life's affairs. In school settings, spirituality may be at work when students choose not to study because they believe that if God wants them to pass, they will pass or that failing the test must have been God's will or plan. Although one's spirituality should be respected, this belief may be misinterpreted as laziness or uncaring or making excuses for performance.

Harmony. Many people within the African American culture have a high sensitivity to and appreciation for rhythm and harmony—being in sync with the environment. This characteristic is displayed in a multitude of ways. For instance, it may be displayed within the classroom whereby an African American student feels unwelcome, like an outsider, by a teacher or classmate(s) who fails to make a personal connection with him/her. This student might go to great pains to be noticed by the teacher or classmates. This might lead teacher candidates to feel that the student is emotionally or socially immature.

Movement. African American students often express a strong desire to move and be actively involved. They tend to have kinesthetic (hands-on) learning styles, as well as possessing psychomotor intelligence (e.g., Shade, 1994; Shade, Kelly, & Oberg 1997). The movement characteristic emphasizes the interweaving of movement, rhythm, music, and dance, all of which are considered to be central to the psychological health of African American students. This physical overexcitability may be mistaken for hyperactivity.

Verve. As with movement, African American students tend to be lively and energetic, preferring a high level of stimulation. This may be considered loud and even obnoxious to those not familiar with this cultural pattern. Black students may be considered as rude, off-task, lazy, or unmotivated when they are unresponsive to lecture-type teaching or forced to learn in a way they may consider dull and lifeless.

Affect. Affective students are sensitive to emotional cues. They have a tendency to know when one does not particularly care for them and may react in a way that may be deemed inappropriate. For example, if a teacher moves back as the student approaches or sighs when the student raises his/her hand to ask a question, the student may respond in an emotional manner. The teacher candidate may consider this type of response as insubordinate and the child may be sent out of the classroom, which may reiterate the student's belief that the teacher does not like him/her.

Communalism. Another characteristic of many African American students is that they have a strong commitment to social connectedness; interdependence is high for this population. African American students often believe that the interdependence of people and social bonds and relationships are fundamental and important. They are committed to building, strengthening, and maintaining these social bonds and responsibilities. These students have a need for affiliation and social acceptance or approval and because of this, their communal connections and conscientiousness surpass their individual privileges. This is apparent in classes where an educator may observe that a student performs well when he/she works with others rather than alone. If this characteristic is not understood, the educator may assume that the student is socially needy and incapable of achieving independent of others.

Oral Tradition. Oral tradition can be found throughout African American history. African American students have been found to prefer oral modes of communication. They also enjoy the use of elaborate and exaggerated language, storytelling, and telling jokes. The creation and use of slang terms and the development and popularity of rap music are examples of the oral tradition. Further, the direct, blunt, and metaphorically colorful use of language is common. Teachers unfamiliar with this tradition may become frustrated with joking and embellishments, as well as students' forthrightness, and may misinterpret them as forms of disrespect or impoliteness.

Expressive Individualism. African American students often seek and develop distinctive personalities that denote a uniqueness of personal style. This is displayed through the colorful use of language and dress. In all actuality, these students are displaying creativity. However, they may be considered as impulsive, eccentric, or as attention seekers by those who do not understand their way of expressing. In turn, this misinterpretation may cause students to feel ostracized.

Social Time Perspective. Many African American students emphasize what is occurring at the present . . . the here and now is what tends to matter most. As such, the event is more important than the time. These students tend to treat time as a social and circular phenomenon—there is no beginning or end—so time is not a limited commodity that drives decisions. Teachers may have difficulty adjusting to this characteristic of circular time, especially when deadlines have been set and are not adhered to by the students.

Teacher educators who are not familiar with the characteristics that African American students possess may (mis)interpret their behaviors or learning styles in a negative, deficit-oriented way. These misunderstandings may inadvertently affect the way that teacher candidates interact with African American students, and students who are unable or unwilling to make the necessary adjustments may experience difficulties coming to grips with their academic, social, and emotional needs and expectations.

Other Recommendations for Teacher Education Programs

In this brief chapter, it is impossible to present all issues and recommendations needed to improve the formal preparation of teacher educators so that they can understand and meet the needs of Black and other racially and culturally different students in gifted education and special education settings. Thus, we hone in on a few final suggestions that can, nonetheless, move us in the right direction, the only direction that we ought to go—preparing teachers to work with Black students who are gifted and need special education services.

The implications of the aforementioned information suggest that many changes should be made to provide the appropriate means to adequately prepare teachers for the reality of a very diverse and different student population. These changes include, but are not limited to:

1. Integrating multicultural content into every course.
   This can be done using the multicultural models described earlier in this paper. The Ford-Harris model of multicultural education is exceptional due to its ability to promote actions and knowledge on several levels of multiculturalism. It enables an educator to implement diverse learning ranging from small to medium to large scale.
2. Requiring that all classes focus on multicultural topics and issues.
   Oftentimes, preservice teachers graduate without any multicultural requirements. For most, multicultural classes are not required until they enter a graduate program and in many cases can be substituted for other elective courses. Regardless of the makeup of the university or the population in which the

preservice teacher will teach, it is imperative that their classes focus on multicultural issues of all aspects of education to be better equipped to interact with and educate their gifted and special education students. Math, science, literature, art, music, history, social studies, civics, pedagogy and learning theory, curriculum-lesson plan development, assessment, family involvement, and all other classes must include multicultural information, resources, and strategies (recall the models by Banks, and Ford and Harris).

3. Practicum or internships in gifted and special education should take place in diverse settings.

    Implement programs such as Texas A&M University's Minority Mentorship Project (MMP). This project's conceptual framework educates preservice teachers to reflect the concerns of multicultural student populations (Lark & Wiseman, 1987; Wiseman, Larke, & Bradley, 1989). It also provides them with exposure and experience to work with students and their families whose backgrounds are different from that of the preservice teacher and helps them to confront their attitudes and perceptions of students and families from different cultures. It also moves them from an ethnocentric point of view to some degree of cultural relativism (Larke, Wiseman, & Bradley, 1990).

4. Schedule educators teaching in diverse settings to come and present or lecture in gifted and special education classes.

    a. It is virtually impossible to gain experience with and exposure to every multicultural group. However, universities can secure guest lecturers to visit and speak to classes in an effort to provide preservice teachers with some knowledge in specific cultural groups in the context of their gifted and special education needs and development.

    b. Topics that the lectures from teacher educators and visitors must include:

        1. *Understanding the concept of culture.*
            What is culture and how does it vary across groups and across settings/contexts.

        2. *Cultural biases, values, and so forth, and how they impact students' performance.*
            How teachers' biases and feelings toward children impact students' educational outcomes and career.

        3. *Learning styles and how they differ across cultures.*
            Different groups or cultures learn in different ways, and it is imperative that students are allowed and able to utilize a style most comfortable or familiar to them so they can obtain and maintain success. This support makes learning culturally responsive. When teacher candidates in special and gifted education classrooms understand and respect culturally influenced learning, communication, and behavioral styles, there is likely to be less misidentification and mislabeling.

        4. *Communication (both verbal and nonverbal) and how communication varies across different cultures.*
            a. Certain cultures have verbal and nonverbal communication skills that may differ from traditional skills of classmates and those of their teachers. These characteristics must be understood and appreciated to prevent misconceptions and miscommunication among teachers, parents, and students (recall the works of Boykin).

b. Understand how behavior is socially determined and judgmental; that is to say, what one teacher candidate deems as "abnormal" may not be viewed as such by another teacher candidate, individual, or group. Readings on culturally responsive classroom or behavior management holds promise for decreasing special education mislabeling, like behavior disordered, disruptive, inattentive, distracted, and so forth. It can also help teacher candidates in gifted education to see gifts and talents despite differences in behaviors.

c. Teaching teacher candidates how to develop and design research projects (e.g., for class assignments, theses, dissertations) guided by best practices in culturally responsive research (e.g., design, questions, instrument development or adoption, data collection, interpretation) (see Ford, Moore, Whiting, & Grantham, 2008).

5. *Understand Black family structures and roles of primary caregivers when children are gifted or have special education needs.*

Familial structure and roles vary across households and cultures. Teaching and parenting styles may conflict, with the student caught in the middle. Both parties need to understand and work through these differences so that students can succeed. Beth Harry's work may be the most extensive in the area of working with Black and Hispanic families of children in special education. Topics include how families hold similar and different views about disability, seeking medical assistance, seeking counseling, and family involvement at school. Few people have focused their work on Black families with gifted children, but Ford (1996) has addressed this to some degree. Black parents have been found to have different and similar concerns about having gifted children than White parents have about their children. For Black parents and families, concerns focus on finding diverse gifted and AP classes, hoping that teachers have high expectations of their children, and helping their children cope with negative peer pressures from both Black and White students and classmates.

6. *Cultural perceptions and values toward education and achievement.*

Too many Black students perceive achievement and success in ways that may differ from the "norm" or what is familiar. For example, a Black student who is in the ninety-fifth percentile may be failing in class for social-emotional or racial identity reasons. However, teacher candidates may attribute low performance to some other factor. Teacher education programs can help these candidates by focusing on the importance of and need to build relationships and respect with Black students as a way to open the lines of communication and, thus, achievement.

A FINAL NOTE

Teacher education programs must prepare teachers to work with racially and culturally different students. In order to do so, professors and instructors of teacher preparation programs must recognize and accept that we live in a culturally diverse society and that "all teachers must be knowledgeable, about cultural diversity, even if they do not teach in multicultural communities" (Kea & Utley, 1998, p. 45). Therefore, teacher candidates must spend their time in university classrooms learning to create equitable learning environments for Black and other racially and culturally different student populations.

Unfortunately, preservice teachers' preparation for multicultural education is very limited. It is not integrated in a thorough, persistent manner and is delivered covertly in program requirements (e.g., Banks, 2008; Grant, 1994). This all-too-common approach leads to teacher candidates' lacking awareness or not taking ownership of their ethnocentric views, stereotypes, and biases and their limited cultural competence regarding students whose culture differs from their own. This lack of multicultural competence or efficacy hinders their adopting affective practices with students and families from diverse backgrounds. A lingering and looming question, then, is "if the goal of education is to help students acquire the necessary tools in order to be successful in society, why, then, is it common practice to graduate preservice teachers without any experience, knowledge, or teachings from a multicultural perspective?"

Teacher training programs must help students to recognize and understand their own worldviews so that they are able to improve their ability to understand the different worldviews of their students. These candidates must confront their own biases (Banks, 2007; Ford, Grantham, & Whiting, 2008; Gillette & Boyle-Baise, 1995; Nieto & Rolon, 1995), learn more about their students' cultures, and perceive the world through other cultural lenses (Banks, 1997, 2007; Gay, 2000, 2002; Ladson-Billings, 2009; Nieto & Rolon, 1995). However, without formal multicultural preparation that is ongoing and in most, if not all, coursework, it is virtually impossible for teacher candidates to change in their attitudes, values, and practice. With formal knowledge in cultural differences (e.g., via teacher education programs or professional development), teachers will be better equipped to help racially and culturally different students, increase their advocacy for such students, increase their self-understanding and empathy, decrease prejudice and stereotypes, and build a much-needed sense of community in their special education and gifted education classrooms.

Over the past few decades, several authors, including Banks (1994, 1997, 2008), Bennett (1990), Garcia (1994), Gollnick and Chin (1998), Grant and Sleeter (1998), and Heid (1988), have focused on the vital need to reform education from one that is Euro-centric or ethnocentric to one that is multicultural and otherwise culturally responsive. When teacher education students are formally trained in multicultural education, they can:

1. develop multicultural curriculum and instruction in all subject areas and courses;
2. integrate a philosophy of multiculturalism into educational practices, policies, and programs;
3. adopt multiculturalism in all educational systems and institutions, regardless of racial and cultural composition;
4. help to recruit and retain a more racially and culturally diverse and different teaching force; and

5. evaluate the quality of multicultural education (curriculum and instruction) to ensure that it is substantive and integral.

It is frightening and alarming to know that teachers graduate from higher education and are placed in gifted education and special education classrooms in which they have no prior knowledge and skills. Yet, they are expected to teach all students to achieve and succeed. Such a goal is difficult to attain when teachers are not prepared to adequately do so. If colleges and universities do not change the way they are preparing current and future educators, we will continue to witness unnecessary dropout rates, school failure, and academic apathy or disengagement among Black and some other culturally different students. For purposes of this chapter, the most obvious impact is the denial of Black students opportunities and the right to participate in gifted education and their often unnecessary placement in special education. Educators and those who prepare them must accept the ever-increasing diversity of our student population and then do what is necessary to become culturally competent or efficacious.

The long-fought battle to achieve equality, equity, and excellence in school settings, as promised by *Brown v. Board of Education* (1954), is not over. Daily, Black students face unnecessary barriers to receiving a high-quality education and accessing an education that is rigorous and responsive. Special education and gifted education are not exempt from this law and must do all they can, legally and ethically, to live up to the promises of desegregation. It is not only Black students who benefit—educators and society at large are also the beneficiaries!

NOTE

1. In this chapter, we use the term *culturally different* rather than *culturally diverse* based on our belief that everyone has a culture. We maintain that our differences contribute to problems. Further, when discussing overrepresentation in special education and underrepresentation in gifted education, we are focusing on African American and Latino students. In many cases, we devote more attention to issues facing African American students because they are the most disenfranchised group of students in school settings, an argument that we develop in the chapter.

REFERENCES

Banks, J. A. (1994). *Multiethnic education: Theory and practice.* Needham Heights, MA: Allyn & Bacon.

Banks, J. A. (1997). *Teaching strategies for ethnic studies* (6th ed.). New York: Allyn & Bacon.

Banks, J. A. (2006). *Diversity in American education: Foundations, curriculum and teaching.* Boston: Allyn & Bacon.

Banks, J. A. (2007). *An introduction to multicultural education* (4th ed.). Boston: Allyn & Bacon.

Banks, J. A. (2008). *Teaching strategies for ethnic studies.* Boston: Allyn & Bacon.

Bennett, C. I. (1990). *Comprehensive multicultural education: Theory and practice* (2nd ed.). Boston: Allyn & Bacon.

Blackorby, J., & Wagner, M. (1996). Longitudinal postschool outcomes of youth with disabilities: Findings from the national transition study. *Exceptional Children, 62(5),* 399–414.

Bloom, B. (Ed.). (1956). *Taxonomy of educational objectives. Handbook I: Cognitive domain.* New York: Wiley.

Boykin, A. W. (1994). Afrocultural expression and its implications for schooling. In Hollins, E. R., King, J. E., & Hayman, W. C. (Eds.). *Teaching diverse populations: Formulating a knowledge base* (pp. 243–56). Albany: State University of New York Press.

Boykin, A. W., Tyler, K. M., & Miller, O. A. (2005). In search of cultural themes and their expressions in the dynamics of classroom life. *Urban Education, 40,* 521–49.

Brown v. Board of Education of Topeka. (1954). 347 U.S. 483.

Davidman, L., & Davidman, P. T. (1994). *Teaching with a multicultural perspective: A practical guide.* New York: Longman.

Davis, G. A., & Rimm, S. B. (2003). *Education of the gifted and talented* (5th ed.). Boston: Allyn & Bacon.

Ford, D. Y. (1996). *Reversing underachievement among gifted black students: Promising practices and programs.* New York: Teachers College Press.

Ford, D. Y., Grantham, T. C., & Whiting, G. W. (2008). Culturally and linguistically diverse students in gifted education: Recruitment and retention issues. *Exceptional Children, 74(3),* 289–308.

Ford, D. Y., & Harris, J. J. (1999). *Multicultural gifted education.* New York: Teachers College Press.

Ford, D. Y., Moore III, J. J., Whiting, G. W., & Grantham, T. C. (2008). Conducting cross-cultural research: Cautions, concerns, and considerations. *Roeper Review, 30(1),* 1–11.

Ford, D. Y., & Webb, K. S. (1994). Desegregation of gifted educational programs: The impact of *Brown* on underachieving children of color. *Journal of Negro Education, 63(3),* 358–75.

Ford, D. Y., & Whiting, G. W. (2006). Under-representation of diverse students in gifted education: Recommendations for nondiscriminatory assessment (pt. 1). *Gifted Education Press Quarterly, 20(2),* 2–6.

Garcia, F. (1994). *Understanding and meeting the challenge of student cultural diversity.* New York: Houghton Mifflin.

García, S. B., & Guerra, P. L. (2004). Deconstructing deficit thinking: Working with educators to create more equitable learning environments. *Education and Urban Society, 36(2),* 150–68.

Gay, G. (1993). Ethnic minorities and educational equality. In Banks, J. A., and Banks, C. A. M. (Eds.), *Multicultural education: Issues and perspectives* (2nd ed.), (pp. 171–94). Boston: Allyn & Bacon.

Gay, G. (2000). *Culturally responsive teaching: Theory, research, & practice.* New York: Teachers College Press.

Gay, G. (2002). Preparing for culturally responsive teaching. *Journal of Teacher Education, 53 (2),* 106–16.

Gillette, M., & Boyle-Baise, M. (1995, April). *Multicultural education at the graduate level: Assisting teaching in developing multicultural perspectives.* Paper presented at the annual meeting of the American Education Research Association. San Francisco, CA.

Gollnick, D. M., & Chinn, P. C. (1998). *Multicultural education in a pluralistic society* (5th ed.). New York: Merrill.

Gould, S. J. (1981). *The mismeasure of man.* New York: Norton.

Gould, S. J. (1995). *The mismeasure of man* (Rev. ed.). New York: Norton.

Grant, C. (1994). Best practices in teacher preparation for urban schools: Lessons from the multicultural education literature. *Action in Teacher Education, 16(3),* 1–18.

Grant, C. A., & Sleeter, C. E. (1998). *Turning on learning: Five approaches for multicultural teaching plans for race, class, gender, and disability* (2nd ed.). New York: Merrill.

Heid, C. A. (Ed). (1988). *Multicultural education: Knowledge and perspectives.* Bloomington: Indiana University, Center for Urban and Multicultural Education.

Horn, L., & Berktold, J. (1999). *Students with disabilities in postsecondary education: A profile of preparation, participation, and outcomes (Statistical Analysis Report No. NCES 199–18).* Washington, DC: U.S. Department of Education Center for Education Statistics.

Kaufman, A. S. (1994). *Intelligent testing with the WISC-III.* New York: John Wiley & Sons.

Kauffman, J. M. (2002). *Characteristics of emotional and behavioral disorders of children and youth* (7th ed.). Columbus, OH: Merrill.

Kea, C., & Utley, C. (1998). To teach me is to know me. *Journal of Special Education, 32,* 44–47.

Ladson-Billings, G. (2009). *The dreamkeepers: Successful teachers of African-American children.* San Francisco: Jossey-Bass.

Larke, P., & Wiseman, D. (1987, November). *Minority mentorship project.* Paper presented at the Instructional Research Laboratory Seminar at Texas A&M University, College Station, TX.

Larke, P., Wiseman, D., & Bradley, C. (1990). The minority mentorship project. *Action in Teacher Education, 12(3),* 23–30.

Losen, D., & Orfield, G. (Eds.). (2002). *Racial inequality in special education.* Boston: Harvard Education Publishing Group.

Menchaca, M. (1997). Early racist discourses: The roots of deficit thinking. In Valencia, R. R. (Ed.), *The evolution of deficit thinking: Educational thought and practice* (pp. 13–40). New York: Falmer.

Naglieri, J. A., & Ford, D. Y. (2005). Increasing minority children's participation in gifted classes using the NNAT: A response to Lohman. *Gifted Child Quarterly, 49(1),* 29–36.

National Association for Gifted Children. (2009). *State directors' report on the gifted.* Washington, D.C.

National Research Council. (2002). *Minority students in special and gifted education.* Washington, DC: National Academy Press.

Nieto, S., & Rolon, C. (1995, November). *The preparation and professional development of teachers: A perspective from two Latinas.* Paper presented at the invitational conference on Defining the Knowledge Base for Urban Teacher Education, Emory University, Atlanta, GA.

No Child Left Behind Act. (2001) 20 U.S.C. § 6319 (2008).

Oakes, J. (1985). *Keeping track: How schools structure inequality.* New Haven, CT: Yale University Press.

Oberg, K. (1960). Culture shock adjustment to new cultural environments. *Practical Anthropology, 7,* 177–82.

Perry, T. (2003) *Young, gifted, and black: Promoting high achievement among African-American students.* Perry, T., Steele, C., & Hilliard III, A. G. (Eds.). Boston: Beacon Press.

Plessy v. Ferguson. (1896). 163, U.S. 537, 16 S. Ct. 1138; 41 L. Ed. 256.

Saccuzzo, D. P., Johnson, N. E., & Guertin, T. L. (1994). *Identifying underrepresented disadvantaged gifted and talented children: A multifaceted approach* (vols. 1 & 2). San Diego: San Diego State University.

Shade, B., Kelly, C., & Oberg, M. (1997). *Creating culturally responsive classrooms.* Washington, DC: American Psychological Association.

Steele, C. (2010). *Whistling Vivaldi: And other clues to how stereotypes affect us.* New York: W. W. Norton & Co.

Trout, A. L., Nordness, P. D., Pierce, C. D., & Epstein, M. H. (2003). Research on the academic status of children with emotional and behavioral disorders: A review of the literature from 1961 to 2000. *Journal of Emotional and Behavioral Disorders, 11,* 198–210.

U.S. Department of Education. (2003). *Twenty-fourth annual report to Congress on the implementation of the Individuals with Disabilities Education Act.* Washington, DC: U.S. Government Printing Office.

U.S. Department of Education. (2009). *Condition of education 2009.* Washington, DC: Author.

Valencia, R., & Solórzano, D. (1997). Contemporary deficit thinking. In Valencia, R. (Ed.), *The evolution of deficit thinking* (pp. 160–210). London: Falmer.

Van Tassel-Baska, J. L. (2006). *Serving gifted learners beyond the traditional classroom: A guide to alternative programs and services.* Austin, TX: Prufrock Press.

Whiting, G. W., & Ford, D. Y. (2006). Under-representation of diverse students in gifted education: Recommendations for nondiscriminatory assessment (pt. 2). *Gifted Education Press Quarterly, 20(3),* 6–10.

Wiseman, D., Larke, P., & Bradley, C. (1989). The minority mentorship project: Educating teachers for a diverse society. *Mentoring International, 3(3),* 37–40.

10

Researching Speakers of Nondominant Languages in Teacher Education Programs

Tapping Into Perceived Barriers to Promote Teaching and Learning in Diverse Contexts

Mandie Uys, Maryna Reyneke, and Kotie Kaiser

When South Africa became a free democratic country in 1994, one of the most advanced constitutions was introduced, a constitution that acknowledged the diversity of its numerous cultures, religions, socioeconomic classes, eleven official languages, and respect for all people. The architects of these changes envisioned access and equity to all South African learners and theoretically allowed all children to receive education through the medium of their home languages. However laudable such declarations may seem, the constitution also states that education in an official language will only occur where it is *reasonably practical*. The result of this caveat was that due to complex issues of multilingualism and multiculturalism in South African classrooms, English emerged as the preferred medium of instruction in most South African schools (Horne, 2005, p. 2; Kgosana, 2006, p. 17). This reality resulted in multiple complex challenges for teacher education programs and their charge to prepare a new generation of teachers for speakers of nondominant languages within the South African context specifically and with implications for teacher education programs globally that are faced with the challenge of preparing teachers from multilingual and multicultural backgrounds.

These issues are the focus of much debate by scholars and practitioners who advocate for mother-tongue instruction in one's own home language versus those who argue that all formal instruction must take place in "standard academic English" (see Balfour, 2007; De Varennes, 2009, p. 9; Heugh, 2002 for further discussion). Second-language medium of instruction is often seen as a barrier to learning and is seldom acknowledged in teacher education programs—even in those programs that exist in the heart of multilingual settings where teachers are often held responsible for poor academic performance, high drop-out rates, and a general loss of cultural pride (Burkett, Clegg, Langdon, Reilly, Verster, 2001; De Varennes, 2009). In order to fully understand this phenomenon, more research is needed on this complex issue. This chapter provides a discussion of a focused and socially responsible approach to researching professional development of teachers who are speakers of nondominant languages, an issue that is often overlooked in the research on diversity in teacher education. The model provided in this chapter is useful for considering future work with teachers from diverse linguistic backgrounds and can be useful in forming a conceptual framework for future research within a global context.

While the authors of this chapter do not underestimate the value of mother-tongue instruction, they argue that the sociocultural, sociopolitical, and socioeconomic constraints on South African classrooms at this time must be considered. Given the current South African context, English as a medium of instruction may provide a viable solution to some of the challenges now facing teacher education programs that serve multilingual populations. In this chapter, the authors offer a close description of a teacher education program that promotes the teaching of different official languages as autonomous subjects while simultaneously introducing English as medium of instruction in other subjects as a case study for consideration by researchers who are seeking alternative ways of examining a very complex issue. After closely describing the program, the authors offer an alternative perspective to regarding English as an obstacle or barrier to teaching and learning and encourage educationists to view English as an instrument for effecting economic mobility and social transformation (Balfour, 2007).

This chapter has implications for further research on programs that provide in-service training to teachers with the goal of accommodating the linguistic diversity of teachers in training who must address their students' content-area needs within linguistically complex educational contexts. The purpose of this chapter is to:

- examine how English may be perceived as a benefit rather than a barrier to promoting diversity;
- discuss the need for a focused and socially responsible approach to researching professional development of teachers who are speakers of nondominant languages;
- propose a model for training in-service teachers to enable effective English medium of instruction in order to tap into the strengths of diverse classrooms;
- provide a framework for future work with teachers from diverse linguistic backgrounds within a global context.

EXAMINING THE STRENGTHS OF
ENGLISH AS A MEDIUM OF INSTRUCTION

Apart from the well-known advantages of additive bilingualism (Burkett et al., 2001), Ward and Ward (2003) report that "using a second language provides one with more opportunities to interact in cross-cultural settings as second-language use increases one's awareness of values, family traditions, and the perceptions of other cultures" (p. 534). One of the most important strengths of using English as a medium of instruction may be the fact that a majority of the parents and learners within the South African educational context are opting for English as the preferred medium of instruction (Probyn, 2005; Kgosana, 2006, p. 17). Probyn notes that the language attitudes of the learners in her research were reflected in their strong preference for English as the language of learning and teaching (LOLT), despite the difficulties this choice may entail for second-language learners who do not have mastery of the preferred language of instruction. While access to competent speakers of a language and opportunities to learn a second language are the most obvious factors that determine a person's successful acquisition of a target language, some language acquisition experts note that one's intrinsic motivation for learning a particular language may be one of the most important differences between individuals who acquire a second language and those who do not. Lightbown and Spada (2006) define motivation in second language acquisition (SLA) as "a complex phenomenon which can be defined in terms of two factors: learners' communicative needs and their attitudes towards the second language community" (p. 201).

National and Global Perspectives on English

Most South African parents and learners seem to believe that proficiency in English will grant them access to the global market and employment (Rademeyer, 2006, p. 15). Since the unions have been arguing that South African learners are not leaving school equipped for the labor market, it can be argued that one of the strengths of English as a medium of instruction is that it may be imperative for creating common ground and communication in the workplace and across cultures.

Van der Walt (2004) reports that English is *the* preferred education language of learning, teaching, and research worldwide and stresses the importance of competency in English. In South Africa, English is generally viewed as *the* language of business, politics, and the media as well (RSA, 2009). This language, already spoken by more South Africans than any other single language, albeit with varying levels of proficiency, creates common ground for communication and interaction across cultures that are almost impossible in any of the other official languages.

The most relevant argument for viewing English as a benefit rather than a barrier may be Johnson's (1992, p. 281) argument that appears in his review on the partiality to English medium of instruction in Hong Kong. He states that "educating students through their native language perhaps becomes irrelevant if it is a major requirement of the society the education system serves that it should produce students with high levels of English proficiency" (Johnson, 1992, p. 281). Some scholars and educationists feel that this is the case within the South African context.

THE NEED FOR SOCIALLY RESPONSIBLE APPROACHES TO RESEARCHING PROFESSIONAL DEVELOPMENT

The issue of mother-tongue instruction is a topic of much debate by scholars and practitioners alike (see Balfour, 2007; De Varennes, 2009, p. 9; Heugh, 2002 for further discussion). Although a great deal of research exists on mother-tongue instruction and curriculum development for students who are speakers of nondominant languages in our schools, very little research exists on professional development for teachers who are themselves speakers of nondominant languages. Second-language medium of instruction is often seen as a barrier to teaching and learning and is seldom acknowledged as a challenge for teacher candidates within teacher preparation programs. This chapter presents a descriptive study of one approach that was used for professional development with teachers who were speakers of nondominant languages within the South African context. This case is used as the focus of a discussion of a socially responsible inquiry concerning professional development for nondominant-language-speaking teachers. Since there exists a need for systematic inquiry concerning professional development of teachers who are speakers of nondominant languages in classrooms around the globe, this is a discussion that has global implications.

A MODEL FOR IN-SERVICE TRAINING THAT ENABLES EFFECTIVE ENGLISH INSTRUCTION IN DIVERSE CLASSROOMS

In the South African context, the constitution allows the learner population within an institutional context to choose the medium of instruction that will be used. The research project reported on in this section focuses on a training model that emerged as part of a collaboration between the Education Quality Improvement Partnership Program (EQUIP), North-West University, and a group of feeder schools who use English as the medium of instruction and who serve students from economically disadvantaged communities. The primary goal of EQUIP is to enhance the capacity of feeder schools to deliver more effective teaching and learning and so to increase the pool of potentially successful students, especially from disadvantaged communities. The EQUIP project achieves this goal by helping participating schools to formulate their own strategies for school development, with support provided in the form of training for governing bodies, school management teams, and educators. North-West University (NWU) is recognized as one of the most stable and successful mergers in the higher education sector in South Africa that strives to establish itself as a vibrant and entrepreneurial university, with a balance between teaching, learning, and research. This collaborative project was designed to meet the need for a whole-school professional development program for educators within the feeder schools surrounding North-West University campuses in order to consolidate, build onto, integrate, and expand the capacity of schools, teachers, and learners within the school community. One of the aims of the project was the facilitation of a participatory, sustainable, and socially responsible approach to the professional development of educators who were held responsible for improving learner outcomes in the schools' mathematics, science, and technology programs. This chapter describes the first phase in the development of a model and the implementation of an in-service teacher training program. A second and third phase is planned for 2010 and 2011.

Research Population

The research involved five secondary schools in three school districts of the North West Province in South Africa and was funded by the Thuthuka Programme of the National Research Foundation (NRF) and the United Kingdom Trust of North-West University. Twenty grade eight science, technology, and mathematics teachers from these schools volunteered to take part in the project. All of the teachers in the project were English second-language speakers. The purposeful sampling for this study was based on the following criteria:

- Science, technology, and mathematics teachers were targeted as these have proved to be the most problematic subjects in the school curriculum.
- Grade eight teachers were targeted as research has proved that learners in this grade find the conceptual gap that exists between primary and secondary school very challenging. The majority of grade eight learners whose mother tongue is not English are not equipped to learn through medium of English as a second language (Burkett et al., 2001; Probyn, 2005).
- Grade eight learners were targeted as this will allow for a possible longitudinal study to follow the learners in the project from grade eight to grade ten in order to see whether the intervention had an impact on the learners' progress.

Research Methodology

Since intervention strategies in the form of one-time workshops are generally considered ineffective (Echevarria, Vogt, & Short, 2004, p. 19), this research introduced an intervention strategy that anticipated measurable, long-term effects. The program was divided into three phases and entailed regular workshops over a period of three years. During phase 1 of the program, teachers at one of the selected schools also received on-site training three times a week. This sustained contact was conducted by a language assistant who helped teachers to implement strategies and techniques demonstrated and discussed during the workshops. Regular feedback from the language assistant on the problems encountered by teachers fulfilled a valuable role in planning for subsequent workshops.

Action research methodology was selected because of its dynamic and interactive approach, where teachers become collaborators in research. The research is depicted in a spiral model that follows certain stages of action research as described by Costello (2003, pp. 8–9) and Seale, Wilkinson, and Erasmus (2005, pp. 215–16). These stages include:

- **Defining the inquiry.** For purposes of this research the enquiry was based on the initial question: Why is second-language medium of instruction (L2MI) seen as a barrier to teaching and learning in the South African context?
- **Describing the educational situation.** The research was guided by the question: How effectively is English as a medium of instruction used in some science, mathematics, and technology classrooms?
- **Data collection and analysis.** This included a literature review and capturing the stakeholders' experiences and perspectives through interviews, observation, surveys, and artifact reviews. Analysis was done by means of categorizing and coding and constructing category systems.
- **Reviewing the data and looking for contradictions.** This focused on the discrepancy between what teachers professed to know about language teaching and what their practice revealed about their knowledge and skills.
- **Taking action.** This involved introducing an in-service training program to supplement or augment the content teachers' language teaching skills.
- **Monitoring the change.** As a strategy for both monitoring and professional development, the researchers introduced professional development portfolios and a mentoring system.

- **Analyzing evaluative data concerning the change.** This is an ongoing process within the spiral model. Data from the first two workshops and feedback received from the language assistant as well as evidence of performance in the teachers' developmental portfolios were used to determine the outcomes and content of the follow-up workshops, which lead to the next stage.
- **Reviewing the change and deciding what to do next.**

Initial Findings

Initial research and observations conducted in the five schools participating in the project revealed results in four categories before the intervention program began: medium of instruction, instructional strategies, conceptual knowledge, and presentation skills.

Medium of Instruction. Questionnaires revealed that teachers were either unaware of the importance of language in the content classroom or did not know how to implement language teaching in the content classroom. Observation revealed a general lack of proficiency and inability to explain concepts through medium of English. All the teachers took a standardized second-language proficiency test (the ELSA test), and only four of the twenty-two participants tested on an intermediate level of proficiency or above.

Instructional Strategies. The lack of a variety of teaching skills was observed. Learners were expected to copy long passages from a blackboard with no attempt from teachers to explain either the difficult words or concepts; for example, the following illustration of longitude or latitude was copied from a blackboard: "For example, Johannesburg lies close to the place where the line of latitude 26°S of the Equator and the line of longitude 28°E of the Greenwich meridian meet or intersect." The teacher who wrote on the blackboard left the class to allow the children to quietly copy down this incomprehensible information.

Teaching practice was adapted to accommodate mostly rote learning of definitions that contained difficult words such as "photosynthesis" in natural science and "adjacent angles" in mathematics. Learners were expected to chant one-word answers to questions or to complete sentences started by the teachers. As far as assessment of the comprehension of content was concerned, the majority of the teachers resorted to questions such as, "Do you understand?" This was repeated until all the pupils acquiesced, regardless of whether real understanding had taken place.

Teacher files consisted of policy documents and documentation sent to the school by the national and provincial departments of education. Except for the official, generic documentation, the files did not contain any specific lesson plans, assessment plans, or examples of additional learning materials suited to accommodating specific needs of learners in particular communities. It furthermore became clear that teachers still had problems implementing the outcomes-based national curriculum. The initial aim of outcomes-based education was to allow teachers more freedom to adapt learning materials to accommodate diversity in their classrooms. However, due to factors such as insufficient training and lack of support, resources, and guidance, teachers were reluctant to develop their own materials and reverted back to using unsuitable and generic textbooks (Reyneke, 2008, pp. 159–60).

Except for one or two strategies that were almost intuitively employed at times, none of the teachers revealed a structured and scientific approach to the teaching of second-language learners. Although they were second-language learners themselves, most teachers seemed unaware that, in the case of providing instruction to second-language learners, the teacher needed to adapt the methodology used for explaining subject content. Since they had not received such instruction in their own experiences as learners or in their teacher training programs, none of the subject area teachers deliberately introduced language learning activities into their content classes. The silence in most of the classrooms corroborates Weideman and Van Rensburg's (2002) findings regarding the lack of communicative activities in the typical African culture of silent classrooms. The researchers realized that, even in the training of teaching language, across the curriculum they had to train teachers to become aware of their learners' strengths and to build on the knowledge different groups bring to the classroom.

Conceptual Knowledge. Although highly qualified college graduates, many of these teachers were not necessarily trained to teach the subjects they had been assigned. A good example is the fact that none of the technology teachers in the population had formal undergraduate training in the subject as it only officially became part of the school curriculum in 1998. These teachers had formal training in areas like agricultural sciences, religious studies, and natural sciences, and they often grappled with the content area materials because technology was not their area of expertise.

Presentation Skills. Both Klaassen (2002) and Johnson, Yin, and Bunton (1996) reported on the adverse effect of poor presentation skills on second-language learners. In many of the classes presentational skills were adapted to suit rote-learning methodology, resulting in countless repetitions and continuous choral responses. This rote-learning methodology is the norm in most South African classrooms, regardless of the background of the students. Teachers also completely disregarded rate of delivery to such an extent that the pace of the lesson sometimes adversely affected instructional effectiveness.

TRAINING IN-SERVICE TEACHERS TO ENABLE EFFECTIVE ENGLISH MEDIUM OF INSTRUCTION

Conducting the First Workshop and Addressing Methodological Problems

Based on the needs analysis and the input of the teachers, the researchers developed a lesson-planning tool. During the first workshop teachers were briefed on the use of the lesson planning tool. This lesson planning tool, designed in the form of a wheel, is particularly suitable for implementing an English medium of instruction approach in the classroom. The lesson planning wheel was developed using principles of a task-based methodology, an approach particularly useful where both content and language outcomes need to be attained in a single lesson. It consists of eight color-coded segments that refer to the following elements of a well-planned lesson:

- learning outcomes, assessment standards, and content (as stipulated by the national curriculum);

- designing specific, measurable, attainable, relevant, and traceable lesson outcomes for both content and language;
- assessment of the set outcomes;
- planning the learner activities;
- selecting suitable teaching strategies;
- planning for effective resources;
- activating learners' prior knowledge of both the content and language of the lesson;
- tailor-making a lesson to meet the diverse needs of different classrooms.

Part of the workshop focused on training the teachers how to integrate assessment with teaching and learning by introducing assessment as an integral part of the ordinary planning, teaching, and learning activities. Initially, the majority of teachers found the tool cumbersome and time-consuming. They commented that it was impossible for a teacher to plan every lesson in such detail due to heavy workloads associated with understaffed schools. Some teachers also held the belief that an experienced teacher and subject specialist does not need to prepare a lesson in detail as such a teacher would obviously have superior knowledge. However, after the first lessons had been planned and presented, teachers became aware of the various aspects that need to be taken into consideration when planning an English medium of instruction lesson in an outcomes-based curriculum. Many "how to" questions emerged from this session. These included:

- Which strategies can you use to integrate language in the content classroom?
- How do you formulate your lesson outcomes based on the Learning Outcomes and Assessment Standards in the National Curriculum?
- How do you create an atmosphere conducive to learning?
- How do you motivate your learners?
- How do you assess?

Focusing on Diversity

After the lecture "Learners—Our Country's Number One Resource," teachers were asked to reflect on the strengths of their learners and to report back on what they thought their learners brought into the classroom. The teachers came up with a list of rich resources that students generally bring into the classroom, including multilingualism, the ability to envision the use of resources in creative ways, and the ability to multitask and take on added responsibilities as exemplified in their need to assume added responsibilities in the home. After taking time to think about the unique attributes of their learners, teachers returned the following day with new perspectives and insights concerning their learners.

This feedback brought a new dimension to the workshops as teachers now realized how irrelevant content in a textbook may be as it often disregards the diversity of individual communities. They became actively involved in identifying relevant subject content tailored to their learners' needs. The "so what?" question (i.e., why would my learners want to know this?) became a reverberating echo among the teachers, which focused them on acknowledging their pupils' diverse backgrounds, interests, and situations. By learning how to contextualize teaching and learning, teachers, for the first time, managed to interpret the essence of the national curriculum instead of getting lost in the theory of learning outcomes, assessment standards, and competencies.

Preparing for the Second Workshop

It became clear from questions and feedback during the first workshop that teachers battled to explain academic concepts and interpret the national curriculum. They requested the involvement of subject specialists in science, technology, and mathematics during the next workshop. The language assistant reported that teachers still struggled with the concept of back mapping or the backward design of lessons, and they also needed to be reminded of the value of the language diversity their pupils brought to the classroom in order to keep them from reverting back to textbook-only content and topics. As a result, the lesson planning wheel was adapted and refined.

In order to measure the effect of the workshops, teachers were required to compile a portfolio of their lessons between the first and second workshop. The language assistant reported that the teachers found it difficult and cumbersome to use the portfolio as a working document. Reports from the language assistant also indicated that much prompting was required to get teachers to conduct meetings on a regular basis and share experiences. It appeared that teachers lost momentum, partly due to a lack of understanding and support from their school's management team (the principal and heads of department). The research team, therefore, envisaged that the effect of the first workshop could be wearing off even more rapidly at the schools where there was no sustained contact.

An interesting development was the extent to which teachers were implementing the model lessons that had been planned and presented during the workshops. Feedback from other schools at the second workshop reported the same trend. Although the researchers suspected that this was because the teachers found it very useful to have a well-planned lesson at hand as it saved considerable time, it also provided them with meaningful feedback. Another development was that teachers, now more aware of the fact that content should be developed to accommodate and optimize their learners' strengths, expressed a desire to gain access to Internet sources and other resources. Based on the feedback between the workshops, the researchers decided to:

- invite members of the schools' senior management teams to attend the workshop with the teachers in order to provide better support in between workshops;
- invite subject specialists in science, technology, and mathematics to become part of the project in order to support teachers in terms of their content-specific needs;
- supply each of the teachers with a 2 gigabyte flash drive to store electronic resource materials and arranged for the teachers to have university-supported email accounts.

Conducting the Second Workshop

The second workshop was planned and offered to each of the participating schools. Only one of the headmasters (from the school where the language assistant worked) accepted the invitation. In addition, some of the teachers from schools where there had been no sustained contact between workshops did not attend the second workshop. Yet, the teachers at the school where the language assistant was posted not only responded enthusiastically but also enquired whether more of their staff could attend. The earlier feedback data revealed that few of the teachers could show evidence in their portfolios of altered lesson plans. However, in their later feedback, it was clear that they had become more aware of the role that language played in teaching and learning for nondominant-language-speaking students. One participating workshop teacher from an urban and more privileged school, who had expressed doubts about the effectiveness of group work in his multicultural, multilingual mathematics classroom, reported how he had allowed his learners to bake pancakes during one of his recent lessons. He deliberately grouped learners from different backgrounds and social groups together to force them to communicate and plan toward a shared goal. They had to adapt and calculate the amount of ingredients required for each group. This exercise not only encouraged communication but also provided opportunities for the application of mathematical skills in a relevant and interesting situation. One learner who had miscalculated the amount of oil required for sixteen pancakes and ended up adding a cup of oil to the batter provided the opportunity to stress the importance of peer assessment for formative purposes. This teacher also reported that he was amazed to see to what extent these learners were willing to work together and cooperate once they had discovered common ground and a mutual purpose.

During the second workshop, subject specialists helped teachers with the planning of lessons and the interpretation of the national curriculum. Teachers were subsequently taken to the university library and shown how to surf the Internet. The resources they found on the Internet were then incorporated into their lesson plans. Aided by subject specialists, teachers were now more confident in using the lesson wheel. During presentations of the lessons teachers had designed, it was clear that the tool had a positive effect on the focus of delivery and that it served to remind teachers about their language responsibility. As the data were analyzed, new professional development needs were also identified. Some of those new needs included the following:

- Teachers expressed uncertainty about the implementation of ongoing and formative assessment.
- Teachers were uncertain about how language should be assessed (if at all) and were now asking more directed questions about the specific language required for each subject.
- Teachers' paradigms shifted from a focus on pronunciation and terminology instruction to asking more pertinent questions, such as: "What should I teach pupils about the tenses they are supposed to use in the science classroom?" or "How should I phrase proper questions that will allow learners to think?"
- Teachers expressed the need for suitable resources (e.g., portable blackboards).

Planning for the Third Workshop

Written reflective comments by participants after the second workshop indicated that the majority of the participants found the second workshop "very informative" or "very helpful." The teachers reported that learners were more confident to actively take part in lessons, and they seemed to be "enjoying the opportunity to express themselves" in English. Many of the teachers reflected that the workshops should continue, and they indicated that they would like their colleagues to attend as well. Furthermore, they suggested that the project also be phased in on the primary-school level. Feedback from the language assistant after the second workshop suggested that teachers were still not implementing the lesson wheel consistently but that almost all the lessons they planned showed evidence of language awareness. In addition to planning for language outcomes the mathematics teachers, specifically, had started to incorporate worksheets that required language outcomes; for example, crossword puzzles to explain terminology and concepts. Other teachers deliberately included exercises that required more than one of the language skills; for example, oral presentations as well as written answers.

Although the language assistant could give positive feedback regarding teachers' planning for the third quarter of the year, no evidence regarding the use of either the portable blackboards or Internet sources was reported. This may be due to the fact that the second workshop came at the end of the second quarter and that when teachers went back to school the following Monday, children were sitting for examinations. Examinations were then followed by the three-week midyear recess. This reinforces observations by Echevarria et al. (2004) that the influence of a workshop diminishes after approximately three days. The researchers realized that intervention workshops would have to be planned with such detail in mind. The third workshop was thus scheduled closer to the beginning of the third quarter. In anticipation of the third workshop, the research team developed an assessment tool. The aim was to introduce a hands-on tool in order to support the teachers to effectively implement assessment as an integral part of teaching and learning.

Conducting the Third Workshop

The third workshop consisted of a series of sessions. During this workshop, the assessment tool was introduced to the participants. The tool prompted teachers to consider assessment tasks, assessment tools, and the phrasing of typical questions. By showing teachers how to phrase questions and how to vary the level of cognitive response required from their learners, we hoped to create a greater awareness of not only the language of assessment but also how to develop the different cognitive and metacognitive skills that learners need to employ for successful learning. During several sessions teachers were trained in developing rubrics that acknowledged diversity in terms of several factors, such as the context, the learners, and the available resources. The aim of the sessions was to tailor-make assessment tools for their specific situations, subjects, and students without compromising on standards. During subsequent sessions, teachers dealt with the assessment of language in the content classroom and the design of rubrics that incorporated criteria for both content and language outcomes. They also had sessions at the university library and computer laboratory that focused on rubric design.

The participants also had the opportunity to collaborate once again with subject specialists from the NWU Faculty of Education. They worked in subject groups across the five schools in order to generate an end-of-year examination paper for their grade eight learners based on the principles discussed during the workshop. In a final session, participants were given the opportunity to critically evaluate one another's rubrics and end-of-year examination papers. During this session, the researchers became the observers and facilitators while the teachers exhibited the application of the knowledge and skills they acquired over the course of the workshops.

Planning for the Fourth Workshop

During reflection based on the implementation of workshops one through three and on the feedback received from the teachers and language assistant, the researchers decided to visit teachers at their schools instead of conducting a final formal workshop. The teachers were observed while they presented their lessons, and follow-up interviews were done to discuss their progress since the beginning of the year. The teachers also completed questionnaires in which they shared best practices and specific examples of how they incorporated effective language instruction in their content classrooms. The data from these visits are still being analyzed in order to plan for phase 2 of the project, which will resume in 2010.

The researchers plan to continue with the same model of training for grade nine science, technology, and mathematics teachers in phase 2. The dynamic and fluid character of the proposed training model is illustrated in figure 10.1, which was adapted from work done by Costello (2003, pp. 8–9) and Seale et al. (2005, pp. 215–16). It clearly indicates that in-service training should be continuous and should tap into the resources that the teachers bring to the table. This process is best illustrated by means of a spiral as illustrated in figure 10.1. This illustration also serves to give a summary of phase 1 of the project.

THE WAY FORWARD: A FRAMEWORK FOR FUTURE WORK WITH TEACHERS FROM DIVERSE LINGUISTIC BACKGROUNDS WITHIN A GLOBAL CONTEXT

In view of the recently announced Five-Year Plan for the improvement of learning and teaching (Department of Education, 2009a), as well as the Ministerial Committee's report (Department of Education, 2009b) on the importance of English as a medium of instruction, it is evident that this project is particularly well timed and relevant. The value of in-service training cannot be overestimated. Experience from these workshops has shown that teachers could hardly be prepared during preservice training for the diversity they have to face once they start teaching. The fact that this project focuses on accommodating diversity in specific school districts, as opposed to using generic material generated by textbook writers, has brought teachers to a new appreciation of the strengths their learners bring to the classroom—least of which is the fact that they *want* to receive instruction through the medium of English.

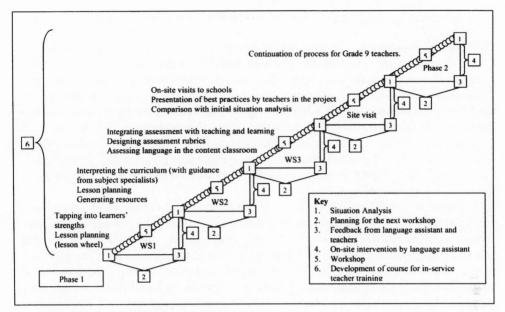

Figure 10.1   Training model for in-service teachers.

The long-term effect of workshops can be promoted by having sustained contact and providing sustained support by means of a language specialist who reinforces new knowledge and skills. This sustained contact in between workshops allowed teachers to become active collaborators and designers in the research process. As a result these teachers have become so motivated that other members of their staff, who were not part of the project, have asked for permission to attend the workshops. Valuable input and suggestions for the content of workshops are also generated in this manner. One of the most significant findings, however, may be that the contact between the language assistant and the teachers can be much less than the three times a week that we stipulated. It is clear that it could be more economical to allocate a language assistant to five schools in a district. One day per week per school on a regular basis may be all that is required to assist teachers in implementing workshop ideas and methodology. The appointment of a language assistant to a district may have more than one beneficial effect as it may also become a way for teachers to cluster information regarding their learners. As one of the problems of outcomes-based education is to define levels of attainment without becoming norm-referenced, contact with other schools may help in this regard.

This research confirms that teachers prefer hands-on tools that enable them to implement complex policy statements. In collaboration with the teachers, hands-on tools were developed (e.g., a lesson wheel and an assessment tool). These manual and portable tools could be used while planning and teaching. They could also be used as a continuous reminder to the teacher of the different strategies that can be used to integrate language teaching in content area classrooms. Using the lesson wheel enabled teachers to plan for diverse South African classrooms (taking demographics, language, and lesson-planning design into consideration).

CONCLUSION

This chapter provides a rich description of one approach to an in-service professional development program for teachers who were themselves mother-tongue
speakers of nondominant languages. This research confirmed that English as a medium of instruction posed no threat to the indigenous languages and cultures of the
teachers or to their students if adequate support and resources are provided—since
it was merely used as a tool of instruction across the curriculum. While this thick
description of one in-service teacher education program highlights a look at professional development for nondominant-language-speaking teachers and pupils, this
research has implications for further inquiry and can promote effective teaching and
learning in a global context.

   If content-area teachers can be enabled to respond to their students' educational
needs using English as the medium of instruction, learners can experience the benefits of additive multilingualism. With adequate support, sufficient resources, and
effective implementation, English language instruction might be seen not as a barrier but rather as a tool for effecting educational and social equity in South African
classrooms and in other linguistically complex contexts. Within this model, the concept of lifelong learning is emphasized, especially when teachers can become active
collaborators and coresearchers, learning from one another. It is our hope that as
teachers are given adequate support to begin to integrate the knowledge they gain
from in-service workshops into their lesson plans and teaching approaches, they
will become more generative in their teaching.

   According to Ball (2009), *generativity* plays a critical role in the preparation of
teachers to work effectively in multilingual and multicultural classrooms. Ball notes
that teachers must develop the ability to add to their understanding by connecting
their personal and professional knowledge with their students' knowledge. In the
case of teachers who are mother-tongue speakers of nondominant languages who
teach students who are mother-tongue speakers of nondominant languages as well,
teachers must be supported in developing the ability to build upon and add to
their understanding of multilingualism by connecting their personal and professional knowledge with their students' knowledge and needs. This will allow them
to produce new knowledge that is useful in curricular planning and pedagogical
problem solving, thus meeting the educational needs of their students. She argues
that through such generativity teachers can begin to envision their classrooms as
communities of change, where transformative learning and emancipatory teaching
can take place. Such teaching serves the purpose of educating not only a generation
of teachers who are generative thinkers but also a new generation of student learners
who will themselves become generative in their thinking and literacy practices. In
this way, we can begin to transform teacher training within the South African context in truly powerful ways. This transformation examined within a global context
can provide a new place for the research on diversity in teacher education.

   The model discussed in this chapter not only introduces an alternative way of
training in-service teachers but also introduces an approach for training teachers to
accommodate diversity in their classrooms. Here, teachers are active collaborators
in the research, helping to design a curriculum and tools that acknowledge and
build on the diverse resources of the school population and the community. The

model proposed in the form of sustained fluid workshops is not a mere repetition of a set or generic curriculum. The upward spiral nature of this model allows for constant reflection that fuels transformation and serves as a promising paradigm for use in the research on diversity in teacher education, particularly when working with teachers who are speakers of nondominant languages. This socially responsible approach to research on teachers from diverse linguistic backgrounds is useful for considering future work with indigenous-language-speaking teachers and students within diverse classrooms and can be useful in charting future directions for research on diversity in teacher education within a global context.

REFERENCES

Balfour, R. (2007). Mother-tongue education or bilingual education for South Africa: Theories, pedagogies and sustainability. *Journal for Language Teaching, 41(2)*, 1–14.

Ball, A. F. (2009). Toward a theory of generative change in culturally and linguistically complex classrooms. *American Educational Research Journal, 46(1)*, 45–72.

Burkett, B., Clegg, J., Landon, J., Reilly, T., & Verster, S. (2001). The Language for Learning Project: Developing language-sensitive subject teaching in South African secondary schools. *Southern African Linguistics and Applied Language Studies, 19*, 149–61.

Costello, P. J. M. (2003). *Action research*. London: Continuum.

Department of Education. (2009a, December). Improving the quality of learning and teaching. Planning for 2010 and beyond. *Curriculum news*. Pretoria, South Africa: Department of Education.

Department of Education. (2009b). *Report of the task team for the review of the implementation of the National Curriculum Statement*. Pretoria, South Africa: Department of Education.

De Varennes, F. (2009, April). Can the language of instruction influence the higher education landscape? *Muratho*, 3–9.

Echevarria, J., Vogt, M., & Short, D. J. (2004). *Making content comprehensible for English language learners*. Needham Heights, MA: Allyn & Bacon.

Heugh, K. (2002). The case against bilingual and multilingual education in South Africa: Laying bare the myths. *Perspectives in Education, 20(1)*, 171–98.

Horne, T. J. (2005, November 13). The big question: Is a matric certificate worth the paper that it is written on? [Television interview]. Johannesburg: South African Broadcasting Services.

Johnson, K. J. (1992). Developing teachers' language resources. In Richards, J., & Nunan, D. (Eds.), *Second language teacher education* (pp. 269–81). Cambridge: Cambridge University Press.

Johnson, K. J., Yin, W. K., & Bunton, D. 1996. *Common methods: Classroom English*. Hong Kong: University of Hong Kong.

Klaassen, R. G. (2002). *The international university curriculum. Challenges in English medium engineering education*. PhD dissertation, Delft University, Delft, The Netherlands.

Kgosana, C. (2006, February 19). Moedertaal eerste: Liewer Engels. Die grootste weerstand kom van swart ouers. *Beeld*, p. 17.

Lightbown, P. M., & Spada, N. (2006). *How languages are learned*. Oxford: Oxford University Press.

Probyn, M. (2005). Learning science through the medium of English: What do grade 8 learners say? *Southern African Linguistics and Applied Language Studies, 23(4)*, 369–92.

Rademeyer, A. (2006, May 15). Meeste in SA verkies Engels as skooltaal. *Beeld*.

Reyneke, E. M. R. (2008). *A model for outcomes-based assessment of English first additional language in the Further Education and Training band*. PhD dissertation, North-West University, Potchefstroom, South Africa.

RSA International Marketing Council of South Africa. (2009). The languages of South Africa. Retrieved August 18, 2009, from http://www.southafrica.info/

Seale, I., Wilkinson, A., & Erasmus, M. (2005). A step-up action-research model for the revitalisation of service-learning modules. *Acta Academica Supplement, (3),* 203–29.

Van der Walt, C. (2004). The challenge of multilingualism: In response to the language policy for higher education. *South African Journal of Higher Education, 18(1),* 140–52.

Ward, M. J., & Ward, C. J. (2003). Promoting cross-cultural competence in pre-service teachers through a second language. *Education, 123 (3),* 532–36.

Weideman, A., & Van Rensburg, C. (2002). Language proficiency: Current strategies, future remedies. *Journal for Language Teaching, 36(1).*

Section B

Frameworks, Perspectives, and Paradigms in Research on Diversity

Implications for Research in Teacher Education

11

A Critical Race Theory Analysis of Past and Present Institutional Processes and Policies in Teacher Education

Thandeka K. Chapman

INTRODUCTION

Peyton's first day of kindergarten was exciting. I took pictures of the entire family—Mom (my sister), Dad (her husband), Peyton (my niece), and her little brother Jared (my nephew) as we walked the three blocks from my sister's million-dollar suburban home to the elementary school. In this school district, boundaries are strictly upheld and children attend the neighborhood school. In this suburban school district that shares a border with the city of Chicago, there is a statistical relationship between the low number of apartment units and high test scores for the corresponding neighborhood school, the low number of black students and high test scores, the low number of students receiving free and reduced lunches and high test scores. Upper-middle-class folks choose their home *after* they choose their elementary school so that they can find the right balance of racial and socioeconomic diversity for their children. By all accounts, Peyton's school, with a majority white, upper-middle-class student population, significant black, middle-class population, a highly respected black principal, and a handful of Latino and Asian kids, is a good school for a smart, pretty, light-skinned black girl with lots of cultural capital to attend.

In the schoolyard the principal greeted us warmly. We had, of course, met her during the open house and other district events while my sister researched each of the seven elementary schools. The bell rang and the five—yes, five—of us went into Peyton's first day of kindergarten. My presence was hardly noticed since most students had multiple adults with them, relatives as well as hired help for their children. But one boy, one dark-skinned, quiet black boy with cornrows, a neatly pressed outfit and shiny white and red gym shoes had no adult with him. The principal brought him to the door after the morning began. She explained to the elderly white teacher that his brother dropped him off in the office before going to his third-grade class. The teacher's body barred the boy's entrance into the classroom.

"He's alone! *[sigh]* Very well," the teacher exclaimed loudly as she moved to let the boy into the room. That's when I spotted Randy.

The classroom was packed with activities that required an adult's help—fill out your home information, write your name on your cubby, find the different learning spaces around the room, color a map, and so on. Word around the neighborhood and among the mommies with older children was that this veteran teacher, known for her highly organized classroom and instructional technique, "did not do well" with boys, especially black boys.

The teacher gave Randy the materials, set him down in a chair, and left to move around the room. He sat at the table with his hands in his lap and looked down around the room. He stared at the paper and markers and watched other students with their parents. My sister and I stepped in to help. My sister wrote his name on his cubby after he whispered it to her. I moved him along through the various stations and helped him complete the tasks. Only once did the teacher come to check on him during the activity or even seem cognizant of his presence.

Later the students sat down on the carpet to sing a song. Randy sat down in the front. As the teacher pointed to different articles of clothing and their colors, the children raised their hands to fill in the answers. Randy never raised his hand. The teacher pointed to something blue in the picture and asked the children to give the answer; the children answered shoes, but the teacher was looking for something more specific.

"They're sneakers," she explained. "Who has on sneakers?" Some students hesitantly raised their hands. Randy did not raise his hand. "Sneakers" is a dated term for athletic shoes that Randy did not recognize as pertaining to his footwear.

"Randy, do you have on sneakers?" she asked. Randy shook his head, "no." The teacher paused, looked at Randy, and took a deep breath. "Okay then, let's continue," she stated. Randy did indeed have on new red and white sneakers.

Two weeks later, Randy's beautiful braids were gone. I barely recognized him on the school playground. The following year, when we took Peyton back to school, I asked her which first-grade class list had Randy's name on it. She told me that Randy was repeating kindergarten with a new teacher.

This incident, my standing witness to Randy's poor treatment in the classroom, left me sick and heartbroken. Did his mother eventually show for class? Yes. She came to pick up her son, spoke to the teacher, and spoke to the principal. Regardless of her circumstances, she made sure that Randy was at school, clean, dressed, and ready to learn. Did his parent attempt to "fit him into the school"? Yes. She shaved his beautiful braids so that he looked like all the other "clean cut"—code for middle class—kids.

So what happened to Randy? Randy's story is not particularly new or shocking to teacher educators who have been trying to change the ways in which we cultivate new teachers for racially and socioeconomically diverse classrooms. There are many elements in this story that beg for a critical race analysis. The fact that Randy's teacher is a veteran hardly makes a difference to the present analysis because teacher demographics and teacher education programs have not been substantially altered in the past thirty years to produce a radically different pedagogue (Sleeter, 2001). Moreover, calls for teacher education reform remain fixated on increasing content knowledge, exit examinations, and greater homogenization among standards for teachers. The skills that would make a student a better teacher than this veteran teacher have been minimized and assumed under benign educational discourses that reflect perennial and essential philosophies of education (Grant, 1994; Zeichner et al., 1998). These philosophies of education stem from Western European perspectives of the educated citizen and contain hierarchies of official knowledge and assimilationist goals for cultivating America's future workforce (Deschenes, Cuban, & Tyack, 2001; Rury, 2002; Tyack, 1990). The hierarchies of official knowledge are sustained through traditional curricular discourses that serve to maintain racial, gender, and class inequality (Yosso, 2002).

When I first began writing this paper, I saw it as a review of the research and a guide to exploring the possibilities of using critical race theory (CRT) in teacher education research. However, as I reread the literature, it has occurred to me that much of what this paper needs to say takes the "what's old is new again approach." This means that much of what we already know about struggles in teacher education programs speak to issues of race, class, and gender that are deeply embedded in questions of the nature of education and the role(s) of the educator in the United States. Using the tenets of critical race theory, this paper will explore how current and historical contexts of higher education and teacher education policies limit the reform of teacher education in order to maintain the core assimilationist principles of whiteness and middle-class morality that normalize particular values, behaviors, and ways of knowing the world. These limitations continue to produce teachers who marginalize children of color, particularly poor children of color, in public schools and who fail to recruit students of color and nontraditional white students into these programs.

CRITICAL RACE THEORY AND EDUCATION

The use of CRT in education becomes both a blessing and a curse because the proliferation of the application of the theory may also result in the dissolution of it as well. Ladson-Billings encourages researchers to use CRT to positively impact the lives of children of color in public classrooms and not trivialize the theory in ways that lessen its potential for facilitating change (Ladson-Billings, 1998). Ladson-Billings nor I would discourage new scholars from using the theory to build new and challenge old knowledge about families of color and their experiences with the institution of schooling. However, scholars should be mindful to value the guiding principles associated with CRT and commit to using the theory in total, so it does not become diluted and ineffective (Ladson-Billings, 2004).

Conceptualizations of CRT

Various conceptual papers define and explain the theoretical components of CRT and serve as helpful guides when discussing how scholars can utilize the theory to explore classroom experiences, preservice and practicing teachers' perceptions and beliefs, teacher education programs, and institutional structures that comprise the body of scholarship found in CRT and teachers and teacher education (Gillborn, 2006; Ladson-Billings, 1998; Lopez, 2003; Milner, 2008; Solorzano & Yosso, 2001b; Tate, 1997). Articles that explain and advocate for CRT in education are a significant portion of the works published on CRT in peer-reviewed journals, edited books, and handbook chapters. This body of scholarship helps readers to understand the origins, concepts, and language being used by critical race theorists. Conceptualizations of CRT are often political acts because they challenge traditional methodologies and modes of scholarship (Ladson-Billings, 2003; Parker, 1998; Solorzano & Yosso, 2001a; Yosso, 2002). These lengthy explanations of CRT "speak to power" in that they reinstantiate the theory and solidify its place in the field of education.

Conceptualizations of CRT show how the theory aligns with and opposes various other paradigms in education research, theory, and practice (Tate, 1997). Lopez (2003), Carbado (2002), Ladson-Billings (1998, 2005), and Dixson and Rousseau (2005) evaluate critical race theory's first decade of scholarship in education and provide readers with timely critiques of CRT applications to issues in education. These scholars offer that the connections to administrative leadership, curriculum and instruction, and policy allow readers to view the development of ideas in education as nonlinear, interconnected, and interdisciplinary. In their overview of CRT, Lynn and Parker (2006) suggest that CRT has had a dramatic effect on the field of education because it reasserted a focus on race and racism that had become less discernible in the field of education.

Yosso (2002) critiques the traditional high school curriculum to reenvision a critical race curriculum. She argues that "traditional curricula under-prepare students of color to go on to attain a higher education" (p. 93). She believes that a critical race curriculum "challenges educators to recognize deficit-based practices that deny students of color access to 'college bound' knowledge" (2002, p. 93). To further clarify the connections between CRT and education, Yosso suggests five concepts that bridge CRT to education:

1. Intersectionality of race and racism with gender, class, and sexuality,
2. Challenge to dominant ideology,
3. Commitment to social justice,
4. Centrality of experiential knowledge,
5. Utilization of interdisciplinary approaches (2002, p. 95).

Yosso uses the principles of CRT to challenge the "business as usual" model of schooling for students of color and poor children; she replaces it with an empowering vision of schooling that helps these same students make higher education a viable goal. These concepts parallel the principles written by Tate (1997). Scholars have applied the branches of CRT to issues of access and equity in education as a means to shed light on continued injustices that are supported through school finance, teacher dispositions and pedagogy, state and federal education policies, and societal inequities that impact a student's ability to be successful. The formation of CRT also parallels the coming of age of critical theory in education scholarship in the United States from the early 1980s, and it is preceded by multicultural education in the United States from the 1970s. In this CRT analysis, the inability to infuse and support principles of multicultural education into teacher education programs is a primary concern and a rationale for the production of teachers who are not equipped to work in racially diverse and economically depressed school communities.

CRT AND TEACHER EDUCATION

Critical race theory emphasizes the intersectionality of racism, classism, sexism, and sexuality as sliding and often situational social and institutional constructs. These grand "isms" work together in disharmonious and irrational ways to form and challenge notions of homogeneity among racially marginalized groups. Critical race theory is an intricate theoretical framework that has been used in education to discuss issues of whiteness and privilege (Bergerson, 2003), education policy (Revilla & Asato, 2002; Solorzano & Ornelas, 2002), curriculum (Yosso, 2002), classroom events (Chapman, 2007), and school finance (Aleman Jr., 2006; Aleman Jr., 2007). Studies by Duncan (2000, 2001), Solorzano and Delgado Bernal (2001), Fernandez (2002), Teranishi (2002), Rolon-Dow (2005), Snipes & Waters (2005), and Rogers and Mosley (2006) focus on K–12 students and public school classrooms. Other studies (Andre-Bechely, 2005; Auerbach, 2002; Villenas & Deyhle, 1999) focus on the counterstories of families of color negotiating various education pathways. Scholars using CRT have focused on administrators' (Aleman Jr., 2006; Evans, 2007; McCray, Wright, & Beachum, 2007; Parker & Villalpando, 2007) and teachers' experiences and beliefs (Chapman, 2007; DeCuir & Dixson, 2004; Lynn, 2002; Morris, 2001) that impact the classroom experiences of students of color. Scholars may utilize one or two of the principles of CRT to highlight particular themes and combine them with queer theory (Blackburn, 2003; Loutzenheiser & MacIntosh, 2004) and other critical frameworks (Gutierrez, Asato, Santos, & Gotanda, 2002).

Over the past three decades, much of the work focused on changing teacher education to reflect pre-K through 12 students' racial, socioeconomic, and cultural backgrounds has been championed by multicultural teacher educators who believe that teacher education students need to be more prepared to address issues of race, culture, class, and gender in curriculum and instruction (Gayles, 1979; Grant, 1994; Haberman, 1991; Hilliard, 1974; Lesko & Bloom, 1998; Sleeter, 1985; Zeichner et al., 1998). The move to create culturally relevant teachers is a field of study that is strongly connected to the use of critical race theory, but the two should not be collapsed into one category. As Ladson-Billings states,

> Of course, critical pedagogy must be performed by critical pedagogues, and few, if any, teacher preparation programs systematically prepare such teachers. CRT's project is to uncover the way pedagogy is racialized and selectively offered to students according to the setting, rather than to produce critical pedagogy. (Ladson-Billings, 2004, p. 60)

Critical race theory is the tool of analysis that leads to the production of critical pedagogy, not the pedagogy itself. Therefore, when CRT scholars ask questions concerning teacher education, the inquiries must explore multiple facets of the context to provide answers that can lead to reform. Milner states,

> Shifting the process of inquiry from the more personalized level to consider policy, institutional, systemic, and collective issues is important in this framework. In the practice of research, researchers take into considerations, for example, how history and politics shape their racialized and cultural systems of knowing and those of the research participants. From a critical race theory perspective, issues of race and racism

need to be situated in the broader context, not just on an individual or personalized level. (Milner, 2008, p. 397)

Thus teacher education cannot be interrogated at the individual or classroom levels without an analysis of how race and racism work in the larger contexts of institutions of higher education, teacher education policies, and state and federal mandates. There are three large areas of research in teacher education that call for a CRT analysis: the contexts of teacher education programs with regard to schools of education and institutions of higher education, the cost of the (in)effective nature of certification programs, and state and institutional policies in teacher education. These three areas beg the larger questions asked by Solorzano and Yosso:

- How do educational structures function to maintain racism, sexism, and classism?
- How do educational processes function to maintain racism, sexism, and classism?
- How do educational discourses function to maintain racism, sexism, and classism? (Solorzano & Yosso, 2001a, p. 3)

In answering these questions with regard to higher education and, more specifically, teacher education, the adage "what's old is new again" fits because the articulated debates are old, with the positioning of race at the center of the analysis possibly contributing a new perspective to the literature. Lopez (2003) suggests that four concepts, power, policy, government, and conflict, are valuable ways to analyze articulations of race and racism in educational institutions. After discussing the use of conceptualizations of whiteness in CRT, I will use these four concepts to structure the paper and frame the discussion of the ways in which majoritarian ideologies, beliefs, and behaviors valued by white middle-class America and given societal privilege over other racial and cultural groups' values are manifested and reinforced in teacher education.

Whiteness Studies and CRT in Teacher Education

Teacher education research that uses CRT has reduced the conversation to a focused look at the way whiteness functions in teacher education programs (Boyce, 2001; Cooper, Massey, & Graham, 2006; Marx, 2004; Marx & Pennington, 2002, 2003; Pennington, 2007). These articles frame the preservice teacher as an ultrapowerful agent that must be reprogrammed through an understanding of whiteness and the prevalence of racism before he or she is allowed to teach children (McCarty, 2003). This "agent" makes it difficult for professors of color to feel successful or relevant in their classrooms, makes white teachers fail to accomplish their own social justice goals, and calls into question the nature of multicultural course work at the program level (Dixson & Dingus, 2007; Dowdy, Givens, Murillo Jr., Shenoy, & Villenas, 2000; Scon, 2003). While these articles attack significant issues in teacher education they privilege the experiences of white, female preservice students and overshadow the larger systemic questions concerning the nature of teacher education programs as reproducers of the status quo. And I don't mean to be harsh to these hardworking and dedicated colleagues who struggle and are indeed marginalized for doing critical work that looks at their classes and students. But I say that the quest for social justice in teacher education is not about the teacher educator or the preservice student. In the realm of CRT, the quest for social justice is about changing the institutions that allow manifestations of whiteness to maintain power and disrupting the uncontested discourses that prevent radical and necessary reforms in teacher education that would help preK–12 children reach their full academic potential. Using the "defining elements" and the conceptual maps of CRT, I will articulate how multiple processes of teacher education continue to maintain white supremacist constructs of knowledge and professional status and what steps educators need to take to push teacher education programs to significantly change.

POWER: HIGHER EDUCATION, SCHOOLS OF EDUCATION, AND TEACHER EDUCATION

In the realm of higher education, schools of education have always held a precarious, powerless position in universities and colleges. Goodlad's (1991) five-year study of educators and teacher education sparked extensive conversations about the status of teacher education programs and the faculty members administering them. This plight is shared by many departments, such as those in the humanities, social sciences, and arts. High status in higher education is based on a number of tangible and intangible factors such as patent generation, research paradigms, and occupational status in society. The hierarchy of departments and programs is strongly tied to the generation of outside grants and funding; yet there are faculty issues of race and gender that impact the status of college departments and programs. The subtle hierarchy of departments and programs, coupled with society's views of particular professions, affects how college disciplines are viewed by students.

It is not accidental that many departments that struggle with low status in universities are also the departments with high numbers of black and brown scholars and women. In a study of efforts to diversify faculty at three top-tier institutions, scholars found

> that the long-standing use of the term "excellence" in opposition to "diversity" has reflected less a commitment to academic quality than an enactment of academic privilege; that is, it reflected the power of established elites to control the norms of the academic enterprise to keep new people, new topics, and new methodologies at bay. (Maher & Tetreault, 2009, p. 17)

Under the Equal Protection Clause, universities and college are mandated to have nondiscriminatory affirmative action plans that can be employed when the institution can show that the race-based policy is a compelling state interest and that the plan is narrowly tailored to achieve the compelling state interest. For instance, according to Executive Order Number 11246 (1964–1965), "Universities receiving federal funds are required 'to take affirmative action' regarding race as a factor in employment" (Igwebuike, 2006, p. 197). Affirmative action plans have led to greater numbers of white women and African American and Latino scholars in the social sciences and humanities; but because the various academic gate-keeping policies and practices that narrow the funnel of higher education attainment become even more miniscule in the applied sciences, women and African American and Latino scholars are rare in departments with high university status.

For example, in a study of over more than 500,000 full-time faculty members, Finkelstein, Seal, and Schuster (1998) found significant increases in the numbers of scholars of color and white women over the past two decades. However, African American and Latino scholars and white women remain overrepresented in the social sciences, humanities, and field of education (Bradley, 2000; Eckes, 2005) and Asian American scholars overrepresented in the applied sciences. To maintain their elitist racialized status and to seemingly comply with affirmative action policies, the applied sciences hire Asian American professors through special diversity initiatives called "targets of opportunity" and continue to hire white scientists through regular application processes. As part of the university backlash of perceived racial preferencing, two white plaintiffs have attempted to overturn university hiring decisions that were made with race-based justifications without success.[1]

Women faculty members often run teacher education programs, with the majority of them being white women. The field of education is home to significant numbers of black and Latino scholars, with white women and women of color being overrepresented in programs tied to teacher certification. "Teacher educators are little respected within higher education, where teacher education remains an embarrassing poor relation who nonetheless subsidizes those better off" (Bullough Jr., 2002, p. 237). Education programs are often found in older buildings or small, cramped spaces on college campuses. The buildings themselves may be less equipped and isolated than other new buildings and resources found in other departments. Their compliance and allegiance to the university is taken for granted, leaving these programs virtually powerless in the university structure (Shipp, 1999).

Students are not blind to the subtle and overt status hierarchies in their universities and colleges. They relate these hierarchies of career status to the larger society based on career salaries, media depictions, social status, and a host of social markers students deem as important. Their interpretations of these physical signs and university discourses influence their choice of major and career pathways. Goodlad observed,

> Increasing attention to research has not brought professors of education greater prestige on campus, nor improved the image of teacher education within schools and colleges of education. A few stars in education enjoy personal prestige, quite apart from the widespread denigration of their field, but students do not enjoy daily association with them as they do with the shadow faculty of adjunct, temporary, part-time personnel who teach the courses required for certification and have little or no say about the conduct and well-being of the enterprise, even though they keep the programs alive. Many students resent this situation. (Goodlad, 1991, p. 3)

Students, especially those who have reaped the rewards of academic success, may not reject the idea of teaching, but they reject the status and lack of tangible rewards that are an integral part of the profession. Programs such as Teach for America offer students a chance to teach on emergency licensure, with the understanding that they are in temporary positions. These teachers are expected to move on to other careers that are more in line with their Ivy League degrees. Additionally, researchers found that students with higher ACT and SAT scores and stronger grade averages tend to leave teaching more quickly than their counterparts with average scores and grade point averages (Podgursky, Monroe, & Watson, 2004; Shipp, 1999).

The low status of teacher education programs also has been linked to the lack of professional standards and sets of common practices in teacher certification programs. In the 1990s, various teacher educators sought to create "rigorous" standards for teacher education in an effort to improve the status of the departments. The former National Association of Education (NEA) president stated, "Our profession lacks a commonly accepted quality control mechanism. And that's one reason—in fact, a primary reason—we lack the full public confidence that is essential to the success of our mission" (Geiger, 1993, p. 2). The teacher standards that have been pushed by professional organizations such as the NEA, the National Council of Accreditation for Teacher Education (NCATE), and the American Association of Colleges for Teacher Education (AACTE) were primarily content based and standardized-test driven. Standardized assessments do not address the pedagogical dispositions for cultivating cultural empathy; the ability to teach the historical and present-day circumstances that are complicated by issues of race, gender, and class; the ability to maintain positive relationships between teachers and families; a substantial knowledge of diverse cultures; or an attention to community contexts (Sleeter, 2001; Yosso, 2002). Just recently, newly appointed Secretary of Education Arne Duncan reiterated this promise to change the status of teaching through higher education standards and assessments. He promised that the American Recovery and Reinstatement Act of 2009: Education Jobs and Reform would "invest heavily in teacher quality and principal quality initiatives that both elevate the teaching profession and help retain great teachers and principals for underserved schools and communities" (Duncan, 2009).

As the debate moves forward, preservice teachers now develop performance portfolios with evidence of instructional techniques and lesson planning. The professional standards incorporate issues of culture, community, and language into their standards, but they do not address the challenges of teaching students who are not the same race as the teacher. These points of inclusion are broadly constructed and can be applied in a generalizable fashion for teachers. For example, the National Board for Professional Teaching Standards (NBPTS) proposes five benign teaching propositions with only one possible reference to cultural diversity. In "Proposition I, Teachers Are Committed to Students and Their Learning," it states that teachers should be able to "respect the cultural and family differences students bring to their classroom." In some content areas, such as the language arts (NBPTS, 2003), teachers are encouraged to discuss issues of culture, stereotyping, morals, and values. These discussions remain at the lower levels of multicultural education as discreet or linear knowledge through the inclusion of books, historical events, and various thematic topics. Similarly, the board references to students' community ties obfuscate the conflict between schools and communities with regard to community perceptions of and relationships with formal educational institutions.

> Accomplished teachers know that a school is not isolated from the larger community, and they recognize the pervasive influence the community can have in shaping and enhancing a student's education. Their awareness of the importance of community relations leads these teachers to inform the community about school goals, projects,

and successes. Accomplished teachers also seek opportunities within the community to expand students' experiences, especially when thinking about future careers. (Standards, 2003, p. 78)

What the "professionalization" of teacher education actually does is support color-blind discourses of content and pedagogy that ignore the challenges of teaching and learning in classrooms where the teacher does not share the same race or cultural background as all of her students and reinstantiates teacher performances that are discursively white. Hobbel, when discussing "conceptions of multiculturalism that appear in national policy" (2003, p. 1876), states,

> Naming professional knowledge as a social operation and illuminating the "rites of institutions" through which it is vivified outline how the cultural struggle to maintain the professional teacher as a class of person takes place. This cultural struggle is particular to the maintenance of whiteness as a class in this field: the shield of difference acts to "make" the good teacher. Whiteness is at the center of professional knowledge so long as the good teacher must know her own privilege and racial characteristics and how they collide with those characteristics of her imagined students. (p. 1884)

Thus the unspoken convergence of interest in teacher education between the government that wants highly trained teachers and the programs that wish to raise the status of the teaching profession is the creation of standards and testing that maintain and solidify white supremacist ideals of a contextualized teaching and learning.

POLICY: NATURE OF CERTIFICATION PROGRAMS

Cost (In)effectiveness of Certification Programs

Critical race theory examines the multiple contexts of events and circumstances to create a more comprehensive and descriptive picture of what has occurred. In the case of teacher education, the design of the program inhibits working-class students, first-generation students, and low-income students from matriculating through these programs. Because a significant number of the students with these class and income demographics are students of color, the reason the preservice teaching population is white and middle class is all too apparent. Teacher certification programs are at worst elitist and at best designed for the exceptionally independent, highly focused college student. Students who need to work during college find it difficult, if not impossible, to complete their certification. Fieldwork curriculum components require that students spend substantial amounts of time in schools during the day, or perhaps during the early evening for tutoring programs. The critique does not lie with the need for field experiences but problematizes the assumptions that underlie unpaid work. Students who cannot afford to lose work hours to unpaid labor struggle to remain in these programs. Those who try to complete their student teaching during the day often work nights and weekends to generate income. Many of these students drop out or fail because they do not have enough time to do either task properly. Additionally, students with small children share these same challenges and possibly more if the student is a single parent with little home support.

The challenges of completing the field curriculum in teacher education programs are only one aspect of a flawed design. Certification programs require an extensive number of credit hours to be completed before students start their practicum. Students who have not had career counseling in college or before they enter higher education often have to add a fifth year to their program of studies to complete teacher certification. These students may have been able to take particular preservice courses as electives to defer the need for additional semesters, but they did not have proper guidance during their first and second years of college. Many savvy preservice students, namely, middle-class students whose parents are college educated, take classes at the community college in the summer, and at a lower price point, to avoid extra semesters. Even if students who are new to higher education were to take the community college route, these classes, which also cost money, must comply with busy summer schedules that are filled with work and perhaps care giving for younger siblings who are out of school or family members who need one-on-one care.

Over the past thirty years, some scholars have pointed to alternative certification programs or masters-certification programs as a means to widen the teacher education funnel. These programs often require students to have a bachelor's degree, and some students are more eligible than others for the program depending on their initial degree. Students with degrees in traditional subject areas are easily placed into alternative certification programs, but students with degrees in social science and human service areas may find themselves close to doing a second bachelor's degree. Researchers found that alternative certification programs are not drastically different from traditional programs in course requirements and field experiences (Podgursky, 2005; Walsh, Jacobs, & Thomas B. Fordham Foundation, 2007). These programs range from no cost to $30,000 for students (Walsh & Jacobs, 2007). Unless the program is tied to a funding stream, the participants may pay the equivalent of a masters program without gaining the actual degree. From a CRT perspective, the financial burden of obtaining the degree, coupled with low teacher salaries comparable to other career options for a baccalaureate degree, significantly dissuades students of color from choosing to be teachers. This institutional structure creates an uncontested barrier to creating more teachers of color.

Students who look toward teaching as a career must weigh the amount of loan monies they will incur over four to five years against the salary they would make as a teacher. For students in higher paid professional fields, the end justifies the means; however, this may not be the case for teachers. Low-income students are more hesitant and less willing to attend college when faced with twenty years of high loan payments (Horwedel, 2006). The majority of students who are willing to accumulate significant debt decide to get their degree in a more financially lucrative field that will help them manage the loan payments.

These circumstances beg the question, whose lifestyle is a teacher education program geared to serve? In a patriarchal society such as the United States, the clear answer is women—women whose jobs contribute to the household budget but do not financially surpass or career supersede that of a male spouse. Following this line of reasoning leads to the question, who gets married in college or the U.S. society most often—white men and women? According the U.S. Census Bureau, 72 percent of white, non-Hispanic men have been married, with 16 percent of those marriages taking place between the college-years ages of twenty to twenty-four and 52 percent of married white men are married between the ages of twenty-five to twenty-nine right after college; 80 percent of white women have been married with 29 percent of those marriages taking place between the ages of twenty to twenty-four and 66 percent between the ages of twenty-five to twenty-nine (Krieder, 2001). These statistics compare to 57 percent of black men and 60 percent of Hispanic men and 58 percent black women and 70 percent of Hispanic women ever being married. Black and Hispanic populations have similar percentages of marriage to whites for the two age periods; however, the differences in population numbers demonstrates that significantly more white families are being created.

Given the connection between the creation of new white family units, the flexibility of teaching careers, and ever-prevalent gender roles assigned to women, it seems likely that teacher education programs are designed for white, heterosexual women who wish to start families after college. The choice for white women to become teachers, or choose other low-status careers, is supported by research that examines the social and economic factors affecting the career choices of men and women. Bradley (2000) posits that men and women's career choices have remained virtually static due to societal norms that place value on women being care givers and homemakers rather than the primary breadwinner. As always in CRT, the issue of race complicates the gender dynamic because educated black and Latino women are less likely to marry for reasons too complex to explain in this paper.

Teacher Education Program Design

Several of the concerns with the costs of teacher education programs are associated with the design of teacher education programs. The step-by-step process to complete teacher education programs often prevents nontraditional, working students from being able to afford the program. However, within teacher education curricula lies a significant problem as well. Many teacher education programs that wish to create multicultural programs do not successfully implement the necessary curricula to infuse multicultural education into the program. Barriers such as limited multicultural education course offerings, qualified teaching staff, marginalization of faculty of color, limited exemplary cooperating teachers, limited quality field placements, and service-learning programs with deficit ideologies all contribute to the under-education of preservice teachers.

Multicultural teacher education asserts that programs must infuse the teaching of race, class, gender, and culture throughout the program curriculum. The "infusion discourse" (Dixson & Dingus, 2007) assumes that every teacher knows and understands concepts of race, class, and culture and how they are manifested in students' learning and teacher pedagogy. It assumes that teacher educators are not passing on deficit notions of students of color and students living in poverty that are often revealed in teacher education research. It assumes that teacher educators share a definition of multicultural education that moves toward social critique and societal change, when in fact most teacher educators espouse more color-blind than color-conscious ideologies that further submerge issues of race and racism in the curriculum. Teacher education programs often have large numbers of adjunct instructors who are not privy to internal conversations about the mission and vision of programs and the process of multicultural education infusion.

The most common program accommodation for multicultural education is the insertion of one "diversity" course that is mandated by the state. This course is often taught by a faculty member of color who has been hired to facilitate the multicultural portion of teacher education curriculum (Dixson & Dingus, 2007). Given other stressors on the curriculum, the course becomes the sole space in the curriculum for discussing a host of diversity issues that are conflated with race, class, and gender in a way that dilutes the impact of issues of racism, sexism, and classism in preK–12 classrooms. Dixson and Dingus state,

> Moreover, given the limited experiences of faculty with these issues, and the limits of the infusion model, students may not have the opportunity in their other courses to further interrogate their understanding of and discomfort with the issues and topics in the token multicultural education course. (Dixson & Dingus, 2007, p. 650)

Students may engage with difficult issues of racism in the diversity class, but subsequent courses do not build upon the diversity course. The lack of infusion of multicultural education prohibits students from developing a more comprehensive knowledge of students' lives and teacher pedagogy.

Similarly, students are unable to unpack the experiential information they gain through field experiences. At the preservice level, teacher education programs suffer from a lack of exemplary cooperative teacher placements where students can observe quality pedagogy. The majority of cooperative teacher placements are with white female teachers whose teaching styles resonate with the teacher educators in charge of the placements, but these programmers may not be the best judges of culturally relevant placements or successful African American and Latino teacher practices (Swetnam & Blocker, 1995).

Unsuccessful field placements also occur in service-learning programs. Many teacher education programs use service-learning programs to connect their preservice students with field experiences in communities of color. Poor field experience placements station students in community organizations and after-school programs where the white student helps the unsuccessful person of color become successful. This dynamic does not provide white students with the opportunity to observe the beauty and strengths of different communities; rather, it reinforces their deficit notions of these communities and the people living in them (Cipolle, 2004). CRT advocates for preservice students to have experiences that promote a discourse of difference and community strength, while many of these programs reinforce a deficit perspective of students of color and their communities (Solorzano, 1997).

GOVERNMENT: STATE INVOLVEMENT IN TEACHER EDUCATION

Much of the operations of teacher education programs can be directly linked to state accountability measures for teacher certification and professional development. When discussing the limited role of multicultural courses and the faculty who teach them, Dixson and Dingus state,

> This limitation of course offerings, coupled with increasing state licensure requirements, constrains the course schedule and thus devalues and limits time for students to engage

in meaningful experiences with difference other than the interactions with us [faculty of color], which they resist. (2007, p. 649)

Programs that desire a multicultural education focus struggle to accommodate state certification requirements and to attend to a more extensive exploration of race and racism.

The weak policies of the state and federal government concerning diversity in teacher education further marginalizes conversations of race, class, and gender that would produce better teachers for impoverished communities and communities of color. Although many states require students to have multiple fieldwork experiences and some course work focused on diversity, their teacher licensure standards do not discuss the teacher's need to understand race and racism, marginalization, classism, or sexism as an integral set of skills for teaching children in the United States (Morrier, Irving, Dandy, Dmitriyev, & Ukeje, 2007). The primary thrust of teacher licensure standards is the need for teachers to develop diverse instructional tools to facilitate students learning substantial amounts of content. This point is difficult to defend without producing a massive document showing the various states and their teacher certification standards. Perhaps a few examples will demonstrate this point. California is in the process of revising its 1997 teaching standards document. The outdated document mentions students from diverse backgrounds several times in the foreword, but it does not further articulate issues of race, culture, or class in the six overarching standards (California Credentialing of Teachers 1997). Wisconsin's ten standards specifically do not address culturally relevant teaching. Instead; the standards reference good teaching practices to serve all students (Burmaster, 2008). Virginia's six standards for professional practice are broadly conceived, with minimal references to students' communities and families in two of the standards and an overall emphasis on differentiated instruction and assessment (Virginia Standards for the Professional Practice of Teachers, 2008).

At the state and federal levels, funding for undergraduate scholarships across higher education has dwindled over the years only to be replaced with public and private loans. State and federal loan forgiveness programs for teaching in areas of need have also become a minimal means of addressing teacher shortages and the dearth of teachers of color. According to a study by the Project on Student Debt, high-level borrowing to fund higher education has grown much faster than low-level, or supplementary, borrowing (Horwedel, 2006). Experts say economically disadvantaged students of all races are worse off if the only aid they receive comes in the form of student loans. Many students graduate only to face immediate and staggering loan debt. Additionally, the processes for applying for and receiving state and federal funds for college tuition need to be streamlined and more transparent to encourage the maximum student access (Perna, Rowan-Kenyon, Bell, Thomas, & Chunyan, 2008).

CONFLICT: CHANGING TEACHER EDUCATION

At a time when state and federal institutions want to standardize education by making the standardized tests more difficult and instruction and content more homogenous, a critical race theory perspective calls for more diversity in teacher certification and programming, not less. Although it may be an "unpopular position" (Ladson-Billings, 1998), CRT scholars must call into question the discourses of homogeneity and sameness that undergird teacher standards, given that those goals are reappropriations of essentialist and perennialist philosophies of education that stem from white elitist doctrines describing assimilationist outcomes and goals of education (Beyer, 2002; Zuzovsky & Libman, 2006). Diversity in teacher education means more racially and ideologically diverse faculty to teach all courses, not just the one or two courses that focus on diversity. In critiquing the institutional structures and daily unexamined practices of teacher education programs, CRT questions who decides how the adjunct teachers, cooperating teachers, and fieldwork supervisors are solicited and are these teachers diverse in race, gender, religion, sexuality, or ideology (Ladson-Billings, 2000). These are difficult conversations to hold in schools of education where certain aspects of programming are seen as the fiefdom of particular faculty members. Program diversity also means creating programs that fit the lives of nontraditional students who have family responsibilities or are responsible for their own financial situations.

Teacher educators need to reject the idea that students with average academic performance cannot be quality teachers and reintroduce the concept of the good educator as someone who poses a host of academic and nonacademic skills that make children and young adults want to learn with him/her. This means searching for students who hold academic possibilities and unproven potential rather than those who have proven themselves successful. Students with potential may be struggling in community colleges or not in a higher education program. They will need academic support and financial support. These are the teachers that many urban students might identify with as community members, family members, and mentors. These are the teachers who will likely understand the financial struggles of low-income students and do not see their communities as deficit spaces devoid of rich cultural practices.

Programs need to be created that allow students' flexibility and that provide them with financial incentives. More loan forgiveness and scholarship monies need to be attached to programs of teacher education. Information on current loan forgiveness programs, federal and by state, can be accessed through the American Teacher Federation website (American Federation of Teachers, 2009). Currently, Stafford and Perkins loan-forgiveness programs only forgive a percentage of the loan, with Stafford not to exceed $17,500. Other programs such as the Public Service Loan Forgiveness Program only dissolves a person's loans after the person has served the public good for ten years and made 120 loan payments. The dollar limits on the programs do not encourage students at highly ranked and more expensive colleges to become teachers. A better opportunity for teachers is the TEACH grant. TEACH grants pay for student tuition with a contractual agreement that students will teach for four years in high-need areas (American Federation of Teachers, 2009). An alternate suggestion for decreasing the financial burden associated with teacher certification is to decrease the number of program course credits required or provide paid internships that can be completed in various educational settings (Podgursky, 2005). Additionally, monies for increasing the numbers of students in teacher certification programs must include the dissemination of information to junior high and high school students that highlights the strengths and joys of the teaching profession. Teachers should be financially rewarded for creating and maintaining programs to support different groups of students that go beyond traditional extracurricular clubs and sports.

In Wisconsin, law students do not take the bar exam to practice in the state. The state has shown incredible trust in the Wisconsin university system to produce quality lawyers without an exit exam. Why can't this same relationship be extended to schools of education? If students maintain a B+ average or better in both their content and pedagogical courses and received similar grades on their performance assessments, why aren't they exempt from the exam? Only those students who have not proven themselves competent through their course work and students who wish to move to a different state should be made to take an exit exam.

Finally, the binary between quality and diversity must be aggressively challenged and dissolved in order for more students to enter the ranks of the teaching profession. As Stovall (2005) observes, "Referencing this work [CRT] as a 'challenge' to traditional theoretical constructs critiques the 'one-size-fits-all' approach to education" (p. 106). Critical race theory sees the official curriculum as a "culturally specific artifact designed to maintain a white supremacist master script" (Ladson-Billings, 1998, p. 18). In the case of teacher education, the master script discourse of standards and rigor is designed to maintain ideological privilege over the K–12 curriculum. If teacher education scholars continue to align "rigor" and "high standards" with homogenous ways of knowing and teaching children and "low status" and "low standards" with diversity and flexibility, teacher education programs will remain rigid programs that continue to produce white, female candidates who have very little understanding of racism, sexism, and classism. The teachers will continue to struggle to serve children of color, and the Randys of the world, clean and ready to learn, will continue to suffer at the hands of new kindergarten teachers with the same old skills and dispositions.

NOTE

1. 56 F. Supp.2d 419

REFERENCES

Aleman, E. (2006). Is Robin Hood the "prince of thieves" or a pathway to equity? Applying critical race theory to school finance political discourse. *Educational Policy, 20(1)*, 113–42.

Aleman Jr., E. (2007). Situating Texas school finance policy in a CRT framework: How "substantially equal" yields racial inequity. *Educational Administration Quarterly, 43(5)*, 525.

American Federation of Teachers (2009). Tools for Teachers AFT–CIO. Retrieved August 11, 2009, from http://www.aft.org/tools4teachers/loan-forgiveness.htm

Andre-Bechely, L. (2005). Public school choice at the intersection of voluntary integration and not-so-good neighborhood schools: Lessons from parents' experiences. *Educational Administration Quarterly, 41(2)*, 267–305.

Auerbach, S. (2002). "Why do they give the good classes to some and not to others?" Latino parent narratives of struggle in a college access program. *Teachers College Record, 104(7)*, 1369–92.

Bergerson, A. A. (2003). Critical race theory and white racism: Is there room for white scholars in fighting racism in education. *Qualitative Studies in Education, 16(1),* 51–63.

Beyer, L. E. (2002). The politics of standardization: Teacher education in the USA. *Journal of Education for Teaching, 28(3),* 239–45.

Blackburn, M. (2003). Exploring literacy performances and power dynamics at the loft: Queer youth reading the world and the word. *Research in the Teaching of English, 37(4),* 467.

Boyce, B. A. (2001). Dilemmas for teacher education programs. *JOPERD: Journal of Physical Education, Recreation & Dance,* p. 6. Retrieved from https://ezproxy.lib.uwm.edu/login?url=http://search.ebscohost.com/login.aspx?direct=true&db=tfh&AN=5150769&loginpage=login.asp&site=ehost-live

Bradley, K. (2000). The incorporation of women into higher education: Paradoxical outcomes? *Sociology of Education, 73(1),* 1–18.

Bullough Jr., R. V. (2002). Thoughts on teacher education in the USA. *Journal of Education for Teaching, 28(3),* 233–37.

Burmaster, E. (2008). *Wisconsin Educator standards—Teachers. Ten standards for teacher development and licensure.* Retrieved from http://dpi.wi.gov/tepdl/stand10.html

California Credentialing of Teachers, C. C. o. T. (1997). California Standards for the Teaching Profession [Electronic Version]. Retrieved August 11, 2009 from http://www.ctc.ca.gov/reports/cstpreport.pdf

Carbado, D. W. (2002). Afterward: (E)racing education. *Equity & Excellence in Education, 35(2),* 181–95.

Chapman, T. K. (2007). Interrogating classroom relationships and events: Using portraiture and critical race theory in education research. *Educational Researcher, 36(3),* 156.

Cipolle, S. (2004). Service-learning as a counter-hegemonic practice evidence pro and con. *Multicultural Education, 11(3),* 12–23.

Cooper, J. E., Massey, D., & Graham, A. (2006). Being "Dixie" at a historically black university: A white faculty member's exploration of whiteness through the narratives of two black faculty members. *Negro Educational Review, 57,* 117–35.

DeCuir, J. T., & Dixson, A. D. (2004). "So when it comes out, they aren't that surprised that it is there": Using critical race theory as a tool of analysis of race and racism in education. *Educational Researcher, 33(5),* 26–31.

Deschenes, S., Cuban, L., & Tyack, D. (2001). Mismatch: Historical perspectives on schools and students who don't fit them. *Teachers College Record, 103(4),* 525.

Dixson, A., & Dingus, J. (2007). Tyranny of the majority: Re-enfranchisement of African-American teacher educators teaching for democracy. *International Journal of Qualitative Studies in Education (QSE), 20(6),* 639–54.

Dixson, A. D., & Rousseau, C. K. (2005). And we still are not saved: Critical race theory in education ten years later. *Race Ethnicity and Education, 8(1),* 1–6.

Dowdy, J. K., Givens, G., Murillo Jr., E. G., Shenoy, D., & Villenas, S. (2000). Noises in the attic: The legacy of expectations in the academy. *International Journal of Qualitative Studies in Education (QSE), 13(5),* 429–46.

Duncan, A. (2009). *FACTSHEET: The American Recovery and Reinstatement Act of 2009: Education Jobs and Reform.* Retrieved February 18, 2009, from http://www.ed.gov/print/policy/gen/leg/recovery/factsheet/overview.html

Duncan, G. A. (2000). Theorizing race, gender, and violence in urban ethnographic research. *Urban Education, 34(5),* 623–44.

Duncan, G. A. (2001). Beyond love: A critical race ethnography of schooling of adolescent black males. *Equity and Excellence in Education, 35(2),* 131–43.

Eckes, S. E. (2005). Diversity in higher education: The consideration of race in hiring university faculty. *Brigham Young University Education & Law Journal, (1),* 33–51.

Evans, A. E. (2007). School leaders and their sensemaking about race and demographic change. *Educational Administration Quarterly, 43(2)*, 159–88.

Fernandez, L. (2002). Telling stories about school: Using critical race theories to document Latina/Latino education and resistance. *Qualitative Inquiry, 8(1)*, 45–65.

Finkelstein, M. J., Seal, R. K., & Schuster, J. H. (1998). *The new academic generation: A profession in transformation*. Baltimore: Johns Hopkins University Press.

Gayles, A. R. (1979). An analysis and cataloging of multicultural teacher education curricula in colleges and universities. *Approved by the American Association of Colleges for Teacher Education*, Document No. ED173338.

Geiger, K. (1993). The integrity of our profession. *NEA Today*, p. 2. Retrieved from https://ezproxy.lib.uwm.edu/login?url=http://search.ebscohost.com/login.aspx?direct=true&db=tfh&AN=9303090095&loginpage=login.asp&site=ehost-live

Gillborn, D. (2006). Critical race theory and education: Racism and anti-racism in educational theory and praxis. *Discourse: Studies in the Cultural Politics of Education, 27(1)*, 11–32.

Goodlad, J. I. (1991). Better teachers for our nation's schools. *Education Digest, 56(6)*, 3–7.

Grant, C. A. (1994). Best practices in teacher preparation for urban schools: Lessons from the multicultural teacher education literature. *Action in Teacher Education, 16(3)*, 1–18.

Gutierrez, K. D., Asato, J., Santos, M., & Gotanda, N. (2002). Backlash pedagogy: Language and culture and the politics of reform. *Review of Education, Pedagogy, & Cultural Studies, 24(4)*, 335–51.

Haberman, M. (1991). Can cultural awareness be taught in teacher education programs? *Teaching Education, 4(1)*, 25–31.

Hilliard, A. G. (1974). *Restructuring teacher education for multicultural imperatives*. Document No. ED091380. U.S. Department of Health, Education and Welfare.

Hobbel, N. (2003). Imagining the good teacher: The nature of professional knowledge main description. *International Journal of Learning, 10*, 1875–84.

Horwedel, D. M. (2006). The misinformation about financial aid. *Diverse: Issues in Higher Education, 23(14)*, 34–37.

Igwebuike, J. G. (2006). Legal and policy implications for faculty diversification in higher education. *Negro Educational Review, 57(3/4)*, 189–201.

Krieder, R. M. (2001). *Number, Timing, and Duration of Marriages and Divorces: 2001*. Retrieved August 11, 2009 from http://www.census.gov/prod/2005pubs/p70-97.pdf

Ladson-Billings, G. (1998). Just what is critical race theory and what's it doing in a *nice* field like education? *Qualitative Studies in Education, 11(1)*, 7–24.

Ladson-Billings, G. (2000). Fighting for our lives: Preparing teachers to teach African American students. *Journal of Teacher Education, 51(3)*, 206–14.

Ladson-Billings, G. (2003). It's your world, I'm just trying to explain it: Understanding our epistemological and methodological challenges. *Qualitative Inquiry, 9(1)*, 5.

Ladson-Billings, G. (2004). New directions in multicultural education: Complexities, boundaries, and critical race theory. In Banks, J. A. (Ed.), *Handbook of research on multicultural education* (vol. 2), (pp. 50–68). San Francisco: Jossey-Bass.

Ladson-Billings, G. (2005). The evolving role of critical race theory in educational scholarship. *Race Ethnicity and Education, 8(1)*, 115–20.

Lesko, N., & Bloom, R. L. (1998). Close encounters: Truth, experience, and interpretation in multicultural teacher education. *Journal of Curriculum Studies, 30(4)*, 375–95.

Lopez, G. R. (2003). The (racially neutral) politics of education: A critical race theory perspective. *Educational Administration Quarterly, 39*, 68.

Loutzenheiser, L. W., & MacIntosh, L. B. (2004). Citizenships, sexualities, and education. *Theory into Practice, 43*, 151–58.

Lynn, M. (2002). Critical race theory and the perspectives of black men teachers in the Los Angeles public schools. *Equity & Excellence in Education, 35(2)*, 119.

Lynn, M., & Parker, L. (2006). Critical race studies in education: Examining a decade of research on U.S. schools. *Urban Review: Issues and Ideas in Public Education, 38(4ov)*, 257.

Maher, F. A., & Tetreault, M. K. (2009). Diversity and privilege. *Academe, 95(1)*, 17–20.

Marx, S. (2004). Regarding whiteness: Exploring and intervening in the effects of white racism in teacher education. *Equity and Excellence in Education, 37(1)*, 31–43.

Marx, S., & Pennington, J. (2002). *Experimentations with critical Race Theory and teacher Education students*. ERIC Document No. 469941.

Marx, S., & Pennington, J. (2003). Pedagogies of critical race theory: Experimentations with white pre-service teachers. *International Journal of Qualitative Studies in Education (QSE), 16(1)*, 91.

McCarty, C. (2003). Contradictions of power and identity: Whiteness studies and the call of teacher education. *International Journal of Qualitative Studies in Education (QSE), 16(1)*, 127.

McCray, C. R., Wright, J. V., & Beachum, F. D. (2007). Beyond *Brown*: Examining the perplexing plight of African American principals. *Journal of Instructional Psychology, 34(4)*, 247–55.

Milner, H. R. I. V. (2008). Critical race theory and interest convergence as analytic tools in teacher education policies and practices. *Journal of Teacher Education, 59(4)*, 332–46.

Morrier, M. J., Irving, M. A., Dandy, E., Dmitriyev, G., & Ukeje, I. C. (2007). Teaching and learning within and across cultures: Educator requirements across the United States. *Multicultural Education, 14(3)*, 32–40.

Morris, J. E. (2001). Forgotten voices of black educators: Critical race perspectives on the implementation of a desegregation plan. *Educational Policy, 15(4)*, 575.

National Board for Professional Teaching (2003). Adolescence and Young Adulthood/English Language Arts STANDARDS (for teachers of students ages 14–18+) [Electronic Version], 2. Retrieved August 11, 2009 from http://www.nbpts.org/userfiles/File/aya_ela_standards.pdf

Parker, L. (1998). "Race is . . . race ain't": An exploration of the utility of critical race theory in qualitative research. *Qualitative Studies in Education, 11(1)*, 43–55.

Parker, L., & Villalpando, O. (2007). A Race(cialized) perspective on education leadership: Critical race theory in educational administration. *Educational Administration Quarterly, 43(5)*, 519–24.

Pennington, J. L. (2007). Silence in the classroom/whispers in the halls: Autoethnography as pedagogy in white pre-service teacher education. *Race, Ethnicity and Education, 10(1)*, 93–113.

Perna, L. W., Rowan-Kenyon, H., Bell, A., Thomas, S. L., & Chunyan, L. (2008). A typology of federal and state programs designed to promote college enrollment. *Journal of Higher Education, 79(3)*, 243–67.

Podgursky, M. (2005). Teacher licensing in U.S. public schools: The case for simplicity and flexibility. *PJE. Peabody Journal of Education, 80(3)*, 15–43.

Podgursky, M., Monroe, R., & Watson, D. (2004). The academic quality of public school teachers: An analysis of entry and exit behavior. *Economics of Education Review, 23(5)*, 507–18.

Revilla, A. T., & Asato, J. (2002). The implementation of Proposition 227 in California schools: A critical analysis of the effect on teacher beliefs and classroom practices. *Equity & Excellence in Education, 35(2)*, 108–18.

Rogers, R., & Mosley, M. (2006). Racial literacy in a second-grade classroom: Critical race theory, whiteness studies, and literacy research. *Reading Research Quarterly, 41(4)*, 462–95.

Rolon-Dow, R. (2005). Critical care: A color(full) analysis of care narratives in the schooling experiences of Puerto Rican girls. *American Educational Research Journal, 42(1)*, 77.

Rury, J. L. (2002). Democracy's high school? Social change and American secondary education in the post-Conant era. *American Educational Research Journal, 39(2)*, 307–36.

Scon, K. A. (2003). My students think I'm Indian: The presentation of an African-American self to pre-service teachers. *Race, Ethnicity & Education, 6(3)*, 211.

Shipp, V. H. (1999). Factors influencing the career choices of African American collegians: Implications for minority. *Journal of Negro Education, 68(3)*, 343.

Sleeter, C. E. (1985). A need for research on pre-service teacher education for mainstreaming and multicultural education. *Journal of Educational Equity and Leadership, 5(3)*, 205–15.

Sleeter, C. E. (2001). Preparing teachers for culturally diverse schools: Research and the overwhelming presence of whiteness. *Journal of Teacher Education, 52(2)*, 94–106.

Snipes, V. T., & Waters, R. D. (2005). The mathematics education of African Americans in North Carolina: From the *Brown* decision to No Child Left Behind. *Negro Educational Review, 56(2–3)*, 107.

Solorzano, D. (1997). Images and words that wound: Critical race theory, racial stereotyping, and teacher education. *Teacher Education Quarterly, 24(3)*, 5–19.

Solorzano, D. G., & Delgado Bernal, D. (2001). Examining transformational resistance through a critical race and Latcrit theory framework: Chicana and Chicano students in an urban context. *Urban Education, 36(3)*, 308–42.

Solorzano, D. G., & Ornelas, A. (2002). A critical race analysis of advanced placement classes: A case of educational inequality. *Journal of Latinos and Education, 1(4)*, 215–29.

Solorzano, D. G., & Yosso, T. J. (2001a). Critical race and LatCrit theory and method: Counter-storytelling. *International Journal of Qualitative Studies in Education, 14(4)*, 471–95.

Solorzano, D. G., & Yosso, T. J. (2001b). From racial stereotyping and deficit discourse toward a critical race theory in teacher education. *Multicultural Education, 9(1)*, 2–8.

Stovall, D. (2005). A challenge to traditional theory: Critical race theory, African-American community organizers, and education. *Discourse: Studies in the Cultural Politics of Education, 26(1)*, 95–108.

Swetnam, L. A., & Blocker, L. S. (1995). The selection and evaluation of cooperating teachers: A status report. *Teacher Educator, 30(3)*, 19–30.

Tate, W. F. (1997). Critical race theory and education: History, theory, and implications. In Apple, M. (Ed.), *Review of Research in Education* (vol. 22), (pp. 191–243). Washington, DC: American Education Research Association.

Teranishi, R. T. (2002). Asian Pacific Americans and critical race theory: An examination of school racial climate. *Equity & Excellence in Education, 35(2)*, 144.

Tyack, D. (1990). Restructuring in historical perspective: Tinkering toward utopia. *Teachers College Record, 92(2)*, 170–91.

Villenas, S., & Deyhle, D. (1999). Critical race theory and ethnographies challenging the stereotypes: Latino families, schooling, resilience and resistance. *Qualitative Inquiry, 29(4)*, 413–45.

Virginia Standards for the Professional Practice of Teachers. (2008). [Electronic Version]. Retrieved February 23, 2009, from http://www.doe.virginia.gov/VDOE/newvdoe/virginia_prof_practice_standards.pdf

Walsh, K., & Jacobs, S. (2007). *Alternative certification isn't alternative*: Thomas B. Fordham Institute. Washington, D.C., ED498382.

Yosso, T. J. (2002). Toward a critical race curriculum. *Equity and Excellence in Education, 35(2)*, 93–107.

Zeichner, K. M., Grant, C., Gay, G., Gillette, M., Valli, L., & Villegas, A. M. (1998). A research informed vision of good practice in multicultural teacher education: Design principles. *Theory into Practice, 37(2)*, 163–71.

Zuzovsky, R., & Libman, Z. (2006). Standards of teaching and teaching tests: Is this the right way to go? *Studies in Educational Evaluation, 32(1)*, 37–52.

12

"I Am Large, I Contain Multitudes"

Teacher Identity as a Useful Frame for Research, Practice, and Diversity in Teacher Education

Brad Olsen

All . . . experience enters into you.

—Jazz pianist Bill Evans[1]

TEACHER IDENTITY AS GROUNDED THEORY

Since about two decades ago, a few dozen education researchers have employed teacher identity as a tool to investigate topics such as teachers' locations in the profession (Britzman, 1991; Coldron & Smith, 1999; Day et al., 2006; Knowles, 2005), teacher development contradictions (Britzman, 1990; Cooper & Olson, 1996; Sexton, 2008), teacher knowledge (Beijaard & Verloop, 1996), narrative features of teachers and teaching (Alsup, 2006; Connelly & Clandinin, 2006; McVee, 2004; Sfard & Prusak, 2005), and the professional life cycle of teachers (Fessler & Christensen, 1992). At least one article has already examined the emerging body of teacher identity research (Beijard, Meijer, & Verloop, 2004). My own review of the existing studies on teacher identity reveals a loose, tacit consensus holding that a teacher's professional identity is (1) dynamic, and not fixed; (2) a relation between some kind of core identity and multiple selves; (3) both a process and a product; (4) an ongoing and situated dialectic among person, others, history, and professional contexts; (5) a political project as much as an ontological frame; (6) socially situated and therefore not traditionally psychological; (7) clearly differentiated from a teacher's "role"; and (8) not clearly differentiated from a teacher's "self."

I consider teacher identity to be a conceptual tool—a more or less coherently formulated theoretical frame for use in viewing teachers, teacher learning, and teacher practice in nuanced, complex ways. Teacher identity is emerging as a promising way to offer fuller, richer, context-sensitive accounts of teachers and teaching. It captures teachers as always engaged in situated interactions that rely on prior iterations of a self while at the same time recreating themselves as professionals in relation to others. It offers a useful frame for investigating any number of research questions related to teaching and teachers. For example, Coldron and Smith (1999) examine teachers' professional identities in order to investigate structure versus agency: a teacher has agency to make choices but those choices exist within the framework of relatively intractable cognitive, social, and institutional structures such as educational policies, school practices, dominant discourses, and social hierarchies. They point out that, for example, any "school's particular ethos affects the room [and so] an individual [teacher] has to negotiate his or her identity within a [preexisting] community bound by its own customs and traditions" (p. 715). Identifying four long-standing traditions of teaching (the craft, the moral, the artistic, and the scientific), the authors illuminate how teachers' agency exists inside particularized, rigid frameworks.

Teacher identity has been employed to interrogate ways teachers understand themselves in relation to the "role" of the teacher against their own incoming conceptions (Mockler, 2004; Sexton, 2008). Teacher identity has been used to understand how novice educators construct their professional selves by integrating multiple self-perceptions around categories such as content knowledge, personality conceptions, teacher education contexts, pedagogical practices, and biography (Flores & Day, 2006; Ronfeldt & Grossman, 2008). Identity has also been employed to critically interrogate ways that culture is inscribed on teachers and how diversity gets treated within teacher education, for example, in terms of gender, race, and power (McIntyre, 1997); ethnicity and language (Florio-Ruane & Niu, 2008; Tellez, 1999); and the influence of social discourses on teacher development (Juzwik, 2006; Mockler, 2004).

Like many researchers who enter the domain of identity studies (a point made in Beijaard et al., 2004), my own work began as a study of teacher knowledge. Studying the professional learning of eight beginning teachers over two years I found "knowledge" to be an insufficient analytical frame since it suggests a static, rationalistic, transferable product (Olsen, 2008a). Instead, I found that the prior experiences of preservice teachers produced deeply embedded conceptions and attitudes about subject matter, teaching, diversity, and students that proved mostly resilient against programmatic intervention, and that most professional learning was in fact a recursive process of negotiation among personal but often unexamined "life themes." These findings led me to pursue teacher identity. Subsequently, in one study teacher identity was employed to analyze fifteen early career urban elementary teachers' decisions about whether to stay in or leave their jobs (Olsen & Anderson, 2007). In another study teacher identity was used to investigate how a group of first-year teachers interpreted and enacted their preparation program's emphasis on Freirian forms of praxis (Hoffman-Kipp & Olsen, 2007). And a third study examined interrelationships between teachers' reasons for entering the profession and the kinds of beginning teachers they were becoming (Olsen, 2008b). Within these studies, teacher identity proved a useful tool because it allowed me to identify multiple, interrelating, situated personal and professional dimensions of teachers and teaching and examine them deeply—both individually as influences and together as an embedded process of professional development.

Important, teacher-identity framings capture, value, and yet critically attend to the diverse experiences of all beginning teachers. Research and practice on teacher education has for too long viewed teachers in broad strokes (e.g., "teachers of color," "women in teaching," or "the teachers from Hawthorne High") or in reductionist terms (such as "all teachers should . . . ," "an effective teacher will . . . ," or "any so-cial justice educator must . . ."). Instead, teacher identity proponents can treat teach-ers both as three-dimensional individuals (with particular sets of lived experiences that become personal or professional influences and effects) and as social beings simultaneously constrained and empowered in relation to the groups, structures, and roles in which they participate (and even those in which they do not). A teacher identity focus ensures that the active diversity and complex power of teachers' lived experiences and varied perspectives is acknowledged and made available for study and productive use by researchers and teacher educators.

DEFINING IDENTITY

The current literature on teacher identity is useful for introducing the topic and high-lighting teachers as complicated, whole beings who actively alter—and are altered by—the personal and professional contexts and demands of their work. Yet I have found that the research has not adequately explained what is meant by "teacher iden-tity" or what kinds of theoretical beliefs undergird topics in identity. What is missing is a treatment of teacher identity that offers a nuanced and complex discussion of identity as a concept or theory. To fill that gap, I present such a discussion here.

Figure 12.1 is meant to both present five theoretical tenets that I believe constitute a theory of identity and highlight their interrelation.

The graphic begins on the upper-left side with the point that mind cannot neces-sarily be separated from matter: we and our experiences inextricably blend together. In this diagram, "person" and "experience" are represented by two broad arrows with permeable boundaries. It is impossible to understand a human being indepen-dent of the world he or she inhabits: we cannot even talk about human beings in isolation because there is no such thing.

This philosophical tenet leads into the remainder of the graphic: identity as a complex mélange of influences and effects in which macro- and microsocial his-tories, contexts, and positionings combine with the uniqueness of any individual person to create a situated, ever-developing self that both guides—and results from—experience. This framing could be applied to any of several dimensions of a life: for example, the romantic lives of college-going women (Holland et al., 1998), men's relationships to the natural environment (Myers & Russell, 2003), or changed perspectives among members of Alcoholics Anonymous (Lave & Wenger, 1991). We could apply the frame to the professional identities of firefighters, medical doctors, ship captains, Vai tailors, masseuses, or teachers. A person's identity is multifaceted (an individual can simultaneously be a romantically involved woman, a recovering alcoholic, a volunteer firefighter, and a midcareer third-grade teacher).

Tenet 1: No Mind-Body Dualism

The view that there is no separation between mind and matter—that we construct our conscious reality rather than just perceive it or interact with it—can be aligned with twentieth-century European philosophy (Gadamer, 1985; Heidegger 1997/1927). It is often cast as a refutation of Descartes' (1637) famous mind-body split. Heidegger,

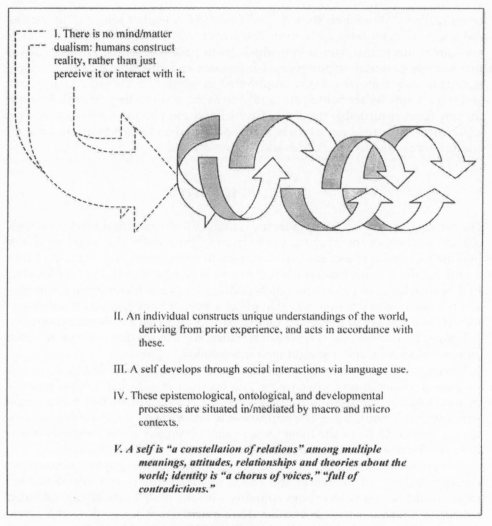

I. There is no mind/matter
dualism: humans construct
reality, rather than just
perceive it or interact with it.

II. An individual constructs unique understandings of the world,
deriving from prior experience, and acts in accordance with
these.

III. A self develops through social interactions via language use.

IV. These epistemological, ontological, and developmental
processes are situated in/mediated by macro and micro
contexts.

V. A self is "a constellation of relations" among multiple
meanings, attitudes, relationships and theories about the
world; identity is "a chorus of voices," "full of
contradictions."

Figure 12.1   Conceptual landscape of identity theory.

for example, argued that humans do not live apart from existence—observing and interacting with it—but rather humans *are* their existence, creating the worlds they inhabit out of their interpretations of events. Heidegger held that as we go through life, we are continually evaluating and reevaluating, assembling and reassembling ourselves in an attempt to carve out authentic existence in relation to the ground-level circumstances with which we are confronted (Heidegger, 1997/1927).

This tenet also emerges from social psychology and literary studies. George Mead famously asserted that our sense of self—what distinguishes humans from all other species—is our ability to be an object to ourselves. In other words, each of us is not only a subject that lives a life, but an object, too, that can be reflected upon by its possessor. Mead posited an inherent and ongoing social process whereby any human develops a self by participating in various early back-and-forth social exchanges with other humans—learning to anticipate, predict, and accommodate in relation to the actions of others. Through this process, he believed, a person becomes aware of herself as a person; she develops a self.

This conception dovetails into the sociocultural-constructivist tradition of viewing identity as "an explicit theory of one's own self as a person," to paraphrase David Moshman (1999). From constructivists like G. H. Mead and Lev Vygotsky to activity theorists like Michael Cole and James Wertsch comes a view of a self forming over time inside social situations. These socioculturalists consider that a self is constructed via both additive and mediating fashions, and it is part individually directed and part the product of both larger cultural and historical forces and the more immediate, specific circumstances of any individual's life. Such a view holds that we create and recreate our selves as selves during our ongoing participation in social practices and discourses. Mead identified activities like informal play and structured games as complex processes by which children become self-aware—subtly internalizing dominant social norms, perspectives, and understandings while constructing themselves as selves.

Others have written about those kinds of micro self-experiences being located inside larger intersections regarding gender, class, race, sexual orientation, religious beliefs, language, and physical ability, to name a few. For example Mary Belenky and her colleagues (1986) studied the ways women's knowledge is shaped by their lived experiences as women: typically being deprived of complex play, being restrictively stereotyped, and required to be obedient as children and then slowly finding their own inflection points toward self-awareness, voice, and empowerment as they experienced childbirth, recognized breakdowns in male authority, and created their own family structures. Belenky and colleagues found that these women's deep views of themselves and what it means to "be" and "know" in the world were fundamentally shaped by how they were treated as women. In fact, whole domains of analysis exist around the intersectional ways that humans' lived experiences fundamentally shape how they come to know themselves in the world: for examples, see black feminism, LatCrit, postcolonial studies, or queer theory.

Applied to teachers, this identity tenet informs us that a teacher's personal history, life experiences, and sociocultural positionings deeply and somewhat firmly shape his or her consciousness. Who we are as people has a lot to do with who we become as teachers (Hamachek, 1999). Researchers and teacher educators who treat incoming teachers as "blank slates" are destined to fail because they are presuming a professional development process that is straightforward and solely additive. Instead, education should centralize the embedded conceptions that teachers already possess, unearth their connections to the teachers' professional perspectives, understand that teacher learning is a process of negotiating and mediating multiple (often conflicting) identity sources, and help teachers critically interrogate and adjust the conceptions on which their professional learning rests. This is acutely significant for issues of culture, race, ethnicity, and power.

Tenet 2: The Role of Language

A self develops through social interactions via language use. This makes language and language study useful locations for understanding identity. Spurred on by

Ferdinand de Saussure's (1998/1913) linguistic formalism and Noam Chomsky's (1957) universal grammar, sociolinguists have long considered ways that language and social practices are inseparable. Many other theorists have too. Mead posited language to be the primary means through which selves interrelate. Central to many philosophers are questions that inextricably link language to identity construction (e.g., Rorty, 1989; Taylor, 1992; Wittingstein, 1991). Language figures prominently in how Mikhail Bakhtin and Lev Vygotsky discussed the social development of the self. And language and language study loom large in psychology (psychoanalysis even frequently called "the talking cure"), education research, and many other branches of social science and the humanities. Language (writ large to also include body language, semiotics, and facial expressions) is the social practice through which one self divines the intents and actions of other selves and similarly makes his or her own intentions and actions understood.

For teacher identity this means that any view of teacher identity should central-ize roles of language and language practices in identity formation. This is because language in use (or "discourse" as it might better be termed), as it relates to identity, possesses both dialogic and representational possibilities. The dialogic view is that identity *arises out of* language use; that is, any self is defined, made, and continually remade by participation in language and language practices. The representational view is that an identity *gets represented by* language use—that language is a kind of "window into" any person's identity. Investigating these two central functions of language in identity deepens views of how language is connected to identity, either dialogically (language as ontological process) or representationally (language as methodology).

One dialogic example of language and identity comes from Mikhail Bakhtin (Bakhtin, 1990; Holquist, 1990), who argued that an individual "authors himself" as both object and subject—the *plot* of the novel of one's self as well as its *writer*. This theory considers that any self develops in (or by way of) constant conversation with others, history, what has been said before, and how language is employed. Bakhtin conceived that human existence emerges out of the "constant, ceaseless cre-ation of exchange of meaning" among self, other, and the relationship between the two (Holquist, 1991, p. 41). Bakhtin treats language simultaneously as the *means* of those interrelationships, the *visible product* of the interrelationships, and the *stage* on which they are enacted. This conception illuminates not only how language simul-taneously co-constitutes identity (the dialogic function from above) but also how it renders identity visible (the representational function).

Extending the ideas of Bakhtin, Anna Sfard and Anna Prusak (2005) bring discourse and identity even closer together—arguing not that language (or "dis-course") shapes or reveals identity but that stories by and about people *are* identity. This particular kind of discourse identity theory takes Bakhtin's "self-authoring" out of the metaphorical and makes it literal: the stories we tell about ourselves along with the stories told about us, in fact, are our identity. Sfard and Prusak (2005) consider that identities "may be defined as collections of stories about per-sons or, more specifically, as those narratives about individuals that are reifying, endorsable, and significant[:] . . . stories told by the identified person . . . stories told to the identifying person . . . [and] stories told about the identified person by a third party to a third party" (pp. 16–17). This hypothesis not only sharpens identity and language as inextricable but in fact argues they are synonymous: stories do not merely *inform* or *offer access* into one's identity—they actually are the identity. Though I am not ready to fully accept this framing, such an assertion warrants serious consideration.[2]

Related to teacher identity development, this tenet underscores the need to acknowledge the power of language in teacher education research and practice. Researchers can benefit from examining language use as a way to capture and more deeply understand teachers' identities, beliefs, relational selves, and educational practices. People who work with teachers should educate them on the subtle but profound influence that language has on their own identity development as well as on that of their students. And teacher education as a whole benefits from deep, thoughtful analyses of inextricable links among cultural histories, power struggles, language use, and identity development (e.g., Bourdieu, 1995; Delpit & Kilgore, 2002; Foucault, 1977).

Tenet 3: The Self as Constructed Project

Any individual constructs unique understandings of the world, deriving from prior experience, and acts in accordance with these. Identity as a conceptual tool considers both *the process of* that situated self-construction and *the resulting, tangled product*. Heidegger named his philosophical version of this process-product that directs how people organize meaning out of lived experience the "fore-structure of understanding" (Heidegger, 1997/1927). It sits before (and below) understanding: performing a function that orients a self in particular ways to the larger world and selects from the total range of what is available to that which is considered significant. Within this process, the present always links to the past since each of us remains in part bound by our historical condition(s) while we are reconstructing our selves within any present experience. The present, Heidegger argued, involves a dynamic interplay of past, present, and future. It is related to a past-made-present in memories and views of the world and a future-already-possessed in the anticipation of events and consequences to be encountered.

A more psychological conception of this theory is George Kelly's (1963) notion of the "personality construct," which he used to explain how any individual uniquely chooses and organizes a subset of phenomena from the totality of possible characteristics of existence and assembles it in ways consistent with the person's prior understanding of the world. Kelly's point is that our lived experiences direct us to see the world in our own particular ways and, because we always test our hypotheses about the world *from within* our particular personality construct, we typically conclude that what we are seeing is, indeed, what exists.

Psychologist Karl Scheibe (1995) borrows the cosmological term *epigenesis* to describe how an individual develops. A person is born with specific attributes (a name, a body and genetic system, a location in history, a family)—"what is given"—and then begins to confront and participate in the situated circumstances of a life. How one participates in those circumstances depends greatly on one's prior self, and yet, as well, participating in those encounters alters the self and so, next time, different circumstances are encountered by a slightly different self. And so on. This constructivist conception of identity as self-development holds that, over time, per-

son and circumstances—what Scheibe terms *self* and *identity*, respectively—continue
to alter each other, and both become entwined:

> As it applies to self and identity, the suggestion is that the initial gift of self combines
> with the initial givens of circumstantial identity, and that self and identity are from that
> moment complexly intertwined. . . . The two kinds of gifts [of personhood]—initial
> endowment and accretions—produce a formed and presentable individual, changing,
> of course, throughout lived time. Roughly speaking, a self is given, about which identity
> characteristics are continuously acquired, some of which are transient (e.g., high school
> student), and some of which are quite permanent (e.g., female.). (1995, p. 18)

Although the process of *how* we develop may be generalizable, and the circumstances of a life are always shared with others past and present, *who* each of us
develops into is unique.

Any program of research or teacher development that adopts this theoretical tenet
can make productive use of the complex, situated process of identity development.
It also benefits from taking the position that any teacher is unique (though goals
and processes of teacher development may be common). A teacher's upbringing,
student experiences, prior work, and current life details are all actively involved in
how she is interpreting, accepting (or rejecting), and using the professional learning
to which she is exposed. This view clarifies why beginning teachers are not always
changed much by teacher education (Zeichner & Tabachnick, 1981), why teachers
often teach the way they were taught (Lortie, 1975), or why teachers sometimes
presume shared identity between themselves and their students (Jackson, 1986).
Teacher education research that starts from the premise that teachers actively, often
automatically, negotiate among past and present, personal and professional strands
of influence to construct their professional selves should yield important, case-
sensitive findings.

Tenet 4: Identity as a Cultural Study of Persons-in-Practice

The processes of identity construction are situated in macro- and microcontexts. As
traditional anthropology and sociology have emphasized, these processes of identity development are located in, and mediated by, the many layers of social context
in which humans participate. Though there is value to a broad framing of identity
as resulting from cultural strata such as race, gender, class, sexual orientation, or
religious beliefs—just to name a few—I am concerned that these macrostructural
treatments overdetermine or essentialize identity.

More helpful, then, is anthropologist Dorothy Holland and her colleagues
(Holland et al., 1998) who locate identity inside a kind of "cultural studies of the
person"—or what Holland and Lave (2001) term *social practice theory*. This angle of
inquiry comes on the heels of inroads made by various social and historical perspectives (i.e., poststructuralism and the critical disruption in the social sciences of
the 1960s) and builds on sociocultural theories and theories of the self-in-practice
(cf. Bakhtin; Lave & Wenger; Rogoff; Vygotsky). Generally, a sociocultural model
of identity considers that people are both products of their social histories, and—
through things like hope, desperation, imagining, play, art, and mindfulness—move

themselves from one subjectivity to the next, from one facet of one's identity to another, and can in some limited sense choose to act in certain ways considered by them to be coherent with self-understandings (Holland et al., 1998). This highlights that one central value of teacher identity is to illuminate levers for active agency in individual teachers and reveal a process—a lighted path, of sorts—by which teachers and teacher educators alike can become more conscious, and in more control, of the contours of their own professional development:

> One's history-in-person is the sediment from past experiences upon which one improvises, using the cultural resources available, in response to the subject positions afforded one in the present. The constraints are overpowering, yet not hermetically sealed. Improvisation can become the bases for a reformed subjectivity. (Holland et al., 1998, p. 18)

This conception of identity does not ignore the view of people as products of major societal, structural features of society such as race, ethnicity, and class. Yet, to avoid the trap of some of traditional sociology's and anthropology's more determinist treatments of identity, I posit two—not one—general strands of influence on an individual's subjectivity. The first is composed of these macrosocial strata (like race, gender, language, sexuality, and class) that dominate sociological notions of cultural identity. The second we might call the microstructures: those specific and immediate contexts, practices, and social relationships any person engages in (of course, themselves influenced by history and macrostructures, but also possessed of their own site-specific contours), and the mediated patterns of power, discourse, and agency they wield.

Identity as a conceptual tool focuses on the coordination of these multiple influences for any individual. It focuses on the process by which a person constantly negotiates among sets of sociohistorical and context-specific influences in order to assemble understandings of and for himself. It is how a self—located in time and space—continually makes sense of herself, the world, and her place in the world. The macrosociohistorical structuring of personhood, then, is constituted in the concrete, daily practices of individuals who participate in social contexts which, themselves, participate loosely in ever-widening positionings and histories. Consider dozens of concentric circles moving out from the immediate, local context in which a specific person might find herself.

One way of understanding this arrangement is to look at social role theory. Social role theory (e.g., Sarbin & Allen, 1968) posits that any person's identity derives in large part from his or her legitimated social positions as already defined by the world. In other words, a person's identity is not only self-referential ("Who am I?") but assigned by others, too ("Who are you?" "Who do others think I am?"). Yet even this self ←→ other identity process does not exist in a vacuum but is, itself, shaped by the available roles and attached histories that we inhabit and the validity with which we are "allowed" to inhabit them. For example, I may be defined as a professor in relation to already established characteristics of what a professor is: I can accept, ignore, or subvert those characteristics—adhere to or break them, or make them an object of contemplation (like I am doing here)—but when I am acting in the role of professor I will be always somehow determined in relation to them (perhaps a pedantic-speaking style, corduroy jacket, sanctimony, or a tendency to overvalue one's own ideas). And, to some extent, I cannot ignore these embedded characteristics of professorhood even as I might attempt to define myself on my own terms. Conversely, I if act like a professor but I am not actually one, I will not be considered a professor because the legitimacy of the role, in fact, is defined without respect to me; it is a technical designation that must be conferred.[3]

Moreover, social role theory holds that identity—being in part marked relative to other people and contexts—changes as the role system changes. I am mostly a professor with my students, mostly a colleague or subordinate with my dean, mostly a son with my parents, and mostly a mediocre drummer with my band. Even though I am all of those things, specific facets of my complex identity are highlighted or shaded, brought to the fore or placed in the background based on which role system I find myself participating in at any given time. (This echoes Bourdieu's [1995] notion of the *habitus* or, I suppose, Gee's [1995] concept of Discourse.) A social identity is the complex overlapping, kaleidoscopic attempt to locate—and define—oneself in mosaics of shifting role systems. Likewise, teachers are teachers not because they say they are or because they act like teachers, but because they fit into a socially, institutionally sanctioned role that allows them, with legitimacy, to call themselves (and "behave like") teachers. A teacher exists within that role: his identity is being partly defined by what it is to be a teacher, irrespective of him as an individual (and yet folding back to influence his self).

In terms of teacher identity, this theoretical tenet reminds us that to be a teacher in this day and age is not a tabula rasa but is enacted in accordance with (or against) predetermined notions of who teachers are, how they act, and what they do. It is this reciprocal negotiation among self, role, and world that forms the crux of professional identity for teachers. And, of course, notions of diversity are a central part of the process: culture, race, and gender influence how roles for teachers are established and maintained; teachers unconsciously rely on beliefs about culture, race, and gender to understand students; and educational structures always preposition participants by way of cultural affiliations and racial-gender-otherwise characteristics. Teacher identity as conceptual tool captures and illuminates the dynamic complexity of all this.

Tenet 5: Self as "a Constellation of Relations" Among Multiple Meanings

An identity, therefore, is "a constellation of relations" (Holland & Lave, 2001) among multiple meanings, attitudes, relationships, and theories about the world, "a chorus of voices" (Beijaard, et al., 2004) that is "full of contradictions" (Britzman, 1991). Identity is the process of constructing a self—one that is considered (consciously or not) to be meaningful and coherent by its owner—out of the innumerable, often contradictory, only partially understood influences that are available to a person. This is how an individual acts inside socially constructed worlds guided by self-understandings. There must surely be stable elements of a person's identity—they emerge from some combination of prior macro- and microsocio-historical influences on the one hand and a person's genetic makeup and upbringing on the other—the "stuff that is given" that Scheibe writes about. An old friend not seen in a long time still seems rather the same. A person's genome remains (mostly) unchanged. Yet, there are also active, dynamic, shifting parts to one's identity that are constantly reinterpreting one's self, reevaluating one's self, and reassembling one's self out of previous incarnations (and memories) and inside the current contexts and relationships that make up a life.

This tenet encourages healthy skepticism toward research that finds teacher development to be mostly rational or linear. It dissuades researchers from believing a teacher's perspectives will always be coherent or knowledge-based. Instead, it should remind teacher education researchers (and practitioners) that any teacher self is multifaceted, frequently composed of competing parts, and as much about emotions and ideologies as about rational bodies of intellectual knowledge. It highlights that teachers learn by way of working through sequences of identity conflicts. Looking for the various values debates, contradictions, and political struggles inherent in any teacher's identity—and viewing teacher development as negotiating tensions, not solving problems—becomes a promising starting point for teacher identity research.

TEACHER IDENTITY'S DUAL FOCUS ON DIVERSITY

I believe that making use of teacher identity as a conceptual tool is essential in order to capture, celebrate, and make positive use of the inherent diversity of all teachers, students, and educational settings. This is because teacher identity opens up the diversity of everyone for scrutiny. That is not to say that all kinds of diversity are equal in terms of the power and privilege to which members are offered; any look at sociohistory reveals certain social groups, discourses, and categories to be negatively affected by oppression and discrimination, while other groups and categories receive surplus power, prestige, and capital. Teacher identity does not deny that. But a significant advantage of teacher identity as analytical frame is its theoretical ability to bridge the individual with the social and simultaneously accept that any educator is always both unique and like others in multiple ways. From this theoretical contribution come two valuable implications: (1) teacher identity foregrounds a view of all teachers as always diverse in intersecting, complex, but identifiable ways; and (2) teacher identity offers a holistic framework for how teachers can identify and adjust their own professional identities in relation to dimensions of diversity (such as race, culture, language, class, sexuality, religion, sexuality, physical ability, national origin, and geography, just to name a few).

That first implication is useful for education researchers, teacher educators, and policy makers alike. It emphasizes a holistic view of teachers as three-dimensional human beings who make complex and often automatic but identifiable use of their personal histories and past experiences—as well as their professional preparation and current contexts—to construct ongoing understandings of and for themselves in relation to diversity. Such a view discourages broad or determinist framings of social strata in relation to teachers and teaching. For example, an early twenties, white, middle-class, monolingual woman who teaches within forty miles of her birthplace (the "typical" teacher candidate, according to research in the 1980s and 1990s [e.g., Calderhead, 1988; Wideen, Mayer-Smith, and Moon, 1998]) cannot or should not be reduced to her assemblage of social strata. Teacher identity illuminates how she is more than "just" a product of those overarching dimensions and that, moreover, she is always organizing and negotiating the multiple parts of herself into a somewhat coherent whole in the flow of situated practice. The educators who work with her, the researchers who study her, and the policy makers whose reforms intend to influence her neglect the active, constantly evolving, intermediated nature of her diversity at their own peril.

That second implication—that teacher identity offers its own pedagogy of consciousness-raising—is significant for teacher education. Teacher identity provides a theoretical tool for use with democratic pedagogies of possibility and diversity. Teacher educators can use the theories and framing of teacher identity to create coherent curricula and instructional approaches that scaffold teachers to (1) acknowledge the active but often hidden roles their own ethnic, cultural, racial, sexual, and socioeconomic experiences (for example) play in their professional perspectives and practices; (2) make those deeply embedded identity dimensions visible for critical, collective interrogation; (3) examine and adjust those dimensions in accordance with existing research, perspectives of mentors, and their own professional goals for students; and (4) position themselves to continually engage in and monitor the results of this iterative, now conscious, professional identity process. As John Dewey wrote, "[Education] is that reconstruction or reorganization of experience which adds to the meaning of experience, and which increases [one's] ability to direct the course of subsequent experience" (Dewey, 1916, p. 82). Teacher identity formulates a holistic framework for making just such a notion possible.

For example, we might imagine a teacher education program where novices construct teacher identity autobiographies in which each candidate uses writing, video, audio, and digital collages to excavate multiple, intersecting parts of their own personal history in relation to diversity and then consider how those parts are currently mediating (and being mediated by) their professional preparation. Explicitly framed by teacher identity readings and conversations, such an assignment could be the foundation for a pedagogical process in which each beginning teacher consciously engages his or her own embedded conceptions in dialog with peers, mentors, and the educational practices the program advocates. This identity autobiography could travel with the teacher throughout the program—used in different classes and experiences in different ways and continually being added to, adjusted, and critically reflected on. The artifact, then, becomes the linchpin of a critical teacher-learning process that begins with the uniqueness of individual teachers, stresses the always-social nature of development, and demands attention to ways diversity plays a role in every nook and cranny of a teacher's professional identity growth.

A CORRESPONDING RESEARCH APPROACH

There are, of course, dozens of ways to conceptualize teacher identity, and each carries its own nuances for how to collect and analyze empirical data. Equally large is the number of research methodologies available for studying teacher education. So, matching conceptual frames to congruent methodology can be vexing. Below, four methodological recommendations are offered that follow the particular contours of how teacher identity has been delineated in this paper. These following suggestions might orient researchers who wish to use teacher identity as the basis of their teacher education research: (1) embrace an ecological paradigm; (2) centralize new teachers' language interactions; (3) privilege teachers in practice; and (4) treat research participants as collaborators, not subjects.

Embrace an ecological paradigm. Ecological research is an important paradigm in education that seeks to capture the integrated webs of influence on any aspect of educational life—the overarching "ecology" or "ecosystem" in which an educational phenomenon exists (LeCompte & Schensul, 1990; Wideen, Mayer-Smith, & Moon, 1998). As a methodological perspective, ecological research considers that the broader ecology that influences—and is influenced by—developing teachers includes multiple levels of educational context; past, present, personal, and professional influences; and affective, intellectual, technical, and moral dimensions of teachers' selves and work. Working within the ecological tradition encourages mixed methods studies; collecting multiple types of naturalistic data on different (and same) beginning teachers in different (and same) settings; longitudinal studies, process narratives, and cross-case ethnographies. Such an approach also benefits from research questions focused on changes in novice teachers over time, examining multiple influences on teacher education and measuring teacher education's effects on K–12 student achievement. To highlight diversity within this model of ecology, consider that life sciences researchers find that a diverse ecosystem adds significant value to the planet: biodiversity stabilizes ecological processes; offers more medicines, foods, and other useful products; and contributes to increased economic and social opportunities (Wilson, 2002). Just as with environmental science, then, diversity in education is inherently beneficial.

Centralize the study of teachers' language interactions. Identity appears to be hard to fully capture or represent—and probably impossible to view directly. Yet, the language practices of developing teachers offer a deep, if perhaps indirect, lens into identity. Sociolinguistics is well suited for teacher identity research in teacher education because it foregrounds the contextualized study of language use as a fundamental part of social existence. Audio- and videotaped conversations with (and among) novice teachers and naturalistic classroom interactions are recommended. Studying the stories new teachers tell about themselves and their professional growth can be quite useful. Applying data analytic procedures such as conversation analysis (Sacks et al., 1974), sociolinguistic pragmatics (Grice, 1975), a life-stories approach (Linde, 1993; Olsen, 2006), and critical discourse analysis (Fairclough, 1989) provides methodological tools well-suited to grasp the complexities, holism, and interconnectedness of professional identities enacted in situated practice.

Privilege teachers in practice. James Gee (1992) wrote that, because cognition is social, the mind does not really exist except when in use: he offered the analogy of a car that is merely a pile of metal until it is activated and driven. Similarly, teacher identity has no real value by itself. It should be employed as a way to better understand and support actual novices learning to teach in actual contexts. The contours of teacher identity are useful to the extent that they can illuminate and support student teachers in practice. Teacher identity can be used to capture and investigate empirical, situated, longitudinal dimensions of teacher learning. Purely theoretical treatments of teacher identity should be resisted in favor of empirical research and grounded theory. Likewise, teacher identity has value not only as a research analytic but also it offers promise as a pedagogical tool in teacher education. Using the explicit frame of teacher identity orients teacher educators and professional development specialists to scaffold concrete activities in which beginning teachers can more critically interrogate personal influences, more deeply direct the contours of their own professional development, and continually appreciate the reciprocal relationships among diversity, teaching, and professional growth.

Teacher identity encourages consideration of teacher education researchers and student teachers as equal collaborators in research-practice. Given the assortment of ways teachers, teacher educators, and researchers are positioned vis-à-vis any study, an analytical frame as complex and intradependent as identity benefits from multiple perspectives. Making identity research a partnership offers an inherent member check: since we never view ourselves the way others view us, but others' views of us are also limiting, both sets of views—the "I" and the "you" of teacher identity—together provide a useful vantage point. And framing this research as collaborative nicely encourages researchers not only to collect information and issue findings but also work closely with practitioners over time to implement what is found together. Teachers and teacher educators can become more conscious of their own identities and more intentionally direct the contours of their own professional growth. Researchers can develop fuller, more nuanced views of teaching while also learning about their own identities as researchers. In fact, the boundaries separating researchers, teacher educators, and teachers can be nicely blurred as each makes use of the other ways of being: researching, educating, and learning can become inextricable. In this complementary way, collaborative spirals of research-implementation-reflection-and-repeat around teacher identity might offer a whole (and holistic) model toward theoretically grounded, empirically driven views of teachers and teacher education in service of the kinds of empowering diversity that contemporary democratic education requires.

NOTES

1. This Bill Evans quote comes from Peter Pettinger's *Bill Evans: How My Heart Sings* (New Haven, CT: Yale University Press, 1998).

2. For more about discursive theories of identity, see Juzwik (2006); and for examples of representational treatments of language and teachers, see Casey (1996) and Clandinin and Connolly (2004).

3. There is of course another dimension to social roles pertaining to strata of identity we do not "choose" and that we do not put on and take off depending on the particular role system we inhabit. These include racial, cultural, physical, religious, sexual, and gender identities and various asymmetrical power relations attached to them. They are in no way unimportant—in fact they are the primary concern of this chapter—and certainly play into my example of being a professor, but I have left them, and the connected topic of identity politics, out of this present discussion. Interested readers see Appiah, 2006; Solorzano and Delgado Bernal, 2001; and hooks, 1994.

REFERENCES

Alsup, J. (2006). *Teacher identity discourses: Negotiating personal and professional spaces.* Mahwah, NJ: Lawrence Erlbaum Associates.

Bakhtin, M. (1990). *Art and answerability: Early philosophical essays.* Austin: University of Texas Press.

Beijaard, D., Meijer, P. C., and Verloop, N. (2004). Reconsidering research on teachers' professional identity. *Teaching and Teacher Education, 20,* 107–28.

Belenky, M., Clinchy, B., Goldberger, N., and Tarule, J. (1986). *Women's ways of knowing: The development of self, voice, and mind.* New York: Basic Books.

Bourdieu, P. (1995). *Language and symbolic power.* Cambridge, MA: Harvard University Press.

Britzman, D. (1990). Is there a problem with knowing thyself? Toward a poststructuralist view of teacher identity. In Shanahan, T. (Ed.), *Teachers thinking, teachers knowing: Reflections on literacy and language.* Urbana IL: NCTE.

Britzman, D. (1991). *Practice makes practice: A critical study of learning to teach.* Albany: State University of New York Press.

Casey, K. (1996). The new narrative research in education. In Apple, M. (Ed.), *Review of research in education* (pp. 21, 211–53). Washington, DC: AERA.

Chomsky, N. (1957). *Syntactic structures.* New York: Mouton.

Clandinin, D. J., and Connelly, M. (2004). *Narrative inquiry: Experience and story in qualitative research.* San Francisco: Jossey-Bass.

Coldron, J., and Smith, R. (1999). Active location in teachers' construction of their professional identities. *Journal of Curriculum Studies, 31(6),* 711–26.

Cooper, K., and Olson, M. R. (1996). The multiple I's of teacher identity. In Kompf, Bond, Dworet, and Boak (Eds.), *Changing research and practice: Teachers' professionalism, identities, and knowledge.* Briston, PA: Falmer Press.

Day, C., Kington, A., Stobart, G., and Sammons, P. (2006). The personal and professional selves of teachers: Stable and unstable identities. *British Educational Research Journal, 32(4),* 601–16.

Delpit, L., and Kilgore, J. K. (2002). *The skin that we speak: Thoughts on language and culture in the classroom.* New York: New Press.

Dewey, J. (1916). *Democracy and education.* New York: Free Press.

Fairclough, N. (1989). *Language and power.* London: Longman.

Fessler, R., & Christensen, J. (Eds.). (1992). *The teacher career cycle: Understanding and guiding the professional development of teachers.* Boston: Allyn & Bacon.

Florio-Ruane, S., and Niu, R. (2008). *When the Coopville Teachers learned Chinese: Transforming teacher identity to teach all learners.* Paper presented at the annual meeting of the American Educational Research Association, New York.

Foucault, M. (1977). *Discipline and punish.* Gordin, C. et al. (Trans.). New York: Vintage Books.

Gadamer, H. (1985). *Philosophical apprenticeships.* Sullivan, R. R. (Trans.). Cambridge, MA: MIT Press.

Gee, J. (1992). *The social mind: Language, ideology and social practice.* New York: Bergin & Garvey.

Gee, J. (2000). *Social linguistics and literacies: Ideologies in discourses.* London: Falmer.

Goodson, I. (Ed.). (1992). *Studying teachers' lives.* New York: Teachers College Press.

Grice, H. P. (1975). Logic and conversation. In Cole, P., and Morgan, J. (Eds.), *Syntax and semantics 3: Speech acts* (pp. 41–48). New York: Academic Press.

Heiddeger, M. (1997/1927). *Being and time: A translation of sein and zeit.* Stambaugh, J. (Trans.). Albany: State University of New York Press.

Hoffman-Kipp, P., and Olsen, B. (2007). Accessing praxis, practicing theory: Theorizing practice in social justice teachers' first year of teaching. In Finn, M. and P. (Eds.), *Teacher education with an attitude* (pp. 141–56). Albany: State University of New York Press.

Holland, D., Lachiocotte, W., Skinner, D., and Cain, C. (1998). *Identity and agency in cultural worlds.* Cambridge, MA: Harvard University Press.

Holquist, M. (1990). *Dialogism: Bakhtin and his world.* London: Routledge.

hooks, b. (1994). *Teaching to transgress.* New York: Routledge.

Jackson, P. (1986). *The practice of teaching.* New York: Teachers College Press.

Juzwik, M. (2006). Situating narrative-minded research: A response to Anna Sfard's and Anna Prusak's "Telling identities." *Educational Researcher, 25(9),* 13–21.

Kelly, G. (1955). *The psychology of personal constructs.* New York: W. W. Norton & Co.

Kelly, G. (1963). *A theory of personality.* New York: W. W. Norton & Co.

Lave, J., and Holland, D. (2001). History in person: An introduction. In Lave and Holland (Eds.), *History in person: Enduring struggles, contentious practice, intimate identities* (pp. 3–33). Santa Fe, NM: School of American Research Press.

Lave, J., and Wenger, E. (1991). *Situated learning.* Cambridge: Cambridge University Press.

LeCompte, M., and Schensul, J. (1990). Paradigms for thinking about ethnographic research. In LeCompte, M., and Schensul, J. (Eds.), *Designing and conducting ethnographic research* (pp. 41–60). Walnut Creek, CA: Altamira.

Linde, C. (1993). *Life stories: The creation of coherence.* New York: Oxford University Press.

Lortie, D. (1975). *Schoolteacher: A sociological study.* Chicago: University of Chicago Press.

McIntyre, A. (1997). *Making meaning of whiteness.* Albany: State University of New York Press.

McVee, M. (2004). Narrative and the exploration of culture in teachers' discussions of literacy, identity self, and other. *Teaching and Teacher Education, 20,* 881–99.

Mead, G. H. (1964/1932). *Mind, self, and society from the standpoint of a social behaviorist.* Chicago: University of Chicago Press.

Mockler, N. (2004). *Architects, travel agents, and bus drivers: Images of teacher professional identity in public discourse.* Paper presented to the Australian Association for Educational Research, Annual Conference, University of Melbourne.

Moshman, D. (1999). *Adolescent psychological development: Rationality, morality, and identity.* Mahwah, NJ: Lawrence Erlbaum Associates.

Myers, G., and Russell, A. (2003). Human identity in relation to wild black bears: A natural-social ecology of subjective creatures. In Clayton, S., and Opotow, S. (Eds.), *Identity and the natural environment: The psychological significance of nature.* Cambridge, MA: MIT Press.

Olsen, B. (2006). Using sociolinguistic methods to uncover speaker meaning in teacher interview transcripts. *International Journal of Qualitative Studies in Education, 19(2),* 147–61.

Olsen, B. (2008a). *Teaching what they learn, learning what they live: How teachers' personal histories shape their professional development.* Boulder, CO: Paradigm Publishers.

Olsen, B. (2008b). How reasons for entry into the profession illuminate teacher identity development. *Teacher Education Quarterly, 35(3),* 23–40.

Olsen, B., and Anderson, L. (2007). Courses of action: A qualitative investigation into urban teacher retention and career development. *Urban Education, 42(1),* 5–29.

Ronfeldt, M., and Grossman, P. (2008) Becoming a professional: Experimenting with possible selves in professional preparation. *Teacher Education Quarterly, 35(3),* 41–60.

Rorty, R. (1989). *Contingency, irony, and solidarity.* Cambridge: Cambridge University Press.

Sacks, H., Schegloff, E., and Jefferson, G. (1974). A simplest systematics of the organization of turn-taking in conversation. *Language, 50,* 696–735.

Sarbin, T. R., and Allen, V. I. (1968). Role theory. In Lindzey, G., and Aronson, E. (Eds.), *Handbook of social psychology* (pp. 488–567). Reading, MA: Adisson-Wesley.

Saussure, F. (1998/1913). *Course in general linguistics.* Chicago: Open Court Publishing.

Scheibe, K. E. (1995). *Self studies: The psychology of self and identity.* Westport, CT: Praeger.

Sexton, D. (2008). Student teachers negotiating identity, role, and agency. *Teacher Education Quarterly, 35(3),* 73–88.

Sfard, A., and Prusak, A. (2005). Telling identities: In search of an analytic tool. *Educational Researcher, 34(4)*, 14–22.

Solorzano, D., and Delgado Bernal, D. (2001). Examining transformational resistance through a critical race and LatCrit theory framework: Chicana and Chicano students in an urban context. *Urban Education, 36*, 308–42.

Taylor, C. (1992). *Sources of the self: The making of the modern identity*. Cambridge, MA: Harvard University Press.

Tellez, K. (1999). Mexican-American preservice teachers and the intransigency of the elementary school curriculum. *Teachers and Teacher Education, 15*, 555–70.

Wideen, M., Mayer-Smith, J., and Moon, B. (1998). A critical analysis of the research on learning to teach: Making the case for an ecological perspective on inquiry. *Review of Educational Research, 68(2)*, 130–78.

Wilson, E. O. (2002). *The future of life*. New York: Alfred Knopf.

Wittingstein, L. (1991). *Philosophical investigations* (50th anniversary ed.). Anscombe, G. E. M., and Anscombe, E. (Trans.). Malden, MA: Wiley-Blackwell.

Zeichner, K., and Tabachnick, B. (1981). Are the effects of teacher education washed out by school experience? *Journal of Teacher Education, 32(3)*, 7–11.

13

Teaching Native Youth, Teaching about Native Peoples

Shifting the Paradigm to Socioculturally Responsive Education

Tiffany S. Lee

In the spring of 2008, I was sitting in a middle school language arts classroom in New Mexico. The school was a public school located in a small town that borders several Pueblo communities.[1] About 28 percent of the school's student population is of Native American[2] heritage predominantly from the surrounding Pueblo communities (New Mexico Public Education Department [NMPED], 2008). About 40 percent of the students in the entire district are Native American (NMPED, 2008). I was speaking with a group of teachers about their experiences teaching Native students, their preparation, their ideas, their struggles, and their successes. I asked the teachers, "If you were to have all the funding that you could possibly have, all the resources . . . You could even change the school structure and environment as you know it now, completely re-envision what the school and what the education would be like. What would that ideal classroom or school look like particularly for you to serve Native students?"

One enthusiastic, white, male teacher said, "Boarding schools . . . From kindergarten or first grade they go and live just like prep schools. They go and live on the school site for the whole school year. But not geared towards, you know, the whole idea of Indian education." I responded, "You mean remove them from their families and community?" He said, "Yes" (Indigenous Education Study Group [IESG], 2009, p. 29). Earlier he had stated "it's not our job to what, indulge in their culture" (IESG, 2009, p. 19). My heart sank at both comments. When asked to envision the best education he could imagine, here was a teacher who felt it was better to forsake the culture, family, and heritage of his students and to indoctrinate and assimilate them into Western culture, values, and the English language, much like Colonel Richard Henry Pratt in the late nineteenth century (Adams, 2008). Pratt was responsible for creating disastrous boarding-school policies with goals of assimilation by removing students from families, enforcing English-only rules, and utilizing harsh punishment techniques, including solitary confinement and beatings (Child, 1998; Pewewardy, 2005). Here was Pratt and this teacher's belief—one hundred years later—that cultural assimilation into Western dominant culture was necessary for citizenship and national belonging. Native students' culture and community were expendable and required abandonment for entrance into the national community. In essence, these teachers were saying that to be American is to be white and to conform to Western cultural values and life ways.

The comments made by this teacher are indicative of the presence of a paradigm of Western culture and assimilationist perspectives that is perpetuated in schools serving Native students. While not all the teachers shared such strongly worded assimilationist perspectives as the teacher quoted above, many expressed similar sentiments about finding a place for Native culture and, for some, they felt Native culture is a distraction from students' education. The comments above are also per-petuated in what is generally taught (or not taught) about Native peoples, which is often uncritical and stereotypical representations of Native peoples' lives, histories, and contributions. On the other hand, there were many teachers in this study who expressed a desire to include their students' sociocultural identity and experiences in the curriculum. It is just that they felt constrained and unsure about how to incor-porate students' heritage and lived experience into their classrooms (IESG, 2009). The purpose of this chapter is to address the need for a paradigm shift in education from one based on the insinuated superiority of Western society, which promotes assimilation, to one that is more inclusive of authentic representations of Native peoples, that is socially, culturally, and locally respectful and that is responsive to all students. With the latter approach, Native peoples are visible and included in the curriculum and content in authentic ways. Education becomes transformative by responding to students' sociocultural and local experiences and their environment. Educational systems are also transformed through the incorporation of realistic and accurate portrayals of who Native people are today. We are learning from this study on Native education in New Mexico (called the New Mexico Indian Educa-tion Study[3]) that, while we have observed tremendous progress when it comes to Indigenous education, there is still so much work to be done to create classrooms that honor and respect the heritage of their students. This chapter intends to offer suggestions for research on diversity in teacher education that can fill that void, particularly in the area of preparing teachers to teach Native students and to teach about Native peoples.

DILEMMAS FOR TEACHER EDUCATION
AND THE TEACHING OF NATIVE STUDENTS

There is a dilemma in teacher education regarding how our schools and teachers can construct their classrooms to reflect and incorporate the diversity of their students and yet also encourage a common set of shared values, ideals, and goals to which all their students are committed as members of their local, state, and national com-munities. Balancing unity and diversity is not only a challenge in schools but also in multicultural nation-states (Banks, 2008).

Part of the problem is in seeing Native peoples as fellow citizens. Albeit we are recognized as First Americans but often not as citizens with contemporary lives who simultaneously participate in our Native family and community life and in the larger mainstream American life. This misunderstanding largely stems from the lack of education about Native peoples at a realistic, appropriate, and humanistic level in our schools. Teaching about Native peoples in our schools mainly falls on Columbus Day and Thanksgiving holidays, which largely perpetuate stereotypes, myths, and fictional, romanticized stories of Native peoples' experiences and that tend to position us as people of the past (Reese, 1996).

The dilemma for teacher education as it pertains to Indigenous peoples is in the ways teachers teach Native students and teach about Native peoples. I argue that to address this dilemma, the essential issue for teachers and teacher educators is to learn about and draw upon the community and identity of Native students through socioculturally responsive education. Socioculturally responsive (SCR) education includes pedagogy that utilizes students' lived experiences, home-based knowledge, and local environment to inform curriculum and relationships with students (Belgarde, Mitchell, & Moquino-Arquero, 2002; Demmert & Towner, 2003). While researchers have generally called it culturally responsive or culturally based education, I distinguish and broaden the term to socioculturally responsive education because Native youth's lives are also inclusive of social influences not solely defined by their Native culture, such as mainstream media, family income and occupations, tribal economic development, off-reservation residence, and peer influences. Socioculturally responsive education is comprehensive in recognizing the breadth of Native students' lived experiences today.

For teaching about Native peoples, teacher education should support critical inquiry into the scholarship, multimedia representations, and historical positioning of Native peoples. Teachers must be prepared with inclusive and accurate portrayals of who Native peoples are today and their unique cultural and political sovereignty over their lands in addition to their distinct political relationships with the United States.

Overall, it is important to create classrooms that promote transformative academic knowledge (Ball, 2004; Banks, 2008; Smith, 2003), which enables all students' feelings of belonging at community, state, national, and international levels. It provides a way to create unity among diversity in that it challenges students to be critically conscious and inclusive of our diversity, especially among less recognized populations like Native peoples. Socioculturally responsive education and transformative academic knowledge necessitate students to recognize the importance of all communities in the world, thereby validating the cultural identities of individual students in their classrooms.

WHAT WE KNOW ABOUT TEACHING NATIVE STUDENTS

With regard to Native students, we know the current trends of their successes and challenges in education. "We" in this context and in the following sections includes educators and researchers interested in Indigenous education. This section will give a brief overview of important research that discusses those trends and that provides insight into effective current practices for teaching Native students. But first, it is important to understand the demographic picture of Native peoples and students in the United States. There are 562 federally recognized Native Nations in the United States and approximately 4.5 million citizens with American Indian, Alaskan Native, or Native Hawaiian heritage, which is about 1.4 percent of the entire population in the United States. Native people live all across the country, but four out of ten live in the West. One in four Native people live below the poverty level, and 30 percent of the population is under the age of eighteen (U.S. Census Bureau, 2007).

Twelve states have more than 100,000 Native students, and across the United States, approximately 624,000 Native students are enrolled in K–12 schools. About 93 percent of these students attend public schools; however, the national graduation rate for Native students in 2003–2004 was 49 percent compared to 76 percent for white students (National Center for Education Statistics as cited by the National Indian Education Association [NIEA], 2007). Approximately 77 percent of the total Native population over age twenty-five has graduated from high school, and about 14 percent have earned a bachelor's degree or higher, compared to 89 percent graduated and 30 percent with bachelor's degrees and higher among white populations (U.S. Census Bureau, 2007).

The diversity of Native peoples is most reflected in the variety of languages and cultural practices, which make up half of all of the U.S. linguistic and cultural diversity (NIEA, 2007). Yet, Native people's languages are largely being lost due to language shift (Fishman, 1991; Nettles & Romaine, 2000), where a Native child's first language is no longer their heritage language but is replaced by English. In 1998, Krauss reported that only about 20 of the 155 Native languages still being spoken in the United States have child speakers.

Retention of teachers in schools serving Native students is another challenge (NIEA, 2007). NIEA cites low retention rates due to rural isolation, low salaries, high poverty areas, and linguistic and cultural differences. In addition, safety is an issue with reports of threats and injuries from fights and weapons at a greater level than black, Latino, and white student populations.

While the NIEA report does not specifically share teachers' reasons for leaving, the focus group I referred to in the introduction and subsequent ones across the state of New Mexico have provided some detail as to the experiences of teachers of Native students (IESG, 2009). Teachers expressed a range of emotion from genuine interest to real frustrations in learning how to best teach Native students, particularly Native students who resist them and who resist school. There is also a true lack of understanding about Native children's lives outside of school, such as the misperception that Native people do not pay taxes, or that their reservation life completely isolates them from the world, or that they do not have rich and diverse cultural, social, and familial experiences outside of school (IESG, 2009). These misperceptions largely stem from a lack of direct experience with Native communities and families and from misunderstandings about the nature of the political relationship that Native Nations hold with the federal government. This relationship is considered Nation to Nation (United States to Native Nation) based on past treaties, agreements, and current laws that recognize the inherent sovereignty of Native Nations (Deloria & Lytle, 1984). Native Nations hold rights to self-governance, rights to their homelands, rights to their cultural and natural resources, and rights to practice their cultural and religious traditions (Wilkins, 2002). These rights of Indigenous peoples were recently acknowledged by the United Nations with the passage of the UN Declaration on the Rights of Indigenous Peoples (United Nations, 2007).

Additionally, there exists the strong sentiment that there is not a place for Native cultural knowledge in schools, thereby perpetuating assimilationist, whitestream[4] perspectives. For example, the Arizona state legislature in 2008 proposed a bill to eliminate "anti-Western" education from publicly funded schools. The measure also hoped to forbid college students in the state from forming support groups based on their race or culture, targeting specifically Native, black, Latino, and Asian (or any non-Western European) students (Benson, 2008). The proposed bill, SB 1108, stated, "A primary purpose of public education is to inculcate values of American citizenship. Public tax dollars used in public schools should not be used to denigrate American values and the teachings of Western civilization" (as cited by Benson, 2008). It was a reactionary position that declared the inclusion of diverse perspectives in schools as anti-Western.

This example from Arizona adds another to the policy initiatives that began with boarding school policies that labeled Native cultures as culturally deficient and, thus, as intellectually damaging (Adams, 1995; Colemant et al., 2004; Demmert & Bell, 1991; Pewewardy, 2005). These type of policies and the generations of Native people being told their Native culture, language, and identity were inferior can explain much of the student resistance the teachers in our focus groups perceived. The multiple ways in which Native youth resist has been revealed or demonstrated in several studies (Deyhle, 1995; Dozier Enos, 2001; Foley, 1996; Martinez, 2010). The common thread in this research has been the resistance to Western cultural assimilation and resistance to the abandonment of one's Native heritage.

So what does work for engaging and effectively teaching Native students? One argument of this chapter is that socioculturally responsive (SCR) education is an effective approach for teaching Native students (Demmert & Towner, 2003; Pewewardy & Hammer, 2003). As stated earlier, I broaden the name to include the social environment not solely defined by cultural practices or beliefs, such as economic indicators. SCR education is inclusive of all the social and cultural influences and experiences in a student's life and recognizes the diversity of experiences of Native students that are not only culturally defined.

Integration of SCR education in teacher education programs has been effective for preparing teachers of Native students (Belgarde, Mitchell, & Moquino-Arquero, 2002; Cleary & Peacock, 1998). For example, in an effort to give their student teachers more than a classroom-based student teaching experience, Indiana University initiated the American Indian Reservation Project to offer their students' opportunities to make important school and community connections in reservation-based locations. They found that "a focus on *both* professional and cultural topics and issues during student teaching, wherever the placements may be, enhances beginning teachers' understandings of the multiple realities that characterize many classroom and community settings and strengthens their ability to respond effectively to people's whose worldview may differ from their own" (Stachowski & Frey, 2003, p. 2 [emphasis is in original]).

Castagno and Brayboy (2008) further analyzed the impact SCR education (called culturally responsive schooling in their review) with a comprehensive literature review of SCR scholarship pertaining to Indigenous youth. Drawing on various scholars' discussions of culturally responsive schooling, Castagno and Brayboy describe it as education that draws on the heritage language and culture Indigenous to particular places, communities, and Native Nations and is fundamental to students' intellectual, social, emotional, and spiritual development and connection to those places. Their review demonstrates that SCR teaching is more than being sensitive and aware of a students' cultural background, but it is also recognizing how cultures are contextually based and necessitates educators become culturally competent in order to meaningfully and appropriately incorporate students' cultural and linguistic backgrounds into their teaching. This incorporation thereby validates students' home-based knowledge and experiences and allows them to participate in constructing what counts as knowledge in their classrooms and schools (Castagno & Brayboy, 2008).

While Castagno and Brayboy found that the literature lacks in its discussion of culturally responsive schooling as it relates to tribal sovereignty, racism, and Indigenous epistemologies, the literature is broad in connecting culturally responsive schooling to learning styles of Native youth, cultural differences, and anticipated beneficial outcomes. However, they critically question much of this scholarship in that it "encourages educational approaches that assume culture to be something that can and should be taught as a discrete school subject" (Castagno & Brayboy, 2008, p. 957) and consequently reduces students' lived experiences and heritage to material aspects of their cultures. Perhaps much of the misunderstanding about being socioculturally responsive on the part of educators, like the one mentioned in the introduction of this chapter, can be explained in part by past scholarship that positions the problems with the achievement gap on a lack of teaching about Native cultures as a school subject, rather than understanding how to respond and include students' diverse backgrounds along with the need for systemic reform of institutional structures and larger social inequities.

SCR education is also inclusive of caring about students' cultural heritage and everyday lives. Many scholars have written about the significance of caring relationships in teacher–student interactions (Noddings, 1984; Valenzuela, 1999), and many have written about its particular importance in teacher interactions with Native youth (McCarty, Romero, & Zepeda, 2006; Quijada, 2008). These authors demonstrate that caring about students involves learning about their daily lives, establishing a relationship of trust with them and their families, and using that deeper social and emotional knowledge in assessment or evaluation of their performance and behavior in school. The New Mexico Indian Education Study (NMIES), which has conducted multiple focus groups and interviews with teachers, Native students, and Native community members statewide, has learned from many participants' perspectives that building on sociocultural knowledge and current lived experiences of students in teaching fosters that relationship of trust and care and creates more meaningful, rewarding, and valuable learning experiences for Native students (IESG, 2009). In addition, that knowledge of students' daily lives should be used in teachers' assessment of their performance and behavior. Evaluation should extend not only beyond academic achievement but also how students' demonstrate their knowledge outside of class. One Native language teacher participant from a charter school that emphasizes Native perspectives discussed it this way.

> The first day of Lakota class, I talked about in Lakota society, the way the structure is created is that it's your uncles and your aunties that will discipline you and that will teach you—they will take upon the teaching opportunities to point things out. So I said

"with that, the relationship we're gonna have in this classroom, I'm gonna treat you like one of my nieces or nephews so that it doesn't end once we are out of this class." . . . Another way I evaluate if they're receiving some of the things that I'm teaching them is how they treat each other out here when they're not in class. I think our teachers here are very intentional about how they teach the kids and that they should care for each other. . . . We encourage the students to embody some of these virtues that we know and we've grown up with when they haven't grown up with them. We can talk about *respect* all we want and how to live it, but we gotta give them the opportunity to act on it . . . I think that's a perfect way to evaluate and to give them experience is to see how they act in the societies, in their communities. (IESG, 2009, pp. 13–15)

In essence, the teacher is describing the inclusion of Lakota family values and structure to inform his own teaching methods and assessment practices. SCR pedagogy is not about teaching a particular material aspect of Lakota culture, but instead he is drawing on Lakota traditional values and knowledge, which can be applied and related to all students as they experience life today.

Similar to these thoughts by this teacher, SCR education includes community-based education. Community-based education (CBE) is experiential education that places the community at the center of learning and decision making with regard to the content that is shared and taught (Ball, 2004; Lee, 2007). Much like service learning, CBE allows students to learn through their direct experience and through service to the community. But CBE for Native students moves beyond service learning by applying tenets of Indigenous educational philosophy. Indigenous education is about learning who you are based on your role and contribution to your community. It is holistic by emphasizing your development intellectually, socially, emotionally, physically, and spiritually (Cajete, 1994). CBE has been successful in stimulating, motivating, and developing students' sense of self because it makes their education relevant to their lives, it validates their community's knowledge and experiences, and it provides a direct opportunity for contribution to their community (Corson, 1999; Kawagley & Barnhardt, 2004; Lee, 2006, 2007; May, 1999).

While the majority of teachers of Native students are non-Native and their role will always be important to nurture and support, there is another type of significance regarding training Native teachers to teach Native students. Research has documented the important role of teachers who share the heritage of their Native students (Beaulieu & Figueira, 2006). Beaulieu and Figueira discussed that Native teachers, by virtue of a life experience that is shared with their students, bring with them knowledge and attributes that are not learned through formal training. Their knowledge and attributes are useful instructionally because they can use them to employ teaching methods that are culturally responsive, sensitive, and appropriate. He argues that training programs should focus on assisting Native teachers with using their cultural and community knowledge effectively in the classroom.

Johnson (2006) extends the discussion further to state that being Native, however, does not automatically ensure one will be aware of or know how to utilize their cultural knowledge in instructional strategies. Additionally, being Native does not ensure the teacher's acceptance to promote changes that are responsive to the values, goals, and ideas of Native communities. Thus, training as SCR teachers is also necessary for Native American teachers.

WHAT WE KNOW REGARDING TEACHING ABOUT NATIVE PEOPLES

With regard to teaching about Native people, we know that there is a large void of curriculum incorporated into public schools that addresses basically who Native people are in today's society and, more specifically, that does this in respectful and appropriate ways (Bigelow & Peterson, 1998; Caracciolo, 2008; Locke & Lindley, 2007; Zehr, 2008). A large part of the problem comes from the dearth of instruction and support given to teachers in schools and in their teacher education programs to learn about Native peoples and seek out or develop SCR curriculum and pedagogy (Kelting-Gibson, 2006; Starnes, 2006).

Native peoples have been portrayed as a part of the American landscape, as a part of the past, and as a part of wild America since the first colonizers came to North America (P. J. Deloria, 1998; Green, 2001; Trask, 2001). They have been dehumanized in this sense and are positioned as vanishing and marginalized, while the dominant, whitestream culture is positioned as progressing and advancing (May, 1999). This positioning reaches down to our schools with a perpetuation of an uncritical colonizer's history of Native peoples. Textbooks, literature, and multimedia materials have relied on noble savage stereotypes and whitewashing of the past to limit and ignore the contributions of Native peoples and celebrate the vantage point of the conquerors (Au, 2008; Peterson, 2008; Reese, 2007). The story of Thanksgiving is a good example. Thanksgiving is often taught using racist and biased language to depict an historical event where the Wampanoag peoples welcomed the occupation of their lands and were willing providers of the Pilgrims' sustenance (Reese, 2006). Ignored are the resistance and massacre of Native peoples and the questions of the validity of colonization of Native peoples' homelands (Little Soldier, 1982).

The field of multicultural education can also apply to and benefit teaching about Native peoples because it requires teachers to become knowledgeable of multiple perspectives and inclusive of Native peoples' viewpoints (Sleeter & Grant, 2009). SCR education and multicultural education are connected in that they both engage students in critical thinking with regard to what counts as knowledge and in challenging Eurocentric curriculum (Au, 2008; Villegas & Luca, 2002). To be inclusive of Native perspectives and avoid the use of stereotypical material when teaching about Native peoples, it is important for teachers and teacher education programs to learn about the changing and vibrant cultures and life ways of Native peoples (Martinez, 2009).

It is also vital not to rely solely on social-scientific understandings of Native peoples because of the problematic nature of many of these studies, including methodologies and interpretations (P. J. Deloria, 1997; L. Smith, 1999). It is essential for purposes of authentic perspectives based on lived experience to include a range of Native voices from academics to community members when learning about the historical and contemporary issues of Indigenous populations (Cook-Lynn, 1996; Mihesuah, 1998). It requires teachers to become the first critical readers and thinkers in their classrooms when utilizing various sources and experts on Native peoples, and then teach their students these same strategies for critically analyzing material on Native peoples. Additionally, it is very important to be honest about our history in this country and its violence and continued oppression toward Native peoples. This encourages students to question, reflect, and understand their country in ways that equip and motivate them to transform their country into a better place (Banks, 2008; Bigelow & Peterson, 1998). Loewen stated this idea well when he said, "The antidote to feel-good history is not feel-bad history, but honest and inclusive history" (1998, p. 82).

WHAT WE NEED TO KNOW ABOUT TEACHING NATIVE STUDENTS

For those teaching Native students, there are three compelling and critical areas that we need to know more about through educational research. One is the necessity and impact of professional development on socioculturally responsive schooling. How can SCR schooling be taught to teachers of Native students given its contextually, politically, culturally, and linguistically based nature? Second, how can we convince educators that cultural assimilation at the expense of Native students' heritage and life ways is not the answer for educational achievement? While an abundance of research and policy has demonstrated its ineffectiveness, we continue to see this idea perpetuated at individual and policy levels. Third, we need to learn how we can balance unity and diversity for Native students when Native people still live in a colonized state and attend schools that represent Western worldviews and whitestream ideologies.

Although there is a wide variety of scholarship on SCR education, there is limited research specific to teachers of Native students on professional preservice or in-service development opportunities that help teachers connect school, community, and cultural knowledge. A special issue on Indigenous perspectives in teacher education in *Action in Teacher Education* (2002) provides many Native scholars perspectives who remarked on the importance of teachers getting to know their Native students, of connecting home life and cultural identity to learning in their classrooms, and to connecting Native community values (such as respect and contribution to community) to school-based values. However, the teachers in the NMIES discussed these types of teaching strategies as something they learned on their own based on individual experiences with their students (IESG, 2009). All teachers do not practice such strategies and should be encouraged to do so through professional development.

Many teachers also expressed the desire to interact more with parents and community members outside of school in order to learn more about the community. One Native teacher in the NMIES described her attempt to create this type of cultural immersion for the non-Native teachers at her school. She led a group of teachers on hiking trips in the community surrounding the school (her home community) and taught them about significant historical and contemporary sites. She created this event in order to broaden the cultural knowledge and competence of teachers in her community. She explained how her colleagues need to incorporate community knowledge and lived experience into their curriculum. If they did, "that would make the student appreciate the teacher more" (IESG, 2009, p. 8). When describing the need for teachers to learn about the home and community life of their students, she said she made that commitment when learning about the whitestream world, so she argued that teachers should make that commitment to learn the Native history and life ways of the community. She said, "I think for the longest time, I've lived in the western white world. That's what these teachers need to do. They need to take classes in history, language, and culture. A lot of these teachers come in from *Planton*[5] in the morning and then are out the door after school. Only a handful of teachers put in the extra effort. You can't get to these kids in that method" (IESG, 2009, p. 8). This study is providing needed research on this type of professional development need for teachers in schools with a majority of Native students. However, more research on effective opportunities and the impact of such professional development would be tremendously valuable.

Professional development on creating culturally responsive schools and educators could transform the beliefs that Western cultural assimilation and reduced involvement in Native cultures is necessary for high academic achievement. These beliefs continue to drive current practice and policy. Despite the research and government reports that have demonstrated its ineffectiveness at improving academic performance, and its demoralizing and devastating impact on Native students' cultural identity, this idea still perpetuates as the NMIES found and as documented by policy initiatives such as the Arizona bill described earlier in this chapter.

The National Indian Education Association has reported that the No Child Left Behind (NCLB) policy has limited the inclusion of cultural and community knowledge and Native languages, and they have called for amendments to NCLB that "strengthen tribal and parent involvement in the education of Native students, and promotes culturally based education, emphasizing Native languages and history instruction" (NIEA, 2008). Problematically however, for all the research on CRS among Indigenous populations, Castagno and Brayboy (2008) point out there is not much implementation at state and federal levels in part due to a lack of decisive data and scientific evidence to link CRS with improved academic achievement among Native youth. The research mostly represents "case-studies, program descriptions, and anecdotal calls for CRS, but many have noted that the causal links in this work are weak and that very few studies make strong claims about how students' academic performance is affected by efforts at CRS" (Castagno & Brayboy, 2008, p. 982). One plausible reason for this lack of evidence may be due to the fact that CRS requires systemic reform and transformation in educational ideologies. Such a task is not easily accomplished in our rigid public school structures bound by state and federal laws. Clearly more research to demonstrate the direct connections between SCR education and academic performance among Native student populations is a strong area of need.

Another area of needed inquiry is learning how to support Native students in school systems that represent a society that continues to oppress them and change them (Battiste, 1998; G. Smith, 2003). Banks (2008) discussed the challenge of schools and multicultural nation-states to create unity among their diversity of students and citizens in order to create a sense of belonging, inclusive of various perspectives, and equity in opportunity and participation. For Native peoples, the challenge is unique and more complex because our lands are still occupied and our tribal sovereignty is still continually challenged. These conditions foster resistance to inclusion in U.S. citizenry and ideals (Dozier Enos, 2001; Waziyatawin & Yellow Bird, 2005). Dozier Enos found that the issue is twofold among Pueblo nations. The Pueblo participants in her study sought to affirm their Pueblo identity through participation in Pueblo traditions, a highly prioritized form of participation in the community. School complicates this because school takes the people away from their traditions. Second, she determined that while Pueblo people try to honor their attachment to their Pueblos, they also try to incorporate aspects of the dominant American culture as well. Consequently, she said, "Part of this, then, becomes the struggle of how to include or reject school in the lives of Pueblo students" (p. 96). Balancing unity among diversity in this respect is a two-way endeavor on the part of the school system and on the part of the Native students' beliefs in unity among diversity.

For teaching about Native peoples, the critical area of research is in how to support and educate teachers to become specifically critically minded in order to recognize, access, and incorporate truly representative, respectful, and appropriate materials and resources about Native peoples. Accessing appropriate materials and learning teaching strategies that do not dehumanize, trivialize, or marginalize Native peoples is culturally respectful and responsive. However, are teachers in their preservice or in-service programs offered opportunities to learn about these issues specific to curriculum and pedagogy about Native peoples? What is the level of interest and commitment among teachers to incorporate this level of scrutinized content to teach about Native peoples, particularly if they do not have any Native students? Do teachers and curriculum writers feel Native peoples' histories and contemporary lives in this country are as important to tell as immigrant and enslaved peoples' histories, despite our smaller population and decreased visibility among the American public? Is our connection to this land and status as First Americans vital to understanding the development of the United States in their perspective? Educational research in this area can help us to understand these questions and tell those of us concerned with these issues where to prioritize our efforts.

SHIFTING THE PARADIGM
TO SOCIOCULTURALLY RESPONSIVE EDUCATION

Given the limited amount of research on teacher education specific to Native peoples, the New Mexico Indian Education study is an important contribution to this body of knowledge. The study has shown us that teachers want to know how to fully engage their students, especially those who resist the school structure and ideologies it represents. One suggestion is for teachers and schools to focus on creating transformative educational experiences and critical consciousness among their students (Smith, 2003). Critical consciousness is an awareness and knowledge of one's self within the realm of a critical understanding of the nature and causes of surrounding social and political conditions. It enables self-direction in education and activates an individual's sense of learning (Freire, 1993; Giroux, 2001). For Native students, stimulating a critical consciousness is very important because it is complicated by experiences of colonization (Brayboy, 2005; Grande, 2004). But for all students, enabling critical consciousness allows students to become aware of social justice, race, and equity issues in all that they learn about in school. It also enables students to become critical thinkers and make connections to learning in more compelling and meaningful ways (Martinez, 2009).

Indigenous scholars, such as Marie Battiste and Graham Smith, have been at the forefront of defining and discussing the importance of transformative education and critical consciousness among Native youth to inspire positive change in their communities. In these discussions, many speak of a return to or an adaptation of Indigenous epistemologies or knowledge systems as a way to engage students for the benefit of their education and for the benefit of Native communities (Battiste, 1998; Benham & Cooper, 2000; Brayboy, 2005; Cajete, 1994; Deloria & Wildcat, 2001; Kawagley, 1995; Smith, 2003). Inclusion of Indigenous knowledge systems (IKS) in current educational institutions requires thought of how both Native and Western worldviews can coexist in an educational setting that values the holistic nature of IKS, including connections to land, language, and cultural heritage. Such inclusion "must be rooted in social action, which seeks to transform our current educational system, one that has for so long silenced Native peoples" (Benham & Cooper, 2000, p. xix).

Similarly, research in multicultural and social justice education has discussed the importance of prioritizing transformative academic knowledge over whitestream knowledge for all students (Nieto, 2000; Sleeter & Grant, 2009). Transformative academic knowledge is a knowledge system that "consists of paradigms and explanations that challenge some of the key epistemological assumptions of mainstream knowledge" (Banks, 2008, p. 135). This may be one approach for accomplishing unity among diversity for Native American students in order to improve the school's connection to their lives and the students' investment in their school. Transformative academic knowledge is inclusive of Indigenous knowledge systems and Indigenous perspectives (Smith, 2003). Incorporation of Indigenous knowledge and SCR schooling provide the means for transformative education and the development of critical consciousness. Brayboy (2005) explained that Indigenous knowledge systems and academic knowledge acquired from Western educational institutions need not be in conflict, and instead, they can complement one another to create a knowledge base that is important for survival and success in a constantly changing global world.

How do we begin to create this type of pedagogical change in our schools that serve Native students and in teaching about Native peoples? The states of Montana and New Mexico have tried to legislate change through Montana's Indian Education for All Act (IEFA) and the New Mexico Indian Education Act (NMIEA). The Montana legislation requires all schools in Montana to teach all Montana students, "whether Indian or non-Indian" about Native peoples of their state. The intent of the legislation was to recognize the cultural heritage of the Native people in Montana and to contribute to their cultural continuity by requiring all state schools to teach about Native peoples in a "culturally responsive manner" (Montana Legislature, 1999). Additionally, the act requires all school personnel "have an understanding and awareness of Indian tribes to help them relate effectively with Indian students and parents," and they are required to work with Montana Native Nations to implement these goals.

Implementation has had its challenges. The act was passed in 1999, but it was not funded until 2004. Then, IEFA funds were diverted by some districts to cover budgetary shortfalls in other areas. They were not legally required to use the funds for implementation of IEFA. For those schools actually trying to implement IEFA, accessing historically accurate and culturally appropriate materials was difficult and problematic because this material needed to be created (Starnes, 2006).

New Mexico has a similar legislation with NMIEA whose goals are to increase the number of Native educators; increase services to schools with Native students and to the twenty-two Native Nations in the state; develop materials, curriculum, and resources that include Native perspectives, language, history, and culture; and develop partnerships with the twenty-two Native Nations in the state (NMPED, 2003). The partnerships are especially important because the NMIEA recognizes the sovereign relationship the Nations have with the United States and attempts to include this important factor in the relationships and partnerships between the state and New Mexico's Native Nations.

The impact in New Mexico has been great in some areas but minimal in others. The greatest benefit of NMIEA has been the increase in the number of Native teachers who have received licensure, the support of $1.6 million in the last three years to fourteen of New Mexico's Native Nations for language revitalization programs, the recent support of $1 million to ten school sites to implement a rural literacy and nutrition program, the support for the New Mexico Indian Education Study, and the memorandum of agreements (MOA) between the state and fourteen of New Mexico's Native Nations. The MOAs signify and detail the specific expectations in the partnerships between the NM Public Education Department and these Native Nations.

While this impact is noteworthy, the teachers across the majority of schools in the New Mexico Indian Education Study reported that they had never heard of the NMIEA or how it might be implemented in their schools. This raises concern about the lack of passage down from policy levels to classroom practices. One of the members of NMIEA's Advisory Council recognized this in a report to one of the school districts regarding its implementation of NMIEA (Emerson, 2008). Emerson asserted that the MOAs between the Public Education Department and Native Nations provide the best means for bridging the gap between school and community. Yet, there was concern that school districts were not acknowledging and implementing the Nation to state MOAs in their schools and classrooms because they felt a Nation to state MOA did not involve school districts. He called for clearer communication and measures to facilitate collaboration, including Native Nation decision making and self-determination. The issue at hand for the Advisory Council is how to hold school districts accountable to Native communities through the MOAs. The MOAs can provide one way to ensure school districts implement SCR education as it applies to their particular students and communities.

CONCLUSION

Early in the chapter, I discussed a dilemma in teacher education regarding how our schools and teachers can construct their classrooms to reflect and incorporate the diversity of their students, and yet also encourage a common set of shared values, ideals, and goals to which all their students are committed as members of their local, state, and national communities. Research in diversity in teacher education that demonstrates examples of these efforts regarding Native peoples is vitally needed because of the dearth of literature in this area. While there is some research in teacher education relating to teachers of Native heritage specifically (Beaulieu & Figueira, 2006; Belgarde, Mitchell, & Moquino-Arquero, 2002), there is minimal research regarding teacher education for Native students and about Native peoples. The examples in Montana and New Mexico are important for demonstrating the transformative change efforts by and on behalf of Native peoples' education and education about Native peoples. Teacher education programs and research on diversity in teacher education can contribute to these efforts by articulating the beneficial and practical implementations of socioculturally responsive (SCR) education.

It is necessary for researchers on diversity in teacher education to attend to SCR education and transformative academic knowledge, specifically for and about Native peoples. Research often creates and unquestioningly perpetuates theoretical paradigms (Deloria, 1997). In this case, the bias toward Western thought and assimilation in curriculum, content, and pedagogy represents an educational paradigm perpetuated in public schools. This chapter has cited important research that teacher candidates and teacher educators must be exposed to in order to learn from and begin to shift toward a paradigm that is more inclusive and socioculturally responsive. For Indigenous peoples, research on teacher education must take a stronger stance to address the marginalization of Native peoples in curriculum, content, and pedagogy in order to ignite SCR education on behalf of Native peoples. This type of research agenda allows for reclamation of what it means to be Native. It includes authentic representations of Native peoples and acknowledgment of their contemporary lived experiences. It also contributes to the dearth of academic knowledge in teacher education regarding SCR education for and about Native peoples.

An important area for future teacher education research that has policy implications is research on professional development that creates SCR teachers, curriculum, and schools. Student, teacher, and community perspectives reflected in the New Mexico Indian Education Study demonstrated the importance they each place on SCR education and on relationships between students, teachers, administrators, parents, and community members. These relationships influence the quality of the educational experience for Native students (IESG, 2009). An SCR education would necessitate a community-based relevant education and foster quality relationships that acknowledge, respect, and include stakeholders' perspectives, knowledge, and lived experiences.

An ongoing dilemma for implementing research and policies of SCR education is situated within the larger context of research on diversity in teacher education. Stimulating and creating the belief in SCR and other models of transformative education among educators continues to present a challenge. Further research on diversity in teacher education is needed that can decisively link SCR education with improved academic performance. Drawing on the New Mexico Indian Education Study and other empirical research, there are three compelling and critical areas for further research. Research is needed in the area of professional development on how socioculturally responsive schooling can be taught to teachers of Native students; on how we can convince educators that cultural assimilation at the expense of Native students' heritage is not the answer for improving their educational achievement; and on how we can engage Native students educationally when Native people still live in a colonized state and attend schools that represent Western worldviews and ideologies. While policy makers may have the best of intentions educationally for meeting the needs of learners within our democratic society, it is the students and the teachers who must be the first to practice it, believe in it, and benefit from it. As researchers, we must build on the common thread that runs through this research—the resistance to Western cultural assimilation—and continue to develop frameworks that push the field forward to deal with the complex issues that warrant further investigations as they relate to diversity in teacher education.

NOTES

1. Pueblo, or Puebloan, is the shared anthropological name for several Indigenous or Native communities of New Mexico who express similar cultural traits, such as language, subsistence, and cultural practices. There are nineteen Pueblo Nations in New Mexico, each separately governed and distinct in their sense of community to one another. Other Native nations in New Mexico include Navajo and Apache. Many other Indigenous peoples from across the United States, Canada, Latin America, and abroad also reside in New Mexico, where they make up 10 percent of the state's population.

2. I use the terms *Native American, Native, American Indian, Indian,* and *Indigenous* interchangeably as they are commonly used in this respect among Native peoples of the Southwest, where I am from as well. In addition, I use the terms *Indigenous* and *Native* as proper nouns (with a capital *I* and *N*) to respect and refer to Native communities throughout the country and the world who assert their rights as sovereign nations and peoples. This is also in common with the United Nations' use of the term, recognizing Indigenous peoples as the original inhabitants of the land.

3. The New Mexico Indian Education study is still in progress. We are analyzing data at the writing of this chapter. Thus, my inclusion of the findings from the study is limited to what our research group has discussed until we have a more complete analysis.

4. I am employing Grande's (2000) use of the term *whitestream* (p. 343) to represent how American society remains structured primarily on the basis of Anglo-European experiences, although not all of America is ethnically white.

5. Planton is a town along the border of the reservation where many teachers live and commute to work. All personal and community names quoted or described as part of the New Mexico Indian Education Study are pseudonyms.

REFERENCES

Adams, D. W. (1995). *Education for extinction: Native Americans and the boarding school experience 1875–1928.* Lawrence: University Press of Kansas.

Adams, D. W. (2008). Fundamental considerations: The deep meaning of Native American schooling, 1880–1900. In Villegas, M., Neugebauer, S. R., & Venegas, K. (Eds.), *Indigenous knowledge and education: Sites of struggle, strength, and survivance* (pp. 9–39). Cambridge, MA: Harvard Educational Review.

Au, W. (2008). Decolonizing the classroom: Lessons in multicultural education. *Rethinking Schools, 23(2),* 27–30.

Ball, Jessica. (2004). As if Indigenous knowledge and communities mattered: Transformative education in First Nations communities in Canada. *American Indian Quarterly, 28(3 & 4),* 454–79.

Banks, J. A. (2008). Diversity, group identity, and citizenship education in a global age. *Educational Researcher, 37(3),* 129–39.

Battiste, M. (1998). Enabling the autumn seed: Toward a decolonized approach to aboriginal knowledge, language, and education. *Canadian Journal of Native Education, 22(1)*, 16–27.

Beaulieu, D. (2006). Re-envisioning Indigenous teacher education. In Beaulieu, D., & Figueira, A. M. (Eds.), *The Power of Native Teachers*. (pp. 113–28). Tempe: Center for Indian Education, Arizona State University.

Beaulieu, D., and Figueira, A. (Eds.). (2006). *The power of Native teachers*. Tempe: Center for Indian Education, Arizona State University.

Belgarde, M. J., Mitchell, R., Moquino-Arquero, A. (2002). What do we have to do to Create culturally-responsive programs?: A story about American Indian teacher education. Special Issue: Indigenous Perspectives of Teacher Education: Beyond Perceived Borders. *Action in Teacher Education, 25(2)*, 42–54.

Benham, M., & Cooper, J. (Eds.). (2000). *Indigenous educational models for contemporary practice: In our mother's voice*. Mahwah, NJ: Lawrence Erlbaum.

Benson, M. (2008). Plan targets anti-Western lesson: Some fear loss of diversity in lawmakers' education proposal. *Arizona Republic*, April 17.

Bigelow, B., and Peterson, B. (Eds.). (1998). *Why rethink Columbus? Introduction to rethinking Columbus: The next 500 years*. Milwaukee, WI: Rethinking Schools, 10–11.

Brayboy, B. M. J. (2005). Toward a tribal critical race theory in education. *Urban Review, 37(5)*, 425–46.

Cajete, G. (1994). *Look to the mountain: An ecology of Indigenous education*. Skyland, NC: Kivaki Press.

Caracciolo, D. (2008). Addressing anti-Indianism in the mainstream curriculum: A partnership model. *Multicultural Perspectives, 10(4)*, 224–28.

Castagno, A., & Brayboy, B. (2008). Culturally responsive schooling for indigenous youth: A review of the literature. *Review of Educational Research, 78 (4)*, 941–93.

Child, B. (1998). *Boarding school seasons*. Lincoln: University of Nebraska Press.

Cleary, L. M., and Peacock, T. D. (1998). *Collected wisdom: American Indian education*. Needham Heights, MA: Allyn & Bacon.

Colemant, S., Schultz, L., Robbins, R., Ciali, P., Dorton, J., & Rivera-Colmant, Y. (2004). Constructing meaning to the Indian boarding school experience. *Journal of American Indian Education, 43(3)*, 22–40.

Cook-Lynn, E. (1996). *Why I can't read Wallace Stegner and other essay: A tribal voice*. Madison: University of Wisconsin Press.

Corson, D. (1999). Community-based education for Indigenous cultures. In May, S. (Ed.), *Indigenous community-based education* (pp. 8–19). England: Multilingual Matters, Ltd.

Deloria, P. J. (1998). *Playing Indian*. New Haven, CT: Yale University.

Deloria, Jr., V. (1997). *Red earth, White lies: Native Americans and the myth of scientific fact*. Golden, CO: Fulcrum Publishing.

Deloria, Jr., V., and Lytle, C. (1984). *The Nations within: The past and future of American Indian sovereignty*. New York: Pantheon Books.

Deloria, Jr., V., & Wildcat, D. (2001). *Power and place: Indian education in America*. Golden, CO: American Indian Graduate Center and Fulcrum Resources.

Demmert, W., and Bell, T. (1991) *Indian Nations at risk: An educational strategy for action*. Final report of the Indian Nations at Risk Task Force. Washington, DC: U.S. Department of Education.

Demmert, W. G., and Towner, J. C. (2003). *A review of the research literature on the influences of culturally based education on the academic performance of Native American students*. Portland, OR: Northwest Regional Educational Laboratory.

Deyhle, D. (1995). Navajo youth and Anglo racism: Cultural integrity and resistance. *Harvard Educational Review, 65(3)*, 403–44.

Dozier Enos, A. (2001). A landscape with multiple views: Research in Pueblo communities. In Merchant, B., & Willis, A. (Ed.). *Multiple and intersecting identities in qualitative research.* (pp. 83–101). Mahwah, NJ: Erlbaum Associates.

Emerson, L. (2008). New Mexico Indian Education Government to Government and New Mexico Indian Education Advisory Council Report to *Western Unified* School District. Delivered May 15, 2008.

Fishman, J. A. (1991). *Reversing language shift.* Frankfurt Lodge, UK: Multilingual Matters.

Foley, D. E. (1996). The silent Indian as a cultural production. In Levinson, B., Foley, D., & Holland, D. (Eds.), *The cultural production of the educated person: Critical ethnographies of schooling and local practice* (pp. 70–91). Albany: SUNY.

Freire, P. (1993). *Pedagogy of the oppressed.* (30th anniversary ed.). New York: Continuum.

Giroux, H. (2001). *Theory and resistance in education: Toward a pedagogy for the opposition.* Westport, CT: Bergin & Garvey.

Grande, S. (2000). American Indian identity and intellectualism: The quest for a new red pedagogy. *International Journal of Qualitative Studies in Education, 13(4),* 343–59.

Grande, S. (2004). *Red pedagogy: Native American social and political thought.* Lanham, MD: Rowman & Littlefield Publishers.

Green, R. (2001). The Pocahontas perplex: The image of Indian women in American culture. In Lobo, S., & Talbot, S. (Eds.), *Native American voices: A reader* (pp. 203–11). Upper Saddle River, NJ: Prentice Hall.

Indigenous Education Study Group (IESG). (2009). Transcript, computer notes, and initial codes from data analysis—to be published in Atlas of Indian Education, 2025, NM.

Johnson, J. (2006). Exercising our power as Native teachers. In Beaulieu, D., & Figueira, A. M. (Eds.), *The power of Native teachers.* (pp. 129–42). Tempe: Center for Indian Education, Arizona State University.

Kawagley, A. O. (1995). *A Yupiaq worldview: A pathway to ecology and spirit.* Prospect Heights, IL: Waveland Press.

Kawagley, O., & Barnhardt, R. (2004). *Education Indigenous to place: Western science meets Native reality.* Fairbanks: Alaska Native Knowledge Network. Retrieved January 8, 2006, from www.ankn.uaf.edu/EIP

Kelting-Gibson, L. (2006). Preparing educators to meet the challenge of Indian Education for All. *Phi Delta Kappan, 88(3),* 204–7.

Krauss, M. (1998). The condition of Native North American languages: The need for realistic assessment and action. *International Journal of the Sociology of Language, 132,* 9–21.

Lee, T. S. (2006, January). "I came here to learn how to be a leader": An intersection of critical pedagogy and Indigenous education. *InterActions: UCLA Journal of Education and Information Studies, 12(1).* Retrieved from http://repositories.cdlib.org/gseis/interactions/vol2/iss1/art3

Lee, T. S. (2007). Connecting academics, indigenous knowledge, and commitment to community: High school students' perceptions of a community based education model. *Canadian Journal of Native Education, 30(2),* 196–216.

Little Soldier, L. (1982). Now's the time to dispel the myths about Indians. *Learning, 11(4),* 44–45, 47.

Locke, S., & Lindley, L. (2007). Rethinking social studies for a critical democracy in American Indian/Alaska Native education. *Journal of American Indian Education, 46(1),* 1–19.

Loewen, J. W. (1998). Plagues and pilgrims: The truth about the first Thanksgiving. In Bigelow, B., & Peterson, B. (Eds.), *Rethinking Columbus: The next 500 years* (p. 82). Milwaukee, WI: Rethinking Schools.

Martinez, G. (2009). Representation, power and stereotyping: A lesson on Indigenous people and sports mascots. In Missias, M., Heilman, E., & Fruja, R. (Eds.), *Social studies and diversity teacher education.* (pp. 176–78). New York: Routledge Press.

Martinez, G. (2010). *Native pride: The politics of curriculum and instruction in an urban, public high school.* Cresskill, NJ: Hampton Press.

May, S. (1999). Language and education rights for Indigenous peoples. In May, S. (Ed.), *Indigenous community-based education* (pp. 42–66). Frankfurt Lodge, England: Multilingual Matters.

McCarty, T., Romero, M. E., and Zepeda, O. (2006). Reclaiming the gift: Indigenous youth counter-narratives on Native language loss and revitalization. *American Indian Quarterly, 30(2),* 28–48.

Mihesuah, D. (Ed.). (1998). *Natives and academics: Researching and writing about American Indians.* Lincoln: University of Nebraska Press.

Montana Legislature. (1999). HB 528. Retrieved February 12, 2009, from data.opi.state.mt.us/bills/billhtml/HB0528.html

National Indian Education Association (NIEA). (2007). *Native education 101: Basic facts about American Indian, Alaska Native, and Native Hawaiian education.* Washington, DC: author.

National Indian Education Association (NIEA). (2008). Indian education provisions for the No Child Left Behind Act. NIEA Resolution 08–04. Retrieved February 9, 2009, from http://www.niea.org/profile/resolutions.php

Nettles, D., and Romainc, S. (2000). *Vanishing voices.* Oxford: Oxford University Press.

New Mexico Public Education Department (NMPED). (2003). Article 23A: Indian education. Retrieved on August 7, 2009, from http://www.ped.state.nm.us/indian.ed/dl08/ARTICLE.23A.pdf

New Mexico Public Education Department (NMPED). (2003). HB 892: Indian Education Act: Amended April 2007. Santa Fe: author.

New Mexico Public Education Department (NMPED). (2005). Indian Education Status Report: 2003–2004 School Year. Santa Fe: NMPED Indian Education Division.

New Mexico Public Education Department (NMPED). (2008). Indian Education Status Report: 2006–2007 School Year. Santa Fe: NMPED Indian Education Division, p. 11.

Nieto, S. (2000). *Affirming diversity: The sociopolitical context of multicultural education.* New York: Longman.

Noddings, N. (1984). *Caring: A feminine approach to ethics and moral education.* Berkeley: University of California Press.

Peterson, B. (2008). Whitewashing the past: A proposal for a national campaign to rethink textbooks. *Rethinking Schools, 23(1),* 34–37.

Pewewardy, C. (2005). Ideology, power, and the miseducation of Indigenous peoples in the United States. In Wilson, W. A., & Yellow Bird, M. (Eds.), *For Indigenous eyes only: A decolonization handbook* (pp. 139–56.) Santa Fe, NM: School of American Research.

Pewewardy, C., and Hammer, P. (2003). *Culturally responsive teaching for American Indian students.* (ED482325). Charleston, WV: ERIC Clearinghouse on Rural Education and Small Schools.

Quijada, P. (2008). *Tribal critical race theory and educational spaces: (Re)examining schooling experiences of Indigenous youth.* Paper presented March 2008 at the annual meeting of the American Educational Research Association, New York.

Reese, D. (1996). *Teaching young children about Native Americans.* Publication no. DERR93002007. Urbana-Champagne: University of Illinois Children's Research Center. Retrieved August 7, 2009, from http://alkek.library.txstate.edu/swwc/cdv/further_study/teaching_children_na.pdf

Reese, D. (2006). *Those Thanksgiving lesson plans.* Retrieved August 7, 2009, from http://americanindiansinchildrensliterature.blogspot.com/2006_11_21_archive

Reese, D. (2007). Proceed with caution: Using Native American folktales in the classroom. *Language Arts, 84(3),* 245–56.

Sleeter, C., & Grant, C. (2009). *Making choices for multicultural education: Five approaches to race, class, and gender* (6th ed.). Hoboken, NJ: John Wiley & Sons.

Smith, G. (2003). *Indigenous struggle for the transformation of education and schooling.* Keynote address to the Alaskan Federation of Natives (AFN) Convention, Anchorage, AK. Retrieved June 16, 2005, from http://www.ankn.uaf.edu/curriculum/Articles/GrahamSmith/

Smith, L. (1999). *Decolonizing methodologies: research and indigenous peoples.* New York: Zed Books.

Stachowski, L., and Frey, C. (2003). *Lessons learned on Navajo land: Student teachers reflect on professional and cultural learning in reservation schools and communities.* Paper presented at the 83rd annual meeting of the Association of Teacher Educators, February 15–19, 2002.

Starnes, B. (2006). Montana's Indian education for all: Toward an education worthy of American ideals. *Phi Delta Kappan, 8(3).* Retrieved on February 12, 2009, from http://www. pdkintl.org/kappan/k_v88/k0611sta.htm

Trask, H.-K. (2001). Lovely hula hands: Corporate tourism and the prostitution of Hawaiian culture. In Lobo, S., & Talbot, S. (Eds.), *Native American voices: A reader* (pp. 393–4014). Upper Saddle River, NJ: Prentice Hall.

United Nations. (2007, September 12). *United Nations declaration on the rights of Indigenous peoples.* 61st session, Agenda item 68, Report of the Human Rights Council.

U.S. Census Bureau. (2007). *The American community—American Indians and Alaska Natives: 2004.* Washington, DC: U.S. Department of Commerce, Economic, and Statistics Administration, U.S. Census Bureau.

Valenzuela, A. (1999). *Subtractive schooling: U.S.–Mexican youth and the politics of caring.* Albany: State University of New York Press.

Villegas, A. M., and Luca, T. (2002). Preparing culturally responsive teachers: Rethinking the curriculum. *Journal of Teacher Education, 53(20),* 20–32.

Waziyatawin, and Yellow Bird, M. (2005). Beginning decolonization. In Wilson, W. A., & Yellow Bird, M. (Eds.), *For Indigenous eyes only: A decolonization handbook.* (pp. 1–7). Santa Fe, NM: School of American Research.

Wilkins, D. (2002). *American Indian politics and the American political system.* Lanham, MD: Rowman & Littlefield Publishers.

Zehr, M. A. (2008). Native American history, culture gaining traction in state curricula. *Education Week, 28(11),* 1, 12.

14

Worthy Witnessing

Collaborative Research in Urban Classrooms

Maisha T. Winn and Joseph R. Ubiles

When we first started our work together in the Bronx, New York, at University Heights High School in the fall 2003 semester, we seemingly wanted different things. Maisha, a university professor and researcher, wanted to learn more about the pedagogical practices of teachers who adopted out-of-school literacy practices in urban high schools. She approached the work with a belief that English language arts teachers who were engaged in writing and reading communities beyond school walls were able to create a forum for young writers that fostered democratic engagement. Joseph, a poet and a teacher grounded in Pan-Africanism and Freirian theory, wanted support for students in his Power Writing Seminar at an urban public high school in the Bronx. He also wanted someone to bear witness to the many truths his students shared through their original poetry and prose. Soon the objectives merged, creating a synergy of research, pedagogy, and practice (Fisher, 2007). Joe's classroom became more than a site in Maisha's study; this writing community became a space in which she witnessed the "pedagogy of possibility" in action (Fisher, 2009). Maisha's research, namely, ethnographic video, interview transcripts, and field notes, became both a mirror and a window for Joseph to reflect and map new directions for practice with his students. After reading a draft of Maisha's article, "From the Coffee House to the School House: The Promise and Potential of Spoken Word Poetry in School Contexts" (Fisher, 2005b) about Joseph's teaching and his students' learning, Joseph shared his reflections on what he thought Maisha's role was in his classroom:

> I feel valued and I feel like you witnessed things and you were a legitimate witness. You are a *worthy* witness. It is a witnessing.

For Joseph, Maisha's presence and subsequent involvement was a witnessing of sorts. Both Joseph and Maisha believed their work together had larger implications for researchers who sought to work in urban classrooms. The purpose of this chapter is to define worthy witnessing and examine its role in teaching and teacher education. In defining worthy witnessing we introduce a methodology that privileges student and teacher voices while building relationships between classroom teachers, students, and researchers. This work, we argue, is important to address issues of diversity in teacher education. First we offer a brief review of scholarship committed to teacher and student-centered methodologies. Next we share our journey as teachers and researchers that shaped how we approached our work. After our purposeful narratives, we examine the four phases of worthy witnessing, including: (1) Admission, (2) Declaration, (3) Revelation, and (4) Confidentiality, and how these dimensions unfolded in our work with ninth–twelfth grade students in an urban public high school in the Bronx, New York. Finally we reflect on what we consider to be the next phase of worthy witnessing, which is our work with preservice and in-service middle grades and secondary English language arts and social studies teachers. Our work has been guided by the following questions:

- What are the pathways for a researcher to enter a literacy classroom in an urban high school that support a dialectical relationship? In what ways can classroom teachers and researchers reconsider research methodologies that encourage reflection and inform teacher education in literacy-centered classrooms?
- What role does "worthy witnessing" play in the professional development of preservice and in-service teachers?

Joseph's class, the Power Writing Seminar, was a cross-generational community of poets and writers who met at least three days a week in spite of the fact that only one day was formally part of University Heights High School's extended day program. Students met Tuesdays after school, Friday mornings, and Saturdays throughout New York City. Saturday classes were sometimes held at a coteacher's loft in the East Village, New York City Botanical Gardens, the Cloisters, Hamilton Grange House, and various libraries, museums, and cultural centers throughout New York City. Since the initial study, Power Writing has found a new Saturday home in the Nuyorican Poets Café, which has been a cultural institution for literary arts, music, and theater in New York City since its doors opened in 1980 (prior to that the café started in Miguel Algarin's living room in 1973). Power Writing has also been implemented in high schools in Brooklyn and Manhattan, and Joseph has created workshops for students in the juvenile justice and alternative school systems.

Joseph works with two additional teaching artists, Amy Sultan and Roland Legiardi-Laura. Amy is a grant writer and filmmaker, and Roland is a poet and filmmaker. School personnel also joined this class at different times at its original site, including the school counselor, attendance officer, and the principal. Elsewhere, Joseph has described Power Writing as having "the traditional elements of a family" (Fisher, 2007). Maisha was inducted into the family in fall 2003 through a process referred to as "worthy witnessing," which is defined in this chapter. However, first we will examine other studies that examine diversity in urban schools and thus have implications for teacher education that embrace methods that demonstrate the three Rs—responsibility, respect, and reciprocity, which we argue are essential to studying diversity in teacher education.

WORTHY WITNESSING IN LITERACY RESEARCH

In an examination of educational research, Duncan-Andrade argues that conventional research methods in education can be problematic. Arguing that "carino," or care and affection, should be central to research, Duncan-Andrade posits:

> The value of this type of critical research is its focus on empowering individuals as agents of meaningful, sustainable change. The direct aim of this kind of research agenda is to positively impact the material conditions of those involved with the study; it is an approach to research that gives more than it receives. (2006, p. 455)

Indeed, there is a growing body of research that seeks to "give more than it receives" by placing youth at the center of the work. Duncan-Andrade's call ushers a new movement of scholars who are both researchers and practitioners devoted to improving the lives of urban youth in school and in out-of-school contexts. Part of this movement includes an area that scholars have referred to as "youth studies" (Ginwright & Cammarota, 2006). In an introduction to their edited volume of studies that employ participatory action research methodology, Ginwright and Cammarota contextualize the work of youth-centered research with four guiding principles:

1. Young people should be conceptualized in relationship to specific economic, political, and social conditions.
2. The youth development process should be conceptualized as a collective response to the marginalization of young people.
3. Young people are agents of change, not simply subject to change.
4. Young people have basic rights. (Ginwright & Cammarota, xvii–xix, 2006)

Contributing scholars to Ginwright and Cammarota's volume used an inquiry approach to learn what issues impacted the youth with whom they worked. They allowed themselves to be guided by young people on their journey to fighting injustices in their schools and communities.

While the aforementioned volume examines educational research broadly, other studies have placed students at the center specifically on teaching and learning literacy. All of these studies can inform the work teacher educators do with preservice teachers and specifically those who will teach English language arts. For example, in an edited volume of scholarship examining literacy as a "civil right" (Greene, 2008), contributors challenge literacy researchers to use a "sociocritical" lens—that is, a lens that privileges the voices and histories of communities while seeking to honor the hybrid language practices of youth, help students of color create a toolkit, and develop "college-going trajectories" (Gutierrez, 2008). Gutierrez's research on Latino youth in Southern California addresses institutional and systemic forces that attempt to silence and block young people while also providing resources to help them navigate their way through the maze of higher education. What scholars in this review and others understand is that youth must be literate in as many ways as possible, and one aspect of that literacy is the ability to exercise agency and fight for their rights and the rights of their peers.

In a study of Harlem youth performing narratives of community, Kinloch (2007) examines "how the lived experiences of urban youth embody a way of telling narratives about place, struggle, and identity that often times are not a part of the work students do, or perform in schools" (pp. 61–62). Through her work, Kinloch introduces Quentin, an African American young man confronting gentrification or the "white-ification" of his hood in Harlem. Using a methodology that includes analyzing narratives of young people, Kinloch codefined the objectives of the project with Quentin. Kinloch was a "worthy witness" to the youth in her study as she created opportunities for Quentin and his peers to engage in critical dialogue about the displacement of his neighbors. Kinloch asserts, "Together, Quentin and I participated in local community meetings, interviewed teachers and students, and analyzed signs of struggle and culture in Harlem" (Kinloch, 2007, p. xx). Kinloch moves away from the false promise of giving voice to young people that some scholarship in diversity in teacher education claims to do. Youth in urban schools and communities already have voices—bold, courageous, and full of wisdom and insight. Rather than "giving voice" to youth, a new generation of literacy scholars seeks to use their privilege as professors at colleges and universities to generate and sustain forums to share and exchange voices.

Morrell's (2008) study of teaching critical literacy to urban youth in California depicts a researcher's dilemma. At the end of a program, Morrell chooses not to "collect" student journals that probably could have informed his research because he believed that students would benefit more from holding on to them. Morrell writes courageously:

> On this occasion, I am reminded by a research colleague to try to gather the students' notebooks for analysis. I think to myself that the notebooks belong to the students and not the research team. The 100+-page philosophical, social, and analytical texts that the students have created over the preceding five weeks are mementos of a prolific time and will serve the students well as reminders of the past and predictors of a future of possibilities for writing and action. (p. 1)

Morrell's narrative captures the tensions of worthy witnessing. At times scholars will have access to rich data; however, scholars must make difficult decisions that require integrity and humanity. Here, Morrell refuses to reify the power dynamic between a researcher and participants by recognizing that these journals truly belong to the young people.

Perhaps no other community of teachers and students are in need of worthy witnessing more than the tireless soldiers and literacy activists in New Orleans. In a critical study of a community of young writers and "neo-griots" in New Orleans, Buras (2009) examines the efforts of a literary community working with "text, sound, and light" to illuminate the lived experiences of young men and women who continue to endure the injustices that were magnified by Hurricane Katrina and the fragile levees that at one time protected the city. Buras's work is essential because of her deep commitment to contextualize the current discussion of post-Katrina New Orleans in a broader conversation about the rich histories of the city and the traditions its residents have graciously shared with the world. However, Buras's work also uncovers the painful reality of the work ahead for teachers like Jim Randels and Kalamu ya Salaam, who struggle to keep their program, Students at the Center, alive. Students at the Center (SAC) is a small class at Frederick Douglass High School where students bring original writing and have an opportunity to exchange their work, much like the Power Writers in the Bronx who we discuss at length later in this article. A community like SAC is even more important because many students have chosen to return to New Orleans without their families due to their deep love for their communities and desire to graduate in the city that has been a part of their identity.

Duncan-Andrade, Kinloch, Morrell, and Buras are in the center of the struggles in the communities in which they work, yet they gracefully move to the margins, allowing the stories to unfold so scholars, teacher educators, and practitioners can actually hear the youth and the committed team of teachers who share their lives with them. Collectively these scholars challenge the current paradigm of research in teacher education. First, they are more than participant observers; they are engaged in the work of their respective communities by building partnerships with classrooms and teachers in schools and in out-of-school settings. In some cases these scholars are actual teachers, calling attention to the important role of teacher research. Additionally this work does not mention diversity in passing; race, class, and agency are central to the work. In the following sections, the authors return to their stories as a practitioner and researcher. In the spirit of the aforementioned scholars, the authors approach their work with reverence for the youth they encounter. Additionally they offer a model for scholarship dedicated to studying diversity in teacher education.

JOSEPH'S JOURNEY: A SOCIAL HISTORY OF POWER WRITING

My students watched the Twin Towers burn and fall from the southern windows of Nichols Hall, on the campus of Bronx Community College, which is located in University Heights. Albert Einstein used to teach in this building, a fact not often shared with students and certainly not celebrated. The education system depends on the notion of separate worlds. Watching the great buildings fall and then walking home with colleagues and students, we observed New Yorkers in our great mosaic of beauty and strength, tragedy and sorrow, and I thought of my poets-writers-students. How can we create a safe space beyond the conventions of public education where education would be a relevant, potent, and liberating experience? And how can this space inform a new generation of teachers and the teacher educators who serve them? The fifty-minute period, one day a week for my poetry club was clearly inadequate and yet contained many elements of a solution.

When Amy Sultan, then the executive director of Early Stages, arrived in my classroom with Roland Legiardi-Laura, an artist and public intellectual in tow, more of the issues of our struggle for a humane and innovative literacy forum were crystallized. In fact, the distance between our students and the site of the fall of the towers could not be measured in linear miles alone but rather in the forces of history and the class and caste contradictions of American society. Our students, whose backgrounds are Nuyorican (New York Puerto Rican) and Afro-American, Dominican and Haitian, Central and South American, African and European American, are all trapped in what Franz Fanon, in his classic description of oppression, called "mutual obscurity." We needed to develop a process through which our students would engage in a true education, where teacher and student would be both fluid and interchangeable, and where all participants are of equal value, mutually engaged in what Paolo Freire (1998, p. 90) called "an intervention in the world."

One of the most valuable lessons was how critical teacher collaboration was to the program. Teachers have few opportunities to collaborate after their teacher education programs; however, we learned that community partnerships provided a way to reflect on our own practices, challenge ourselves, and expand. Part of this collaboration meant we extended the traditional classroom to include the entire city. Amy brought resources and ideas including field trips to Broadway plays and art films, museums, and major cultural institutions. We developed a commitment to unswerving intellectual rigor and geographic and mathematic literacy. We recognized the imperative that our students acquire a genuine literacy, which we define as the ability to read the world, write the world, and speak the world. We asserted that the mastery of the language is not merely a source of power but is power itself and as such is essential to the survival of our community. Our students learn to examine the world critically, to ideate, and to write and speak their own truths.

We evolved from one, fifty-minute period per week into fourteen hours of class per week spread across two school days and Saturdays. Our students learn to take ownership of their own lives and educations, to travel throughout New York City, and to fearlessly present their ideas and worldviews in many artistic and intellectual venues. We study Bronx history as well as world history and claim the right to define our space and our place in it.

In the third year of our praxis, Maisha began attending class as a postdoctoral researcher at Teachers College, Columbia University, and subsequently published *Writing in Rhythm: Spoken Word Poetry in Urban Classrooms* (2007), in which she analyzed the Power Writing seminar from a socially and politically aware academic perspective. Her continued collaboration has been critical to our self-assessment process and issues clarification. Her support and intellectual contributions have been invaluable in the continuation of the work. Perhaps most important for me as a teacher was having a living example of a code-switching woman of color who was accessible to my black and Latino female students. We expected much from her; in addition to asking her to join our team of teachers, we also wanted a systematic examination of our program that asked compelling questions that would help us think about how we might use our methods in other teaching contexts.

Many of the award-winning poets and scholars that the program has produced were once "hooky queens" and "hallway kings" for whom school was an oppressive and dehumanizing environment. Together we witnessed and continue to witness that the transition and transformation of these young people is the product of vigorous, visionary, and relentless work. As former students graduate from college and return to the program to teach and mentor, the institution achieves a life of its own. It is our hope to help other teachers in urban, public classrooms transform schools into safety nets for children and to demonstrate how teacher and researcher collaborations can begin this dialogue.

MAISHA'S JOURNEY

When I first visited Joseph's Power Writing class at UHHS in the Bronx, New York, I was ill prepared for the hazing I would receive from his students as part of my education in the circle. In Joseph's classroom, it was ultimately the students' decision whether or not I would be invited to stay. In Joseph's words, I had to become "more than the professor who wanted to study them." I had to be a "truth-sayer" and eventually a "worthy witness" in a classroom community where students shared their life experiences through poetry and prose. While I have written about my experiences with Joe and his Power Writers, I have always wanted to work with Joseph in co-constructing a methodology that synthesizes the objectives of students, teachers, and researchers in this literacy-centered community. Additionally, I wanted for us to consider ways in which we could share this work with ELA preservice teachers. As a researcher in the Power Writing seminar, I first had to experience what it means to be a part of this writing community. In my experiences as an educator and teacher educator, I have never entered an urban school that did not need some kind of assistance, whether it be volunteering, mentoring, or tutoring.

I remember my first time conducting a study of an after-school program as a graduate student for one of my courses. My plan was to "observe" the program by sitting quietly in the back of the room and record notes. While there were opportunities for me to do just that, I could also see an urgent need for someone to help students and teachers. I realized early in my research trajectory that I could never accept the luxury of just sitting and watching when there was so much work to do in our schools.

One thing that I learned from Joseph rather quickly was that he was an avid reader. He and I exchanged literature and academic journal articles as easily as lesson plans or literature guides. We wanted to be sure we developed a foundation for our knowledge as we worked together. I was also committed to getting education research into the hands of classroom teachers. There is often an unspoken, and sometimes spoken, concern that education research does not find its way into the everyday classroom or into a teacher's hands. However, I believe that scholars can get these projects into the worlds of classroom teachers and invite them to be a part of the conversation. Of course, this model is not new; the M-Class teams (Freedman, et al., 1999) began their journey as teacher researchers with a common set of readings and attending a symposium addressing intersections of race, class, and literacy teaching and learning. Additionally, teachers in the M-Class teams participated in a forum that introduced them to some of the ideas that have been analyzed in education research circles. Much of Joseph's work reminded me of the Carol Lee's Cultural Modeling Project. I remember Joe calling me after reading Lee's work and how enthusiastic he was to read about someone conducting research in which he could locate himself and his work with the Power Writers. Additionally, Joseph found the work of Kris Gutierrez and the concept of "Third Space" useful for conceptualizing the work of his student poets. Joseph also found it helpful to read the writing of English and social studies teachers in Freedman's 1999 edited volume, *Inside City Schools*, and was keenly interested in the ways these teacher researchers generated research questions about their own practice.

FOUR PHASES OF SERIOUS ETHNOGRAPHIC INQUIRY

Scholars, teacher researchers, and teacher educators must be aware that ethnography and cultural anthropology have evolved in concert with a complex order of domination. They have been the dominant classes that traditionally practice these methodologies. This fact is central to our work involving urban literacy; we wanted to return the power to define process, structure, and function to the group being "studied." As we considered the role of the ethnographer in the recording, interpretation, and analysis of our student-controlled literacy project, a protocol evolved out of our praxis. How could we intrude yet be unobtrusive? In what ways could we understand our affect in and effects upon the social construct we are studying? How could we insure that our inquiries and analytical formats enhanced and did not arrest the development of the social entity that we sought to understand? How could our work be repositioned and redefined so as not to be voyeuristic, colonial, and paternalistic in its structure and function? And most important, how could our work be used to help teachers in other urban classrooms throughout the country? These, we claim, are the essential questions involving ethnography in studying diversity in teacher education.

In their seminal work, *Literacy: Reading the Word and the World* (1987), Freire and Macedo reject the deficit model of "Banking Education" by offering the observation that "no one is ignorant of everything, no one knows nothing." This is an important concept for the ethnographer to bear in mind. In our work with literacy-based Power Writing, in the South Bronx and the Lower East Side of Manhattan, urban youth practice a liberation-driven model of literacy acquisition. It is in this setting that the ethnographic inquiry, worthy witnessing, has evolved: Admission; Declaration; Revelation; and Confidentiality. We believe this method of inquiry is essential to collaborative research between and among researchers who are also teacher educators and classroom teachers.

Admission. Admission, the first phase of worthy witnessing, certainly has a price. For a scholar to enter a community as a stranger and expect to "conduct a study" can be problematic. Conversely, a scholar who enters a particular community with guiding questions about the teaching and learning taking place, with an openness to be "schooled" by students and teacher, will have more to offer to the larger polylogue. The need to critically examine the classroom communities and pedagogical practices of educators who are committed to their students and to provide opportunities for students to develop critical literacies is undoubtedly urgent. There are many "soldiers"—literacy activists and advocates who work with our youth in schools and in out-of-school contexts throughout the United States (Fisher, 2007). In the context of the Power Writing seminar, the researcher, an African American middle-class woman from California, sought admission to a community of student writers—ninth–twelfth graders of African American, Dominican, Puerto Rican, and West Indian descent and largely from working-class families from the Bronx. Initially, Maisha believed her ticket for admission had already been purchased; when she saw the students she saw herself. What Maisha did not take into account was the ways in which students would read her in terms of speech, way of communication, and style of dress. While she carried the ethic of "carino" in her heart and her approach to her work, Maisha still had to demonstrate to this collective of student poets that she would learn how to follow their lead.

Admission emerged in three phases. Initially there was admission to the school and classroom, which was in large part dictated by the principal and classroom teacher as well as institutional review boards for the university and the school district. Next, there was admission to Joseph's world, which involved extensive dialogue about teaching philosophies, common readings, and pedagogical models.

Last, there was admission to the Power Writing circle. While the group accepted Maisha's presence and participation, she still had to forge relationships on her own. Most important, there was admission into individual student lives, which eventually led to interviews that were conducted at the end of the academic year after relationships had been established throughout the school year.

Declaration. The second phase, declaration, involves the researcher introducing him- or herself and introducing his or her ideas. Where declaration diverges with a typical introduction of a research project is the unmasking of social and political ideologies that frame the work. Power Writing was political in nature; Joseph's orientation toward his work as a teacher in urban high schools was to resist attempts to colonize youth and thus colonize the teaching of reading, writing, and speaking. Joseph and his students deserved and demanded to know my philosophy of education and my family history, which was grounded in a commitment to Independent Black Institutions (IBIs) (Fisher, 2009).

Revelation. Revelation refers to the process of students and researchers achieving an equilibrium of acceptance through the bonds of mutual respect that can only be reached when the research is engaged in classroom activities. When students and researchers work side by side, the bonds of mutual respect and understanding allow a new practice to evolve in which the researcher is fellow traveler, journalist, critic, and contributor. Additionally, students begin to see themselves in analytical and reciprocal roles in relationship to the researcher. In many ways this process mirrors Rogoff's notion of apprenticeship, in which she argues that the learning process occurs on three planes, including apprenticeship, guided participation, and participatory appropriation (1994). Students realize that there are implications for what they are doing that can inform students and teachers in other schools and regions. This realization then leads to the development of relationships that extend far beyond the project, characterized by mutual respect, caring, and, dare we say, friendship.

Confidentiality. All teacher researchers and university researchers have to make decisions about what aspects of the findings make final reports, articles, and publications. While teachers and students provided signed consent forms to participate in my project with the Power Writers, Joseph and I still discussed which poems and which conversations around particular poems exposed too much of our students' lives. The last thing either of us wanted was to create a culture around sensationalizing the heartache and frustration many of our youth endured. We also felt a strong sense of responsibility given the trust and faith they held in us. It was quite possible they thought they wanted particular poems that revealed their multiple and shared truths accessible to the public; however, we erred on the side of caution that they may not foresee possible regrets they may have about sharing certain aspects of their lives.

THE ROLE OF ETHNOGRAPHIC VIDEO IN WORTHY WITNESSING

In the context of the Power Writing study, ethnographic video included the uninterrupted filming of class sessions, unexpected sounds, noises, and unrehearsed moments. This notion of uninterrupted filming is important because that is where many potentially useful lessons for preservice and in-service teachers began to unfold.

While the camera was seemingly unobtrusive—Maisha often set it on a windowsill or somewhere out of the way—students began to pass the camera around and film each other at different points during the read and feed process. In many ways the camera was a part of the circle, being passed from the hands of one student to the hands of another, eventually finding its way back to the sill when it grew too heavy or cumbersome. Joseph began to use the camera as a second pair of eyes. According to Joseph, student interactions with the camera represented the many encounters students would have with strangers and people who were unfamiliar with their styles, "Bronxonics," and other elements of the circle. The camera, much like the stage where the Power Writers sometimes shared their work, was a metaphor for the reality that someone would always be listening and watching. Joseph encouraged students to be prepared for any possible scenario, and it was his desire that students exhibit confidence in their communication abilities. One unforeseen benefit of using ethnographic video was that teachers used footage to reflect on their pedagogical practices and language with the students. Since the tapes were not edited for "best practices" or used as "highlight reels," the data reflect the real classroom community—unrehearsed and honest. Power Writers also appreciated being able to watch and hear themselves, often using the LCD screen as a mirror and a window for where to go next.

In our work with preservice teachers in teacher education programs we have been able to use the footage not only to demonstrate the ways in which the Power Writing process fosters democratic engagement and positive peer networks but also to offer educators a window to view the way we worked through difficult issues such as race, class, and religion, raised by student poets in their poetry and prose. Employing these pedagogical portraits has been a way for us to begin conversations with novice and experienced teachers about building community, learning when and where teachers' voices enter, and when teachers should move out of their students' way.

"AT HOME WITH BOOKS": WORTHY WITNESSING WITH PRESERVICE AND IN-SERVICE TEACHERS

One of the prevailing questions during and after the ethnographic study of the Power Writers was how Joseph's, Amy's, and Roland's work with the Power Writers could best be replicated by teachers in urban classrooms. As Joseph often said to the Power Writers, "I can't teach you what I know, but I can teach you how I know." In sum, Joseph was invested in the process of cultivating new writers who could make decisions about where they wanted to go after being equipped with the necessary tools. Additionally, Joseph wanted to assist new and experienced teachers with this process. While the Power Writing teaching team was a dynamic collective of educators who shared similar ideals, the collective sensed this work could be adopted in different settings. When Joseph and Maisha first planned a Power Writing workshop for preservice teachers, they spent a lot of time discussing the key components of the process. One thing that they agreed on was that many who dared to teach language arts were often men and women who at some point in our lives became intimate with words both spoken and written. In other words, many of the preservice teachers shared memories of sitting in parent's laps while being read to, taking trips to the local library and bookstore, or a single teacher taking time to make sure reading was a joyous experience for his or her students. It was Joseph and Maisha's desire to create that same sense of intimacy for students in literacy classrooms in urban schools. The worthy-witnessing workshop encouraged preservice teachers to explore how they acquired literacy and a fondness for reading, writing, and speaking in order to think about how their experiences impacted their teaching. In workshops for preservice and in-service teachers, Joseph and Maisha asked teachers to create a footprint map of their neighborhood or community in which they acquired literacy. On 11x14 sheets of paper, workshop participants reconstructed these communities while unearthing memories of their first experiences with words and language. Some maps focused on individual homes or buildings, while others show an entire block or streetscape. Participants sometimes labeled relevant buildings, including corner stores and libraries, or do not include any words at all. After participants completed their maps they wrote a short piece using poetry or prose that described their experiences learning to read, write, and speak. Once everyone completed their maps and their writing project, Joseph and Maisha gathered the group into a circle, giving everyone a chance to talk through their map, pass it around, and read their poem. Joseph and Maisha used the same format used in the Power Writing class; everyone chose one "feeder" or a person who provides feedback after they read their piece. The feeder was selected prior to reading their piece (you can have more than one "feeder" if time permits). One of the Power Writing rituals was to "clap" the reader in to welcome him or her as well as to offer encouragement. We typically asked someone to be an emcee who introduced each reader and his or her poem, which helped participants get to know each other's work. All of us read and we discussed the experience as well as the ways we can see it working in our classes. Joseph's "At Home with Books," depicting his mother's and grandmother's pursuit of literacy for themselves and their children, was used as an example during the process:

> One door opens
> Another closes
> Somewhere
> A door slams shut
> Somewhere
> Sirens scream
> Still sounds sound
> Silently
> Memory shimmers with
> Colors and darkness
> Grandma had the alphabet up
> Written on brown paper
> Taped to a wall
> It hung long after
> We had learned
> To read and write
> I see the letters
> The kitchen wall
> Hear moms reading to us
> Everyday
> Sometimes folktales

Sometimes fairytales
Adventures and mysteries
We had books
Laboriously towed
From the Salvation Army
Red wagon
With hard rubber wheels
And ungreased axles
Squeaking into the wind
I read everything
Once I had learned the code
Letter-sound-silent letter-sound
Diphthong-sound-letter-word
Image
Idea
Object
Subject
Feeling
Thought
Emotion
Expression
Impression
Damn, I love these books and stories
They make me what I am

In these circles we have had teachers experience themselves and others in new ways. For example, teachers reconnected with the vulnerability one feels when asked to share their work aloud as often is the case in classrooms. Teachers also learned about traditions, customs, and experiences of fellow teachers that did not mirror their own. Most important, teachers were able to trace their trajectory with literacy learning and consider the ways in which these experiences influence their teaching. The most powerful workshops have taken place with Power Writing alumni or student poets who participated in the Power Writing seminar at University Heights High School. Amanda, Arline, Ramon, and Ron Jay,[1] along with Joseph and Maisha, led workshops at the University of Puerto Rico, Mayagüez, for the "English as a Field of Change and Flow" conference.[2] This collective of Power Writing alumni taught workshops in high school classrooms in Mayagüez as well as for graduate students and teachers at the "collegio" or the college. Worthy witnessing with Amanda, Arline, Ramon, and Ron Jay created another critical layer to the process. Not only did workshop participants learn to use their lived experiences as a mirror and a window to improve their work in urban classrooms from students but Joseph and Maisha also were able to reflect on their practice and learn from former students.

WITNESSING THE FUTURE

In this chapter we attempted to show a movement in educational research that focuses on the lives of urban youth in school and in out-of-school contexts throughout the United States. More specifically, we focused on studies in language, literacy, and culture that inform teachers, teacher educators, and researchers while having implications for studying diversity in teacher education. We urge future studies that are committed to addressing diversity in teacher education and urban classrooms to consider the following:

- **Demonstrate responsibility in the research community.** Responsibility comes in many forms, but one of the most important aspects includes dependability and accountability. Teachers and students open their classrooms—in school and out of school—to researchers and thus their personal lives and experiences through the work witnessed and heard. In some contexts responsibility comes in the form of advocacy work around issues that impact the lives of youth and their families.
- **Establish an opportunity to exercise reciprocity.** Exercising reciprocity for teachers may come in the form of coauthoring studies, professional development opportunities at universities and with national organizations at conferences, volunteering in other classes, and sharing books, journal articles, and other resources that may be relevant to the particular teacher's life and work. For students, exercising reciprocity may include an ongoing relationship that may include editing and proofreading personal statements, college essays, and other kinds of writing and assisting students in establishing ongoing social networks and meaningful work.
- **Ritualize respect.** "Respect" is a word that can be taken for granted but it has profound consequences when it is not established mutually. Showing responsibility in a research community and exercising reciprocity are at the foundation of respect. However, the road to respect does not end here. One thing that we established early is that there would be opportunities for us to present the work we do as teachers and researchers, and other times students from the Power Writers would present the work. Joseph did not want students to be "specimens" or in the audience if their lives were a part of the materials being presented. We want to foster opportunities for Power Writers to speak for themselves about the ways in which their participation impacted their lives beyond high school. A last but critical component of ritualizing respect is being open to the work with preservice and in-service teachers.

In order for scholarship to have an impact on studying diversity in teacher education, classroom teachers, university researchers, and students' work have to be collaborative and rooted in the aforementioned components. Participant observation is a witnessing of sorts; researchers have an opportunity to be a part of a classroom community, quite often a sacred space where he or she is initially a stranger and attempting to translate lessons learned to a new generation of educators. Being a *worthy* witness entails being actively engaged in the community.

NOTES

1. Amanda, Arline, Ramon, and Ron Jay were a part of Fisher's (2007) ethnography of the Power Writers, *Writing in Rhythm: Spoken Word Poetry in Urban Classrooms*.

2. The University of Puerto Rico, Mayagüez, "English as a Field of Change and Flow" conference took place in February 2009.

REFERENCES

Buras, K. L. (2009). "We have to tell our story": Neo-Griots, racial resistance, and schooling in the other south. *Race Ethnicity and Education, 12 (4)*, 427–53.

Duncan-Andrade, J. (2006). Utilizing cariño in the development of research methodologies. In Kenchloe, J., Hayes, K., Rose, K., & Anderson, P. (Eds.), *The Praeger handbook of urban education* (pp. 451–60). Westport, CT: Greenwood Press.

Fisher, M. T. (2005a). Literocracy: Liberating language and creating possibilities. *English Education, 37(2)*, 92–95.

Fisher, M. T. (2005b). From the coffee house to the school house: The promise and potential of spoken poetry in school contexts. *English Education, 37(2)*, 115–31.

Fisher, M. T. (2007). *Writing in rhythm: Spoken word poetry in urban classrooms*. New York: Teachers College Press.

Fisher, M. T. (2009). *Black literate lives: Historical and contemporary perspectives*. New York: Routledge.

Freedman, S. W., Simons, E. R., Kalnin, J. S., Casereno, A., & the M-Class Teams. (1999). *Inside city schools: Investigating literacy in multicultural classrooms*. New York: Teachers College Press.

Freire, P. (1998). *Pedagogy of freedom: Ethics, democracy, and civil courage* (pp. 139–64). Lanham: MD: Rowman & Littlefield.

Freire, P., & Macedo, D. (1987). *Literacy: Reading the word and the world*. Westport, CT: Bergin & Garvey.

Ginwright, S., & Noguera, P. (Eds.). (2006). *Beyond resistance! Youth activism and community change*. New York: Routledge.

Greene, S. (Ed). (2008). *Literacy as a civil right: Reclaiming social justice in literacy teaching and learning*. New York: Peter Lang.

Gutierrez, K. (2008). Language and literacies as civil rights. In Greene, S. (Ed.), *Literacy as a civil right: Reclaiming social justice in literacy teaching and learning* (pp. 169–84). New York: Peter Lang.

Kinloch, V. (2007). "The white-ification of the hood": Power, politics, and youth performing narratives of community. *Language Arts, 85(1)*, 61–68.

Morrell, E. (2008). *Critical literacy and urban youth: Pedagogies of access, dissent, and liberation*. New York: Routledge.

Rogoff, B. (1994). Observing sociocultural activity on three planes: Participatory appropriation, guided participation, and apprenticeship. In Wertsch, J. V., d' Rio, P., & Alvarez, A. (Eds.), *Sociocultural studies of the mind*. Cambridge: Cambridge University Press.

15

The Principal Facts

New Directions for Teacher Education

Jeffrey M. R. Duncan-Andrade

> I may not change the world, but I will set the spark off in the mind that does.
>
> —Tupac Shakur

INTRODUCTION

As we consider new directions for teacher education, we would do well to heed the following excerpt from James Baldwin's essay, "Nobody knows my name":

> What it comes to, finally, is that the nation has spent a large part of its time and energy looking away from one of the principal facts of its life. This failure to look reality in the face diminishes a nation as it diminishes a person . . . Any honest examination of the national life proves how far we are from the standard of human freedom with which we began. The recovery of this standard demands of everyone who loves this country a hard look at [their self], for the greatest achievement must begin somewhere, and they always begin with the person. If we are not capable of this examination, we may yet become one of the most distinguished and monumental failures in the history of nations. (2004, p. 96)

Baldwin's essay offers a strategy for the nation to live up to its lofty ideals, one that demands the courage to confront the principal facts of our shortcomings and the creativity to correct them. Were we to engage such an endeavor, schools would need to play a significantly different role in our society, shifting from reinforcing the status quo to redefining it. Any such discussion of creating schools that prepare young people to take on the seemingly intractable forms of inequity facing our society will require us to seriously rethink our approach to teacher education.

The new direction for teacher education proposed in this chapter acknowledges the important progress we have made in our research on diversity in teacher education over the last several decades. The chapter pulls from important ideas such as critical pedagogy (Duncan-Andrade & Morrell, 2008; Freire, 1970), social

309

justice (Ayers, Quinn, & Stovall, 2009; Oakes & Lipton, 2002), multiculturalism (Banks, 2001; Darling-Hammond, French, & García-Lopez, 2002; Nieto, 1992), cultural relevance (Akom, 2003; Delpit, 1995; Howard, 2001; Ladson-Billings, 1994; Moll, Amanti, Neff, & Gonzalez, 1992), and caring (Noddings, 1992; Valenzuela, 1999) to make the argument that we must pay closer attention to the research on the social indicators of health if we are going to prepare educators to meet the challenges of working in urban and poor environments. To this end, this chapter examines some of the most cutting-edge, and also some of the most established, research in fields such as public health, community psychology, social epidemiology, and medical sociology to make the case that teacher education must engage with this research to improve our ability to address diversity in teacher education. This approach constitutes a rethinking of how we talk about research on diversity in our field. By extension, it shifts our approach in teacher education toward one that aims to develop educators better equipped to respond to the "socially toxic environments" (Garbarino, 1995) that emerge from racism, poverty, and other forms of oppression. Given the abysmal performance record of schools serving our nation's most impoverished youth, it seems high time that those of us working to prepare teachers for those schools heed Baldwin's advice and take a long look at ourselves. What we are doing is not working, and if we are honest, we will admit that it has not been working for some time—some might even argue it has never worked.

From this perspective, this chapter argues for teacher education to make a change of course. It begins by examining recent research breakthroughs in the aforementioned fields that are rarely discussed in teacher education. These fields have increasingly turned their attention to identifying and understanding the social indicators of health and well-being—for education, this is the idea that "place," the conditions in which our students live, must be understood for teachers to be effective (Adelman, 2008). This research reveals clearly identifiable social toxins that young people face in the broader society and these are the "principal facts" for teacher education to confront. Drawing from these analyses, this paper chapter presents a pedagogical framework for educators to respond, treating the classroom as a microecosystem committed to "radical healing" (Ginwright, 2009) and "critical hope" (Duncan-Andrade, 2009). The chapter concludes with a discussion of pragmatic steps to be taken by teacher education to develop teachers that can meet the challenge of delivering this type of pedagogy.

The chapter is split into three sections, addressing the following three core questions respectively: (1) What are the material conditions that effect urban youth before they even step foot in our classrooms? (2) What does it mean to develop educational environments that are relevant and responsive to these conditions? (3) What conditions are necessary in teacher recruitment, training, and support to develop educators that can create these types of classrooms? Answers to these questions pose a challenge that must be met with vigor in every school, but the approach to such efforts must be specific to the context where that work is taking place. This chapter will focus on key principles for teacher educators that aim to prepare teachers to work in urban schools. Many of these principles are applicable for educators working in contexts outside of urban poverty, but I would argue they must be adjusted for that context by similarly committed experts in those communities.

SECTION 1: THE PRINCIPAL FACTS

Youth living in areas that are entrenched in persistent cross-generational poverty—typically overrepresented by youth of color—where the rate of violence (physical and institutional) is high and legitimate living-wage employment options are low, frequently attend public schools that are underresourced and have disturbingly low completion rates. David Williams, of the Harvard School of Public Health, argues that these conditions result in the "accumulation of multiple negative stressors, and there are so many of them [that it's] as if someone is being hit from every single side. And, it's not only that they are dealing with a lot of stress, [it's that] they have few resources to cope" (Adelman, 2008). The accumulation of these negative social stressors can threaten hope for youth and inhibit academic performance (Finn, 1999; MacLeod, 1995; Valenzuela, 1999; Willis, 1977), social development (Adelman, 2008; Garbarino, 1995), and have serious long-term health implications (Syme, 2004; Wilson et al., 2008). The exposure to chronic stress associated with living in these types of "socially toxic environments" (Garbarino, 1995) is now thought of as one of the most, if not *the* most, significant contributor to poor health and academic difficulties for youth. By logical extension, teachers' ability to pedagogically respond to these "unnatural causes" (Adelman, 2008) of inequality will deeply impact educational outcomes for students.[1]

The implications of students' exposure to chronic stress for teaching and learning are profound. Consider Maslow's (1943) hierarchy of needs, which defined a person's primary human needs (food, clothing, shelter, safety) as prerequisites for pursuing needs higher up on the scale (such as education). When we connect the dots between Maslow's framework and the latest research on unequal access to the social indicators of health (Adelman, 2008), a serious dilemma is revealed for urban youth whose exposure to unremitting stressors leaves most (sometimes all) of their primary human needs under constant attack.

According to Williams (as quoted in Adelman, 2008), "in our society today, everybody experiences stress. In fact, the person who has no stress is the person who is dead." The body's stress response "calls forth the release of adrenaline and renocritical hormones" (such as cortizol) that have positive adaptive and protective functions for the body, including increased memory and muscle function (McEwen & Seeman, 1999, p. 2). Under normal conditions (see figure 15.1), the body's heightened response is maintained for an appropriate amount of time and then slowly recedes during a recovery period. However, urban youth of color are often faced with repeated or unremitting stressors such that their bodies are denied the necessary recovery period (see figures 15.2 and 15.3).

New research (Adelman, 2008; Geronimus et al., 2006) has reinforced findings that under these social conditions, the normally protective and adaptive function of the stress response is lost, as the overproduction of "stress mediators" is toxic to the body. According to medical and public health researchers, these conditions produce an "allostatic load" (McEwen & Seeman, 1999) that results in "weathering" (Geronimus et al., 2006). Allostatic load refers to the "cumulative negative effects, or the price the body pays for being forced to adapt to various psychosocial challenges and adverse environments" (McEwen & Seeman 1999, p. 3). Over time, this load stacks up and produces the effect of weathering on the body, which recent re-

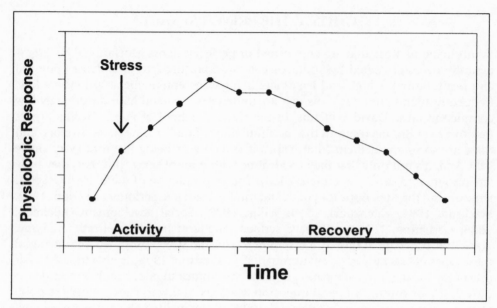

Figure 15.1   Normal stress response. *Source:* McEwen & Seeman, 1999, p. 6.

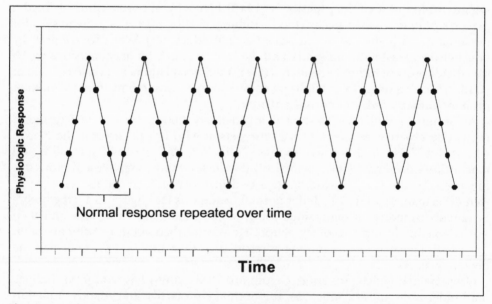

Figure 15.2   Repeated hits from "novel stressors." *Source:* McEwen & Seeman, 1999, p. 6.

search (Adelman, 2008) has shown to be a major cause of diseases plaguing modern society (heart disease, cancer, type II diabetes, and hypertension).

For young people whose lives are replete with social stressors over which they feel little control (racism, poverty, violence, environmental toxins, gentrification, police

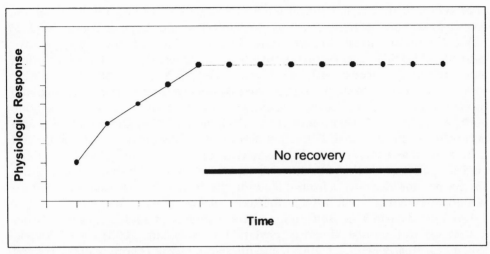

Figure 15.3 Prolonged response due to delayed shutdown. *Source:* McEwen & Seeman, 1999, p. 6.

brutality, xenophobia, language discrimination, lack of access to nutrition, substandard education, substandard housing, substandard health care) their systems are forced to work overtime all the time. This is where we can return to Baldwin for advice on how to confront these principal facts of our lives as educators of urban youth. The fact is, we live in a racist, xenophobic, classist, patriarchal, homophobic society, and this results in our students' overexposure to social toxins. Once we are willing to admit these facts, we can plot a course for teacher education that will prepare teachers to recognize and respond to the conditions that threaten their students' well-being and, by extension, their achievement.

According to Freire (1970, 1997), the project of developing pedagogy dedicated to freedom and hope for students living in these social conditions has two phases. The first of these requires educators to identify and analyze the oppressive conditions facing their students. The second phase consists of developing a pedagogy that uses education as a pathway to develop, implement, and evaluate action plans that respond to those conditions.

The remainder of this section provides a cross-disciplinary discussion of the research that should inform engagement with the first of these two phases. Drawing from recent research in the fields of health, psychology, and social science, I describe four major sources of traumatic stress in students' lives that educators must be prepared to address: (1) institutional violence; (2) physical violence; (3) root shock; and (4) wealth inequality. To address the second phase, section 2 of this chapter presents a framework for pedagogical response that combines solutions from health and educational researchers.

Institutional violence. When we think about the ways that violence impacts urban youth, it is important to understand that violence operates through institutional norms as well as through interpersonal physical conflict. The list of forms of institutional violence is long and cannot be covered comprehensively here. Instead, I will highlight some of the most pernicious and pervasive forms of institutional violence to which educators should be prepared to respond.

In efforts to understand institutional violence, "one should not look for the gross and obvious" (Pierce, 1974, as cited in Solórzano, Ceja, & Yosso, 2000, p. 60). Rather, institutional violence tends to take the shape of "micro-aggressions," defined as "subtle insults (verbal, nonverbal, and/or visual) . . . [that occur] often automatically or unconsciously" (Solórzano, Ceja, & Yosso, p. 60). In isolation, these events may seem harmless, but their cumulative impact is debilitating, and numerous studies identify these as leading causes of persistent social stress (Akom, 2008; Adelman, 2008; Geronimus et al., 2006; Pierce, 1995). Research in this area is conclusive. In each area that someone's identity falls outside of the dominant cultural norms of this country (white-heterosexual-male middle class or wealthy-English-speaking able bodied), they will experience forms of institutional violence. The further one's identity is from this norm, the greater the potential that their institutional experiences will result in the accumulation of social stressors.

Three specific terms are worth noting here as important additions to the teacher lexicon on institutional violence: poverty tax (Adelman, 2008), eco-apartheid (Akom, Cheung, & Bettinger, 2009), and infraracial racism (Akom, 2008). "Poverty tax" is a term describing the hidden tax poor communities pay as a result of limited options to virtually every essential service (banking, groceries, health care, housing, transportation).

Eco-apartheid describes the disproportionate stacking of ecologically toxic conditions in poor communities of color. Extending Jones's (2000) original definition, Akom and colleagues (2009) describe eco-apartheid as:

> the unequal distribution of environmental and educational benefits and burdens based on race, class, gender, ability, immigration status, as well as the inter-connections between these factors. Eco-apartheid is a more powerful definition than environmental racism or environmental inequality precisely because it captures inequalities beyond just race, (including space, place, and waste) while simultaneously, centering race and racism and their political implications.

Finally, infraracial racism describes "the actual mental, physical, epistemological, and ontological harm, beyond the visible end of the spectrum, that racism does to black people/people of color in everyday life; as well as accounting for how cumulative advantages are gained by whites and lighter skinned people" (Akom, 2008, p. 211).

Each of these ideas narrates institutional violence in a way that helps us understand it as a phenomenon that has a cumulative impact over time, threatening essential forms of institutional security: citizenship, jobs, schools, neighborhoods, hospitals, health care, and legal outcomes (Akom, 2008, p. 211).

Physical violence. The fact that witnessing or experiencing physical violence contributes to a person's traumatic stress load is common sense. What is not often clear to educators is the frequency and intensity with which this happens to urban youth and the medical research that suggests this may be one of the biggest inhibitors to academic success. Recent studies suggest that as many as one-third of children living in urban poverty show the symptoms of posttraumatic stress disorder (PTSD), a rate nearly twice that found in soldiers returning from Iraq (Tucker, 2007, p. 1). Complexifying the issue is the fact that while soldiers leave the battlefield, young people do not. This suggests that for youth that are repeatedly exposed to violent traumatic events, modifiers like "perpetual" or "persistent" would more accurately describe their experiences than the commonly used "post" traumatic stress.

Public health research has identified physical violence as one the biggest threats to well-being among urban youth. According to Robert Prentice, Senior Associate for Public Health Policy and Practice at the Public Health Institute (CA):

> the specter of community violence has completely transformed the way people live in certain neighborhoods. So, it's a public health issue not only for the prevention of early death through homicide, but for the ripple effects it has on the other things that contribute to people's poor health—the ability to go out, to go shopping, to live a normal life. (Adelman, 2008)

Jack Shonkoff, a pediatrician at Harvard's Center on the Developing Child, argues that studies indicate that exposure to violence "triggers physiological responses in a child and can actually be disruptive to the developing brain and immune system such that you are primed to be more vulnerable to physical and mental health problems throughout your life" (Adelman, 2008). These concerns are echoed by findings from Stanford University's Early Life Stress Research Program (Carrion et al., 2007; Kletter et al., 2009). The program's director, Victor Carrion, argues that PTSD "feeds on avoidance. The more you avoid it, the worse it gets" (Tucker, 2007). His belief that schools have an important role to play in healing this trauma in youth has led him to begin trainings with urban schools to help educators identify the symptoms of PTSD so they can get their students access to treatment. This level of training should be standard fare for all educators being prepared to work in urban schools.

Root shock. Root shock is a metaphor borrowed from botany to describe "the traumatic stress reaction to the destruction of all or part of one's emotional ecosystem" (Fullilove, 2004, p. 11). Plants suffer from root shock when they are relocated. The loss of familiar soil and its balanced nutrients is damaging to the root system. The term was coined by Fullilove to describe the impact of gentrification projects (often referred to as "urban renewal") that create neighborhood displacement. Other studies have shown the harmful impacts of being ripped from roots by analyzing groups that have suffered losses of language, land, or culture (Adelman, 2008; Milne, 2004, 2010). Educators should understand the impact of historical cultural genocide, ongoing cultural disenfranchisement, and recent thrusts of urban gentrification projects on their students so they can develop pedagogical responses *and* avoid contributing to those conditions.

Wealth inequality. Although I am convinced that wealth inequality is a form of structural violence, I have separated it out for the purposes of distinguishing it from traditional notions of poverty. According to health researchers, the unremitting stress of childhood poverty produces a toxic daily burden from not knowing whether you will have a roof over your head, food on the table, electricity, heat, or clean water (Adelman, 2008). Shonkoff (Adelman, 2008) describes this effect as a "pile up of risk: the cumulative burden of things that increase your chances of having problems, as opposed to the cumulative protection of having things in your life that increase the likelihood that you are going to have better outcomes."

However, poverty alone does not explain the fact that at the turn of the century, the World Health Organization (WHO, 2000) ranked the United States dead last in health outcomes among the world's industrialized nations, despite spending $2 trillion on health care per year (nearly half the health dollars spent globally) (Adelman, 2008). The position of the United States is one of the major surprises of the new rating system. "Basically, you die earlier and spend more time disabled if you're an American rather than a member of most other advanced countries" (p. 2), says Christopher Murray, director of WHO's Global Programme on Evidence for Health Policy. He goes on to identify a clear racialized pattern in these seemingly inexplicable results:

> In the United States, some groups, such as Native Americans, rural African Americans and the inner city poor, have extremely poor health, more characteristic of a poor developing country rather than a rich industrialized one. (p. 2)

Research suggests that these conditions of poverty are exacerbated when they occur in the face of great wealth. Despite wealth inequality reaching record lows in 1976, the United States is now "far and away the most unequal of the world's rich democracies" (Adelman, 2008) and getting worse. To be entrenched in intergenerational poverty in a country where wealth is flaunted and constantly visible, and the rhetoric of meritocracy reigns supreme, adds an additional layer of stress by intensifying awareness of one's poverty. Akom (2008) describes this as a by-product of "Ameritocracy," a largely U.S. phenomenon where the nation preserves the rhetoric of meritocracy, despite a reality that presents us with overwhelming evidence of stark inequality and unearned privilege. In this sense, wealth inequality is different than poverty, because wealth inequality accounts for the additional stress experienced by urban youth who, based on their proximity to financial centers, are constantly aware of all the things they do not have in their lives as result of their poverty.[2]

Don't Get It Twisted

Such an "honest examination of the national life" can be mind-numbing and paralyzing for some. To be sure, the task in front of us is monumental and growing—in short, we are facing a crisis state. Our willingness to be honest about the gravity of these conditions is the first step out of this hole, but we must not twist this examination to create justifications for poor teaching and rationales for student failure. Quite the contrary, an examination of the array of inequalities facing urban communities suggests that we should be all the more inspired as educators, knowing that we are working with young people that Tupac Shakur (1999) referred to as the "roses that grow from concrete." They are the ones that prove society's rule wrong by keeping the dream of a better society alive, growing in spite of the cold, uncaring, unnurturing environment of the concrete. According to Shakur, educators should not "ask why the rose that [grows] from concrete [has] damaged petals. On the contrary, we [should] all celebrate its tenacity. We [should] all love its will to reach the sun."

We must be critical of efforts that deny the tenacity and capacity of urban youth and families, aiming to distort discussions of unequal social conditions to support models of cultural deficiency (see D'Souza, 1995; Herrnstein & Murray, 1994; Ogbu & Davis, 2003; Payne, 2005; Thernstrom & Thernstrom, 2004). Any truthful adherence to Baldwin's challenge will: (1) be *honest* about the complicity of dominant institutional forces in the disproportionate displacement of inequality onto poor communities of color, (2) be *honest* about the incredible resilience and capacity of individuals and communities that persist despite these inequalities, and (3) be *honest* about the ways in which individuals from *all* communities can be complicit in the maintenance of an unequal social order.

Simply put, people that ascribe to deficit models, blaming students and families for unequal social conditions, should not be permitted to teach in urban communities. In my experience and research (Duncan-Andrade, 2007), these teachers are present in schools and teacher education programs, but they are rare. The majority of teachers and teacher education students that I come across feel overwhelmed by the challenges urban youth face in their lives and consider themselves ill-equipped to respond with a pedagogy that will develop hope in the face of such daunting hardships. They are liberal minded enough to avoid "blaming the victim," turning instead to blaming the "system" (the economy, the violence in society, the lack of social services). These teachers have a critique of social inequality but cannot manifest this critique in any kind of transformative pedagogical project (Solórzano & Delgado-Bernal, 2001). They "hope" for change in its most deferred forms: either a collective utopia of a future reformed society or, more often, the individual student's future ascension to the middle class (Duncan-Andrade, 2009).

Eventually, many students come to perceive a significant gap between their most pressing needs and the things being emphasized in the schooling these educators offer them (test scores, grades, college). When they figure out that the teacher is unwilling or unable to close this gap, their hope that school would be relevant in the context of their everyday lives is deferred. And, just as Martin Luther King Jr. foretold of justice, hope too long deferred is hope denied.

We will not end inequity tomorrow. But, we can develop more effective strategies for responding to it in classrooms, which may very well seed the generation that brings to fruition a more equitable society. According to S. Leonard Syme, Professor Emeritus at UC Berkeley's School of Public Health, recent research into the development of hope in urban youth shows the most promise for creating these kinds of classroom spaces (2004; Wilson et al., 2008). Syme describes hope as "sense of control of destiny," an actively present sense of agency to manage the immediate stressors in one's daily life; and he calls the research community's growing attention to strategies for cultivating hope in youth facing intense social stressors a "major breakthrough in thinking" (p. 3).

Other researchers have theorized hope as having two key components: (1) identifying pathways toward a desired goal, and (2) motivating oneself to begin and sustain goal-directed behavior (Snyder, 2002). Snyder calls this "hope theory," and numerous studies show hope to be one of the best indicators we have for predicting student resiliency, success, and well-being (Curry, Snyder, et al., 1997; Edwards, Ong, & Lopez, 2007; Snyder, Hoza, et al., 1997; Snyder, Sympson, et al., 2001).

One would be hard pressed to find a successful educator that would disagree with the importance of developing hope in the lives of young people as a principal pathway to raising engagement and achievement. Despite this acknowledgement

by our most accomplished teachers, it is my sense that very few teacher education programs explicitly discuss hope as a pedagogical concept. The insistence by
educational policy makers (see No Child Left Behind Act of 2001[3]) that educational practice guided by "scientifically based research" presents an opportunity
to change this trend if teacher education has the foresight to utilize recent breakthroughs in research on the social indicators of health (Adelman, 2008). The findings from this research are clear that closing the glaring disparities in the health-
wealth gradient is the major challenge of the twenty-first century and schools are
one of the most important institutions in proposed solutions to this dilemma. If
teacher education can capitalize on this trend, we can swing the pendulum toward
teacher preparation that emphasizes the principles that we know matter the most
for teaching and learning. The next section of this chapter uses a cross-disciplinary
research base to describe a classroom pedagogy framework that can be used to
guide this type of urban teacher preparation.

SECTION 2: CLASSROOMS AS MICROECOSYSTEMS: THE PAINFUL PATH IS THE HOPEFUL PATH[4]

In my previous work (Duncan-Andrade 2007, 2008, 2009), I have described
hope as a bedrock principle for developing effective urban classroom pedagogues. My most recent work extends this discussion by examining theory and
research on hope to develop an educator's framework on critical hope (Duncan-
Andrade, 2009). I make the argument that our nation expends a good deal of
effort trying to avoid what Carl Jung referred to as "legitimate suffering," or the
pain of the human experience. The stockpiling of resources in privileged portions
of the population so that they may be "immune" to suffering, while isolating the
unnatural causes of socially toxic environments onto others, creates undeserved
suffering while simultaneously delegitimizing it. In the face of these conditions,
critical hope boldly stands in solidarity with urban communities, sharing the
burden of their underserved suffering as a humanizing hope in our collective
capacity for healing.

An educator's critical hope also defies the dominant ideology of defense, entitle-
ment, and preservation of privileged bodies at the expense of the policing, disposal,
and dispossession of marginalized "others." We cannot treat our students as "other
people's children" (Delpit, 1995)—their pain *is* our pain. False hope would have
us believe in individualized notions of success and suffering, but critical hope demands that we reconnect to the collective by struggling alongside of one another,
sharing in the victories *and* the pain. This solidarity is the essential ingredient for
"radical healing" (Ginwright, 2009), and healing is an often overlooked factor for
raising hope and achievement in urban schools.

Moving From Coping to Hoping—Reflections on Seventeen Years in Urban Classrooms

There is an inescapable challenge before us as urban educators, and it is often misun-
derstood. Too many of us try to create classroom spaces that are safe from righteous

rage or, worse, we design plans to "weed out" children that display it. The question we should be grappling with is not how to manage students with these emotions but how we will help students channel them. The inevitable moments of despair and rage that urban youth feel are understandable and an "appropriate response to an absurd situation" (West, 2004, p. 295). West argues that youth

are saying they want to see a sermon, not hear one. They want an example. They want to be able to perceive in palpable concrete form how these channels will allow them to vent their rage constructively and make sure that it will have an impact. (296)

If the accumulation of stressors is like having a boot on your neck, then coping strategies are the strengthening of one's neck to handle the pressure of the boot. This is an important strategy, one in which many of our students are well practiced. However, as suggested by the expanding research on the social indicators of health, a lifetime of coping atrophies the body and can deteriorate into hopelessness (Adelman, 2008). To capitalize on students' coping resiliency without trapping them there means engaging the project of moving from coping to hoping. When teachers show the sermon with how we live our lives, rather than just preaching it as a way for our students to live theirs, students see living proof of the transition from just coping to hoping.

The way I take on this challenge is by thinking about my classroom as a micro-ecosystem. Ecologists would tell me that to build a healthy microecosystem, I would need to understand the principle of interdependency—in short, both pain and healing are transferable from person to person inside the classroom.

I'd like to use two metaphors here to help educators understand how I think about this idea of my classroom as a microecosystem. The first is an allegory presented by Camara Jones (2000) in the *American Journal of Public Health* to provide a common sense analysis of the health impacts of racism. Jones describes two flower boxes that sat outside her newly purchased home. One box was empty, and the other was filled with soil. Jones and her husband bought new potting soil and filled the empty box and, assuming the soil in the second box was fine, they equally distributed a seed packet into the boxes. The seeds in the new rich and fertile soil sprang up quickly. They grew tall and strong with vibrant colors. The seeds in the other box did not fare as well, most growing only to middling height or dying early. It turned out that the soil in that box was rocky and lacked essential nutrients for growth. Jones describes this as "vivid, real-life illustration of the importance of environment" (p. 1213). Our classrooms are the microecosystem of a flower box, and we can control the type of soil we offer our students in which to grow.

The second metaphor is borrowed from Tupac Shakur's reference to young people who emerge in defiance of socially toxic environments as the "roses that grow from concrete." Concrete is one of the worst imaginable surfaces to grow something in: devoid of essential nutrients and frequently contaminated by pollutants. As with the Jones's' second flower box, growth in such an environment is painful because all of the basic requirements for healthy development (sun, water, nutrient-rich soil) must be hard won. The ability to control, in a material way, the litany of social stressors that result from growing up in the concrete is nearly impossible for urban youth. As educators, then, we must find and create cracks in the concrete. The quality of our teaching, along with the resources and networks we connect our students to, are those cracks. They do not create an ideal environment for growth, but they afford some leakage of sunlight, water, and other resources that provide a justification to hope. Teacher education programs should make it plain that it takes courage to be a gardener in the concrete. It requires a willingness to embrace a painful path, the only one available when we move in solidarity with our students through those jagged cracks in the concrete.

Tupac's metaphor complicates the application of Jones's analogy to our classrooms because our students do not only live in our classrooms. They also live in the concrete, where they experience chronic exposure to social toxins. The pain that results from this is carried in the bodies of young people, and it crosses the threshold of our classrooms. There is no getting around this principal fact of teaching, and the fewer resources the young person has to cope with those social stressors, the more intense their pain will be. I have virtually no control over the array of social toxins that my students are exposed to in the metaecosystem of our society, but I can control how I respond to them in my classroom and this gives me, and my students, the audacity to hope (Wright, 1990).

This pain that our young people carry manifests in my classroom in a variety of ways. Sometimes it takes an obvious form like an outpouring of emotion, which might even be directed at me or another student. Usually, the signs are more subtle, manifesting in classic signs of depression (fatigue, sadness, self-deprecation). In these moments when a child can no longer contain the pain they feel, my response has the potential to add to it—or begin the healing process. We may think that if we send the "disobedient" child out that we have removed the pain from our system. It simply does not work that way. Rather, when we exclude a child we introduce another social stressor into the microecosystem of our class. We rationalize the exclusion by telling ourselves that we have pulled a weed from the garden, allowing for a healthier environment for the other children to grow. This ignores the fact that every student in our classroom is part of a delicate balance built on interdependency. Wayne Yang, an urban science and math teacher of more than seventeen years and one of the finest educators I have known in my career, put it this way: "All my students are indigenous to my classroom and therefore there are no weeds in my classroom." From this perspective, the decision to remove a child, rather than to heal them, is not only bad for the child, it is destructive to the social ecosystem of the classroom.[5]

I have been teaching long enough to know the enormity of this challenge, particularly because these moments almost always happen when I am convinced we are doing something of the utmost importance in the classroom. But, then I think to myself, how did I get to a place where I am prioritizing lesson plans over healing a child in pain? This not only ignores my most basic sensibilities as a teacher, it also disregards years of research documenting the importance of caring, self-esteem, trust, and hope as preconditions for positive educational outcomes (Delpit, 1995; Duncan-Andrade, 2007; Kohl, 1995; Ladson-Billings, 1994; Nieto, 1992; Noddings, 1992; Valenzuela, 1999).

As educators, we also tend to seriously underestimate the impact our response has on the other students in the class. They are watching us when we interact with their peers. When we become frustrated and punish youth who manifest symptoms of righteous rage or social misery, we give way to legitimate doubts among other students about our capacity to meet their needs if they are ever in pain.

At the end of the day, effective teaching depends most heavily on one thing— deep and caring relationships. Herb Kohl (1995) describes "willed not learning" as the phenomena by which students try *not* to learn from teachers who do not "authentically care" (Valenzuela, 1999) about them. The adage "students don't care what you know until they know that you care" is supported by numerous studies of effective educators (Akom, 2003; Delpit, 1995; Duncan-Andrade, 2007; Ladson-Billings, 1994; Valdes, 1996; Valenzuela, 1999). To provide the authentic care that students require from us as a precondition for learning from us, we must connect our indignation over all forms of oppression with a critical hope that we can act to change them.

False hope would have us believe this change will not cost us anything. This kind of false hope is mendacious; it never acknowledges pain. Critical hope stares down the painful path, and despite the overwhelming odds against us making it down that path to change, we make the journey, again and again. There is no other choice. Acceptance of this fact allows us to find the courage and the commitment to cajole our students to join us on that journey. This makes us better people as it makes us better teachers, and it models for our students that the painful path *is* the hopeful path.

TEACHER EDUCATION FOR WHAT?

A person's answer to the question of the course for urban teacher education will be framed by how they see the *purpose* of the teacher in communities that are, and almost always have been, denied quality schools. Freire (1997) argued that the primary purpose of education should be to inscribe hope in the lives of the students. He described hope as an "ontological need" (p. 8), especially in the lives and the pedagogy of educators working in communities where forms of social misery seem to have taken up permanent residence. Hope has always been a theme in the lives and movements of the poor and dispossessed in this country. During the civil rights era, as well as other key historical moments of social change, the nation's hope connected moral outrage to action aimed at resolving undeserved suffering. Educators cannot simply call an end to the conditions of inequality in our society. However, we can develop pedagogy that is responsive to those conditions *and* academically rigorous, such that we begin to rebuild the critical hope that has been worn down in these communities. Such educators deliver us from false hope by teaching in ways that connect the moral outrage of young people to actions that relieve the undeserved suffering in their communities. The spread of this kind of educational practice in our schools adds to the hopefulness because it develops transgenerational capacity for long-term, sustainable, critical hope in communities.

This chapter has been an effort to honestly confront the enormity of the challenge before us, honor the resilient commitment of urban youth and families to meet that challenge, and advance discussions about how urban educators can share that struggle. If teacher education is going to do its part, our field will need to make changes in three key areas: recruitment, curriculum and instruction, and mentoring.

Rethinking Recruitment

Teacher education continues to fail to recruit and attract students of color, particularly candidates from the racial groups that struggle the most in our schools (Native Americans, Latinos, African Americans, and Pacific Islanders). Oddly enough, this same challenge (especially for the latter three groups) does not seem to present itself to the athletic programs on our college and university campuses. Teacher education would do well to learn from sports programs that have successfully recruited from communities of color for decades. This will require us to get into schools, as early as elementary school, to start forming relationships with young people, families, and educators, encouraging and incentivizing their matriculation into teaching. The recent advents of programs such as Clemson University's Call Me Mister[6] or San Francisco State University's Urban Teacher Pipeline[7] are steps in the right direction.

In addition to more aggressive recruitment of teacher candidates that more closely represent the racial and social background of urban students, schools of education should also pay greater attention to screening applicants for a desire to work in urban schools. Not every program needs to commit to preparing teachers to work in urban schools, but for those that do, it should be their only focus. This allows for targeted recruitment of candidates with that specific purpose for joining the profession and more focused allocation of department resources to develop that purpose. Several programs around the country have made this exclusive commitment to urban education, the most prominent of which may be UCLA's Center X.[8]

Curriculum and Instruction

It is virtually impossible to teach someone how to teach in a university classroom. We should be more honest with our students about this fact. From the university classroom, we can give teacher candidates three things: (1) cutting-edge theory and research, (2) critical and supportive dialogue with peers and mentors, and (3) a preliminary credential. To do these most effectively, teacher educators should have firsthand knowledge of the conditions in the schools where they are sending students and the practices that work there. They should also be able to carry out that effective practice themselves. Urban teacher education would do well to change its faculty recruitment criteria by prioritizing context-specific, ongoing, field-based successful practice as a primary requisite for teaching future teachers. This would require collaborating with doctoral programs and local school districts to actively recruit faculty candidates with these qualifications.[9]

If we grow the number of teacher educators that are active in urban classrooms, the curriculum in teacher education will change just based on the faculty's practical experience in the field. However, we should also make an explicit effort to include relevant cutting-edge research that raises understanding of the conditions to which classroom pedagogy must respond. These can be coupled with forums with righteous scholars and practitioners from an array of other disciplines, including public health, medicine, child services, immigration advocacy, and law. Finally, the curriculum should involve regular discussions with community members, students, parents, and effective teachers that come from the schools and communities where these teachers in training are headed.

From Mentoring to Apprenticeship

Teacher education should move toward an apprenticeship model where future teachers apprentice under master pedagogues for multiple years. To accomplish this, each program will first need to develop rigorous criteria for selecting exceptional teachers to become mentors. This effort can proceed using a two-pronged approach that includes a community nomination model (see Ladson-Billings, 1994; Duncan-Andrade, 2007, for examples) and an urban teacher quality index.[10] If my previous advice is followed to recruit potential teachers earlier, then these relationships are more likely to take the form of actual apprenticeships, evolving over multiple years. The relationship would ideally begin in a student's first or second university year and continue throughout their career. The premiere program would allow teacher candidates and master teachers to select each other, forming a more natural and invested start to their relationship. The limited number of master pedagogues will require careful planning such that cohorts of apprentices progress through different levels with their master pedagogue (as we see in the trades, law, business, medicine, and the martial arts).

The upsides of an apprenticeship model are numerous. First, this will create a steady inflow of undergraduates (with cultural competency if the aforementioned recruitment strategy is followed) that are committed to multiple years of service in our highest-need schools. If instructional methods are inclusive of students' apprenticeship experiences, it creates the opportunity for applied discussions of course readings and fertile ground for meaningful problem-solving exercises and sharing of firsthand experiences with master pedagogues. Apprenticeship models are also more likely to create formal and lasting partnerships between teacher education programs and the strongest teachers in the area. Finally, this approach stands to cultivate meaningful, and likely lasting, mentorship relationships between early career and veteran teachers in the community—something sorely lacking that contributes to higher rates of early career teacher turnover (Quartz, Olsen, & Duncan-Andrade, 2008).

PARTING THOUGHTS

I'd like to end this chapter by quoting from three of my mentors, people whose lives changed the world *and* set off sparks in the minds of others to try to do the same. The first of these mentors is Malcolm X, whose concluding remarks at the prestigious Oxford Union Debate in 1964 I will quote at length here, because I cannot think of a more profound way to describe the challenge in front of our field:

> I believe that when a human being is exercising extremism in defense of liberty for human beings, it's no vice. And when one is moderate in pursuit of justice for human beings, he is a sinner. . . . I read once about a man named Shakespeare . . . He was in doubt about something. Whether it was nobler in the mind of man to suffer the slings and arrows of outrageous fortune—moderation. Or, to take up arms against a sea of troubles and by opposing, end them. I go for that. If you take up arms, you will end it. But, if you sit around and wait for the one who is in power to make up his mind that he should end it, you will be waiting a long time.
>
> In my opinion, the young generation of whites, blacks, browns . . . you are living in a time of extremism, a time of revolution, a time when there has got to be a change.

People in power have misused it and now there has to be a change and a better world has to be built and the only way it is going to be built is with extreme methods. I, for one, will join in with *anyone*. I do not care what color you are, as long as you want to change this miserable condition that exists on this earth.

For those considering moderation, the alternative to Malcolm's preference, I would remind you of the example set for us by Harriet Tubman, who said in response to detractors of the "extreme" methods for which she advocated by freeing herself and leading the underground railroad:

I had reasoned this out in my mind; there was one of two things I had a right to, liberty, or death; if I could not have one, I would have the other; for no man should take me alive; I should fight for my liberty as long as my strength lasted, and when the time came for me to go, the Lord would let them take me. (Clinton, 2004. p. 32)

This is undoubtedly what Gloria Anzaldúa (2003) meant when she wrote: "What we say and what we do ultimately comes back to us so let us own our responsibility, place it in our hands, and carry it with dignity and strength" (p. 87).

Our field can reach the level of commitment to human dignity put forth by these three individuals by preparing our next generation of educators to meet Camangian's (2009) expectation that we "teach like our lives depend on it." When we do, we will spark the minds that change the world.

NOTES

1. I am indebted to Nance Wilson, Len Syme, and Shawn Ginwright for their advice, patience, and wisdom in the development this chapter.

2. It should be noted that the Internet and mass media are quickly intensifying this effect for all poor youth, but these will probably never have the same impact as firsthand accounts of wealth inequality.

3. In June 2008, AERA convened a working group to provide a concrete definition of "scientifically based research." The group recently released its definition, which can be found at: http://www.aera.net/opportunities/?id=6790.

4. This section draws directly from my recently published article "Note to Educators: Hope Required When Growing Roses in Concrete" (Duncan-Andrade, 2009).

5. Yang (2009) has written on this idea of inclusionary practice, creating a framework for classroom discipline that critiques traditional models of school discipline as nothing more than exclusionary models of punishment that are bad for teachers and students.

6. http://www.clemson.edu/hehd/departments/education/research-service/callmemister/

7. http://cci.sfsu.edu/taxonomy/term/66

8. http://www.centerx.gseis.ucla.edu

9. It should be noted that there are a growing number of scholars in schools of education (many of whom are faculty of color) that continue to teach in urban schools while maintaining tenure, track faculty positions (see Stovall and Majors at University of Illinois Chicago, and Akom at San Francisco State University). Most of these faculty members do this work with little to no additional university support, an issue that should be taken up with universities that espouse a commitment to urban communities.

10. A collection of scholars from San Francisco State, Arizona State, and the University of Nebraska are currently working on developing an urban teacher quality index tool that

draws from leading research to identify the characteristics of effective urban teachers but is also context sensitive by responding to input from key local stakeholders (students, families, administrators, and educators).

REFERENCES

Akom, A. A. (2003). "Re-examining resistance as oppositional behavior: The Nation of Islam and the creation of a black achievement ideology." *Sociology of Education, 76(4),* 305–25.

Akom, A. A. (2008). Ameritocracy and infra-racial racism: Racializing social and cultural reproduction theory in the twenty-first century. *Race Ethnicity and Education, 11(3),* 205–30.

Akom, A. A., Cheung, R., & Bettinger, C. (2009). Eco-Apartheid or educational equity: Rethinking school desegregation through the lens of environmental justice. *Teachers College Record* (in press/forthcoming).

Anzaldúa, G. (2003). Speaking in tongues: A letter to third world women writers. In Browdy de Hernández, J. (Ed.), *Women writing resistance: Essays on Latin American and the Carribean.* New York: South End Press.

Ayers, W., Quinn, T., & Stovall, S. (Eds.). (2009). *The handbook of social justice in education.* New York: Routledge.

Baldwin, J. (2004). *Vintage Baldwin.* New York: Random House.

Banks, J. (2001). *An introduction to multicultural education.* Boston: Allyn & Bacon.

Carrion, V., Weems, C., & Reiss, A. (2007). Stress predicts brain changes in children: A pilot longitudinal study on youth stress, posttraumatic stress disorder, and the hippocampus. *Pediatrics, 119(3),* 509–16.

Clinton, C. (2004). *Harriet Tubman: The road to freedom.* New York: Back Bay Books.

Curry, L. A., Snyder, C. R., Cook, D. L., Ruby, B. C., & Rehm, M. (1997). The role of hope in student-athlete academic and sport achievement. *Journal of Personality and Social Psychology, 73,* 1257–67.

Darling-Hammond, L., French, J., & García-Lopez, S. (Eds.). (2002). *Learning to teach for social justice.* New York: Teachers College Press.

D'Souza, D. (1995). *The end of racism: Principles for a multiracial society.* New York: Free Press.

Duncan-Andrade, J. (2007, November–December). Gangstas, wankstas, and ridas: Defining, developing, and supporting effective teachers in urban schools. *International Journal of Qualitative Studies in Education, 20(6),* 617–38.

Duncan-Andrade, J. M. R. (2009). Note to educators: Hope required when growing roses in concrete. *Harvard Educational Review, 79(2),* 181–94.

Duncan-Andrade, J., & Morrell, E. (2008). *The art of critical pedagogy: Possibilities for moving from theory to practice in urban schools.* New York: Peter Lang.

Edwards, L., Ong, A., & Lopez, S. (2007). Hope measurement in Mexican American youth. *Journal of Behavioral Sciences, 29(2),* 225–41.

Freire, P. (1970). *Pedagogy of the oppressed.* New York: Continuum.

Freire, P. (1997). *Pedagogy of hope.* New York: Continuum.

Garbarino, J. (1995). *Raising children in a socially toxic environment.* San Francisco: Jossey-Bass.

Geronimus, A., Hicken, M., Keene, D., & Bound, J. (2006, May). "Weathering" and age patterns of allostatic load scores among Blacks and Whites in the United States. *American Journal of Public Health, 96(5),* 826–33.

Herrnstein, R., & Murray, C. (1994). *The bell curve.* New York: Free Press.

Howard, T. C. (2001). Telling their side of the story: African American students' perceptions of culturally relevant pedagogy. *Urban Review, 33(2),* 131–49.

Jones, C. (2000). Levels of racism: A theoretic framework and a gardener's tale. *American Journal of Public Health, 90,* 1212–15.

Kletter, H., Weems, C., & Carrion, V. (2009). Guilt and posttraumatic stress symptoms in child victims of interpersonal violence. *Journal of Clinical Child Psychology and Psychiatry, 14(1),* 71–83.

Ladson-Billings, G. (1994). *The dreamkeepers: Successful teachers of African American children.* San Francisco: Jossey-Bass.

Lazin, L. (Writer). (2003). *Tupac: Resurrection.* Atlanta, GA: Amaru Entertainment.

Maslow, A. H. (1943). A Theory of Human Motivation. *Psychological Review, 50(4),* 370–96.

Milne, A. (2004). "They didn't care about normal kids like me": Restructuring a school to fit the kids. Unpublished master's thesis. Massey University, Palmerston North, New Zealand.

Milne, A. (2010). Colouring in the White spaces: Developing cultural identity in mainstream schools. Unpublished doctoral thesis. University of Waikato, Hamilton, New Zealand.

Moll, L. C., Amanti, C., Neff, D., & Gonzalez, N. (1992). Funds of knowledge for teaching: Using a qualitative approach to connect homes and classrooms. *Theory into Practice, 31,* 132–41.

Nieto, S. (1992). *Affirming diversity: The sociopolitical context of multicultural education.* New York: Longman.

Noddings, N. (1992). *The challenge to care in schools: An alternative approach to education.* New York: Teachers College Press.

Oakes, J., & Lipton, M. (2002). *Teaching to change the world.* New York: McGraw Hill.

Ogbu, J., & Davis, A. (2003). *Black American students in an affluent suburb.* Mahwah, NJ: Lawrence Erlbaum Associates.

Payne, R. (2005). *A framework for understanding poverty.* Highlands, TX: Aha Process.

Pierce, C. 1995. Stress analogs of racism and sexism: Terrorism, torture, and disaster. In Willie, C., Rieker, P., Kramer, B., & Brown, B., (Eds.), *Mental health, racism, and sexism* (pp. 277–93). Pittsburgh: University of Pittsburgh Press.

Quartz, K. H., Olsen, B., & Duncan-Andrade, J. (2008). The fragility of urban teaching: A longitudinal study of career development and activism. In Peterman, F. (Ed.), *Partnering to prepare urban teachers: A call to activism.* New York: Peter Lang.

Snyder, C. R. (2002). Hope theory: Rainbows in the mind. *Psychological Inquiry, 13,* 249, 275.

Snyder, C. R., Hoza, B., Pelham, W. E., Rapoff, M., Ware, L., Danovsky, M., et al. (1997). The development and validation of the Children's Hope Scale. *Journal of Pediatric Psychology, 22,* 399–421.

Snyder, C. R., Sympson, S. C., Michael, S. T., & Cheavens, J. (2001). The optimism and hope constructs: Variants on a positive expectancy theme. In Chang, E. C. (Ed.), *Optimism and pessimism* (pp. 101–25). Washington, DC: American Psychological Association.

Solorzano, D., Ceja, M., and Yosso, T. (2000). Knocking at freedom's door: Race, equity, and Affirmative Action in U.S. higher education. *Journal of Negro Education, 69(1/2),* 60–73.

Thernstrom, A., and Thernstrom, S. (2004). *No excuses: Closing the racial gap in learning.* New York: Simon & Schuster.

Tucker, J. (2007, August 26). Children who survive urban warfare suffer from PTSD, too. *San Francisco Gate,* pp. 1–7.

Valdes, G. (1996). *Con respeto: Bridging the distances between culturally diverse families and schools.* New York: Teachers College Press.

West, C. (2004). The impossible will take a little while. In Rogat, P. (Ed.), *The impossible will take a little while: A citizen's guide to hope in a time of fear* (pp. 293–97). New York: Basic Books.

Williams, D. (2005). The health of U.S. racial and ethnic populations. *Journals of Gerontology, 60B* (Special Issue II), 53–62.

Wilson, N., Minkler, M., Dasho, S., Wallerstein, N., & Martin, A. (2008). Getting to social action: The youth empowerment strategies (YES!) project. *Health Promotion Practice, 9(4),* 395–403.

III

FUTURE TRENDS AND DIRECTIONS

An Agenda for the Work That Still Needs to be Done

Where should we be going and what is the nature of the work that still needs to be done in order to address the challenges that are currently facing our field?

Part III of this volume provides insights on future trends and directions for the research on diversity in teacher education as well as an agenda for the work that still needs to be done. As seasoned scholars in the field, the contributing authors in this section recognize the need to move beyond the practice of "navel gazing" and take the field to task for failing to address the most critical issues in teacher education head on. Authors in this section present a *call to action* in the research on diversity in teacher education—focusing attention on identifying *what works* and addressing the persisting issues that continue to elude and perplex both scholars and practitioners in our field. Addressing these challenges from their respective areas of specialization, these scholars provide explicit direction and a discourse for interrogating the status quo with the goal of providing a focused and socially conscious research agenda for the twenty-first century.

Zeichner begins the section by focusing specifically on two aspects of the research on diversity in teacher education: the need to connect individual studies to one another in programs of research within communities of researchers in ways that enable the accumulation of knowledge over time and the need to design research in ways that reflect the complexity of what is being studied. Cochran-Smith and Fries, Nieto and McDonough, Ladson Billings, and Ball and Tyson broaden the discussion on what we still need to know in order to move the field forward. These authors challenge educational researchers to continue to examine their research agendas and teacher education programs to ensure that today's and tomorrow's teachers can meet the complexities of teaching in diverse settings. They further underscore the need for using better methodologies in our research, examine continuing controversies from a critical lens, and challenge the profession to "place equity front and center" in every aspect of our work. Finally, these scholars outline a research agenda for diversity in teacher education that includes both theoretical and empirical components and focuses our attention toward preparing teachers for diversity in twenty-first century classrooms within the broader social, political, and socioeconomic context of a global society.

Complementing the contributions made by prior scholars who focus on issues of content and pedagogy in the teacher education profession, these authors move beyond earlier work to broaden the frame in which we consider what it means to "prepare teachers to teach in diverse classrooms" and to consider scholarship related to studying diversity in teacher education. In order to reverse the cycle of under-achievement experienced by many students of color, these authors seek to empower teacher educators and teachers alike with the research necessary to understand what the scholarship tells us and what we still need to know.

Ultimately, these contributing authors have helped us to rethink the articulation of issues of diversity in teacher education, interrogate some of the myths that under-pin ineffective curricular and pedagogical routines that take place in teacher education programs when it comes to diverse student populations, and help us to think clearly about the creation of equitable and inclusionary classrooms for *all* students in our increasingly diverse society.

16

Embracing Complexity and Community in Research on Multicultural Teacher Education

Kenneth Zeichner

This chapter builds on work that I have done over the past few years alone and with colleagues to examine the nature and quality of research in U.S. teacher education (e.g., Cochran-Smith & Zeichner, 2005; Zeichner, 2005; Zeichner & Conklin, 2008).[1] In these analyses, we have examined research on different issues in teacher education, have attempted to assess what is known and not known from existing studies, and have made recommendations for improving the quality and usefulness of the research. In this chapter, I will focus on two aspects of the research on multicultural teacher education: the need to connect individual studies to one another in programs of research within communities of researchers in ways that enable the accumulation of knowledge over time, and the need to design research in ways that reflect the complexity of what is being studied.

Existing reviews of research on diversity in teacher education in the United States (e.g., Cochran-Smith, Davis, & Fries, 2003; Hollins & Guzman, 2005; Ladson-Billings, 1995; Sleeter, 2009; Zeichner & Hoeft, 1996) have concluded that much of the research in this area consists of individual studies by teacher educators that are often about their own teaching. Regardless of whether the research has been focused on one's own teaching or that of other teacher educators, researchers in these individual studies often define terminology (e.g., culturally responsive teaching, cultural competence, prejudice reduction) in different ways and collect their data using instruments and protocols that they design themselves, often with no visible attention to issues of reliability and validity of the research instruments. It is very difficult to look across a set of studies on a given topic like the role of methods courses or field experiences in preparing culturally responsive teachers and draw any conclusions about what has been learned. Researchers most often have not explicitly built upon one another's work and shown how their research connects to and adds to the findings of related work (Zeichner, 2005).

The typical study reported in the literature involves an examination of some intervention with teacher candidates (e.g., an instructional method, a particular curriculum, a specific set of experiences in courses, schools, or communities) and an attempt to assess the impact of the intervention on teacher candidates. Impact is usually defined in terms of how the attitudes or beliefs of the candidates change over a course or field experience. Surveys, interviews, and the analysis of candidates' course assignments are typically used to assess their attitudes and beliefs. Teaching practice, if it is addressed at all, is usually understood through the self-reports of the candidates or the reports of their teacher educators. Rarely is there direct observation of candidate's teaching and any follow-up to examine how specific approaches impact teaching candidates beyond the course or field experience. Studies attempting to link interventions in teacher education programs to pupil learning are almost nonexistent.

Although the interventions under study are usually described as being embedded in particular courses or field experiences, there is very rarely attention in reports of research to describing the programs and the institutional and state policy contexts in which the interventions are situated. Furthermore, the interventions themselves are often very minimally described so that it is often not possible to discern the particular features of an intervention. Similarly, what teacher candidates bring to the course or field experience in relation to what is being studied is frequently not described. The consequence of the lack of attention to what candidates bring and to the specific features of interventions prevents researchers from being able to adequately explain their research findings.

For example, if a researcher examines the impact of a particular kind of community field experience on the sociocultural consciousness of teacher candidates[2] without examining the sociocultural consciousness that prospective teachers bring to the field experience, he or she is not in a position to assert that the field experience is responsible for the outcomes that emerge. To be in a position to attribute changes in teacher candidate attitudes, beliefs, or practices to particular experiences that are provided in a teacher education program, one must be able to distinguish selection effects and the impact of the personal characteristics of candidates from those of the teacher education experiences that are provided to them.

Also, to be able to understand the particular aspects of the intervention that are connected to the outcomes, one must describe the specific features of the experiences as they are enacted. For example, both the purposes and structures for community-based learning vary a great deal across teacher education programs (Zeichner & Melnick, 1996). Some community field experiences emphasize service learning and involve teacher candidates in activities such as tutoring students, while in other programs community field experiences emphasize candidates learning how to educate themselves about the funds of knowledge and social networks in the communities in which their students live. Some community field experiences are situated in community-based organizations, religious organizations, or schools, while others involve a broader immersion into communities and interactions with adults. The preparation for and debriefing of these experiences also varies within and across programs. Without a description of the purposes and features of these experiences as they are enacted in particular programs, it becomes very difficult to accumulate knowledge across individual studies.

The fragmented nature of many teacher education programs and differences in courses with the same labels even with the same teacher education institution often depending upon who is teaching them at a given time, underline the importance of researchers fully describing the situations they study in their reports of their research.

The typical conclusion that emerges in discussions of research on the preparation of teachers for diversity is that an intervention (type of course or field experience or instructional method) has a particular kind of impact on teacher candidates without attention to the specific features of intervention. It then gets reported in the literature that community field experiences, case studies, participatory action research, and so on have particular effects on the attitudes, beliefs, or practices of teacher candidates, and the implication is that this is true regardless of how the interventions are conceived or enacted and the contexts in which they exist. This uncritical glorification of concepts and practices has been a problem in teacher education research generally as concepts and practices such as reflection, professional development schools, and so on are offered as panaceas for accomplishing certain goals as if it does not matter how they are conceived and enacted.

I will begin with a discussion of the issue of doing research on issues of diversity in teacher education that reflects the complexity of the issues being studied and then move to a discussion of doing research that consciously builds on related research and contributes to the accumulation of knowledge about particular issues over time.

AN ECOLOGICAL APPROACH TO STUDYING DIVERSITY IN TEACHER EDUCATION

There are many different factors that need to be taken into account when attempting to understand the nature and impact of particular teacher education practices on the learning of teacher candidates, their teaching practices, and the learning of their pupils. Figure 16.1 illustrates some of the dimensions of the complex ecology that are related to how teacher education program practices impact candidate and pupil learning (also see Zeichner & Conklin, 2008). I will use the common practice of requiring teacher candidates to engage in student teaching, internship, or residency experiences in diverse schools where at least some of the students they will teach come from backgrounds very different from the candidate's background as the example of a teacher education practice as I discuss this ecology.

First, teacher candidates come to their teacher education programs with certain knowledge, skills, and dispositions, attitudes and beliefs, as well as demographic characteristics that will influence their actions in the classroom during and after their teacher education program. Some of the nondemographic entering characteristics may change during the course of the teacher education program, but others may not be substantially different at program completion from what they were when candidates entered. Researchers who want to understand the impact of a school-based field experience on particular aspects of teacher and pupil learning need to assess what teacher candidates bring to the experience. If the issue under study is how a ten-week student-teaching experience in one school has impacted the candidates' ability to enact teaching practices that are culturally responsive, then there needs to be some investigation of candidates' abilities to enact culturally responsive teaching when they begin the experience.

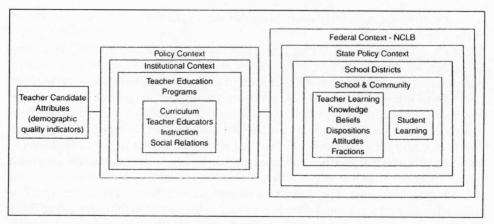

Figure 16.1 Studying the relationships between teacher education and teacher and student learning. *Note:* NCLB stands for No Child Left Behind legislation.

The school-based field experience is not a freestanding course that impacts teacher candidates independent of the social and institutional contexts in which it exists. In order to understand the nature of the field experience that is being studied, researchers need to situate it in a teacher education program, the institution(s) that house the program, and the state policy context in which the institution(s) exist. Goodlad's (1990) national study of teacher education in the United States showed significant diversity in the way in which teacher education is treated in different kinds of higher education institutions (e.g., liberal arts colleges versus research universities versus regional universities), and the landscape of teacher education today includes a number of providers of teacher education other than colleges and universities (Grossman & Loeb, 2008). Teacher education programs are significantly influenced by the institutional structures and cultures in which they exist.

Furthermore, although most teacher candidates work under the guidance of an experienced teacher before assuming full responsibility for students, an increasing number of teacher candidates in early-entry programs complete a significant portion of their "preservice" preparation while serving as teachers of record fully responsible for classroom(s) of students (Wilson & Tamir, 2008).

There are also significant variations in the state policy context for teacher education that influence teacher education programs. For example, several states, such as Texas, have placed severe limits on the number of professional education credits that can exist in preservice teacher education programs while other states, such as Wisconsin, have required an increasing number of preservice coursework in schools and departments of education (Darling-Hammond & Chung, 2009).

Within the context of the field experience itself, a number of things need to be taken into account. These include the relationship between the classroom(s) in which the candidate has been placed and the curriculum and instructional practices in the rest of the teacher education program. For example, to what degree does the kind of culturally responsive teaching encouraged in the program exist in the classroom and school, and what are the attitudes and beliefs of the cooperating teacher(s) and other staff in the school about the desirability of teaching in this way? What kind of mentoring and guidance are provided to candidates by school- and university-based supervisors with regard to culturally responsive teaching? To what extent are school-based teacher educators knowledgeable of the specific content of the various courses in which culturally responsive teaching is discussed? To what degree do campus-based teacher educators and field supervisors make connections between coursework and candidates' experiences in schools? To what extent are the campus-based teacher educators aware of what the other is doing in their courses and develop links across courses? All of these kinds of things matter in one's attempt to understand the nature and impact of any aspect of a teacher education program.

The nature of the classroom and school also needs to be considered. Enacting culturally responsive teaching is very different in a homogeneous classroom in which the linguistic, socioeconomic, ethnic, and racial backgrounds of the students are similar to one another versus a classroom with a lot of linguistic, ethnic, and racial diversity. Teacher candidates in most preservice teacher education programs are placed in situations where they work under the direct supervision of a fully licensed classroom teacher, and the classroom culture and organization established by the cooperating or mentor teacher prior to the candidates' arrival will greatly influence what the candidate is able to do in the classroom and how it will be experienced by students.

All of these factors and more need to be considered when examining the impact of a methods course or field experience on teacher candidates' capabilities to engage in teaching that is culturally responsive. Obviously, it is not possible for individual researchers to address all of the ecological aspects of a situation under investigation in any given study. Funding for research in teacher education in the United States has been and will probably continue to be in very short supply. Even when funding for research has been substantial in studies like those conducted by the National Center for Research on Teacher Education (e.g., Kennedy, 1998), the National Council for Teaching and America's Future (e.g., Darling-Hammond, 2006), and the New York City Pathways into Teaching Study (e.g., Boyd et al. 2008), it has still been a challenge to understand the ecological environment in which teacher education programs under study are situated. I will now discuss how the idea of programs of research in teacher education can help address the problem of complexity in the ecology of teacher education.

COMMUNITIES OF RESEARCHERS AND PROGRAMS OF RESEARCH

Although individual research studies cannot investigate all of the complex ecology that influences the nature and impact of every aspect of a teacher education program, this complexity can be addressed over time within coherent programs of research (Shulman, 2002). Programs of research involve researchers taking on the study of various aspects of a general problem or issue and adding new understandings with each new study.

For example, with regard to the broad field of research on multicultural teacher education, the growing body of studies that have been focused on the role of community-based field experiences on teacher and pupil learning is one of the many programs of research that has developed. Since at least the 1960s, researchers have studied a variety of approaches to both conceptualizing and implementing community-based field experiences and have examined how particular kinds of community-based learning for teacher candidates impacts their development as teachers (e.g., Lucas, 2007; McDonald et al., in press; Seidel, 2007; Sleeter, 2008).[3]

One consequence of researchers seeing themselves as part of a community of researchers working on a research program is that they consciously build upon the work of other researchers who are working on similar issues. This results in researchers attempting to situate their work in relation to the theoretical and methodological approaches in similar research, a discussion of how the purposes and design features of the field experiences differ across studies, and a discussion of how the findings add to the findings of others. Ideally, researchers within a research program move toward clear and more common definitions of the same terms and draw upon the research instruments and protocols of other researchers and adapt them for their own purposes. Research instruments and protocols from a number of the major studies of teacher education include attention to issues of diversity and are available for use by others (e.g., Kennedy, Ball, & McDiarmid, 1993).[4] I believe that if researchers who study issues related to diversity in teacher education would begin to develop greater commonality in the ways in which concepts were defined and examined, it would be far more possible than at present to build upon the research of others.

The sharing of research instruments and protocols and of the theoretical lenses used by researchers should include the ways in which teacher learning are conceptualized and examined and the ways in which teacher practice is assessed. There are a wide variety of ways in which the quality of the teaching performance of teacher candidates and program graduates has been assessed in research, including surveys of principals; supervisors and mentors; the use of classroom observation instruments with varying degrees of reliability and validity; self reports by teachers; ratings of teachers by pupils; and the examination of teacher performance assessments. Because there is very little overlap in the ways in which teacher performance has been assessed across studies, it is very difficult to look across a set of studies and determine what has been learned.

There are currently a number of different theoretical lenses that have been utilized in studying various aspects of teacher learning, including those related to issues of diversity (e.g., see Grossman, Smagorinsky, & Valencia, 2001; Hamerness et al. 2005; Smagorinsky, Cook, & Johnson, 2003). Frequently studies of the nature and impact of particular approaches to educating teachers for diversity examine how a course or experience in a program impacts teacher candidates, but the learning of the teachers is not situated in relation to a more general theory of teacher learning such as those based in activity theory or other theories of teacher development and change. The consequence of this failure to ground a piece of research in a broader theoretical perspective is the inability to adequately explain one's findings and difficulty in seeing how each individual study contributes to the development of a greater cumulative understanding of teacher learning in relation to issues of diversity.

CONCLUSION

In this chapter, I have attempted to draw on recent analyses of what has been learned about the nature and impact of different components of teacher education and different program models in the United States and discuss a few aspects of how I think research on issues of diversity in teacher education can be strengthened. The failure of much existing research to address the ecological complexity of teacher education and to explicitly build upon research on similar issues within research programs has resulted in a situation where research has not been able to disentangle the impact of courses and programs from the characteristics, perspectives, and capabilities that prospective teachers bring to teacher education and from the settings in which they teach. Because of the lack of common definitions of terms, and the lack of overlap in how researchers have gathered data about certain social or individual characteristics, it has been difficult to draw conclusions about what is known about a given issue across studies. Generally, there have been few efforts to assess the impact of a teacher education intervention beyond the course or experience, and there have been almost no attempts to connect particular approaches to educating teachers for diversity to pupil learning of any kind (Hollins & Guzman, 2005).

Despite these problems and the lack of a serious interest currently on the part of foundations and the government to invest in research in teacher education, including studies of diversity in teacher education, I am hopeful about our ability to work together as a research community to improve the quality of the research in our field. The key, I believe, will be in our willingness to share our resources such as our research instruments and protocols and to coordinate our research studies within and across institutions within the context of distinct programs of research.

Currently we are in a situation where investments are being made in models for the preparation of teachers in and outside of colleges and universities based on very little empirical evidence about the ability of these various models to prepare teachers who will be successful in our diverse public schools and stay there over time. As good as some of these models may seem on the surface, it is irresponsible to make policy with such little empirical support for an approach. One of the most recent examples of this problem is the teacher residency model that the Obama administration has invested substantial amounts of money to spread without the existence of any peer-reviewed studies that would support this investment (Sawchuck, 2009). As good as this model may sound on the surface, the stakes are very high for pupils in the teacher education models and approaches we choose to support with our limited resources. Those of us who do research in issues of diversity in teacher education need to own up to the problems that have existed in research in our field for a long time and work together to address them.

NOTES

1. This work has focused on empirical studies that have sought to examine the nature and impact of particular components of teacher education or pathways into teaching. There are other kinds of research in teacher education (e.g., conceptual, historical) that were not part of our analysis.

2. Villegas and Lucas (2002) define sociocultural consciousness as the degree to which an individual is aware that one's social location and positions of power and privilege influence the ways in which one interprets issues and events.

3. The connection between teachers and communities has been identified as an important aspect of successful teaching for many years (e.g., Cuban, 1969) and community-based field experiences have been a strategy used for more than sixty years for strengthening the connection between teachers and the communities in which their students live (Flowers et al. 1948).

4. Another example of available research instruments is the surveys from the Pathways into Teaching in New York City studies (teacherpolicyresearch.org).

REFERENCES

Boyd, D., Grossman, P., Hamerness, K., Lankford, R. H., Loeb, S., McDonald, M., Reininger, M., Ronfeldt, M., & Wyckoff, J. (2008). Surveying the landscape of teacher education in New York City: Constrained variation and the challenge of innovation. *Educational Evaluation and Policy Analysis, 30(4),* 319–43.

Cochran-Smith, & Zeichner, K. (Eds.) (2005). *Studying teacher education.* New York: Routledge.

Cochran-Smith, M., Davis, D., & Fries, M. K. (2003). Multicultural teacher education: Research, practice and policy. In Banks, J., & Banks, C. M. (Eds.), *Handbook of research on multicultural education.* San Francisco: Jossey-Bass.

Cuban, L. (1969). Teachers and community. *Harvard Educational Review, 39(2),* 253–72.

Darling-Hammond, L. (2006). *Powerful teacher education.* San Francisco: Jossey-Bass.

Darling-Hammond, L., & Wei Chung, R. (2009). Teacher preparation and teacher learning: A changing policy landscape. In Sykes, G., Schneider, B., & Plank, D. (Eds.), *Handbook of education policy research* (pp. 613–36). New York: Routledge.

Flowers, J. G., Patterson, A., Stratemeyer, F., & Lindsey, M. (1948). *School and community laboratory experiences in teacher education.* Oneonta, NY: American Association of Teachers Colleges.

Goodlad, J. (1990). *Teachers for our nation's schools.* San Francisco: Jossey-Bass.

Grossman, P., & Loeb, S. (2008). *Alternative certification: Mapping the new landscape of teacher education.* Cambridge, MA: Harvard Education Press.

Grossman, P., Smagorinsky, P., & Valencia, S. (2001). Appropriating tools for teaching English: A theoretical framework for learning to teach. *American Educational Research Journal, 108,* 1–29.

Hammerness, K., et al. (2005). How teachers learn and develop. In Darling-Hammond, L. & Bransford, J. (Eds.), *Preparing teachers for a changing world* (pp. 358–89). San Francisco: Jossey Bass.

Hammerness, K., Darling-Hammond, L., Grossman, P., Rust, F., & Shulman, L. (2005). Implementing curriculum renewal in teacher education: Managing organizational and polisy change. In L. Darling-Hammond & J. Bransford (Eds.). *Preparing teachers for a changing world* (pp. 442–79). San Francisco: Jossey-Bass.

Hollins, E., & Guzman, M. T. (2005). Research on preparing teachers for diverse populations. In Cochran-Smith, M., & Zeichner, K. (Eds.), *Studying teacher education.* (pp. 477–548). Mahwah, NJ: Lawrence Erlbaum Associates.

Kennedy, M. (1998). *Learning to teach writing: Does teacher education make a difference?* New York: Teachers College Press.

Kennedy, M., Ball, D., & McDiarmid, G. W. (1993). *A study package for examining and tracking changes in teacher knowledge.* East Lansing, MI: National Center for Research on Teacher Learning.

Ladson-Billings, G. (1995). Multicultural teacher education: Research, policy and practice. In Banks, J., & Banks, C. M. (Eds.), *Handbook of research on multicultural education* (pp. 747–61). New York: Macmillan.

Lucan, T. (2005). Fostering a commitment to social justice through service learning in a teacher education course. In N. Michell & D. L. Keiser (Eds.). *Teacher education for democracy and social justice* (pp. 167–88). New York: Routledge.

Lucas, T. (2007). Fostering a commitment to social justice through service learning in a teacher education course. In Michelli, N., & Keiser, D. L. (Eds.), *Teacher education for democracy and social justice* (pp. 167–88). New York: Routledge.

McDonald, M., Tyson, K., Brayko, K., Bowman, M., & Shimomura, F. (in press). Innovation and impact in teacher education: Community-based organizations as field placements for pre-service teachers. *Teachers College Record.*

McDonald, M., Tyson, K., Brayko, K., Bowman, M., Delport, J., & Shimomura, F. (in press). Innovation and impact in teacher education: Community based organizations as field placements for preservice teachers. *Teachers College Record.*

Sawchuck, S. (2009, October 14). Teacher residencies get federal funding to augment training. *Education Week*, p. 8.

Seidel, B. (2007). Working with communities to explore and personalize culturally relevant pedagogies. *Journal of Teacher Education, 58(2)*, 168–83.

Shulman, L. (2002). Truth and consequences: Inquiry and policy in research on teacher education. *Journal of Teacher Education, 53*, 248–53.

Sleeter, C. (2009). Preparing white teachers for diverse students. In Cochran-Smith, M., Feiman-Nemser, S., & McIntyre, D. J. (Eds.), *Handbook of research on teacher education* (3rd ed.), (pp. 559–82). New York: Routledge.

Smagorinsky, P., Cook, L. S., & Johnson, T. S. (2003). The twisting path of concept development in learning to teach. *Teachers College Record, 105(8)*, 1399–436.

Villegas, A. M., & Lucas, T. (2002). Preparing culturally responsive teachers. *Journal of Teacher Education, 53(1)*, 20–32.

Wilson, S., & Tamir, E. (2008). The evolving field of teacher education. In Cochran-Smith, M., Feiman-Nemser, S., and McIntyre, D. J. (Eds.), *Handbook of research on teacher education* (3rd ed.), (pp. 908–35). New York: Routledge.

Zeichner, K. (2005). A research agenda for teacher education. In Cochran-Smith, M., & Zeichner, K. (Eds.), *Studying teacher education* (pp. 737–60). New York: Routledge.

Zeichner, K. (2005). Studying teacher education programs: Enriching and enlarging the inquiry. In Conrad, C., & Serlin, R. (Eds.). *The Sage handbook on research in education* (pp. 79–94). Thousand Oaks, CA: Sage.

Zeichner, K., & Conklin, H. (2008). Programs as sites for teacher preparation. In Cochran-Smith, M., Feiman-Nemser, S., & McIntyre, D. J. (Eds.), *Handbook of research on teacher education* (3rd ed.), (pp. 269–89). New York: Routledge.

Zeichner, K., & Hoeft, K. (1996). Teacher socialization for cultural diversity. In Sikula, J., Buttery, T., & Guyton, E. (Eds.), *Handbook of research on teacher education.* (2nd ed.), (pp. 525–47). New York: Macmillan.

Zeichner, K., & Melnick, S. (1996). The role of community field experiences in preparing teachers for cultural diversity. In Zeichner, K., Melnick, S., & Gomez, M. L. (Eds.), *Currents of reform in pre-service teacher education* (pp. 176–98). New York: Teachers College Press.

17

Teacher Education for Diversity

Policy and Politics

Marilyn Cochran-Smith and Kim Fries

POLICY AS DISCOURSE AND THE POLICY WEB

Since the 1990s, a discourse approach to policy analysis has been used in a number of social science fields, including political science, sociology, linguistics, planning and environmental policy, nursing, and education (e.g., Bacchi, 2000; Ball, 2008; Cheek & Gibson, 1997; Fischer & Forester, 1993; Joshee, 2007; Luke, 2002; Popkewitz & Lindbled, 2000; Sharp & Richardson, 2001).[1] Generally speaking, those who take a discourse perspective reject the idea that policymaking is the result of the objective and nonbiased assessment by experts about how to obtain clear and fixed goals; they also reject the idea that policymaking is an apolitical, strictly rational process. Rather, from a discourse perspective, it is understood that goals themselves are competing and protean. Problems are constructed by multiple actors through language and deed rather than discovered "out there" through universal and scientific methods. From a discourse perspective, it is assumed that policymaking involves many agents at multiple levels, all of whom are engaged in constructing meaning (Bacchi, 2000). This means, as Deborah Stone (1997) suggests, that policy making is a struggle over ideas: "Each idea is an argument . . . in favor of different ways of seeing the world . . . There are multiple understandings of what appears to be a single concept, how these understandings are created, and how they are manipulated as part of political strategy" (p. 11).

Echoing the language of the "interpretive" and "linguistic" turns in twentieth-century philosophy, Fischer and Forester (1993) use the term *the argumentative turn* to emphasize that policymaking and policy analysis are argument-making processes. Like Stone, they emphasize that policy actors must first formulate and construct what "the problem" is before they can propose plausible solutions and recommendations. In political terms, they suggest:

> Policy and planning arguments are intimately involved with relations of power and the exercise of power, including the concerns of some and excluding others, distributing

responsibility as well as causality, imputing praise and blame as well as efficacy, and employing particular political strategies of problem framing and not others. (p. 7)

A central way groups, individuals, and agencies promote their definitions of problems and their conclusions about who is praise- and blameworthy is through metaphor and analogy, emblematic language, symbols, stories, and literary devices along with recurring arguments that forward their own positions and discredit others. All of these can be understood, discursively, as attempts by the proponents of particular positions to garner support—not simply for the solutions they favor but also for their ways of understanding the issues in the first place (Stone, 1997). Viewing policy through a discursive lens means that policy controversies are struggles over values, worldviews, and underlying ideologies as well as agreements and disagreements over strategies.

Consistent with a discourse perspective on policy, in our examination of teacher quality and teacher education policy, we use the notion of a "policy web," as developed by Reva Joshee and Laurie Johnson (Joshee, 2007, 2009; Joshee & Johnson, 2005), who in turn built on Hogwood and Gunn's (1990) suggestion that policies are made "by the interactions of many policy influentials operating in a power network" (cited in Joshee & Johnson, 2005, p. 55). Joshee and Johnson suggest that the web image conveys the idea that policies are developed formally on multiple levels and in multiple forms, like the rings of a web, and that policy discourses are both discrete and interconnected, like the cross-cutting, but nonlinear, threads of a web. The web image also suggests that specific policy issues must be interpreted within a larger network of related policies. As Joshee and Johnson point out, the notion of a policy web calls attention to the relationships between and among discourses, who the actors are, how new ideas and competing agendas enter into the larger arena, and which discourses are predominant, silenced, valorized, and marginalized.

THE TEACHER QUALITY-TEACHER EDUCATION POLICY WEB

Increasingly over the last decade, major policy discussions about the preparation and education of teachers have been part of, or intertwined with, larger discussions about teacher quality. In fact, at this juncture, it is impossible to understand teacher education policy without understanding larger teacher quality issues. Thus the focus of this analysis is what we refer to here as the "teacher quality-teacher education policy web." Like policy regarding other public services in the United States, policies related to teacher quality and teacher education are not developed and enacted at a single level by a single agency but at multiple levels and by many actors, including federal, state, and local agencies. In addition, teacher quality-teacher education policy is developed and enacted by professional organizations and national and regional accreditors, as well as by individual higher education institutions (or higher education systems) and by alternate providers of preservice preparation who make decisions related to recruitment, admissions, placement, curriculum, program completion, and graduation.

Sorting out the overlap and interplay of federal, state, local or institutional, and professional-organizational levels is central to understanding teacher quality-teacher education policy. Identifying the official actors and agencies at these levels is relatively straightforward, and their formal policy statements and related documents are generally easy to access. Just as important to understanding the teacher quality-teacher education policy web, however, are the multiple alliances, advocacy groups, research organizations, centers, consortiums, commissions, think tanks, and other individuals and groups, which are organized on an ad hoc or longer-term basis to inform and influence policy at various levels. These are somewhat more difficult to enumerate and sort out. To identify the major "influencers" in debates about teacher quality and teacher education, we drew on Swanson and Barlage's (2006) study of people, organizations, and reports that have influenced the educational policy landscape during the past decade; Wilson and Tamir's (2008) notion of the players in the "social field" of teacher education; and DeBray-Pelot and McGuinn's (2009) analysis of the new politics of post-NCLB education policy. Additionally, we noted what expert witnesses were called before congressional committees that had been assigned the task of considering, instituting, and reauthorizing federal policies related to teacher quality-teacher education and which groups or individuals were cited by policy makers and others to buttress their positions. The multiple levels, actors, and agencies involved in the teacher quality-teacher education policy web are represented in table 17.1.

To establish an initial list of pertinent documents, texts, and other items for this analysis of the teacher quality-teacher education policy web, we conducted a Boolean literature search using the terms *policy, teacher education,* and/or *teacher quality* in the United States between 2005 and 2009, using major databases (e.g., ERIC, Academic Search Premier, JSTOR, Books in Print). In keeping with a discourse perspective, however, we did not simply review official documents and formal policy statements. Rather, the web involves multiple channels and modes of discourse, many of which are texts or text analogues, but also including actions and instantiations. Thus we also located news articles, blogs, op ed pieces, podcasts, transcriptions of videotaped speeches, congressional testimony, public position statements, and reports. We also reviewed the websites and major documents of the actors and agencies identified in table 17.1. Here we performed a "quick read" of items and documents to determine which were pertinent to teacher quality-teacher education and whether and how diversity, social justice, equity, or multiculturalism were constructed. In addition, because we were specifically interested in diversity, we reviewed a selection of articles in major teacher education journals related to multicultural, diversity, and social justice–oriented teacher education policy and practice. We added to and subtracted from our list based on hand searches of major texts, references cited in other sources, and newly released reports and documents. Eventually we accumulated more than 225 policy statements, press releases, reports, research studies, news articles, positions statements, editorials, transcripts of debates, testimonies, speeches, and journal articles. Although space limitations prevent us from including the entire list, table 17.2 lists selected documents and texts for each of the actors and agencies in the policy web to provide a sense of the material we used.

To identify major discourses, we read and reread these materials, paying particular attention to the language, metaphors, and logic of the arguments that were constructed as well as noting which arguments were most prominent in which

Table 17.1   The Teacher Education/Teacher Quality Policy Web: Multiple Levels, Actors, and Agencies

FEDERAL LEVEL	STATE LEVEL	LOCAL/ INSTITUTIONAL LEVEL	PROFESSIONAL/ ORGANIZATIONAL LEVEL
Federal Mandates/ Programs ESEA (NCLB)– Title II–teacher quality mandates relative to teachers in the classroom; Title I and III–includes provisions relative to qualifications for teachers who work with students with limited English proficiency HEA–Title II– mandates relative to teacher preparation IDEA–includes mandates relative to special education	State DOE Regulations regarding teacher licensure, certification, program approval, teacher testing, alternate routes	Local school districts: policies and practices regarding recruitment, hiring, placement, retention, assessment of new teachers, including collective bargaining agreements	National/regional accreditors and licensing agencies: regulations and standards regarding regional/ national accreditation of universities and/or professional preparation programs or professional licensing of teachers (e.g., NCATE, TEAC, NBPTS, CHEA)
	Interstate New Teacher Assessment and Support Consortium (INTASC) accountability requirements relative to teacher preparation, licensing, and ongoing professional development	Higher education institutions: policies and practices related to teacher preparation program selection, preparation, assessment, completion of teacher candidates in college/university-recommending programs	Professional organizations: standards and positions regarding teacher preparation (e.g., AACTE) including in specific subject matter areas or school levels (e.g., NCTE, NCTM, TESOL, ACEI)
Funding opportunities: for example: ARRA (Stimulus funds) Race-to-the-Top Funds Innovation Funds Teacher Quality Grants			
Position statements regarding the administrations' education agenda, related to teacher education/teacher quality	State-advisory agencies: Provides technical support as well as policy analysis and research to state governors and state DOE (e.g., NGA, ECS)	Other teacher recruitment/ preparation providers: policies and practices related to selection, preparation, assessment, completion of teacher candidates in alternate recruitment and preparation routes	Teachers associations/ federations: positions related to collective bargaining agreements at local/state levels (e.g., AFT, NEA)
Congressional Committees on Education: U.S. Senate Committee on Health, Education, Labor, and Pensions and the U.S. House of Representative's Committee on Education and Labor			

INFLUENCERS:
Think tanks, agencies, commissions, professional organizations, centers, alliances, advocacy groups, research organizations, and consortiums that have as one of their major goals influencing or informing policymaking related to teacher quality/teacher education at any of the above levels, **and/or** individual analysts whose work is intended to influence one or more of these levels, for example: Achieve Inc., American Association of Colleges for Teacher Education, American Enterprise Institute, Center for American Progress, Center for Teaching Quality, Economic Policy Institute, Education Trust, Fordham Foundation, Hoover Institute, National Academy of Sciences, National Center on Education and the Economy, National Commission on Teaching and America's Future, National Comprehensive Center for Teacher Quality, National Council on Teaching Quality, Progressive Policy Institute, Public Agenda, Teach for America, and Urban Institute.

Table17.2   Selected/Sample Documents at Each Level

Federal	U.S. Department of Education Reports: • U.S. Department of Education. (2002). *Meeting the highly qualified teachers challenge: The Secretary's annual report on teacher quality.* Washington, DC: Author. • U.S. Department of Education. (2003). *Meeting the highly qualified teachers challenge: The Secretary's second annual report on teacher quality.* Washington, DC: Author. Hearings before the U.S. Senate and House of Representatives. For example: • ESEA Reauthorization: Boosting quality in the teaching profession. (2007). • Protecting America's Competitive Edge Act (S. 2198). *Finding, training, and keeping talented math and science teachers.* (2006). • Speeches by President Obama and Secretary of Education Duncan • Duncan, A. (2009c). Teacher preparation: Reforming the uncertain profession. (Remarks made at Teachers College, Columbia University, October 22). Retrieved from http://www.ed.gov • Obama, B. (2009). Taking on education: Speech before the Hispanic Chamber of Commerce. Retrieved from http://www.whitehouse.gov
State	• Feistritzer, E. (2005, September). *State policy trends for alternative routes to teacher certification: A moving target.* Paper presented at the Conference on Alternative Certification: A Forum for Highlighting Rigorous Research, Washington, DC. • National Council on Teacher Quality. (2008). *State teacher policy yearbook: What states can do to retain effective new teachers.* Washington, DC: Author. • National Governors Association, CCSSO, & Achieve. (2008). *Benchmarking for success: Ensuring U.S. students receive a world-class education.* Washington, DC: National Governors Association.
Local/ Institutional	• Cochran-Smith, M., & Zeichner, K. (Eds.). (2005). *Studying teacher education: The report of the AERA panel on research and teacher education.* Mahwah, NJ: Lawrence Erlbaum. • Darling-Hammond, L., & Bransford, J. (Eds.). (2005). *Preparing teachers for a changing world: What teachers should learn and be able to do.* San Francisco, CA: Jossey Bass. • Wineburg, M. (2006). Evidence in teacher preparation: Establishing a framework for accountability. *Journal of Teacher Education, 57*(1), 51–64.
Professional/ Organizational	• AACTE. (2009). AACTE's resolutions toward policy development. Washington, DC: Author. • NCATE. (2008, Fall). NCATE Professional Standards for the Accreditation of Teacher Preparation Programs. Retrieved from www.ncate.org
Influencers	• Ayers, W., Quinn, T., & Stovall, D. (Eds.). (2009). *Handbook of social justice in education.* Philadelphia: Taylor & Francis. • Darling-Hammond, L. (2007). The flat earth and education: How America's commitment to equity will determine our future. *Educational Researcher, 36*(6), 318–34. • Economic Policy Institute. (2008). A broader, bolder approach to education. Retrieved from http://www.boldapproach.org • Hess, R., & Petrilli, M. (2009). Wrong turn on school reform. *Policy Review,* 55–68. • National Academy of Education. (2009). *White Paper: Teacher quality and distribution.* Washington, DC: Author. • Peske, H., & Haycock, K. (2006). *Teaching inequality: How poor and minority students are shortchanged on teacher quality: A report and recommendations by the Education Trust* (No. ED 494820-ERIC Document). • Walsh, K., & Jacobs, S. (2007d). *Alternative certification isn't alternative.* Washington, DC: Thomas B. Fordham Institute.

debates and how the various ideas were connected to or disconnected from each other. We examined the strategies of persuasion and argumentation the various actors, agencies, and stakeholders used to support, extend, authorize, or undermine various constructions of the problems of teacher quality-teacher education. We also noted how the threads and cross-threads of the various discourses overlapped and intersected, but also sharply diverged.

TEACHER QUALITY AND TEACHER EDUCATION: MAJOR DISCOURSES IN THE POLICY WEB

Not surprisingly, our analysis of a large number of documents revealed that in the United States there is not a single policy discourse surrounding controversies related to teacher education and teacher quality but multiple discourses that sometimes compete, but are also sometimes combined, for political expediency. We also found that some discourses and actors were much more influential than others in current debates; indeed, some have gained substantially in influence over the last decade while others have been marginalized. We identified five major discourses, as follows:

- **Discourse #1:** The Teacher Quality Gap and Educational Inequality
- **Discourse #2:** Teacher Quality and the Market
- **Discourse #3:** Teacher Quality in a Globalized Society
- **Discourse #4:** Teacher Quality and Professional Teacher Education
- **Discourse #5:** Teacher Quality and Social Justice

The argumentative structure of each of these discourses is based on particular constructions of the problems and issues regarding teacher education and quality, which lead more or less logically to particular policy solutions and recommendations. These discourses reflect larger worldviews and ideologies related to difference and diversity. Below we discuss each of the five discourses, including its argumentation, the major actors and larger agendas with which each is associated, underlying ideologies and worldviews, commonalities and differences in relation to other discourses, and how each discourse constructs diversity.

Discourse #1: The Teacher Quality Gap and Educational Inequality

In policy debates about teacher quality and preparation, the "teacher quality gap" has emerged as a powerful idea that builds on the imagery, connotations, and language of the very familiar "achievement gap" between students of color, poor students, and immigrants and others whose first language is not English, on one hand, and their white, middle-class counterparts, on the other. The argumentation goes something like this: (1) Research has shown that teacher quality and effectiveness are among the most important factors in students' achievement. (2) Schools with large numbers of poor and minority students are most likely to have teachers who are inexperienced, assigned to teach in areas outside their fields, or otherwise not well qualified. (3) Thus the teacher quality gap exacerbates the achievement gap.

(4) Direct action targeted at school factors will redress the inequality of educational opportunities and outcomes, particularly distribution of quality teachers.

The *teacher quality gap* discourse uses the rhetoric and logic of civil rights to appeal to the long American struggle against injustice in the form of discrimination and exclusion of diverse and minority groups. The concept of "justice for all" emphasizes that all students have the right to equal educational opportunities and, presumably as a result, equal educational outcomes. This is dramatically different from simply claiming that all students must achieve to the same high standards despite unequal opportunities. Rather, from this perspective, opportunity is a key part of equality, and the argument is that opportunity to be taught by well-educated teachers has too long been denied to students in hard-to-staff and low-performing schools.

The *teacher quality gap* discourse is illustrated in a number of highly influential reports and analyses about teacher distribution patterns and states' responses to No Child Left Behind's (NCLB) equity requirements (e.g., Education Trust, 2008; National Comprehensive Center for Teacher Quality, 2009; Peske, Crawford, & Pick, 2006; Peske & Haycock, 2006; Walsh, 2007a, b, c), as this excerpt illustrates:

> Poor and minority children don't underachieve in school just because they often enter behind; but, also because the schools that are supposed to serve them actually *short-change* them in the one resource they most need to reach their potential—high-quality teachers. Research has shown that when it comes to the distribution of the best teachers, poor and minority students do not get their fair share. (Peske & Haycock, 2006, p. 1)

Reports like this one urge the federal government to demand that states comply with NCLB's teacher quality equity requirements and urge states to ensure poor and minority students' access to teacher quality.

From this perspective, blame for inequalities goes to federal, state, and school district policies—especially teacher-licensing policies and teachers' union contracts (Hess, Rotherham, & Walsh, 2004)—and other "anti-performance structures" that preserve a "failed system" (Education Equality Project, 2008, 2009). Here, university-based preparation programs are regarded as a barrier in part because they "make excuses" for teachers' failure to close achievement gaps, despite evidence that teachers and leaders can turn around failing schools (Haycock, 2004). The argument here is for replacing the status quo with "progress-based" rather than "inputs-based" approaches (Educational Equality Project, 2008, 2009), such as: alternate entry routes into teaching; new data systems tracking teachers' effectiveness, students' achievement scores, and teacher preparation; revised hiring and assignment practices; rewards connected to effectiveness; and improved mentoring.

The teacher quality gap discourse can be understood in relation to a larger, primarily Democratic agenda for educational equality, reflected in the Education Equality Project[2] (EEP) (2008, 2009), a coalition of civil rights activists and urban educators, including Al Sharpton, Joel Klein, Katie Haycock, and Michelle Rhee. Here school factors are identified as both the root cause of educational inequality and its fundamental solution. Underlying this agenda is a distributive notion of justice (Fraser & Honneth, 2003; North, 2006), wherein teacher quality and effective schools are regarded as goods and services that have hitherto been unequally distributed in society. It is important to note, however, that there is little acknowledgement in this discourse that educational inequality could be rooted in and sustained by larger societal inequalities (Fraser, 2003), manifested in unequal access to health care, early childhood services, housing and transportation, and job development initiatives (Anyon, 2005). There is also little recognition that curricula and educational goals might need to be revised in ways that reflect the values and knowledge traditions of marginalized groups. Rather, a premise of this discourse is that the remedy for inequality is ensuring that everybody has access to the existing system, more or less assuming that those who are currently "unequal" want to be like the dominant group and will be like that group once they have equal access to teacher quality and effective schools. Ultimately, this discourse represents an ideology of liberal democracy (Joshee, 2007) with an underlying view of diversity as something to be overcome or neutralized.

Discourse #2: Teacher Quality and the Market

A second discourse that is very visible in debates about teacher quality and teacher preparation is what we call "teacher quality and the market," which is part of larger agendas related to educational deregulation and privatization. The market discourse is almost always dressed in the verbal clothing of core American concepts—freedom, choice, individual opportunity, entrepreneurship, and competition. The structure of the argument is this: (1) Teachers are the most important determiners of school success. (2) However, the current system of recruiting, preparing, licensing, and rewarding teachers is not producing the teacher workforce the nation needs (including teachers for high-poverty schools), but its proponents resist reform to preserve their own self-interests. (3) This means the "invisible hand" of the market cannot operate naturally to correct a failing system. (4) A deregulated system based on tight accountability and loose methods is needed to attract new talent into teaching, reward teachers based on performance, and focus on individual student progress.

The market ideology has been prominent in debates about teacher quality and preparation for more than a decade (e.g., Hess, 2001; Thomas Fordham Foundation, 1999). Deborah Stone (1997) characterized the market model of society as a social system where individuals compete for scarce resources and pursue self-interest through exchange of mutually beneficial items. Here, problems requiring collective social action for the greater good are seen as exceptions. From this perspective, the ultimate freedom is the freedom of the market, and change is assumed to occur through informed self-interest, prompted by competition and the prospect of rewards and punishments.

The fundamental tenets and current implications of this ideology are well illustrated in Hess and Petrilli's (2009) analysis of the "wrong turn" of education reform after NCLB and their list of priorities for redirecting reform:

- A school accountability system that emphasizes individual student progress over time, without regard to race
- An accountability system that incentivizes schools to help all students make gains, including high achievers
- Dramatically fewer mandates and a lot more incentives
- Embrace competition, not just choice
- Promote "supply side" solutions and entrepreneurial problem solving (pp. 65–67)

Regarding teacher quality and preparation specifically, advocates of the market discourse champion teacher accountability based on students' achievement (Hess & Petrilli, 2009); elimination of teacher preparation or certification "barriers" at state and institutional levels (Feistritzer, 2005; Hess, 2009); "real" alternate routes into teaching (Walsh & Jacobs, 2007); pay for performance (Walsh, 2007c); and emphasis on individual student progress, not race- or other group-based averages (Hess & Petrilli, 2009).

In the market discourse, the rhetorical strategy is nearly always to construct the "status quo" as the cause of educational failure, thus making the case for new choices and alternatives. The argument for choice in terms of teacher preparation depends on the prior conclusion that the "status quo," which includes all college- and university-based preparation programs, plus state licensing and certification regulations, is inefficient and ineffective. The groundwork for this conclusion was laid in reports and analyses during the late 1990s and early 2000s wherein teacher education was consistently described as a "broken system" without empirical support, and alternate routes were consistently forwarded as the solution to the problem (e.g., U.S. Department of Education, 2002, 2003). This same conclusion is bolstered by current reports, such as those asserting that university-based teacher education fails to focus on the "science" of reading and math (Greenberg & Walsh, 2008; Walsh, Glaser, & Wilcox, 2006), issued by the National Center on Teacher Quality.

The market discourse on teacher quality is most remarkable not for the positions it holds about the education of diverse populations but for the positions it explicitly rejects. Hess and Petrilli (2009), for example, argue that the uneasy coalition between the Bush administration and civil rights groups and other liberals "led conservative education-reformers to embrace . . . an explicitly race-based conception of school accountability; a focus on closing achievement gaps to the exclusion of all other objectives; [and] a pie-in-the-sky, civil rights oriented approach" (p. 57). This analysis, which describes NCLB's approach to accountability as "obsess[ed] with race" (p. 64) highlights differences between the *teacher quality gap* discourse, described earlier, and the discourse of the market, even though these two agree on some of the solutions (i.e., alternate routes, test-based accountability) to the teacher quality problem and thus have often been on the same side of policy debates. However, the *teacher quality gap* discourse and the *market* discourse have enormous ideological differences as well. The rights-based *teacher quality gap* discourse, which is committed to public education, is intended to insure the common good in the form of equality of school-based opportunities and outcomes. In contrast, the market discourse focuses on the freedom of the market, which depends on everyone pursuing their informed self-interests, which presumably results in what is best for all. Implicit in the market discourse is a notion of educational progress as a matter of private self-interest rather than public trust and a firm belief in "letting the market decide" who gets access to well-qualified and effective teachers.

Discourse #3: Teacher Quality in a Globalized Society

The discourse we refer to here as "teacher quality in a globalized society" is prominent in many state and federal discussions about teacher quality and preparation and is sometimes present in the language and logic of national professional organizations, accreditors, and other teacher education leaders as well. Its argumentation is as follows: (1) We live in a globalized society with a knowledge economy that requires world-class academic standards and cognitively complex skills for problem solving and decision making. (2) The robustness of the U.S. economy depends on the country's educational achievements, which in turn depend on the quality of its teachers and schools. (3) However, both international comparisons and national assessments indicate that teachers are not teaching to world-class standards, nor producing the labor force needed, particularly in math and science. In fact, large segments of the school population are not prepared for work or higher education, which costs the country in individual productivity and economic growth. (4) Radical changes are needed, including rigorous new standards and assessments for all students, a more effective teaching force, and a drastically revamped system of continuous, evidence-based teacher education.

The steady repetition of this discourse since the release of *A Nation at Risk* (National Commission on Excellence in Education, 1983) has made the link between quality of teaching and educational achievement, on one hand, and the American values of progress, global leadership, and economic prosperity for all, on the other, appear inextricable and almost self-evident (e.g., Kennedy, 2006). This discourse is the foundation of the rationale for all of the education monies in the American Recovery and Reinvestment Act (2009) and is replete in statements by the Obama administration and others, as this excerpt from President Obama's 2009 speech to the U.S. Hispanic Chamber of Commerce illustrates:

> America will not remain true to its highest ideals—and America's place as a global economic leader will be put at risk—unless we . . . do a far better job than we've been doing of educating our sons and daughters; unless we give them the knowledge and skills they need in this new and changing world. For we know that economic progress and educational achievement have always gone hand in hand in America.

This discourse is also evident in the Common Core State Standards Initiative, a project to adopt rigorous common standards for high school students across the states, which is being developed by the National Governors Association; Achieve, Incorporated; ACT; the Council of Chief State School Officers; and the College Board.

The globalized society discourse uses a "story of decline" (Stone, 2002) to construct the educational status quo as both the cause of the current deterioration of the country's international standing and the major obstacle to change (e.g., National Center on Education and the Economy, 2006; Vagelos, 2006). From this perspective, business as usual at schools of education is constructed as part of the problem of national economic decline. Specific solutions to the problem of teacher quality and preparation include systematic state-level data systems that link student data with data about teacher effectiveness and teacher preparation, alternate pathways into teaching, teacher residency programs, training teachers to use data for continuous improvement, national assessment of teacher candidates, accreditation standards dependent on student outcomes, explicit teacher training in practices focused on cognitively complex material, quality supervision during clinical experiences, and state and institutional policy decisions about teacher preparation programs and pathways based on evidence about outcomes (e.g., Cochran-Smith & Zeichner, 2005; Duncan, 2009a, b, c; National Academy of Education, 2009; Wineburg,

2006). All of these proposed solutions to the teacher quality problem zero in on outcomes and accountability for students' learning.

Some of the new outcomes and accountability emphases of professional organizations such as NCATE and AACTE, which have long been regarded as "the establishment" of teacher education, reflect the global society discourse. These new directions may be understood, at least in part, as efforts to align with the powerful globalization discourse that dominates many policy debates and the now firmly entrenched system of accountability that is driving it. These efforts may also be seen as what Penny Earley (2000) once described as avoiding being "cast as a culprit" in the larger phenomenon of lower scores on international competitions.

Interestingly the global society discourse (Discourse #3) is often linked with the rights-based teacher quality gap discourse (Discourse #1) we described earlier in this chapter (e.g., Duncan, 2009a; McKinsey & Company, 2009; National Governors Association, the Council of Chief State School Officers, and Achieve, 2008). The braiding of these two discourses results in a message about diversity that goes something like this: Everybody in America, including the nation's increasingly diverse population, has the right to a good education and to high-quality teachers; these rights must be fulfilled so that everybody is prepared for work and is thus able to contribute to the nation's economic health. We would note, however, that what is missing from this discourse is emphasis on access to high-quality teachers as a human right and access to a rich and cognitively complex curriculum as an essential ingredient for deliberative participation in a democratic society. Like the teacher quality gap discourse, then, the ideology underlying the globalized discourse is consistent with capitalism and competitive individualism. This ideology has been critiqued for its focus on the economic need for an educated (and thus competitive) workforce, rather than a focus on education as a fundamental human right in a democratic society. Perkins (2004) uses the term *corporatocracy* to refer to the alignment of business, government, and financial interests and institutions and contrasts this with democracy. Building on Perkins, Sleeter (2009) argues that corporatocracy is aimed at consolidating global economic power for the benefit of the elite and is thus antithetical to the fundamental principles of democracy. We return to these ideas in the next two sections of this chapter.

Discourse #4: Teacher Quality and Professional Teacher Education

Like all of the discourses so far, the "teacher quality and professional teacher education" discourse is wrapped in language and concepts that resonate with certain aspects of the American tradition—excellence, high standards, equal opportunity, and the capacity of educated professionals with special expertise to solve problems in specific areas of social life. The basic argumentation is this: (1) Teachers are central to school success, with professional preparation and certification among the strongest correlates of teachers' effectiveness. (2) However, current policies and practices disproportionately place the least well-prepared teachers in high poverty and minority schools and classrooms. (3) This exacerbates achievement gaps and also contributes to the mediocre performance of American students on international comparisons. (4) Radical revisions in professional and governmental policies regarding preservice teacher preparation, certification, licensure, and ongoing development will redress inequalities, particularly distribution of teacher quality.

Although it has deeper roots, this professionalization discourse grew out of the 1980s education reform movement, especially the emphasis on standards, and was instantiated in the alliance of multiple professional organizations seeking a common system of performance-based standards for teacher preparation, licensing, and certification. As Linda Darling-Hammond's (2007) words illustrate, the current professionalization discourse has important similarities to both the rights-based discourse of the teacher quality gap (Discourse #1) and the standards- and accountability-based discourse of the globalized society (Discourse #3):

> To substantially improve both educational quality and equality in the United States, a comprehensive approach is needed. We cannot remain a first class power in the new world that is emerging around us simply by calling for higher achievement and establishing more tests. We need to ensure that resources for education are adequate in every community, that curriculum and assessment support the kind of transferable learning that matters in the 21st century, and that investments in teaching produce highly skillful teachers for all students. This policy agenda must be approached systemically at the federal, state and local levels if it is to succeed. (p. 329)

What the professionalization discourse (Discourse #4) shares with the teacher quality gap discourse (Discourse #1) is the position that students from diverse groups (e.g., children of poverty, minority students, special education students, English language learners) cannot achieve to high standards without reasonable opportunities in the first place, including access to teacher quality (Darling-Hammond, 2006). Although there are other differences, the major dividing line here is that at the heart of the professionalization discourse is a definition of teacher quality as professional preparation and full certification prior to the point when teachers become the teacher of record in K–12 schools (AACTE, 2009a; NCATE, 2008). In sharp contrast, Discourse #1 (teacher quality gap) constructs teacher preparation and certification as not only *not* essential to teacher quality, but in fact, barriers to it.

The professionalization discourse (Discourse #4) is also somewhat similar to the globalized society discourse (Discourse #3), in the sense that both emphasize rigorous standards, the need for a more effective teaching force, and accountability for student-learning outcomes (AACTE, 2009b). Again, however, the differences are important. As we noted earlier, the globalization discourse uses a narrative of national economic decline to cast "traditional" teacher education and certification as major culprits. In contrast, the professionalization discourse uses what Stone 2002) calls a "story of control," which suggests possibility and hope rather than despair to cast radically improved teacher preparation as part of the solution to the achievement gap and the problem of global competition (Cibulka, 2009). This means that all teachers need strong and coherent preparation (as well as ongoing professional development) centered on content knowledge, pedagogical and assessment skills, supervised fieldwork in schools organized for learning, and theoretical as well as practical understandings of the relationships among culture, language, and learning (AACTE, 2009b; Darling-Hammond & Bransford, 2005; NCATE, 2008). The professionalization discourse also shares certain ideas about diversity as an asset with Discourse #5 (social justice), which is discussed in the next section of this chapter.

It is important to note that the professionalization discourse has been marginalized in state and federal policy discussions in part because of its insistence that all teachers must be professionally prepared *prior to* their work with school students. This constructs alternate routes into teaching, which are now permitted in nearly all of the states, as a problem rather than a solution to the teacher quality problem and thus flies in the face of all three of the dominant policy discourses discussed so far, which champion alternate routes. More important, perhaps, the professional discourse has been marginalized because of its prevalence in AACTE and NCATE, professional organizations that are associated with teachers' unions, the National Education Association (NEA), and the American Federation of Teachers (AFT). Although for somewhat different reasons, in all three of the dominant state and federal discourses, teachers' unions have consistently been constructed as a root cause of the teacher quality problem because they presumably support the status quo, obstruct rather than support reform, and interfere with the functioning of the market. This creates a major tension for the profession since it is trying to be aligned with two discourses, one of which (globalization, Discourse #3) generally casts preservice teacher preparation as a culprit and the other (professionalization, Discourse #4) casts it as a solution.

Discourse #5: Teacher Quality and Social Justice

Discourse #5, "teacher quality and social justice," is based on the core American values of respect for differences, equal opportunities for all, and democratic participation. The argumentation goes like this: (1) There are significant disparities in the distribution of educational and other resources to minority and low-income students and their white, middle-class counterparts. (2) In addition, long-standing policies, practices, and systemic structures—including traditional curricula and school norms as well as health care and employment policies—privilege dominant groups and disadvantage others. (3) Inequities in distribution of resources and lack of recognition of the knowledge traditions of minority groups run counter to the democratic ideal, which depends on widespread participation and deliberation. (4) Thus, part of the job of teaching is enhancing students' learning and life chances by building on their resources and allying with others to challenge school and societal inequities.

This social justice discourse grows out of the civil rights movement and various critical perspectives on education and society writ large. A central premise is that diversity is an asset—not a deficit—in students' learning, a perspective that has been reflected in AACTE and NCATE positions since the 1970s.

Although the social justice discourse (Discourse #5) shares the goal of challenging inequality with Discourse #1 and Discourse #4, there are important differences. The argument of Discourse #1 (the teacher quality gap) is that poor and minority students—who enter school "behind" (Peske & Haycock, 2006)—need high-quality teachers to raise their achievement levels within the existing accountability system. From this perspective, diversity can be seen as a kind of deficit, existing curricula and teaching goals are fine as they are, and what is needed is to make sure everybody has access. From a social justice perspective, however, these premises have been critiqued as untenable because, as Joyce King (2006) suggests, "equal access to a faulty curriculum" (p. 337) does not constitute justice.

Both Discourse #4 (professionalization) and Discourse #5 (social justice) explicitly reject a deficit view of diversity. Rather, the assumption is that teachers must utilize students' cultural resources to build new knowledge and skills and broaden the curriculum (e.g., Lee & Ball, 2005). For example, teachers must incorporate the "funds of knowledge" of local communities and cultural groups (e.g., Moll, 2009), build on the language skills and identities of English learners (e.g., Brisk, 2007), and assume a "capacity framework" regarding students with special needs (El-Haj & Rubin, 2009). Discourses #4 and #5 both assume that a central purpose of schooling is the preparation of all students for democratic participation (e.g., Darling-Hammond & Bransford, 2005; Lucas & Grinberg, 2008; Sleeter, 2009; Villegas, 2008; Villegas & Davis, 2008).

Although the social justice discourse converges in many ways with the professionalization discourse, it is important to note that the former also critiques the latter's notion of a universal knowledge base and its inadequate acknowledgement of the structural and systemic forces that perpetuate inequities. This excerpt from Christine Sleeter (2009) captures some of the major ideas underlying the social justice discourse (Discourse #5):

> Social justice in teacher education can be conceptualized as comprising three strands: (1) supporting access for all students to high-quality, intellectually rich teaching that builds on their cultural and linguistic backgrounds, (2) preparing teachers to foster democratic engagement among young people, and (3) preparing teachers to advocate for children and youth by situating inequities within a systemic socio-political analysis. . . . Reflected in the first strand above, teachers must be able to teach such children effectively so they can master that [dominant] culture . . . the culture of power must also be critiqued, particularly for processes by which oppressive relationships are perpetuated. All of this must involve dialogue—the second strand—in which those who occupy positions of privilege—including teachers and teacher educators—learn to listen to, hear, and work with those who do not.

A similar social justice discourse is threaded throughout the teacher education section (Cochran-Smith et al., 2008; MacDonald & Zeichner, 2008; Richert, Donahue, & LaBoskey, 2008; Sleeter, 2008; Westheimer & Suurtamm, 2008) of the *Handbook of Social Justice in Education* (Ayres, Quinn, & Stovall, 2008).

One way to understand the social justice discourse is in terms of its contrast with the Education Equality Project, noted in our discussion of Discourse #1 (the teacher quality gap), and its consistency with the widely disseminated "Broader Bolder Agenda" (BBA) (2008), a primarily Democratic coalition of social scientists, educators, and policy experts, including Helen Ladd, Pedro Noguera, Tom Payzant, and Richard Rothstein. BBA explicitly rejects NCLB-type accountability frameworks because they work from false premises: that school factors are the major reason for low achievement and that policies targeting standards, testing, and teacher quality can overcome the impact of poverty. Instead, BBA argues that a bolder approach is needed that focuses on teacher quality and other school reforms at the same time it targets early childhood, antipoverty, and health programs and also incorporates new ideas about assessment and accountability.

The social justice discourse has been critiqued because of its supposed preoccupation with social goals, its failure to account for achievement, and its obsession with ideology (Cochran-Smith et al., 2009). As such, it is marginalized in many of the current major discussions about federal and state policy related to teacher quality and teacher education. Its marginalization is also related to the fundamental inconsistency between education where the bottom line is economic growth, on one hand, and education where the bottom line is democratic participation, on the other (Sleeter, 2009).

TEACHER QUALITY-TEACHER EDUCATION POLICY: LOOKING ACROSS THE DISCOURSES

Understanding policy as discourse is a powerful theoretical lens for unpacking co-existing, and often competing, ideas about "the problem" of teacher quality and teacher preparation in the United States as well as how diversity is constructed as part of that problem. As our analysis indicates, different discourses about teacher quality reflect different ideas, ideals, and worldviews at the same time that they differently assign blame and praise regarding the problem of teacher quality and thus advocate specific strategies and solutions. A discourse lens helps to explain why certain discourses are prominent while others are marginalized as well as how diverging discourses are at certain times sutured together but at other times explicitly split apart. This lens also helps to reveal how relations of power and the exercise of power influence policy within the complex and continuously changing education policy landscape. Below we offer several concluding points that cut across the discourses.

Teacher Quality as Common Ground

At this political and policy juncture, it is almost a truism to say that teacher quality is an essential ingredient—if not the central determining factor—in students' achievement and other school outcomes. Part of the reason this claim seems so thoroughly self-evident at this time is that it has been so consistently and frequently repeated over the last decade by policymakers, pundits, researchers, and policy influencers from all points across the political spectrum. This is evident in the countless reports and public statements that begin with some version of the mantra, "teachers matter."

All of the discourses we analyzed in this chapter assume that teachers—and teacher quality—matter, and all of them assume that there is some essential connection between teacher quality and students' learning and other school outcomes. However, although teacher quality may appear at first glance to be a single concept, it is not. In fact, across the five discourses are widely differing views about what is or is not encompassed in the term *teacher quality*. Implicit in Discourse #2 (teacher quality and the market), for example, is the (supposedly) simple and straightforward definition of teacher quality as the ability of teachers to raise students' test scores. In contrast, although Discourse #1 (the teacher quality gap) is also grounded in test-based evidence of students' learning, it specifically includes teachers' qualifications in its notion of teacher quality, especially teachers' subject matter knowledge credentials and their years of teaching experience, but at the same time, it specifically excludes teacher preparation in "traditional" college- or university-based programs from this definition. Again, in contrast, Discourse #4 (teacher quality and professional preparation) assumes a definition of teacher quality that encompasses an array of teachers' credentials, experiences, certification status, and classroom performance and, most important, preservice teacher preparation grounded in a rich and multidisciplinary professional knowledge base. These and other variations in meaning notwithstanding, the notion of teacher quality can appear to be—and sometimes is regarded as—common ground in policy debates and controversies, which makes certain powerful alliances possible. At other times, however, fundamental discrepancies in the meaning of the term *teacher quality* are immediately surfaced, which results in the polarization of various constituencies and makes coalitions unlikely.

Core American Values

One of the most interesting things our analysis reveals is that despite major differences in underlying ideologies and specific policy recommendations, each of the five discourses we identified comes to the policy table dressed in the verbal garments of core American values and traditions. This apparent paradox is possible because the nation has more than one set of core values—even though some of these are inconsistent with one another—and also because what are sometimes taken to be single concepts really have multiple meanings. For example, Discourse #3 (globalized society) is wrapped in the verbal clothing of world leadership, competition, economic prosperity for all, and the steady march of Western progress, all of which are dear to Americans. Along somewhat different (but simultaneously somewhat similar) lines, Discourse #2 (teacher quality and the market) appeals to freedom, choice, competition, individual progress, and free enterprise, ideals that are also at the forefront of national consciousness. On the other hand, Discourse #1 (the teacher quality gap), Discourse #4 (professional preparation), and Discourse #5 (social justice) all wear the verbal attire of equality, fairness, justice, and civil rights, although Discourse #1 completes the outfit with progress-based assessment measures, Discourse #4 completes it with professional performance, and Discourse #5 emphasizes societal redistribution and social recognition. Appealing to core American values is a rhetorical strategy as old as American politics itself; however, overlapping interests and the multiple meanings of values-oriented language sometimes make for unexpected coalitions and divisions around issues of teacher quality and preparation.

Constructions of Diversity

Within the five discourses, diversity is constructed in a variety of ways, some of which are made much more explicit than others. Discourse #1 (teacher quality gap), for example, focuses explicitly on inequalities in the distribution of teacher quality to schools with large numbers of poor students and students who are members of minority racial groups. Here, equality is defined as "same," and inequality is just the opposite. Thus it is assumed that the problem of inequality will be resolved when diverse school populations have the same access to teacher quality as do those in majority populations. As we noted earlier, from the perspective of this discourse, the emphasis is not on changing the existing arrangements of schooling (e.g., curriculum, instructional goals, and accountability measures) but rather making sure everybody has the same access to the existing arrangements.

In contrast, Discourse #2 (market) explicitly rejects race-based notions of accountability and eschews efforts to ensure equal opportunities based on racial and other kinds of diversity. Rather, Discourse #2 emphasizes individual progress, based on the assumption that societal change is the result of all persons pursuing their own informed self-interests. Discourse #3 (globalized society) defines the problem of diversity in terms of the increasing numbers of school students (especially those in poor and minority schools) who are not prepared for work or tertiary education, which threatens the economic prosperity of the nation and its ability to compete in the knowledge economy. Here diversity is constructed as a problem that interferes with the robustness of the economy in a globalized society. On the other hand, solving this problem by making sure that diverse groups have opportunities to be taught by high-quality teachers is regarded as not only good for individuals, who will then be able to find a place in today's work force, but also good for the economy.

As we have shown, both Discourse #4 (professionalization) and Discourse #5 (social justice) explicitly reject a view of diversity as deficit, which is implicit in the first three discourses. Instead, Discourses #4 and 5 construct diversity as an asset, emphasizing that quality teaching means building on all students' diverse cultural, linguistic, and experiential resources in order to develop new knowledge and skills and respond to specific learning needs. In addition, Discourse #5 directly challenges the current system, making it clear that better access to a faulty curriculum and universal application of a flawed sense of educational purpose to which many social groups have not contributed in the first place is not the solution to problems of inequality and inequity.

Coalitions, Culprits, and Relations of Power

It is important to note that although the five discourses we discuss in this chapter are identifiable and distinctive, they are not mutually exclusive. Rather, some strands of certain discourses are at times braided and intertwined with strands of other discourses that share some, but not all, of their assumptions and conclusions. The braiding (but also unbraiding) of these discourses reflect the recent history of education policy writ large, which features not only unprecedented policies but also the emergence of unprecedented formal and informal coalitions, compromises, and strategizing for expediency. For example, Discourse #2 (market) has tenets that are fundamentally inconsistent with the civil rights orientation of the teacher quality gap (Discourse #1). These differences notwithstanding, certain strands of these two discourses, especially praise for alternate routes into teaching and blame for university-based teacher education and teachers' union policies, have been braided together in many debates about teacher preparation with highly effective results. On the other hand, these two discourses may also be deliberately unbraided, as we indicated in our discussion of Discourse #2, if and when it becomes clear that their coalition requires too many compromises and concessions from one side and not enough political payoff.

Along somewhat different lines, it is important to note that the rights-based orientation of Discourse #1 (teacher quality gap) and the knowledge economy theme of Discourse #3 (globalized society) share a fundamental commitment to public education, while Discourse #2 (market), which is aligned with larger privatization agendas, does not. However, all three of these discourses emphasize accountability and outcomes, and all three reach some of the same conclusions about who is to blame (e.g., teachers unions, current state and federal policies) and who should be praised (e.g., alternate routes, state-level data systems linking students, teachers, and teacher education programs) when it comes to teacher quality. This helps explain why these discourses are prominent in federal- and state-level debates and why their proponents have sometimes formed powerful alliances.

As we noted in our discussions of some of the discourses, a powerful motivator for political maneuvering around policies related to teacher quality and preparation is avoiding being cast as a "culprit" in whatever framing of the problem has gained ground, or, on the flip side, casting one's opponent as a culprit in order to marginalize a viewpoint. This is part of what explains the gradual shift in teacher education's higher education and professional communities toward evidence- and accountability-based standards for accreditation and licensure. It also helps to explain the brouhaha surrounding President Obama's choice for Secretary of Education, in which Linda Darling-Hammond was cast as culprit and painted with the brush of "status quo/antireform," despite more than two decades of crusading for change in schools, licensing and certification standards, and teacher preparation programs.

Teacher Quality and Teacher Education: The Politics of Policy

Throughout this chapter, we have taken an explicitly political perspective on policy by assuming that ambiguity, conflict, and competing goals are inherent in human societies. From this perspective, politics is a "creative and valued feature of social existence" (Stone, 2002, p. x) and the "process by which citizens with varied interests and opinions can negotiate differences and clarify places where values conflict" (Westheimer, 2004, p. 231). This view of the politics of policy is quite different from the view that "being political" about teacher quality and teacher education is equated with being partisan and is, thus, a barrier to understanding or to improvement. From our perspective, it is impossible to debate teacher quality-teacher education policy while remaining politically neutral, value free, and outside of larger debates about educational goals and means.

To the contrary, our analysis in this chapter makes it clear that policy debates about teacher quality and preparation are inherently and unavoidably political. Whether made explicit or not, these debates involve the negotiation of conflicting values and ideologies about teaching and learning, curriculum, difference and diversity, accountability, individual and group progress, the role of schooling in democracies, the relationship between education and national economic health, and the persons and structures that govern and regulate all of these.

NOTES

1. There are multiple branches within this approach, and various analysts draw upon diverse theoretical traditions, some of which are related to controversies surrounding poststructuralism. These issues are not within the scope of the discussion here.

2. Arne Duncan was an original signatory of this agenda; he is also a signatory of the Broader, Bolder Agenda, which is discussed under Discourse #5. Duncan was the only signer of both of these documents.

REFERENCES

American Association of Colleges for Teacher Education. (2009a). AACTE's resolutions toward policy development. Retrieved Retrieved December 13, 2009 from http://www.aacte.org

American Association of Colleges for Teacher Education. (2009b). Teacher preparation makes a difference. Retrieved December 12, 2009 from http://www.aacte.org

American Recovery and Reinvestment Act. (2009). Retrieved December 13, 2009 from http://www.recovery.gov

Anyon, J. (2005). *Radical possibilities: Public policy, urban education, and a new social movement.* New York: Routledge.

Ayers, W., Quinn, T., & Stovall, D. (Eds.). (2008). *Handbook of social justice in education.* Philadelphia: Taylor & Francis.

Bacchi, C. (2000). Policy as discourse: What does it mean? Where does it get us? *Discourse: Studies in the Cultural Politics of Education, 21(1),* 45–57.

Ball, S. (2008). *The education debate: Policy and politics in the twenty-first century.* Bristol, England: Policy Press.

Brisk, M. (Ed.). (2007). *Language, culture, and community in teacher education.* Mahwah, NJ: Lawrence Erlbaum Publishers.

Cheek, J., & Gibson, T. (1997). Policy matters: Critical policy analysis and nursing. *Journal of Advanced Nursing, 25,* 668–72.

Cibulka, J. (2009). How institutions can leverage change as an opportunity for educator preparation. *NCATE: Quality Teaching, 19(1),* 1–3.

Cochran-Smith, M., Barnatt, J., Lahann, R., Shakman, K., & Terrell, D. (2008). Teacher education for social justice: Critiquing the critiques. In Ayers, W., Quinn, T., & Stovall, D. (Eds.), *Handbook of social justice in education* (pp. 625–39). Philadelphia: Taylor & Francis.

Cochran-Smith, M., Feiman-Nemser, S., McIntyre, J., & Demers, K. (Eds.). (2008). *Handbook of research on teacher education: Enduring questions in changing contexts* (3rd ed.). New York: Routledge, Taylor & Francis.

Cochran-Smith, M., & Fries, K. (2005). Researching teacher education in changing times: Politics and paradigms. In Cochran-Smith, M., & Zeichner, K. (Eds.), *Studying teacher education: The report of the AERA panel on research and teaching* (pp. 69–110). Mahwah, NJ: Lawrence Erlbaum Associates.

Cochran-Smith, M., & Zeichner, K. (Eds.). (2005). *Studying teacher education: The report of the AERA panel on research and teacher education.* Mahwah, NJ: Lawrence Erlbaum Associates.

Darling-Hammond, L. (2006). Constructing 21st-century teacher education. *Journal of Teacher Education, 57(3),* 300–314.

Darling-Hammond, L. (2007). The flat earth and education: How America's commitment to equity will determine our future. *Educational Researcher, 36(6),* 318–34.

Darling-Hammond, L., & Bransford, J. (Eds.). (2005). *Preparing teachers for a changing world: What teachers should learn and be able to do.* San Francisco: Jossey-Bass.

DeBray-Pelot, E., & McGuinn, P. (2009). The new politics of education: Analyzing the federal education policy landscape in the post-NCLB era. *Educational Policy, 23(1),* 15–42.

Duncan, A. (2009a, May 5). Press Release: Education secretary launches national discussion on education reform. Retrieved July 8, 2009 from http://www.ed.gov

Duncan, A. (2009b). Press Release: Remarks of Arne Duncan to the National Education Association—Partners in reform. Retrieved May 5, 2009 from http://www.ed.gov

Duncan, A. (2009c, October 22). Teacher preparation: Reforming the uncertain profession (Remarks made at Teachers College, Columbia University). Retrieved October 25, 2009 from http://www.ed.gov

Earley, P. (2000). Finding the culprit: Federal policy and teacher education. *Educational Policy, 14(1)*, 25–39.

Economic Policy Institute. (2008). A broader, bolder approach to education. Retrieved December 12, 2008 from http://www.boldapproach.org

Economic Policy Institute. (2009). School accountability: A broader, bolder approach to education. Retrieved December 13, 2009 from http://www.boldapproach.org

Education Equality Project. (2009). On improving teacher quality. Retrieved December 27, 2009 from http://www.educationqualityproject.org

Education Trust. (2008). *Core problems: Out-of-field teaching persists in key academic courses and high-poverty schools*. Washington, DC: Author.

El-Haj, T., & Rubin, B. (2009). Realizing the equity-minded aspirations of detracking and inclusion: Toward a capacity-oriented framework for teacher education. *Curriculum Inquiry, 39(3)*, 435–62.

ESEA reauthorization: Boosting quality in the teaching profession, 110th Congress: U.S. House of Representatives, 1st Sess. (2007).

Feistritzer, E. (2005, September). *State policy trends for alternative routes to teacher certification: A moving target*. Paper presented at the Conference on Alternative Certification: A Forum for Highlighting Rigorous Research, Washington, DC.

Fischer, F., & Forester, J. (Eds.). (1993). *The argumentative turn in policy analysis and planning*. Durham, NC: Duke University Press.

Fraser, N. (2003). Social justice in an age of identity politics: Redistribution, recognition and participation. In Fraser, N., & Honneth, A. (Eds.), *Redistribution or recognition: A political-philosophical debate* (pp. 7–109). London: Verso.

Fraser, N., & Honneth, A. (2003). *Redistribution or recognition? A political-philosophical exchange*. London: Verso.

Greenberg, J., & Walsh, K. (2008). *No common denominator: The preparation of elementary teachers in mathematics by America's education schools*. Washington, DC: National Council on Teacher Quality.

Gutman, A. (1999). *Democratic education*. Princeton, NJ: Princeton University Press.

Haycock, K. (2004). The real value of teachers: If good teachers matter, why don't we act like it? *Thinking K–16: A Publication of the Education Trust, 8(1)* 3–4.

Hess, F. (2001, November 27). Tear down this wall: The case for a radical overhaul of teacher certification. Retrieved May 21, 2003, from http://www.ppionline.org

Hess, F. (2009). Increasing access to effective teachers. *Statement before the House Education and Labor Committee on "Teacher Equity: Effective Teachers for All Children."* Retrieved March 15, 2010 from http://edlabor.house.gov/education

Hess, R., & Petrilli, M. (2009). Wrong turn on school reform. *Policy Review*, 55–68.

Hess, F., Rotherham, A., & Walsh, K. (2004). *A qualified teacher in every classroom: Appraising old answers and new ideas*. Cambridge, MA: Harvard Education Press.

Hogwood, B., & Gunn, L. (1990). *Policy analysis for the real world*. Toronto, Canada: Oxford University Press.

Joshee, R. (2007). Opportunities for social justice work: The Ontario diversity policy web. *Journal of Educational Administration and Foundations, 18(1/2)*, 171–99.

Joshee, R. (2009). Multicultural education policy in Canada: Competing ideologies, interconnected discourses. In Banks, J. (Ed.), *The Routledge international companion to multicultural education* (pp. 96–108). New York: Routledge.

Joshee, R., & Johnson, L. (2005). Multicultural education in the United States and Canada: The importance of national policies. In Bascia, N., Cumming, A., Datnow, A., Leithwood,

K., & Livingstone, D. (Eds.), *International handbook of educational policy* (pp. 53–74). New York: Springer.

Kennedy, M. (2006). Knowledge and vision in teaching. *Journal of Teacher Education, 57(3)*, 205–11.

King, J. (2006). If our objective is justice: Diaspora literacy, heritage knowledge, and the praxis of critical studying for human freedom. In Ball, A. (Ed.), *With more deliberate speed: Achieving equity and excellence in education—Realizing the full potential of Brown v. Board of Education* (pp. 337–57). Chicago: University of Chicago Press.

Lee, C., & Ball, A. (2005). "All that glitters ain't gold": CHAT as a design and analytic tool in literacy research. In Beach, R., & Green, J. (Eds.), *Multidisciplinary perspectives on literacy research*. Cresskill, NJ: Hampton Press.

Lucas, T., & Grinberg, J. (2008). Responding to the linguistic reality of mainstream classrooms: Preparing all teachers to teach English language learners. In Cochran-Smith, M., Feiman-Nemser, S., McIntyre, J., & Demers, K. (Eds.), *Handbook of research on teacher education: Enduring questions in changing contexts* (3rd ed.), (pp. 606–36). New York: Routledge, Taylor & Francis.

Luke, A. (2002). Beyond science and ideology critique: Developments in critical discourse analysis. *Annual Review of Applied Linguistics, 22*, 96–110.

McDonald, M., & Zeichner, K. (2008). Social justice teacher education. In Ayers, W., Quinn, T., & Stovall, D. (Eds.), *Handbook of social justice in education* (pp. 595–610). Philadelphia: Taylor & Francis.

McKinsey & Company. (2009). *The economic impact of the achievement gap in America's schools.* Author.

Moll, L. (2009). *6th Annual Brown Lecture: Mobilizing culture, language and education practices: Fulfilling the promises of Mendez and Brown.* Washington, DC: American Educational Research Association.

National Academy of Education. (2009). *White Paper: Teacher quality and distribution.* Washington, DC: Author.

National Center on Education and the Economy. (2006). *Tough choices or tough times: The report of the new commission on the skills of the American workforce (Executive Summary).* San Francisco: Jossey-Bass.

National Commission on Excellence in Education. (1983). *A nation at risk: The imperative for educational reform.* Washington, DC: U.S. Government Printing Office.

National Comprehensive Center on Teacher Quality. (2009). *Thinking systematically: Steps for states to improve equity in the distribution of teachers: An action-planning workbook to help guide regional comprehensive center and state education agency conversation to address the inequitable distribution of teachers.* Washington, DC: NCCTQ, ETS, Learning Points, and Vanderbilt University.

National Council for Accreditation of Teacher Education. (2008). NCATE professional standards for the accreditation of teacher preparation programs. (Fall). Retrieved February 20, 2009 from http://www.ncate.org

National Council on Teacher Quality. (2008). *State teacher policy yearbook: What states can do to retain effective new teachers.* Washington, DC: Author.

National Governors Association, Council of Chief State School Officers, & Achieve, I. (2008). *Benchmarking for success: Ensuring U.S. students receive a world-class education.* Washington, DC: National Governors Association.

North, C. (2006). More than words? Delving into the substantive meaning(s) of "social justice" in education. *Review of Educational Research, 76(4)*, 507–36.

Oakes, J., Lipton, M., & Renee, M. (2006, July). *Research as a tool for democratizing education policymaking.* Paper presented at the International Invitational Symposium on Figuring and Re-configuring Research, Policy and Practice for the Knowledge Society, Dublin, Ireland.

Obama, B. (2009). Taking on education: Speech before the Hispanic Chamber of Commerce. Retrieved March 25, 2009 from http://www.whitehouse.gov

Perkins, J. (2004). *Confessions of an economic hit man.* San Francisco: Berrett Koehler Publishers.

Peske, H., Crawford, C., & Pick, B. (2006). Missing the mark: An education trust analysis of teacher-equity plans. Retrieved January 7, 2007 from http://www.edtrust.org

Peske, H., & Haycock, K. (2006). *Teaching inequality: How poor and minority students are short-changed on teacher quality: A report and recommendations by the Education Trust.* (No. ED 494820–ERIC Document).

Popkewitz, T., & Lindblad, S. (2000). Educational governance and social inclusion and exclusion: Some conceptual difficulties and problematics in policy research. *Discourse: Studies in the Cultural Politics of Education, 21(1),* 5–44.

Protecting America's Competitive Edge Act (S. 2198): Finding, training, and keeping talented math and science teachers. (2006). Hearing before the United States Senate, 109th Congress, 2nd. Sess.

Richert, A., Donahue, R., & LaBoskey, V. (2008). Preparing white teachers to teach in a racist nation: What do they need to know and be able to do? In Ayers, W., Quinn, T., & Stovall, D. (Eds.), *Handbook of social justice in education* (pp. 640–53). Philadelphia: Taylor & Francis.

Sharp, L., & Richardson, T. (2001). Reflections on Foucauldian discourse analysis in planning and environmental research. *Journal of Environmental Policy and Planning, 3(3),* 193–210.

Sleeter, C. (2008). Teacher education, neoliberalism, and social justice. In Ayers, W., Quinn, T., & Stovall, D. (Eds.), *The handbook of social justice in education* (pp. 611–24). Philadelphia: Taylor & Francis.

Stone, D. (2002). *Policy paradox: The art of political decision making* (Second edition). New York: Norton.

Swanson, C., & Barlage, J. (2006). *Influence: A study of the factors shaping education policy.* Washington, DC: Editorial Projects in Education Research.

Thomas B. Fordham Foundation. (1999). The teachers we need and how to get more of them Retrieved January 1, 2008 from http://www.edexcellence.net

U.S. Department of Education. (2002). *Meeting the highly qualified teachers challenge: The Secretary's annual report on teacher quality.* Washington, DC: Author.

U.S. Department of Education. (2003). *Meeting the highly qualified teachers challenge: The Secretary's second annual report on teacher quality.* Washington, DC: Author.

Vagelos, R. (2006). Rising above the gathering storm: Energizing and employing America for a brighter economic future. U.S. Senate's Subcommittee on Education and Early Childhood Development. Retrieved March 10, 2008 from http://www7.nationalacademies.org

Villegas, A. (2008). Diversity and teacher education. In Cochran-Smith, M., Feiman-Nemser, S., McIntyre, J., & Demers, K. (Eds.), *Handbook of research on teacher education: Enduring questions in changing contexts* (3rd ed.), (pp. 551–58). New York: Routledge, Taylor & Francis.

Villegas, A., & Davis, D. (2008). Preparing teachers of color to confront racial/ethnic disparities in educational outcomes. In Cochran-Smith, M., Feiman-Nemser, S., McIntyre, J., & Demers, K. (Eds.), *Handbook of research on teacher education: Enduring questions in changing contexts* (3rd ed.), (pp. 583–605). New York: Routledge, Taylor & Francis.

Walsh, K. (2007a). If wishes were horses: The reality behind teacher quality findings. Retrieved December 28, 2007 from http://www.nctq.org

Walsh, K. (2007b). Steps that Congress can take to improve teacher quality without overstepping its bounds. Retrieved December 28, 2007 from http://www.nctq.org

Walsh, K. (2007c). Robbing Peter to pay Paul: The case against "comparability." Retrieved December 28, 2007 from http://www.nctq.org

Walsh, K., Glaser, D., & Wilcox, D. (2006). *What education schools aren't teaching about reading and what elementary teachers aren't learning.* Washington, DC: National Council on Teacher Quality.

Walsh, K., & Jacobs, S. (2007). *Alternative certification isn't alternative.* Washington, DC: Thomas B. Fordham Institute.

Westheimer, J. (2004). The politics of civic education. *Political Science and Politics, 37(2),* 231–34.

Westheimer, J., & Suurtamm, E. (2008). The politics of social justice meets practice: Teacher education and social change. In Ayers, W., Quinn, T., & Stovall, D. (Eds.), *Handbook of social justice in education* (pp. 589–94). Philadelphia: Taylor & Francis.

Wilson, S., & Tamir, E. (2008). The evolving field of teacher education: How understanding challenge(r)s might improve the preparation of teachers. In Cochran-Smith, M., Feiman-Nemser, S., McIntyre, J., & Demers, K. (Eds.), *Handbook of research on teacher education: Enduring questions in changing contexts* (3rd ed.), (pp. 908–36). New York: Routledge, Taylor & Francis.

Wineburg, M. (2006). Evidence in teacher preparation: Establishing a framework for accountability. *Journal of Teacher Education 57(1):* 51–64.

18

"Placing Equity Front and Center" Revisited

Sonia Nieto and Kathy McDonough

A critical question facing public education today is whether preservice teachers are adequately prepared to teach students of diverse backgrounds. Given the rapidly growing number of students of color and immigrants in U.S. public schools, as well as the lagging number of teachers and administrators of color, this is a question worth addressing for considerations of both policy and practice. Moreover, the abysmal gap between the achievement of white students and students of color, particularly African American, American Indian, and Latino/a students, is reason enough to analyze what can be done to prepare teachers and other educators to be successful with students of diverse backgrounds.

A number of years ago, Sonia Nieto wrote an article on just this question. The article, "Placing Equity Front and Center: Some Thoughts on Transforming Teacher Education for a New Century" (2000), was published in the inaugural issue of Marilyn Cochran-Smith's editorship of the *Journal of Teacher Education*. In the article, Nieto suggested how teacher education programs could "place equity front and center" by reconceptualizing teacher preparation curricula and pedagogy, making student field placements more congruent with the needs and realities of the future work of preservice teachers, and changing the nature of faculty work and rewards to prioritize collaborative relationships.

A decade has passed since that article was published, and in the intervening years many changes have taken place in our nation and our schools. As we will document following, the number of students of diverse backgrounds has continued to grow while the teaching profession has remained largely white and monolingual. In addition to shifting demographics, the political climate has also changed quite dramatically. The election of the nation's first African American president in 2008 is emblematic of this change, although it is still too early to tell the long-term impact of this administration's education policies.

Given the changes mentioned above, in this chapter coauthors Sonia Nieto and Kathy McDonough revisit the 2000 article to see where we are in terms of the issues addressed in it. We review some recent efforts to reconceptualize teacher preparation curriculum and pedagogy and promote collaborative relationships among faculty in teacher preparation programs. We also discuss whether such changes have been sufficient to prepare preservice teachers to work in diverse settings. We end with a cautionary note concerning recent efforts to create more equitable teacher preparation programs. We begin with a demographic description of the nation's schools and universities.

THE DEMOGRAPHICS OF SCHOOLS AND UNIVERSITIES: A BRIEF PORTRAIT

In order to effectively address the current status of the preparation of teachers for diverse classrooms, we first need to answer some key questions, namely:

- Who are the children in our public schools, and who is teaching them?
- What is the nature of the faculty in teacher education programs, and who are their students?

In this section, we review some salient demographics to help answer these questions.

The nation's K–12 student population has changed significantly in the past half century. In 1970, at the height of the public school enrollment of the "baby boom" generation, white students were 79 percent of total enrollment, followed by 14 percent African American, 6 percent Hispanic, and 1 percent Asian and Pacific Islander and other races. The situation is vastly different now: currently, only about 60 percent of students in U.S. public schools are white, while 18 percent are Hispanic, 16 percent are African American, and 4 percent are Asian and other races (U.S. Census, 2009). Although students of color traditionally have been most visible in urban schools, this is not the case today; now, every suburb and small town can expect to have students of diverse backgrounds, including immigrants and English learners. Moreover, the demographics of every region in the nation are changing as formerly monocultural or bicultural areas are becoming more multicultural. For instance, the South—a region where white and African American students were typically the majority—is now home to a vastly growing number of Hispanics. From 2000 to 2006, for example, Arkansas saw a 69.3 percent increase in Hispanics, while the increases in Georgia (60 percent), North and South Carolina (about 58 percent each), and Virginia (40 percent) were also dramatic. In addition to the Southeast, tremendous increases in the Latino/a population are evident in the Northwest and Midwest (Pew Hispanic Center, 2006).

While the demographics of the nation's student population have changed considerably, the same is not true of the teacher population. The National Education Association reports that the average U.S. teacher is a forty-three-year-old, married, white female (Pytel, 2006). More concretely, according to the Census Bureau (2004), just over 17 percent of teachers in the United States are people of color, an improvement over the statistics in the previous decade where about 10 percent were people of color. Of these, 8.4 percent were black, 5.5 percent were Hispanic, 2.9 percent were Asian, and 0.5 percent were American Indian and Alaska native. In spite of the growing number of teachers of color, however, the discrepancy in race and ethnicity between students and teachers is enormous.

Growth in the enrollment of students of color in higher education, according to the American Council on Education (2008), has been disappointing. Despite significant gains in college enrollment rates for young people of all races, progress was uneven and gaps widened. In its annual report on people of color in higher education, the American Council on Education (2008) found that while 61 percent of Asian Americans and 44 percent of whites aged eighteen to twenty-four were in college, the rate for African Americans was only 32 percent and it was even lower, 25 percent, for both Hispanics and American Indians. It is hard to know how many of these students were pursuing degrees in education, but the increased enrollment in business and computer science probably means that fewer students of color are pursuing education, which had been a traditionally chosen field for many.

The growth in the number and percentage of faculty of color in institutions of higher education has also been disappointing. In the same report cited above, the American Council on Education (2008) reported that although progress has been made, whites are still the overwhelming majority of faculty throughout the nation. Specifically, people of color were just 16 percent of full-time faculty.

What are the implications of these numbers? For one, given the tremendous racial and ethnic imbalance between students in K–12 schools and their teachers, it is evident that most teachers will need appropriate education and training to work effectively with students who are different from them. In addition, because those who prepare teachers—faculty at colleges and universities and professional developers in school systems—generally do not reflect the backgrounds of most K–12 students, it is safe to say that they too are many times not prepared to teach preservice and practicing teachers about the diversity they will face in the classroom. This means that serious recruitment of candidates of diverse backgrounds for both preservice teachers and university faculty needs to be undertaken. In addition, teacher preparation curriculum and pedagogy need to be reconceptualized, a topic to which we now turn.

Reconceptualizing Teacher Preparation Curriculum and Pedagogy

The demographics reviewed above, as well as the level of discomfort and the lack of knowledge and preparation of many teachers concerning diversity, means that reconceptualizing teacher education today is an even more urgent challenge than it was in 2000. It is now commonplace for schools and colleges of education to name social justice as an integrative thread in their programs and for some professors to research preservice teacher attitudes and beliefs. In addition, a growing number of teacher preparation programs are experimenting with new models of faculty collaboration to promote a focus on equity. In spite of these advances, consistent and satisfactory achievement of typically marginalized K–12 students has yet to be realized. In addition, there is little research evidence that preservice teachers maintain revised beliefs about diversity and social justice beyond their teacher education experience.

Curriculum and pedagogy that focus on moving preservice teachers toward critical consciousness may help them to understand the complexities of identity and to confront racism and other inequalities. In what follows, we look at promising practices within the past ten years that demonstrate how teacher education programs are preparing preservice educators to teach for social justice and then discuss if these efforts are sufficient. We begin with the construct of critical consciousness to frame the next section.

DEVELOPING CRITICAL CONSCIOUSNESS

If teaching is always political, then teaching for social justice requires educators to be able to critique every aspect of their craft. Critical consciousness offers a framework for understanding what is involved in this type of critique. Also referred to as *political clarity* (Bartolomé, 2004) and *critical social consciousness* (Grant & Agosto, 2008), critical consciousness involves critiquing relations of power, questioning one's assumptions about reality, and reflecting on the complexities of multiple identities (Freire, 1973; Nieto et al., 2008). Research and pedagogy related to critical consciousness explore the intersection of power in relation to identities and the function of schools. It also positions preservice teachers to be change agents. Educators who demonstrate critical consciousness have the ability and the will to theorize and politicize their experiences. Knowing they are located in a variety of social spaces, critically conscious educators question their own positions (Gatimu, 2009).

Critically conscious projects build on what we know about preservice teachers. Previous literature demonstrated that many white teachers enter preservice programs with negative perceptions of students of color (Terrill & Mark, 2000). Christine Sleeter (2000) noted that many white teachers avoid discussing issues of race by "minimiz[ing] the extent and impact of racial discrimination" (p. 123) and "refus[ing] to examine race openly" (p. 125). Similarly, in her study of white, middle-class, preservice teachers, Alice McIntyre (1997) found that they wanted to be seen as raceless individuals, particularly in the context of working with children of color. McIntyre, as well as Sherry Marx (2006), identified patterns of "white talk," or ways in which white teachers use language to marginalize people of color and avoid discussions of race. In these cases, racial consciousness is either ignored or denied. In an earlier study, Sleeter (1995) found that a number of white teachers uncritically accepted the belief that U.S. society provides equal opportunities for everyone and, therefore, an analysis of racism was unnecessary.

The scholarship on white teachers highlights the experiences, beliefs, and assumptions that many preservice teachers bring to both college and K–12 classrooms. It is essential to draw from and build on this literature. In the studies that follow, teacher educators asked preservice teachers to explore ideology, engage in critical inquiry, and question their assumptions through critical reflection.

The exploration of ideology is a key construct in the work of Lilia Bartolomé (2004, 2008), who employs critical pedagogy in her work with preservice teachers to help them develop political and ideological clarity. Acknowledging teaching as a highly political process, Bartolomé states that teachers must have an understanding of how their ideological orientation shapes their views of students and influences their teaching. She reminds us that teacher beliefs are not purely individually motivated dispositions but also are "ideologies" (p. 100). As a result, teacher education must include the explicit study of ideology in relation to coursework, field placement, and service-learning opportunities. Like Michael Vavrus (2002), Bartolomé believes that naming ideology in relation to oppression is not enough. Teachers must also take action. Hence, she advocates for preparing preservice teachers to take on a "counter-hegemonic stance" (2004, p. 118) so that they learn to challenge the demeaning conditions and inequitable learning opportunities their students face in schools.

Preservice teachers cannot be expected to independently and effectively work with or through experiences designed to unsettle their assumptions. Consequently, it is crucial that teacher educators provide supports for preservice teachers through scaffolding, such as conceptual frameworks that can help them investigate racism or classism, specific guidelines for carrying out inquiry projects, teacher modeling of, for example, constructive listening, and assistance in learning how to question. Like Bartolomé (2004), Sleeter, Torres, and Laughlin (2004) use critical pedagogy to explore connections among ideology, histories, and structures. By using Paulo Freire's (1970) problem-posing pedagogy to frame projects of critical inquiry, Sleeter and her colleagues intentionally provide scaffolding for preservice teachers by asking them to question what they take for granted. Through a cycle of dialogue and inquiry, preservice teachers participate in various assignments and class discussions to name and deconstruct their realities.

Providing models and support for practice in critical reflection is a necessary step toward developing critical consciousness (Gay & Kirkland, 2003). Unfortunately, this is not the case in many programs because teacher reflection is often presented as unproblematic (Grant & Agosto, 2008). In their teacher education courses, Geneva Gay and Kipchonge Kirkland (2003) design opportunities for preservice teachers to practice engaging in cultural critical consciousness and personal reflection. According to them, "This practice should involve concrete situations, guided assistance, and specific contexts and catalysts" (p. 186) using real-life experiences from the preservice educators' classroom practice. By exploring poetry, deconstructing national symbols, and analyzing the pedagogy and dialogue of the professors, preservice teachers learn to question assumptions. Most important, Gay and Kirkland (2003) guide their students to move beyond merely discussing race and racism to transform their newly developing critical thoughts into classroom practice.

Another promising approach to develop preservice teachers' critical consciousness is mentoring by urban high school students as in the work of Ernest Morrell and Anthony Collatos (2002). In the Pacific Beach Project at UCLA, high school students who had been trained in the sociology of education met with preservice teachers for the purpose of engaging in authentic dialogue as proposed by Freire (1970). The project aimed to have both the high school students and preservice teachers grow in consciousness. Thus, the goals of the project were threefold: (1) for preservice teachers, the goals were to help them think differently about themselves in relation to how they imagined their teacher identity and (2) to have them recognize the potential of urban youth; (3) for the teens, the goal was to build their identity as intellectuals. Some preservice teachers shared that they were better able to understand issues they were reading about in class as a result of the dialogue with the high school students.

Another example of youth as mentors is evident in the work of Jason Irizarry (2009), who asserts that teacher educators and preservice teachers should learn *from* youth rather than simply learn *about* youth through course readings and field placements. Using the concept of *representin'* from hip-hop culture, Irizarry demonstrates how a group of teachers who differed by age, race, and experience "did not position themselves as 'missionaries' or 'saviors' but rather understood their roles as members of socially constructed communities that are often marginalized and oppressed" (p. 500). The work of the teachers demonstrates that *representin'* functions as culturally responsive pedagogy and as praxis. Through this research, Irizarry confirms that urban youth can be a resource for teachers. The lesson is clear: the field can benefit by looking to urban youth culture to inform teacher preparation.

The previous studies illustrate that enacting critical consciousness is an ongoing social process of multiple insightful moments (Sleeter, Torres, & Laughlin, 2004) to counter *dysconcious racism*; that is, a limited understanding of racism that lacks social critique (King, 1991). The framework of critical consciousness provides an overarching construct for two of the recommendations made by Nieto in her 2000 article, namely, understanding the complexities of identity and learning to challenge racism.

FACING AND UNDERSTANDING THE COMPLEXITIES OF IDENTITY

In 2000, Nieto recommended that during their teacher preparation, preservice teachers should have the opportunity to reflect on both their identities and their privileges. Identity and privilege are related because how we see the world is connected to how we perform our roles (Grant & Agosto, 2008). Our beliefs, values, and assumptions are culturally formed through socialization within the differing groups with which we affiliate. Thus, cultural identity helps to shape what teachers believe to be right, true, and good in student learning and schools. Because of the complex connection among culture, identity, privilege, and teachers' practices, an important part of learning to teach is to explore who one is culturally and racially. Teachers, particularly if they are young and inexperienced, may not be conscious of their beliefs or values and therefore may need guided exploration and study in clarifying these. What follows is a summary of recent practices to engage preservice teachers in an examination of their identities and privileges.

Cognitive dissonance played an important role in developing critical consciousness in Nelda Barrón's (2008) study with preservice educators in a course designed to explore racial and cultural identities. The initial expectation of the preservice teachers was that they would study cultural "others." As the preservice teachers engaged in course content that asked them to interrogate their own cultural identity in relation to oppression, privilege, and notions of what it means to be American, many became uncomfortable. It is from this discomfort that some of them "destabilized their existing beliefs, allowing them to tolerate ideological disruptions and sustain a heightened consciousness" (p. 194). Barrón is clear that these ideological shifts were just a beginning and that long-lasting change would take sustained work and learning before the preservice teachers could see *how* their cultural frames of reference shaped their perceptions and explanations of student learning and behavior. Interrogating teacher ideology, according to Barrón, needs to occur in tandem with exploring one's cultural identity in order for preservice teachers to learn to work effectively with disenfranchised students.

All teachers and students are socialized similarly in schools and are exposed to many of the same media messages. Dominant ideologies influence teachers from all backgrounds and create a common sense way of doing things in schools. Having opportunities and guidance to explore beliefs and values will assist all teachers in critiquing their own practice and may prompt critical consciousness.

Autobiography. Autobiography is increasingly used as an important tool in teacher education for preservice teachers to consider their beliefs, experiences, and reasons for teaching. Without reflective self-exploration of their attitudes, beliefs, and values, teachers may unwittingly participate in perpetuating the status quo, which often marginalizes students.

Nieto (2003), working with a teachers' inquiry group of mostly veteran high school teachers in Boston, asked them to write their "teaching autobiographies." The resulting autobiographies were powerful examples of how teachers' identities—cultural, racial, and social—as well as their experiences and values influenced their reasons for entering and remaining in the profession. For example, one of the teachers, Junia Yearwood, reflected on how her racial background had a profound impact on her choice of career:

> I was born on the Caribbean Island of Trinidad and was raised and nurtured by my paternal grandmother and aunts on the island of Barbados. My environment instilled in me a strong identity as a woman and as a person of African descent. The value of education and the importance of being able to read and write became clear and urgent when I became fully aware of the history of my ancestors. The story of the enslavement of Africans and the horrors they were forced to endure repulsed and angered me, but the aspect of slavery that most intrigued me was the systematic denial of literacy to my ancestors. As a child of ten or so, I reasoned that if reading and writing were not extremely important, then there would be no need to withhold those skills from the supposed "savage and inferior" African. I concluded that teaching was the most important profession on earth and that the teacher was the Moses of people of African descent.
>
> This revelation made my destiny clear. I had to be a Teacher. (pp. 27–28)

Other researchers have used autobiography with different goals. For example, Virginia Lea (2004) asks preservice teachers to explore their cultural scripts that are "different ways of thinking, feeling, believing and acting that shape our actions" (p. 116). While Lea's focus is on whiteness, a critique of one's cultural scripts has value for preservice teachers from racially diverse backgrounds as well. In Lea's classes, student teachers write short, autobiographical sketches which they believe inform their teaching. Throughout the semester, the preservice teachers, with the assistance of readings and dialogue, explore how public cultural scripts (based, for example, on concepts such as meritocracy or racial harmony) inform their private scripts. The sketches of the preservice teachers often expose contradictions within themselves or between their beliefs and the practices of their schools.

The writing of cultural scripts is similar to the work of Susan Florio-Ruane (2001), who uses autobiography to explore identity with preservice teachers. Initiating a book club to explore their autobiographies, preservice teachers read autobiographical literature to learn about culture. Florio-Ruane extended the project to two years as the novice teachers became increasingly enthusiastic about learning from literature and took on leadership roles in the discussions and book selections. The six women and Florio-Ruane engaged in multifaceted conversations that increasingly uncovered the complexity and dynamism of culture. This group of teachers discovered, over time, that they too are cultural beings.

Whiteness Studies. Increasingly, teacher education is drawing on whiteness studies as an approach for white preservice teachers to deepen an examination of white privilege and to initiate an antiracist stance in their practice (Lawrence & Tatum, 1997). A pedagogy of whiteness is a key, but not the only, framework used by Kathy Hytten and Amee Adkins (2001) to critique how whiteness frames education and schooling in the United States. Hytten and Adkins define whiteness as discursive formations that "reinforce the dominant culture in our institutions" (p. 435) rather than as essentialist representations of all white people. In their pedagogy of whiteness, they use dialogue, in the spirit of the work of Freire, to encourage preservice teachers to "name, act upon, and transform their worlds" (p. 441). Hytten and Adkins strive to develop a climate of questioning, learning, and unlearning where the instructors push and challenge preservice teachers without offering their own positions too strongly. A climate of inquiry assists students to critique their assumptions and positions as well as begin to understand racism as a complex social system. Their goal is for preservice teachers to develop a stance of engagement because it is not enough for them to be able to identify patterns of whiteness; they must also learn to challenge those patterns. Hytten and Adkins (2001) acknowledge that the more difficult and often overlooked work is to interrupt whiteness through the invention of new discursive practices. The goals are more equitable teaching practices and a transformed multicultural education pedagogy.

One question frequently asked by both preservice and in-service teachers is why they should engage in multicultural education if their school or classroom is mostly white. Louise Derman-Sparks and Patricia Ramsey (2006) attempt to answer that question in their informative book, *What If All the Kids Are White?* While not specifically focused on teacher preparation, parallels can be drawn from their recommendations for elementary classrooms to the content of teacher education programs. What is significant is that the authors apply learning about white identity to work with young children.

While whiteness studies is a field that explores the complexity of identity, it can also assist teachers in learning to challenge racism, a topic we discuss next.

LEARNING TO CHALLENGE RACISM

Many preservice teachers typically frame racism as something that has largely been overcome in the United States. If it exists at all, it is seen as individual acts of meanness or general ignorance. Often, however, institutionalized racism is overlooked because of white teachers' attempts to maintain a color-blind stance (Gordon, 2005; Nieto & Bode, 2008). Seemingly, to acknowledge race is to name a deficit, something unwanted or unpleasant. In reality, what some white teachers have not yet come to understand is that the problem is not *race*; the problem is *racism*.

Helping preservice teachers identify and understand the workings of racism presents a particular challenge in an era where color-blindness is framed in a positive way as abstract liberalism or the minimization of racism (Bonilla-Silva, 2006). These color-blind frames as well as "white talk" (McIntyre, 1997), ways of talking to minimize racism and "insulat[e] whites from examining their/our individual and collective role(s) in the perpetuation of racism" (p. 45), are often drawn on by preservice teachers as strategies to resist talking and learning about racism.

Part of the work of teacher educators is to uncover and counter forms of resistance to learning about racism and instead engage preservice teachers in exploring how racism frames all social institutions and, in particular, schools (Case & Hemmings, 2005). Vavrus (2002) recommends including racism as a field of study in teacher education as well as taking an antiracist stance as an essential component of the program. He cautions that if a program strives to engage in transformative education in which teachers are prepared with a social justice perspective, learning to see racism is a step in the right direction; however, it is not enough (Vavrus, 2002). Teacher educators and preservice teachers need to learn not only how to identify differing forms of racism but also how to take an antiracist stance.

In *Everyday Antiracism*, Mica Pollock (2008) offers a number of very specific strategies for educators to create more equitable learning opportunities for all students. Based on the idea that our everyday acts can take on a proactive stance to narrow the achievement gap, the contributors of this edited text write short, focused pieces about designing curriculum, managing classrooms, communicating with families, and interacting with communities. The structure of the text includes core principles, strategies, and "try tomorrow" suggestions, offering concrete actions for educators to include in their daily work. Pollock's text helps to answer preservice teachers' questions about what they can do once they begin to notice institutional practices of racism. Yet Pollock also cautions us that action without reflection can become a dangerous form of activism (Freire, 1970).

As teacher education programs add new content and new field placement sites in order to promote social justice, the racial order is often, unknowingly, reified if these revisions are not carefully critiqued. Focusing on diversity and multiculturalism without attending to issues of power, racism, and whiteness only serves to reproduce systemic inequities under the guise of multicultural education (Cross, 2005). One challenge is that racism has taken on new and often invisible forms. Instead of overt and visible, it operates as a "hidden system of power and domination" (Cross, 2005, p. 267). Without careful analysis of new racism, teacher education programs may unintentionally produce as well as teach racism. What follows are recent examples in teacher education where the focus is on preparing preservice teachers to engage in analyses of racism and power.

Ethnography. Using nontraditional approaches to study racism in addition to assigned readings and class dialogue may provide new opportunities for engaging in conversations that preservice teachers often find challenging (Cochran-Smith & Lytle, 1992; Villegas & Lucas, 2002). For example, performance ethnography may have unrealized potential in providing opportunities for preservice teachers to research and analyze issues of racism and privilege. In his course, Diversity and Inclusion in Schools, Edward Garcia Fierros (2009) led preservice teachers through an eight-week ethnographic exploration of the *Brown vs. Board of Education* decision. The teachers in training worked in groups to interview campus faculty, administration, staff, and peers to explore the participants' memories of the *Brown* decision. They learned ethnographic procedures, analyzed data, and developed a script from excerpts taken from the interviews. Their public performance to more than two hundred college students provided a venue for their learning and a forum for additional campus conversations about race and segregation. This assignment served as both an alternative assessment and a novel approach to integrating research, history, and teacher education.

Autoethnographic pedagogy is a method used by Pennington (2007) to engage white preservice teachers in conversations about race and education. Beginning by asking the preservice educators to share narratives about their student-teaching experiences, Pennington also shares her own development around race talk and understanding whiteness. Her autobiographical sharing, framed as counternarrative bridging, helped offset the student narratives that skirted around race. Reflexive engagement around issues of race offers a beginning place to explore how racism functions in schools.

Bridging narratives and ethnography, both as writing process and as methodology, is an intentional design in the collaborative work at Boise State University to prepare teachers to work with English language learners. Aileen Hale and her colleagues (2008) begin with narrative writing and research to aid preservice teachers in self-discovery. The preservice teachers use tools of narrative to explore who they are and how their cultural identity influences classroom practice. Narrative is then bridged to ethnography as a methodology for preservice teachers to learn who their students are as cultural beings. This process of awareness of self first and awareness of others later led some preservice educators to transformative action and advocacy as they developed "consciousness of educational issues and their implications" (p. 1422).

Counterstories. *Counterstories* are narratives that share a person's reality while also challenging or disrupting taken-for-granted beliefs formed by dominant ideologies. Counterstories, a core element of Critical Race Theory, or CRT (Delgado & Stefancic, 2001), provide a space for faculty of color and preservice teachers of color to be validated because they often report comments of disbelief from their white classmates when sharing their experiences with racism. A number of teacher educators have used counterstories to analyze their efforts in using a race-explicit pedagogy. H. Richard Milner (2007) provides one salient example of his work with predominantly white preservice teachers as he explored what he, as a black teacher educator, brings to a classroom to help preservice teachers learn about race and teaching. Milner found that his "racialized experience outside of the classroom emerged in the classroom and enhanced [his] teaching" (p. 591). By sharing some of his own race-related narratives in class as one avenue to help preservice teachers understand the course content, he found that some were better able to engage in dialogue about racism. He also explicitly shared his decision-making process of planning the class and how he made connections between his personal narrative and the goals of each class session. Milner (2007) reminds us that the lived experiences and realities of teachers and teacher educators themselves become part of the classroom curriculum.

Milner's (2007) counterstories also opened up possibilities and presented alternative realities to his mostly white graduate students. As a result of this experience, while some students maintained their positions of resistance, others began to acknowledge that racism exists.

Preservice teachers of color tend to bring "racialized self understandings" to the work of reflection and are often discouraged from doing so. Denise Baszile (2008) shares her experience as an African American woman teaching *The Adventures of Huckleberry Finn* to a group of white eleventh grade students. In reviewing her student-teaching journal, Baszile noticed that at times she used reflection to rationalize her decisions rather than as a means to explore her intentions. This "pseudo-reflection . . . directs teachers to reflect on certain things and not others; on, for instance, how well they are demonstrating their competencies as opposed to perhaps the cultural literacy that informs such competencies" (Baszile, 2008, p. 377).

Baszile's college supervisor often commented that Baszile should not focus as much on race issues but instead on her teaching. In this case, as Baszile notes, the work of reflection was not for transformation but for surveillance. This counterstory serves to ask how the "purpose and politics of teacher reflection" (p. 383) can be reimagined, an important question since teacher preparation often relies on the reflection of preservice teachers as they learn to work with diverse populations. Baszile's (2008) counterstory raises important questions about the role of reflection in teacher education.

Critical Analysis of Research and History. It is rare for research findings about preservice teachers' beliefs to be shared with the participants for the purpose of intervening in their thinking and teaching. In her research, Sherry Marx (2006) did just that. She identified patterns of whiteness and racism among her teacher education students and then shared the data she collected with them. Her hope was to engage them in critical reflection concerning their own beliefs.

Marx worked with nine preservice teachers who, during a semester of tutoring children of Mexican descent, espoused negative ideologies about the children they were tutoring. Often their behavior took the form of "passive racism" (p. 37), for example, as when they held low expectations or when they equated students' race with deficits. Marx's decision to intervene was motivated by her awareness that sending the preservice teachers to tutor the children was causing the children both emotional and academic harm. During the course that supported the tutoring sessions, Marx shared transcripts of their talk in class. As a result of their analysis and dialogue, Marx found that the preservice teachers tended to use "politically correct" language when exploring their feelings and questions, and she encouraged them to avoid doing so. Some experienced discomfort while others continued to resist, yet Marx was encouraged by those who took some ownership of their whiteness and racism.

Another useful framework for studying racism in teacher education coursework is exploring how historical context shapes existing conditions (Hill, 2009). Hill drew on a historical analysis of race divisions between Detroit and a nearby suburb to illustrate reasons for current inequities and to make the case that all teachers, whether in urban or suburban schools, need to learn culturally relevant pedagogy. She situated a middle school ethnography in its historical context by drawing on post 1940's documents to illustrate school and housing segregation as well as negative attitudes about integration. Her findings imply that preservice teachers need many opportunities to engage in dialogue that takes them outside of their comfort zone. It also reinforces the importance of culturally relevant pedagogy (Ladson-Billings, 1995).

In her work with preservice teachers, Sleeter (2008a) used family history projects as an entry point to help teachers understand themselves as cultural beings. She found that often the preservice teachers crafted family stories that exemplified the myth of individualism, rather than uncover—as she had hoped they would—historical patterns of institutional discrimination. Currently, Sleeter is working on *critical family history*, an approach that shows promise in engaging preservice teachers in a deeper level of analysis of self, family, and history. Her personal genealogical project aligns the historical and political context with events and persons in her own family history. For example, uncovering the nineteenth-century U.S. laws that provided easy access to land ownership for European immigrants helps to highlight the ways that white privilege has worked historically. By contextualizing family history stories, preservice teachers may learn information that transforms their ways of thinking about identity, privilege, and institutional discrimination. On the other hand, without connecting history to the present, as both Sleeter and Hill do, preservice teachers are likely to frame the study of racism in history as proof that racism is a mere memory of our past.

After reviewing these studies, the question that remains is what supports preservice teachers receive after participating in courses such as those reviewed above. Work such as this must be continuous because unlearning years of socialization cannot be accomplished in a single course or even a series of courses. As Sleeter (2008b) points out, preparing teachers to close the achievement gap is challenged by socializing forces that are a part of teachers' everyday context. For white teachers, these socializing influences include the messages they receive about being white by living in a relatively homogeneous neighborhood as well as what they learned and continue to learn about teaching and schools as K–12 students, and now as practicing teachers. As a result, their socializing experiences solidify common sense understandings they have of teaching, learning, and schooling, leaving little room to imagine new possibilities.

GETTING TO KNOW STUDENTS AND THEIR COMMUNITIES

Teaching is not just about communicating content to students. It also includes learning to know who students are and developing strong and meaningful relationships with them. This means that learning about their students does not consist solely of reading books on cultural differences or adding a unit on families of diverse backgrounds to the curriculum, although of course, both of these can help. Nevertheless, such activities may do little to help teachers learn about the specific children in their classrooms. Getting to know one's students also means learning about the sociocultural realities of their students and the sociopolitical conditions in which they live. The late Brazilian educator Paulo Freire addressed this question eloquently when he wrote,

> Educators need to know what happens in the world of the children with whom they work. They need to know the universe of their dreams, the language with which they skillfully defend themselves from the aggressiveness of their world, what they know independently of the school, and how they know it. (Freire, 1998, pp. 72–73)

As mentioned previously, teachers who share their students' backgrounds and experiences may have an easier time of relating to them. A good example comes from Juan Figueroa, a young Boston public high school teacher who knew "what happens in the world of the children" because he shared similar experiences with his urban students. Juan said,

These kids were *me*. You know, I grew up in the city too, and that's what keeps me going. All the other stuff you had was crazy, but it's when you make that one-to-one connection with a kid and a kid finally says, *"Now* I get it!"*,* that just makes everything else seem so right. (Nieto, 2003, p. 42)

Most teachers who work with diverse populations, however, do not share their students' backgrounds or experiences. For these teachers, professional development must include learning about young people whose lives are different from theirs. In this case, teachers need to learn to, in the words of Paulo Freire (1998), read "a class of students as if it were a *text* to be decoded, comprehended" (p. 49). How do teachers learn to "read" their students and their students' communities? A first step is to learn to be comfortable with families, and this is one of the great gaps in teacher education. That is, preservice teachers need to learn explicit skills in communicating with families. These include having parent-teacher conferences, contacting family members in culturally appropriate and respectful ways, and learning how to make home visits. Most essential is learning about the histories and realities of the communities in which they work and developing a true respect and solidarity with them.

In addition to specific skills in meeting with families, learning about students also means developing an open mind about what families have to offer. The work of Norma Gonzalez, Luis Moll, and Cathy Amanti (2005) is instructive here. By teaching preservice and practicing teachers to do ethnographic research with the families of their students, in the process teachers learn to incorporate the families' "funds of knowledge" into the curriculum. This process recognizes that all families have talents, strengths, and skills that can be used in the curriculum. Given the positive results such research has shown, incorporating funds of knowledge research into teacher preparation is clearly a more productive and promising approach than is viewing families as if all they have to offer are deficits that teachers and schools must repair.

More recently, another approach that has gained prominence in teacher preparation is participatory action research (PAR), and its offshoot, youth participatory action research (YPAR). Both PAR and YPAR are based on the assumption that participants—whether families, community members, or students—have significant insights and experiences that can have a decisive influence on student learning. For example, in a study of urban high school students who became critical researchers, Ernest Morrell (2008) documented how the students' experiences, insights, and knowledge helped make them active and engaged participants in their own learning. Other recent YPAR efforts to collaborate with students and their families to improve education are found in research by Duncan-Andrade (2007), Cammarota and Fine (2008), and Irizarry (2009). Such research serves as a powerful antidote to deficit-centered research that views students, their families, and their communities as having little to offer.

CHANGING THE NATURE OF FACULTY WORK

Reforming faculty work can strengthen and sustain teaching for social justice. Heavy teaching loads, busy research agendas, and expectations of service to their department, university, and professional community make it imperative that collaborative faculty work be re-imagined as integrated rather than an add-on to already full schedules. Beverly Cross's (2005) analysis of the insidious ways that racism is both present in, and an outcome of, teacher education programs provides a strong case for rethinking the nature of faculty work typical in institutions of higher education. Her findings indicate that teacher education, even when revised, continues to reproduce racism. True transformation requires new visions about the business of teacher education because course revisions and self-studies by individual teacher educators are not enough. Collaboration within and across institutions offers multiple perspectives to emerge and opportunities to challenge entrenched systems and curriculum.

Collaboration at the Program Level. The Bilingual/ESL/Multicultural Education (BEM) program at the University of Massachusetts, Amherst, is a collaborative model with unique elements designed to respond to the growing numbers of English language learners in grades P–12. Unique to the program is its student selection criteria, program structure, and the collaborative work of the faculty. Admitting graduate students who demonstrate a commitment to social justice education and who speak languages other than English, the program does not divide students according to the licensure they seek. Instead, preservice and in-service teachers, elementary education teachers, and language specialists all take classes together. The program is designed around three core concepts: social justice, a dialogic stance, and a praxis orientation. Coursework is designed to prompt students to take action both inside and outside of their classrooms and to be shared with local schools, community centers, and parents. Some of these collaborative projects include a video about the Latino community that was created for new staff, a presentation to a local school committee about the problems inherent in using Native American images as school mascots and professional development workshops for teachers about working with bilingual students. The BEM faculty also engage in collaborative research to evaluate the effectiveness of the program. For example, interviews of BEM alumni revealed that the program was meeting faculty goals in some areas but not others. The participants of these interviews demonstrated comfort in talking about their raced and classed identities as well as an understanding of teaching as intellectual work, as political, and as sociocultural mediation. The faculty research also indicated that further work was needed to help the BEM students develop counterdiscourses to some typical misunderstandings of working with English learners (Gebhard et al., 2002).

Collaboration at the Institution Level. Collaborative relationships among faculty are necessary if teacher education programs want to strengthen their approaches to social justice education. If Cross's (2005) prediction holds true, that in the future, "teacher educators will be called well intentioned yet fraudulent because we reproduce racism, power, and whiteness through new forms of racism" (p. 271), then collaborative models are essential to identify and deconstruct the ways in which racism and whiteness exist in teacher education program ideology, content, and practice. The normalcy of whiteness renders it invisible to many (Frankenburg, 1997), and thus individual efforts to identify whiteness are hindered.

Coupled with the challenge of failing to see whiteness is the discomfort that many whites experience when talking about racism. One way to address the invisibility of whiteness is for multiracial teams of faculty to design and revise courses and create models to support one another. Working in multiracial teams does not guarantee that faculty will identify whiteness in the curriculum or that preservice teachers will develop a consciousness of whiteness and racism, but the collaboration of persons from different subject positions helps to increase opportunities for reflexivity and it holds faculty accountable for their work in this area.

At UCLA, Tyrone Howard (2003) and his colleagues designed *Identity and Teaching*, a mandatory course for all preservice teachers in their teacher education program. This course encouraged participants to explore their own identities and identify realms of privilege. As a result of difficult and emotionally demanding conversations about racial identity and racism, the faculty learned to support one another as well as their own learning by participating in a three-day workshop that included many activities they required of their preservice teachers. This workshop also serves to train faculty new to teaching the course.

In another example, faculty, staff, and administrators at Wheelock College in Boston have participated in a monthly antiracist seminar for more than ten years which, since its inception, has had a number of variations. Unique to this forum is the participation of staff and administration, its multidisciplinary focus (i.e., participants are generally from the fields of social work and education but the seminar is open to all), and its long tenure. The goal of the seminar is to support and challenge members in the exploration of racism and privilege in the culture of the institution, the college's professional programs, and individual members of the seminar (Cox Suarez, 2008).

While whites can and must take responsibility for unlearning racism, to do so without participation by faculty of color is naïve and potentially dangerous. Both the UCLA and Wheelock College collaborative models are strengthened by diverse faculty participation because they are based on the understanding that to overlook implications of the overrepresentation of white teacher educators is, in and of itself, a blindness to whiteness. Thus, to continue to reform teacher education for socially just teaching, recruiting and retaining faculty of color is imperative (Irvine, 2003). As Marilyn Cochran-Smith (1995) warns, "Unless we unflinchingly interrogate the explicit and implicit images in our pre-service pedagogy and then work to alter our own teaching and programs, it is unlikely that we can help student teachers do the same" (p. 568).

Other models that hold promise are faculty collaboration with teacher education students as coresearchers and collaboration with the community (Murrell, 2006). The Elementary Education Masters program at Ohio State University does both. By joining preservice teachers to explore questions, phenomena, and dilemmas related to teacher practice, Barbara Seidl (2007) models as well as participates in cooperative inquiry with the preservice teachers in her program. In addition, the teacher education program collaborated with the Mt. Olivet Baptist Church, and Minister Gloria Friend, for more than seven years. The graduate students volunteered at a variety of youth programs provided by the church and debriefed in weekly meetings facilitated by both faculty and church members. Alongside Siedl, the preservice teachers read about African American history and issues of racism and privilege and wrote stories of their experiences at the church. These narratives were revisited to identify themes as well as to name what cultural and political information they were learning about in this particular context.

Collaboration across Institutions. Opportunities for faculty to work together across institutions to provide unique programming for preservice and in-service teachers is worth consideration. Project QUEST linked seven institutions of higher education in Massachusetts to provide support for new urban teachers. Twenty-three classroom teachers from three urban school districts and seven university faculty members met a few Saturdays each term from 2002 to 2005. What began as general mentoring evolved to specifically focus on disparities in achievement as the classroom teachers voiced frustrations about the educational inequities their students faced. The QUEST group engaged in both unstructured time for "teacher talk" and structured activities to address the following questions: *What does it take to retain new teachers in urban schools?* and *How can the disparities in student achievement among racial-ethnic, socioeconomic, and linguistic-cultural groups be narrowed?* (Alkins et al., 2006).

THE CONTINUING CHALLENGES OF "PLACING EQUITY FRONT AND CENTER"

Our review of some of the programmatic changes taking place in teacher preparation leads us to sound a cautionary note. For one, we are concerned that efforts to decenter whiteness can, and often do, result in just the opposite; that is, in centering whiteness. As Cameron McCarthy (2003) has pointed out, a number of whiteness studies in teacher education decontextualize whiteness while they construct it as stable. In the process, they exclude teachers and students of color in their analysis. The fact that teacher educators are attempting to explicitly talk about and study the constructs of race and whiteness is a positive sign, but future work must situate studies within a historic and contemporary context. They must also include more complex portraits of preservice teachers to examine the intersection of race with gender and class (McCarthy, 2003).

There are a number of additional challenges to identity work with preservice teachers. We will briefly mention three here. The first two are related to how society shapes and constructs commonplace definitions of identity and culture. Teacher education students often define identity as characteristics of an individual, isolated from social systems and power. The myth of American individualism is replete with success stories of people who have "made it" against all odds, and these myths contribute to the challenge of understanding identity as relational. Yet, who we are is *both* how we see ourselves *and* also how others define us (Tatum, 1997). One challenge in teacher education programs is therefore to help preservice teachers understand the complexities of identity: its relation to group membership, its hybridity, and its flux within changing contexts.

The second challenge is for teacher educators to help preservice teachers understand the complexities of the concept of culture. Again, the everyday discourse of media, schools, and institutions often reifies culture as synonymous with the celebrations and "ways of being" of ethnic groups. Understandably then, it is difficult for preservice teachers to move away from essentializing the identities of students and their families. In preservice teachers' efforts to understand culture, they sometimes overdetermine its effects to explain everything from behaviors to celebrations to learning (Ladson-Billings, 2006). Instead, teacher education programs need to help preservice teachers learn how cultural knowledge is shaped in relation to social, historical, and political contexts. Rather than focus on cultural practices of groups (a heroes and holidays approach), teacher education programs would do better to assist preservice teachers to explore themselves as cultural beings and to critically analyze the representation of cultural knowledge and traditions (Duesterberg, 1998; Gutierrez & Rogoff, 2003).

A third challenge is to better design teacher education programs for *both* white teachers and teachers of color. Most teacher education is framed around preparing white teachers and understanding white identity. Since the majority of preservice teachers are white, this seems at first glance to make good sense. Yet, this approach leaves out and continues to marginalize future teachers of color (Knight, 2002; Meacham, 2000), perhaps in this way contributing to the low numbers of teachers of color in the field. Some potential frames for addressing identity with diverse groups are *intersectionality* (Collins, 2001), *positionality* (Martin & Van Gunten 2002), and the *hybridity of identity*.

Given their invisibility in teacher preparation programs, it is imperative that the unique perspectives and needs of preservice teachers of color, which may differ from those of white teachers, not be overlooked. The process of exploring one's racial and cultural identities is important for both white teachers and teachers of color because teachers' beliefs and values influence their practice. For preservice and practicing teachers of color, the assumption is often made that as a group they are better able to successfully teach children of color. This assumption, if applied in a blanket fashion, can be erroneous and does little to prepare preservice and practicing teachers of color for diverse classrooms. For example, in a review of literature, Ana María Villegas and Danné Davis (2008) reported that studies measuring success by test scores have found no definitive correlation between teacher and student identity and better learning. Nevertheless, Villegas and Davis also found that the literature suggests favorable academic *effects* when teacher and student identities are similar. In addition, studies other than test scores have found evidence that students of color are likely to benefit from exposure to teachers of color (Villegas & Davis, 2008).

Finally, teacher education programs willing to revise course work should take a look at Cross's (2005) work for helpful strategies and questions for critiquing what we do in the context of racism and whiteness. Course revisions may help reconceptualize teacher education pedagogy and curriculum by using a "systemic analysis of how these invisible operations shape programs and unintended program outcomes" (p. 265).

FINAL THOUGHTS

Public schools in the United States are now more diverse in terms of culture, race, language, and immigration status than ever before, yet our schools and colleges of education, as Nieto pointed out in her 2000 article, have not adequately met this challenge. Nevertheless, the number and variety of approaches, strategies, research studies, and programmatic changes in the past decade that we have reviewed in this chapter are heartening. In addition, the fact that young scholars—many of whom are people of color themselves—are pushing the profession beyond its former boundaries concerning race and diversity is great cause for hope. Also, in some cases, teacher education has become more relevant and inclusive in terms of the focus of programs, kinds of courses, and recruitment of students and faculty of diverse backgrounds, among other changes. Because of these developments, our analysis of efforts to "place equity front and center" in teacher education leads us to conclude that some progress has indeed been made in the past decade in preparing teachers for the schools of the twenty-first century.

At the same time, our investigation makes it clear that schools and colleges of education have just scratched the surface of change. Most glaring in terms of problems that are yet to be addressed are data concerning the continuing variability in student achievement (the "achievement gap") and the persistently high dropout rates among Latinos, African Americans, and Native Americans that belie efforts to prepare teachers adequately for different student populations. In addition, while the field has integrated and considered issues of power in some courses, course readings, and student placements, this change is not enough. For example, in an extensive review of syllabi in multicultural education, Paul Gorski (2009) found that many courses are still at a very basic, and sometimes superficial, level of understanding diversity. Also problematic is the one-course approach; that is, the practice of offering just one course in diversity as if that were enough to prepare preservice teachers for the tremendous variety of ethnicities, languages, cultures, and social-class backgrounds they will be facing in their classrooms.

Our review also found that there are too few studies on programmatic approaches. While the studies we reviewed are a promising beginning, we found that in too many cases, changes have been individual, sporadic, and inconsistent. There are also still too few studies concerning teacher practice in diverse classrooms. As a result, we will not know what is effective until there is more research of teacher practice in actual classrooms. An even greater challenge for changing teacher education so that it focuses more directly on social justice and equity is the so-called "reform movement" of the past decade that has resulted in an obsession with standardized testing. When this is the case, teachers' time is too often taken up with preparing students for mindless tasks that will do little to prepare them for their future.

As teacher educators, we are not so naïve as to believe that the changes we make in courses, readings, assignments, and field placements to address issues of equity and social justice always result in changes in actual teacher attitudes or practices. Despite our best efforts to have them confront issues of racism, classism, and privilege, preservice teachers' attitudes and beliefs, and consequently their practice, may show little change. It is humbling to realize that realistic and comprehensive change may take more than changing individual courses and programs; indeed, it will probably take an overhaul not only of teacher education but also of the priorities and goals of our nation.

In spite of the gaps in theory and practice in placing social justice and equity at the center of teacher preparation, we believe that some initial progress has been made. We remain hopeful that if we return to this topic again in another ten years, we will have made more progress than we have made since the original article was first published. Our nation's children deserve no less.

REFERENCES

Alkins, K., Banks-Santilli, L., Elliott, P., Guttenberg, N., Kami, M. (2006). Project Quest: A journey of discovery with beginning teachers in urban schools. *Equity and Excellence in Education, 39*, 65–80.

American Council on Education. (2008). *Minorities in higher education 2008. Twenty-third status report.* Washington, DC: Author.

Barrón, N. (2008). Reflections from beneath the veil: Mainstream preservice teachers (dis) covering their cultural identities. In Bartolomé, L. (Ed.), *Ideologies in education: Unmaking the trap of teacher neutrality* (pp. 181–205). New York: Peter Lang.

Bartolomé, L. (2004). Critical pedagogy and teacher education: Radicalizing prospective teachers. *Teacher Education Quarterly, 31(1)*, 97–122.

Bartolomé, L. (2008). *Ideologies in education: Unmaking the trap of teacher neutrality.* New York: Peter Lang.

Baszile, D. (2008). The oppressor within: A counterstory of race, repression, and teacher reflection. *Urban Review, 40*, 371–85.

Bonilla-Silva, E. (2001). *White supremacy and racism in the post-civil rights era.* Boulder, CO: Lynne Rienner Publishers.

Bonilla-Silva, E. (2006). *Racism without racists: Color-blind racism and the persistence of racial inequality in the United States.* Lanham, MD: Rowman & Littlefield.

Cammarota, J., & Fine, M. (Eds.). (2008). *Revolutionizing education: Youth participatory action research in motion.* New York: Routledge.

Case, K., & Hemmings, A. (2005). Distancing strategies: White women preservice teachers and antiracist curriculum. *Urban Education, 40(6)*, 606–26.

Cochran-Smith, M. (1995). Uncertain allies: Understanding the boundaries of race and teaching. *Harvard Educational Review, 65*, 541–70.

Cochran-Smith, M., & Lytle, S. (1992). Interrogating cultural diversity: Inquiry and action. *Journal of Teacher Education, 43(2)*, 104–15.

Collins, P. H. (2000). *Black feminist thought: Knowledge, consciousness and the politics of empowerment* (2nd ed.). New York: Routledge.

Cox Suárez, S. (2008). Can the academy live the work and walk the talk? Lessons learned from a long-term faculty dialogue about racism. *American Academic, 4(1)*, 45–64.

Cross, B. (2005). New racism, reformed teacher education, and the same ole' oppression. *Educational Studies, 38(3)*, 263–74.

Delgado, R., & Stefancic, J. (2001). *Critical race theory: An introduction.* New York: New York University Press.

Derman-Sparks, L., & Ramsey, P. (2006). *What if all the kids are white?: Anti-bias multicultural education with young children and families.* New York: Teachers College Press.

Duesterberg, L. (1998). Rethinking culture in the pedagogy and practices of teacher education. *Teaching and Teacher Education, 14(5)*, 497–512.

Duncan-Andrade, J. M. R. (2007). Urban youth and the counter-narration of inequality. *Transforming Anthropology, 15(1)*, 26–37.

Florio-Ruane, S. (2001). *Teacher education and the cultural imagination: Autobiography, conversation, and narrative.* Mahwah, NJ: Lawrence Erlbaum.

Frankenburg, R. (1997). Introduction: Local whitenesses, localizing whiteness. In Frankenburg, R. (Ed.), *Displacing Whiteness: Essays in social and cultural criticism* (pp. 1–34). Durham, NC: Duke University Press.

Freire, P. (1970). *Pedagogy of the oppressed.* New York: Seabury Press.

Freire, P. (1973). *Education for critical consciousness.* New York: Seabury Press.

Freire, P. (1998). *Teachers as cultural workers: Letters to those who dare teach.* Boulder, CO: Westview Press.

Garcia Fierros, E. (2009). Using performance ethnography to confront issues of privilege, race, and institutional racism: An account of an arts-based teacher education project. *Multicultural Perspectives, 11(1)*, 3–11.

Gatimu, M. W. (2009). Undermining critical consciousness unconsciously: Restoring hope in the multicultural education idea. *Journal of Educational Change, 10*, 47–61.

Gay, G., & Kirkland, K. (2003). Developing cultural critical consciousness and self-reflection in preservice teacher education. *Theory into Practice, 42(3)*, 181–87.

Gebhard, M., Austin, T., Nieto, S., Willett, J. (2002). "You can't step on someone else's words": Preparing all teachers to teach language minority students. In Beykont, L. (Ed.), *The power of culture: Teaching across language difference* (pp. 219–43). Cambridge, MA: Harvard Publishing Group.

Gonzalez, N., Moll, L. C., & Amanti, C. (2005). *Funds of knowledge: Theorizing practices in households and classrooms.* Mahwah, NJ: Lawrence Erlbaum Associates.

Gordon, J. (2005). Inadvertent complicity: Colorblindness in teacher education. *Educational Studies, 38(2)*, 135–53.

Gorski, P. (2009). What we're teaching teachers: An analysis of multicultural teacher education coursework syllabi. *Teaching and Teacher Education 25*, 309–18.

Grant, C., & Agosto, V. (2008). Teacher capacity and social justice in teacher education. In Cochran-Smith, M., Feiman-Nemser, S., & McIntyre, D. (Eds.), *Handbook of research on teacher education* (3rd ed.), (pp. 175–200). New York: Routledge.

Gutierrez, K., & Rogoff, B. (2003). Cultural ways of learning: Individual traits or repertoires of practice. *Educational Researcher, 32(5)*, 19–15.

Hale, A., Snow-Gerono, J., & Morales, F. (2008). Transformative education for culturally diverse learners through narrative and ethnography. *Teaching and Teacher Education, 24*, 1413–25.

Hill, K. D. (2009). A historical analysis of desegregation and racism in a racially polarized region: Implications for the historical construct, a diversity problem, and transforming teacher education toward culturally relevant pedagogy. *Urban Education, 44 (1)*, 106–39.

Howard, T. (2003). Culturally relevant pedagogy: Ingredients for critical teacher reflection. *Theory into Practice, 42(3)*, 195–202.

Hytten, K., & Adkins, A. (2001). Thinking through a pedagogy of whiteness. *Educational Theory, 51(4)*, 433–50.

Irizarry, J. (2009). Representin': Drawing from hip hop and urban youth culture to inform teacher education. *Education and Urban Society, 41(4)*, 489–515.

Irvine, J. J. (2003). *Educating teachers for diversity: Seeing with a cultural eye.* New York: Teachers College Press.

King, J. (1991). Dysconscious racism: Ideology, identity, and the miseducation of teachers. *Journal of Negro Education, 60(2)*, 133–46.

Knight, M. (2002). The intersections of race, class, and gender in the teacher preparation of an African American social justice educator. *Equity & Excellence in Education, 35(3)*, 212–24.

Ladson-Billings, G. (1995). Toward a theory of culturally relevant pedagogy. *American Educational Research Journal, 32(3)*, 465–91.

Ladson-Billings, G. (2006). It's not the culture of poverty, it's the poverty of culture: The problem with teacher education. *Anthropology and Education Quarterly, 37(2)*, 104–9.

Lawrence, S., & Tatum, B. D. (1997). Teachers in transition: The impact of antiracist professional development on classroom practice. *Teachers College Record, 99(1)*, 162–78.

Lea, V. (2004). The reflective cultural portfolio: Identifying public cultural scripts in the private voices of white student teachers. *Journal of Teacher Education, 55*, 116–27.

Martin, R., & Van Gunten, D. (2002). Reflected identities: Applying positionality and multicultural reconstructionism in teacher education. *Journal of Teacher Education, 53(1)*, 44–54.

Marx, S. (2006). *Revealing the invisible: Confronting passive racism in teacher education.* New York: Routledge.

McCarthy, C. (2003). Contradictions of power and identity: Whiteness studies and the call of teacher education. *Qualitative Studies in Education, 16(1)*, 127–33.

McIntyre, A. (1997). *Making meaning of Whiteness: Exploring the racial identity of white teachers*. Albany: SUNY Press.

Meacham, S. (2000). Black self-love, language, and the teacher education dilemma: The cultural denial and cultural limbo of African American preservice teachers. *Urban Education, 34(5)*, 571–96.

Milner, H. R. (2007). Race, narrative inquiry, and self-study in curriculum and teacher education. *Education and Urban Society, 39*, 584–609.

Morrell, E. (2008). *Critical literacy and urban youth: Pedagogies of access, dissent, and liberation*. New York: Routledge.

Morrell, E., & Collatos, A. (2002). Toward a critical teacher education. *Social Justice, 29(4)*, 60–70.

Murrell, P. (2006). Toward social justice in urban education: A model of cultural collaborative inquiry in urban schools. *Equity and Excellence in Education, 39(1)*, 81–90.

Nieto, S. (2000). Placing equity front and center: Some thoughts on transforming teacher education for a new century. *Journal of Teacher Education, 51(3)*, 180–87.

Nieto, S. (2003). *What keeps teachers going?* New York: Teachers College Press.

Nieto, S., & Bode, P. (2008). *Affirming diversity. The sociopolitical context of multicultural education* (5th ed.). New York: Allyn & Bacon.

Nieto, S., Bode, P., Kang, E., & Raible, J. (2008). Identity, community and diversity: Retheorizing multicultural curriculum for the postmodern era. In Connelly, F. M., He, M. F., & Phillion, J. (Eds.), *The Sage handbook of curriculum and instruction* (pp. 176–97). Thousand Oaks, CA: Sage.

Pennington, J. (2007). Silence in the classroom/whispers in the halls: Autoethnography as pedagogy in White pre-service teacher education. *Race, Ethnicity, and Education, 10(1)*, 93–113.

Pew Hispanic Center. (2006). *Statistical portrait of Hispanics in the United States*. Washington, DC: Author.

Pollock, M. (2008). Everyday antiracism: Getting real about race in schools. New York: New Press.

Pytel, B. (2006, July 9). NEA: Today's teacher issues. Suite 101.com. Washington, DC: National Education Association.

Seidl, B. (2007). Working with communities to explore and personalize culturally relevant pedagogies: "Push, doubled images and race talk." *Journal of Teacher Education, 58(2)*, 168–83.

Sleeter, C. (1995). White preservice students and multicultural education coursework. In Larkin, J., & Sleeter, C. (Eds.), *Developing multicultural teacher education curricula* (pp. 17–30). Albany: State University of New York Press.

Sleeter, C. (2000). Multicultural education, social positionality, and whiteness. In Duarte, E., Smith, S. (Eds.), *Foundational Perspectives in multicultural education* (pp. 118–34). New York: Longman.

Sleeter, C. (2008a). Critical family history, identity, and historical memory. *Educational Studies, 43*, 1–11.

Sleeter, C. (2008b). Preparing white teachers for diverse students. In Cochran-Smith, M., Feiman-Nemser, S., & McIntyre, D. (Eds.), *Handbook of research on teacher education: Enduring questions in changing contexts* (3rd ed.), (pp. 559–82). New York: Routledge.

Sleeter, C., Torres, M., & Laughlin, P. (2004). Scaffolding conscientization through inquiry in teacher education. *Teacher Education Quarterly, 31(1)*, 81–96.

Tatum, B. (1997). *"Why are all the black kids sitting together in the cafeteria?" And other conversations about race*. New York: Basic Books.

Terrill, M., & Mark, D. L. H. (2000). Preservice teachers' expectations for schools with children of color and second-language learners. *Journal of Teacher Education, 51(2)*, 149–55.

U.S. Census Bureau. (2004, 22 April). *Facts for features*. Washington, DC: Author.

U.S. Census Bureau. (2009, March 5). *Current population survey*. Washington, DC: Author.

Vavrus, M. (2002). *Transforming the multicultural education of teachers: Theory, research and practice*. New York: Teachers College Press.

Villegas, A. M., & Davis, D. (2008). Preparing teachers of color to confront racial/ethnic disparities in educational outcomes. In Cochran-Smith, M., Feiman-Nemser, S., & McIntyre, D. (Eds.), *Handbook of research on teacher education* (3rd ed.), (pp. 583–605). New York: Routledge.

Villegas, A., & Lucas, T. (2002). Preparing culturally responsive teachers: Rethinking the curriculum. *Journal of Teacher Education, 53(1)*, 20–32.

19

Asking the Right Questions

A Research Agenda for Studying Diversity in Teacher Education

Gloria Ladson-Billings

INTRODUCTION

One of the more pressing issues facing public education in the United States is how to ensure the academic success of an increasingly diverse student population (Planty et al., 2009). Students from a variety of racial, ethnic, linguistic, national, ability, and familial structure backgrounds populate our schools and classrooms. Teachers regularly raise concerns about the ability to effectively teach such a diverse group of students (Cornbleth, 2008). The challenge that the nation's teachers face is also apparent in our teacher education programs. More recently, critics of education schools and teacher education programs in particular have argued that the problem with student performance can be traced to the low quality of teachers and the inadequate preparation they receive in traditional teacher education programs (Cochran-Smith & Fries, 2001).

I have written on the issue of diversity in teacher education in some form on at least four occasions (Ladson-Billings, 1995, 1999a, 2000, 2005). In each instance I have talked about diversity in teacher education or multicultural teacher education in relation to what we know about (regular) teacher education. Until we improve teacher education we have no hope of improving diversity in teacher education. Indeed, how scholars and practitioners go about improving teacher education must include a plan for making the issue of diversity a constituent component of that improvement. In this chapter I will attempt to outline a research agenda for studying diversity in teacher education. I will begin with the demographic questions, the program structure questions, the clinical experiences questions, the professional development questions, and the alternative certification questions.

UNDERSTANDING THE NUMBERS

The U.S. Census Bureau (Jones & Overberg, 2008) reports that white populations have declined in more than half of U.S. counties since 2000. These data reflect how immigration, particularly of Latinos, combined with the slowing growth of an aging white population is changing the racial and ethnic faces of America. People of color make up more than half of the population in 302 of the nation's 3,141 counties. Although whites are 66 percent of the population nationwide, the Latino and Asian communities are growing rapidly and are dispersing throughout the nation. California is a particularly interesting state with a growing population of more than 39 million (Garofoli, 2009). White registered voters in the state comprise 65 percent of the electorate—18 percent fewer than they were in 1978. Latino voters grew to 21 percent of the state's voters, up 13 percent since 1978.

U.S. schools and classrooms are experiencing some of the most dramatic racial-ethnic shifts of any social institutions. Close to four million documented immigrants settled in the United States between 2000 and 2004. Given the rapid pace of globalization the United States should expect to see school-aged children from all over the world show up in the nation's schools. War-torn regions like Iraq, Afghanistan, Sudan, and Somalia are likely to continue to have citizens who will seek refuge in the United States. Natural and economic disasters will force still others to look to the United States as a safe haven. The increased globalization of manufacturing, commerce, and services means that people from all over the world will see the United States as a place of opportunity and innovation. While many Western nations are looking for ways to close their borders, the United States, at least in principle, continues to advertise itself with open arms. The iconic Statue of Liberty declares, "Give me your tired, your poor" (Lazarus, 1889).

The research questions that emerge from these changing demographics are more conceptual than empirical. We will want to know how teacher education conceptualizes this changing diversity. Will we draw sharp lines of demarcation between citizens and recent immigrants? Will the established notions of race prevail over those of national origin? Rather than becoming preoccupied with counting we will want to know more about the meaning of that difference. We must also leave open the possibility that different kinds of diversity will become more salient in future classrooms. And finally, we will want to know what role can (and should) teacher education play in this changing demographic landscape.

As we consider our more global and diverse future, rather than an emphasis on race and ethnicity we may become more focused on language, gender, and religion. What impact does an increasingly female teaching profession have on the learning and achievement of boys? How do religious practices (e.g., female students wearing hijab or male students wearing turbans) influence what teachers and schools teach and how they interact with families? All of these questions have empirical possibilities, but they are nested in the conceptual question I posed previously: "How do teachers conceptualize diversity?" If a teacher stands before a room filled with Latino students and declares she works in a "diverse" classroom, we know that her conceptualization of diversity is rooted in notions of otherness or difference from that which is perceived to be the norm. On the other hand, if that same teacher were to explain that the class was diverse because she had students from several nations—Mexico, Honduras, Guatemala, Panama, and El Salvador—several different areas of immigration and some who were native born, and a wide spectrum of schooling experiences—some having attended school in their country of origin and others attending school for the first time—then we would understand that teacher to have a complex understanding of diversity. She does not presume the fact that the students speak a common language to be a strong enough marker of a common identity. The complexities of identity will continue to mark our understanding of diversity in teacher education.

HOW TO MAKE A TEACHER

Medical schools prepare doctors. Law schools prepare lawyers. Veterinarian schools prepare veterinarians. Everybody prepares teachers. Of course this is an overstatement. However, a large part of the current debate about teacher education is unmooring teachers from teacher education programs (Hess, 2001). Why do we believe that teachers would be so much better if they were not prepared in teacher education programs? In this discussion I look at two issues—the argument against teacher education and the structure of teacher education programs that make them vulnerable to regular critique.

Teachers have been the focus of much of the debate about how to improve our schools (Darling-Hammond, 2002). However, what teachers actually do has not been the primary focus of the debate. Instead, much of the debate has focused on what teachers teach (curriculum) and how well students learn it (assessment) (see figure 19.1). The actual work of teaching has received scant attention. The notion that pedagogy might actually matter seems lost in most discussions about teaching and learning.

In general the anti-teacher-education argument looks at teachers' qualifications as solely constituted of teacher subject-matter knowledge. The argument posits, the more content knowledge the teacher has, the better she is. Thus, a good English teacher is someone who has a high-quality English degree. A good biology teacher has extensive knowledge of biology. Of course, no one would argue that teachers should not have deep subject-matter knowledge, but scholars and practitioners in teacher education understand subject-matter knowledge as a necessary but not sufficient condition for good teaching (Shulman, 1986, 1987). The argument against teacher education suggests that too much time is taken up with "how to teach" courses that lack intellectual substance and rigor. Thus, anti-teacher-education voices see teacher education as a barrier rather than an aid to preparing people for the profession. Interesting, the backlash against teacher education comes as a result of teachers' lack of success with diverse groups of students—poor children, children of color, students whose first language is other than English. Most middle- to upper-middle-class communities have schools that are almost exclusively staffed by teachers who have received conventional teacher preparation. Schools serving poor children, children of color, children whose first language is other than English struggle to find certified teachers and become dependent on alternatively prepared teachers.

Many of the conventionally prepared teachers prefer not to work in communities serving poor, working-class students of color and recent immigrant students. When their job opportunities are limited to working in the very communities they prefer not to work in, they struggle not only with teaching but also feeling comfortable and efficacious in those communities. Research suggests that there exists a "revolv-

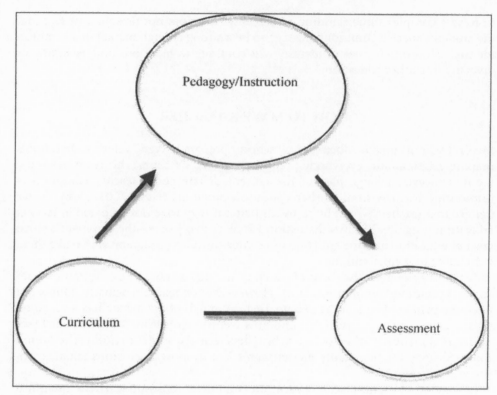

Figure 19.1   Classroom learning triad.

ing door" of teachers coming into the profession and leaving soon after (Ingersoll, 2001, 2002). The problem of teacher retention is especially acute among new teachers of color (Ingersoll & Connor, 2008). This loss of teachers of color is particularly frustrating because research indicates that teachers of color, more than their white counterparts, choose to work in so-called hard to staff schools (Darling-Hammond, Dilworth, & Bullmaster, 1996; Hanushek, Kain, & Rivkin, 2004; Kirby, Berends, & Naftel, 1999). However, research also indicates that having more teachers of color is not enough to alleviate the achievement disparities that exist between students of color and their white peers (Achinstein & Ogawa, 2008). These teachers need the support of school administrators and organizational structures that will allow them to their use cultural knowledge and skills to enhance teaching and learning (Ladson-Billings, 2009).

In this discussion I will necessarily focus on a generic conception of teacher education. This is not meant to discount the variety of teacher education programs that specialize and customize preparation for teachers. However, the majority of teachers are prepared in programs that include the following elements: general education or introductory courses, a major concentration (for secondary teachers) or a minor concentration (for elementary teachers), and a professional sequence that consists of foundation courses such as history, philosophy, sociology or psychology of education, teaching methods courses, and field experiences (that may include observations, practica, and student teaching). This model of teacher preparation (with some minor variations) has held sway for at least fifty years. In states that require teacher preparation to be a postbaccalaureate certification, prospective students begin with a degree in an approved major (i.e., some content area commonly taught in K–12 schools) and then complete a professional sequence. However, the professional sequence is remarkably similar to that taken by their four-year undergraduate teacher education counterparts.

Teacher educators who are committed to issues of diversity in teacher education have a number of "leverage points" to consider in their practice. The first leverage point is at admissions—those we admit into the teacher education program. For many years Martin Haberman (1995) argued that in the case of teachers who will teach in urban schools, we need to think differently about whom to recruit. Instead of continuing to recruit nineteen- to twenty-year-olds with limited experience outside of suburban communities, the better candidates for urban schools may be those who themselves have experienced lives similar to urban students. Such teacher candidates may be more mature and better understand the life circumstances of students who are struggling with poverty and other family and community challenges.

We should not assume that being an older, urban person makes one qualified to be an urban teacher. However, we should question the repeated practice of preparing young, white, suburban, middle-class, monolingual English speakers to teach an increasingly diverse student population. Also, we should question how helpful it is to expose white, middle-class school students to only white, middle-class teachers. How are they disadvantaged by a view of education as the sole purview of whites?

In addition to addressing the demographics of teaching we should also consider the intellectual interests and strengths of those we recruit to become teachers. In instances where gaining admission into teacher education programs is limited and programs require high grade point average, we find students loading their transcripts with less challenging courses to produce those high grade point averages. In instances where gaining admission into teacher education programs is relatively easy, we have to ask whether it is better to have no teacher education program than to have one that accepts poorer performing college students. Perhaps the best way to address the quality of candidates issue is to provide generous scholarships and loan forgiveness for the best students. For example, a student with high academic performance in rigorous courses in mathematics, science, social sciences, and humanities could be guaranteed a full scholarship should she choose teaching as a career.

The second leverage point in teacher education could be just before candidates are assigned to student teach. Having successfully completed course work may not indicate that a candidate is prepared to work with students, even under the supervision of a knowledgeable mentor. Students who have expressed grave concerns about whether particular groups of students are capable of learning or entitled to an education may not be ready to assume responsibility for teaching. Each student teacher assigned to teach in an urban school should go through a careful assessment to determine his readiness for the assignment. Instead of merely being pleased to find a location for student teachers, teacher educators have to carefully match the student teacher to the student-teaching placement. Perhaps teacher educators need to rethink the student-teaching placement process to parallel the way medical schools place interns. Medical students seek out internships based on their interests and the reputation of the teaching hospital. Their matches do not always reflect their first choices. Instead they reflect a selection by a more experienced practitioner about what would be a good fit for the novice.

The third leverage point is at the completion of the teacher education program and prior to recommendation for certification. Teacher licensure is a responsibility of the state. However, states approve teacher education programs to prepare and then recommend candidates for licensure. Again, as mentioned above regarding assignment to student teaching, recommendation for licensure should not be regarded as a guarantee of program completion. Careful consideration on the part of program officials—faculty, supervisors, cooperating teachers, and school principals—should contribute to the decision to recommend a teacher candidate for licensure. The reality is this decision is regularly made by one to two people (e.g., a university supervisor and a cooperating teacher) who have limited organizational authority.

A possible fourth leverage point happens during the probationary period, namely, the first two years of teaching. Unfortunately, most teacher education programs assume no responsibility for novice teachers once they complete the certification program. Hard-to-staff schools rarely have the resources to adequately supervise novice teachers. Thus, those teachers who are willing to stay for two years may automatically receive tenure. Unlike medical school where prospective doctors go from medical students to interns and from interns to residents on a trajectory of increasing responsibility, prospective teachers generally go from students to teachers in a relatively short time.

By making the probationary period a time of guided practice with close supervision, college and university teacher education programs could work in close contact with their graduates and receive valuable feedback on program effectiveness and serve as an important source of professional development for novice teachers.

THE "MULTICULTURAL" REQUIREMENT

Almost every preservice teacher education program has some requirement for students to fulfill a diversity or multicultural component. Unfortunately, many teacher education programs do not have adequate capacity to make this requirement an integral part of the program, and the requirement is handled by a single course, a workshop, or a program module (Cochran-Smith, 2003). Preservice programs that make the multicultural (or diversity) requirement a single course tend to segregate the course from other aspects of the program. It is not connected to methods courses or field experiences, and some faculty members would rather not teach it because of student resistance to the ideas expressed in the course and fear of poor course evaluations.

In programs that make the requirement either a workshop or module, preservice students take away the not-so-subtle message that issues of diversity, equity, and multiculturalism are not particularly important and they just have to endure these experiences because of state requirements. The students do not believe there is anything of intellectual or pedagogical value to be taken from such experiences. Even in those programs where issues of diversity, multiculturalism, equity, and social justice are well integrated into the entire program, students may express resistance and question its value in helping them to become effective teachers. This resistance may reflect prospective teachers' unspoken intentions to avoid teaching in school communities that serve diverse groups of students. The current emphasis on standards and accountability make preservice teachers believe that focusing on diversity and equity are counterproductive and unrelated to student achievement.

The unspoken issue in diversity and teacher education is the low participation of scholars of color in teacher education (Ladson-Billings, 1999b). With the exception of those employed at the approximately one hundred historically black colleges and universities, few blacks were (are) employed as teacher educators. Eighty-eight percent of the full time education professors (AACTE, 1994) in the United States are white. Eighty-one percent of this faculty is between the ages of forty-five and sixty (or older). Thus, a profession that is trying to diversify and "multiculturalize" its students finds itself in the embarrassing and awkward position of remaining overwhelmingly white, monolingual, and middle class.

STUDENT TEACHING AS A PROXY FOR TEACHING

In general, teacher education students regard the student-teaching experience as the single most valuable component of their preparation program (Hollins, 2008). Students regularly complain that foundations courses such as History of Education, Philosophy of Education, or Educational Psychology are "irrelevant" and unrelated to their practice. Students also complain that methods courses such as methods of teaching reading, mathematics, science, or social studies are little more than activity courses that fail to consider the actual experiences students will encounter as teachers. Structurally, most methods professors do not supervise students in the field, and those assigned to supervise often are either graduate students or experienced practitioners who serve as adjunct faculty members. Neither of these conditions necessarily means those who work in these areas are not competent. Rather, their disconnection reminds us, just as Meyer and Rowan (1977) did more than three decades ago, that schools are loosely coupled organizations, and teacher education may be more so.

Student teaching takes place in real classrooms, not ideal classrooms. The great need to find clinical sites for preparing teachers means that teacher education programs often function at the mercy of school districts, principals, and individual teachers. Since the primary mission of schools is to educate their K–12 constituents, college and university requests can be seen as just another demand on an already filled agenda. Selection of cooperating teachers runs the gamut from careful matching of teacher candidates to highly skilled teachers to arbitrary and ambiguous assignment as a result of volunteers and administrative perks. In the best programs a student-teaching placement coordinator maintains a cadre of exceptional cooperating teachers and allows prospective teachers to visit and interview with cooperating teachers. The match—of teaching styles, personal philosophy, and personality— creates a positive working arrangement that hopefully ensures the growth of the new professional.

Unfortunately, many teacher education programs routinely solicit placements for student teachers and administrators announce the availability of student teachers.

Individual teachers decide to accept a student teacher based on their own needs—interest in nurturing new professionals, access to learning latest curriculum and pedagogical knowledge and skills, or another set of hands to help in the classroom. In some schools principals assign student teachers to their favorite teachers as a form of no-cost rewards. The teachers' expertise and suitability are not considered in this type of assignment.

Increasingly, teacher education programs require that students have field experiences in "diverse" classrooms. This requirement typically means that prospective teachers are assigned to schools with racial, ethnic, linguistic, or socioeconomic differences (as determined by metrics such as the proportion of students receiving free and reduced lunches). This is a desirable feature of teacher preparation; however, it is not coupled with a demand for outstanding cooperating teachers. The data clearly demonstrate that students in these "diverse" schools are more likely to have teachers who are less qualified (or at least less qualified for the job to which they have been assigned) (Lankford, Loeb, & Wycoff, 2002). Thus, the admirable goal of placing prospective teachers in classrooms serving diverse learners is thwarted by the reality that their mentorship may be controlled by less desirable cooperating teachers.

The danger of placing student teachers in settings with poor quality cooperating teachers is the inordinate influence that student teaching has on prospective teachers. Unable to integrate the theoretical and research knowledge from university-based courses, student teachers quickly fall into the folkways and prevailing discourses of the field experience (Cornbleth, 2008; Zeichner & Tabachnick, 1981). Currently, urban schools serving low-income and working-class communities (many of which are overwhelming schools serving children of color) are awash in a discourse of the "culture of poverty." This discourse suggests that the problem of school achievement resides in the status characteristics of the students and their families and not the ineffective performance of schools. As a consequence schools become a place where the major responsibility of teachers is to demand compliance and keep order. Despite more nuanced and scholarly critiques of this perspective (Bomer et al., 2008; Sato & Lensmire, 2009), teachers and, by default, many student teachers accept the explanation of school failure as the sole purview of students, their families, their communities, and something loosely cobbled together as their "culture." However, almost twenty years ago Haberman (1991) pointed out that rather than a culture of poverty, what urban students suffer from is the "pedagogy of poverty." In his description of the strategies employed by ineffective urban teachers, Haberman points out that the focus on regimentation and control belie a teacher who most likely did not have deep intellectual engagement as a student, is afraid of the urban poor, and has a limited pedagogical repertoire.

EXAMINING ALTERNATIVES

Given the ongoing problems of preparing teachers to be successful in schools serving diverse communities, it would appear that alternatives would be plentiful and readily embraced. The data suggest the first—plenty—is the case (Feistritzer, 2005), while the second—embracement—is a mixed bag (Darling-Hammond, 2002). In 2007 all fifty states and the District of Columbia had alternative certification routes to teaching. Originally, alternative certification encompassed a wide range of state practices, from issuing emergency certificates to specific alternative programs.

It is important to note that alternative teaching certification is not a new practice. In 1965 the National Teacher Corps (NTC) was a federally funded program of the Johnson administration included in the Higher Education Act. Senator Gaylord Nelson (Wisconsin) and Senator Edward M. Kennedy (Massachusetts) proposed the original legislation. The purpose of the program was to provide teachers for schools in low-income and poverty-stricken communities.

The Corps recruited liberal arts graduates and students of color to teach in urban communities. After an eight-week summer program, Corps interns were assigned to urban classrooms and required to enroll in a two-year university-based program and participate in community activities such as after-school programs and recreation centers. This threefold approach, on-the-job training, professional development, and community involvement, seemed to be an important strategy for inducting new professionals into the field. The program survived until 1981 when the Reagan administration folded it into an educational block grant that was a part of the new federalism.

In 1990 Wendy Kopp, a Princeton University graduate, launched the first cohort of Teach for America (TFA) teachers. This alternative included many features of the National Teacher Corps—recruit bright liberal arts graduates, provide summer training, and place recruits in hard-to-staff schools serving poor and low-income school communities. One difference between NTC and TFA is TFA's independence from university-based professional development (although more recently a number of universities have contracted with TFA to provide professional development). The second difference is that TFA graduates make a two-year commitment to teaching (although many stay longer) similar to that of Peace Corps volunteers. Critics point to this short-term commitment as one of the program flaws (Laczko-Kerr & Berliner, 2002). More pointedly, critics cite the failure of TFA program members to produce significantly better student outcomes than their peers without certificates (Darling-Hammond, 1994).

Despite the apparent shortcomings of Teach for America it seems that the program is a permanent fixture on the alternative certification landscape. The program may have started out as one that depended on private and corporate donors, but in the new Obama administration it has received a $20 million allocation to meet its goal of placing 7,500 teachers in thirty-three states and regions to serve what it projects as more than 600,000 underserved students from poor and low-income communities (see Teach for America website, http://www.teachforamerica.org/newsroom/documents/020808_HEA_Amendment.htm). However, Teach for America is not the most concerning development in alternative teacher certification. Online or computer-based certification programs are an increasing proportion of the alternative certification strategy. Historically black colleges and universities (HBCUs) are moving into online education as a way to preserve enrollment (Roach, 2002), and large for-profit entities such as the University of Phoenix, Cappella University, and Western Governor's Teachers University are making increasing inroads in teacher certification. However, the majority of alternative certification programs are run by states to determine who can receive a teaching license. According to Feistritzer (2005), 70 percent of those who pursue teaching certification through alternative routes are more than thirty years of age. Thirty-eight percent are male, 30 percent are nonwhite, and 46 percent are teaching in large cities. Nearly half of the alternative-route teachers were working in a non-education-related field prior to seeking certification, and nearly half indicated that they would not have become teachers without access to an alternative route. One of the main reasons for choosing an alternative route is the ability to teach and receive a salary and benefits while completing certification requirements.

About 35,000 teachers enter the field through alternative routes each year. Given that TFA produces a maximum of 7,500 teachers, it seems that state-sponsored programs are the primary source of such teachers and it seems that their outreach to nontraditional communities is more effective than that of traditional university-based programs. The ability to recruit more males, more people of color, and more candidates who choose to teach in urban schools makes such programs attractive to administrators in urban school districts.

Currently the data are unclear concerning the effectiveness of alternative certification for improving academic achievement for urban schools. One of the major problems in comparing traditional and alternative programs is definitional. What constitutes an "alternative" teacher preparation program? Some university-based programs are small, boutiquelike programs that share many of the features of alternative certification programs. Some alternative programs are housed in universities and carry the imprimatur of the academy. If increasing the diversity of the teaching force is one of the goals of teacher education, it seems that alternative routes to teaching will continue to be a necessary component of preparing teachers.

THE CHALLENGE TO COME

The point of this chapter is to outline the research agenda for diversity in teacher education. I have attempted to detail the state of teacher education and the concerns about certification. In this final section I want to address what the research agenda for diversity in teacher education could be. It should be noted that a research agenda aimed at looking at practice needs both theoretical and empirical components, and some of that empirical work should be in the form of experimentation. Below is a decidedly short list of research studies that should help sharpen our focus and advance diversity in teacher education.

1. **Establish what role, if any, issues of diversity play in helping new teachers become effective with all learners.** In general, discussions about diversity focus on the social and civic good that diversity performs in society. That good is rarely debated. However, little research points to the scholastic good that results from diversity. We need to design research studies that allow us to trace the academic benefit of diversity for prospective teachers and later for the students they teach. Such studies may look at levels of student engagement and attention to school tasks as proxies for the benefits of diversity.
2. **Establish clearer definitions for what we mean by diversity.** As discussed in the early part of this chapter, we carry multiple meanings of the term *diversity*. We talk about diversity in terms of race, class, gender, language, religion, na-

tional origin, ability, and sexuality. Those categories are important and salient in everyday life—in communities, in the workplace, in commerce. However, because school is a place that can and should serve to minimize social differences, diversity categories should be regulated by academic performance categories. A close look at achievement measures can tell teachers which groups are performing at lower levels than others. Are boys performing at lower levels than girls? Are African American students performing at lower levels than white students? Are second-language learners performing at lower levels than native speakers? These empirical data that are available to teachers in every classroom should become the data from which we shape our notions of diversity. This is not to suggest that other forms of diversity are not important. Rather, it is to align diversity with the central mission of the school.

3. **Examine the practice of diverse groups of novice teachers from both traditional and alternative certification routes to determine their satisfaction with their preparation.** In general, we guess at what makes a prospective teacher of color choose teaching as a profession and a particular form of preparation. Closer inspection of their decision-making processes and program supports will add to our knowledge base and improve our practice.

4. **Experiment with models of teacher education to determine which forms are more effective for preparing prospective teachers for teaching in diverse settings.** University teacher education programs rarely experiment to determine effectiveness. Instead, they add or subtract according to state mandates and faculty decision making. However, experimentation is crucial to continuous improvement. University-based teacher education programs can use the occasion of their program reviews as an opportunity to conduct small design experiments to determine more effective ways to improve practice.

5. **Examine the procedures and strategies of alternative programs that are successful in recruiting more diverse teacher candidates.** Despite the critiques of alternative routes to teacher education, the data show that some alternatives are more successful in recruiting a diverse teaching force. We need better information about their success in recruiting and retaining candidates of color, male candidates, and candidates willing to teach in urban settings serving low-income and poor students.

6. **Experiment with models that increase the number of diverse teacher educators to increase the likelihood prospective teachers will experience diverse intellectual and pedagogical perspectives.** The "dirty little secret" of teacher education is that as much as it champions diversity for its students, it is not a diverse field. What makes this especially problematic is the fact that education is the primary field in which people of color hold earned doctorates. However, most of those holding doctorates work in school-district, county-, and state-level education agencies. These people form a ready-made cadre of professionals who can help increase the diversity of the teacher education program.

7. **Look for "existence proofs" and "lesson studies" of diversity in teacher education.** Given all of the negative discourse around the usefulness of teacher education, it is important to identify those teacher education programs that take seriously the challenge of preparing teachers who can be successful with diverse groups of students. Even when these programs are small, we should be able to

isolate relevant components and determine whether they can be scaled up for replication. The idea of lesson study is to look at small but constituent aspects of a program and study it systematically. For example, a careful study of admissions procedures might yield valuable information about who chooses a particular program, what their academic and background profile looks like, and how diversifying the pool might initiate change in other aspects of the program.

No agenda focused on ongoing practice can be definitive. In many ways we are looking at making changes on a moving target, or as Cochran-Smith (1995) argues, "We are trying to build a boat while we are already in a boat." However, the challenges of defining diversity, establishing its role in teacher education, experimenting with various models of teacher education, recruiting a more diverse pool of teacher educators, looking more carefully at alternative certification, and looking at outstanding programs and program components all help in the ultimate improvement of the field. We must move past intuitive notions of what diversity means for teaching and teacher education to more research-based approaches to innovation and improvement.

REFERENCES

Achinstein, B., & Ogawa, R. (2008). *Beyond retaining new teachers of color: Survival and the loss of vision for culturally relevant teachers and agents of change.* Paper presented at the Annual Meeting of the American Educational Research Association, New York.

American Association of Colleges of Teacher Education. (1994). *Briefing books.* Washington, DC: Author.

Bomer, R., Dworin, J., May, L., & Semingson, P. (2008). Miseducating teachers about the poor: A critical analysis of Ruby Payne's claims about poverty. *Teachers College Record, 110(12)*, 2497–31.

Cochran-Smith, M. (1995). Uncertain allies: Understanding the boundaries of race and teaching. *Harvard Educational Review, 65(4)*, 541–70.

Cochran-Smith, M. (2003). The multiple meanings of multicultural teacher education: A conceptual framework. *Teacher Education Quarterly, 30(2)*, 7–26.

Cochran-Smith, M., & Fries, K. (2001, November). Sticks, stones, and ideologies: The discourse of reform in teacher education. *Educational Researcher, 30*, 3–15.

Cornbleth, C. (2008). *Diversity and the new teacher.* New York: Teachers College Press.

Darling-Hammond, L. (1994). Who will speak for the children: How "Teach for America" hurts urban schools and students. *Phi Delta Kappan, 76*, 21–34.

Darling-Hammond, L. (2002). Research and rhetoric on teacher certification: A response to "Teacher certification reconsidered." *Educational Policy Analysis Archives, 10(36)*. Retrieved November 22, 2009, from http://epaa.asu.edu/epaa/v10n36.html

Darling-Hammond, L., Dilworth, M. E., Bullmaster, M. (1996). *Educators of color: A background paper for the invitational conference, "Recruiting, preparing and retaining persons of color in the teaching profession."* National Alliance of Black School Educators. Washington, DC: Phi Delta Kappa Educational Foundation; Bloomington, IN: Recruiting New Teachers.

Feistritzer, C. E. (2005). *Profile of alternative route teachers.* Washington, DC: National Center for Education Information.

Garofoli, J. (2009, August 4). Demographic shifts may shape governor's race. *San Francisco Chronicle*, p. A–6.

Haberman, M. (1991). The pedagogy of poverty versus good teaching. *Phi Delta Kappan, 73(4),* 260–64.

Haberman, M. (1995). *Star teachers of children in poverty.* Indianapolis, IN: Kappa Delta Pi.

Hanushek, E., Kain, J. F., & Rivkin, S. G. (2004). Why public schools lose teachers. *Journal of Human Resources, 39(2),* 326–54.

Hess, F. (2001). *Tear down this wall: The case for a radical overhaul of teacher certification.* Report of the Progressive Policy Institute. Retrieved November 11, 2009, from http://www.ppionline.org/ppi_ci.cfm?knlgAreaID=110&subsecID=135&contentID=3964

Hollins, E. (2008). *Culture in school learning: Discovering the deep meaning.* New York: Routledge.

Ingersoll, R. (2001). Teacher turnover and teacher shortages: An organizational analysis. *American Educational Research Journal, 38(3),* 499–534.

Ingersoll, R. (2002). The teacher shortage: A case of wrong diagnosis and wrong prescription. *NAASP Bulletin, 86(631),* 16–31.

Ingersoll, R., & Connor, R. (2008). *National data on minority and black teacher turnover.* Paper presented at the Annual Meeting of the American Educational Research Association, New York.

Jones, C., & Overberg, P. (2008, August 7). Demographic landscape shifts across United States. *USA Today,* p. A–1.

Kirby, S. N., Berends, M., & Naftel, S. (1999). Supply and demand of minority teachers in Texas: Problems and prospects. *Educational Evaluation and Policy Analysis, 21(1),* 47–66.

Laczko-Kerr, I., & Berliner, D. C. (2002, September 6). The effectiveness of "Teach for America" and other under-certified teachers on student academic achievement: A case of harmful public policy." *Education Policy Analysis Archives, 10(37).* Retrieved November 11, 2009, from http://epaa.asu.edu/epaa/v10n37/

Ladson-Billings, G. (1995). Multicultural teacher education: Issues, policies, and practices. In Banks, J. A., & Banks, C. M. (Eds.), *Handbook of research on multicultural education* (pp. 747–59). New York: Macmillan.

Ladson-Billings, G. (1999a). Preparing teachers for diversity: Historical perspectives, current trends, and future directions. In Pearson, P. D. & and Iran-Najed, A. (Eds.), *Review of Research in Education* (Vol. 24), (pp. 211–47). Washington, DC: American Educational Research Association.

Ladson-Billings, G. (1999b). Is the team alright? Diversity and teacher education. *Journal of Teacher Education, 56(3),* 229–34.

Ladson-Billings, G. (2000). Fighting for our lives: Preparing teachers to teach African American students. *Journal of Teacher Education, 51(3),* 206–15.

Ladson-Billings, G. (2005). What's the matter with the team? Diversity in teacher education. *Journal of Teacher Education, 56,* 229–34.

Ladson-Billings, G. (2009). *The dreamkeepers: Successful teachers of African American children,* 2nd ed. San Francisco: Jossey-Bass.

Lankford, H., Loeb, S., & Wycoff, J. (2002). Teacher sorting and the plight of urban schools: A descriptive analysis. *Educational Evaluation and Policy Analysis, 24,* 37–62.

Lazarus, E. (1888). *The poems of Emma Lazarus.* New York: Houghton Mifflin.

Meyer, J., & Rowan, B. (1977). Institutional organizations: Formal structure as myth and ceremony. *American Journal of Sociology, 83,* 340–63.

Planty, M., Hussar, W., Snyder, T., Kena, G., KewalRamani, A., Kemp, J., Bianco, K., Dinkes, R. (2009). *The condition of education 2009* (NCES 2009–081). National Center for Education Statistics, Institute of Education Sciences, U.S. Department of Education. Washington, DC.

Roach, R. (2002, April 25). Going online with V–HBCU. *Black Issues in Higher Education.* Retrieved November 23, 2009, from FindArticles.com, http://findarticles.com/p/articles/mi_m0DXK/is_5_19/ai_85880317/

Sato, M., & Lensmire, T. (2009). Poverty and Payne: Supporting teachers to work with children of poverty. *Phi Delta Kappan, 90(5)*, 365–70.

Shulman, L. (1986). Those who understand: Knowledge growth in teaching. *Educational Researcher, 15(2)*, 4–14.

Shulman, L. (1987). Knowledge and teaching: Foundations of the new reform. *Harvard Educational Review, 57(1)*, 1–22.

Zeichner, K. M., & Tabachnick, B. R. (1981). Are the effects of university teacher education "washed out" by school experience? *Journal of Teacher Education, 32(3)*, 7–11.

20

Preparing Teachers for Diversity in the Twenty-first Century

Arnetha F. Ball and Cynthia A. Tyson

In this volume, the contributing authors have discussed many of the pressing and persistent challenges facing teacher education today. Part I of the volume highlights the historical trajectory of research on diversity in teacher education. These authors make a call for more empirical, longitudinal, and large-scale studies that place multicultural knowledge and equity study at the center of individual teacher education programs. The contributing authors make connections between high-quality teacher education for diverse students (Grant et al.), identity development (Hollins), reconceptualizations of core values in teacher preparation and the juxtapositioning of induction, recruitment, and retention for teachers of color (Sleeter & Milner), and the need for supporting an equity agenda over the entire spectrum of our educational system—from kindergarten through graduate school—in twenty-first-century classrooms (Pang & Park).

In structuring this volume, contributing authors were asked to take up the critical questions of our times as they relate to research on diversity in education *and* research on diversity in teacher education and to highlight critical recommendations for future research. After a review of the historical timeline of research on diversity in teacher education, Grant and colleagues highlight the need for more empirical, longitudinal, and large-scale studies that address the following questions:

- How do we assess high-quality teacher education for diversity?
- What are the roles of supervisors and cooperating teachers—the teacher educators who, arguably, have the largest impact on preservice teachers and yet are understudied and undertrained on issues of diversity in teacher education?
- What do we find when we follow multicultural teacher education program graduates into their classrooms?
- What effect does the deregulation of teacher education have on the quality of multicultural and culturally relevant teaching?
- What programs and pathways are successful at educating culturally competent teachers, and what distinguishes these programs and pathways?

- What can be learned from global and transnational teacher education work on diversity and equity?

Anderson and Olsen (2006), Ball (2006, 2009), Cornbleth (2008), and Watson and colleagues (2006) are examples of studies that have begun to move the field in the direction of responding to these questions.

In chapter 2, Pang and Park propose that improving diversity in teacher education programs will require that all participating faculty and administrators have a cognate area of specialization that focuses on equity studies and that this training should begin with those faculty in charge of training the teacher educators of tomorrow. These faculty and administrators would then be better equipped to prepare future teachers and other educational practitioners through graduate education. According to Pang and Park, professional development for existing faculty should consist of the appropriate knowledge, theories, principles, and practices to support equity over the entire spectrum of our educational system from kindergarten through graduate school. They also recommend that establishing multicultural teacher education as a discipline in its own right would increase the probability that faculty and administrators in colleges and schools of education will become more fully qualified to train prospective teacher educators, credentialed teachers, and graduate students for effective service in twenty-first-century schools. They further propose that equity must be at the core of every teacher education program and that equity must be valued in order for education—as we now know it—to improve. These authors note that the implementation of this new paradigm would require structural changes in higher education, necessitate continual professional development aimed at the creation of a spiral curriculum, and involve continuing individual development on the part of all stakeholders.

Based on their review, Sleeter and Milner propose four interrelated areas of focus that can move the field forward: (1) more and deeper situated internal self-studies; (2) more and deeper contextualized external evaluations; (3) more and deeper long-term and longitudinal studies on teaching and teacher education; and (4) studies that investigate linkages between teacher ethnicity and student outcomes. They suggest that future studies might continue an examination of various ways to increase the number of teachers of color in public schools and propose deeper questioning about what it means for teachers of color to teach increasingly diverse students, how well these teachers fare with all their students, including white ones, what support structures enable and hinder their success, and what qualities about these teachers ensure meaningful learning opportunities for their students.

The basic premise of Hollins's discussion is that culture is central to social interaction, communication, and cognition. She further notes that the challenge for teacher educators is to develop an approach that will engender habits of mind to mitigate or replace the ideology of power and privilege in learning to teach. One approach to changing this discourse is to involve candidates, cooperating teachers, and university faculty in a process of shared observations, collaborative inquiry, and problem solving based on evidence from classrooms with diverse and underserved students. In this dialogue the focus is on the relationship among learning, learners, pedagogy, and learning outcomes. The goal of this process is for candidates and cooperating teachers to develop authentic and contextualized *knowledge in practice* and for university faculty to gain new perspectives and insights into classroom practices.

Part II of this volume focuses on current trends and innovations in the research on diversity in teacher education and sets in motion a dialogue on the interrogation of teacher preparation in the context of the diverse lives of the current student demographics. Realizing that it is not enough to discuss the gap in achievement through the lens of standardized assessment and curriculum standards, these authors provide theoretical exemplars that can be used when reconceptualizing our research through existing theoretical frameworks such as critical race theory and Tribal Critical Race Theory (Chapman; Lee). They also call for models of rigorous research that utilize expansive theoretical frameworks and complex methodological designs (Kinloch), research with teachers and students in classrooms (Kirkland; Quijada Cerecer), consideration of approaches to in-service teacher professional development within a global context (Uys, Kaiser, & Reyneke), and the consideration of contexts of urban ecologies (Duncan-Andrade).

Absent from the content of much of the research on teaching and teacher education are the voices and perspectives of marginalized student populations. Each of the researchers in part II emphasizes the importance of placing at the center of our research and analyses the voices and perspectives of the marginalized students themselves. Chapters 5 to 10 highlight voices and perspectives that every teacher educator and every teacher should be exposed to in order to prepare them to work effectively within culturally and linguistically complex educational contexts. In chapter 5, Quinn and Meiners highlight the educational research literature on sexuality in teacher education and propose that if taken up more broadly within teacher education, their suggested move from cultural to political clarity (awareness of the relationship between education and society and the educator's role as a political actor) could be paired with political competency (familiarity with collective histories and strategies of political action) to meet parallel and interlocking goals. They propose that if we would put political clarity and competency together as aims, dispositions, or standards in teacher education this could result in the fostering of more-aware teachers and more-activist teacher educators and, ultimately, could help preserve a fully public education system. In chapter 6, Kinloch turns our attention toward research that focuses on African American youth and a critical pedagogy of place in teacher education. Some of the implications emerging from Kinloch's chapter include: authoring new ways of learning and new selves that speak against inequitable educational practices and institutional structures; refiguring school spaces from sites where banking forms of education are experienced to sites of inquiry, exchange, and experimentation; and conceptualizing teaching and learning in frameworks that theorize equity pedagogy, multiculturalism, and social change. In her chapter, Kinloch calls for privileging the voices, perspectives, and critical insights of teachers (pre- and in-service) and students, even if those insights appear multiple, complex, contradictory, and divergent. And finally she calls for rigorous research that utilizes expansive theoretical frameworks and complex methodological designs that is inclusive of a multivoice approach and that provides specific, yet critical, directions for preparing teachers and students to live, work, and participate in a diverse, multicultural world.

In chapter 7, Quijada Cerecer engages readers in the lives of indigenous youth and their understandings of youth-adult relationships. She emphasizes their voices in her writing and moves beyond theory in an effort to challenge our thinking about youth by first listening to their voices and then by posing questions about how we can develop our understandings about youth-adult relationships. Through her analysis of a group of American Indian youth who attend a rural public high school, this author accomplishes what few other researchers have accomplished: she places Indigenous youth narratives at the center of analysis to demonstrate how these youth discussed and advocated for ways to improve their productive engagement in schools and enhance their learning experiences in those schools. In doing so she contributes to and extends our current understanding and conceptions of Indigenous youths' schooling experiences and encourages others to do so as well. Kirkland then turns our attention to the notion that teachers must also be prepared to attend to the complexities of students who are growing up black and male in their classrooms. He offers four suggestions for accomplishing this:

1. through courses that examine theories on black masculinities (cf. Brown, 1999; Young, 2007);
2. through targeted field experiences (within black neighborhoods as opposed to schools) working with young black men (cf. Morrell, 2005);
3. through research-training skills in ethnography or critical discourse analysis so that teachers can draw informed and systematic conclusions about their students to better teach them (cf. Alim, 2005; Heath, 1983; hooks, 2004); and
4. through assessment tools that measure whether or not a teacher can adequately demonstrate complex and sophisticated cultural knowledge of her or his students. This assessment of social and cultural content and pedagogical knowledge must be matched equally with an assessment of culturally relevant content and pedagogies (cf. Dixson, 2003; Greene & Abt-Perkins, 2003; Irvine & Armento, 2001).

Scott and Ford begin by focusing on the preparation of teachers to work with students with disabilities and gifts and talents. They highlight the fact that in many cases black students are denied opportunities to participate in gifted education and often they are unnecessarily placed in special education. They also highlight a lingering and looming question that needs to be addressed in their field: If the goal of education is to help students acquire the necessary tools in order to be successful in society, why, then, is it common practice to graduate preservice teachers without any experience, knowledge, or teachings from a multicultural perspective?

In chapter 10, Uys, Reyneke, and Kaiser highlight the value of in-service training while researching speakers of nondominant languages to contribute to a foundational base of research about diverse populations to which every teacher educator and teacher candidate must be exposed in order to begin the journey toward preparing a force of teachers that are prepared to teach diverse learners. The authors offer a close description—a case study for consideration by researchers who are seeking alternative ways of examining a very complex issue. The professional development model introduced in this chapter can be useful for considering future work with teachers from diverse linguistic backgrounds, forming a conceptual framework for future research within a global context with particular implications for further research on programs that provide in-service training to teachers with the goal of accommodating the linguistic diversity of teachers in training who must address their students' content-area needs within linguistically complex educational contexts.

Chapters 11–15 focus our attention on frameworks, perspectives, and paradigms in research on diversity in teacher education. In chapter 11, Chapman highlights the notion that teacher education cannot be interrogated at the individual or classroom levels without an analysis of how race and racism work in the larger contexts of institutions of higher education, teacher education policies, and state and federal mandates. She proposes that programs need to be created that allow students' flexibility and that provide them with financial incentives. The author also notes that within the realm of CRT, the quest for social justice is about changing the institutions that allow manifestations of whiteness to maintain power and disrupting the uncontested discourses that prevent radical and necessary reforms in teacher education that would help pre-K–12 children reach their full academic potential. Finally, she notes that the binary between quality and diversity must be aggressively challenged and dissolved in order for more students to enter the ranks of the teaching profession.

Olsen offers a framework for thinking about research on teachers and teaching in situ presenting *teacher identity* as a conceptual framework as well as a conceptual tool that carries implications for both educational practice and research, particularly as they relate to issues of diversity. He suggests the following to orient researchers who are considering embarking on research that employs teacher identity as a frame for research, practice, and diversity in education. They must (1) embrace an ecological paradigm; (2) centralize research on the study of teachers' language interactions; (3) privilege teachers in practice; and (4) treat research participants as collaborators, not subjects.

Lee provides another perspective by highlighting the need for a paradigm shift in education from one based on the insinuated superiority of Western society—which promotes assimilation—to one more inclusive of authentic representations of Native peoples and one that is socioculturally and locally respectful and responsive for all students. Lee notes that education becomes transformative by responding to students' sociocultural and local experiences and environments. However, according to Lee, socioculturally responsive (SCR) research must take a stronger stance to address the marginalization of Native peoples in curriculum, content, and pedagogy in order to ignite SCR education on behalf of Native peoples. This type of research agenda allows for reclamation of what it means to be Native because it includes authentic representations of Native peoples and acknowledges their contemporary lived experiences.

In chapter 14, Winn and Ubiles propose a movement in educational research that focuses on the lives of urban youth in schools and in out-of-school contexts throughout the United States. More specifically they focus on studies in language, literacy, and culture that inform teachers, teacher educators, and researchers while having implications for studying diversity in teacher education. Building on their collaborative research in urban classrooms, these authors introduce a methodology that privileges student and teacher voices while building relationships among classroom teachers, students, and researchers. After explicating the four phases of that research methodology, these authors urge future researchers who are committed to addressing diversity in teacher education and urban classrooms to consider the need to demonstrate responsibility within the research community and to establish opportunities to exercise reciprocity and to ritualize respect in the conduct of their research.

Duncan-Andrade rounds out this section by offering a rethinking about research on diversity in teacher education by strategizing about an approach to teacher education that develops educators who are better equipped to respond to the "socially toxic environments" (Garbarino, 1995) they exist in. This author notes that we live in a racist, xenophobic, classist, patriarchal, homophobic society and this results in our students' overexposure to social toxins. According to Duncan-Andrade, once we are willing to admit this reality, we can plot a course for teacher education that will prepare teachers to recognize and respond to the conditions that threaten their students' well-being and, by extension, their achievement.

The third and final part of this volume considers the sociocultural and sociopolitical contexts and consequences as well as future trends and directions for research on diversity in teacher education. The authors in this part of the volume have honed in on one very important factor in educational research in general and teacher education in particular: that is, the highly political nature of teacher preparation. Through a discussion of discourses, Cochran-Smith and Fries provide an analysis that yields a framework for the discussion of teacher quality and teacher preparation. These authors note that the bipartisan façade of an apolitical context within which these discussion are happening is misleading at best and disingenuous at worse. Therefore, these authors call for a politicized examination of federal, state, and local policies and funding of teacher education research while simultaneously taking the field to task for the lack of its ability to research the ecological complexity of teacher education or to create a solid empirical body of literature. Zeichner contributes to this discussion by pointing out our need to explicitly disentangle the impact of courses and programs from the characteristics, perspectives, and capabilities that prospective teachers bring to teacher education in our research. In addition, we must begin to share our research instruments and protocols and coordinate our research studies within and across institutions in this field. Another challenge to the field is highlighted by Nieto and McDonough in their discussions of our need to explore the creation and recreation of teacher education programs for both white teachers and teachers of color. While some programs have worked to explicitly prepare white teachers, little attention has been given to the expressed preparation of teachers of color. This invisibility may be the reason why so few teachers of color are enrolled in existing teacher preparation programs and ultimately in classrooms and why those who do matriculate to the classroom are ill prepared to meet the challenges of the classrooms they enter.

More explicitly, in chapter 16, Zeichner focuses on two aspects of the research on multicultural teacher education: the need to connect individual studies to one another in programs of research within communities of researchers in ways that enable the accumulation of knowledge over time and the need to design research in ways that reflect the complexity of what is being studied. He concludes that the failure of much existing research to address the ecological complexity of teacher education and to explicitly build upon research on similar issues within research programs has resulted in a situation where research has not been able to disentangle the impact of courses and programs from the characteristics, perspectives, and capabilities that prospective teachers bring to teacher education and to the settings in which they teach. He notes that because of the lack of common definitions of terms and the lack of overlap in how researchers have gathered data about certain social or individual characteristics, it has been difficult to draw conclusions about what is known about a given issue across studies. In chapter 17, Cochran-Smith and Fries identify and unpack five major discourses that are currently shaping policy and policy controversies in the United States regarding teacher quality and teacher preparation. They suggest that differences in these five discourses are not simply the result of different conclusions about how best to reach certain goals. Rather, they argue that these discourses are based on different ideas about what the goals should be in the first place. Embedded in these different constructions of "the problem" of teacher quality and teacher education are different values and assumptions about diversity and diverse groups. They suggest that different outcomes and consequences emerge from particular constructions of the problems to be solved and the larger agendas to which they are attached. Finally, they conclude that it is impossible to debate teacher quality or teacher education policy while remaining politically neutral, value free, and outside of larger debates about educational goals and means. It is high time that we move into an era of more truthful and forthright discussions about the political nature of teacher education and about solutions to the challenges that we face. In chapter 18, Nieto and McDonough highlight the notion that often teachers of color are rendered to a place of invisibility in teacher preparation programs because most programs focus on preparing white teachers for the classroom. It is imperative, however, that the unique perspectives and needs of preservice teachers of color be considered as well, since they often differ from those of white teachers. These authors challenge teacher education programs to do a better job of designing programs to meet the needs of teachers of color. The process of exploring one's racial and cultural identities is important for both white teachers and teachers of color because teachers' beliefs and values influence their practice. For preservice and practicing teachers of color, the assumption is often made that, as a group, they are better able to successfully teach children of color. This assumption, if applied in a blanket fashion, can be erroneous and does little to prepare preservice and practicing teachers of color for diverse classrooms. Therefore, we must seriously explore the creation of effective teacher education programs for both white teachers and for teachers of color. In chapter 19, Ladson-Billings calls for a research agenda that highlights the challenges of defining diversity, establishes the role of diversity in teacher education, experiments with various models of teacher education that prepares teachers for diversity, recruits a more diverse pool of teacher educators, looks more carefully at alternative certification, and looks at outstanding programs and program components in order to help improve the field. However, according to Ladson-Billings, the challenge remains for us to move beyond intuitive notions of what diversity means for teaching and teacher education toward more research-based approaches to innovation and improvements to the field.

These authors do an exceptional job of providing opportunities for readers to engage with an in-depth, intellectually stimulating analysis of the literature on diversity in teacher education and with new information that allows them to consider recent research from multiple perspectives. This information is designed to inform and facilitate the self-actualizing empowerment of researchers, teacher educators, policymakers, and practitioners, and to move them out of their zones of comfort while at the same time equipping them with the information needed to imagine new possibilities for the success of diverse students in classrooms within a rapidly changing global society. Complementing the contributions of earlier scholars who focused on issues of content and pedagogy in teacher education, these authors stand on the shoulders of and transcend the earlier work in the field to broaden the frame in which we consider what it means to "prepare teachers to teach in diverse classrooms" and to consider scholarship related to studying diversity in teacher education. In order to reverse the cycle of underachievement experienced by many students of color, these authors seek to provide the information necessary for teachers, teacher educators, and researchers to empower themselves with a deeper understanding of what the scholarship tells us and what we still need to know. Ultimately, these contributing authors help us to rethink the articulation of issues of diversity in teacher education so that our theories and practices might enable us to prepare teachers for effective classroom practices and provide educational researchers with direction for new inquiry. These authors interrogate some of the myths that underlie and drive so many of the ineffective curricular and pedagogical conventions that take place in teacher education programs when it comes to preparing teachers for diverse student populations. This interrogation will help us to think clearly about the creation of classrooms as places of equity, excellence, and achievement for all students in our increasingly diverse society.

A FEW CLOSING THOUGHTS

As the authors contributing to this volume have pointed out, many issues—including changing demographics in rural, urban, and inner-city schools, global migration of diverse populations to urban areas, persistent trends of academic underachievement for particular (stigmatized) student groups, and criticisms of current university models of teacher education by policymakers, teachers, students, and other stakeholders—challenge us to reconceptualize how we think about research and its impact on the delivery of instruction in teacher education programs. In particular, these issues challenge us to reconceptualize the way we think about research on diversity in teacher education programs and the impact of that research on the preparation of teachers for twenty-first century classrooms.

Before closing this volume, we would like to further emphasize three important areas of research that can support the teacher education community in reconceptualizing our thinking about diversity in teacher education programs and our approaches to preparing teachers for culturally and linguistically diverse classrooms. We feel that it is critically important that every educator have the ability to meet the needs of historically marginalized students; to identify the challenges and contradictions that are impacting the classroom lives and literacy development of underachieving students from culturally and linguistically diverse backgrounds; and to consider how their classroom practices and notions of "appropriate" instructional goals and outcomes are impacted by their engagement with research on radical citizenship, by policy development, and by their commitment to action for social change. One important area of research that can contribute to our reconceptualization of issues related to diversity in teacher education and our approaches to preparing teachers for culturally and linguistically complex classrooms is the way we think about the important role that *language* plays in teaching and learning and in our efforts to prepare teachers to teach diverse student populations. A second important area of research that can contribute to our reconceptualization of these issues is the way we think about the important role that *generativity* plays in teaching and learning and in our efforts to prepare teachers to teach in diverse classrooms. A third important area is the way we think about *globalization* and its impact on our research relating to issues of preparing teachers for diversity. Educators and teacher educators must come to better understand that today's educators around the globe are faced with similar challenges concerning their need to prepare teachers to teach diverse, underserved, and underachieving populations. We are citizens of a global community, which requires that we investigate further how we can address issues of diversity in teacher education as "scholar-activists"—that is, scholars who are openly interested in the processes of becoming change agents and engaged in research that is social-justice oriented. This requires more than an affinity with what has become the rhetoric of "interdependence" on a global level. Levstick and Tyson (2008) state that "recognizing interdependence, however, offers little help in working across borders, sorting out local, national, and global interest, recognizing fundamental differences as well as similarities, or having enough information and understanding to participate intelligently and humanely in related decision making." Therefore, the research community must move beyond the rhetoric of "interdependence" and keep the notions of language, generativity, and globalization in mind as they plan a research agenda that informs and supports diversity in teacher education and addresses the pressing challenges facing our field.

Research on the Centrality of Language in the Preparation of Teachers for Diversity

First, we propose that researchers must contemplate further the critical role that language plays in the preparation of teachers to teach diverse student populations and in the conduct of research that can inform the redesign of teacher education programs. According to Halliday (1993), "Language is *the* essential condition of knowing, the process by which experience becomes knowledge" (p. 94). In particular, we propose that every educator needs to contemplate how we come to understandings of the abstract kinds of knowledge that schooling aims to develop. Through serious contemplation they will come to realize that it is through language that all school subjects are taught and through language students' understandings of all concepts are displayed and evaluated within the school context. That is why teachers' knowledge about language itself is such a critical part of their schooling— because language *is* the content as well as the medium through which schooling occurs. Although schooling is primarily a linguistic process, language often serves as an *unconscious* means of evaluating and differentiating students. Both content and disciplinary knowledge are constituted and presented through language. Sadly, however, most teacher education candidates are not explicitly taught that *language is the medium through which we are taught, it is the medium through which we demonstrate what we have learned, and it is through language that we challenge, support, and evaluate learning.* Language is what Delpit (2002) refers to as *The Skin We Speak*. That is because through language we present ourselves as *knowers* and as *sharers of knowledge*—

not just for ESL learners, but for *all* students. Unfortunately, however, language itself is rarely the focus of attention within the general context of education programs—not for students or for student teachers—and a teacher's expectations for language education are seldom made explicit. That is because most teacher educators—and as a result, most teachers—do not understand language, how language develops, its relationship to literacy development, or the critical links that exist among language, identity, power, and school achievement.

All too often students have difficulties understanding a teacher's linguistic reasoning because there is a disconnect between the familiar processes of linguistic reasoning they bring from home and the linguistic processes they are expected to use at school. And teachers are unable to assist students with difficulties because of their limited understanding of the language and linguistic processes. In addition, teachers often have difficulties understanding the intent or meaning of a student's comment because of their lack of cultural understanding of the students' language use or their linguistic styles and modes of expression. The linguistic judgments that are unconsciously made to maintain status quo values are often not made explicit. All of this suggests it is critically important that teachers know more about language and that they have the ability to conduct a careful analysis of the linguistic challenges and opportunities that exist in their classrooms each day. In particular, it is critically important that teachers have an understanding of language and its role in teaching and learning if they expect to become effective teachers in urban and inner-city schools and in culturally and linguistically complex classrooms.

In order to address these challenges, teachers must come to understand that learning, learning language, and learning through language are simultaneous processes (see Halliday, 1993). While they are within the safe contexts of teacher education programs, teachers should have opportunities to investigate how the knowledge and social practices that constitute schooling are construed in great part through language. They need greater knowledge about the linguistic basis of what they are teaching and the tools they need for helping students achieve greater facility with the ways language is used in creating the kinds of texts that constitute specialized knowledge at school. If teachers lack this understanding, is there any wonder that linguistically diverse students are faring poorly in our schools?

Most teachers are unprepared to make the linguistic expectations of schooling explicit to their students. In addition, most teacher educators lack an understanding of how language works and the need to raise teachers' consciousness about the power of different linguistic choices in constituting different kinds of meaning making. Teachers and teacher educators need to receive explicit research-based training in order to raise students' consciousness about the power of language and linguistics in teaching and learning. In the absence of an explicit focus on language, students from certain socioeconomic and class backgrounds will continue to be privileged and others will continue to be disadvantaged in learning, assessment, and promotion—perpetrating the obvious inequalities that exist in our schools today. Our schools serve students who speak different languages and dialects, who have been socialized in different ways, and who face different kinds of challenges in their daily lives. Students whose cultural practices are similar to those of the school may be able to transfer those practices to the school setting, but students from other backgrounds may need to focus much more explicitly on the ways that language contributes to meaning-making as they engage in new social and cultural practices in order to succeed in achieving advanced literacy. Teachers and teacher educators who have not studied language are unaware of this and unprepared to integrate activities into their teaching that can support students in achievement in these areas.

We need to bring teacher education programs into the twenty-first century. Due to the historic development of teacher education programs in this country, most teachers receive coursework and instruction in the psychological foundations of education and coursework on the sociological foundations of education. However, given what we now know about the centrality of language in the teaching and learning of our increasingly diverse student populations, it is clear that a series of research-based courses in the language foundations of education must also be included in all teacher education programs. That series of courses would require teachers to engage with notions of:

A. An understanding of language and its development in students, with links to issues of language and identity
B. An understanding of the centrality of language in teaching and learning
C. Critical language study
   a. The relationship among language, ideology, power, and teacher professional development
   b. The relationship among discourses, Discourse, sociocultural theory, and generative change
   c. The language series should include a critical language awareness action research project that builds on the work of Foucault, Derrida, Bourdieu, Habermas, Smitherman, Rickford, Baugh, Ball, Alim, Ngugi wa Thiong'o, and others

While scholars like Fairclough and others talk about the central role of *critical language study* in teaching, most teacher education programs marginalize this work and instead move to the center of their programs a focus on content knowledge and pedagogical knowledge alone. In reality, cultural and linguistic knowledge must stand equally alongside content knowledge and pedagogical knowledge in every teacher education program and particularly in those teacher education programs that are attempting to prepare teachers to teach in today's culturally and linguistically complex classrooms. Given what we now know about the centrality of language in the teaching and learning of our increasingly diverse student population, a series of courses in the language foundations of education must be included in all teacher education programs. These courses should build on the large body of research that currently exists as well as newly emerging research on critical language study. Finally, research must be conducted on the increases in teacher effectiveness as a result of their expanded understanding of the critical role that language plays in the education of culturally and linguistically diverse students.

Research on the Role of Generativity in the Preparation of Teachers for Diversity

Second, we propose that researchers need to further contemplate the critical role that generativity plays in the preparation of teachers to teach diverse student populations and in the preparation of teachers who not only understand the centrality of language in the teaching and learning but who also are able to use that knowledge effectively in their pedagogical decision making and in their teaching practices. Since teachers *are* the key factor to the successful teaching of *all* students, teacher education programs are compelled to think seriously about the preparation of teachers who can organize their classrooms and diversify their teaching practice so that they can engage every student in learning. This requires further research on generativity, on the part it plays in teacher development as successful agents of change in diverse classrooms, and on what teacher education programs must do to facilitate the development of teachers who are generative thinkers.

Ball (2009) used the term *generativity* to refer to *a teachers' ability to continually add to their understanding by connecting their personal and professional knowledge with the knowledge they gain from their students in order to produce or originate new knowledge that is useful to them in pedagogical problem solving and in meeting the educational needs of their students.* Building on the work of Franke, Carpenter, Levi, and Fennema (2001), Ball presented a *Model of Generative Change* that professional development programs can use to support teachers' growth toward generativity and that teachers themselves can subsequently take up and use in their instruction within their own culturally and linguistically complex classrooms. Ball's decade-long, longitudinal study demonstrated how teachers participating in a carefully designed professional development program can develop metacognitive awareness about the role of language and literacies in their teaching as well as a sense of agency, advocacy, efficacy, personal voice, and generative thinking skills to direct their continued development as teachers within their culturally and linguistically complex classrooms. Building on the work of Vygotsky (1978), Wertsch (1985), and Bakhtin (1981), Ball's model illustrated the notion of mediation as a process involving the strategic use of oral and especially written language as cultural tools to shape and influence teachers' considerations about how to use the knowledge they gain about pedagogical problem solving to become generative agents of change in their classrooms. The process is generative in that once the teachers were exposed to a generative model in their teacher education programs, they were motivated to use the same cultural tools demonstrated in that program to shape their own students' development as problem solvers and as generative thinkers as well. Ball used writing as a pedagogical tool for reflection, introspection, and critique—within her professional development work to facilitate the teachers' development as generative thinkers. Teachers modeling this process subsequently used writing as a pedagogical tool for reflection, introspection, and critique within their culturally and linguistically complex classrooms to create dynamic learning communities in which oral and written discourses were strategically planned to establish environments where the students' cognitive activity was enhanced and where teachers' new knowledge learned about their students was linked to student knowledge on an ongoing basis to help them plan activities designed to facilitate generative thinking, problem solving, and high achievement in their classrooms.

Some of the most challenging teaching in the United States and abroad is taking place in classrooms that serve students from diverse cultural and linguistic backgrounds. The teachers in these classrooms are required to make appropriate pedagogical adjustments to meet the needs of their students each day; however, because many of them come from backgrounds that are very different from their students, they lack the ability to draw heavily on their own personal, cultural, and linguistic experiences as a knowledge base for making those adjustments for many of their students. It is therefore imperative that teacher education programs prepare these teachers to become generative in their thinking as pedagogical problem solvers and effective teachers in culturally and linguistically complex classrooms. Ball's research demonstrates how this can be accomplished. According to Ball (2009),

> Achieving this vision requires changes in teacher education programs that include the development of teachers who are prepared to teach students from backgrounds very different from their own. Achieving this vision also requires changes in teachers' conceptions of themselves as teachers and as learners. Teachers must be prepared to be generative in their thinking and generative in their teaching practices. Professional development programs must be reconceptualized as places where pedagogical approaches that are appropriate for working with diverse populations are modeled to scaffold teachers' development as generative practitioners. (p. 69)

Ball further notes that we need to reconceptualize current notions of professional development so that we place the preparation of teachers to teach in culturally and linguistically complex classrooms at the center, rather than at the margins, of current reform efforts in teacher education. Further research is needed on this model and its application in teacher education programs in the United States and abroad. Since the challenge to prepare teachers for culturally and linguistically complex classrooms is one that faces teachers cross-nationally, Ball recommends that further research on the implementation of this model must take place not only in U.S. classrooms but also in international contexts as well because, "Moving forward, we must begin to view the preparation of teachers to teach diverse students as a global challenge and look to the international community for ways to address the challenges we face."

RESEARCH ON DIVERSITY IN TEACHER EDUCATION AND GLOBAL PERSPECTIVES

Our third proposal is for further research on the place of diversity in teacher education from a global perspective—a perspective from which poor students, students of color, and underserved students are viewed as the majority population rather than as "minorities." The need to prepare more researchers from diverse communities around the globe is a growing phenomenon, and researchers on diversity in teacher education must embrace a global and comparative perspective as an important ideological orientation. These researchers must bring with them diverse perspectives that grow out of their circumstances and experiences. These perspectives will allow a new generation of scholars and researchers to look at global issues with perspectives that are enriched by multiple local visions. These researchers must also bring together innovative thinking on how teaching and researching for equity and social justice can facilitate the development, implementation, and evaluation of teacher education programs within a global society. The fact that today's educators and teacher educators face similar challenges globally in their efforts to prepare teachers to teach diverse and underserved populations underscores the need for inquiry into the best methodologies, techniques, conditions, and materials for bringing equity and social justice to student populations in classrooms across the globe. We further emphasize the need for researchers to recognize teachers, teacher educators, and teacher education programs not as the subjects of their research but as collaborators and as citizens of a global community.

Situating issues of research on diversity in teacher education within a global perspective would require that we look more broadly at the systemic improvement of urban education, the integration of new information and communication technologies in education, and the examination of the roll of linguistic resources, representational multimodal media, and ethnic, racial, and cultural diversity in urban education. Researchers must begin to imagine the ways that mobilization and reallocation of these urban resources can help students to become fully prepared for participation within a global society.

The fact that today's educators face similar challenges globally in their efforts to prepare teachers to teach diverse and underserved populations underscores the need for inquiry into the best methodologies, techniques, conditions, and materials for bringing equity and social justice issues to public attention through critical comparative studies conducted around the globe. We recommend pulling together the field's best thinking on how teaching and researching for equity and social justice can facilitate the development, implementation, and evaluation of teacher education programs within a global society so that we can begin to:

- cultivate a network of global scholars, researchers, and practitioners interested in working within cross-national collaborations on the study of teacher education;
- challenge the field to identify generativity in teachers' thinking and teachers' practices as a primary goal for the profession to work toward;
- advance the quantity and quality of research in the field by strengthening global collaborations on setting a mutually beneficial research agenda and by broadening the methodological approaches used in the field; and
- identify action steps that can engage scholars in "innovative research activities" that can advance the research on diversity in teaching and teacher education.

Moving toward a research vision that has the power to influence policies and practices that impact citizens of the global teacher education community will require that we conduct top-notch scholarship on issues of teacher change and on the process of changing teacher education programs; cast issues of diversity within a global context where people of color are the majority rather than the minority population; and recast the negative image of scholar activists into a more positive light. This top-notch scholarship will facilitate "radical thought; radical thought supports; radical action; and radical action [that] can advance a transformative . . . agenda" (Tyson, 2006) in educational research on teacher education in a global context.

However, taking a global perspective as activist scholars in teacher education will motivate us to put new issues on the research agenda as well as a public and global agenda that will open opportunities for us to address the needs of specific constituencies around the world.

In this volume we have highlighted theoretical frameworks—critical race theory (Chapman), teacher identity (Olsen), critical pedagogy (Kinloch), and urban ecologies (Andrade)—that support scholarship and activism. Often in education we evoke examples from the medical field. Being a medical activist involves working to improve health care, especially in the area of preventive care. Illnesses diagnosed too late can result in debilitating conditions and fatalities. While educational research for some may not be an arena for discussions of medical diagnosis, it should be a place for discussions concerning theory to practice for the overall improvement of the teaching and learning for those who are the underserved in our nation and the world's schools, with an eye to the "preventative care" needed to confront the blight of low academic achievement, especially for diverse students in the world's urban centers.

This is especially true given the increase in urban centers around the globe. The migration patterns of many people in search of jobs and substance is resulting in increases and changes in the demographics as well as the population of urban centers. These shifts have unique challenges when we think about preparing teachers. The preparation of teachers for these twenty-first-century schools and classrooms requires specialized training. We must ask ourselves, "What does it mean to teach children in urban centers from East Palo Alto, California, to Alexandra, South Africa?" Both have students that are economically fragile, both have the challenges of children without health care, both have parents and caregivers of these children and young people who are dually challenged with the cyclical nature of undereducation and poverty.

What we need is a movement toward alternative hybrid models that are generative in nature, sensitive to the context in which they are grounded, and organic. We need the best research to inform the development of programs that can creatively and effectively meet the needs of the ever-changing contexts of school in general and in urban schools in particular. This would have a profound impact on research agendas in teacher education as they relate to the complex issues facing urban education. The unique focus of these inquiries would be found at the intersection of two principal research agendas: (1) research on issues of curriculum and instruction in urban schools, and (2) policy analysis research on broader social, political, and economic issues that determine the context of urban education globally.

The issues related to curriculum and instruction in urban schools within a paradigm of global perspectives would require that we conduct research that supports the development of courses, field experiences, and internships that look at the systemic renewal of urban education; the integration of new information and communication technologies in education; examination of the role and issues of language and representational multimodal media for ethnic, racial, and cultural diversity in urban education; and at schools and teacher education programs as learning organizations (see Anthony & Ball, 2010). A new generation of researchers must begin to imagine the ways that research on the mobilization of urban resources will help teachers as well as the children they teach to become fully prepared for participation in a global society.

This new generation of researchers will need to simultaneously make epistemological and methodological moves as they carry out new lines of inquiry in teacher education. Tyson (1998) more than ten years ago made a call for an "epistemology of dismantling and dissecting" (p. 22). This dismantling of both epistemological and methodological moves would require that researchers displace the center of what has been privileged in the research on teaching and teacher education and giving attention to the margins. There is a cautionary note, however. Tyson stated,

Although the deconstructions project is not to reconstruct dominant hierarchs, something is reconstructed, much like a puzzle that can be taken apart but put together again and again while the picture remains the same. The pieces, though deconstructed, can be reconstructed, recreating a privileging of one race-based epistemology over the other. (p. 23)

As new lines of inquiry result in a grounded theory that arises from the "specificity of the day-to-day experiences of oppressed people" (Tyson, 2006), it is the hope that the "puzzle" of studying diversity in teaching and teacher education does not result in the pieces being reconstructed in research agendas again and again while the picture remains the same. The "picture" of the study of diversity in teaching and teacher education must interrogate existing theories, methodologies, and epistemologies to produce new lines of inquiry that support policies and practice for the diverse learners around the globe.

A CLOSING THOUGHT

As students from diverse racial, ethnic, and language groups across the globe seek access to quality educational opportunities in twenty-first-century classrooms, it is more imperative than ever that teachers be prepared with the attitudes, skills, knowledge, and dispositions necessary to become excellent teachers for students from racial, ethnic, and linguistic backgrounds that differ from their own. Many educators, administrators, policymakers, and students around the globe lament the fact that schools are having relatively little success in educating students who are poor, members of socially, culturally, or racially marginalized and disenfranchised groups, and speakers of first languages that differ from the mainstream or academic varieties of English. As these realities become more evident, educational researchers are challenged to provide the scholarship that combines research on diversity in education and research on diversity in teacher education necessary to a new generation of teachers who have the knowledge, attitudes, and skills necessary to work effectively with students who are culturally and linguistically diverse. In order for this to occur, first, it is necessary to investigate *approaches* to teacher education that can serve to motivate teachers to consider the option of teaching students from diverse racial, ethnic, and language groups in marginalized schools as well as the *mechanisms* through which teachers become more confident, more efficacious teachers for *all* students. Second, it is important that teachers be exposed to research-based transformative academic knowledge in their teacher preparation programs. It is our hope that the work of the scholars presented in this book will have an impact on discussions related to educational reform and efforts for social change and that this work, along with the work of other small groups of thoughtful scholars, can change the world. Indeed, as Margaret Meade has noted, it's the only thing that ever has.

REFERENCES

Alim, H. S. (2005). Critical language awareness in the United States: Revisiting issues and revising pedagogies in a resegregated society. *Educational Researcher, 34*(7), 24–31.

Anderson, L., & Olsen, B. (2006). Investigating early career urban teachers' perspectives on and experiences in professional development. *Journal of Teacher Education. 57*, 359–77.

Anthony, A., & Ball, A. F. (2010). Preparing teachers for twenty-first century schools: Organizational learning as a means to improving the relevance of teacher preparation programs. In Issa, M. S., & Khine, M. S. (Eds.), *Teaching teachers: Approaches in improving quality of education*. Hauppauge, NY: Nova Science Publishers.

Bakhtin, M. (1981). Discourse in the novel. In Bakhtin, M. M., *The dialogic imagination* (pp. 259–422). Austin: University of Texas Press.

Ball, A. F. (2006). *Multicultural strategies for education and social change: Carriers of the torch in the U.S. and South Africa*. New York: Teachers College Press.

Ball, A. F. (2009). Toward a theory of generative change in culturally and linguistically complex classrooms. *American Educational Research Journal, 46(1).* 45–72.

Brown, J. A. (1999). Comic book masculinity and the new black superhero. *African American Review, 33(1),* 25–42.

Cornbleth, C. (2008). *Diversity and the new teacher: Learning from experience in urban schools.* New York: Teachers College Press.

Daisaku, I. (1996). *Thoughts on education for global citizenship*. Speech delivered at Teachers College, Columbia University, June 13, 1996.

Delpit, L. (2002). *The skin that we speak: Thoughts on language and culture in the classroom*. New York: New Press.

Dixson, A. (2003). 'Lets' do this!': Black women teachers' politics and pedagogy. *Urban Education, 38(2),* 217.

Falk, R. (1994). The making of global citizenship. In van Steenbergen, B. (Ed.), *The condition of citizenship* (pp. 127–40). Sage Publications: London.

Franke, M., Carpenter, T., Levi, L., & Fennema, E. (2001). Capturing teachers' generative change: A follow-up study of professional development in mathematics. *American Educational Research Journal, 38(3),* 653–89.

Garbarino, J. (1995). *Raising children in a socially toxic environment*. San Francisco: Jossey-Bass.

Greene, S., & Abt-Perkins, D. (Eds.). (2003). *Making race visible: Literacy research for racial understanding*. New York: Teachers College Press.

Hale, J. (2008). Children, racial disparities and status. In Moore, J. (Ed.), *Encyclopedia of race and racism*. Detroit: Macmillan Reference.

Halliday, M. A. K. (1993). Towards a language-based theory of learning. *Linguistics and Education, 5,* 93–116.

Heath, S. B. (1983). *Ways with words language, life and work in communities and classrooms*. UK: Cambridge University Press.

hooks, b. (2004). Culture to culture: Ethnography and cultural studies as critical intervention. In Hesse-Biber, S., & Leavy, P. (Eds.), *Approaches to qualitative research*. New York: Oxford University Press.

Irvine, J. J., & Armento, B. (2001). (Eds.), *Culturally responsive teaching: Lesson planning for elementary and middle grades*. Boston: McGraw-Hill.

Keck, M., & Sikkink, K. (1998). *Activists beyond borders: Advocacy networks in international politics*. New York: Cornell University Press.

Levstick, L., & Tyson, C. (Eds.). (2008). *Handbook of research in social studies*. New York: Rutledge Publishing.

Morrell, E. (2005). Critical English education. *English Education, 37(4),* 312–21.

Tyson, C. (1998). A response to coloring epistemology: Are our qualitative research epistemologies racially biased? *Educational Researcher, 27(9),* 21–22.

Tyson, C. (2006). Research, race, and the social studies. In Barton, K. (Ed.), *Research methods in social studies education: Contemporary issues and perspectives* (pp. 39–56). Charlotte, NC: Information Age Publishing.

Vygotsky, L. S. (1978). *Mind in society: The development of higher psychological processes*. Cambridge, MA: Harvard University Press.

Watson, D., Charner-Laird, M., Kirkpatrick, C., Szczesiul, S., & Gordon, P. (2006). Grappling with definitions, grappling with difference. *Journal of Teacher Education, 57(4)*, 395–409.

Wertsch, J. V. (1985). *Vygotsky and the social formation of mind*. Cambridge, MA: Harvard University Press.

Woodson, C. G. (1937/1977). *Mis-education of the Negro*. New York: AMS Press.

Young, V. A. (2007). *Your average nigga: Performing race, literacy, and masculinity*. Detroit, MI: Wayne State University Press.

Index

AACTE. *See* American Association of Colleges for Teacher Education
Academy for Teaching Excellence, 86
accreditation, of teachers, 136; by communities, 136
achievement gap, 22; for African American males, 183; in multicultural education, 65; teacher quality gap and, 344–46
Action in Teacher Education, 283
activity theory, 334
additive approach, to multicultural education, 207
Adkins, Amee, 370
admission phase, in worthy witnessing, 296, 302–4
AERA. *See* American Educational Research Association
affirmative action, CRT and, 243–44
African American communities: communalism within, 209; diversity research projects in, 168n1; individualism within, 210; movement in learning styles for, 209; oral traditions within, 209–10; sense of harmony within, 209; social time perspective within, 210; spirituality within, 208–9; stimulation as learning factor for, 209; "white-ification" of, 7, 298
African American males, teacher education and, 183–97; achievement gaps and, 184; for affective students, 209; through

assessment tools, 195; bragging for, as mode of discourse, 186–87; through critical discourse analysis, 195; CRT and, 237–38; cultural labeling and, 185; culturally responsive curriculum and, 208–10; deficit perspectives and, 184; devaluation of, 194; diversity within teacher education and, 183–97; hip hop culture as influence on, 189–99; identity and, 8; interventions in, 184; literacy for, 8, 183–97; literacy gap for, 194; masculinity for, 183, 188–91; materialism and, iconography in, 191–94; modes of discourse for, 185–87, 196n2; NAEP literacy levels, 184; overreference of, as learning disabled, 201–203; programs for, 194–95; reading for, cultural myths about, 185; research frameworks for, 8; ritual insult among, 75; self-denial for, 185; sex themes and, 189–91; study methodologies for, 186–87; through targeted field experiences, 195; voyeurism and, 189–91; writing for, cultural myths about, 185
African Americans, cultural assimilation of, 109
African American teachers, 82–92; CRT and, 242–43; culturally specific pedagogy for, 26; recruitment of, 25–27; retention of, 26. *See also* teacher(s) of color
African Genome Project, 73

About the Contributors

Arnetha F. Ball is a Stanford University education professor who is a language, literacy, teacher education, and urban studies expert, and is president-elect of the American Educational Research Association (AERA). She is the Visiting Barbara A. Sizemore Distinguished Professor of Urban Education at Duquesne University. Her research centers on the writing and writing instruction of culturally and linguistically diverse students, the preparation of teachers to teach diverse student populations, and the linking of sociocultural and linguistic theory with educational practice.

Cynthia A. Tyson is a professor in the School of Teaching and Learning at The Ohio State University. Her research and scholarship interests include teaching for social justice, early childhood social studies, and multicultural children's literature. She also has an interest in the examination of race/racism in qualitative research.

Linda Darling-Hammond is Charles E. Ducommun Professor of Education at Stanford University, where she has launched the Stanford Center for Opportunity Policy in Education and served as faculty sponsor for the Stanford Teacher Education Program. She served as executive director of the National Commission on Teaching and America's Future, a blue-ribbon panel whose 1996 report, *What Matters Most: Teaching for America's Future*, led to sweeping policy changes affecting teaching in the United States. She recently served as the leader of President Barack Obama's education policy transition team.

Gloria Ladson-Billings is the Kellner Family Chair of Urban Education at the University of Wisconsin, Madison, and faculty affiliate in the Departments of Educational Policy Studies and Afro-American Studies. Her research investigates successful teachers of African American students and critical race theory applications to education.

Thandeka K. Chapman is an associate professor in the Department of Curriculum and Instruction at the University of Wisconsin, Milwaukee, where she teaches courses in education research and curriculum for the master's program and PhD Urban Education Doctoral Program. She has worked on a number of research projects that focus on matters of access and equity in urban schools. These projects have explored how confounded issues of race, class, gender, and language continue to marginalize students of color and hinder their opportunities for success.

Marilyn Cochran-Smith is the Cawthorne Professor of Teacher Education for Urban Schools and director of the doctoral program in curriculum and instruction at the Lynch School of Education at Boston College. A former president of the American Educational Research Association, she is an elected member of the National Academy of Education. She has authored or coauthored more than 150 articles, chapters, and editorials as well as nine books, four of which have won national awards.

Jeffrey M. R. Duncan-Andrade is associate professor of raza studies and education administration and interdisciplinary studies. In addition to these duties, he continues as a high school teacher in East Oakland, where for the past eighteen years he has practiced and studied the use of critical pedagogy in urban schools. He works with teachers and school leaders around the world and has authored three books as well as numerous journal articles and book chapters on effective pedagogy in urban settings and urban teacher support and development.

Donna Y. Ford is a professor in the Department of Special Education at Vanderbilt University. Her scholarship focuses mainly on closing the achievement gap, reversing underachievement among gifted African American students, improving the representation of black students in gifted education and advanced placement classes, and creating culturally responsive education for all students. She has written several books and numerous articles on these topics and has received many awards for her scholarship.

Kim Fries is an associate professor in the Department of Education at the University of New Hampshire. Her research interests include preservice and in-service teacher education, teacher quality, and the politics and policies surrounding the professional development of teachers.

Melissa Gibson is a doctoral student and teacher educator in the Department of Curriculum & Instruction at the University of Wisconsin, Madison. Her research focuses on social justice education and teacher education, urban school communities and reform, and the purposes and philosophies of education in a multicultural democracy.

Carl Grant is Hoefs-Bascom Professor of Teacher Education in the Department of Curriculum and Instruction at the University of Wisconsin, Madison. He has been editor of the *Review of Education Research* and the chair of the AERA Publications Committee. His most recent publications include *Teach! Change! Empower!* (2009) and the six-volume set *History of Multicultural Education* (2008, coedited by Thandeka K. Chapman).

Etta R. Hollins is Professor and Kaufman Endowed Chair in Urban Teacher Education at the University of Missouri at Kansas City. She was a contributor to the report of the AERA panel on research and teacher education, "Studying Teacher Education." She is the author of the award-winning book *Culture in School Learning*.

Kotie Kaiser is a lecturer in the Department of English in the Faculty of Education at the North-West University in Cape Town, South Africa. Her research focus is English for specific purposes and English across the curriculum.

Valerie Kinloch is associate professor of literacy studies in the School of Teaching and Learning at Ohio State University. She is author of various publications, including *Harlem on Our Minds: Place, Race, and the Literacies of Urban Youth* (2010), and is the 2010 recipient of the AERA Scholars of Color Early Career Award.

David E. Kirkland is an assistant professor of English education at New York University's Steinhardt School of Culture, Education, and Human Development in the Department of Teaching and Learning. His research focuses on urban youth culture, African American language and literacy, digital identities, and urban teacher education. He is a recipient of the 2008 AERA Division G Outstanding Dissertation Award.

Tiffany S. Lee is an assistant professor in Native American studies at the University of New Mexico. She teaches courses related to Indigenous education and language issues. She is Navajo from Crystal, New Mexico, and Lakota from Pine Ridge, South Dakota.

Kathy McDonough is an instructor in the Integrated Elementary and Special Education Program at Wheelock College, Boston, Massachusetts, and a doctoral student in the Language, Literacy, and Culture Concentration of the School of Education at the University of Massachusetts.

Erica R. Meiners writes and participates in antiprison organizing and immigrant, queer, and educational justice work. A professor of education and women's studies at Northeastern Illinois University, she is the author of four books, including *Right to be Hostile: Schools, Prisons and the Making of Public Enemies* (2007). She was the 2010 Lillian J. Robinson Scholar at the Simone de Beauvoir Institute in Montreal.

H. Richard Milner IV is associate professor of education in the Department of Teaching and Learning at Vanderbilt University, Nashville, Tennessee. He is also a faculty affiliate in the teacher education program at Fisk University in Nashville. His research, policy, and teaching interests are urban education, the sociology of race in education and society, and teacher education.

Sonia Nieto is Professor Emerita of Language, Literacy, and Culture at the University of Massachusetts, Amherst, and has written widely on multicultural education, teacher education, and the education of students of culturally and linguistically diverse backgrounds. She has taught at all levels from elementary school through graduate school, and she has been recognized for her research, advocacy, and service with many awards, including four honorary degrees.

Brad Olsen is associate professor of education at the University of California, Santa Cruz. His research focuses primarily on teachers, teaching, and teacher education. His most recent book is *Teaching for Success: Developing Your Teacher Identity in Today's Classroom* (2010).

Valerie Ooka Pang is a professor in the School of Teacher Education at San Diego State University. Her latest text, *Multicultural Education: A Caring-centered, Reflective Approach*, is published by Montezuma Publishing. She has been a consultant with organizations such as the Children's Television Workshop and has published in numerous journals.

Cynthia D. Park began her university career as an educational evaluator of bilingual programs and has led the development and implementation of bilingual teacher preparation programs. She currently directs the Pre-College Institute, whose mission is to increase college access and success for low-income, underrepresented public school students.

Patricia D. Quijada Cerecer is an assistant professor of educational psychology at the University of Texas at San Antonio. Her research interests include Indigenous identity development in home, community, and school contexts; Indigenous epistemologies; and multicultural education in community and school contexts.

Therese Quinn is an associate professor of art education at the School of the Art Institute of Chicago (SAIC). Her most recent publications are *Flaunt It! Queers Organizing for Public Education and Justice*, which was cowritten with Erica Meiners (2009), and *Handbook of Social Justice in Education* (2009). She coedits the Teachers College Press Series, *Teaching for Social Justice*; serves as president of the SAIC American Association of University Professors (AAUP) Chapter; and writes about public and art education at her occasional blog, *The Other Eye*.

Maryna Reyneke is a senior lecturer in the Department of English (Faculty of Education) at North-West University in Cape Town, South Africa. Her research focus is educational assessment and English across the curriculum.

Michelle Trotman Scott is an assistant professor at the University of West Georgia. A former teacher and administrator, Dr. Trotman Scott's research focuses on the areas of the achievement gap, overrepresentation in special education, underrepresentation in gifted education, and parent involvement.

Christine E. Sleeter is professor emerita in the College of Professional Studies at California State University, Monterey Bay, and currently a visiting professor at San Francisco State University. She is president-elect of the National Association for Multicultural Education and previously served as vice president of Division K of the American Educational Research Association. Her research focuses on antiracist multicultural education and multicultural teacher education. Her recent books include *Critical Multiculturalism: Theory and Praxis* (with Stephen May, 2010) and *Doing Multicultural Education for Achievement and Equity* (with Carl Grant, 2007).

Joseph R. Ubiles is a poet, educator, and cofounder and codirector of Power Writing at the Nuyorican Poets Café located in the Loisada of Manhattan in New York City. Power Writing is a revolutionary literacy project in its approach to literacy and urban youth. He has been awarded a Soros Open Society Institute Social Justice fellowship for his work with Power Writing, and his work is the subject of Maisha Winn's study, *Writing N Rhythm*.

Mandie Uys is on the Faculty of Education of the University of the North-West, Potchefstroom Campus, Cape Town, South Africa. Her research agenda is primarily focused on inquiry into the development of English medium of instruction programs for preservice and in-service teachers, where the focus is on training subject teachers to be language sensitive in the content classroom.

Maisha T. Winn (formerly Maisha T. Fisher) is an associate professor in language, literacy, and culture in the Division of Educational Studies at Emory University. Her research examines the intersections of literacy and the lives of urban youth and has been published in numerous journals. Her forthcoming book, *Girl Time*, is a multisited ethnography of incarcerated and formerly incarcerated girls' participation in a theater program.

Kenneth Zeichner is the Boeing Professor of Teacher Education and director of teacher education, University of Washington, Seattle.

Printed in Great Britain
by Amazon.co.uk, Ltd.,
Marston Gate.